REGIME OF
OBSTRUCTION

REGIME OF
OBSTRUCTION

HOW CORPORATE POWER
BLOCKS ENERGY DEMOCRACY

EDITED BY
WILLIAM K. CARROLL

◊ **AU PRESS**

Copyright © 2021 William Carroll

Published by AU Press, Athabasca University

1200, 10011 – 109 Street, Edmonton, AB T5J 3S8

https://doi.org/10.15215/aupress/9781771992893.01

Cover image: Voyata/Shutterstock.com
Cover design by Marvin Harder
Interior design by Sergiy Kozakov
Printed and bound in Canada

Library and Archives Canada Cataloguing in Publication

Title: Regime of obstruction : how corporate power blocks energy democracy /
    edited by William K. Carroll.

Names: Carroll, William K., editor.

Description: Includes bibliographical references.

Identifiers: Canadiana (print) 20200198262 | Canadiana (ebook) 20200199331
        ISBN 9781771992893 (softcover) | ISBN 9781771992909 (pdf)
        ISBN 9781771992916 (epub)

Subjects: LCSH: Energy policy—Canada. | LCSH: Oil sands industry—
    Environmental aspects—Canada. | LCSH: Fossil fuels—Environmental
    aspects—Canada. | LCSH: Oil sands industry—Economic aspects—Canada. |
    LCSH: Oil sands industry—Government policy—Canada. | LCSH: Corporate
    power—Canada. | LCSH: Business and politics—Canada.

Classification: LCC HD9574.C22 R44 2021 | DDC 338.2/72820971—dc23

This book has been published with the help of a grant from the Federation for the
Humanities and Social Sciences, through the Awards to Scholarly Publications
Program, using funds provided by the Social Sciences and Humanities Research
Council of Canada.

We acknowledge the financial support of the Government of Canada through the
Canada Book Fund (CBF) for our publishing activities and the assistance provided
by the Government of Alberta through the Alberta Media Fund.

Canada   Alberta
          Government

Contents

Acknowledgements

All edited volumes are collective efforts by nature, but this one is special. Since 2014, the authors of the chapters collected herein have worked as a team within the Corporate Mapping Project (CMP), a research and community-engagement partnership co-directed by Shannon Daub and me. Shannon, who is director of the Canadian Centre for Policy Alternatives, BC Office (CCPA-BC), has made an enormous contribution to the CMP and to virtually all of its products, including this one. Her intellectual and organizational leadership has been indispensable to the success of our efforts. As editor of this book, I am eternally grateful to Shannon and thankful for the opportunity to work closely with her over the past few years, during which I have learned a lot about how to make social science research come alive in policy and practice.

Back in the autumn of 2013, when we first conceived of the project behind this book, we envisaged building a "community of practice" that would include academics, policy analysts, movement activists, community-based researchers, and community leaders. Within an integrated program of social science research, we would expose the undue power and influence of the fossil fuel industry in Canada while developing feasible alternatives to the continued hegemony of corporate capital in and around the energy sector. But, of equal import, our community of practice would mobilize that critical knowledge via a wide array of platforms reaching a wide array of publics—concerned citizens, social and ecological activists, First Nations, policy networks, and, of course, professional social scientists. And, although the authors featured in this volume have all made crucial contributions to the CMP, the creative efforts of many others in our community of practice—which by now numbers over a hundred members—have also enhanced the chapters of this book, in many ways.

This volume addresses all the groups mentioned above, but it leans toward the last one: social scientists and students of social science. The chapters in the book highlight research conducted during the first three years of the project, from 2015 to 2018.

The University of Victoria, my academic home since 1981, has served as host of the Corporate Mapping Project. I am grateful to administrative staff in my home department, Sociology, for the many ways in which they have provided support for the project and this book in particular. Big thanks to Zoe Lu, Aileen Chong, Carole Rains, and Ann Hamilton. Their efforts have been complemented by those of two successive department chairs, Sean Hier and Steve Garlick, and by senior administrators, in particular Peter Keller and Catherine Krull, successive deans of the Faculty of Social Sciences; Valerie Kuehne, Vice-President Academic; and David Castle and Lisa Kalynchuk, successive Vice-Presidents Research.

The CMP has functioned as a community-university partnership, and the efforts of partner organizations have been crucial to its success and to the realization of this volume. In particular, I thank Seth Klein, director of the CCPA-BC until 2018; Ricardo Acuña, executive director of the Parkland Institute until 2020, and Trevor Harrison, director of the Parkland Institute; and Kevin Connor and Michael "Ziggy" Mintz, at the Public Accountability Initiative. Thi Vu, who served as project director from 2014 through 2019 from her desk at the CCPA-BC, deserves special thanks for her unflagging dedication and diligence.

Our community of practice has been enabled by a grant from the Social Sciences and Humanities Research Council of Canada, whose commitment to academic freedom is even more precious than the funds it dispenses.

Our publisher, Athabasca University Press, has been a source of indefatigable support. Senior editor Pamela Holway enthusiastically steered the manuscript through the review process and made extensive and thoughtful editorial contributions after an initial round of copyediting by Alison Jacques. Karyn Wisselink offered excellent support on the production and marketing side. A leader among university presses in making its books freely available online, AU Press has been a perfect fit for the CMP, given our strong commitment to open-access publishing.

Last but certainly not least, a great many student researchers and research assistants at UVic and at other university partners to the CMP have made splendid contributions to the chapters of this volume, in some cases as co-authors. In the Sociology Department at UVic, I am thrilled to have worked with graduate students Ryan Butler, David Chen, Nicolas Graham, Robyn Hlatky, Jouke Huijzer, Mike Lang, Zach Lewis, Kevin McCartney, Jason Miller, Sara Naderi, Mark Shakespear, and Zoë Yunker, and post-doctoral fellows J. P. Sapinski and Bob Neubauer.

As I write these acknowledgements, the world has plunged into a deep public health crisis, revealing the injustices and irrationalities of neoliberal capitalism. This crisis is a foretaste of what awaits us if business-as-usual continues for much longer. The climate emergency is also a massive public health crisis, although its impacts are less acute. Coastal inundation, inland desertification, flooding, superstorms, heat waves, and other forms of extreme weather will have public health effects far more severe than a disease that runs its brutal course. The COVID-19 pandemic only intensifies the need to transition from a fossil-fueled way of life organized under the thumb of corporate power to a socially just and ecologically healthy future. I hope that this volume will be of value in clarifying the nature of the problem before us, and its possible solution.

REGIME OF
OBSTRUCTION

Introduction

The intensifying development of western Canada's fossil fuel resources has far-reaching implications for our economic and ecological well-being, for the trajectory of global climate change, and for recognition of the rights and title of Indigenous peoples. Large corporations play a central role in managing fossil fuel resources, yet the industry's internal organization and its evolving relationships to other sectors of society are not well understood, nor are they easily visible to scholars, students, and citizens. Drawing on a varied array of empirical research in and around Canada's carbon-extractive sector, this volume integrates new knowledge of the modalities of corporate control within an overarching perspective that problematizes and dissects the concentrated power of fossil capital.

Our goal is to probe the multifaceted ways in which the organization of corporate power blocks a transition from fossil capitalism to energy democracy. By *fossil capitalism* we mean a form of capitalism "predicated on the growing consumption of fossil fuels, and therefore generating a sustained growth in emissions of carbon dioxide" (Malm 2016, 11). When we speak of *energy democracy*, we have in mind a double shift of power, from the energy of fossil fuels to the power of renewables (decarbonization) and from social power concentrated in a corporate oligarchy to public, democratic control of economic decisions (democratization). Corporate control of the production of energy—most of it currently in the form of fossil fuels—and the reach of corporate power into other social fields pose the greatest obstacles to addressing the ecological and economic challenges that humanity faces today.

Portions of this chapter were previously published in "Fossil Capitalism, Climate Capitalism, Energy Democracy: The Struggle for Hegemony in an era of Climate Crisis," *Socialist Studies / Études socialistes* 14, no. 1 (2020): 1–26. They are reprinted here by permission of the journal.

In Canada and globally, such a transition is technically feasible, particularly as new energy-storage technologies are refined. Yet the organization of economic power, concretized in large corporations and extending into political and cultural life in complex, multifaceted ways, presents a set of blockages. To move toward a just transition to energy democracy, we need to understand how these blockages function as a *regime of obstruction*, rooted in the political economy of fossil capitalism and expressed through a panoply of hegemonic practices that reach into civil and political society and into Indigenous communities whose land claims and world views challenge state-mandated property rights. This book maps the relations and contours of the regime of obstruction as it operates in contemporary Canada.

Fossil Capital and the Climate Emergency

According to leading climate scientist James Hansen, "Global warming has reached a level such that we can ascribe with a high degree of confidence a cause and effect relationship between the greenhouse effect and observed warming. It is already happening now." Hansen's definitive diagnosis was not made last week, or last year. He offered it in June 1988, before a US Senate committee (see Shabecoff 1988). In the three ensuing decades, global warming has become a climate emergency. Rapidly rising carbon emissions from the burning of fossil fuels have enhanced the greenhouse effect, leading directly to increased temperatures and melting polar ice caps. The knock-on effects include sea-level rise, extreme weather (droughts, heat waves, hurricanes, floods, and cyclones), ocean acidification, losses in biodiversity, and the spread of diseases once confined to the tropics (United Nations Framework Convention on Climate Change 2007, 8–9). Certain of these impacts create feedback effects, further amplifying climate change. For instance, the loss of ice caps reduces the planet's reflective capacity, trapping more heat; rising temperatures near the poles thaw permafrost, releasing methane, a greenhouse gas (GHG) estimated to be eighty-six times more potent a warming agent over a 20-year period than carbon dioxide; droughts and heat waves fuel wildfires that release CO_2 while decreasing forests' capacities to absorb carbon; and ocean acidification compromises the marine food chain, reducing the ocean's capacity to absorb carbon from the atmosphere.[1]

Carbon dioxide (CO_2) remains in the atmosphere for decades after it is emitted. These amplifying mechanisms would therefore drive global warming for some time even if humanity were to choose a path of rapid decarboniz-ation, through renewable energy and overall reductions in energy use. Yet carbon emissions continue to rise—by 2.0 percent globally in 2018, a year when even emissions from coal, the dirtiest fossil fuel, increased by 1.4 per-cent.[2] Thanks to the feedback effects mentioned above, increasing emissions are pushing the Earth system toward multiple tipping points, beyond which catastrophic climate change becomes unavoidable (Steffen et al. 2018). The implications for human lives are dire. We already glimpse them in crop fail-ures and famine, in deaths from heat waves, wildfires, and extreme storms, in growing numbers of climate refugees, and in increasing rates of suicide (Burke et al. 2018; Miller 2018).

If climate science has isolated the primary cause of global warming in human-induced GHG emissions, Richard Heede (2013) has identified the leading social forces behind those emissions. Ninety corporations (including petro-state organizations) have been responsible for the lion's share of GHG emissions since the mid-nineteenth century. Indeed, the global ascent of cap-italism as the dominant way of life has been fuelled by carbon energy, which enables capital to accumulate on an extended scale but releases CO_2 on the same scale, leading inevitably to climate crisis (Malm 2016).

Capital has always boosted its profitability by appropriating what Jason Moore (2015) memorably christened "Cheap Nature," including the buried sunshine of fossil fuels, which concentrate enormous quantities of energy. For capital, he argues, nature has been both "tap" and "sink." From cod and beaver pelts in early colonial Canada to oil and gas in post–World War II Alberta, business has *tapped* nature's bounty. At the same time, nature has been a *sink*, absorbing waste. As long as capital claimed only a small part of the planet, these ecologically destructive tendencies had only local impacts: a ravaged forest here, a polluted river there. But since the closing decades of the twentieth cen-tury, with full-fledged globalization and the closing of resource frontiers, the sink has overflowed with GHGs and other pollutants, and the tap has started to run dry—not only in declining agricultural productivity gains (portending the end of "cheap food") but in depletion of high-grade oil. The latter provokes recourse to "extreme oil"—tar sands, fracked oil and gas, deepwater drilling—carrying greater emissions and ecological risk (Pineault 2018). What Allan Schnaiberg (1980) called the "treadmill of production" spins out of control.

Fossil capital has been deeply implicated in the political and cultural forms of corporate capitalism. Timothy Mitchell (2011, 18) notes ironically that from the 1870s on, the age of democratization coincided with the age of empire: "the rise of coal produced democracy at some sites and colonial domination at others." Within the core of the world system, coal mining brought workers together at a key point in the commodity chain, enhancing their power and enabling the working class in the Global North to demand concessions that led to "carbon democracy." In the Global South, however, colonial domination became further consolidated with the twentieth-century transition from coal to oil, as seven oil majors came to control supply, engendering "a geopolitics of domination in which the US figured prominently" (Williams 2018, 237).

In an astute case study of the United States as epicentre of carbon democracy, Matthew Huber (2013) explores how, after World War II, fossil capital's hegemony was cemented in the rise of suburbanized consumerism. Through the acquisition of cars, single detached houses, and appliances, certain segments of the working class were "energized, afforded enormous power over machines, space, and everyday life in navigating the practices of reproduction" (159). Within this assemblage, the individual comes to experience automobility as empowering and liberating and the single detached house as a domain of personal sovereignty. The long-range result has been to constrain politics within narrow limits "focused on the family, private property, and anticollectivist sentiments" (79)—the stock-in-trade of neoliberalism. Even if the American Dream is a hoax, however, it continues to carry heavy affective and ideological ballast and poses a great barrier, psychoculturally, to movements for climate justice. Nor is the dream uniquely American. In Canada, automobility and suburbanization have also underwritten popular allegiances to fossil capitalism, although arguably a social-democratic political current, grounded in a more robust labour movement, has to some extent tempered the tendency toward atomized individualism.

Canada as Climate Laggard

Although Canada has long been a producer and exporter of fossil fuels, under the Conservative federal government of Stephen Harper (2006–15) the country was propelled, according to Harper himself, into the ranks of "energy superpower" (Taber 2006). This was accomplished in part through extremely low royalty rates and a host of state subsidies to the oil and gas industry: Canada's subsidies are the highest per capita among the G7 countries (McSheffrey 2018). With the exception of a few Middle East petro-states and two small

Caribbean countries, Canada also has the dubious honour of producing the highest per capita level of carbon emissions in the world (Janssens-Maenhout et al. 2017). It has been a regular recipient of the Climate Action Network's satirical Fossil of the Day awards, earning a "Fossil of the Year" award at the UN Climate Change Conference in 2009, before garnering a "Lifetime Unachievement" Fossil award in 2013.

In an apparent reversal of this trend (and having just formed a majority government), at the opening of the December 2015 UN Climate Change Conference in Paris Justin Trudeau vowed that "Canada will take on a new leadership role internationally" and declared, "Canada is back, my good friends. We are here to help." Yet the actual policy framework barely shifted at all. By March 2017, Trudeau was reassuring top fossil capitalists assembled in Texas that "no country would find 173 billion barrels of oil in the ground and just leave them there."[3] A year later, Canada's federal government announced that it would purchase Kinder Morgan's Trans Mountain Pipeline, contentiously slated to be twinned by a new pipeline that would triple capacity to pump bitumen to Burnaby, British Columbia. Meanwhile, in November 2016, the federal government released its Pan-Canadian Framework on Clean Growth and Climate Change. But as earth scientist David Hughes (2018, 159) points out, the government's own projections under the plan will see an overall decrease in emissions of only 0.7 percent from 2005 levels by 2030 (with oil and gas emissions increasing by 46.5 percent). Hughes concludes that oil and gas resources

> are non-renewable and finite, and production of oil and gas is the largest source of Canadian emissions, yet current policy is to extract them as fast as possible and sell them at rock-bottom prices with diminishing returns for the Canadian economy. This compromises emissions-reduction commitments and imposes long-term risks for Canadian energy security. (165)

Indeed, a climate action plan that mandates major new oil and gas pipelines, which can only serve to massively expand emissions, is fundamentally incoherent.

Apparent reversals of Canada's climate-laggard record at the provincial level are equally dubious. Alberta's vaunted "cap" on tar sands production, initiated by an NDP government in 2016, called for a 47.5 percent *increase* from 2014 levels before the cap would be reached (Hussey 2017). But, three year later, even this cap was swiftly removed, along with all the rest of the province's recently enacted climate legislation, by the newly elected United Conservative Party government of Premier Jason Kenney. Such a shift—from bad to worse on the climate action front—simply repeats what has been happening in Ontario, as a Conservative government, elected in June 2018, eliminates virtually all of the modest climate action reforms introduced in 2016 by the Liberal government of Kathleen Wynne. In fact, incoherent as it is, the Trudeau government's national climate plan may be unravelling, as climate-laggard provinces—notably Saskatchewan, Ontario, and Alberta—refuse to play ball, evidently preferring legal action to climate action.

The Corporate Mapping Project as Public Sociology and Action Research

Canada thus presents the interesting case of a climate laggard and, in some respects, a First World petro-state (Adkin 2016). Although actual jobs in the fossil-capital sector account for a tiny fraction of the national workforce, and although state revenues from that sector have plunged in recent years to negligible levels (Hughes 2018, 164), political and corporate leadership is solidly behind a slightly modified version of "business as usual," with carbon extraction continuing to increase (even as other measures partly mitigate ever-growing emissions). But the case of Canada is of more than academic interest. The urgency of the situation, globally, demands not only scholarly understanding but effective action. As the authors of a recent study of climate change conclude, if we are to avoid the "Hothouse Earth" scenario of runaway climate change, "a deep transformation based on a fundamental reorientation of human values, equity, behavior, institutions, economies, and technologies is required" (Steffen et al. 2018, 7).

This book features research findings from the first three years (2015–18) of a seven-year SSHRC-funded partnership that I co-direct with Shannon Daub, associate director of the British Columbia office of the Canadian Centre for Policy Alternatives (CCPA)."Mapping the Power of the Carbon-Extractive Corporate Resource Sector"—also known as the Corporate Mapping Project (CMP)—involves six western Canadian universities and several civil society organizations, including the CCPA, the Parkland Institute, Unifor, and the Public Accountability Initiative. The partnership is founded in a shared commitment to advancing reliable knowledge that supports citizen action and transparent public policy toward a just transition away from fossil capitalism.

As researchers with the CMP, contributors to this volume see *corporate power* as a key factor in the chasm between climate science and climate action. The CMP is a case study of the forces that shape Canada's climate policy, one that partners social scientists with progressive policy researchers, journalists, and activist movements (including environmentalism, labour, and Indigenous leadership). Our approach is centred on a family of techniques that map the organization of power, socially, economically, politically, and culturally. These include analyses of the social networks through which power and influence flow; the commodity chains along which carbon extraction, transport, processing, and consumption occur; and the discursive structures that frame issues and narratives in the struggle to persuade publics, governments, and communities as to the desirability or inevitability of fossil capitalism as a way of life. But the project's scope extends to counter-power, as popular resistance to the regime of obstruction reveals how corporate power operates while also pointing toward alternatives.

As a community-university partnership, the CMP combines social science research with popular education and democratic advocacy in a continuing program of public sociology and action research. As public sociology, the CMP brings sociology and kindred disciplines into conversation with communities and movements about the obstacles that corporate power and fossil capital pose to ecological well-being, economic justice, and democracy. As action research, the CMP helps to build a transdisciplinary community of practice capable of monitoring and challenging corporate power and influence on an ongoing basis. Our efforts have involved:

- exposing and problematizing corporate power in its various modalities, to various publics

- providing evidence-based ammunition to allies in social justice, Indigenous, and ecological movements, to bolster their counter-power

- offering policy analyses that propose feasible alternatives for a just transition from fossil capitalism—evoked in such projects as climate justice and energy democracy.

As action research, the CMP puts at the centre of its mission the production of critical knowledge that can inform effective political practice. In mapping the carbon-extractive sector's organization, its political and cultural reach, and the resistance to its power, we offer a relational analysis attuned to both political-economic and discursive structures and practices. At the core of the analysis is the idea that corporate power is wielded through a number of distinct *modalities*.

Modalities of Corporate Power

In *Organizing the 1%: How Corporate Power Works*, J. P. Sapinski and I argue that contemporary corporate power is at once economic and hegemonic, manifesting itself not merely as an economic force grounded in accumulation but also as a political and cultural force. As figure I.1 shows, this power stretches across the capitalist economy, the state, and civil society, expressing itself in various modalities within three overlapping spheres (see figure I.1).

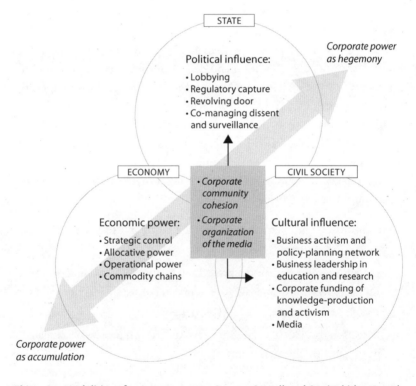

Figure I.1 Modalities of corporate power. *Source*: Carroll and Sapinski (2018, 101).

In its economic aspect, corporate power is coterminous with the entire process of capital accumulation, from the labour entailed in extraction, manufacturing, and transport through to marketing and finance. The popular imagery of "free" markets obscures the cardinal reality that capitalism is an economic system in which a dominant class of business owners and top executives appropriates the wealth created by a subordinate class of wage and salary earners. The economic surplus that labour generates in production forms the basis for profit, interest, and rent and for the ultra-high salaries of CEOs (some of whom earn in excess of $10 million annually).[4] Capital's competitive dynamic means that each firm, including large corporations, must grow or eventually die, as other enterprises overtake it. Thus, most of the surplus that capital appropriates from labour is reinvested, giving capitalists power not only within current economic practices but also over the future. As capital accumulates, giant corporations and massive pools of capital concentrate power in the capitalist class's top tier—those who own and/or control large corporations. The economic power of corporate capital is reflected in the economic dependence of workers, communities, and states on corporate investments to generate jobs and government revenue.

As figure I.1 suggests, there are several distinct modalities of economic power. *Operational* power is the power of management, flowing through a chain of command in which the scope of decision making is narrowed as we move from top management to shop floor. Operational power is also wielded along commodity chains, from resource extraction through processes of transport, processing, manufacturing, and distribution. *Strategic* power, the power to set business strategies for the company, involves control of the corporation itself, often by acquiring the largest bloc of shares. This power is lodged in the board of directors but rooted in the nondemocratic character of corporate capital. Corporate directors are annually "elected" but by shareholders only. The majority of those with a stake in the enterprise—workers, communities, consumers—are thus disenfranchised. Moreover, elections are typically based not on one vote per person but on one vote per corporate share owned, thereby enabling large shareholders to wield strategic control, as Jouke Huijzer and I show in chapter 4. Finally, *allocative* power stems from the control of credit, the money-capital on which large corporations depend. This power, which accrues to financial institutions of all sorts (banks, life insurers, asset managers, hedge funds), is crucial in expanding or retooling operations, launching takeover bids, or coping with cash squeezes during crises (see Carroll and Sapinski 2018, 39–40).

Figure I.1 also depicts the *hegemonic* face of corporate power, as it extends into the political and cultural fields of state and civil society. Hegemony can be defined as rule with the consent of the ruled; hence, hegemonic power refers to how that consent is secured, organized, and maintained, from the visceral level of everyday life up to the top tiers of state institutions. Although capitalists themselves dominate in accumulation, within political and civil society corporate power is exercised by capital's *organic intellectuals*, "deputies" or members of the capitalist class who are entrusted with the activity of "organising the general system of relationships external to . . . business itself" (Gramsci 1971, 6). As Giuseppe Vacca (1982) has noted, such intellectuals are "organic" in a double sense. On one hand, they are "organizers" of an advanced capitalist way of life, providing leadership within the core institutions of capitalist society. On the other hand, their efforts are functionally (organically) predicated on the dominance of capital in human affairs and serve to reproduce that dominance. The agency of corporate capitalists as "business leaders" and "business activists" promoting the virtues of one or another aspect of corporate capitalism is an important expression of the organic relationship between the business of capital accumulation and wider world of politics and cultural life. However, most organic intellectuals are not major shareholders or high-level executives but well-placed and highly skilled professionals whose agency legitimates and facilitates the corporate system, through their involvement in areas such as public relations and media, policy formation, lobbying, higher education, accounting, and corporate law (Carroll and Shaw 2001).

Such experts can also be found on the directorates of leading corporations, where they function in an advisory capacity and often help to integrate the corporate elite by serving on multiple boards. Indeed, as I show in chapter 5, a dense network of interlocking directorates among Canada's leading fossil-capital companies pulls together capitalists and organic intellectuals as an elite within the wider Canadian corporate community (and the even wider transnational capitalist class). Within this elite, power is centralized, as top capitalists and their advisors interact frequently, maintaining a sense of solidarity and common purpose even as they compete over the division of spoils appropriated from labour and nature. The corporate community's *cohesiveness* is an important modality of hegemony, as it enables corporate capital to reach a consensus on long-term goals and vision and, on that basis, to speak politically with a single voice and thus to lead.

Complementing elite integration is the *reach* of corporate power into the public sphere, effectively seeking to dominate the institutions, agendas, policies, discourses, and values that add up to an entire way of life. Doris Fuchs and Markus Lederer (2007, 4) have distinguished three forms of such power. Grounded in the vast resources that corporations control, *instrumental* power involves investing those resources in order to exercise influence in the political process, as in lobbying and campaign or party finance activities. *Structural* power, grounded in capitalists' control of investment, is the power to set the agenda and make the rules, with the threat of possible capital withdrawal keeping some options (such as rapid decarbonization that would threaten immediate profits) off the table. Finally, business wields *discursive* power, shaping norms, values, and beliefs through image campaigns that trumpet corporate social responsibility and "corporate citizenship," as well as through the wider promotion of consumer and entertainment culture, the wellspring of popular desires and concerns. These forms often operate in conjunction. For instance, in August 2018, Canada's federal government, after what was described as extensive "consultation" with industry (a veiled reference to instrumental power), announced that it was walking back its plan for a national carbon tax. Environment minister Catherine McKenna explained, "We don't want to drive industry out of our country" (an acknowledgement of structural power) (quoted in Rabson 2018). In this volume, we focus on the instrumental and discursive forms, although capital's structural power is always in the background.

As illustrated in figure I.1, corporate reach is a many splendoured thing. Vis-à-vis civil society, it includes, among other things:

- business leadership exercised by corporate elites as they govern business councils, industry groups, policy-planning organizations, and institutions of higher education and research
- selective allocation of funds to business-friendly think tanks, advocacy groups, political parties, etc.
- public relations (PR) and corporate social responsibility (CSR) initiatives

- the framing of news and other media content to privilege business interests (who as advertisers selectively fund that content)
- the corporate organization of communications media, whose goal of profit maximization trumps the public interest.

Corporate funding of organizations and activities in civil society is itself an expression of allocative power reaching into and colonizing the public sphere. Funds accumulated as capital are selectively directed, often through private foundations, to initiatives aligned with corporate business, including policy-planning groups, political parties, lobbies and industry groups, universities and research centres, community organizations, and "astroturf" advocacy groups such as Canada's Energy Citizens. Corporate power reaches into the state via such relations and practices as

- intensive and sustained lobbying (in the five years ending in early 2016, the Canadian Association of Petroleum Producers lobbied the federal government on nearly a daily basis)
- regulatory capture (for example, Canada's National Energy Board rubber-stamped industry proposals for years, leading an investigative panel to observe in 2017 that "Canadians have serious concerns that the NEB has been 'captured' by the oil and gas industry, with many Board members who come from the industry that the NEB regulates, and who—at the very least appear to—have an innate bias toward that industry" [McCarthy 2017])
- revolving doors, through which business leaders become political leaders and vice versa.

A final aspect of corporate reach into political society aligns corporations with the repressive arm of the state, as co-managers of dissent and surveillance. Although it is business as usual to govern with popular consent, when hegemony fails—when dissent becomes well organized and potentially effective—the state turns to more repressive strategies of social control.

In the realm of fossil capital, this began to happen under the Harper regime, as coalitions of Indigenous, environmental, and social justice activists rose up in opposition to proposed pipelines such as Northern Gateway and Keystone XL (both first proposed in the mid-2000s). In response, the state mobilized its security agencies in order to protect "critical infrastructure," working in collaboration with fossil fuel corporations (Crosby and Monaghan 2018). In 2014, in its *Action Plan for Critical Infrastructure*, Public Safety Canada recommended that "private sector stakeholders" be granted special security clearance "to enable increased sharing of sensitive information" (Public Safety Canada 2014, 6). Then came Bill C-51, introduced by the Harper government in January 2015 (and passed six months later). Otherwise known as the Anti-terrorism Act, 2015, the bill included "interference with critical infrastructure" in its definition of activities that undermine the country's security. That "critical infrastructure" included pipelines and other oil and gas industry facilities was clear from a January 2014 RCMP report, "Critical Infrastructure Intelligence Assessment: Criminal Threats to the Petroleum Industry," in which "violent anti-petroleum extremists" were essentially tagged as terrorists (Linnitt 2015). Although the Trudeau government's Bill C-59, introduced in June 2017 (and passed two years later), softened the language of Bill C-51, it continues to target "significant or widespread interference with critical infrastructure" as a threat to national security and to allow authorities to detain or arrest someone if they have reasonable grounds to believe that doing so "is necessary to" prevent the occurrence of terrorist activity.[5]

These various modalities can be placed within an even wider framework that recognizes that power implies resistance (Barbalet 1985). Resistance can take different forms, including

- shop-floor struggles of workers against the lash of management

- protests, boycotts, and blockades at key junctures along commodity chains

- shareholder activism and divestment campaigns, which engage the power of investors

- calls for the private allocative power of finance to be brought under public control

- critiques of the concentration of power within old boys' clubs and among corporate elites

- demands to remove big money from politics and to end the institutional corruption that infects practices of business lobbying

- media activism pushing to democratize public communication while fostering community-based media

- counterhegemonic projects to transform our way of life—as in the 2015 Leap Manifesto, which proposes to shift from fossil capitalism to energy democracy.[6]

Although the Corporate Mapping Project has focused on domination, issues of resistance (and even transformation) are never far below the surface of our investigations, and they figure prominently in this collection's third part.

Structure of the Book

In the chapters that follow, we show how these modalities of corporate power in and around Canada's fossil-capital sector comprise a regime of obstruction. The analysis is presented in three parts:

- "The Organization of Fossil Capital," through networks and commodity chains in which a few large corporations dominate the scene
- "The Struggle for Hearts and Minds," as corporate power reaches into political and civil society and into Indigenous communities, via various instrumental and discursive relations
- "Resistance and Beyond," as counter-power builds, opening space for transformative policies and practices that can move toward energy democracy.

The Organization of Fossil Capital

Part 1 highlights the structure and dynamics of Canada's fossil-capital sector, its internal organization and links to national and transnational capitalist structures and agencies, its extractivist logic of accumulation by dispossession, and the business strategies that carbon-extractive corporations are adopting in the current era of decreased fossil fuel prices and increasing risks (to fossil-capital investors) of stranded assets.

Two chapters focus on the core of fossil capital in Canada and the exercise of operational and strategic power within the accumulation process. In "Boom, Bust, and Consolidation: Corporate Restructuring in the Alberta Oil Sands," Ian Hussey, Éric Pineault, Emma Jackson, and Susan Cake present comparative case studies of the "oligopolistic bloc" that dominates Canada's tar sands and the wider fossil-capital sector. They show how, amid the wild swings of the commodity cycle, five companies have pursued accumulation strategies that reproduce fossil capital by building up and deploying organizational power over material resources, labour, and spaces of circulation. The normalization of ramped-up bitumen extraction and the revenue streams issuing from it have become central to Canada's regime of obstruction.

James Lawson's "Lines of Work, Corridors of Power: Extraction, Obstruction, and Counter-obstruction Along Fossil Fuel Production Networks" presents a complementary analysis of the corporate strategies and practices that maintain and enlarge the flow of fossil fuels from the point of extraction to ports and processing facilities. Lawson focuses on flows of material along commodity chains, noting that the capacity to block and unblock flows also underwrites disruptive counter-power. In effect, obstruction cuts both ways: fossil capital obstructs the political and economic changes that might jeopardize its self-expansion, while anti-pipeline campaigns strive to obstruct the flow of carbon energy that is the basis for that self-expansion.

Mark Hudson's "Landscapes of Risk: Financial Representations of Catastrophe" shifts the focus to the financial sector and its entwinement with fossil capital. Hudson interrogates how the climate crisis, an ecological phenomenon, gets "digested" into the logic of capital and thereby transfigured from a lived, heterogeneous, and qualitative phenomenon into a homogeneous, fictitiously commensurable stream of quantitative values. Moving away from overt climate change denialism, financial institutions have come to construct climate change as a set of risk factors manifested in changing commodity prices, which inspire new financial commodities that recalibrate finance's allocative power. The financial industry's practical responses to climate change depend on a reliable (or at least credible) means for distilling climate change mitigation efforts into quanta. The chapter explores financial capital's early efforts to produce such numbers and raises questions about the implications of this digestion for both capitalism and how we conceive of nature.

The final chapters in part 1 offer social network analyses of the organization of corporate power within fossil capital. In "Who Owns Big Carbon? Mapping the Network of Corporate Ownership," Jouke Huijzer and I take up the issue of strategic power, charting the patterns of share ownership surrounding Canada's carbon-extractive sector. We identify ownership interests—corporate, personal, institutional—and we map the key ownership relations that tie corporations in Canada's fossil-capital sector into networks of national and transnational corporate power. These networks include the global carbon majors that reach into Canada through their subsidiaries, the financial institutions and asset managers that own slices of many companies, and the wealthy Canadian families that own significant stakes in key firms. The substantial holdings of Canada's top five banks create a close symbiosis between fossil capital and financial capital, giving the latter an interest in the vitality of the entire sector and in obstructing efforts to wind down fossil capital before fixed-capital assets are fully valorized.

In "Canada's Fossil-Capital Elite: A Tangled Web of Corporate Power," I map the interlocking directorships through which the directors and top executives of fossil-capital firms are integrated into a Calgary-centred elite and the additional interlocks that link that elite into the financial sector and other segments of corporate capital, both national and transnational. A few dozen well-connected corporate capitalists and their advisors provide much of the network's "inner circle" (Useem 1984), further concentrating corporate power. The architecture of corporate power resembles an entrenched oligarchy. In corporate boardrooms, decisions affecting communities, workers, and ecologies are made by small, often interlocked groups of men prioritizing short-term private profit over public and ecological concerns.

The Struggle for Hearts and Minds

Part 2 of this volume focuses on the struggle for hearts and minds: the practices and relations through which fossil capital strives to secure popular consent and to co-opt, disorganize, or marginalize dissenting perspectives. Integral to obstruction, these practices include the reach of corporate power into Indigenous communities, who have suffered the worst environmental and health impacts from carbon extraction as part of ongoing colonization, and whose land claims and collectivist traditions often stand in the way of oil and gas infrastructure. In many cases, however, these communities face the dilemma of participating in fossil capitalism or forgoing badly needed income and jobs (a quandary not unfamiliar to non-Indigenous workers).

In "Fossil Capital's Reach into Civil Society: The Architecture of Climate Change Denialism," Nicolas Graham, Michael Lang, Kevin McCartney, Zoë Yunker, and I map the Canadian network of fossil-capital corporations whose boards interlock with key knowledge-producing civil society organizations, including think tanks, industry associations, business advocacy organizations, universities, and research institutes. We find a pervasive pattern of carbon-sector reach into these domains of civil society, forming a single, connected network that is centred in Alberta yet linked to the corporate elite of central Canada through hegemonic capitalist organizations, including major financial companies. The many threads of communication and collaboration in civil society afforded by interlocking governance boards enable the fossil-capital elite to define, defend, and advance its profit-driven concerns as "common sense," in the "public interest." This structure thus provides the architecture for a "soft" denial regime that acknowledges climate change while protecting the continued flow of profit to fossil-fuel and related companies. What obstructs serious action are corporate interests, expressed in part through the intricate elite network that reaches from fossil-capital boardrooms to civil society.

In "'Our Oil': Extractive Populism in Canadian Social Media," Shane Gunster, Robert Neubauer, John Bermingham, and Alicia Massie explore how the Canadian fossil fuel industry and its proponents are increasingly using social media to mobilize core constituencies of supporters, to attack industry critics, and to position the sector as a national public good. Their study analyzes the Facebook posts of seven groups active in the promotional and advocacy social media infrastructure for the Canadian fossil fuel sector. The rapid growth of extractivist groups on social media marks a shift away from advertising campaigns that address the general public toward targeted mobilization that aims to convert passive industry stakeholders into engaged issue publics. These groups combine conventional pro-capital tropes (such as jobs versus environment and free market fundamentalism) with more innovative discourses to construct a coherent, accessible, appealing, and easily shared set of legitimating narratives and frames. Concurrently, as they circulate the content of more established commentators, extractivist groups create online "echo chambers" that further insulate industry supporters from the wider world. As Ferguson (2018) points out, the proliferation of such echo chambers accentuates the public sphere's fragmentation, impeding the public conversations that are crucial to democracy.

Our next two chapters map the reach of corporate power into the state and the shaping of public policy. In "Episodes in the New Climate Denialism," CMP co-director Shannon Daub, Gwendolyn Blue, Lise Rajewicz, and Zoë Yunker illustrate the contradictory logic of a policy paradigm that acknowledges fossil capital's central role in the climate crisis while denying the need to decarbonize energy systems at a pace commensurate with what we know from climate science. As a hegemonic intervention, new denialism advocates technological and market-based fixes that leave corporate power intact while creating new profit-making opportunities. In the lead-up to the 2015 Paris Agreement, when the world's carbon majors first embraced this perspective, and in the 2016–17 "climate leadership" efforts in Alberta and British Columbia, when industry submissions to advisory panels underlined the overriding need for fossil-capital "competitiveness" in climate leadership, we witness the capture of climate policy by industry and its use in legitimating continued extraction and burning of carbon. The strategic gambit is to win a measure of popular support, or "social license" (Thompson and Boutilier 2011), while neutralizing opposition to pipelines and tar sands expansion. The Trudeau government's 2016 announcement of the Pan-Canadian Framework on Clean Growth and Climate Change, nine days after federal approval of two major pipeline projects, is a third recent episode in the new denialism and reminds us that governments are not simply passive conveyors of corporate power but active participants. The regime of obstruction is, in this sense, a "power bloc" that takes in core positions of economic and political power, with the capitalist class and the state forming a *"partnership between two different, separate forces*, linked to each other by many threads, yet each with their own sphere of concerns" (Miliband 1983, 65).

The following chapter, "'Doing Things Better Together': Industry Capture of Climate Policy in British Columbia," can be read as a companion piece in which Shannon Daub, Chuka Ejeckam, Nicolas Graham, and Zoë Yunker show how corporate reach into key state organizations leads to regulatory capture and institutional corruption. The mechanisms range from the vast funds that fossil capital contributed to the BC Liberal Party (in power from 2001 to 2017), through the thousands of lobbying contacts between fossil capital and BC public officials (averaging fourteen contacts per business day between 2010 and 2016), to the institutional capture of climate leadership as the BC government and the Canadian Association of Petroleum Producers (CAPP) co-organized a secret, parallel process, at CAPP's Calgary offices, in which leaders from oil and gas companies crafted the actual policy, even as official public consultations were underway in British Columbia. These examples are a measure of the chasm between the current regime of obstruction and what most people would recognize as a functioning democracy. Yet Daub and her co-authors rightly insist that, however much corporate power has captured and corrupted political processes, the state remains a terrain of struggle, and the outcome of that struggle is indeterminate.

One might say the same about the Alberta-based research universities that preoccupy Laurie Adkin in "Petro-universities and the Production of Knowledge for the Post-carbon Future." Here again, the regime of obstruction operates through a number of mechanisms, sometimes grouped under the rubric of "corporatization" (see Brownlee, Hurl, and Walby 2018), but does not go unchallenged. Fossil-capital interests have become entrenched, both within state agencies that provide funding for university-based research and within universities themselves. Even state funding of so-called environmental and clean technology initiatives, such as carbon capture and storage, chiefly support (and legitimate) fossil capital, rather than pointing toward a future energy system. In mapping the flows of funding to the Universities of Alberta and Calgary for energy-related research and development, Adkin illuminates another aspect of the allocative power that corporations wield vis-à-vis the state and civil society while demonstrating how the former, through its own funding bodies, underwrites technological improvements that subsidize the ongoing accumulation of fossil capital. Corporate-state largesse extends to research centres and research chairs, many of them endowed by fossil-capital "partners."

Adkin's detailed analysis of corporate involvement in university governance extends the network analysis in chapter 6, completing a picture of multifaceted corporate influence in shaping knowledge and technology. Yet her recounting of the Suzuki affair again points to contested terrain. In April 2018, the University of Alberta's decision to honour acclaimed environmental scientist David Suzuki with a doctorate of science was met by shrill protest from the deans of both the Faculty of Engineering and the School of Business, as well as from astroturf advocacy groups and CAPP, and by open threats from fossil capitalists to cancel future donations to the university. Despite the moral panic, senior administration held fast to their decision, illustrating that it is still possible for universities to define and serve a public interest distinct from the private interests of capital but also that this requires principled leadership.

Much less contestation can be found in rural prairie communities dependent on fossil capital, the subjects of Emily Eaton and Simon Enoch's chapter. "The Oil Industry Is Us: Hegemonic Community Economic Identity in Saskatchewan's Oil Patch" offers ethnographic insights from small towns where oil is part of the everyday fabric of life. Drawing on in-depth interviews with the residents of three such municipalities, as well as on a content analysis of local newspapers, Eaton and Enoch show how fossil corporations have instilled a sense of "psychological identification" as community members embrace the frames and narratives of the petroleum industry on a range of issues. In these instances, hegemony is deeply lodged in identity and community, as the allocative power of corporations to fund local amenities combines with the discursive power of industry-propagated frames. As communities come to see their fate as inextricably linked to industry's fate, they not only turn to oil companies as the authority through which energy issues are understood, but they also rise to the defence of those companies against threats posed by climate-activist outsiders.

Community also figures strongly in Angele Alook, Ian Hussey, and Nicole Hill's "Indigenous Gendered Experiences of Work in an Oil-Dependent, Rural Alberta Community." Focusing on the experiences of Indigenous workers and their families in Wabasca, Alberta, the authors examine how precarious employment in carbon extraction shapes family and community life. Grounding their analysis in a series of "life story" interviews, they explore the contradiction between the Cree vision of *miyo-pimatisiwin*—a holistic understanding of living the good life—and precarious employment within the boom-and-bust cycle. Their research supports Eaton and Enoch's observation that fossil capital gains community support in part by providing the dominant source of employment. However, companies owned by First Nations bands and private businesses owned by Indigenous capitalists also have a stake in the game, often competing with one another for subcontracts from Big Oil. In addition, the division of labour is highly gendered. Oilfield work is male dominated, while women's paid and unpaid care work, even as it strives to maintain the balance integral to *miyo-pimatisiwin*, marginalizes Indigenous women in the labour market. The study uncovers racist stereotypes that are internalized by some Indigenous workers and resisted by others, while also registering concern about the development on reserves of capitalist class relations, which could divide communities against themselves, co-opting them into extralocal relations of ruling. All these elements comprise a complex articulation of corporate power within Indigenous communities struggling to terminate and recover from a colonialism that is still very much intact.

In "Between a Rock and a Hard Place: Canada's Carbon Economy and Indigenous Ambivalence," Clifford Atleo offers a nuanced analysis of settler colonialism and fossil capitalism in Canada, refusing the romantic (and racist) binary that positions Indigenous peoples on the side of "pristine nature." Indigenous struggles for self-determination coexist with capitalism's powerful capacities to invade "every corner of both the earth *and* our imaginations." Settler capitalism was founded on accumulation by dispossession (Coulthard 2014), and as their land was stolen many Indigenous people lost their livelihoods and migrated to urban settings, where land-based sensibilities may weaken. This has led some, including some Indigenous leaders, to internalize the logic of neoliberal capitalism. Within advanced settler colonialism, one version of self-determination now envisages Indigenous peoples as sovereign participants in a capitalist way of life, garnering the benefits of resource extraction within "a despiritualized world understood simply as a business opportunity" (Coburn and Atleo 2016, 190). Unsurprisingly, First Nations bands are often pulled in two directions. As Atleo notes, in the case of the Trans Mountain Pipeline project, some First Nations joined the Treaty Alliance Against Tar Sands Expansion (Meyer 2018), while others chose to sign "mutual benefit agreements" with the project's proponent, Kinder Morgan. The struggle for hearts and minds, ever at hegemony's core, is no less salient among Indigenous peoples than among the non-Indigenous.

The chapters by Atleo and by Alook, Hussey, and Hill highlight the deep settler-colonial legacy that continues to shape the political ecology and economy of carbon extractivism in Canada and that must be addressed and remediated in any just transition to a post-carbon world.

Resistance and Beyond

Although this collection centres on the reality of corporate power, we strive not to reify that power and to consider prospects for the dual shift in power required for energy democracy—toward the decarbonization of energy and the democratization of control. Part 3 takes up these issues.

In "From Clean Growth to Climate Justice," Marc Lee, director of the Climate Justice Project, presents two alternative pathways for climate action. "Clean growth," which has become the mantra of both the federal government and the environmental mainstream, proposes market-based measures, chiefly in the form of carbon pricing, designed to shift the full cost of the damage done by carbon emissions onto those who contribute directly to them, as producers and consumers, thereby creating a negative incentive that will steer the accumulation process toward decarbonization. As a hegemonic project, clean growth parallels financial capital's "digestion" of the climate crisis (see chapter 4). Premised on the fantasy of endless economic growth, this vision of green capitalism frames climate solutions as new business opportunities. But it also ignores the contradiction between economic growth and ecological health, discounts the increasing inequalities that accompany capital accumulation, and underestimates the scale and scope of the energy transitions actually required to reduce Canada's carbon footprint. In contrast to this new, corporate-friendly version of denialism, a "climate justice" framework combines decarbonization with the integration of social justice principles into climate change policy. Lee reviews a range of research findings from the Climate Justice Project, emphasizing how such integration offers a more inclusive and effective approach that seeks to achieve deeper changes in living patterns and economic structure.

Complementing Lee's policy perspective, our final three chapters focus on the counter-power of social movements as protagonists in the struggle for climate justice and energy democracy. Karena Shaw's "Flashpoints of Possibility: What Resistance Reveals About Pathways Toward Energy Transition" focuses on flashpoints along carbon commodity chains—sites at which resistance becomes visible in ways that challenge the legitimacy and power of the fossil fuel industry. It is in this challenge that fossil capital is exposed as a self-interested actor and its influence is problematized. Shaw's reading of one such flashpoint—popular mobilization in 2018 against the Trans Mountain Pipeline Expansion, as refracted through various news outlets—distills both the obstacles and the more promising developments that may prove critical to the future of climate justice. These include, on the one hand, the hegemonic position of fossil capital in political processes and news discourse, as well as the framing of political issues and identities around federal-provincial and interprovincial conflict, and, on the other, the migration of First Nations claims from the margins to the centre of political contention and the evolution of environmentalism beyond single-issue politics. Perhaps most importantly, the flashpoint reveals the struggle "for a collective public imagination" of life beyond fossil capital, an imaginary that needs to be built in tandem with post-fossil alternatives at community, regional, and national scales.

In "Toward a Typology of Fossil Fuel Flashpoints: The Potential for Coalition Building," Fiona MacPhail and Paul Bowles also interrogate the roots and meaning of flashpoints. With the intention of creating an analytical framework that could contribute to the building of successful resistance campaigns, they advance a typology of these episodes of heightened public contention. The typology identifies three axes of contestation that shape flashpoints at distinct junctures along fossil-capital commodity chains: the distributive axis (how are a project's material benefits to be distributed?), the procedural axis (has the approval process been fair?), and the ecological and recognition axis (what are the environmental risks, as well as the risks to non-capitalist economies?). The successful campaign, which ran from 2010 to 2016, to put a stop to the construction Enbridge's Northern Gateway pipeline illustrates how all three axes of contention can be activated synergistically in a broad oppositional coalition. However, because the underlying reasons for contestation may differ greatly from one node in a commodity chain to another, such convergence is not easily achieved. Understanding the nature of contestation at the local level and how different strands of opposition can be braided together in coalitions can strengthen strategies of resistance, thereby contributing to a move toward energy democracy.

As the climate crisis has deepened, campaigns to persuade institutional investors to divest from fossil capital have proliferated on university campuses and elsewhere. In our final chapter, "Fossil Fuel Divestment, Non-reformist Reforms, and Anti-capitalist Strategy," Emilia Belliveau, James Rowe, and Jessica Dempsey put divestment into critical conversation with André Gorz's concept of a non-reformist reform. Whereas traditional efforts at reform are constrained by what is possible within a given system, the struggle for non-reformist reforms is "determined not in terms of what can be, but what should be" (Gorz 1967, 8). For Gorz, non-reformist reforms are steps along the path toward system change: they disturb the capitalist status quo in ways that build popular power. Divestment's apparently reformist orientation has evoked a lukewarm reception from anti-capitalist critics, who view divestment as a co-opted politics that accomplishes no more than a shift in investment portfolios. Intriguingly, interviews with divestment campaigners across Canada reveal a gap between their anti-capitalist commitments and the movement's pragmatic external messaging. The gap may be a productive one, however, strategically designed to reach broad publics through mainstream media that eschew anti-capitalism. To the extent that it opens conversations that challenge the legitimacy and economic viability of big carbon as a leading economic sector, while attracting new activists (on campuses and off) to climate justice, divestment can serve as a non-reformist reform. Divestment's specific targeting of the fossil fuel industry and its climate obstructionism is a crucial step, but only a step, in the transition to energy democracy and climate justice.

Indeed, the various policies and campaigns discussed in these four chapters add up to a set of non-reformist reforms, not a full-blown project of system change. This reflects the political reality of contemporary Canada, within which capital's hegemony is intact, even if carbon-extractive corporations are increasingly under critical scrutiny. Corporate control of the financing and production of energy, along with the legitimation of that control through the modalities of power that we map in this book, poses the greatest obstruction to our dealing effectively with the ecological and economic challenges we face today. Understanding how that power is continually secured and reproduced—the primary remit of this volume—needs to be conjoined with coordinated efforts, within the accumulation process, in civil society and vis-à-vis the state, to "build a politics on the scale necessary to dismantle fossil capital" (Kinder 2016, 24).

The concept of *energy democracy* neatly condenses the combination of energy decarbonization and economic democratization that is so urgently needed. Energy democracy comprises a bundle of sectorally targeted non-reformist reforms that push toward even broader democratization and decolonization of economic, political, and cultural life. In such a transformation, the various modalities of corporate power we map here would give way to popular power and participatory planning in production, environmental stewardship, public communication, and inclusive community development.

Contemporary struggles for energy democracy offer alternatives, but their viability depends largely on the extent to which an effective mass political base can be built. Building such a base will require a clear and thorough understanding of Canada's fossil fuel complex and the regime of obstruction it currently constitutes. The chapters that follow offer intellectual resources for that socio-political construction project, opening onto broader possible transformations. In the face of climate crisis, the struggle for a world beyond fossil capital may be the leading edge of convergent movements to create a socially and ecologically just world beyond capital itself.

Notes

1. On Canada's methane emissions, see Environment and Climate Change Canada (2017, 9). That methane is estimated to have a global warming potential (GWP) eighty-six times that of CO_2 over a 20-year time horizon was established in 2013 by the Fifth Assessment Report of the United Nations Intergovernmental Panel on Climate Change: see IPCC (2013, 714, table 8.7). Crucially, this figure factors in climate–carbon feedback—that is, the effect of changes in climate on the carbon cycle; if that factor is omitted, the estimated GWP of methane drops to eighty-four.

2. *BP Statistical Review of World Energy 2019*, June 2019, https://www.bp.com/content/dam/bp/business-sites/en/global/corporate/pdfs/energy-economics/statistical-review/bp-stats-review-2019-full-report.pdf, 2. The rate of growth in carbon emissions was the largest in seven years.

3. Trudeau was speaking on March 9, 2017, at the CERAWeek Global Energy Award Dinner, in Houston. See the CBC video clip (posted the following morning) at https://www.cbc.ca/news/world/trudeau-no-country-would-find-173-billion-barrels-of-oil-in-the-ground-and-leave-them-there-1.4019321. For his remarks on the opening day of the Paris talks, see "Canada's National Statement at COP 21," November 30, 2015, https://pm.gc.ca/en/news/speeches/2015/11/30/canadas-national-statement-cop21.

4. According to a report released in 2018 by the CCPA, Canada's one hundred most highly paid CEOs earned a record-breaking average of $10.4 million in 2016—an income 209 times greater than that of the average worker (Macdonald 2018, 4).

5. See Bill C-59, "An Act Respecting National Security Matters," June 21, 2019 (Royal Assent), https://www.parl.ca/DocumentViewer/en/42-1/bill/C-59/royal-assent, s. 115 (3) and ss. 146 (1) and (3). The bill is now known as the National Security Act, SC 2019, c. 13. Compare Bill-51 (now the Anti-terrorism Act, 2015, SC 2015, c. 20), https://parl.ca/DocumentViewer/en/41-2/bill/C-51/royal-assent https://laws-lois.justice.gc.ca/PDF/2015_20.pdf, s. 2(f) and ss. 17(1) and (2). Note that the latter two sections of Bill C-51 read "is likely to," which Bill C-59 then changed to "is necessary to."

6. "The Leap Manifesto: A Call for a Canada Based on Caring for the Earth and One Another," Leap Manifesto, accessed August 2, 2018, http://leapmanifesto.org/en/the-leap-manifesto/.

References

Adkin, Laurie E., ed. 2016. *First World Petro-Politics: The Political Ecology and Governance of Alberta*. Toronto: University of Toronto Press.

Barbalet, J. M. 1985. "Power and Resistance." *British Journal of Sociology* 36: 531–48.

Brownlee, Jamie, Chris Hurl, and Kevin Walby. 2018. *Corporatizing Canada: Making Business out of Public Service*. Toronto: Between the Lines.

Burke, Marshall, Felipe González, Patrick Baylis, Sam Heft-Neal, Ceren Baysan, Sanjay Basu, and Solomon Hsiang. 2018. "Higher Temperatures Increase Suicide Rates in the United States and Mexico." *Nature Climate Change* 8 (August): 723–29. https://doi.org/10.1038/s41558-018-0222-x.

Carroll, William K., and Murray Shaw. 2001. "Consolidating a Neoliberal Policy Bloc in Canada, 1976 to 1996." *Canadian Public Policy* 27, no. 2: 195–217.

Carroll, William K., and J. P. Sapinski. 2018. *Organizing the 1%: How Corporate Power Works*. Halifax: Fernwood.

Coburn, Elaine, and Clifford Atleo. 2016. "Not Just Another Social Movement: Indigenous Resistance and Resurgence." In *A World to Win: Contemporary Social Movements and Counter-Hegemony*, edited by William K. Carroll and Kanchan Sakar, 176–94. Winnipeg: ARP Books.

Coulthard, Glen Sean. 2014. *Red Skin, White Masks: Rejecting the Colonial Politics of Recognition*. Minneapolis: University of Minnesota Press.

Crosby, Andrew, and Jeffrey Monaghan. 2018. *Policing Indigenous Movements: Dissent and the Security State*. Halifax: Fernwood.

Environment and Climate Change Canada. 2017. *Strategy on Short-Lived Climate Pollutants—2017*. Ottawa: Ministry of Environment and Climate Change. http://publications.gc.ca/collections/collection_2018/eccc/En4-299-2017-eng.pdf.

Ferguson, Niall. 2018. "Social Networks Are Creating a Global Crisis of Democracy." *Globe and Mail*, January 19, 2018. https://www.theglobeandmail.com/opinion/niall-ferguson-social-networks-and-the-global-crisis-of-democracy/article37665172/.

Fuchs, Doris, and Markus M. L. Lederer. 2007. "The Power of Business." *Business and Politics* 9, no. 3: 1–17.

Gorz, André. 1967. *Strategy for Labor: A Radical Proposal*. Translated by Martin A. Nicolaus and Victoria Ortiz. Boston: Beacon Press.

Gramsci, Antonio. 1971. *Selections from the Prison Notebooks*. New York: International Publishers.

Heede, Richard. 2013. "Tracing Anthropogenic Carbon Dioxide and Methane Emissions to Fossil Fuel and Cement Producers, 1854–2010." *Climate Change* 122, nos. 1–2: 229–41.

Huber, Matthew T. 2013. *Lifeblood: Oil, Freedom, and the Forces of Capital.* Minneapolis: University of Minnesota Press.

Hughes, J. David. 2018. *Canada's Energy Outlook: Current Realities and Implications for a Carbon-Constrained Future.* Vancouver: Canadian Centre for Policy Alternatives, BC Office. https://www.corporatemapping.ca/energy-outlook/.

Hussey, Ian. 2017. "Five Things to Know About Alberta's Oil Sands Emissions Cap." *Parkland Blog*, Parkland Institute. February 22, 2017. https://www.parklandinstitute. ca/five_things_to_know_about_albertas_oil_sands_emissions_cap.

IPCC (Intergovernmental Panel on Climate Change). 2013. *Climate Change 2013: The Physical Science Basis. Contribution of Working Group I to the Fifth Assessment Report of the Intergovernmental Panel on Climate Change.* Edited by Thomas F. Stocker, Dahe Qin, Gian-Kasper Plattner, Melinda M. B. Tignor, Simon K. Allen, Judith Boschung, Alexander Nauels, Yu Xia, Vincent Bex, and Pauline M. Midgley. Cambridge: Cambridge University Press. https://www.ipcc. ch/report/ar5/wg1/.

Janssens-Maenhout, G., M. Crippa, D. Guizzardi, M. Muntean, E. Schaaf, J. G. J. Olivier, J. A. H. W. Peters, and K. M. Schure. 2017. *Fossil CO2 and GHG Emissions of All World Countries.* Luxembourg: Publications Office of the European Union. https://doi.org/10.2760/709792.

Kinder, Jordan. 2016. "The Coming Transition: Fossil Capital and Our Energy Future." *Socialism and Democracy* 30, no. 2: 8–27.

Linnitt, Carol. 2015. "LEAKED: Internal RCMP Document Names 'Violent Anti-petroleum Extremists' Threat to Government and Industry." *The Narwhal*, February 17, 2015. https://thenarwhal.ca/leaked-internal-rcmp-document-names-anti-petroleum-extremists-threat-government-industry.

Macdonald, David. 2018. *Climbing Up and Kicking Down: Executive Pay in Canada.* Ottawa: Canadian Centre for Policy Alternatives. https://www.policyalternatives. ca/publications/reports/climbing-and-kicking-down.

McCarthy, Shawn. 2017. "National Energy Board Needs Major Overhaul, Panel Says." *Globe and Mail*, May 15, 2017. https://beta.theglobeandmail.com/ report-on-business/industry-news/energy-and-resources/dismantle-neb-create-bodies-for-regulation-growth-panel/article34989230/?ref=http://www. theglobeandmail.com&.

McSheffrey, Elizabeth. 2018. "Environment Canada Urged to Release Its Probe of Fossil Fuel Subsidies." *National Observer*, June 19, 2018. https://www. nationalobserver.com/2018/06/19/news/environment-canada-urged-release-its-probe-fossil-fuel-subsidies.

Malm, Andreas. 2016. *Fossil Capital: The Rise of Steam Power and the Roots of Global Warming.* London: Verso.

Meyer, Carl. 2018. "Chiefs from 133 First Nations Join Fight Against Kinder Morgan Pipeline and Oilsands Expansion." *National Observer*, May 2, 2018. https://www.nationalobserver.com/2018/05/02/news/chiefs-133-first-nations-join-fight-against-kinder-morgan-pipeline-and-oilsands.

Miliband, Ralph. 1983. "State Power and Class Interests." *New Left Review* 138 (March–April): 57–68.

Miller, Nick. 2018. "Europe Burns as Climate Change Fuels 'Forest Fire Danger Extremes.'" *Sydney Morning Herald*, July 25, 2018. https://www.smh.com.au/world/europe/europe-burns-as-climate-change-fuels-forest-fire-danger-extremes-20180725-p4zteh.html.

Mitchell, Timothy. 2011. *Carbon Democracy: Political Power in the Age of Oil.* London: Verso.

Moore, Jason W. 2015. *Capitalism in the Web of Life: Ecology and the Accumulation of Capital.* London: Verso.

Pineault, Éric. 2018. "The Capitalist Pressure to Extract: The Ecological and Political Economy of Extreme Oil in Canada." *Studies in Political Economy* 99, no. 2: 130–50. https://doi.org/10.1080/07078552.2018.1492063.

Public Safety Canada. 2014. *Action Plan for Critical Infrastructure, 2014–2017.* Ottawa: Government of Canada.

Rabson, Mia. 2018. "Citing Competitiveness Pressures, Feds Ease Carbon Tax Thresholds." *National Observer*, August 1, 2018. https://www.nationalobserver.com/2018/08/01/news/citing-competitiveness-pressures-feds-ease-carbon-tax-thresholds.

Shabecoff, Philip. 1988. "Global Warming Has Begun, Expert Tells Senate." *New York Times*, June 24, 1988. https://www.nytimes.com/1988/06/24/us/global-warming-has-begun-expert-tells-senate.html.

Schnaiberg, Allan. 1980. *The Environment: From Surplus to Scarcity.* New York: Oxford University Press.

Steffen, Will, Johan Rockström, Katherine Richardson, Timothy M. Lenton, Carl Folke, Diana Liverman, Colin P. Summerhayes, Anthony D. Barnosky, Sarah E. Cornell, Michel Crucifix, Jonathan F. Donges, Ingo Fetzer, Steven J. Lade, Marten Scheffer, Ricarda Winkelmann, and Hans Joachim Schellnhuber. 2018. "Trajectories of the Earth System in the Anthropocene." *Proceedings of the National Academy of Sciences of the United States of America* 115, no. 33: 8252–59. www.pnas.org/cgi/doi/10.1073/pnas.1810141115.

Taber, Jane. 2006. "PM Brands Canada an 'Energy Superpower.'" *Globe and Mail*, July 15, 2006. https://www.theglobeandmail.com/news/national/pm-brands-canada-an-energy-superpower/article18167474/.

Thomson, Ian, and Robert G. Boutilier. 2011. "Social License to Operate." In *SME Mining Engineering Handbook*, 3rd ed., edited by Peter Darling, 1:1779–96. Littleton, CO: Society for Mining, Metallurgy, and Exploration.

United Nations Framework Convention on Climate Change. 2007. *Climate Change: Impacts, Vulnerabilities and Adaptation in Developing Countries*. Bonn: Climate Change Secretariat.

Useem, Michael. 1984. *The Inner Circle: Large Corporations and the Rise of Business Political Activity in the U.S. and U.K.* New York: Oxford University Press.

Vacca, Giuseppe. 1982. "Intellectuals and the Marxist Theory of the State." In *Approaches to Gramsci*, edited by Anne Showstack Sassoon, 37–69. London: Writers and Readers.

Williams, Michelle. 2018. "Energy, Labour and Democracy in South Africa." In *The Climate Crisis: South African and Global Democratic Eco-socialist Alternatives*, edited by Vishwas Satgar, 231–51. Johannesburg: Wits University Press.

Part I

The Organization of Fossil Capital

1   Boom, Bust, and Consolidation

Corporate Restructuring in the Alberta Oil Sands

Ian Hussey, Éric Pineault, Emma Jackson, and Susan Cake

The Alberta oil sands tend to evoke images of sprawling surface mines worked by giant rope-and-pulley shovels and larger-than-life trucks, extracting and transporting a tarlike substance to immense industrial processing facilities. The oil sands may also conjure up images of tailings ponds and mountains of caustic sand—the by-products of bitumen extraction—and of billowing smokestacks that send greenhouse gases rising into the atmosphere, along with visions of pipelines and trains snaking their way south, east, and west to refining hubs or to ports elsewhere on the continent. Underlying these images, however, is another, more abstract one: that of a massive web of economic power, concentrated in Alberta but linked to policy makers in Ottawa and to central Canadian elites via Bay Street finance. This hegemonic complex, an intricate network of both public and private power, has had an enormous impact on Canadian politics, economics, and society, particularly over the past two decades. It has been able to exert a defining influence in areas as diverse as labour regulations and employment, fiscal policy, interprovincial commerce and international trade, climate and environmental management (including the protection of water resources), funding for scientific research, and relations of the colonial state with Indigenous nations.

This chapter was first published as a Corporate Mapping Project report (Edmonton: Parkland Institute; Vancouver: Canadian Centre for Policy Alternatives, BC Office, 2018). It is reprinted here, in somewhat revised form, by permission of the publishers.

The early years of the twenty-first century were dominated by concerns that the world's supply of oil was running out, which contributed to an upward spiral in oil prices. Over the course of a ten-year commodity boom—prices were high from 2004 to 2014—the oil sands grew into an ever more dominant economic force capable of nourishing and sustaining the hegemonic power of the fossil fuel industry. Then, in the autumn of 2014, oil prices crashed, with a barrel of West Texas Intermediate (WTI) losing nearly half its value in the space of only four months.[1] Yet the key corporations that make up this hegemonic complex managed to emerge from the crisis relatively intact, with the oil sands industry ultimately retaining its status as a decisive economic and political force.

The power of the oil sands industry is grounded in the activities of a surprisingly small number of firms: five extractive corporations dominate bitumen production in Canada. Together with two major pipeline companies, these corporations form the core of this hegemonic complex.[2] Their strategies of capitalist accumulation are embodied in the fixed capital mentioned above—in the equipment, physical structures, and other tangible property bound up in the flow of bitumen from pit to refinery—as well as in the labour and energy required to mobilize these assets. The accumulation of capital has sustained the hegemonic power of the oil sands as an economic and political force, and this power has in turn been exercised to further the accumulation strategies of the major corporate players in the industry. The "Big Five" are Suncor Energy, Canadian Natural Resources Limited (CNRL), Cenovus Energy, Imperial Oil, and Husky Energy.[3]

Of course, the oil sands industry is populated by thousands of businesses, of all sizes. In 2011, at the height of the oil sands boom, the extractive portion of the Canadian oil and gas sector comprised 7,051 firms that actually employed staff (counting employee-less shell firms the number goes up to 14,415). Of these firms, 6,537 (93 percent) were small businesses with fewer than fifty employees. Of the remaining 514 firms, 485 were medium-sized businesses with 50 to 499 employees, while only 29 were large corporations with 500 employees or more. Most of these firms (including roughly two-thirds of the small ones) operated in the area of "services to oil and gas extraction," a category that accounted for 62 percent of the total number of firms with employees. Conventional oil and gas extractors made up another 25 percent of the total number, while 10 percent were oil and gas contract drillers. At that time, firms active in "non-conventional oil extraction" accounted for fewer than 1 percent of the total.[4] Yet it is the investment decisions made by this handful of firms—firms engaged in extracting hydrocarbons from unconventional sources such as oil sands and in exploring for new reserves and developing ways to increase extractive capacity—that determine the overall growth trajectory of the industry.

The accumulation strategies of the Big Five must be examined in the context of the commodity cycles that mark the development of extractive capital. Capitalist development is not a linear and progressive process. Accumulation is, by its very nature, cyclical, and commodity-producing industries are subject to some of the wildest economic gyrations. Price volatility is a hallmark of commodity-producing sectors, all the more so given the existence of vast and deeply rooted financial markets where shipments of basic commodities are bought and sold and options on future transactions traded. The price dynamics of commodity extraction and circulation drive an investment cycle that is prone to immense overshoots, which can have dire economic consequences as the value of fixed capital is destroyed during the inevitable downturns. These cyclical dynamics lie behind the recent development of the Canadian oil sands, and an appreciation of their influence is crucial to the analysis presented in this chapter.

We begin by examining the Big Five's key assets—both financial and organizational—with a view to understanding the nature of their oligopolistic power. The Big Five have, in particular, been developing and implementing their accumulation strategies in an era of "extreme oil," and we go on to outline the industrial, financial, and ecological relations in which bitumen as a commodity is enmeshed. We then turn to the cyclical dynamics that undergird the Big Five's accumulation strategies, focusing on the three phases of the most recent commodity cycle—boom (2004–14), bust (2014–16), and restructuring and consolidation (from 2015 onward). This analysis enables us to offer certain projections about the future direction of the extreme oil industry in a world now gripped by climate change.

Mapping the Oligopolistic Core of the Oil Sands Industry

In the period from 1999 to 2016, bitumen's share of overall oil production in Canada grew by 419 percent, with bitumen (refined and unrefined) accounting in 2016 for roughly 63 percent of the oil produced in the country (Hughes 2018, 55, figure 50)—a figure that had risen to 64 percent by the following year.[5] In 2017, Canada's overall oil production averaged 4.2 million barrels per day (bbl/d), and bitumen accounted for nearly 2.7 million of those barrels.[6] The Big Five alone had the potential to produce even more than that amount: their combined capacity for bitumen production stood at 2.86 million bbl/d in 2017 (see table 1.1). This meant that they controlled 79.4 percent of Canada's total potential capacity for bitumen production, which stood at 3.6 million bbl/d in 2017.[7] Beyond control over supply, however, their production capacity also gave them control over an immense amount of wealth.

Table 1.1. The Big Five's key economic variables, 2017

	Assets *Market capitalization* (TSX ranking)	Total revenue *Net income*[a]	Number of employees	Bitumen production capacity (bbl/d)
Suncor	$89,494,000,000 *$84,375,452,708* (4)	$32,176,000,000 *$4,458,000,000*	12,381	1,175,372 (including 54% stake in Syncrude)[b]
CNRL	$73,867,000,000 *$55,044,350,036* (9)	$17,669,000,000 *$4,640,000,000*	9,973	655,500 (including 70% stake in Athabasca Oil Sands Project)
Imperial	$41,601,000,000 *$34,926,986,855* (18)	$29,125,000,000 *$490,000,000*	5,400	501,750 (including 25% stake in Syncrude)
Husky	$32,927,000,000 *$19,615,752,388* (34)	$18,946,000,000 *$786,000,000*	5,152	90,000
Cenovus	$40,933,000,000 *$16,808,580,856* (40)	$17,314,000,000 *$3,366,000,000*	2,882	440,800

Sources: For assets and net income, FP Infomart; for revenue, data available from Morningstar, Inc.; for market capitalization and ranking, Toronto Stock Exchange (TSX), "Quoted Market Value," May 31, 2018; for number of employees and production capacity, Excel data underlying JWN Energy's *Oilweek 2018 Top 100: An Uneven Recovery* report (prepared by KPMG), June 2018.

[a] *Total revenue* refers to total earnings in a given reporting period, prior to the deduction of any expenses. *Net income* is the amount remaining once all expenses (including the cost of goods sold) have been deducted.

[b] Early in 2018, Suncor acquired Mocal Energy's 5 percent share in Syncrude, bringing Suncor's total Syncrude stake to 58.74 percent (Canadian Press 2018).

In 2017, the Big Five had an aggregate revenue of over $115.2 billion (see table 1.1). Their net income totalled more than $13.7 billion, and the assets they owned were worth in excess of $278.8 billion. (By way of comparison, Alberta's annual gross domestic product is about $325 billion.) As of May 31, 2018, the Big Five represented 7 percent of the total Quoted Market Value of the Toronto Stock Exchange (TSX), with Suncor, by far the largest of the Big Five, ranking fourth among all the companies listed on the TSX. Its Quoted Market Value was $84 billion, such that Suncor alone represented 3 percent of the TSX total. In 2017, the Big Five's aggregate gross profit—a measure of their overall spending capacity—stood at nearly $47 billion. In contrast, the Government of Alberta's total income for 2017 was about $45 billion. The Big Five thus collectively mustered as much spending capacity as the province from which they derive the vast majority of their profits.

In addition to their strategic control of extractive capacity, the Big Five also own a significant proportion of the extractable reserves of oil in Canada (see table 1.2). Bitumen deposits represent 97.4 percent of Canada's remaining extractable oil reserves (Hughes 2018, 63, figure 57). The Big Five are thus positioned to dominate the future development of Canada's oil sector. In a very real sense, they *are* the oil sands.

Table 1.2. The Big Five's proved reserves, 2017 and 2018

	2017 BOE	2018 BOE	2017 oil (bbl)	2018 oil (bbl)	2017 gas (MMcf)	2018 gas (MMcf)
Suncor	4,720,500,000	4,633,000,000	4,717,000,000	4,633,000,000	21,000	0
CNRL	8,660,666,667	9,678500,000	7,539,000,000	8,579,000,000	6,730,000	6,597,000
Imperial	4,196,166,667	4,101,166,667	4,111,000,000	4,008,000,000	511,000	559,000
Husky	1,169,783,333	1,315,883,333	974,100,000	1,101,200,000	1,174,100	1,288,100
Cenovus	5,232,666,667	5,167,166,667	4,881,000,000	4,915,000,000	2,110,000	1,513,000

Source: Daily Oil Bulletin, *Top Operators 2018: Two Steps Forward, One Step Back*, 13.

Note: BOE = barrels of oil equivalent; bbl = barrels; MMcf = million cubic feet. A "proved" reserve is one that is considered to be reliably recoverable under current economic and political conditions.

In terms of their ownership of assets, the Big Five are both vertically and horizontally integrated within the fossil fuel industry, and therein lies the basis of their oligopolistic power. Three of the Big Five—Suncor, Imperial, and Husky—are active from pit to pump: extracting bitumen (upstream), upgrading and refining the bitumen, shipping various grades of petroleum products through commercial circuits across North America (midstream), and finally selling directly to consumers and businesses through downstream assets such as branded gas stations (Petro-Canada, Esso, and Husky, respectively). Their vertical integration is thus complete. Although Cenovus and CNRL do not own any downstream assets, they do have significant midstream assets (see table 1.3).

All five firms are horizontally integrated as well, their activities spread across the full spectrum of the fossil fuel sector. In addition to conventional oil and gas extraction, the Big Five are all active in the recovery of "unconventional" fossil fuels, including not only bitumen but also wet natural gas from the Montney Formation (located in northwestern Alberta and northeastern British Columbia).[8] Most of the Big Five are also involved in deepwater oil and/or gas extraction, and Suncor has owned wind farms since 2002. All five firms are multinationals with subsidiaries operating in Africa, Europe, and Asia, but, more importantly, all five have significant midstream assets, such as refineries and storage facilities, in the United States.

This complex integration gives these large corporations strategic and operational flexibility: they can use their own products as inputs, they can shift activity from one component of the fossil fuel sector to another according to market conditions, and, through internal costing procedures, they can compensate for losses in one of their business operations with gains in another. This strategy was important during the oil price downturn from 2014 to 2016, where losses in the upstream segment of the integrated producers were offset by strong gains in midstream and downstream segments. Finally, because they are multinationals, and in particular because a significant amount of their activities span the Canada-US border, they also adjust their internal costing in response to foreign exchange and commodity-product spreads in order to mitigate the impact of the price discount for relatively low-quality Canadian crude. In short, they are able to minimize their fiscal exposure.

While integration is critical to the economic power of the Big Five, it is just one aspect of the corporate power at their command. As members of an oligopolistic core, they can exercise their economic power outward, effectively exerting control over the myriad of small and medium-sized service firms that depend on their activities. The Big Five can also combine forces, collaborating on research and technology development and forming partnerships for large-scale projects, as well as lobbying jointly with government regulators and public officials—thus transforming economic power into political power.

Table 1.3. The Big Five's sectoral integration, 2017

Ownership[a]	Midstream operations / assets	Downstream operations / assets	Foreign operations / assets	Operations / reserves in sectors other than oil sands
Suncor				
Shares principally held by various North American investors	Refining, upgrading	Petro-Canada	Offshore Norway, offshore UK, Libya, and Syria;[b] refinery in Colorado (US), with pipeline link to storage facilities in Wyoming	Natural gas, conventional oil, ethanol, wind farms
CNRL				
Shares principally held by various North American investors; 9% Royal Dutch Shell (the Netherlands)	Refining, upgrading	No	Offshore UK, offshore Côte d'Ivoire, offshore South Africa	Natural gas, conventional oil
Imperial				
Subsidiary of ExxonMobil (US)	Refining, upgrading	Esso	Parent firm has foreign assets	Natural gas, conventional oil, asphalt
Husky				
Majority of shares (70%) owned by Li Ka-Shing (Hong Kong)	Refining, upgrading	Husky	Offshore China, offshore Indonesia; Lima Refinery (full owner) and Toledo Refinery (50% stake), both in Ohio (US)[c]	Asphalt, natural gas, ethanol
Cenovus				
Shares principally held by various North American investors; 25% ConocoPhillips (US)	Refining, upgrading	No	50% stake in Wood River Refinery (Illinois) and in Borger Refinery (Texas) (US)	Natural gas, conventional oil

[a] Information about ownership is taken from Hulshof et al. (2017).

[b] In December 2011, Suncor suspended its Syrian operations indefinitely. Its operations in Libya were suspended in June 2011 owing to the political turmoil that culminated in the October assassination of Muammar Gaddafi. Operations subsequently resumed but have remained limited.

[c] Late in 2017, Husky acquired a third US refinery—the Superior Refinery, in Wisconsin. The following April, a major fire broke out at the refinery, and Husky is now in the process of rebuilding.

The Economic Base for Capital Accumulation: Gross Profit

The capacity of these corporations to expand their power can be analyzed using two variables—gross profit and capital expenditure (capex)—that together shape the contours of their accumulation strategies. Gross profit is a measure of a corporation's current economic power, and it is the foundation of capital accumulation. It is through gross profit that corporations not only cover their routine expenses but also finance capital expenditures—that is, long-term investments, whether they involve the maintenance or upgrading of existing assets or the acquisition of new ones. The nature of these capital expenditures is the principal signal of the accumulation strategy that a corporation is presently pursuing. In what follows, we examine the first variable, gross profit, before going on, in a subsequent section, to consider capex.

Gross profit is the revenue that remains to a company after direct costs—that is, the cost of goods sold—have been deducted. These are costs, whether of labour, materials, or energy, that can be traced directly to the production and sale of a specific item, such as a barrel of oil. Because these costs are directly linked to production, they will vary with the amount of output. In 2017, the total revenue of the Big Five stood at a little over $115.2 billion (see table 1.4, below), and, overall, direct costs consumed 59.5 percent of this revenue, leaving an aggregate gross profit of $46.7 billion, almost half of which was captured by Suncor. Although, on average, 40.5 percent of the revenue collected by the Big Five was gross profit, this average hides an important disparity. At the top end, Suncor's gross profit, which stood at roughly $21 billion, represented 65.4 percent of its revenue, while, at the other extreme, a mere 17.5 percent of Imperial's revenue ended up as gross profit. Yet, even at this low end, Imperial's gross profit was upwards of $5 billion in 2017.[9]

It is out of gross profit that corporations then cover their indirect costs, or overhead—that is, what the company must spend simply in order to run its business. In contrast to direct costs, which vary with production output, indirect costs tend to be relatively stable, or fixed. They include routine expenses—such as rent and utilities, office equipment and supplies, and the salaries paid to administrative staff—that cannot be associated directly with the manufacture and sale of a specific product. In the case of the Big Five, indirect costs also include expenses necessary to sustain their oligopolistic power within the industry—in particular, the cost of maintaining large and complex corporate bureaucracies responsible for activities such as information gathering, financial strategizing, research and development, company advertising and public relations, and lobbying. Overhead thus covers the costs of both vertical and horizontal integration: it represents the costs associated with maintaining the full depth and breadth of a corporation's operations. In 2017, overhead expenses amounted to $13 billion, or roughly 12 percent of the Big Five's aggregate revenue, $10 billion of which was spent by Suncor alone. Overall, the ratio of overhead to direct costs for the Big Five was 20 percent in 2017, which means that for every dollar spent on direct costs, 20 cents were spent on overhead. But again, this aggregate figure hides a wide disparity, in this case between Suncor, whose ratio is 92 percent, and Cenovus, whose ratio is 3 percent.

It is also out of gross profit that corporations cover financial expenses such as interest on debt, as well as the repayment of loan principal. Debt represents assets that have already been acquired. When the asset in question is a tangible, or material, one (such as a major piece of equipment), which will eventually wear down and need to be upgraded or replaced, the cost of acquiring it is typically spread out its anticipated lifetime of use and, for purposes of accounting, itemized as depreciation. Similarly, loans, as well as expenses related to the acquisition of intangible assets (such as copyrights, trademarks, and other forms of intellectual property), are amortized—that is, paid off in installments.[10] These costs are likewise deducted from gross profit.

Table 1.4 presents a breakdown of these expenses for each of the Big Five in 2017. Suncor appears as an outlier, having the highest revenue, the lowest direct costs by far, and thus the largest gross profit. This gross profit sustains a strikingly high level of overhead (which reflects a very top-heavy corporate structure), significant depreciation and amortization expenses, and a high net income (half of which was transferred to shareholders in the form of dividends in 2017). Imperial offers a clear contrast to Suncor, with very high direct costs and a correspondingly modest gross profit, very low overhead and relatively minor depreciation and amortization expenses, and a negligible net income.

Table 1.4. The Big Five's gross profit, major expenses, and net income relative to total revenue, 2017

	Total revenue (millions)	Direct costs	Gross profit	Over-head	Depreciation and amortization	Net income
Suncor	$32,176	34.56%	65.44%	31.96%	17.41%	13.86%
CNRL	$17,669	53.94%	46.06%	2.56%	29.35%	13.57%
Imperial	$29,125	82.49%	17.51%	3.07%	7.46%	1.68%
Husky	$18,946	67.87%	32.13%	7.86%	15.21%	3.97%
Cenovus	$17,314	63.71%	36.29%	1.78%	11.72%	19.44%
Total ($) or average (%)	$115,230	59.50%	40.50%	11.65%	15.51%	9.95%

Source: Based on data from Morningstar, Inc.

Finally, gross profit is used to cover taxes and royalty expenses. In 2017, the Big Five paid roughly $1.6 billion in income taxes and another $3.1 billion in royalties to various governments (both in Canada and abroad), for a total of $4.7 billion. After all these expenses have been paid, what remains is net income, otherwise known as the bottom line. A portion of net income is then distributed to shareholders in the form of dividends, as well as through offers of share buybacks—an approach that has several advantages, notably the reduction of the number of shares outstanding, which increases the value of those shares. Whereas taxes and royalties represent a transfer of economic power to the state, dividends and buybacks transform industrial capital into financial capital available to investors and thus represent a shift of economic power from the extractive sector to the financial sector. In 2017, the Big Five returned approximately $4.2 billion to their shareholders in the form of dividends. (Figures for each of the five are provided in table 1.6, below.) They spent about another $2.0 billion of their income buying back shares from the market, meaning that the total transfer of value to shareholders in 2017 approached $6.2 billion.

Once funds have been disbursed to shareholders, the remaining portion of net income is held by a company as "retained earnings"—uncommitted capital that can be invested in the accumulation of assets, both tangible and intangible. For the Big Five, retained earnings amounted to $7.3 billion in 2017. These earnings can be used to expand extractive capacity and thus increase production output, which serves to build economic power, as well as to move into new areas of operation, thereby also enhancing strategic flexibility.

To summarize, in terms of capital accumulation, the higher the gross profit of these corporations, the larger the possible scale of their extractive capacity and the broader the possible scope of their business operations (the two economic foundations of the Big Five's corporate power). This snapshot of the Big Five's deployment of gross profit must, however, be complemented by an in-depth analysis of their accumulation strategies over the most recent commodity cycle. As an introduction to the analysis of this commodity cycle, we will begin by examining the nature of the commodities involved—bitumen and its upgraded derivatives—as examples of extreme oil.

The Political Economy of Extreme Oil

Over the past decade or so, concerns about "peak oil"—fears that the supply of oil is running out—have largely waned. As the climate crisis deepens, however, a world dependent on fossil fuels has been confronted with a new problem: oil that can be extracted from known reserves but cannot subsequently be burned. Extractive capitalists have sharpened their knowledge of the location, scope, and nature of these reserves and of possible ways to unlock their value. Yet these reserves consist mainly of unconventional sources of hydrocarbons, notably oil sands and oil shale. Because recovering oil from these sources is far more energy intensive than conventional oil extraction (and hence more expensive), their use increases emissions of greenhouse gases, thereby accelerating climate change. If the Paris Agreement's 2°C limit to global warming is to be met, some 60 percent to 80 percent of global fossil fuel reserves must therefore remain underground, thereby becoming stranded assets (see Muttitt 2016; Thieroff et al. 2017; see also Hussey and Janzen 2018; Lee 2017).

Reliance on "extreme" oil generates a number of additional problems, foremost among them the need for new, and potentially conflict-ridden, industrial development. Accessing unconventional sources of hydrocarbons entails opening up hitherto undisturbed territories to oil extraction and generally requires the use of very invasive forms of extraction. This puts new pressure on ecosystems and communities and provokes new dispossessions and new environmental conflicts. In addition, the knowledge that the supply of oil is not in jeopardy—that vast reserves of unconventional forms of oil exist—creates a cultural and sociopolitical inertia in industrial societies that rely heavily on hydrocarbon combustion, dampening the collective will for transition away from fossil fuels. Finally, in the era of extreme oil, climate change is no longer a distant possibility but a contemporary fact, one that is creating extreme weather and related natural events, including catastrophic fires and unpredictable floods, which come with enormous social and economic costs.

In economic terms, the oil we burn and the plastic we eventually dispose of or recycle have a specifically capitalist use value. The production of fossils fuels is thus managed so as to maintain a rhythm of hydrocarbon consumption (a burn rate) that serves to enhance the value of extractive capital. Maintaining an optimal flow of production depends not only on the state of world markets for oil, where demand and supply are reflexively managed, but also on the development of infrastructure to support the extractive chain, from frontier to corridor to export gateway. The process whereby this capital is valorized is driven by an imperative of accumulation that attempts to anticipate, manage, and plan the acceleration of the extractive flow. Management and planning are necessary in a context in which the amount of fixed capital is large and the cycle of rotation long, such that investments are slow to yield a return. The valorization process thus generates an elongated temporal frame that both conditions demand and locks in the metabolic future of advanced capitalist societies presently in a state of carbon dependency.

Where extraction assumes a massive form, as it does in western Canada, space is likewise configured by the needs of the extractive commodity chain. The spatial and temporal matrix within which extractive industries operate further engenders an ensemble of economic linkages, in the form of related industries, in a process whereby extractive capital draws other sectors of the economy into its expanding circle of influence. Through these linkages—as well as through the development of a working class harnessed to, and hence allied with, fossil capital—extractivism imprints its logic on state priorities and on an economy vulnerable to reprimarization. Finance capital is also tied into this logic: its own accumulation process comes to depend on the expansion of extractive capital, at the same time that it advances this ongoing development. In a financial sector dominated by institutional investors, entrusted with managing funds on behalf of others, and by state-sponsored savings plans, the logic of extractivism effectively mobilizes a broad segment of society in support of extractive capital accumulation, as pensions and savings become dependent on profits generated by the exploitation of extreme oil (see Pineault 2018).

It is within an era shaped by the political economy of extreme oil that the Big Five's accumulation strategies unfold. With this context in mind, let us now turn to a consideration of the most recent commodity cycle, which began with a decade-long boom in the fossil fuel industry.

The Commodity Cycle

The second major factor in our analysis of the Big Five's accumulation strategies is capital expenditure, or capex. A capital expenditure is not an operating expense but rather an investment in the survival and long-term growth of a business. Although such expenditures typically involve the acquisition of tangible assets, they extend to the purchase of intangible assets (such as a licence or copyright) or to funding research and development. These investments may aim to strengthen a company's core business, by augmenting or improving its existing assets, but they may also represent an entry into new areas of operation (as when a firm engaged in bitumen extraction expands into fracking for natural gas). As the most recent commodity cycle moved from boom to bust to recovery, the Big Five adjusted their accumulation strategies accordingly, and these shifts are reflected in their capex.

From Boom to Bust

Early in 2004, oil prices, which had hovered around US$30 per barrel for many years, began a steady climb, with the price of a barrel of WTI reaching record highs of more than US$130 in June and July 2008. The boom lasted almost unbroken until the autumn of 2014, and as it progressed, the aggregate productive capacity of the Big Five surged. In 2005, the Big Five's cumulative capacity for the production of bitumen was 1 million bbl/d; by 2009, it stood at about 1.5 million bbl/d, and, by 2015, it had risen to 2.5 million bbl/d.[11] As table 1.5 illustrates, this expansion of the extractive capacity of the oil sands was spurred by substantial capital expenditures. Our analysis begins in 2009 because that was year in which Cenovus came to exist, when the Encana Corporation split into an oil company (Cenovus) and a natural gas company (Encana).

Table 1.5. The Big Five's capital expenditures, 2009–17 (in millions $)

	2009	2010	2011	2012	2013	2014	2015	2016	2017	Total
Suncor	4,246	5,833	6,850	6,959	6,777	6,961	6,667	6,582	6,551	57,426
CNRL	2,985	5,335	6,201	6,104	7,067	11,398	4,468	3,797	4,698	52,053
Imperial	2,285	3,856	3,919	5,478	6,297	5,290	2,994	1,073	993	32,185
Husky	2,762	3,852	4,800	4,701	5,028	5,023	3,005	1,705	2,220	33,096
Cenovus	1,984	2,208	2,792	3,449	3,269	3,058	1,714	1,034	1,670	21,178
Annual total	14,262	21,084	24,562	26,691	28,438	31,730	18,848	14,191	16,132	195,938

Source: Data from Morningstar, Inc. Figures are in nominal dollars.

Over the period from 2009 to 2014, the aggregate capex of the Big Five totalled nearly $146.8 billion, the figure rising to a whopping $195.9 billion by 2017. Suncor and CNRL are the largest producers of bitumen among the Big Five (see table 1.1), and, unsurprisingly, they consistently outspent the others during the period from 2009 to 2017. Newcomer Cenovus had the lowest capex of the five firms, spending roughly $11 billion less over these nine years than the firm with the second-lowest capex, Imperial Oil.

Over the same period, the Big Five paid substantial dividends to their shareholders, as table 1.6 shows. In the aggregate, the Big Five disbursed $31.76 billion in dividends over the nine years, with one-third of this total coming from Suncor. Suncor's annual dividend total increased substantially every year, even during the downturn. The firm's consistently large capex throughout this period clearly paid off for shareholders. Similarly, CNRL's substantial capex over the nine years resulted in dividend payments in 2017 that were more than 500 percent higher than those in 2009. The firm's dividends grew for the first seven of the nine years and then lost about 40 percent of their value in 2016, before bouncing back in 2017 to match the 2015 total.

Imperial had the smallest nine-year total, although the company's dividend payments rose each year. For a corporation its size, Husky paid out relatively high dividends until 2016 and 2017, when its dividend payments almost dried up completely—although Husky still had the second-highest nine-year total of the Big Five. Cenovus's annual dividend payments increased steadily over the first six years but declined significantly in 2015 and then dropped off quite sharply in 2016. The company's dividend payments bounced back a bit in 2017, but the total was still less than half of what it was in 2015.

Table 1.6. The Big Five's dividends paid to shareholders, 2009–17 (in millions $)

	2009	2010	2011	2012	2013	2014	2015	2016	2017	Total
Suncor	401	611	664	756	1,095	1,490	1,648	1,877	2,124	10,666
CNRL	225	302	378	444	523	955	1,251	758	1,252	6,088
Imperial	341	356	373	398	407	441	449	492	524	3,781
Husky	1,020	1,020	495	574	1,184	1,182	1,203	27	34	6,739
Cenovus	158	601	603	665	732	805	528	166	225	4,483
Annual total	2,145	2,890	2,513	2,837	3,941	4,873	5,079	3,320	4,159	31,757

Source: Data from Morningstar, Inc. Figures are in nominal dollars.

In short, during the years of the boom, the Big Five flourished financially and were able to focus on expanding their oil sands operations. The growth in production was facilitated in part by the development of so-called in situ methods of extraction that use thermal technologies, such as steam-assisted gravity drainage (SAGD), to extract bitumen from deeply buried deposits. As the consistent growth in their capex indicates, the Big Five all made significant investments in fixed assets during this period, through which they could in turn further their capital accumulation—at least as long as oil prices remained high.

The Immediate Impact of the Downturn

In the autumn of 2014, the price of oil fell by nearly half, with the price of WTI dropping from over US$100 a barrel in August to under US$60 by the end of the year, and the aggregate capex of the Big Five quickly followed suit. Between 2014 and 2015, expenditures dropped by about 40 percent and then decreased a further 25 percent in 2016, before recovering slightly in 2017. The one exception to this trend was Suncor, whose capex fell only slightly (see table 1.5). All the same, the Big Five's total capex in 2017 was only 50.8 percent of what it was at the spending peak in 2014.

The abrupt downturn in the oil industry had a devastating impact on employment: 2015 was the worst year for job losses in Alberta since the 1982 recession—a year in which a staggering 45,000 jobs were lost in the province. While the loss of 19,600 jobs in 2015 might seem comparatively modest, the total exceeded the 17,000 jobs lost in Alberta as a result of the 2009 global financial crisis (Parkinson 2016). Overall, employment in Alberta's mining, quarrying, and oil and gas extraction sector declined precipitously, with the number of salaried employees falling by 18.7 percent, from 85,487 in 2014 to 69,516 in 2015. The number of salaried employees working in supporting activities dropped by 38.1 percent, from 34,277 in 2014 to 21,225 in 2015.[12]

At the same time, there was a slight rise in the number of employees paid by the hour. In mining and oil and gas extraction, numbers increased by 4.6 percent, from 42,730 in 2014 to 44,678 in 2015, and, in support industries, by 2.6 percent, from 33,014 in 2014 to 33,875 in 2015.[13] These increases were, however, offset by a steady decline in wages. In the mining, quarrying, and oil and gas extraction sector, the average hourly earnings (including overtime) for employees paid by the hour dropped by 6.5 percent, from $43.42 in 2014 to $40.61 in 2016. Workers in support industries suffered an even larger cut, with the average wage falling by 10.8 percent, from $42.54 in 2014 to $37.95 in 2016. Across Canada, spending on support activities for mining and oil and gas extraction decreased by 38.4 percent from 2014 to 2016, and most of these cuts were in Alberta.[14]

The Big Five reacted to the downturn in somewhat different ways, although all five companies cut costs. In January 2015, Suncor delayed a planned expansion of its MacKay River project (an in situ mining operation) owing to the decline in prices, and, over the course of the year, the company laid off 12 percent of its workforce (roughly 1,700 employees). It also began using automated trucks at some of its oil sands mines, a technology that could eventually replace some eight hundred drivers. At the same time, as table 1.5 shows, Suncor largely maintained its capex during the bust. The company considered the downturn an opportunity and made several significant investments. As part of a larger strategy to focus on its core assets (including its Petro-Canada stations), Suncor sold its 50 percent share of Pioneer Energy, another gasoline retailer, in September 2014. Then, in July 2015, the company traded two of its six wind farms to TransAlta in exchange for TransAlta's stake in the Poplar Creek co-generation facility (which provides steam and electricity for oil sands production). Under the terms of the agreement, Suncor will gain full ownership of the Poplar Creek facility in 2030.

Suncor made its biggest move in 2016, however, when it became the majority shareholder in Syncrude, in which the company already held a 12 percent share. In February, in a deal worth a total of $6.6 billion, Suncor purchased Canadian Oil Sands Limited, the owner of a 37 percent share in Syncrude stock. Then, in April, Suncor acquired an additional 5 percent share from Murphy Oil, giving Suncor 54 percent ownership of Syncrude. (Suncor went on, early in 2018, to acquire another 5 percent of Syncrude by a purchase of shares from Mocal Energy.) In a second substantial move, made in September 2016, Suncor—one of two principal partners in the Fort Hills Oil Sands Project—acquired an additional 10 percent from the project's other major partner, Total E&P Canada, a subsidiary of Paris-based Total SA. Although Total retained roughly a 29 percent share, this purchase gave Suncor nearly a 51 percent share, making it the majority owner of Fort Hills as well.

Unlike Suncor, CNRL substantially reduced capex during the bust (see table 1.5), in addition to cutting $2.4 billion (about 28 percent) from its 2015 budget. As a result, CNRL substantially delayed a planned expansion of its Kirby North Oil Sands Project. The company laid off 5.1 percent of its "permanent" employees in 2015 and 2016, as well as imposing a hiring freeze. It also cut senior managers' salaries by 10 percent and reduced the pay of other salaried employees, although it chose not to cut the hourly wages of oilfield workers. Like Suncor, however, CNRL saw the downturn as an opportunity, in this case to diversify its assets. In February 2014, CNRL had acquired liquids-rich natural gas assets from Devon Energy, along with six natural gas processing plants and related infrastructure. Between 2014 and 2016, CNRL further acquired about twelve thousand natural gas wells, positioning the company as Canada's largest natural gas producer, above Encana. In addition, CNRL continued with the expansion of its Horizon Oil Sands Project, with Phase 2B completed in 2016 and Phase 3 in construction.

Imperial Oil slashed its capex in 2015 by more than 40 percent, and in 2017 its total expenditures were more than 80 percent lower than in 2014 (see table 1.5). In March 2014, Imperial—then in the process of expanding two existing oil sands projects and seeking regulatory approval for a third—sold several of its conventional oil assets to Whitecap Resources for $855 million. During the bust, however, the company delayed the development of Phases 3 and 4 of the Kearl Oil Sands Project and, in 2016, sold 497 Esso-branded gas stations to five fuel distributors for $2.8 billion. In the face of ongoing debates about the future of various pipeline proposals, Imperial opted to develop rail infrastructure. Its Edmonton rail terminal began operating in mid-2015, with the capacity to ship up to 210,000 barrels per day.

Husky's reaction to the oil price decline was likewise to cut its capex by 40 percent, from $5 billion in 2014 to $3 billion in 2015 (see table 1.5), while also reducing administrative expenses by 41 percent, from $156 million in 2014 to $92 million in 2015. Over the course of 2015, Husky also cut 22 percent of its workforce, eliminating about 1,400 jobs. The same year also saw two existing projects come to fruition. In March 2015, Husky's Sunrise Energy Project, located northeast of Fort McMurray, began bitumen production, and, in May, a heavy oil plant at Rush Lake, Saskatchewan, likewise became operational. Husky's planned development of its heavy oil assets in western Saskatchewan continued into 2016. At the start of March, its Edam East plant—a thermal facility located about 115 kilometres east of Lloydminster, Alberta—was brought online, soon followed by two more thermal plants in the same area, the Vawn facility (in May) and the Edam West plant (in June). The company soon suffered a setback, however, when, on July 20, approximately 225,000 litres of heavy oil leaked out of a Husky pipeline near Maidstone, Saskatchewan, not far southeast of Lloydminster—much of it ending up in the North Saskatchewan River, where it polluted the drinking water supply of 70,000 people. Quite apart from the damage done to its reputation, Husky was obliged to undertake a clean-up operation and was eventually fined $3.8 million in connection with the spill.

Cenovus reacted to the downturn largely by cost reductions, slashing its capex by about two-thirds in 2015 and 2016 (see table 1.5). In particular, the firm scaled back spending on oil sands projects: it suspended a pilot project at its Grand Rapids facility, put the Christina Lake Phase G expansion on hold, and deferred development at the Telephone Lake project. It also laid off 25 percent of its workforce in 2014 and 2015, as well as cutting costs through a salary freeze and reductions to discretionary spending. All the same, in January 2016, Cenovus and Suncor announced a $100-million investment—$50 million from each over ten years—directed to Vancouver-based Evok Innovations to accelerate the development of "clean" technologies that reduce the environmental costs of oil sands production, including carbon emissions, water consumption and pollution, and the disposal of toxic waste in the form of tailings.

Restructuring and Consolidation

The 2014 downturn was precipitated by a glut in global oil markets, which proved to be prolonged, extending throughout 2015, 2016, and most of 2017. The resulting depression of oil prices altered the investment environment and drove a restructuring of the Alberta oil sands industry. This restructuring saw several global oil giants sell their oil sands assets, with the Big Five subsequently acquiring much of this productive capacity. In May 2015, Total SA, headquartered in France, indefinitely suspended development of the Joslyn North oil sands mine, an $11-billion project in which it partnered with Suncor, in addition to selling 10 percent of its stake in the Fort Hills Oil Sands Project (the share that Suncor acquired). In late 2016, Norway's Statoil decided to exit the oil sands altogether, selling its assets to the Athabasca Oil Corporation. Early in 2017, Netherlands-based Royal Dutch Shell sold most of its Alberta assets to CNRL (with Shell then acquiring a 9 percent share in CNRL), while the US-based ConocoPhillips sold most of its Canadian assets to Cenovus (with ConocoPhillips then becoming Cenovus's largest single shareholder, with a 25 percent stake in ownership).

During the downturn, banks and other investors in the United States seized on the decline in Canadian stock prices to buy up shares in both Suncor and CNRL (Hulshof at al. 2017). At the same time, the exodus of global oil giants from direct involvement in the Alberta oil sands (apart from retaining certain stock holdings) coincided with a continuing shift in the North American investment market toward shale oil basins in the United States, another unconventional source of hydrocarbons. In 2016, for example, ExxonMobil, the parent company of Imperial Oil, wrote off 3.5 billion barrels of its oil sands reserves in its annual accounting. Then, in January 2017, the firm announced US$5.6 billion in spending to double its shale oil reserves in the Permian Basin in Texas, thereby adding 3.3 billion barrels to its production capacity. Perhaps ironically, the sudden upsurge in shale oil production and hence in the global oil supply was one of the factors centrally responsible for the decline in oil prices that threatened the financial viability of bitumen production.

Royal Dutch Shell made two major transactions on the heels of the moves by ExxonMobil, one of Shell's main competitors. In February 2017, Shell purchased the British oil and gas corporation BG Group for £36 billion (roughly US$53 billion) in a move to strengthen its presence in liquefied natural gas (LNG) production and consolidate its portfolio of offshore deepwater wells. In order to reduce its debt, Shell then made its second major transaction—the sale of its oil sands assets to CNRL. Shell's global strategy bets on LNG and deepwater wells, so it was logical for the firm to divest from the oil sands. Before the sale to CNRL, oil sands holdings represented nearly 43 percent of Shell's global portfolio of proved oil reserves. So the decision to divest amounted to a major shift in Shell's strategy.

Back in Alberta, during the prolonged period in which oil prices remained below $60 per barrel, developing new extractive facilities in the oil sands was not economically feasible, although running existing facilities was, as long as firms controlled production costs. This is precisely the strategy that the Big Five adopted. CNRL led the oil sands industry in cost-cutting efforts, reducing its production costs to the low twenty dollars per barrel. Other oil sands majors—including Syncrude (in which Suncor now owns a majority stake)—also reduced their costs, to somewhere between the mid-twenty to low thirty dollars per barrel. The cost reductions came through improvements to technology and the squeezing down of labour costs. As oil prices gradually climbed back up, hovering in the range of $60 to $70 per barrel throughout most of 2018, oil sands majors saw their existing facilities become increasingly profitable assets, generating stable and predictable returns.

In the years immediately following the downturn, the Big Five were all very vocal about what this phase of consolidation meant for the future of the industry. All five downplayed the possibility of any large-scale expansion of productive capacity through new investments in mining or in situ facilities in the near term. There would be an expansion of production, but this would largely be achieved through an increase in the efficiency of current facilities and through realizing the benefits of past investments. The shift from a booming, high-investment, high-growth, high-innovation environment of intensive capital accumulation to a more gradual pattern of accumulation characterized by cost cutting has indeed proved to be permanent (see Hussey 2020). Even before the price war that began in March 2020 precipitated a new crisis, it was clear that many of the jobs lost during the previous downturn would never return.

Conclusion: The Big Five and the Future of Extreme Oil in Alberta

Extreme oil can be defined as hydrocarbons that should have remained in the ground but were driven into the world economy by the capitalist pressure to extract. During the decade-long boom phase of the commodity cycle that began in 2004, unconventional sources of hydrocarbons, including oil sands, were normalized, and northern Alberta became home to the world's third-largest reserve of oil. In the years from 2008 to 2014, as the price of a barrel of WTI peaked at more than US$130 in the summer of 2008, falling briefly during the global recession only to rise again to over US$100 early in 2012, authorities ranging from state regulators to energy-sector agencies and auditors changed the valuation of oil sands reserves from the status of risky and marginal assets to that of standard exploitable assets. Crucially, as the commodity cycle moved from boom to bust and prices dropped to lows of under US$40 a barrel early in 2015, this process of normalization was not reversed. And when prices slowly began to recover late in 2017, bitumen had survived as an accepted form of crude oil, and the Alberta oil sands had retained their symbolic promise of abundance and future prosperity.

During this process of normalization, an oligopolistic bloc of seven large firms—the Big Five producers plus two pipeline corporations, Enbridge and TransCanada (now TC Energy)—gradually extended their control over the flow that transforms deposits of bitumen into barrels of heavy crude that will eventually become burnable oil. As figure 1.1 illustrates, the capacity to extract bitumen has exploded over the past decade, through massive investments in fixed capital and in research that led to the refinement of in situ extractive technologies, with the pace of this buildup slowing only after 2014. Not only did the Big Five expand their extractive capacity exponentially, but they also consolidated their control over the potential flow of bitumen, marginalizing other corporations in the process.

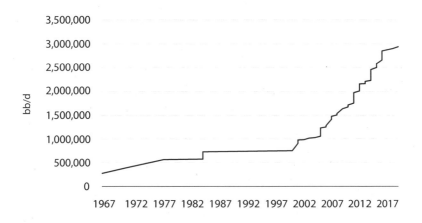

Figure 1.1. Growth in the bitumen output of the Big Five

If the potential output controlled by the Big Five forms the basis of their oligopolistic power over the resource and its capitalist development, the concrete flow of bitumen generates the income that realizes the value locked in the oil sands. Over the commodity cycle, as the boom turned to bust, the Big Five were able to maintain their gross profit, out of which they could continue to repay debt, cover their overhead, and pay out dividends. They did this chiefly by cutting direct production costs. In the case of Suncor, for example, direct costs consumed an average of 54 percent of gross revenue in the years from 2008 to 2015 but fell to 37 percent in 2016 and 2017.

As we have argued, gross profit is the key to accumulation strategies: it is what corporations use to finance past, current, and future investments in fixed capital. Gross profit also provides the economic means by which the Big Five can deploy and reproduce their hegemonic power over the market, the state, and society. The accumulation strategies we have surveyed evolved in reaction to the phases of the commodity cycle. The boom period is characterized by an escalation of extractive capacity, coupled with the development of new, more technologically sophisticated, in situ methods of extraction. The bust and restructuring phases are marked by a wave of concentration of control over the resource base itself and over fixed extractive capital, as well as by the consolidation of ownership and the protection of stock value through share buybacks.

It is this flexibility with regard to accumulation strategies that sustains the hegemonic power of the oil sands industry within the Canadian capitalist landscape. As long as the bitumen flows, it will generate the gross profit that forms the material base of this hegemony. In May 2015, the Alberta New Democratic Party (NDP) came to power with several objectives, including general commitments to improve the province's climate policies and to review royalty rates for various fossil fuels. However, the boom was already becoming a bust before the 2015 election. In this context, and because of stiffening competition from shale oil producers in the United States, the NDP's royalty review resulted in the reduction of some rates. Now, with the United Conservative Party firmly ensconced in power, it seems very unlikely that the generous royalty and tax regime that has existed in Alberta since the late 1990s will change significantly in the foreseeable future.

With the Big Five gradually increasing production while squeezing costs and slowing down investment, a significant chunk of Alberta's (and Canada's) carbon budget is currently reserved for a slow-growing, environmentally destructive sector with weak fiscal, investment, employment, and innovation benefits. To thrive in the long term, the Big Five, along with the two pipeline companies, will require fiscal, energy, and climate policies that suit their needs. To put it bluntly, their survival rests on their ability to capture and control these policies at both the provincial and federal levels, and that ability rests on a sustained deployment of corporate power.

At a time when other jurisdictions are taking steps to transition away from fossil fuels, Canada's current policy trajectory would strengthen the country's ties to oil and gas production over the next three decades. If the oligopolistic bloc that controls fossil fuel production is able to continue steering provincial and federal fiscal, energy, and climate policies, then Canada will not be able to live up to its Paris Agreement obligations, and its professed commitment to the future will be shown to be hollow.

Notes

1. West Texas Intermediate is a crude oil that is used as a benchmark in oil pricing, particularly in North America. In August 2014, WTI was selling at an average price (in US dollars) of $103.54 a barrel; by December, the price was down to $57.24 a barrel—a drop of about 45 percent. During the more recent crash, in the spring of 2020, the price of WTI fell as low as $11.57 a barrel (on April 21), according to https://oilprice.com/oil-price-charts/ (accessed September 2, 2020), before recovering to roughly $42 a barrel by the end of the summer.

2. The two corporations that dominate the pipeline industry in Canada are TC Energy (formerly TransCanada Corporation) and Enbridge. A third company, US-based Kinder Morgan, sold most of its Canadian assets to the Government of Canada in 2018, including the existing Trans Mountain Pipeline (in operation since 1953).

3. On January 4, 2021, Cenovus's takeover of Husky became finalized, reducing the Big Five to four.

4. Figures calculated on the basis of data provided in Table 33-10-0025-01 (formerly CANSIM 551-0001), "Businesses by Industry and Employment, December 2011," Statistics Canada, https://www150.statcan.gc.ca/t1/tbl1/en/tv.action?pid=3310002501&pickMembers%5B0%5D=3.1. The following industry classifications were used in the analysis: "Conventional oil and gas extraction," "Non-conventional oil extraction," "Oil and gas contract drilling," and "Services to oil and gas extraction."

5. In its raw state, bitumen is a thick, tarlike substance that must be partially processed in order to meet pipeline specifications. In some cases, bitumen can

be diluted with lighter hydrocarbons to produce a heavy "sour" crude oil (that is, one with a relatively high sulphur content) and then sold directly to high-conversion refineries, which are able to convert it into petroleum products such as gasoline or lubricants. In other cases, however, bitumen must be further upgraded into relatively sweet synthetic crudes before it can be sold to refineries. (Crude oil is considered "sweet" if its sulphur content is less than 0.5 percent.)

6. National Energy Board, "2017 Estimated Production of Canadian Crude Oil and Equivalent (b/d)," table now archived by the Canada Energy Regulator, available at https://www.cer-rec.gc.ca/nrg/sttstc/crdlndptrlmprdct/stt/archive/stmtdprdctnrchv-eng.html.

7. Calculated from Excel data underlying JWN Energy's *Oilweek 2018 Top 100: An Uneven Recovery* report (prepared by KPMG), June 2018. In addition, with a collective capacity for bitumen upgrading of 1.23 million bbl/d, the Big Five controlled almost 96 percent of the total capacity for upgrading.

8. Conventional "dry" natural gas is basically methane (although it does contain certain impurities that need to be removed). Natural gas is called "wet" when, in addition to methane, it contains NGLs, or natural gas liquids—that is, hydrocarbons such as butane, propane, and ethane. While these additional ingredients have their own uses, they lower the methane content of the gas. Note also that, properly speaking, "unconventional" refers not to the hydrocarbons themselves but to the context and location in which they occur and, by extension, the methods required for their extraction.

9. Here and below, financial data were obtained through Morningstar, Inc.

10. Depreciation and amortization are not expenses per se but are rather accounting manoeuvres that serve to spread costs out over a number of years (rather than assigning these costs only to the year in which a purchase was made). Doing so serves to free up a proportion of gross profit each year for other uses, while also allowing for ongoing annual reductions in taxable income.

11. Calculated from Excel data underlying JWN Energy's *Oilweek 2018 Top 100* report.

12. Table 14-10-0202-01 (formerly CANSIM 281-0024), "Employment by Industry, Annual," Statistics Canada, https://www150.statcan.gc.ca/t1/tbl1/en/tv.action?pid=1410020201.

13. Ibid.

14. Table 14-10-0206-01 (formerly CANSIM 281-0030), "Average Hourly Earnings for Employees Paid by the Hour, by Industry, Annual," Statistics Canada, https://www150.statcan.gc.ca/t1/tbl1/en/tv.action?pid=1410020601.

References

Canadian Press. 2018. "Suncor Hikes Its Stake in Syncrude to 58% in $920 Million Deal." *Financial Post*, February 18, 2018. https://financialpost.com/commodities/ energy/suncor-energy-increases-stake-in-syncrude-acquires-stake-in-fenja-development.

Hughes, J. David. 2018. *Canada's Energy Outlook: Current Realities and Implications for a Carbon-Constrained Future*. Vancouver: Canadian Centre for Policy Alternatives, BC Office. https://www.policyalternatives.ca/energy-outlook.

Hulshof, Menno, Aaron Bilkoski, Juan Jarrah, Josie Ho, and Jin Yan. 2017. *Testing the U.S. Investor 'Capital Drain' Thesis*. Industry Note, July 20, 2017. Equity Research, TD Securities. Toronto: Toronto-Dominion Bank.

Hussey, Ian. 2020. *The Future of Alberta's Oil Sands Industry*. Edmonton: Parkland Institute. https://www.parklandinstitute.ca/the_future_of_albertas_oil_sands_ industry.

Hussey, Ian, and David W. Janzen. 2018. *What the Paris Agreement Means for Alberta's Oil Sands Majors*. Edmonton: Parkland Institute. https://www. parklandinstitute.ca/what_the_paris_agreement_means_for_albertas_oil_sands_ majors.

Lee, Marc. 2017. *Extracted Carbon: Re-examining Canada's Contribution to Climate Change Through Fossil Fuel Exports*. Vancouver: Corporate Mapping Project. https://www.corporatemapping.ca/extracted-carbon-re-examining-canadas-contribution-to-climate-change-through-fossil-fuel-exports/.

Muttitt, Greg. 2016. *The Sky's Limit: Why the Paris Climate Goals Require a Managed Decline of Fossil Fuel Production*. Washington, DC: Oil Change International. http://priceofoil.org/content/uploads/2016/09/OCI_the_skys_limit_2016_ FINAL_2.pdf.

Parkinson, David. 2016. "Alberta Endures Most Annual Job Losses Since Early 1980s Recession." *Globe and Mail*, January 26, 2016. https://www.theglobeandmail.com/ report-on-business/economy/jobs/alberta-job-losses-last-year-worst-since-early-1980s-recession-statscan/article28393681/.

Pineault, Éric. 2018. "The Capitalist Pressure to Extract: The Ecological and Political Economy of Extreme Oil in Canada." *Studies in Political Economy* 99, no. 2: 130–50. https://doi.org/10.1080/07078552.2018.1492063.

Thieroff, John, Rebecca Greenberg, Steven Wood, Brian Cahill, Vikas Halan, and Elena Nadtotchi. 2017. *Oil and Gas Industry Faces Significant Credit Risks from Carbon Transition*. New York City: Moody's Investor Service. https://www. divestinvest.org/wp-content/uploads/2017/09/Moodys.April2017.Oil-and-Gas-Industry-Faces-Significant-Credit-Risks-from-Carbon-transition.pdf.

2   Lines of Work, Corridors of Power

Extraction, Obstruction, and Counter-obstruction Along Fossil Fuel Production Networks

James Lawson

Bring in the workers and bring up the rails
We're gonna lay down the tracks and tear up the trails
Open her heart, let the life blood flow
Gotta get on our way, 'cause we're moving too slow.

Gordon Lightfoot, "Canadian Railroad Trilogy"

The above lines come from a venerable contribution to English-Canadian national mythology, a song commissioned by the CBC to celebrate the country's centennial. Aired in a CBC Radio broadcast on January 1, 1967, Lightfoot's ballad drew on an already well-established theme in Canadian historiography: the central role of mercantile and railway interests in the westward expansion of the Canadian nation following Confederation (Creighton 1956; Naylor 1972).

In these lines, Lightfoot metaphorically links the settlement of the land (and the ability to speed across it) to the flow of blood and, by extension, to blood sacrifice. But the song goes on to invoke a second image of flow, which falls at a triumphant climax in the music just before the closing refrain: "We have opened up the soil / with our teardrops and our toil." Here, Lightfoot speaks of the hard labour of navvies required for this victory over the land, a flow of sweat and tears that presumably justifies the sacrifice. While all but erasing the Indigenous presence, Lightfoot's song nonetheless offers two provocative proposals: that violence is central to settler relations with the land and that resource extraction and transport express that violence.

Metaphors of flow also proliferate in the rhetoric of resource politics, notably in images of the *obstruction* and *release* of flows. The present volume, for example, highlights flow obstructions: corporate power obstructs the flow of democracy and, by locking investments of fixed capital into fossil fuel projects, also blocks the flow of funds into green-energy infrastructure. Yet, for the western Canadian fossil fuel industry and its allies, those same projects release massive positive flows of profit and jobs. For them, protest and regulation merely obstruct flows of profit from existing and potential investments in fossil fuels (see Workman and McCormack 2015, 32).

At the same time, the obstruction of flow can be understood in more generative terms. In *This Changes Everything*, for example, Naomi Klein offers her vision of "Blockadia"—a global archipelago of resistance against the fossil fuel industry that includes many "resource hot spots" in Canada (2014, 298). In Canada, many of Blockadia's more radical denizens are Indigenous peoples fighting to retain sovereignty over their traditional lands and to restore relations of reciprocity and stewardship. In the face of an icy-hearted world-gone-windigo, Indigenous activists obstruct its arterial corridors— pipelines, rails, and roads. But stilling this monster's heart is also a generative act: it makes a greener, more democratic and communitarian world possible. Similar arguments have been made about the potential of Indigenous blockades and occupations to generate a sense of solidarity and political energy in ongoing struggles for Indigenous sovereignty (Belanger and Lackenbauer 2014; Napoleon 2010).

This chapter explores material flows in relationship to power and violence in resource extraction. Beyond the product-in-transformation, the flows at stake include the resources and energy needed for extraction and transportation, the labour force, the wastes released, and materially embodied networks of communication. Flows run to and from nodes of production via transportation and communication infrastructure. These flows do more than supply and relieve individual nodes: they link any one node to others, as well as to the chain's or network's surroundings, and therefore form part of the architecture that binds together the chain or network itself. As this chapter will argue, the geography of contestation depends on this underlying geography of flow.

This proposal stands on solid precedents in macroeconomics and in the sociology of work. Interest in the materiality of flow and in diagnosing the macroeconomic consequences of flow imbalances can be traced back at least to the physiocratic model of circulation presented in François Quesnay's *Tableau économique*, first published in 1758. Quesnay wrote from the assumption that, in material terms, agriculture rather than labour was the source of all wealth, a claim that both reflected the low-growth dynamic of the manufacture of his age and appeared to justify the wealth of the landed aristocracy. Here, the highlight is his interest in tracing the circulation of wealth—an interest that influenced many others. It was an interest that led him to call for *laisser-faire*—the free movement of goods and wealth—a call that drew attention to the manifold flow obstructions.

Flows of physical materials and goods arguably require more attention to physical and geographic conditions. In volume 2 of *Capital*, Marx's attention to the materiality of capital flows is particularly evident in his account, in chapter 8, of fixed capital as distinct from circulating capital. It is also evident in his reflections on the application of his reproduction schemas in the context of "social production"—a future collective economy without markets—and not merely in capitalist production (see Marx [1978] 1992, 434, 470). Although the practicalities of transport are largely absent from his analysis, Wassily Leontief's input-output modelling—extensions of Marx's reproduction schemas—emphasize the problems of balance and imbalance in relation to material flows (see, especially, Leontief 1936, 1937; see also Harvey 2013, 320–21).

Some macroeconomic theorists, notably John Maynard Keynes (1936) and Michal Kalecki (1939), have focused instead on flows of income and capital, particularly in the context of national economies. While still dependent on material infrastructure, such flows are relatively abstract, and their movements are largely independent of spatial constraints.[1] Especially in the decades since the publication of Nicholas Georgescu-Roegen's *The Entropy Law and the Economic Process* (1971), however, other analysts have continued to focus on flows of physical materials, stressing the need to achieve balance and proportionality among such flows, particularly in the face of the depletion of natural resources (see, for example, Daly and Cobb 1989; Brown 2001). The macroeconomic consequences of material imbalances in relation to resource requirements and industrial waste form a core theme in Marina Fischer-Kowalski's materials flow analyses (Fischer-Kowalski 1998;

Fischer-Kowalski and Hüttler 1998), as well as in late Soviet centralized economic planning.

It is only with yet other authors, however, that we see sustained attention to the fixed geographies associated with the transportation of specific materials and with the coordination of material flows. Some of these analysts work in the Canadian staples tradition (for example, Drache 1996; Watkins 2006), while others focus on the logistics of supply-chain management (for example, Bonacich and Wilson 2008; Trace 2001). These approaches attend to the practical orchestration of material flows, especially in relation to transportation and communication infrastructure, which in turn directs attention to the implications should this orchestration fail and disruptions of flow occur. Some of the more radical logistics literature (see Cowen 2010; Alimahomed-Wilson and Ness 2018) explores the political significance of the obstruction of flows and the political and security issues associated with maintaining "free" flows.

The Trans Mountain Expansion Project

As I write, tropes of flow obstruction and release are proliferating around "pipeline politics" in western Canada, in connection with the transportation of both diluted bitumen and liquefied natural gas (LNG). In early February 2020, protests erupted across the country in response to the RCMP's heavily armed clearance of blockades on unceded Wet'suwet'en territory in north-central British Columbia so that construction of the Coastal GasLink pipeline could continue (Canadian Press 2020a)—a sequence of flow-disrupting political actions that requires separate analysis. Following the 2016 demise of another highly contested project, Enbridge's proposed Northern Gateway pipeline, bitumen politics soon came to centre on the Trans Mountain Expansion project. The expansion would roughly triple the quantity of bitumen already flowing along the existing Trans Mountain pipeline from Edmonton, Alberta, to a storage and loading terminal in Burnaby, British Columbia. From there, tankers would take the diluted bitumen past a sensitive, island-studded coastline and then out to sea. New but uncertain Asian markets have been the project's main advertised objective, although the ongoing role of American markets may be understated.

Since its initial public announcement, in February 2012, the Trans Mountain project has survived multiple challenges, including abandonment by the original proponent, US-based Kinder Morgan, and purchase by the Canadian government at a cost of about $4.5 billion in 2018. Several First Nations along both the coast and the project corridor have asserted their rights and interests against it. Environmental groups with varied agendas on the coast and along its interior route have targeted the project as a local menace and as a signal contributor to climate change. Stoutly supported at the outset by the Conservative federal government of Stephen Harper, the project nonetheless met with opposition across a broad section of the political spectrum in coastal British Columbia. Yet, despite public criticism, the project passed review by the National Energy Board and was approved by Justin Trudeau's Liberal government in late November 2016 (at the same time that the Northern Gateway project was scuttled).

But controversy surrounding the project had only begun. First Nations, both on the coast and along the pipeline corridor, asserted their rights and interests against the project, at the same time that environmental groups raised alarms about potential spills and targeted the project as a signal contributor to climate change. During the provincial election campaign in May 2017, the BC New Democratic Party (NDP) government, under the leadership of John Horgan, promised that it would insist on further research and investment in spill cleanup capacity before allowing the project to proceed. The government further argued in court—ultimately unsuccessfully—that the province had a constitutional right to regulate the transport of bitumen within its borders in the interests of the local environment.[2]

By the spring of 2018, delays were driving up costs, prompting Kinder Morgan to announce, in April, that it would withdraw funding for the project at the end of May unless an agreement could be reached that would allow construction to proceed. On May 29, 2018, Ottawa announced a buyout to ensure that the pipeline would be built—"an investment in Canada's future," according to Minister of Finance Bill Morneau, who declined to estimate what the eventual cost would be to the Canadian public (Harris 2018; see also Tencer 2018). At the time, Kinder Morgan's own estimate of the total cost of construction was $7.4 billion—a cost that, by February 2020, had escalated to a projected $12.6 billion (Kapelos and Tasker 2020).

In the meanwhile, lawsuits had been filed both by BC First Nations and by environmental groups in response to the government's November 2016 decision to approve the project. On August 30, 2018, the Federal Court of Appeal upheld these challenges, ruling that the federal government's process of consultation had been inadequate (see Bellrichard 2018) and its environmental assessment incomplete. The government was thus obliged to undertake a supplementary round of consultations as well as to address the environmental shortcomings. The government complied, and the Trans Mountain project was subsequently reapproved, in June 2019. A new challenge was then brought, by a number of the original First Nations applicants, again on the grounds of inadequate consultation.[3] On February 4, 2020, however, the Federal Court of Appeal rejected this new challenge (Canadian Press 2020b), thereby closing down one avenue of opposition.

The project has, however, enjoyed the support of successive governments in Alberta. In the spring of 2018, Rachel Notley's NDP government, in an ongoing effort to avoid alienating business interests, threatened to cut oil and gas deliveries to British Columbia unless the latter permitted construction of the pipeline to proceed (Morgan 2018). This threat was backed by her government's passage of legislation empowering the province to place restrictions on its exports—legislation not formally proclaimed until May 2019, after mid-April provincial elections brought the United Conservative Party (UCP) government of Jason Kenney to power. BC holds Alberta's law to be unconstitutional (Williams 2019).[4] Kenney also repealed the Notley government's climate legislation (which had previously been criticized as insufficiently robust) and, in December 2019, established the UCP's $30-million Canadian Energy Centre (popularly described as its "war room") to counter environmentalist and Indigenous criticism of Alberta's fossil fuel industry (Anderson 2019).

Even if the hour may thus be too late for those who would stop the Trans Mountain Expansion, the struggle is far from over. Major international investors have for the most part withdrawn their investments in oil sands projects, while scientific reports continue to stress the need for a radical and rapid transition away from fossil fuels, as well as Canada's unacceptably high levels of per capita carbon emissions. In this arena of struggle, flows and possible obstructions to flow have a direct bearing not only on contending themes of profit, protest, and transition but also on the strategies adopted by the contending parties.

Flow and Infraction

With respect to the flow of bitumen, at least three broad categories of strategy exist, but only one depends on the industrial geography of production. The first is divestment: persuading investors to withdraw funding for bitumen-related projects, including pipeline construction, and for fossil fuel extraction more generally (see Rowe, Dempsey, and Gibbs 2016, as well as chapter 17 in this volume). Debating the moral legitimacy of such projects may engage the values of specific territorially bound populations, but otherwise this strategy requires little geographic analysis. For this reason, it is bracketed here.

Another type of strategy concerns conflicts among jurisdictions, as an extractive chain or network passes through a jurisdiction's territory and thus becomes the object of its governance. In Canada, one obvious subtype involves conflict among legally constituted state jurisdictions. Examples are BC's two recent legal challenges (discussed above) regarding jurisdiction over the flow of bitumen within and across provinces, specifically in relation to the constitutional division of powers. A second subtype involves conflicts between state jurisdictions and Indigenous authority. In BC, a province in which most First Nations never negotiated treaties with the Canadian state, jurisdictional claims flow from the recognition of Aboriginal title.[5] Regardless of subtype, however, legal strategies founded on competing claims to authority over the space occupied by an extractive chain or network are only tangentially connected to *how* the struggle proceeds on the ground. Consequently, such strategies are also bracketed here.

A third anti-pipeline strategy type, material obstruction, appears to be growing in its frequency of application. Here, the operations of the extractive chain or network itself become the terrain of struggle, not merely its rationale or objective. One such corridor ends at the mouth of the Fraser River, in suburban Vancouver. Although the expansion would alter this part of its route, the existing Trans Mountain Pipeline corridor crosses parkland and upscale neighbourhoods on Burnaby Mountain before terminating at a seaside storage facility, where tankers are then loaded. Anti-pipeline protests in this area began in the late fall of 2017, with protesters and land defenders clustering around a trailer parked near the entrance to the construction site—the origins of what came to be called "Camp Cloud." On March 10, 2018, a large Indigenous-led demonstration that included activists from resource struggles across North America marked the beginning of an organized direct-action campaign. That day, protesters and land defenders constructed a traditional Coast Salish "watch house" near the trailer and lit a sacred fire that would be kept burning continuously. In defiance of a March court injunction ordering protesters to stay away from the construction site, the campaign—punctuated by arrests and charges of criminal contempt—continued until August, when the BC Supreme Court issued a second injunction ordering protesters to dismantle Camp Cloud.

The Tsleil-Waututh Nation, whose lands lie adjacent to the terminus, has provided important leadership in this campaign, working alongside other Vancouver-area First Nations. Their efforts have been joined by First Nations elsewhere along BC's coastlines and in the interior. Echoing the obstruction strategy of the long-standing Unist'ot'en Camp in central British Columbia (see Unist'ot'en Camp 2017), the Tiny House Warrior movement of the Secwepemc Nation, whose lands lie in south-central BC, has undertaken the construction of a series of small houses intended to prevent the Trans Mountain Pipeline corridor from crossing unceded Secwepemc territory.[6] First Nations with analogous stakes have in the past obstructed transportation corridors such as those associated with the Keystone XL, Enbridge Northern Gateway, and Energy East pipelines. The resulting networks have generated a dense environment for mutual support and strategic exchange not only among First Nations but also between Indigenous communities and non-Indigenous environmental groups.

Environmental organizations have long appreciated First Nations' vested interest in safeguarding the integrity of their traditional lands, as well as their superior legal leverage, and authority in resource matters. However frustrating and limited "Aboriginal rights" can be for Indigenous peoples under Canadian constitutional rulings, this difference in leverage can become important for interactions between environmental movements and First Nations. Most BC First Nations retain rights and duties to the land, even under settler constitutional and common law, that settler environmentalists do not have and that many other First Nations in Canada appear to have ceded in the eyes of Canadian law.[7] Freehold tenure is not a constitutional right like Aboriginal and treaty rights, for example; in many parts of the country, freehold tenure specifically excludes subsurface resources, while Aboriginal title does not. Recent settler court decisions have attached growing significance to those rights, though not without limitation, especially since the 1997 Supreme Court ruling on Delgamuukw. Supplementary decisions then followed, including the 2004 *Haida Nation* and *Taku River Tlingit* cases, as well as the 2014 *Tsilhqot'in* case. The *Haida* case established that both federal and provincial governments had obligations to consult that could not be delegated to third parties. The *Tsilhqot'in* decision included a statement from the courts that rejected the doctrine of *terra nullius* in Canadian law (see para. 69), notwithstanding its practical application over decades in government policy.

These facts co-exist with extensive and expensive procedural delays and obstacles, as well as judicial limitations on the practical meaning of Aboriginal rights. The *Taku River Tlingit* ruling established a major limitation on the duty to consult in Canadian law, namely that it did not extend to a duty to reach agreement. These court decisions have also never questioned Crown sovereignty claims in relation to Indigenous sovereignty (for example *Tsilh-qot'in* 2014, para. 69–70). Moreover, inequalities in real power have privileged government and industry interests in eliminating these rights through forced negotiation. These practical limitations have driven some First Nations to negotiate an end to their Aboriginal title, typically in exchange for money and benefits compensation and some more conventional land rights. Tensions have emerged in many communities between Indian Act councils willing to sign such agreements and traditional leaderships. Still, in tactical terms, the existence of this jurisprudence can still link the second obstruction strategy type to the third, particularly prior to the opening of such negotiations.

Some earlier environmental campaigns rested on admirably respectful relations. But in response to Indigenous objections to notably disrespectful or ill-informed relations, many environmental organizations have had to make important adjustments in their approach. As the March 10, 2018, Trans Mountain protest suggests, this situation may be changing (see, for example, Berman 2018), with environmentalists now often seeking to signal heightened deference to Indigenous leadership, procedures, and conceptions of justice. Locally grounded actions, such as blockades, bring people together, both literally and figuratively, it may be that strategies involving material obstruction have helped to foster this growing sense of collaboration.

Toward a Strategic Geography of Obstruction

As suggested earlier, resource-extractive operations most closely resemble chains or networks and, as such, are geographically distinctive. Although they occupy only very small amounts of land, thereby limiting the area directly under corporate control, such chains frequently traverse broad expanses of territory, cutting across national and other jurisdictional boundaries. Their configuration on the land tends to be relatively linear, consisting of concentrated nodes of activity connected by sometimes lengthy transportation corridors along which flow people, equipment, and the product itself. For opponents, this structural linearity invites targeted intervention tactics that can produce cascading effects both upstream and downstream.

The fact that an intervention could, in theory, occur anywhere along the chain inevitably raises the question of why strategic actions take place where they do. Why, for example, did protests against the Trans Mountain pipeline centre on the Burnaby terminus rather than upstream at Fort McMurray or somewhere else? Similarly, why were protests against the Petronas LNG project centred almost exclusively on the proposed terminal at Lelu Island, not far south of Prince Rupert? After all, protests against clearcutting—such as the 1990s "War in the Woods" in Clayoquot Sound—typically focused on the site of extraction, namely, the forests themselves, rather than on sawmills or lumberyards. So why, in the case of oil and gas, do coastal terminals seem to be the preferred targets? More generally, what determines the locations along a given resource-extractive chain that will emerge as sites of protest?

One factor is, of course, the location of those whose livelihoods, lands, and lifeways are most immediately under threat. The Trans Mountain protests at Burnaby were, for example, spearheaded by local Coast Salish peoples, while Lelu Island is the traditional territory of the Gitwilgyoots, a Lax Kw'alaams tribe, who were joined in their struggle against Petronas by both commercial and sport fishers.[8] Similarly, Clayoquot Sound is the traditional home of two Nuu-chah-nulth bands, as well as a popular tourist and recreation site. In other words, struggles may simply break out in places where local residents have reasons for opposition.

Another possible factor is the degree to which the concerns surrounding a project focus on a particular site. The Petronas project met with little opposition, for instance, until alarms were raised about the potential environmental and economic impacts of a LNG terminal specifically at Lelu Island—located, as it is, in the ecologically sensitive Skeena River estuary so vital to the salmon fishery. In contrast, logging-road protests typically emphasized the impact of the logging industry on the forest overall. Similarly, in addition to local concerns, pipeline protests often address issues that extend far beyond the route of the pipeline itself. Moreover, despite relentless stress on the environmental degradation wrought at or near sites of bitumen extraction, only limited, symbolic, and generally non-confrontational actions, such as the former Tar Sands Healing Walk (Leahy 2014), have taken place at such sites. For the most part, then, sites of protest seem only loosely related to the geographic scope of the concern.

A third possible factor is the influence of precedent. One thinks of iconic sites of protest such as the logging roads of the 1980s and 1990s or the coal mine entrances at which striking workers assembled. The possibility that a "trend-setting" site will emerge surely deserves investigation, yet clearly not all issues generate such a shared site of protest.

While such factors may shed light on which protest sites become popular, recent comparisons across chains suggest an additional line of inquiry. Resource-extractive chains or networks may become vulnerable to intervention at specific points owing to the particularities of the work process. Timothy Mitchell (2011) compares coal to conventional oil from the standpoint of the relative effectiveness of coal miners and oil workers in making demands for reform. Given that miners worked directly at the site of extraction, producing the coal itself, striking coal miners could easily obstruct coal flows and subsequently release them—a power of obstruction, he argues, that placed miners at the vanguard of organized labour and of democratic struggle. In contrast, the flow of oil is not so easily interrupted, and the production process is also more complex. As Mitchell (2011, 144) observes, oil has to be "recovered from beneath the ground, stored in tanks, processed in treatment plants, pumped into pipelines, loaded onto tankers and transported across oceans."

Mitchell also points out that British coal served nearby markets, with the result that the buyers could press directly for settlements when strikes broke out. Oil, by contrast, generally has offshore customers (and sometimes foreign owners as well): threats to extractive flows thus require greater transnational, transcultural, and translingual coordination. Finally, work processes favoured organizing by coal miners but not by oil riggers. Room-and-pillar coal mining required intense worker collaboration underground, where workers were hidden from managerial oversight. In addition, miners and their families tended to cluster in homes near the pits, creating intergenerational communities of support. By contrast, conventional oil crews form anew with each project, with workers often housed in temporary camps, and operate above ground under eagle-eyed supervisors.

These patterns are, of course, imperfect: not all coal miners struck successfully, while some oil and gas workers have (Nore and Turner 1981; Wanderley, Mokrani, and Guimaraes 2012). But these examples do suggest that certain flashpoints emerge and prove effective because of the manner in which the work process is organized, as well as the capacity of managers and/or the state to exercise surveillance.

Flow analysis may also suggest why sites that are divorced from the sites of immediate concern can still prove useful to protesters and land defenders (as we will see in the discussion of logistics below). The material flows that allow a geographically dispersed work process to succeed necessarily mediate power both upstream and downstream; intervention on the part of fossil fuel opponents can "piggyback" on this existing power (see also Bernstein and Cashore 2007; Cashore, Auld, and Newsom 2004; Lawson 2009). Much like coal miners, Indigenous and environmental protesters can focus not only on sites associated with specific grievances but also on those least vulnerable to corporate or police surveillance—that is, on sites where protesters enjoy an organizational advantage.

In sum, a clear understanding of the production process and the relations of power associated with it is important not merely in connection with corporate concerns, such as the maximization of efficiency or profit (the focus of much mainstream supply-chain research), or with respect to the implications for public concerns such as climate change or damage to local ecosystems. Above all, these processes and power dynamics need to be understood in the context of the struggle itself, with a view to assessing the strategic potential of disrupting them. Disruption may involve labour relations or relations with interests external to the chain or network. As a strategic terrain, each chain or network thus exhibits a distinctive logic for contention, just as the configuration of a chessboard shapes the playing of the game. The logic underlying the terrain may determine where conflicts or tensions are apt to arise, and, with careful analysis, contenders may also be able to identify especially advantageous sites.

Accordingly, in what follows, I focus on analyzing flows of material along resource chains or networks. Again, these flows require study not merely because they pose an important environmental policy problem in their own right. They demand attention because of the potential of their obstruction or diversion to alter the balance of power in policy debates.

Reading Power Through Chain and Network Literatures

That the technical and economic aspects of material flows, flow obstruction, and other work relations simultaneously entail power relations is not a new claim (see Braverman 1974; Rueschemeyer 1986; Cleaver [1979] 2000). But it does suggest a principle for selective reading of existing chain or network research (on which see Bair 2005; Lawson 2009). Each of the following frameworks emphasizes distinctive features about chains or networks; a limited subset emphasizes different dimensions of chain or network power.

Terence Hopkins and Immanuel Wallerstein's (1986) commodity-chain analysis and the global production network (GPN) literature (Henderson et al. 2002; Hess and Yeung 2006) consider power in labour relations, together with interfirm exchanges and transfers. Hopkins and Wallerstein relate levels of extra-economic coercion to the locations of particular nodes in the commodity chain within the capitalist world system. For Jeffrey Henderson, Martin Hess, and their colleagues, a GPN is a site for (among other things) producing and transferring economic value. This suggests a specifically Marxist reading of GPN power, since value in that tradition implies labour exploitation.

Supply-chain management and global commodity chain (GCC) analyses emphasize power as governance, in a specific era of outsourcing and offshoring, rising interfirm managerial authority, and integrated communications technologies (Gereffi 1994; Lambert 2001). Initially attuned to the chain leadership of particular firms at particular nodes (Gereffi 1994), authors concerned with GCCs later contributed to global value chain (GVC) analysis (Gereffi, Humphrey, and Sturgeon 2005). This hybrid approach drew special attention to the location of monopoly rents (including resource rents) in explaining interfirm governance relations as well as differentiated experiences of globalization (see, for example, Kaplinsky 1998).

GPN and GVC analyses both consider two interpenetrating flow types: *material* flows for production (labour and material inputs, including energy sources and catalytic materials); and *abstract* flows (value and rents) that pass through the material flows, providing for profitable production and growth.

Like supply-chain management research, logistics research, both business oriented (Lambert 2001) and critical (Cowen 2010), emphasizes material flow and its governance. As we have seen, one governance practice, stockpiling, historically served several purposes. First, rates and rhythms of work varied between nodes, with conditions at one node creating knock-on effects for its neighbours. Second, means, rhythms, and rates of transport varied between nodes and among different flow types. Third, strikes and accidental interruptions at one node necessarily created pressures on efficiency and profitability elsewhere. Finally, stockpiles provided convenient sites for public and private governance, such as quality control, inventory, and taxation.

The logistics revolution of the late twentieth century, including numerically controlled monitoring, just-in-time (JIT) systems, and intermodal containerization, dramatically enhanced profitability (see Lambert 2001; Bonacich and Wilson 2008, chap. 1). It diminished the practical day-to-day value of large stockpiles and generally accelerated the passage of goods and therefore the turnover time. Yet this made flow efficiency and thus profitability all the more vulnerable to unanticipated interruptions. Accordingly, supply-chain management increasingly required enhanced managerial control over potentially disruptive forces, such as migrant labour and workers at border operations (Walia 2010; Cowen 2010).

Implications of Frontier Extraction

Beyond these insights from chain and network literatures, at least three additional points concern the special circumstances of frontier extractive sites. First, much chain or network literature either neglects fixed-capital formation or assumes that such capital already exists. The same applies to management's prior need to establish the very possibility of extracting useful materials profitably. But frontier locations often require both kinds of investment before production can begin or a labour force, with its day-to-day needs, can move in and take root.

Fossil fuel extraction tends to be relatively capital intensive and high cost wherever it occurs. This has become all the more true as fossil fuels have grown scarcer and harder to extract, requiring sophisticated technology, and as extraction revives in the Global North (Kellogg 2015). Frontier locations increase this expense. Longer distances and more challenging terrain typically add to per-unit transportation costs, while distance from population centres makes it more difficult to attract and maintain a work force. As Andreas Malm (2016) noted, the historical shift from water-powered rural mills to coal-powered urban factories occurred partly because densely populated areas offered independent capitalist producers an abundant supply of workers in need of employment.

The expense associated with frontier extraction also has certain implications with respect to the exercise of state power. The sheer size of the capital investments needed to set up extractive operations in remote locations tends to privilege large, multinational corporations and to encourage monopoly or oligopoly ownership. This situation may then require state intervention in the form of oversight and regulation. At the same time, increased expenses on the frontier, including above-average wage rates to address the high cost of living, may also stimulate state subsidy or other forms of publicly funded support.[9]

Consideration of cost notwithstanding, waves of extractive capital accumulation, at least on northern resource frontiers, typically display three distinct stages:

1. Technological innovations, geological surveys, and engineering research: these initial activities demonstrate that, with the right combination of technology and technique, hard-to-reach resources can in fact be profitably exploited.

2. Investments of fixed capital in the construction of infrastructure needed for specific nodes of production and social reproduction along the chain or for the transportation and communication corridors that connect nodes.

3. Routine extraction, processing, and transport of the resource.

Several observations can be made about these stages. First, temporal gaps between the stages can open possibilities for disruption. For instance, although extractive operations often use the same transportation network (such as a river system or railway) both to bring equipment, labour, and supplies to the extraction site and to bring out the resulting product (such as timber or wheat) this was not the case for Alberta bitumen. There, the outbound product (created at stage 3) was to be shipped through pipelines, rather than along the same highway used for inbound capital equipment and workers—and, since there was no immediate need for the pipelines, their construction (stage 2) was planned for later. With so much capital already tied up in the infrastructure built at the extraction sites, however, companies became vulnerable to tactics aimed at further delaying pipeline construction. Opponents found this to be an effective means of disruption: the delay prevented companies from bringing their product to market, while, in the meanwhile, costs of materials and labour continued to rise.

In addition, time lags at one node can delay (or accelerate) the realization of fixed-capital investments already complete at other nodes. Éric Pineault and David Murray (2016) draw special attention to such asymmetric time lags in fixed-capital investments for the Energy East bitumen pipeline proposal. Extractive and upgrading nodes were built up first. Pressure then rose to complete the remaining capital investments, chiefly relating to pipeline capacity, to ensure the profitability of extractive and upgrading investments already complete or underway. This only encouraged industry opponents to delay the pipelines.

A second point about stage differentiation concerns the integration of chain or network governance. Briefly, chains vary both in the degree of integration of the stages (and their component elements) into single business plans and in the number of firms involved in any such plans. Breaking up responsibility for planning the different stages may impair chain coherence, but it also may have its uses. Bankruptcy sales or sales at a loss may lessen the burden on firms operating at later stages to realize the full value that others built up in early stages. For now, however, the central strategic point is that both time lags and divisions in leadership across the stages do emerge and have real consequences.

A final point concerns the impact of frontier extractive sites on the spatial configuration of a resource chain or network. The earliest GPN literature rightly argued that the complexity of much contemporary production suggests a "network" rather than a "chain" (Henderson et al. 2002). But, in contrast to the nodes in urban manufacturing networks, frontier extractive sites are spatially distant from other nodes, and the often lengthy connecting corridors between them tend to privilege a certain linearity. As a result, the overall pattern of the infrastructure on the landscape more closely resembles a chain than a network. Moreover, because constructing transportation and communication corridors over long distances and/or rugged terrain is expensive and can be technically difficult, these corridors tend to be relatively few in number (although they may multiply if the resource is extensive and/or extraction prolonged or if multiple destinations become important to profitability).

Flow Imbalance as a Generator and Object of Power Relations

What, then, can be said about flow obstruction and release as expressions of power in fossil fuel extractive chains? This section zeroes in on underlying imperatives to establish and maintain proportionality among related material flows over a period of time, if capitalist production is to be sustained profitably. Here, proportionality refers to a set ratio between different material inputs relative to a given quantity of output. A variation in the quantity of output generally requires a proportional change in the quantity of all the inputs, not merely a change in the quantity of some of them. In a linked series or chain of production processes, balance refers to the changes required elsewhere along the chain when such a variation occurs at one point or node in the chain.

In capitalist production, flow proportionality depends on the specific materials and labour that particular production steps require of one another, as well as on the value and rents that those materials bear. One imperative that drives proportionality is based on simple chemistry and physics, as these operate under given technological and organizational conditions. Producing a given volume and type of concrete, for example, will require the combination of specific quantities of lime, gravel, and other materials, and in a specific number of cement mixers of a certain size. A second imperative that becomes important along a chain that is not vertically integrated rests on the principle (however compromised) of equal exchange in market prices and, as some argue, underlying value flows. Thus, for a set combination of cement mixers, lime, gravel, and other materials, plus the needed type and size of work force, a general understanding will emerge in the cement trade about how much money will typically have to flow out to the providers of these various inputs and about how much income the resulting stretch of sidewalks or of foundation walls will yield.

In places and periods of relative stability, these relationships can be worked out arithmetically, in ledgers and work plans, with a reasonable degree of predictability. But the reasons that balance and proportionality stand in the ratios that they do are specific, enduring physical and societal conditions, which in turn compel particular spatio-temporal patterns for operations (Harvey 2013, 267–86; Lawson 2011).

Particular resource chains or networks could hardly internalize such equilibria and proportions fully, given the importance of fuel and other resources to the wider economy. Outside supplements to (or deductions from) their flows are integral to their operation and require integrated analysis: examples include taxes and tax credits, private-sector transfer pricing, and fiat pricing for royalties. These "articulations" (see Wolpe 1980) may arise as unintended side effects of routine activities or as expressions of the interest that wider capitalist networks, civil-societal initiatives, and political forces have in a chain or network's activities. But even given the possibility of sustaining internal disproportions through such articulations, certain workable patterns are likely necessary to sustain overall chain or network activity.

These patterns matter, and not only for workable production arrangements. It is against the imperatives of balance, proportionality, and symmetry that the introduction of imbalance, disproportion, and asymmetry may acquire disruptive strategic significance. Such disruptions may arise spontaneously from structural contradiction or incoherence or as the consequences (intended or unintended) of intentional acts. Flow imbalance is an important indicator and generator of social inequalities, hierarchical control, and ecological domination, but the introduction of disruptive imbalance can foreshadow or directly trigger democratizing, emancipatory, and pro-ecological counter-power.

Taking the foregoing observations into account, a strategic and power-sensitive research agenda should consider at least three contexts for flow balance and imbalance, obstruction and release.

Within the Ordinary Extractive Stage of Existing Chains or Networks

Power relations and capacities (economic and political) can arise from flow imbalances along established extractive chains or networks. The patterns, as well as chain or network vulnerability to them, are likely to vary by case. They arise spatially, most clearly from the arrangement of the physical environment and built infrastructure established in the two previous stages, and temporally, from such routine work rhythms as turnover times and volumes, daily and seasonal rhythms, capital depreciation rates, and rates of material flows. This type of variation is crucial to the differences in capitalist and labour organizing for conventional oil, coal, and water power (see above).

Dysfunctional bottlenecks and shortfalls arise organically from incompatible rates and rhythms of material flow at the various nodes and entrepôts, and along different transportation corridors. (As we will see below, these are also a concern during fixed-capital formation.) Stockpiling is a simple mechanism responding to this diversity, whether planned or arising organically from routine operations. Supply management reflects more intentional, sophisticated responses. JIT supply-chain management is still more sophisticated intervention in flow rates and rhythms, to reduce the unprofitable stockpiling of value-bearing materials. However, the added vulnerability of JIT management to unexpected interruptions (intended or accidental) encourages costly investment in heightened managerial control and policing of potential disruptions.

Often, managerial intervention at just one point in the chain can also resolve imbalances, whether through modification of existing machinery and reorganization (or "debottlenecking": see Suncor 2014) or through targeted "patches" of capital intensification through the application of higher technology (see Samuel 1977). Either technique extends the useful life of older nodes or corridors. But intentionally introducing technological or organizational heterogeneity into the chain or network may then introduce fresh imbalances with socioeconomic and political consequences. High-tech innovation rents may emerge at the "patches," empowering the firms based there and shifting overall interfirm power relations (see Gereffi, Humphrey, and Sturgeon 2005). New "high-tech" workers at such patches may lack solidarity with surrounding "low-tech" workers at other locations. Patterns of outsourcing versus vertical integration might change, as new leading firms assess the optimal institutional arrangements for their newfound power. That in turn would alter the institutional bases for supply-chain management.

Between Major Stages in Chain or Network Life

The latter points suggest larger patterns of unevenness that implicate earlier chain or network stages. First, as is well known, resource-extractive investment, like capital investment generally, commonly comes in distinct waves rather than incrementally; the global commodities boom of the early 2000s is an example. Second, as mentioned above, resource-investment waves often exhibit at least three stages: research establishing a new pattern of profitable resource extraction; fixed-capital investment in a definite series of production sites and corridors; and routine extraction.

Thinking of resource-extractive chains in terms of multi-stage waves has certain implications:

- *Degrees of stage separation*: More profound time lags between stages generally heighten the risk profile for returns on early-stage investments within a given wave. Higher risks can increase pressures for state or other collective action as well as for disruptive strategic interventions.

- *Political-economic asymmetries within and between the stages*: Each stage requires appropriate financing, material inputs, and labour force and therefore exhibits distinct levels of capital, labour, rent, and land intensity. Each generates distinctive products (in broad terms, geological and engineering services, fixed-capital assemblages, and resource commodities, respectively) and distinct degrees of product commodification.

Each stage may therefore display distinct business and political salience, and the combination of stages may form a distinct pattern for a particular chain or network. GVC research has already recommended competitive positioning at *rent-rich* nodes (Kaplinsky 1998). But some fossil fuel chains or networks are also relatively *job rich* at particular stages and *job poor* in others, as with fixed capital and ordinary extraction stages for bitumen steam-assisted gravity drainage (SAGD), relative to the equivalent stages in bitumen strip mining. Governments pressed for job creation therefore likely derive disproportionate benefits from stimulating job-intensive stages. This could force growth at one stage out of rational alignment with the others.

- *Variations in the mode by which products from one stage become inputs for the next*: Are these sold on open markets, transferred between tightly related firms at nominal rates, or simply forwarded between subunits within a single firm or firm alliance (see Gereffi, Humphrey, and Sturgeon 2005)? Are pipelines and other transportation corridors common carriers or (at the limit), as monopoly services for the firms that own them, based at the extractive or upgrading sites? To what extent does the common-carrier pattern coincide with separate corridor ownership?

Between Nodes and Corridors During Research and Fixed-Capital Construction

The fixed-capital infrastructures for resource extraction, transportation, upgrading, storage, and so on, are rarely built simultaneously or even in a tightly coordinated sequence governed by a single business plan or several closely linked ones.

Undoubtedly, practical construction considerations and business competence play roles in the coherence or incoherence of sequencing, as does whether transportation infrastructure is organized as a monopolized asset, as a single common carrier, or as multiple competing lines. Some variation may also involve corporate responses to regulation. For instance, deliberately presenting construction to regulators in separate stages and/or by separate proponents can block consideration of full life-cycle analysis and cumulative effects (Princen 2002) or ensure that project sections come before the most sympathetic regulatory venues (Pralle 2006; Jang 2017). Outsourcing sections of the whole chain's fixed-capital construction can similarly distance firms from upstream or downstream responsibilities while maintaining control over profitability and lead-firm authority over the wider chain (Princen 2002). All such strategies must be measured against the transaction costs involved in breaking up chain authority (see Hopkins and Wallerstein 1986). Finally, all of the above factors have implications for managerial and strategic exercises of power: they are factors that affect the potential threats to the expected return on invested fixed capital by further disrupting the construction sequence, just as they affect measures to police and prevent such disruptions.

Some of these sociopolitical patterns are arguably evident in the history of Alberta bitumen, which has exhibited marked waves of investment and, within them, discrete research, fixed-capital formation, and extractive stages. For example, in the mid- to late 1990s, Premier Ralph Klein's Progressive Conservative government stimulated fixed-capital and consumer-fund investment at Alberta bitumen-extractive sites through deregulation, reduced resource royalties, and other policies. The purpose of these initiatives was ostensibly to restart the provincial economy and especially to increase jobs, not to prepare for a defined foreseeable level of long-term demand for the final chain product, bitumen. Many of the private actors implicated in this stage had similarly little at stake in the extractive stage to follow. Alberta also had the most direct jurisdiction over specific nodes of the final extractive chain, those directly connected with resource-bearing lands. Interprovincial and international trade—and, thus, transport of saleable bitumen—was more clearly federal. Finally, unlike some other resource-extractive chains, outbound transportation for the bitumen required separate infrastructure from inbound transportation for inputs in fixed-capital construction—respectively, pipelines and rail versus (overburdened) highways and airports.

Extractive capacity therefore arguably moved well ahead of pipeline capacity (and consumer-fund capacity in the extractive region). That capacity also built up according to imperatives that did not line up with final demand for the saleable bitumen, either in overall quantities or at the (mainly American) end of existing and anticipated pipeline corridors. All of this arguably heightened the stakes for any further pipeline delays. It opened the door to critics of pipeline obstruction, and indeed for much broader elite demands to accelerate and expand pipeline construction.

Conclusion

Many environmental critiques of modern capitalist relations with non-human (or extra-human) nature stress the functional and physical linearity of material flows. Matter necessary for production is drawn from hinterlands into social production, and transformed matter is then ejected elsewhere, either post-production or post-consumption, for non-human nature to metabolize. Both radical critiques, such as Foster's (2009, 161–200) elaboration on Marx's theory of "metabolic rift," and more reform-minded life-cycle analyses (Brown 2001) stress the interdependent dangers of resource depletion and "waste" disposal.

A kind of balance or proportionality to material flows, on the one hand, and value and rent flows, on the other, is nonetheless essential to extractive and disposal activities, as it is for the economic system as a whole. In part, flow balance and proportionality are physically and unavoidably determined (as with chemical transformations); in part, they are the product of managerial orchestration, including the obstruction and release of flows. Whether disruptions or imbalance emerge organically from structural contradictions and incoherence or are deliberately provoked as strategic interventions (also often in the form of obstruction or release), they merit our attention.

Regimes of obstruction are institutionalized modes of blocking departures from fossil fuel use and from corporate power. This chapter grounds an understanding of the foundations of these regimes in the complex processes that extract, refine, and transport carbon-based fuels. It also highlights the potential vulnerabilities of these regimes presented by certain characteristics of these processes, and it seeks to understand the possibilities and conditions of counter-obstruction that arise on the strength of those vulnerabilities. Interventions from actors detached from core chain operations may be more effective, and flashpoints of contention over chain or network power may be more transformative at points where corporate power is weakest and counter-powers are strongest, or at points where policy concerns (such as visible pollution) are most acute, or at points associated with broader patterns of protest.

But this chapter has suggested another explanatory factor that may be at work: the balances and imbalances, the blockages and bottlenecks, and the intentional or inadvertent obstruction and release of production flows. Actors situated within the chain—management and labour—as well as those located outside it may piggyback their purposes on flow processes that originate within the chain.

This analysis does not mean that contention over fossil fuels reduces to the conditions along these material corridors. Nor does it argue for studying these chains or networks in isolation from wider economic patterns. Rather, it emphasizes the explanatory potential of flow asymmetries, blockages, or bottlenecks in fuel-extractive work processes with respect to power relations, and it draws attention both to their rhythms and syncopations and to their geography.

Corporate interests profit from long-term investments in current energy systems, and they use their power to manage further expansion and to block a just and green transition. But that power is not absolute: it is founded on a complex capitalist production process that is not perfectly under corporate control. The power to block and unblock flows is simultaneously a basis for disruptive counter-power, which can be mobilized to release and accelerate a just and green transition.

Notes

1. Today, such flows—not only of money but also of information—operate without temporal constraints as well: they proceed at the speed of light, indifferent to time zones or national boundaries. Manuel Castells's (1996) "space of flows" accordingly centres on global telecommunications networks that allow for instantaneous transmission and transaction.

2. The issue of constitutional jurisdiction arose in relation to the Horgan government's proposed amendment to BC's Environmental Management Act that would require shippers of heavy oil to obtain a "hazardous substance permit" (see British Columbia 2018, esp. Backgrounder 1). The province argued that such an amendment was justified under ss. 92(13) and 92(16) of the Constitution Act, 1867, which, respectively, grant provinces authority over property and civil rights within a province and over matters of a merely local or private nature. In a May 2019 ruling, the BC Court of Appeal (2019 BCCA 181)

rejected the province's argument on the grounds that the proposed amendment would contravene federal authority under s. 92(10)(a) of the Constitution Act, which exempts lines of shipping and transport that extend beyond provincial borders from a province's jurisdiction over "local works and undertakings." See *Reference re Environmental Management Act (British Columbia)*, 2019 BCCA 181, https://www.canlii.org/en/bc/bcca/doc/2019/2019bcca181/2019bcca181.html, para. 105. The province appealed the ruling, but, in a decision handed down in January 2020, the Supreme Court of Canada (2020 SCC 1) concurred with the BC court and dismissed the appeal—much to the disappointment of environmentalists (Boynton and Zussman 2020).

3. The applicants in this second case, *Coldwater First Nation v. Canada (Attorney General)*, 2020 FCA 34, were the Coldwater Indian Band, the Squamish Nation, the Tsleil-Waututh Nation, and the Ts'elxwéyeqw Tribe of the Stó:lō Nation. In the 2018 case, *Tsleil-Waututh Nation v. Canada (Attorney General)*, 2018 FCA 153, the applicants also included the Upper Nicola Band and the Stk'emlupsemc Te Secwepemc Nation, as well as the Raincoast Conservation Foundation, the Living Oceans Society, the City of Vancouver, and the City of Burnaby.

4. The BC government argues that the Alberta legislation (rather tendentiously titled the Preserving Canada's Economic Prosperity Act) attempts to regulate interprovincial trade and commerce, thereby contravening federal jurisdiction under s. 91(2) of the Constitution Act, and that the legislation cannot be justified under s. 92A—the section that grants provinces jurisdiction in matters concerning non-renewable resources. Although s. 92A(2) specifically allows provinces to pass laws governing the export of such resources, it also stipulates that such laws cannot be applied in a discriminatory manner. On September 24, 2019, the Federal Court granted BC's request for an injunction prohibiting the Alberta government from issuing orders under the law, pending the court's decision on its constitutional status. See *British Columbia (Attorney General) v. Alberta (Attorney General)*, 2019 FC 1195, https://www.canlii.org/en/ca/fct/doc/2019/2019fc1195/2019fc1195.html.

5. Historically, governments in British Columbia refused to abide by the Royal Proclamation of 1763 and, by extension, to recognize the existence of Aboriginal title. Despite the constitutional affirmation of Aboriginal rights and title (Constitution Act, 1982, s. 35), it has taken a series of Supreme Court rulings—notably its landmark decision in *Delgamuukw v. British Columbia*, [1997] 3 SCR 1010—to establish the existence of Aboriginal title in BC, as well as to oblige government (both federal and provincial) to consult adequately with First Nations before encroaching on their territory. Neither government nor industry have welcomed these developments, preferring to devise ways to persuade BC First Nations to "extinguish" their rights: see Lukacs and Pasternak (2020).

6. See "Tiny House Warriors," Secwepemcul'ecw Assembly, 2017, https://www.secwepemculecw.org/tiny-house-warriors. According to a news release dated July 11, 2018, three such tiny houses had been constructed over the past ten months. "Tiny House Warriors Reclaim Land, Block Trans Mountain Expansion Pipeline Route," Secwepemcul'ecw Assembly, 2018, https://www.secwepemculecw.org/.

7. The written versions of many historic treaties (those dating to the eighteenth and nineteenth centuries) differ sharply from what was agreed upon orally at the time the treaties were negotiated, notably on the question of land cession. Other treaty texts also retain significant resource rights, relative to government implementation practices, even before the orally agreed terms are considered. Examples include protections for ongoing use of non-reserve lands in the 1850s Robinson treaties. Governments since the treaties have notoriously violated and ignored such texts. But for some Indigenous leaders and allies, the texts and underlying oral terms have formed the basis for tactical litigation.

8. For an analysis of the protest against the Petronas project, see chapter 16 in this volume. On the multiple concerns that culminated in the proponent's decision to cancel the project, see Leach (2017); Lee (2017).

9. This often-observed high cost of inputs for frontier production sits in suggestive tension with Jason Moore's (2015) arguments about the frontier as a source of "cheap" labour, resources, energy, and food for the wider economy.

References

Alimahomed-Wilson, Jake, and Immanuel Ness, eds. *Choke Points: Logistics Workers Disrupting the Global Supply Chain*. London: Pluto Press, 2018.

Anderson, Drew. 2019. "Alberta's Energy 'War Room' Launches in Calgary." *CBC News*, December 11, 2019. https://www.cbc.ca/news/canada/calgary/alberta-war-room-launch-calgary-1.5392371.

Bair, Jennifer. 2005. "Global Capitalism and Commodity Chains: Looking Back, Going Forward." *Competition and Change* 9, no. 2: 153–80.

Belanger, Yale D., and P. Whitney Lackenbauer. 2014. *Blockades or Breakthroughs? Aboriginal Peoples Confront the Canadian State*. Montréal and Kingston: McGill-Queen's University Press.

Bellrichard, Chantelle. 2018. "'More Was Required of Canada': Ruling Shows Where Ottawa Fell Short with First Nations on Trans Mountain." *CBC News*, August 31, 2018. https://www.cbc.ca/news/indigenous/trans-mountain-appeal-ruling-first-nations-duty-to-consult-1.4805694.

Berman, Tzeporah. 2018. "Opinion: From Clayoquot Sound to Trans Mountain, the Power of Protest Endures." *Globe and Mail*, April 20, 2018. https://www.theglobeandmail.com/opinion/article-from-clayoquot-sound-to-trans-mountain-the-power-of-protest-endures/.

Bernstein, Stephen, and Benjamin Cashore. 2007. "Can Non-State Global Governance Be Legitimate? An Analytical Framework." *Regulation and Governance* 1, no. 4: 347–71.

Bonacich, Edna, and Jake B. Wilson. 2008. *Getting the Goods: Ports, Labor, and the Logistics Revolution.* Ithaca, NY: Cornell University Press.

Boynton, Sean, and Richard Zussman. 2020. "BC Government, Environmentalists 'Disappointed' over Trans Mountain Court Decision." *Global News*, January 16, 2020. https://globalnews.ca/news/6422611/bc-reax-trans-mountain-pipeline-court-case/.

Braverman, Harry. 1974. "Scientific Management." In *Labour and Monopoly Capitalism: The Degradation of Work in the Twentieth Century*, 85–138. New York: Monthly Review Press.

British Columbia. 2018. "Province Submits Court Reference to Protect B.C.'s Coast." Office of the Premier, Ministry of Attorney General, Ministry of Environment and Climate Change Strategy. April 26, 2018. https://archive.news.gov.bc.ca/releases/news_releases_2017-2021/2018PREM0019-000742.pdf.

Brown, Lester. 2001. "Designing a New Materials Economy." In *Eco-Economy: Building an Economy for the Earth*, 121–43. New York: W. W. Norton.

Canadian Press. 2020a. "The Latest on Protests Across Canada in Support of Anti-Pipeline Demonstrators." *EnergyNow.ca*, February 12, 2020. https://energynow.ca/2020/02/the-latest-on-coastal-gaslink-protests-across-canada/.

———. 2020b. "Trans Mountain Scores a Win as Federal Court Dismisses First Nations' Challenges." *Calgary Herald*, February 4, 2020. https://calgaryherald.com/business/energy/alert-federal-court-of-appeal-dismisses-challenge-to-trans-mountain-pipeline.

Cashore, Benjamin, Graeme Auld, and Deanna Newsom. 2004. *Governing Through Markets: Forest Certification and the Emergence of Non-State Authority.* New Haven: Yale University Press.

Castells, Manuel. 1996. *The Rise of the Network Society.* Vol. 1, *The Information Age: Economy, Society and Culture.* Malden, MA: Blackwell.

Charles, Loïc. 2003. "The Visual History of the *Tableau Économique*." *European Journal of the History of Economic Thought* 10, no. 4: 527–50.

Cleaver, Harry. (1979) 2000. *Reading Capital Politically.* Austin: University of Texas Press.

Cowen, Deborah. 2010. "A Geography of Logistics: Market Authority and the Security of Supply Chains." *Annals of the Association of American Geographers* 100, no. 3: 600–20.

Creighton, Donald G. 1956. *The Empire of the St. Lawrence.* Toronto: Macmillan of Canada.

Daly, Herman E., and John B. Cobb Jr. 1989. *For the Common Good: Redirecting the Economy Toward Community, the Environment, and a Sustainable Future.* Boston: Beacon Press.

Drache, Daniel. 1996. "Introduction—Celebrating Innis: The Man, the Legacy, and Our Future." In *Staples, Markets, and Cultural Change: Selected Essays, Harold A. Innis,* edited by Daniel Drache, xiii–lix. Montréal and Kingston: McGill-Queen's University Press.

Eltis, W. A. 1975a. "François Quesnay: A Reinterpretation. 1. The *Tableau Économique.*" *Oxford Economic Papers,* n.s., 27, no. 2: 167–200.

———. 1975b. "François Quesnay: A Reinterpretation. 2. The Theory of Economic Growth." *Oxford Economic Papers,* n.s., 27, no. 3: 327–51.

Fischer-Kowalski, Marina. 1998. "Society's Metabolism: The Intellectual History of Materials Flow Analysis, Part I, 1860–1970." *Journal of Industrial Ecology* 2, no. 1: 61–78.

Fischer-Kowalski, Marina, and Walter Hüttler. 1998. "Society's Metabolism: The Intellectual History of Materials Flow Analysis, Part II, 1970–1998." *Journal of Industrial Ecology* 2, no. 4: 107–36.

Foster, John Bellamy. 2009. *The Ecological Revolution: Making Peace with the Planet.* New York: Monthly Review Press.

Georgescu-Roegen, Nicholas. 1971. *The Entropy Law and the Economic Process.* Cambridge, MA: Harvard University Press.

Gereffi, Gary. 1994. "The Organization of Buyer-Driven Global Commodity Chains: How US Retailers Shape Overseas Production Networks." In *Commodity Chains and Global Capitalism,* edited by Gary Gereffi and Miguel Korzeniewicz, 95–122. Westport, CT: Praeger.

Gereffi, Gary, John Humphrey, and Timothy Sturgeon. 2005. "The Governance of Global Value Chains." *Review of International Political Economy* 12, no. 1: 78–104.

Harris, Kathleen. 2018. "Liberals to Buy Trans Mountain Pipeline for $4.5B to Ensure Expansion Is Built." *CBC News,* May 29, 2018. https://www.cbc.ca/news/politics/liberals-trans-mountain-pipeline-kinder-morgan-1.4681911.

Harvey, David. 2003. *The New Imperialism.* Oxford: Oxford University Press.

———. 2013. *A Companion to Marx's Capital, Volume 2.* London: Verso.

Henderson, Jeffrey, Peter Dicken, Martin Hess, Neil Coe, and Henry Wai-Chung Yeung. 2002. "Global Production Networks and the Analysis of Economic Development." *Review of International Political Economy* 9, no. 3: 436–64.

Hess, Martin, and Henry Wai-Chung Yeung. 2006. "Whither Global Production Networks in Economic Geography? Past, Present and Future." *Environment and Planning A* 38: 1193–1204.

Hopkins, Terence K., and Immanuel Wallerstein. 1986. "Commodity Chains in the World-Economy Prior to 1800." *Review: A Journal of the Fernand Braudel Center* 10, no. 1: 157–70.

Jang, Brent. 2017. "Court Orders NEB to Examine Proposed TransCanada Pipeline's Jurisdiction." *Globe and Mail*, July 20, 2017. https://www.theglobeandmail.com/report-on-business/industry-news/energy-and-resources/court-orders-neb-to-examine-proposed-transcanada-pipelines-jurisdiction/article35756274/.

Kalecki, Michal. 1939. *Essays in the Theory of Economic Fluctuations*. London: George Allen and Unwin.

Kapelos, Vassy, and John Paul Tasker. 2020. "Cost of Trans Mountain Expansion Soars to $12.6B." *CBC News*, February 7, 2020. https://www.cbc.ca/news/politics/vassy-trans-mountain-pipeline-1.5455387.

Kaplinsky, Raphael. 1998. "Globalisation, Industrialisation and Sustainable Growth: The Pursuit of the Nth Rent." IDS Discussion Paper 365. Brighton, UK: Institute of Development Studies, University of Sussex.

Kellogg, Paul. 2015. "The Political Economy of Oil and Democracy in Venezuela and Alberta." In *Alberta Oil and the Decline of Democracy in Canada*, edited by Meenal Shrivastava and Lorna Stefanick, 139–68. Edmonton: Athabasca University Press.

Keynes, John Maynard. 1936. *The General Theory of Employment, Interest and Money*. London: Macmillan.

Klein, Naomi. 2014. *This Changes Everything: Capitalism vs. the Climate*. Toronto: Knopf Canada.

Lambert, Douglas M. 2001. "The Supply Chain Management and Logistics Controversy." In *Handbook of Logistics and Supply Chain Management*, edited by Ann M. Brewer, Kenneth J. Button, and David A. Hensher, 99–126. Amsterdam: Pergamon.

Lawson, James. 2009. "Power, Political Economy, and Environmental Governance: Staple Chains as Media of Power." *International Journal of Green Economics* 3, no. 1: 28–47.

———. 2011. "Chronotope, Story, and Historical Geography: Mikhail Bakhtin and the Space-Time of Narratives." *Antipode* 43, no. 2: 384–412.

Leach, Andrew. 2017. "Why Petronas Cancelled Its Plans for an LNG Project on B.C.'s Coast." *Maclean's*, July 29, 2017.

Leahy, Derek. 2014. "June 28th: Final 'Tar Sands Healing Walk' Simply a New Beginning, Say Organizers." *The Narwhal*, May 20, 2014. https://thenarwhal.ca/june-28th-final-tar-sands-healing-walk-simply-new-beginning-say-organizers/.

Lee, Marc. 2017. "Opinion: Why Petronas' LNG Cancellation Is a Blessing for B.C." *Vancouver Sun*, August 2, 2017. http://vancouversun.com/opinion/op-ed/opinion-why-petronas-lng-cancellation-is-a-blessing-for-b-c.

Leontief, Wassily W. 1936. "Quantitative Input and Output Relations in the Economic Systems of the United States." *Review of Economics and Statistics* 18, no. 3: 105–25.

———. 1937. "Interrelation of Prices, Output, Savings, and Investment." *Review of Economics and Statistics* 19, no. 3: 109–32.

Lightfoot, Gordon. 1967. "Canadian Railroad Trilogy." *The Way I Feel*, side 2, track 5. United Artists Records (UAS 6587). Vinyl LP, released April 1967.

Lukacs, Martin, and Shiri Pasternak. 2020. "Industry, Government Pushed to Abolish Aboriginal Title at Issue in Wet'suwet'en Stand-off, Docs Reveal." *The Narwhal*, February 7, 2020. https://thenarwhal.ca/industry-government-pushed-to-abolish-aboriginal-title-at-issue-in-wetsuweten-stand-off-docs-reveal/.

Malm, Andreas. 2016. *Fossil Capital: The Rise of Steam Power and the Roots of Global Warming*. London: Verso.

Marx, Karl. (1978) 1992. *Capital*. Volume 2. Translated by David Fernbach. Introduction by Ernest Mandel. London: Penguin Books / New Left Review.

Mitchell, Timothy. 2011. *Carbon Democracy: Political Power in the Age of Oil*. London: Verso.

Moore, Jason W. 2015. *Capitalism in the Web of Life: Ecology and the Accumulation of Capital*. London: Verso.

Morgan, Geoffrey. 2018. "'Ready and Prepared to Turn Off the Taps': Notley Issues Stark Warning to B.C. as Pipeline Fight Escalates." *Financial Post*, May 16, 2018. https://business.financialpost.com/news/ready-and-prepared-to-turn-off-the-taps-notley-issues-stark-warning-to-b-c-as-pipeline-fight-escalates.

Napoleon, Val. 2010. "Behind the Blockades." *Indigenous Law Journal* 9, no. 1: 11.

Naylor, R. T. 1972. "The Rise and Fall of the Third Commercial Empire of the St. Lawrence." In *Capitalism and the National Question in Canada*, edited by Gary Teeple, 1–43. Toronto: University of Toronto Press.

Nijhuis, Michelle. 2018. "'I'm Just More Afraid of Climate Change Than I Am of Prison.'" *New York Times Magazine*, February 13, 2018.

Nore, Petter, and Terisa Turner, eds. 1981. *Oil and Class Struggle*. London: Zed Press.

Pineault, Éric, and David Murray. 2016. *Le piège Énergie Est: Sortir de l'impasse des sables bitumineux*. Montréal: Éditions écosociété.

Pralle, Sarah B. 2006. *Branching Out, Digging In: Environmental Advocacy and Agenda Setting*. Washington, DC: Georgetown University Press.

Princen, Thomas. 2002. "Distancing: Consumption and the Severing of Feedback." In *Confronting Consumption*, edited by Thomas Princen, Michael Maniates, and Ken Conca, 103–31. Cambridge, MA: MIT Press.

Rowe, James, Jessica Dempsey, and Peter Gibbs. 2016. "The Power of Fossil Fuel Divestment (and Its Secret)." In *A World to Win: Contemporary Social Movements and Counter-Hegemony*, edited by William K. Carroll and Kanchan Sarker, 233–49. Winnipeg: ARP Books.

Rueschemeyer, Dietrich. 1986. *Power and the Division of Labour*. Stanford, CA: Stanford University Press.

Samuel, Raphael. 1977. "Workshop of the World: Steam Power and Hand Technology in Mid-Victorian Britain." *History Workshop* 3, no. 1: 6–72.

Schachter, Gustav. 1991. "Francois Quesnay: Interpreters and Critics Revisited." *American Journal of Economics and Sociology* 50, no. 3: 313–22.

Suncor. 2014. "Oil Sands Players No Longer Keeping It All Bottled Up." *OSQAR: Oil Sands Question and Response* (blog). April 17, 2014. http://osqar.suncor. com/2014/04/oil-sands-players-no-longer-keeping-it-all-bottled-up.html.

Tencer, Daniel. 2018. "Kinder Morgan Pipeline Buyout: Analysts Question Trudeau's Move as Activists Vow to Fight On." *Huffington Post*, May 29, 2018. https://www.huffingtonpost.ca/2018/05/29/trans-mountain-buyout-analysts-activists_a_23446150/.

Trace, Keith. 2001. "Bulk Commodity Logistics." In *Handbook of Logistics and Supply-Chain Management*, edited by Ann M. Brewer, Kenneth J. Button, and David A. Hensher, 441–54. Amsterdam: Pergamon.

Unist'ot'en Camp. 2017. "Unist'ot'en Camp: Heal the People, Heal the Land." Accessed August 9, 2017. http://unistoten.camp/wp-content/uploads/2019/01/UZINE_View.pdf.

Walia, Harsha. 2010. "Transient Servitude: Migrant Labour in Canada and the Apartheid of Citizenship." *Race and Class* 52, no. 1: 71–84.

Wanderley, Fernanda, Leila Mokrani, and Alice Guimaraes. 2012. "The Socio-Economic Dynamics of Gas in Bolivia." In *Flammable Societies: Studies on the Socio-Economics of Oil and Gas*, edited by John-Andrew McNeish and Owen Logan, 176–200. London: Pluto.

Watkins, Mel. 2006. *Staples and Beyond*. Montréal and Kingston: McGill-Queen's University Press.

Williams, Nia. 2019. "Court Blocks Alberta Law Curbing Energy Flows to British Columbia." *Reuters*, September 24, 2019. https://www.reuters.com/article/us-canada-energy-alberta-idUSKBN1W929Y.

Wolpe, Harold. 1980. "Introduction." In *The Articulation of Modes of Production: Essays from Economy and Society*, edited by Harold Wolpe, 1–43. London: Routledge.

Workman, Thom, and Geoffrey McCormack. 2015. *The Servant State: Overseeing Capital Accumulation in Canada*. Halifax: Fernwood.

3   Landscapes of Risk

Financial Representations of Catastrophe

Mark Hudson

In late June 2017, the Financial Stability Board's Task Force on Climate-Related Financial Disclosures (TCFD), led by billionaire Michael Bloomberg, founder and CEO of the financial services and data firm Bloomberg LP, released its final report (TCFD 2017). A week later, another financial heavy hitter, Mark Carney—governor of the Bank of England and chair of the Financial Stability Board at the time—presented the report to heads of state at the G20 summit in Hamburg. The report, which was given a considerable amount of space in the mainstream business press, recommended that companies reveal their climate-based risks to investors, in order that consideration of such risks might become a standard part of investment decisions. This has been a goal of climate campaigners for some time—particularly those operating through shareholder activism. On the surface, such disclosure could result in a significant revaluation of firms and their share prices, by making visible what the TCFD report calls the "material risks" of climate change. As one member of the task force put it, by shedding light on "the fact that climate-related risks and opportunities can be material, and increasingly will be material," the report aimed to make these risks "clear and comparable—that is what the investment community wants" (McCarthy 2017).

Disclosure such as this is supposed to make markets work more efficiently. However, acts of revelation often simultaneously serve to obscure, as any decent magician will tell you. While recognizing that a significant shift has occurred in corporate practice and discourse relating to climate change, in what follows I lay out how the modes of revealing climate change currently being developed by financial firms have the potential both to dramatically change the public understanding and the politics of climate change as an environmental problem and to serve to obstruct a robust, democratic political response to the threat of climate catastrophe.

From Denial to Risk Management: Two Fronts of the Corporate Response

Gone are the days when CEOs of major companies or even politicians could publicly deny that climate change is happening or that human activities are the main driver. Even the most notorious agents of climate denial such as Exxon, which obscured what it knew about the connection between its main product and climate change, and which funded the "merchants of doubt" (Oreskes and Conway 2010) in their campaign to sow uncertainty over climate science, can no longer simply say "It's not happening" or even "We don't know if it's happening." Forced to acknowledge that climate change is real and human induced, Exxon publicly endorsed the Paris Agreement and said that it would support a carbon tax. Clearly, what Exxon says and what Exxon does are far from identical. While acknowledging climate change, the corporation remains wedded to a business model that, if it is allowed to continue, will put us well over the 2°C "safe" average global warming threshold. Its demand projections and planning models assume that we will overshoot. Research from the Corporate Mapping Project has unearthed the emergence of a "new denialism" along these lines, describing a shift from good old head-in-the-sand denial that there is a problem or that we are in any way responsible to a public acknowledgement of the problem, its severity, and its genesis in human activity, all the while working the back channels to ensure that no action is taken that would actually address the problem. That is, the denial concerns not the science but what the science implies for policy (Klein and Daub 2016).

Corporate and government inaction aside, acknowledgement of anthropogenic climate change is widespread among political and economic elites globally. It features prominently at elite policy gatherings like the World Economic Forum in Davos, Switzerland. Of course, this consensus on the reality and significance of climate change has emerged within the parameters of another one: that any steps taken toward adaptation and mitigation must occur within current social relations; that is, they must not seriously threaten the conditions for accumulation, and while steps are sure to result in winners and losers across sectors, they will take place within existing relations of property and power. Now that political, industrial, and financial elites have decided that they cannot ignore the unpalatable mess of climate change that they have created (Heede 2014), they are asking how they might attempt to digest it, without causing too much internal damage and, preferably, while getting some joy out of it. In addition to the strategies being worked out by networks of capitalists to obstruct political action on climate change, there is increasing effort to make the biophysical and meteorological effects of climate change comprehensible and actionable (commensurable and exchangeable) to market actors.

So there is a two-front class-based response to climate change, intended to manage the implications of climate change for profitability and accumulation. They align with the two primary ways that capitalists, as a class, must understand and treat nature. The first of these, as Mann and Wainwright (2018) indicate, is as a collection of resources. That is, it is a storehouse of raw materials that can be put to use in the creation of commodities and, in turn, value. In this vein, we see corporations scrambling, through the new denialism, to maintain their access to the fossil fuel storehouse. The second way that nature is apprehended, however, is as an element of uncertainty, risk, and hazard to the production of value. Forests, for example, are increasingly seen as ticking time bombs of value destruction given their (increasingly catastrophic) tendency to catch on fire. Where once there was timber, now there is fuel. Oceanfront once contributed to property value; we may now be at a point where the menace of storm surges and flooding detracts more than the view adds (Luscombe 2017). While some parts of the business lobby are busy staving off any genuine political action that might reduce their ease of access to fossil fuel resources and to the atmosphere, the financial industry has for some time been becoming attuned to the potential threat to profit (and perhaps to accumulation overall) posed by climate change itself. This latter front began to develop with the growing realization among particularly exposed or sensitive elements of capital that, in fact, real economic costs—discussed as "material risks"—were starting to emerge that are related to climate change. In what follows, I attempt to trace the contours of this second front and to consider its implications for the status of nature and for climate justice. Is this transformation of how we see, understand, and act on the problem of climate change a successful "mainstreaming" of climate action, or is it another obstruction on the pathway to just and sustainable societies?

One of the ways we can think about how climate change presents risks for profitability is through the concept of "negative value." This is a concept put forward by Jason Moore (2015a, 2015b) to talk about the possibility that rather than providing appropriable value to capital through the provision of "free work," reorganizations of socioecological arrangements can sometimes actually inhibit accumulation. Moore (2015a, 98) defines negative value (in contrast to surplus value) as "the emergence of historical natures that are increasingly hostile to capital accumulation." In the case of climate change, Moore describes how "capitalism's wastes are now overflowing the sinks, and spilling out over the ledgers of capital" (279).

While Moore argues, I think correctly, that the obstacles to accumulation presented by climate change are unavoidable by capital as a whole because they act to directly increase the costs of production (see Risky Business Project 2014), the *distribution* of negative value among firms (that is, when and where disasters or changes in weather patterns that have cost implications occur) has become the subject of competitive manoeuvring such as efforts to "climate proof" businesses against weather-related supply-chain disruptions or to socialize their costs. Many of the forms taken by capital's response to climate change, which we will sample below, can be understood as efforts to diversify and spread risk or to transfer the costs of climate change (its negative value) onto other parties.

The redistribution of negative value from climate change certainly involves political action. Firms, industries, and associations lobby and backroom deal to reduce political risk by minimizing or displacing costs of regulation. They also, through image management, attempt to maintain or gain market share by greening their corporate images.

It also involves market action—reallocating capital, changing asset mixes and investment portfolios, managing supply chains, and creating new commodities, all of which depend on the creation of credible (not to be confused with accurate) information that firms and investors can act on. This information must eventually take the form of a number, for the simple reason that in order to be of use to market-based actors, it has to be related to a price. The work that goes into the creation of this information I call the work of digestion. It involves the transformation of place-bound, relational, qualitatively heterogeneous effects and phenomena (like wildland fires, or melting arctic sea ice, or drought) into seemingly unbound, isolated, homogeneous quantities that eventually find their way into prices and, through those, into new allocations of social labour and new relationships between humans and extra-human nature. I believe digestion to be an apt metaphor for this because it involves a diverse, qualitatively heterogeneous range of things (think apples and oranges) being inserted at one end and, at the other, the production of what looks and feels like a fairly homogeneous quantity: a substance varying largely by some commensurable unit, like weight or volume. It *may* in fact vary in quality from others of its kind, but we would rather not look closely enough to find out.

In order to get a solid handle on what I mean by digestion, and on how capital is working to translate the messiness of climate change into an order it can handle, we can look at the products of digestion—primarily new kinds of commodities and tools for modifying the value of existing commodities. The most obvious of these are carbon emissions allowances, or offsets. A great deal of ingenuity goes into translating a landscape into separable units of potential carbon sequestration: what is bought and sold as a credit for a tonne of carbon either sequestered or never emitted is in fact a set of modified ecological and social relations, and it requires some intricate accounting and a few fairly heroic assumptions to transform these relations into a tonne of carbon not emitted (or its equivalent in other greenhouse gases, expressed as "CO_2e"). However, while carbon credits get a lot of attention, they are as yet a boutique kind of commodity for which governments and firms are struggling to make and maintain markets. Other products of digestive work have broader consequences, potentially affecting every commodity price and every investment decision.

Climate Change Risk Indexes

One of the functions of digestion is to provide better information to investors and traders. From the perspective of capital, the key questions with regard to climate change are these: What is going to happen to the price of wheat, rice, natural gas, or herring, or the value of land, factories, or real estate, as climate change destabilizes the biological and biophysical conditions of production? How can investors or firms make informed decisions about assets and commodities in the face of this destabilization? Is there a way to turn "climate change" into a number that can modify my net present value calculations? This is the practical dimension through which climate change is a problem for capital.

The "problem" of climate change can, however, be constructed in a number of ways. One of these—certainly one that is plausible—is to construct it as a form of "catastrophe risk" (see Cooper 2008, 82; Haller 2002). In this framework, we are confronted with the dilemma of having to take action in the face of irreducible uncertainty. Having a very strong suspicion that something really terrible is going on, combined with an inability to calculate its likelihood, or to "pinpoint the precise when, where and how of the coming havoc" (Cooper 2008, 83), leaves us in a bind, with no calculable basis for action, but also with the sense (in some cases very well empirically grounded) that terrible things will occur in the absence of action. For that portion of humanity with the most grounded, experiential, or proximate sense of impending, irreversible disaster (pick a small island state whose coastlines are shrinking, for example), this kind of framework makes sense and impels a *moral* requirement to act even in the absence of certainty. Capital, however, has a hard time operating within this framework. Incalculability is just one more limit to overcome. As such, firms reject this construction of climate change in favour of the much more comfortable framework of risk management. Here, morality exits the picture, crowded out by the fetish of numbers. Likelihoods are calculated—partly through the hive mind of insurance and investment markets and partly through increasingly sophisticated modelling techniques, often developed at the outset in universities and then made proprietary and dispensed on a (hefty) fee-for-service basis.

For example, there are a number of efforts to do a coarse-grain, nation-by-nation quantification of climate change risk. This form of digestion attempts to take the multiple forms of material transformations and "vulnerabilities" faced by a particular territory and relate them quantitatively to those faced by all others. All of these rely to some extent on the notion that risk is a product of vulnerability and "readiness" or "resilience." The Notre Dame Global Adaptation Initiative, for example—a project housed at the University of Notre Dame—defines its ND-GAIN Country Index as a "measurement tool that helps governments, businesses and communities examine risks exacerbated by climate change, such as over-crowding, food insecurity, inadequate infrastructure, and civil conflicts."[1] The index assigns countries scores in two broad categories: their vulnerability to climate change and their readiness to adapt to it. Each of these scores is based on forty-five indicators related to food, water, human habitat, ecosystem services, economy, governance, and social readiness. These indicators, of course, embed all sorts of political presumptions about what makes for a "ready" or "resilient" state—things like control over corruption, business climate, educational attainment, or the debt-to-GDP ratio. ND-GAIN, for example, uses the World Bank's "Ease of Doing Business" index as the economic component of its "readiness" indicator. This is an index of how easy it is to start and profitably operate a business in any given country: a country with high levels of investor protection and low levels of regulation and taxation is deemed more "ready" than a country in which regulations (possibly including environmental ones) or licensing processes make setting up and running business operations more risky and difficult. Index scores can be used as intended by the project as a basis for identifying priority locations for climate change adaptation but equally for discounting investments in low-scoring nations. As of 2017, Canada ranked thirteenth out of 181 countries on the global list. Norway was the front-runner, with Somalia coming last.[2]

Figure 3.1. The ND-GAIN Country Index. Source: University of Notre Dame, https://gain.nd.edu/our-work/country-index/.

Other platforms offering the same sort of information are presented more explicitly as tools for investment and corporate risk management in the face of climate change. Investment bank HSBC, for example, developed a climate change scorecard for nations in 2009 (updated in 2011 and again in 2013), which is not too dissimilar from the ND-GAIN: ranking nations (but not actually producing a risk coefficient) according to their exposure (how likely any country is to be adversely effected by climate change) and their sensitivity to climate change (how economically significant any such effects are), as well as on two indicators of resilience, "adaptive potential" and "adaptive capacity."

One interesting aspect of the HSBC research is that, like the ND-GAIN Country Index, while it provides what appears to be neutral information on the state of the world, it simultaneously produces a list of appropriate managerial targets through which governments and multilateral development institutions might influence the investment ratings of a country. Thus, the numbers and their means of generation become active, orienting managerial attention, rather than simply being passive reflections of an existing state of affairs. Education, for example, becomes a way of reducing one's exposure to adverse climate effects. In a particularly ironic twist, increasing a country's GDP per capita (a very good predictor of a country's contribution to climate change) improves its risk ranking, so the more a nation exacerbates the overall problem, the less vulnerable it is. The debt-to-GDP ratio is also included, so the very political process of minimizing debt—which frequently means imposition of austerity and in some cases pressure to increase production of natural resources, including fossil fuels—here translates numerically into a reduction in climate change vulnerability. In short, there should be no false hopes that these kinds of rankings will serve as a device through which financial markets discipline states or firms into taking action to reduce emissions. The rankings actually reflect a nation's ability to insulate *commodity values* from climate change and thus provide only a very rough estimate of predicted negative value.

While the exercise undertaken by HSBC produces only a ranking and not a specific set of national risk coefficients, it is an early effort to make the uncertain effects of climate change visible to banks and investors and integral to investment algorithms. Private firms such as Risk Management Solutions (RMS) and Verisk Maplecroft (a subsidiary of Verisk Analytics) offer tailor-made quantifications of risk to supply chains, operations, and investments around the world, promising to make the complex field of environmental, social, and political risks—including those arising from climate change—transparent to investors. Four Twenty Seven, which integrates the data from ND-GAIN into its analytics, similarly helps its clients to "reduce risks, identify new opportunities, and build resilience in the face of climate change."[3] In addition to gathering market intelligence, the firm offers made-to-order climate risk scores for specific companies based on the precise location of their corporate facilities and on the sectors or industries in which a particular company is active, thereby enabling investors to factor climate change into their portfolio management and investment decisions. In order to enhance its own risk assessment toolkit, Moody's purchased a majority stake in Four Twenty Seven in July 2019.

Apart from mapping the physical risks of climate change for the benefit of investors, effort is also going into calculating political risk. For example, the global asset management company Schroders provides fund managers with analyses of "Carbon Value at Risk" (Carbon VaR), a process that assumes governments will eventually impose (in some form) a $100/ton price of carbon and then provides an estimate of the cost implications of this for any particular firm. This representation translates climate change directly into expected future profit and therefore shareholder value. Climate change is indeed made visible as a material risk, but the implications for action by the firm remain open. One such action would be to minimize exposure in the event of the "worst-case" scenario (from the firms' perspective), in which governments actually act to keep us below a 2°C average global warming. The other, of which we see much greater evidence, is to realistically assess what governments are doing, rather than saying, about establishing a meaningful carbon price and intervening aggressively through lobbying and campaign funding to minimize the likelihood of any political action that would avoid catastrophic global warming but also trigger potentially large losses in value in the short and medium term.

We are thus witnessing the rise of a small, privatized, scientific industry whose purpose is to produce and sell a visible climate risk landscape, which then becomes the salient aspect of climate change for investors, banks, and firms. What is produced and made visible through this work is a geography of negative and positive value, altered according to changing climate patterns and distributions of disruptive events. Each qualitative form of havoc is made commensurable with every other, and the damage done to lives both human and otherwise, to specific communities, to landscapes and eco-systems, becomes identical (in the gaze of capital and, in turn, policy makers, civil-society organizations, NGOs, and the rest of us) with risks to value—always mediated through price and already-existing value. This means, of course, that flood damage to a wealthy Florida neighbourhood is "worse"—*ceteris paribus*—than that done to a Dhaka slum. The possibility that we may lose 50 percent of animal species in "biodiversity hotspots" (Watts 2018) is *in itself* insignificant post-digestion. What matters is how this might transform the landscape of risk and the existing or potential future value of an asset under current projections of warming. Climate change is seen not as an existential threat for particular people, plants, animals, towns, nations, or ways of life but, first and foremost, as an optimization problem. However, as we will see, the numbers generated only ever have an uncertain and probabilistic relationship to the realities they purport to represent. We should be clear that these are representations, whose job is to be credible enough to create value for their producers. They are not climate change. They are a view of climate change as seen through a lens that filters everything but value.

Insurance and Reinsurance

The first group to have recognized climate change as a form of negative value was probably the insurance industry—and its insurers, the reinsurance indus-try. Insurance has been positioned as an important tool for climate adaptation, particularly for low-income nations or governments without the financial wherewithal to cope with the aftermath of disasters, enabling them to trans-fer risk and access funds in greater volumes and more quickly than through other forms of lending or relief (Grove 2010, 541). The insurance industry has considerable expertise in converting various forms of tragedy, disaster, and catastrophe into streams of numbers, and their profitability rests on their ability to do so with a reasonable degree of accuracy. This goes back perhaps as far as the fourteenth century, and certainly as far as the seventeenth, as merchants and lenders were trying to quantify and insure against the risks of getting cargo across the ocean (Martin 1876, 6).

Thanks to this long expertise, the insurance industry has been at the forefront of the attempt to quantify the likely impacts of climate change, par-ticularly as they relate to weather-related property damage and casualties. Reinsurers, who are ultimately holding the bag in the event that the insurers find themselves overexposed, have been attempting to grapple with climate change (as far as it impacts their bottom line) for longer than most other industries and for longer than many governments (Johnson 2011, 2). Since 1980, average insured losses worldwide from extreme weather have doubled each decade, hitting US$50 billion by 2013 (Reguly 2013). Much of this is due to a significant increase in the value and quantity of exposed settlements and infrastructure (McAneney 2014), but a changing climate and increased incidence of natural disasters are also playing an important part (Thomas, Albert, and Hepburn 2014). With regard to Hurricane Harvey, for example—an event that JPMorgan estimated would result in $10 billion to $20 billion in insured losses (Keoun 2017)—climate change researchers suggested that the probability of such an intensity of rainfall in the Houston area was increased by a factor of three on account of global warming (van Oldenborgh et al. 2017, 10).

So one would imagine that the (re)insurance industry is in a particularly sensitive place with regard to the "material risks" of climate change. The industry's public pronouncements would support this view. In an early attempt to draw the attention of insurance executives to the threat to profitability, for example, a 2006 report from specialty insurer Lloyd's declared that "so far, the industry has not taken changing catastrophe trends seriously enough. Climate change is likely to bring us all an even more uncertain future. If we do not take action now to understand the risks and their impact, the changing climate could kill us" (Lloyd's 360 Risk Project 2006, 3).

Despite this dire early warning, the extent to which (re)insurers are integrating climate change into their corporate practices is unclear. In a study of the reinsurance market, Leigh Johnson (2011, 53) concluded that, "by and large, firms have not developed formal or informal methods for integrating climate change impacts into their underwriting and pricing decisions." She attributes this in part to the uncertainties that plague the process of digestion. The implications of climate change, at least in 2010, when Johnson was writing, were understood to be uncertain as well as small relative to other sources of variation and uncertainty. Catastrophe models are made up of modules that aim to predict not only the likelihood of a hazard but also how it will interact with the built environment, and with the financial value of elements within that environment, so uncertainties are stacked. As a result, the public commitment to integrate climate change into pricing and underwriting was not reflected in actual practice (Johnson 2011). Since then, the quantifying practice of "probabilistic event attribution" has advanced considerably, to the point that litigators are interested in their use in assigning specific blame for specific, climate-related harms (Dzieza 2018; for a more skeptical view, see Lusk 2017). Climate models have improved in their degree of resolution. Nonetheless, (re)insurers and the catastrophe-modelling firms upon which many of them rely still find themselves facing considerable challenges because probabilities assigned to weather events—to their severity, their combination, and the likely property damage associated with them—are no longer stable, and different climate models vary considerably in their forecasts. They realize that the models based on historic data underestimate the costs they will likely have to pay out now or in the future, so they are trying to turn from historical to predictive modelling, relying on processes of "expert elicitation." The latter involves asking a handful of climate scientists for their best guesses as to the future of, for example, hurricane frequency and severity over the next five years and using those as a basis for modelling. That may be a step forward but leaves (re)insurers stuck with another source of uncertainty. The Geneva Association (a think tank for insurers and reinsurers) puts it this way:

> The lack of historical and observational data and the existence of competing theories formalized in competing forecasting models, leads to a multitude of different answers for the return periods of certain extreme events in today's transient environment. Unfortunately, it is difficult to assign confidence or the probability of one answer being better than the other, a situation which can be described as ambiguity. (Geneva Association 2013, 17)

It should also be noted that the prices of insurance products, as a reflection of the "costs" of climate change, involve only the costs of damage to insured property and life. For the developed world, it is estimated that about 40 percent of the property value at risk is actually insured. For a region like South Asia, it is more like 8 percent. The distribution of insurance coverage worldwide is profoundly unequal. In 2017, the United States accounted for 50 percent of total losses, which was unusually large, but even on a long-term average basis, it makes up 32 percent of the total. While the media were riveted to the flooding of Houston that year, 2,700 people died in flooding in a heavy South Asian monsoon, the economic losses from which were estimated at $3.5 billion. With only a tiny fraction of that insured, the disaster will hardly appear on the ledgers of (re)insurers. (Munich RE 2018). This non-alignment of insured costs and actual harm is further illustrated by the fact that only one of the top forty most deadly catastrophes also ranks among the forty most costly (Johnson 2011, 20).

The example of insurance suggests that the business of digestion is very much incomplete and plagued by huge uncertainty. While the (re)insurers are publicly proclaiming the need for and their commitment to improved risk modelling, and while they have remained profitable so far despite the ballooning costs, the best valuations of even the most straightforward effects of climate change remain ambiguous. Nonetheless, (re)insurers have a clear material interest in calculating the distributions of "negative value" threatened by climate change and so are active participants in the process of digestion. Riddled with problems though it is, the representation of climate change's consequences as value at risk is becoming a widely used frame for the politics of climate change.

Cat Bonds

(Re)insurers are not the only ones trying to turn a profit off of the quantification of climate change. Catastrophes and extreme weather have burst the boundaries of insurance markets and made the leap into global bond markets. The global pool of capital operative in insurance and reinsurance is about $350 billion to $400 billion. That sounds like a lot, but one Hurricane Katrina costs about $60 billion, so a few of those in a year can seriously strain, or even break, the market's capacity to adequately spread risk. Hence the more recent turn to getting financial and bond markets to shoulder some of this risk by designing new financial instruments based on insurance, known as insurance-linked securities. In terms of climate change risk, the key instrument is the catastrophe bond, or "cat bond" for short. Cat bond issuance is about $28 billion to date, though the rate of growth has not been steady. The market originated in the 1990s, grew very quickly in the early 2000s until 2007, collapsed in 2008–9, grew steadily if not spectacularly until 2014, and then dropped moderately until 2017.

Cat bonds work as follows. If you have, say, $200 million lying around looking for a decent return, you can opt to make a bet that a particular event— in this case, a catastrophe of some kind—is not going to happen in a particular place over a particular period of time. If indeed it does not happen, you get a pretty good return—8 or 9 percent. If it does happen, you lose a portion or the entire amount invested, which goes to whoever issued the bond (usually an insurer) in order to help them cover their losses. The triggers vary among bonds: it could be an actual weather event, or an indemnity amount, or a mortality index, or an industry loss. As an example, you might bet that a named storm on the eastern seaboard of the United States is not going to surpass a certain storm surge high-water mark. If during the relevant window of time a storm surge does go over the threshold, the bond issuer uses your money to pay off claims. If not, you are sitting on a healthy return, based on the premiums paid by the insured (plus an additional return on the principle, which is usually invested during the relevant period of the bet). Of course, constructing these offerings requires a substantial amount of digestive labour—transforming a possible future weather disaster into a price-bearing commodity that can be bought and sold. Companies such as RMS and AIR (Applied Insurance Research, another Verisk company) provide the risk analyses that form the bases of cat bond offerings. Through this work, the catastrophic consequences of climate change appear to be financially tamed. Havoc gives way to the orderly world of probability and price.

The risk analyses that form the substance of the bonds are in some ways very sophisticated, and each bond circular provides an incredible amount of detail to potential investors about how measuring gets done (for example, what kinds of gauges are used to measure the height of the storm surge, and where they are located, and how they work) and about the simulation modelling that predicts the indemnity. However, as sophisticated and as high-resolution as the models are, the translation of disaster into value still occurs through the classic definition of risk as the probability of a hazard multiplied by the consequences—in dollar terms, of course. The first part of that equation, the actual probability of the trigger events themselves, remains rooted in historical data—data that, as we have seen, are unlikely to have much actual predictive value as climate change sets in. This may help to explain the frequent disclaimers in bond circulars about the irreducible uncertainties involved.

Is digestion a technique of revelation or obstruction? Here I want to avoid decrying the "violence of abstraction" or presenting a blanket critique of reductionism through modelling, because abstraction and reductionism are key aspects of how humans think. We categorize the world in order to make sense of it, and we must abstract from specificity in order to discern patterns. These general abstractions then form the basis for explorations of their different, historically and spatially specific, forms, as well as the fuzziness of their boundaries. Rather than critiquing abstraction and representation, we need to pay attention to who creates our abstractions and for what purpose, whether they misrepresent the world, and whether they are used to remake something in the image of the abstraction. We need to ask, do our models *of* the world become models *for* the world? Moore (2017, 182–83), looking at cartography's role in empire, has (after Donna Haraway) called this capitalism's "God trick," namely, "to re-present the world in 'objective' form. This trick accomplished two big things: it concealed capital's desire for domination under the guise of objectivity, and in the same breath, it enabled the practical tasks of world domination." Part of capital's response to climate change has been to engage in a new round of cartography and representation. What do the new maps reveal, and what do they hide?

Leigh Johnson (2011, 98) asks the crucial question of "whether model output can be rendered in terms other than the expected loss of exchange value." If it cannot, it is a technique of obstruction, since it allows the politics of climate change to occur only in the register of the market, at the level of the firm or the individual responding to changes in relative values and prices. Given the uses to which modelling has been put—notably, *not* attempting to minimize the aggregate production of "negative value" but positioning firms strategically within its distribution over time and space—its outputs are forced to speak in the language of exchange value. Importantly, this realization should move us away from targeting the modellers, the scientists, and the "experts" who generate the numbers as the problematic and powerful actors and force us to recognize that they produce what a market-based system demands. They are (highly paid) workers producing a product whose generation is driven by the systemic requirements of capitalism. (Re)insurers and investors, who are increasingly positioned as the key actors in any kind of transition to low-carbon economies, can only speak the language of price. In this way, taking the metaphor of digestion one step further, we might speak of "autocoprophagia."[4] This might be more apt because not only does capital dedicate energy through the social allocation of labour to producing what I am here comparing to feces, but it also goes one better and consumes it, closing the circle. Capital must produce streams of numbers, turning qualities into quantities to represent risk, hazard, and opportunity, and then treat those same uncertain quantities as real and credible enough to consume—to plug into calculations and algorithms that in turn condition the pricing of real assets and commodities and that therefore condition landscapes, socio-natural relations, and the fortunes of human and non-human lives.

The work that goes into turning qualities into quantities not only creates a passive representation. In some cases (as with insurance products or carbon credits) it actively produces new commodities, instead of just *enabling* their production. The numbers so created form, for example, the actual substance of the financial commodities generated as capital's primary market-based responses to climate change. Johnson (2013, 35) points in this direction when she claims that "a bond does not become a tradable commodity or income stream unless and until it has been modeled and assigned an expected loss." In the case of capital's digestion of climate change, actual, specific, and differentiated forms of danger (in this case, the capacity of weather to destroy value) must be transformed by labour into exchangeable packets of risk—a transformation that Brett Christophers (2016) argues is constitutive of the commodity. That is, it is the translation of physical or political risk into exchangeable, abstract risk that allows the commodity to bear value.

The generation of these abstractions is part of a historical progression rather than a complete novelty or a sudden break. Cartography, accounting, botany, and zoology, among other forms of intellectual and abstracting labour, made aspects of the world—land, labour, energy, species—more easily available, or available at all, for appropriation and for capitalization (Moore 2015a). According to Christian Parenti (2015), this is what makes analysis of the state so important to understanding the metabolic relations of capitalism. States are, in his view, "crucial membranes" in this relationship because they are responsible for delivering to capital the use values of extra-human nature. While states do indeed serve this function, it is increasingly also undertaken by private consulting firms, as discussed above.

As climate change is digested, it is depicted as a map of values (both negative and surplus) unevenly scattered over time and place, and each capitalist's primary interest is in placing him or herself strategically within that matrix. Indeed, the very characteristic of the catastrophe risk mentioned above, that "no mass of information will help us pinpoint the precise when, where, and how of the coming havoc" (Cooper 2008, 83), is precisely the basis of an insurance market in which actors bet on and hedge against the uncertainty of when, where, and upon whom disasters will fall. Capital, in the face of the increasing certainty of large-scale damages from climate change, chooses *not* to maximally preclude the source of harm, or do what can be done to spare human and non-human life from catastrophes we know will result (by leaving fossil fuels in the ground, for example), but to place itself advantageously within the "havoc" to come, minimizing costs relative to competitors and finding new spaces for valorization.

How does this change the policy environment around climate change? What happens to our understanding of the problem? At issue is not the act of quantification itself. It is the open question of whether capital's way of seeing climate change becomes the way that we all see climate change—whether the models' output, expressed as expected exchange value, dominates our view of both the problem and our responses to it. While the claim made in favour of this is that it makes climate change "visible," we need to bear in mind that climate change is already visible to billions of people. People see and experience it through water scarcity, rising sea levels, storm surges, wildfires, and typhoons. I'm sure that non-human life experiences it as well, though I cannot say how. It is only capital that cannot see these things until they are translated into value terms. The rest of us already get it. The much more basic mathematics of the carbon budget inform us that we must begin a rapid process of transition to zero carbon economies, which involves leaving fossil fuels in the ground. Failure to do so will mean that the suffering already being experienced bodily in many different ways will be hugely amplified. However, through digestion—a supposed act of revelation—the complex entanglements of social and "natural" relations that actually make up the world we live in are, in their qualitative dimension, lost. The actual consequences of climate change for human and non-human life—hunger, thirst, sickness, extinction, homelessness, death—are obscured, replaced with streams of expected value expressed ultimately as price. Human suffering, species loss, the erasure of particular kinds of landscapes in favour of others, all of this vanishes under the streams of numbers that are the only actionable information markets can handle, since they are the among the abstractions upon which exchange rests. Representations of the world and the construction of problems (Is the problem the floods, or threats to supply chains?) always suggest a specific politics and therefore limit or preclude others. It is only if we move the politics of climate change and transition out of the exclusive register of the market that it might be guided by principles like justice, democracy, or survival understood as non-commensurable with other "values."

Notes

1. "Our Work," ND-GAIN, University of Notre Dame, n.d., accessed November 6, 2019, https://gain.nd.edu/our-work/.
2. "Rankings," ND-GAIN, University of Notre Dame, n.d., accessed November 6, 2019, https://gain.nd.edu/our-work/country-index/rankings/ (scores are for 2017). Canada ranked sixth on the "vulnerability" scale, but it was in eighteenth place in terms of "readiness." For information about methodology, including the indicators used, see the "Technical Document," https://gain.nd.edu/assets/254377/nd_gain_technical_document_2015.pdf.
3. Home page, Four Twenty Seven, n.d., accessed November 6, 2019, http://427mt.com/.
4. Inasmuch as one can be thankful for having knowledge of this phenomenon, I'm indebted to Jeff Masuda for introducing me to it and suggesting its metaphorical uses. For those of you who have been spared up until now, coprophagia is the consumption of feces.

References

Christophers, Brett. 2016. "Risking Value Theory in the Political Economy of Finance and Nature." *Progress in Human Geography* 42, no. 3: 330–49. https://doi.org/10.1177/0309132516679268.

Cooper, Melinda. 2008. *Life as Surplus: Biotechnology and Capitalism in the Neoliberal Era*. Seattle: University of Washington Press.

Dzieza, Josh. 2018. "If Climate Change Wrecks Your City, Can It Sue Exxon?" *The Verge*, February 20, 2018. https://www.theverge.com/2018/2/20/17031676/climate-change-lawsuits-fossil-fuel-new-york-santa-cruz.

Geneva Association. 2013. *Warming of the Oceans and Implications for the (Re)insurance Industry*. Geneva: Geneva Association.

Grove, Kevin J. 2010. "Insuring 'Our Common Future?' Dangerous Climate Change and the Biopolitics of Environmental Security." *Geopolitics* 15, no. 3: 536–63.

Haller, Stephen. 2002. *Apocalypse Soon? Wagering on Warnings of Global Catastrophe*. Montréal and Kingston: McGill-Queen's University Press.

Heede, Richard. 2014. "Tracing Anthropogenic Carbon Dioxide and Methane Emissions to Fossil Fuel and Cement Producers, 1854–2010." *Climatic Change* 122: 229–41.

Johnson, Leigh. 2011. "Insuring Climate Change? Science, Fear, and Value in Reinsurance Markets." PhD diss., University of California, Berkeley.

Johnson, Leigh. 2013. "Index Insurance and the Articulation of Risk-Bearing Subjects." *Environment and Planning A* 45, no. 1: 2663–81.

Keoun, Bradley. 2017. "Hurricane Harvey to Bring up to $20 Billion in Insurer Losses, JPMorgan Predicts." *TheStreet*, August 29, 2017. https://www.thestreet.com/story/14286338/1/harvey-to-bring-up-to-20-billion-in-insurer-losses-jpmorgan-says.html.

Klein, Seth, and Shannon Daub. 2016. "The New Climate Denialism: Time for an Intervention." *Policy Note* (blog). Canadian Centre for Policy Alternatives, BC Office. September 22, 2016. http://www.policynote.ca/the-new-climate-denialism-time-for-an-intervention/.

Lloyd's 360 Risk Project. 2006. *Climate Change: Adapt or Bust*. London: Lloyd's. https://www.lloyds.com/_test/library/natural-environment/adapt-or-bust.

Luscombe, Richard. 2017. "How Climate Change Could Turn US Real Estate Prices Upside Down." *The Guardian*, August 29, 2017. https://www.theguardian.com/environment/2017/aug/29/hurricane-harvey-climate-change-real-estate-florida.

Lusk, Greg. 2017. "The Social Utility of Event Attribution: Liability, Adaptation, and Justice-Based Loss and Damage." *Climate Change* 143, nos. 1–2: 201–12.

Mann, Geoff, and Joel Wainwright. 2018. *Climate Leviathan: A Political Theory of Our Planetary Future*. London: Verso.

Martin, Frederick. 1876. *The History of Lloyd's and of Marine Insurance in Great Britain*. London: Macmillan.

McAneney, John. 2014. "What Is Driving the Rising Cost of Natural Disasters?" *Risk Frontiers Quarterly Newsletter* 14, no. 2: 3–4.

McCarthy, Shawn. 2017. "Task Force Report Puts 'Material Risks' of Climate Change in Focus." *Globe and Mail*, June 29, 2017. https://www.theglobeandmail.com/report-on-business/task-force-report-puts-material-risks-of-climate-change-in-focus/article35493217/.

Moore, Jason W. 2015a. *Capitalism in the Web of Life: Ecology and the Accumulation of Capital*. London: Verso.

———. 2015b. "Cheap Food and Bad Climate: From Surplus Value to Negative Value in the Capitalist World-Ecology." *Critical Historical Studies* 2, no. 1: 1–43.

Munich RE. 2018. "Natural Catastrophe Review: Series of Hurricanes Makes 2017 Year of Highest Insured Losses Ever." Press release. January 4, 2018. https://www.munichre.com/en/media-relations/publications/press-releases/2018/2018-01-04-press-release/index.html.

Oreskes, Naomi, and Erik M. Conway. 2010. *Merchants of Doubt*. New York: Bloomsbury.

Parenti, Christian. 2015. "The Environment-Making State: Territory, Nature, and Value." *Antipode* 47, no. 4: 829–48.

Reguly, Eric. 2013. "No Climate-Change Deniers to Be Found in the Reinsurance Business." *Globe and Mail*, November 28, 2013. https://www.theglobeandmail.com/report-on-business/rob-magazine/an-industry-that-has-woken-up-to-climate-change-no-deniers-at-global-resinsurance-giant/article15635331/.

Risky Business Project. 2014. *Risky Business: The Economic Risks of Climate Change in the United States: A Climate Risk Assessment for the United States.* https://riskybusiness.org/site/assets/uploads/2015/09/RiskyBusiness_Report_WEB_09_08_14.pdf.

TCFD (Task Force on Climate-Related Financial Disclosures). 2017. *Final Report: Recommendations of the Task Force on Climate-Related Financial Disclosures.* Basel: Financial Stability Board. https://www.fsb-tcfd.org/publications/final-recommendations-report/.

Thomas, Vinod, Jose Ramon G. Albert, and Cameron Hepburn. 2014. "Contributors to the Frequency of Intense Climate Disasters in Asia-Pacific Countries." *Climate Change* 126, nos. 3–4: 381–98.

van Oldenborgh, Geert Jan, Karin van der Wiel, Antonia Sebastian, Roop Singh, Julie Arrighi, Friederike Otto, Karsten Haustein, Sihan Li, Gabriel Vecchi, and Heidi Cullen. 2017. "Attribution of Extreme Rainfall from Hurricane Harvey, August 2017." *Environmental Research Letters* 12, no. 12: 1–11.

Watts, Jonathan. 2018. "World's Great Forests Could Lose Half of All Wildlife as Planet Warms—Report." *The Guardian*, March 14, 2018. https://www.theguardian.com/environment/2018/mar/14/worlds-great-forests-could-lose-half-of-all-wildlife-as-planet-warms-report.

4   Who Owns Big Carbon?
Mapping the Network of Corporate Ownership

William K. Carroll and Jouke Huijzer

Advocates for continued expansion of fossil fuel production tend to represent the carbon-extractive sector as a "black box," out of which flows what Matthew Huber (2013) aptly describes as the lifeblood for our consumer-capitalist ways. In addition to powering our cars and homes with the "buried sunshine" of carbon energy, the black box, these advocates claim, provides jobs and income for legions of workers. According to this narrative, all Canadians benefit from the production and consumption of fossil fuels. Yet the carbon-extractive sector is actually a complex of corporations, each owned by specific moneyed interests who claim the profits and are the central beneficiaries of sectoral activity. In this chapter, we look inside the black box to identify the investors who own substantial share blocs in Canada's leading carbon-extractive companies and who have the most compelling stake in continuing to expand fossil fuel production. Aided by a network analysis of ownership relations, we offer several views of the powerful interests that dominate carbon-extractive activities in Canada.

In mapping who owns and controls Canada's fossil-capital sector we identify which agents have both an *interest* in the sector's continued growth and the *economic power* to shape the future of that sector. This in turn raises

This chapter was first published as a Corporate Mapping Project report (Vancouver: Canadian Centre for Policy Alternatives, BC Office, 2018), under the title "Who Owns Canada's Fossil-Fuel Sector? Mapping the Network of Ownership and Control." It is reprinted here, with minor revisions, by permission of the publisher.

the question of how ownership of corporate shares confers economic power upon certain agents. As mentioned in this volume's introduction, the parcelling of share ownership offering limited liability to investors is integral to corporate capitalism and to its structure of economic power. Each share is a title to part ownership in the company, entitling its owner to a portion of profit (as dividends) and a vote at the annual general meeting, at which the board of directors is elected and key policy proposals (including mergers and acquisitions and shareholder resolutions) are put to the vote. Who owns those shares is thus of great consequence. Although most corporations are not listed on stock exchanges—their shares are privately held either by persons, states, or other corporations—the shares of many of the largest corporations are publicly traded and thus distributed among multiple owners, including wealthy individuals, other corporations, small shareholders, and institutional investors. The last category, whose shareholdings have increased with the financialization of capitalism (Durand 2017), includes banks and life insurance companies, pension funds, asset managers, and hedge funds.

According to some scholars, the dispersal of corporate shares among many investors dilutes the power of capital owners, leaving salaried managers in charge. In their classic analysis of the "managerial revolution" in the largest US-based corporations, Adolf Berle and Gardiner Means (1932) discerned such a trend, portending a separation of owners of capital (mostly small investors) from actual controllers of capital, namely, professional managers. In the 1950s, Rolf Dahrendorf (1959) and other sociologists argued that this separation of corporate ownership and control had brought about a "decomposition of capital," as the owners of capital no longer controlled corporate business. Yet scholars soon demonstrated that there was (and still is) reason to question the validity of these accounts (Scott 1997). For the vast majority of corporations in Canada and elsewhere, whose shares are not listed on stock exchanges, one owner or a few associated investors wield absolute strategic power over the corporation. But what of the largest corporations, most of which issue shares that are publicly listed on stock exchanges? In these cases, it is typical for the wealthiest of investors to amass strategic blocs of shares. By holding, say, 10 percent or more of a company's shares an investor can (if the rest of the share capital is scattered among many small investors) control a corporation whose capital is many times greater than the value of the shares held. This further concentrates corporate power in the hands of people and corporations that assemble such blocs. *Strategic control* refers to the ability to control the composition of the board of directors based on ownership of such blocs.

In Canada, beginning with John Porter's research based on data from 1960 (1965, 591–95), studies have consistently shown that most publicly traded corporations are controlled by individuals, families, and other corporations (Niosi 1978; Morck, Strangeland, and Yeung 2000; Carroll 2004). As William Burgess (2002, 249) noted, "the Canadian corporate network is character-ized by the large degree of majority or strong minority control, and by the incorporation of many firms within larger corporate groups," whether the controlling interest be a family or another corporation. In a study of corporate ownership and control in Canada conducted more than a decade ago, Yoser Gadhoum (2006, 180) reported that, among 1,120 Canadian-controlled cor-porations whose shares were publicly listed on stock exchanges at the time, 56.17 percent were ultimately controlled by wealthy families, while only 17.79 percent were without a clearly identifiable controlling interest.

Economic Concentration and Foreign Control

Economic concentration and the foreign control of Canadian corporations are key issues in understanding who owns Canada's carbon-extractive sector. Overall, the Canadian economy is dominated by a relative few giant corpora-tions, into which the lion's share of capital has been concentrated. Economist Jordan Brennan (2012, 19, figure 5) found that in the half-century after 1960, the share of total net business profits in Canada claimed by the sixty largest firms listed on the Toronto Stock Exchange grew from 35 percent to an aston-ishing 60 percent. In 2000, slightly more than one million Canada-based firms reported under the Corporations Returns Act. Of these, just 1,434 (0.139 percent) were large enterprises (revenue greater than $75 million), yet they claimed 45.69 percent of all corporate operating revenue. By 2017, the total number of corporations had grown to 1.8 million, of which large enterprises, now numbering 2,979, constituted only 0.165 percent but garnered 48.86 percent of revenue.[1] Concentration in the oil and gas sector is especially pro-nounced, as we show below.

A related concern is whether ownership and control is lodged within Canada or in foreign domains (and if the latter, where). In Canadian studies, a pivotal issue has been the role of foreign-based centres of strategic control in structuring corporate power within Canada. Concern about high levels of foreign control in key sectors, including oil and gas, goes back to the 1956–57 Royal Commission on Canada's Economic Prospects, and although levels have fallen since then, the issue retains salience. Kari Levitt (1970) identified high levels of foreign control as a threat to Canada's economic sovereignty, the seeds of what she projected would be a bitter "harvest of lengthening dependency." But a large body of research has pointed to the success of Canadian capitalists in maintaining their own positions and even expanding internationally (Niosi 1981; Carroll 1986; Klassen 2014; Kellogg 2015). In an era of capitalist globalization, each local capitalist class cedes some control of its home market but as quid pro quo is able to accumulate capital more effectively outside that market, in a multilateral cross-penetration of capital (Carroll and Klassen 2010). One indisputable fact in all this is the strong alignment of foreign ownership with economic concentration. As of 2017, 0.615 percent of all corporations based in Canada were foreign controlled (down from 0.751 percent in 2000), but these firms earned 27.54 percent of all corporate revenues (down from 29.72 percent in 2000). Foreign control is concentrated among the Canadian subsidiaries of giant transnational corporations, which themselves tend to be big companies. In 2017, among large enterprises (with revenues exceeding $75 million), foreign-controlled firms comprised 39.07 percent of companies and 41.52 percent of revenue.[2] Similarly, as of 2015, foreign-controlled firms operating specifically in oil and gas extraction and in supporting industries accounted for 39.5 percent of revenue and 44.3 percent of assets, with enterprises based in the United States (39.0 percent) and the European Union (24.3 percent) together owning a majority of all assets under foreign control.[3]

In this chapter, we focus on the investors that own substantial share blocs in the leading carbon-extractive companies in Canada. The analysis offers several views of the powerful interests that dominate carbon-extractive activities in Canada. This chapter has four objectives:

- to identify *who owns the lion's share of the carbon-extractive sector* and to track trends in overall ownership over a recent five-year period

- to provide an overview of the mechanisms through which significant shareholders—corporate, personal, institutional—wield *strategic control over individual corporations in the sector*

- to map, more closely, the key ownership relations that tie the largest corporations in the sector into a *national and transnational network of corporate power*
- to take up the *implications* for our understanding of corporate power in Canada's carbon-capital sector.

Who Owns the Largest Players in the Sector?

To identify the ownership interests that dominate in Canada's carbon-extractive sector, we selected 103 carbon-extractive firms that numbered among the largest fifty in Canada at some point between 2010 and 2015 and identified their shareholders in each year. (For details on our methods, see the appendix at the end of this chapter.) Longitudinal analysis is of value here because Canada's carbon sector has been in the throes of ongoing capital restructuring. After the financial crisis of 2008, oil prices were subject to tremendous fluctuations, reaching a peak in 2011 and then crashing to unexpected lows in 2014 before a partial recovery. As a consequence, companies saw much of their revenues vaporize, and some struggled to keep their businesses afloat.

We identified a total of 1,061 owners with substantial holdings in one or more of the companies within the window under examination, with the total number of identified owners in any given year varying from 459 in 2010 to 595 in 2015. To determine how large a share of total annual sectoral revenue each owning interest claimed in a given year, we first aggregated the annual revenues of all the carbon-extractive companies in our sample and calculated the percentage of total sectoral revenue that each carbon-extractive firm claimed. For each owner, we then multiplied the percentage of shares that the owner held in each carbon-extractive company by that firm's percentage share of total sectoral revenue. Summing these values for each owner, we determined what percentage of the entire sector's revenue each owning interest claimed.[4] If, for example, a company is responsible for 4 percent of the sectoral revenue, and 5 percent of its shares are owned by one owner, such as Royal Bank of Canada (RBC), that stake gives the owner 0.2 percent (that is, 5 percent of 4 percent) of sectoral revenue overall. As can be seen in table 4.1, in 2015, RBC's holdings in the companies in our sample gave it a 3.83 percent share in the total sectoral revenue that year.

Table 4.1. Leading owners of Canada's oil and gas sector

	2010		2011		2012	
	Control	Share	Control	Share	Control	Share
Top 10 owners	28.0	26.1	31.0	26.8	28.1	25.6
Top 25 owners	43.0	40.9	49.0	44.4	45.8	42.3
Top 50 owners	52.2	49.9	58.5	53.9	55.9	52.3
Largest owners	**Rank**	**Share**	**Rank**	**Share**	**Rank**	**Share**
Exxon Mobil Corporation	1	6.59	1	4.9	1	6.98
Royal Bank of Canada	3	2.97	3	3.21	2	3.23
Desmarais Family Residuary Trust	4	2.6	4	3.04	5	2.31
Blackrock Inc.	2	3.72	2	3.75	14	1.16
Capital Group Companies Inc.	7	2.07	8	2.17	7	2.11
Toronto-Dominion Bank	8	1.96	11	1.74	10	1.87
FMR LLC	6	2.17	9	2.13	8	1.94
Royal Dutch Shell PLC	9	1.74	7	2.27	6	2.15
Bank of Montreal	5	2.26	10	1.91	11	1.85
CK Hutchison Holdings Ltd.	—	—	6	2.59	4	2.45
Bank of Nova Scotia	10	1.71	12	1.63	12	1.76
L.F. Investments Ltd.	—	—	5	2.72	3	2.56
CIBC	14	1.13	16	1.21	13	1.52
Korea National Oil Corporation	12	1.5	13	1.37	9	1.88
Province of Québec	13	1.23	15	1.24	17	0.97
Jarislowsky Fraser Ltd.	11	1.56	14	1.35	15	1.12
Franklin Resources Inc.	28	0.51	23	0.66	19	0.83
Keevil Holding Corporation	15	1	18	1.05	18	0.95
Sentgraf Enterprises Ltd.	24	0.6	28	0.57	16	1.07
Trencap LP	16	0.81	19	0.86	21	0.8
Spectra Energy Corporation	19	0.69	17	1.14	20	0.81
Wellington Management Group LLP	20	0.66	21	0.73	25	0.59
People's Republic of China	18	0.75	20	0.78	22	0.71
Invesco Ltd.	25	0.58	27	0.59	23	0.66
Government of Canada	22	0.62	25	0.61	24	0.6
Concerned Parents and Teachers of Wycocomagh and Area	21	0.66	24	0.62	26	0.59
Norway	31	0.42	32	0.43	31	0.51
Goldring Capital Corporation	17	0.77	22	0.71	28	0.55
Chevron Corporation	—	—	—	—	27	0.57
Manulife Financial Corporation	33	0.39	33	0.43	40	0.33
Vanguard Group Inc.	240	0.01	84	0.12	65	0.17

2013		2014		2015	
Control	**Share**	**Control**	**Share**	**Control**	**Share**
29.6	27.1	28.4	26	27.8	25.6
48.3	44.7	46.8	43	44.6	40.7
57.3	53.8	56.0	52.2	53.6	49.7
Rank	**Share**	**Rank**	**Share**	**Rank**	**Share**
1	6.99	1	7.03	1	6.92
2	3.41	2	3.47	2	3.83
7	2.19	3	2.34	4	2.26
3	3.23	13	1.36	12	1.44
9	2.05	10	1.96	3	2.90
8	2.06	5	2.31	5	2.22
10	1.9	7	2.1	8	1.86
6	2.21	8	2.08	9	1.66
11	1.9	9	2.07	7	1.91
5	2.4	6	2.24	6	2.07
12	1.79	11	1.88	10	1.46
4	2.52	4	2.34	—	—
14	1.49	12	1.52	11	1.45
13	1.5	16	1.02	147	0.05
18	0.94	17	0.97	13	1.26
23	0.71	24	0.65	22	0.64
16	1.05	14	1.22	14	1.04
19	0.8	23	0.67	19	0.88
15	1.07	21	0.74	17	0.91
17	0.98	15	1.03	28	0.45
21	0.78	22	0.71	20	0.73
20	0.78	19	0.92	16	0.93
24	0.66	18	0.93	21	0.71
22	0.71	20	0.86	18	0.9
26	0.57	26	0.58	34	0.39
25	0.6	29	0.43	42	0.32
27	0.56	25	0.6	23	0.63
29	0.47	37	0.37	58	0.22
28	0.53	27	0.57	24	0.58
50	0.23	72	0.16	25	0.55
58	0.21	46	0.27	15	0.94

Note: Owners are listed in descending order of their average rank over the entire period. Figures for "Share" and "Control" are percentages. "Share" refers to an owner's share of the aggregate revenue of the companies in our sample in a particular year. Figures in the "Control" column (in the first section of the table) reflect an additional analysis conducted to take account of the fact that majority ownership confers effective control over a company, essentially giving an owner control of effectively 100 percent of the firm's revenue. For details, see the chapter appendix.

It is worth noting that revenue in the sector is quite concentrated. The three largest companies (Enbridge, Suncor, and Imperial Oil) earn over 30 percent of the total revenue in the sample each year. About 60 percent of the total is claimed by top ten revenue earners, and the figure increases to over 80 percent when one considers the top twenty-five. In short, we find that, in terms of revenue, the market is already dominated by a handful of players. As table 4.1 indicates, ownership and control in the sector are also highly concentrated. Although approximately five hundred owners of share blocs can be identified in any given year, the top ten owners together account for over 25 percent of the sector's total revenue. This share increases to over 40 percent for the top twenty-five owners and to 50 percent when the top fifty shareholders are considered. The numbers are even higher if we consider any majority shareholder to wholly "own" a company, given that shareholder's uncontestable control over it.

Table 4.1 lists the shareholders who numbered among the top twenty-five in at least one year of the period under study. That the list of the largest individual owners includes only thirty-one such shareholders points to long-standing relationships between investors and companies, not quickly broken. Amid many thousands of investors, a small group has had a prominent and enduring presence, remaining largely unchallenged in the aftermath of the financial crisis and following the sudden drop in oil prices. The largest owners include foreign-based carbon transnationals (notably, Exxon Mobil, owner of both Imperial Oil and ExxonMobil Canada, and Royal Dutch Shell, owner of Shell Canada); Canadian banks (notably, RBC, the Toronto-Dominion Bank, and the Bank of Montreal); wealthy families such as the Montréal-based Desmaraises, who control the investment company Power Corporation of Canada; and asset managers such as Blackrock and Capital Group (both based in the United States).

In view of the high concentration of share ownership among a relatively small number of owners, figure 4.1 offers a graphical overview that focuses on the seventy-seven owners that have been in the "Top 50" largest owners in any year. Here we see the relative share of total revenue claimed by each type of investor. As a group, these leading investors account for approximately 70 percent of the revenue of the Top 50 in each year (the rest is divided among many thousands of small investors). The largest share is controlled through majority ownership by foreign corporations, closely followed by mainly US-based asset managers and investment funds. The third major type of shareholder is banks that, like most insurance companies and pension funds, are predominantly based in Canada. The "big five" Canadian banks are continuously present among the Top 50 investors, together accounting for over 10 percent ownership of the total sector.

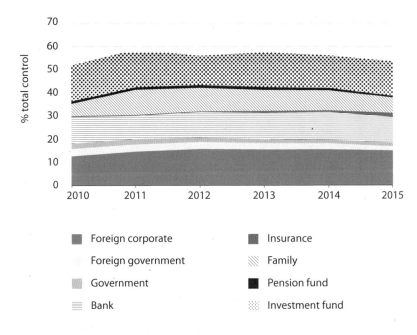

Figure 4.1. Control of Top 50 investors aggregated by each type of investor

The holdings of wealthy families account for another tranche of the sector's capital, although in recent years their share has declined somewhat. Among those owning families are the Desmaraises, the Southern family (which by pyramidal shareholdings owns ATCO and Canadian Utilities through their holding company Sentgraf Enterprises), and Hong Kong's richest man, Li Ka-shing (majority owner, through various holdings, of Husky Energy). In addition, foreign governments are represented via sovereign wealth funds, in the case of Norway and Japan, and via the China National Offshore Oil Corporation and the Korea National Oil Corporation, respectively owned by the Chinese and Korean governments. Together, foreign governments own about 3 percent of total revenue of sample firms, closely followed by the combined ownership of the Canadian federal and provincial governments (2 percent).

The difference between foreign and Canadian investment can be seen in more detail in Figure 4.2, which apportions the total revenue earned by the Top 50 investors by geographical locus of control. The overall picture is one of stability rather than change. Neither the eighteen takeovers in the period under study nor the aforementioned fluctuations in oil prices have significantly impacted the geographic distribution in ownership. Canadian investors still control the largest share of sectoral revenue: slightly under 30 percent. They are followed by US investors, with around 25 percent, and those in other countries in the Global North (which includes European countries, Australia, and New Zealand), with approximately 10 percent.[5] Asian investment has decreased recently, from 3 percent to 2 percent. Investors from the Global South were and remain scarcely involved in Canada's carbon-capital sector, although many of the foreign activities of Canadian firms are located in that area. The remaining shareholders of note are based in tax havens or could not be classified because their location or nationality was unknown.

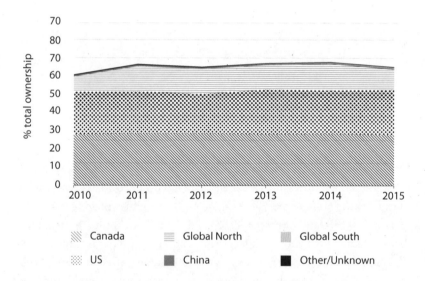

Figure 4.2. Ownership aggregated by geographical region of investors

Ownership and Control in the Top 200

In this section we dig beneath the overall trends revealed above, to provide a snapshot of the strategic control of the two hundred largest-revenue companies in Canada's carbon-extractive sector (including extraction, processing, and transporting of oil, gas, bitumen, and coal) as of March 2017.[6] If, as noted in the introduction, Berle and Means's (1932) hypothesis of a growing separation of ownership and control does not exactly fit the case of Canada, they can still be credited with stimulating a long-standing research program into the *modes* by which corporations are controlled. They drew distinctions between several modes of control:

- companies under the *absolute* (or semi-absolute) control of a single owner
- those controlled by a major shareholder owning a *majority* of shares
- those controlled by a shareholder owning a *minority* of shares sufficiently large to enable strategic control
- those with no identifiable controlling owner (i.e., widely held companies).

Among our Top 200, the most common mode of control is minority control (10 percent to 49.9 percent), which pertains to 51.5 percent of companies. Slightly more than one-quarter of the sample (25.5 percent) has no owner with 10 percent or more shares. The remaining corporations are either wholly owned by a single owner (12 percent) or majority-owned by a single owner (11 percent).

Berle and Means viewed widely held corporations as controlled internally, by management, but the situation is actually more complex, especially in today's financialized capitalism, when institutional investors own significant blocs of shares in many companies (Durand 2017). As John Scott (1997) has documented, a company lacking any one dominant shareholder may be controlled by a *constellation of interests*. Depending on circumstances, such constellations can include key creditors, senior management, and shareholders whose combined share ownership would be large enough to give them at least minority control (that is, greater than 10 percent of shares) but who lack the unity required to wield control in an active way. Admittedly, our use of share ownership as the criterion in designating a company as controlled in this way does not demonstrate whether or not a controlling constellation operates in a coherent and coordinated way. In fact, this mode of strategic control is virtually invisible, unless internal corporate management fails to deliver on profit or an external capitalist makes a hostile takeover bid. In the former case, the controlling constellation might initiate a change in top management; in the latter, the constellation might mobilize its combined share bloc against the unwanted suitor, to protect its collective investment (Scott 1997, 47–50; Carroll and Sapinski 2018).

In these scenarios, institutional investors often play key roles. Since the 1980s, as capitalism has become more financialized, major banks, life insurers, asset managers, and other institutional investors have taken ownership stakes in corporations, sometimes exceeding the 10 percent level that is typically seen as the threshold for strategic control. Yet, unlike corporations that amass share blocs with the intent of control and influence, these investors do not seek representation on the boards of the many companies in which they invest. Although institutional investors are in this sense passive, their investments represent votes of confidence in current management. Conversely, they hold "exit power": divestment from a firm can register as a vote of nonconfidence in corporate management. Moreover, key owning interests sometimes exert influence through "one-on-one meetings between CEOs and institutional investors" (Carroll 2008, 59).

We thus distinguish, as types of controlling interests,

(a) wealthy individuals or families

(b) states or state bodies, including sovereign wealth and similar investment funds

(c) constellations of interests (with no one interest owning more than 10 percent)

(d) control by institutional investors (one of which owns more than 10 percent)

(e) control by another corporation.

These categories are key to determining the country in which control resides. For firms controlled by individuals or families, the country of control is the family's country of principal residence, or domicile.[7] Control by a constellation of interests typically involves a plethora of financial institutions and asset managers each holding stakes ranging from a threshold of 2 percent through to 9 percent. In these cases, we assume that strategic control is in Canada, unless the constellation is entirely based in another country (in which case control resides in that country). The last two types, (d) and (e), invite a further investigation of "ultimate control," to determine which individual/ family, state, or constellation of interests controls the ultimate parent firm in the chain of intercorporate ownership. For the fifty-two firms that we found to be controlled by another corporation, we traced the controlling interest in the parent firm up to the institution, individual/family, or state holding ultimate control—and noted the domicile of that owner. In the case of (d), control by institutional investors (such as financial institutions, asset managers, and pension funds), we noted the domicile of the investor holding the dominant stake, which was typically a bloc greater than 20 percent.

Overall, institutional investors are the most common ultimate controlling interest, accounting for 38.0 percent of the two hundred firms, followed by personal control (30.0 percent), control by a constellation of interests (28.5 percent), and control by a state (or, in one case, a cooperative based in India) (3.5 percent). While wealthy families and individuals have control over a substantial share of Canada's carbon-extractive sector, most corporations are ultimately controlled by various constellations in which institutional investors figure prominently. Moreover, the mean 2016 revenue of the sixty firms ultimately controlled by persons (US$5.2 billion) is substantially less than the mean revenue of firms ultimately controlled by constellations of interests (US$8.6 billion) and institutional investors ($14.6 billion), though greater than the mean for the few state- (and co-op-) controlled companies (US$1.1 billion). As for the country in which ultimate control of these firms resides (see figure 4.3), we find that 65.0 percent are ultimately controlled in Canada, 18.0 percent in the United States, 10.5 percent in other jurisdictions of the Global North, 4.0 percent in China (including Hong Kong), and 2.5 percent in the Global South.

Compared with the ownership analysis in the previous section, US-based investors are less numerous. This is due to two factors: (1) since control by American transnational corporations is concentrated among the largest fossil fuel companies (hereafter, fossils), when we expand the sample to two hundred firms, and consider the number of firms rather than the amount of revenue flowing through them, the US-controlled segment shrinks; and (2) US-based asset managers own small but significant pieces of many Canadian fossils, but most of those investments are not large enough to confer strategic control. Fully 70 percent of the fossil firms controlled in Canada have constellations of interest or institutional investors as their ultimate controlling interests, with the rest controlled mostly by individuals and families. Institutional investors predominate as ultimate controllers of firms controlled in the Global North, including the United States. However, personal control is prominent among the small number of companies ultimately controlled in China and the rest of the Global South, as is state control in the case of China.

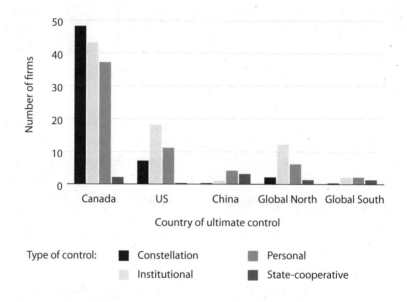

Figure 4.3. Canada's Top 200 carbon-capital companies, by country and type of ultimate control

Given the prevalence of control by constellations of interest and institutional investors, a mapping of the ownership network can reveal who the key players are and how their stakes are configured. We take this up next.

Mapping the 2017 Top 50

In view of the pronounced concentration of capital in the very largest carbon-extractive firms, we now focus on the Top 50 within our core sample of two hundred.[8] As of July 2017, the ORBIS database identified 1,679 ownership blocs into which the shares of the Top 50 have been concentrated, ranging in size from 0.01 percent of a company's share capital (the Soros Fund's stake in CNRL) to 100 percent (for example, Royal Dutch Shell's stake in Shell Canada). However, 1,233 blocs amounted to less than 1 percent of the owned firm's share capital, while 89 blocs comprised at least 5 percent of the owned firm's share capital. Since our interest is in the major lines of ownership, we established 1 percent as a floor criterion and focused on the 446 shareholdings of at least 1 percent that link the Top 50 to a variety of major investors.

Not surprisingly, given the concentration of capital across the corporate economy, the 446 significant blocs were owned by a much smaller number of investors. As of summer 2017, they were directly held by 127 interests external to the Top 50—corporate, institutional, personal, and state.[9] The combination of the Top 50 fossils and these 127 owners constitutes a *network* of 177 entities, with a total of 446 significant ownership ties, 89 of which involve stakes of 5 percent or more in a given carbon-extractive firm.

Most of the Top 50 and their owners—161 of the 177—form a single connected network of 161 nodes (corporations or persons), a "dominant component" in the parlance of network analysis. The other sixteen, consisting of seven of the Top 50 carbon-extractive firms and nine owners, are isolates from the dominant component of 161. Five of these seven are Canadian subsidiaries of non-Canadian companies and are represented only in dyads, each consisting of the subsidiary and its foreign-based parent.[10] The other two Top 50 fossils that are detached from the main ownership network are partly owned by wealthy shareholders or by a combination of wealthy shareholders and financial companies.[11] But, aside from these seven outliers, the other forty-three Top 50 fossils are connected into an intricate network of corporate ownership.

The entire network is mapped in figure 4.4, with the small, isolated networks shown to the right of the dominant component. In this sociogram, fossil-capital firms and their owners appear as points, and ownership blocs appear as directed lines, leading from the owner to the owned. The colour of a symbol indicates the type of entity, while the shape indicates the domicile of ultimate ownership. Line thickness indicates the proportion of shares held by a given owner, as of the summer of 2017. Node size is proportionate to "weighted outdegree" (the sum of a given investor's ownership stakes in the Top 50 firms), highlighting the owners that hold the most substantial stakes in the Top 50.

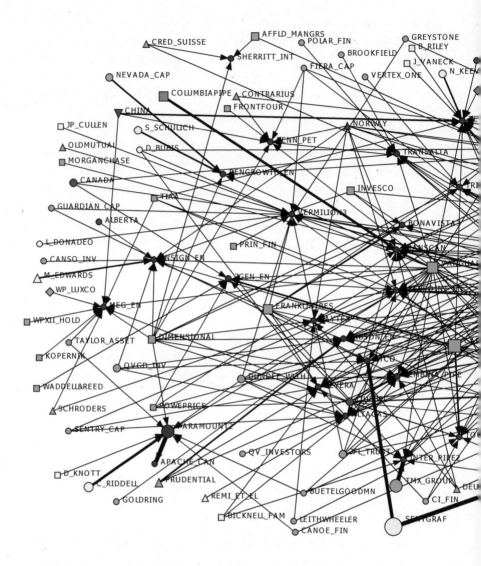

Figure 4.4. Sociogram of Top 50 fossil-capital corporations and their significant owners, 2017. Key: (1) *Type of entity*: brown = Top 50 fossils; orange = corporate owners (n = 9); green = financial company owners (n = 79); yellow = personal owners (n = 31); red = state owners (n = 8). (2) *Domicile of ultimate ownership*: circles = Canada; squares = United States; up-triangles = Europe; diamonds = other Global North; down-triangles = China (including Hong Kong); circles inside boxes = Global South.

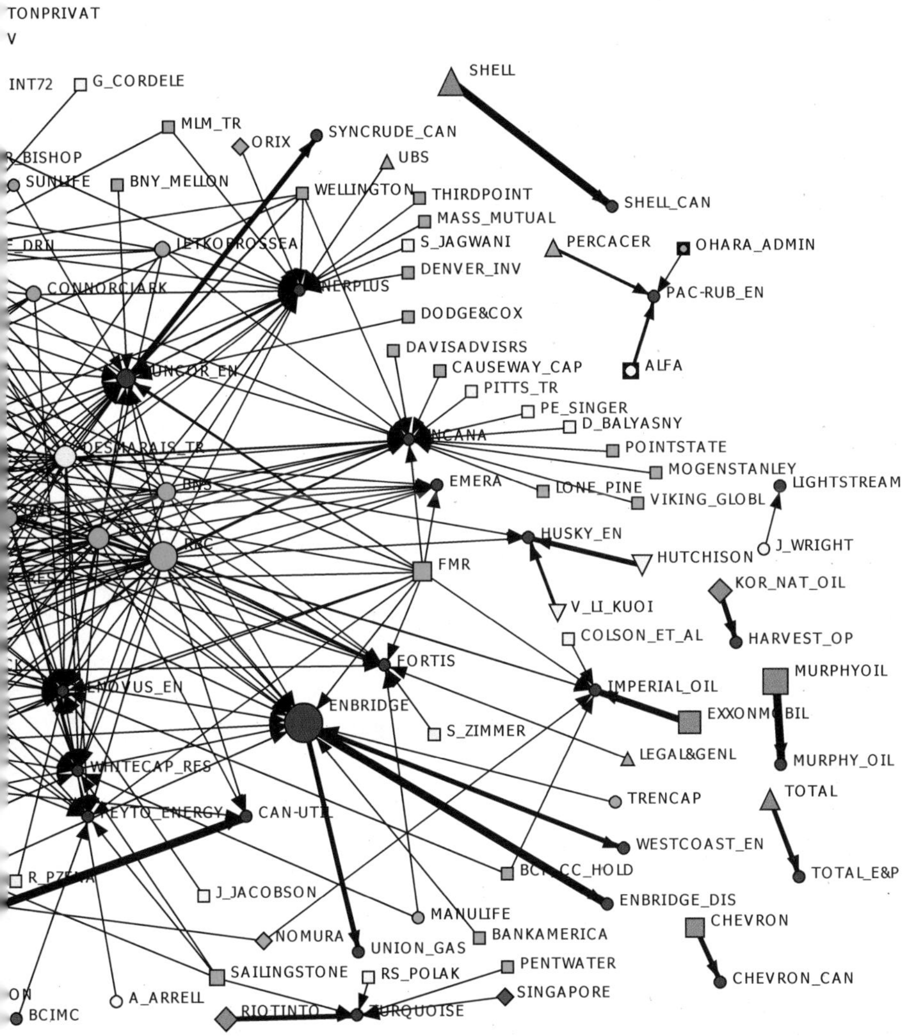
TONPRIVAT
V
INT72
G_CORDELE
SHELL
MLM_TR
ORIX
SYNCRUDE_CAN
BISHOP
UBS
SUNLIFE
BNY_MELLON
WELLINGTON
THIRDPOINT
SHELL_CAN
MASS_MUTUAL
S_JAGWANI
PERCACER
OHARA_ADMIN
DENVER_INV
CONNORCLARK
PAC-RUB_EN
DODGE&COX
DAVISADVISRS
CAUSEWAY_CAP
ALFA
PITTS_TR
PE_SINGER
D_BALYASNY
POINTSTATE
MOGENSTANLEY
EMERA
LONE_PINE
VIKING_GLOBL
LIGHTSTREAM
HUSKY_EN
J_WRIGHT
FMR
HUTCHISON
KOR_NAT_OIL
V_LI_KUOI
COLSON_ET_AL
HARVEST_OP
FORTIS
MURPHYOIL
IMPERIAL_OIL
ENBRIDGE
EXXONMOBIL
S_ZIMMER
LEGAL&GENL
MURPHY_OIL
WHITECAP_RES
TOTAL
CAN-UTIL
TRENCAP
WESTCOAST_EN
TOTAL_E&P
J_JACOBSON
ENBRIDGE_DIS
MANULIFE
CHEVRON
NOMURA
BANKAMERICA
UNION_GAS
SAILINGSTONE
RS_POLAK
PENTWATER
CHEVRON_CAN
SINGAPORE
A_ARRELL
BCIMC
RIOTINTO

The network is a configuration produced by hundreds of weak ties—smaller institutional holdings, mostly owned by financial companies, including banks, asset managers, and life insurers—along with a few dozen large holdings that confer strategic control upon their corporate or personal owners. In the small networks (shown on the right) that are isolated from the dominant component and that exemplify bilateral relations of strategic control, we can see several transnational parents, including Royal Dutch Shell, owner of Shell Canada. What pulls the dominant component together as a connected network are many relatively small holdings, typically owned by institutional investors—the relatively large green circles and squares that form the core of the network. Among them, Canada's top five banks (the circles) are prominent, along with five US-based asset managers (the squares, namely, Capital Group, Vanguard, Franklin Resources, FMR, and Blackrock). These ten major institutional investors have a total of 190 ownership stakes in thirty-six of the Top 50. Their weak ownership ties radiate from the network's core, representing 43 percent of all ownership relations in the entire network. The Montréal-based Desmarais dynasty (represented in the network as the Desmarais Family Residuary Trust) straddles the institutional/personal divide as its majority-controlled investment company, Power Corporation of Canada, ultimately holds controlling interest in a range of Canadian (and European) corporations and also holds smaller stakes in many Canadian corporations across a range of sectors.

The network map shows that, as in the case of control by a constellation of interests, many of the top fossil-capital firms are partly owned by multiple institutional investors. However, this is not to say that personal ownership is unimportant. Through its private investment company, Sentgraf Enterprises, the Southern family controls two major fossil-based power producers: ATCO and Canadian Utilities. Billionaire Clayton Riddell, founder of Paramount Resources, is the major shareholder of that firm (and of several other carbon-capital firms). In summer 2017, Paramount bought controlling interest in Apache Canada from Houston-based Apache Corporation. Both the Southerns and the Riddells (including Clayton's daughter Susan Riddell Rose, CEO of family-controlled Perpetual Energy) are ensconced within Calgary's tightly knit carbon-capital elite, with Clayton (along with Murray Edwards) a part owner of the Calgary Flames.

In sum, the ownership network is constituted through the combination of a relative few highly concentrated share blocs (the thick lines in the sociogram, affording persons and corporations strategic control) and many relatively small blocs owned by financial companies (the thin lines). Individual investors and corporations tend to maintain a small number of strong ownership ties while financial companies maintain a great many weak ownership ties. Two financials (RBC and the US-based Vanguard Group) each hold stakes in a remarkable thirty of the Top 50 fossils, making them the most central investors in the ownership network. Although they have the same number of ownership stakes, RBC's mean ownership blocs are nearly double the size of Vanguard's.

At the other end of the ownership relation, the Top 50 fossils also vary greatly in how their share capital is distributed among significant owners. On average, each Top 50 fossil has 8.88 owners with stakes of at least 1 percent. Although twelve of the Top 50 have only one owning interest (and ten of these are majority-controlled by other corporations), most have multiple owners. Another dozen have fourteen or more (typically institutional) significant shareholders. This dozen includes eight of the largest Canadian-controlled firms: Encana (twenty-three significant shareholders), Cenovus (twenty-one), Suncor Energy (eighteen), Teck Resources (eighteen), TransCanada Corporation (seventeen), CNRL (sixteen), Pembina Pipeline (fifteen), and Enbridge (fourteen). Consistent with our earlier finding that institutional shareholders or constellations of interest predominate in the ownership of most Canadian-controlled fossil-capital firms, all but one of these Canadian-controlled majors are controlled by complex and overlapping constellations of interest involving the chartered banks and other financial institutions.[12]

Figure 4.5 isolates the significant ownership relations that converge upon these eight Canadian-controlled majors. Fifty-nine of the 127 external owners have stakes in one or more of the eight majors, and thirty-seven of them are financial companies. The ownership network is highly integrated by virtue of the overlapping investment portfolios of the big banks and other financial institutions. Four of the five major Canadian banks have significant stakes in all eight carbon majors.[13] Canada's most important financial institutions thus have a common interest in the continued growth of Canada's carbon-extractive sector, but, it must be said, they also have a common interest in one another. Other research has shown that the banks are significant shareholders in one another, with RBC holding an average of 5.1 percent ownership of the other four while the Bank of Nova Scotia, the least invested, holds an average of 3.7 percent (Carroll and Sapinski 2018).

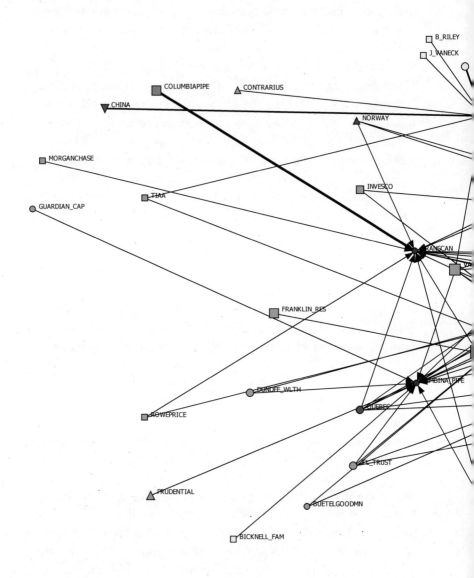

Figure 4.5. Eight Canadian-controlled carbon majors and their owners, 2017. See Figure 4.4 for key.

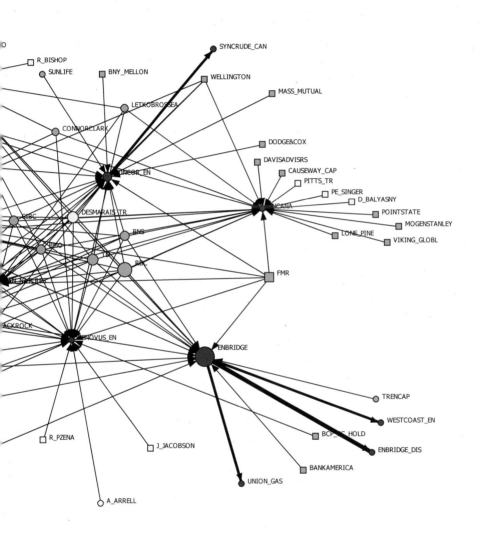

Finally, to isolate the central core of ownership interests, and in view of the variation in the size of ownership stakes in the network, we performed a stepwise reduction of the network, successively ratcheting up the criterion for an ownership stake from 1 percent to 10 percent (see table 4.2).

Table 4.2. Stepwise reduction of the ownership network

Minimum ownership stake (%)	1	2	3	4	5	10
N of ties	446	260	151	108	89	35
N of firms in the network	177	136	517	104	99	65
N of core-sample firms	50	50	50	48	47	35
N of corporate owners	9	9	9	9	9	8
N of financial owners	79	54	41	32	28	11
N of person owners	31	17	12	11	11	8
N of state of owners	8	6	5	4	4	3
Size of dominant component	161	120	95	78	51	14

When the floor criterion for a significant ownership stake is raised to 2 percent, 41.7 percent of the ties and 23.2 percent of firms participating in the network disappear, leaving a network of 136 companies linked by 260 ownership ties. Clearly, many of the connections are well below the level at which strategic control or influence could be asserted. At a floor of 5 percent, the network is reduced to 99 firms linked by 89 ownership stakes, with 51 firms constituting a dominant component. At 10 percent or above, the network breaks into 22 components, each organized around particular strategic-control relations. Financial owners (including banks, insurers, and asset managers) are profusely involved at lower levels of ownership. They make up 63 percent of all owners whose stakes are between 1 percent and 3 percent. But among owners with stakes of 10 percent or more, the proportion of financial companies drops to 37 percent (eleven of thirty). Similarly, but less dramatically, although there are nineteen personal owners with stakes of 1 percent to 2.99 percent, only a dozen personal owners have stakes of 3 percent or more in any one of the Top 50. As is well known, several giant operating companies in the carbon-extractive sector own controlling interest in major Canadian firms. Eight have stakes of 10 percent or more in one of the Top 50.

Isolating the subset of firms linked together by ownership relations of 5 percent or more, we arrive at the map of the dominant component shown in figure 4.6. In this configuration, which includes twenty-eight of the Top 50 fossils, financial companies predominate, making up seventeen of twenty-three owners. Four of Canada's five big banks participate, and US-based institutional investors—particularly Capital Group but also Franklin Resources, FMR, and Sailingstone—have significant stakes in multiple fossil firms. But RBC is by far the major stakeholder, owning 5 percent or more of twelve corporations. Earlier research revealed that RBC, which promotes itself as "Canada's leading energy bank, for conventional, non-conventional and renewable resources," matches many of its ownership stakes in fossil fuel companies with interlocks between its board/senior management and those of the firms it partly owns (Daub and Carroll 2016).

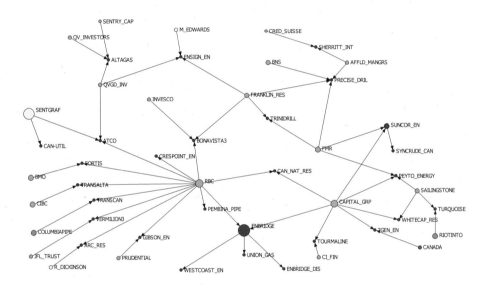

Figure 4.6. Dominant component of 28 carbon-sector firms and 23 owners with stakes of 5 percent or more, 2017. Key: brown = fossil fuel firms based in Canada; red = states; orange = foreign-based corporations; green = financial institutions and asset managers; yellow = persons/families.

Of course, shareholdings are not the only, or even the most weighty, capital relations between high finance and big carbon. Canadian banks are major lenders to the fossil sector. Because detailed data on these relations are not systematically available, however, our mapping is restricted to ownership stakes. Yet, as an illustration of the scale of the loans that are integral to the symbiosis of the two sectors, consider that, since 2017, the troubled Kinder Morgan Trans Mountain Pipeline expansion project has had a $5.5 billion loan facility agreement with the five big Canadian banks, with RBC as administrative agent (Allan 2018). Without such financial enablement (complemented by government largesse, as in the May 2018 federal purchase of Kinder Morgan's Trans Mountain Pipeline assets), megaprojects such as the proposed bitumen pipeline could not be mounted.

Conclusion

Our mapping of ownership and control in Canada's carbon-extractive sector reveals the major interests with stakes in business-as-usual. We find a confluence of Canadian capitalist ownership, via families and financial institutions, and foreign ownership, via transnational corporations and asset managers. These ownership relations are arrayed in a network of many weak ties (smaller institutional holdings) and a few dozen large holdings that confer strategic control upon their corporate or personal owners. As concentrated as the sector is, so are its owners concentrated: a small group of actors has control over much of the sector. The concentration of fossil capital and of its ownership/ control represents a massive centralization of economic power in the hands of private investors accountable only to themselves. Although foreign-based capital figures in the ownership of many corporations, through asset managers and in some cases transnational parent corporations, Canadian capitalists, including bankers, own and control a substantial (and increasing) share of the sector. Yet, far from representing the national interest of Canadians, these proprietors simply pursue their own particular interests in maximizing immediate profits from carbon extraction and processing.

Personal control of fossil capital remains substantial, particularly among mid-sized fossils. Some of the world's largest transnational corporations continue to control several of the largest Canadian fossils. But what stands out are the many comparatively small yet significant holdings of institutional investors (some of them major US-based asset managers), which form constellations of interests, in partnership with top-level management. This pattern is consistent with two sets of related findings. In chapter 5 of this volume, a mapping of the elite network of interlocking directorates around the largest Canada-based fossil firms reveals a well-integrated, east-west configuration of financial institutions (based mainly in Toronto) and fossil corporations (based mainly in Calgary). An earlier mapping of the global corporate ownership network, circa 2007, showed that "the socialization of capital within the capitalist class, mediated by institutional investors and expressed through intercorporate ownership of proportionately small, fluidly held blocs of shares, is now a global phenomenon" (Carroll 2012, 71). Within this form of capitalist socialization, massive financial institutions participate in overlapping constellations of interest, creating a close symbiosis between fossil capital and financial capital. Their many stakes in various firms, sometimes accompanied by board interlocks, give them an obvious interest in the vitality of the entire sector and in obstructing movement to wind down fossil capital and to build up renewables.

In the immediate situation, our findings support a strategy of pressing fossil capital's financial enablers to divest. Divestment does not pre-empt other policy- or movement-based initiatives to reduce or undo the highly concentrated ownership of Canada's carbon sector, and it is not a panacea, as noted in chapter 17. Divestment does not challenge corporate power as it operates across the economy, nor does divestment in itself suggest what will replace fossil fuels or, equally important, how the social relations of a post-carbon economy can be organized democratically rather than oligarchically. What makes divestment (and complementary policies to sunset fossil capital) appealing is its clear focus: "to destroy the most ecological[ly] harmful sector of capitalism, that is, fossil capital" (Holgersen and Warlenius 2016, 523). Although fossil fuel divestment has registered victories elsewhere, Canada's major financial institutions are, as we have seen, so deeply invested in fossil capital that divestment must push especially hard against an entrenched "new denialism" that acknowledges the verdict of climate science yet refuses to take meaningful action (Klein and Daub 2016).[14] Still, even unsuccessful divestment campaigns can have a salutary impact in raising consciousness about the actualities of economic power in fossil capitalism (see chapter 17). Moreover, divestment may gain political traction as fossil majors like Suncor acknowledge that some reserves are best left in the ground (Linnitt 2016), while research highlights emerging risks to fossil fuel investors, as in climate-damage liabilities and stranded assets (Leaton and Grant 2017; Shue 2017).

In the longer term, however, our findings underscore the need to democratize control of energy as we shift from carbon to renewables. Our fossilized system of oligarchic ownership of an ecological time-bomb needs more than fine tuning.

Appendix: Methodological Notes

To conduct a longitudinal tracking of sectoral ownership, we could not simply take a set of companies dominant at one point and trace their owners over time, as we would miss companies that were prominent years ago but went bankrupt, were taken over, or did not grow quickly enough to remain in the Top 50. Instead, we constructed a sample consisting of all companies that, during the period under study, appeared at least once among the top fifty companies listed in Oilweek's annual "Top 100." This yielded an initial sample of 101 companies. We then found that this initial sample included several subsidiaries that were wholly owned by other companies also on the list, as well as a few energy and utility companies not directly involved in carbon-extractive production. At the same time, it excluded several subsidiaries of foreign-based firms. We therefore excluded a total of eight companies but added ten of the largest foreign-owned subsidiaries based in Canada (such as Shell Canada, Total E&P Canada, and Chevron Canada). In total, the sample thus comprised 103 companies. Of these, eighteen were taken over by another company during the period under study. In such cases, we excluded these companies from the analysis in years subsequent to their takeover only if the new owner was already in the sample.

We gathered data on total revenue from the annual reports of these companies and used the ORBIS Bureau van Dijk database to identify their shareholders. The ORBIS database lists only shareholdings of size. Rarely does it include share blocs comprising less than one-tenth of 1 percent of outstanding shares, even though some of these blocs are valued in millions of dollars.[15] As a result, small shareholdings are not represented in our analysis. Our estimates of the ownership shares held by major owners are also rather conservative, but for a different reason. For firms majority-controlled by an identified owner, ORBIS often reports share ownership simply as majority-owned, without indicating the percentage of shares owned. We initially coded these cases as ownership of 50.01 percent, yet actual ownership may range up to 100 percent, and, as noted earlier, majority ownership effectively confers control. In that light, we did an additional analysis of control, taking each majority holding as equivalent to 100 percent ownership while removing all other holdings from the analysis. The results are presented in the "Control" columns in table 4.1.

An additional methodological complication stemmed from the secrecy of financial information pertaining to some wholly owned subsidiaries of foreign-based corporations. For six such firms, we imputed total revenue by benchmarking on the basis of their total production in Canada, using the barrels of oil equivalent (BOE) metric to do so. We estimated the revenue per BOE and used this to estimate the revenue for the companies on which we did not have revenue data. If, as was the case for some of these firms, information about annual production output was also missing, we assumed an annual revenue growth for the firm equal to the average annual growth in the sample.

Notes

1. Calculated from Table 33-10-0005-01, "Foreign-Controlled Enterprises in Canada, Counts by Operating Revenue Size Groups" (formerly CANSIM 179-0005), Statistics Canada, https://www150.statcan.gc.ca/t1/tbl1/en/tv.action?pid=3310000501. In 2000, the total number of corporations stood at 1,033,745; in 2017, the number was 1,801,622.
2. Calculated from Table 33-10-0005-01, "Foreign-Controlled Enterprises in Canada, Counts by Operating Revenue Size Groups" (formerly CANSIM 179-0005), Statistics Canada, https://www150.statcan.gc.ca/t1/tbl1/en/tv.action?pid=3310000501. In comparison, in 1975 foreign control of operating revenue in non-financial industries stood at 36.6 percent, according to Chart 2, "Share of Foreign Control for Non-financial Industries in Canada," in "Foreign Control in the Canadian Economy, 2015," *The Daily*, July 4, 2017, Statistics Canada, https://www150.statcan.gc.ca/n1/daily-quotidien/170704/dq170704a-eng.htm.
3. Table 1, "Assets, Operating Revenue and Operating Profits Under Foreign Control, by Industry," and Table 2, "Total Assets, Operating Revenue and Operating Profits Under Foreign Control, by Major Country of Control, All Industries," in "Foreign Control in the Canadian Economy, 2015."
4. We used revenue, rather than assets, as our criterion because it is the most widely available measure of firm size. Moreover, in the current era, revenue has another advantage over assets as a measure of firm size. Carbon-extractive companies include as assets the reserves of potentially extractable carbon to which they have exclusive access. Yet calculations of Canada's carbon budgets reveal that most of these reserves (particularly of coal and bitumen) will have to stay in the ground if the country is to meet its international obligations regarding climate mitigation (Lee 2018). In this hopeful scenario, a large share of the declared assets of corporations heavily invested in bitumen or coal would be "stranded," bereft of economic value.

5. Currently, available data take us only to year end 2015, before several global carbon majors sold their tar sands stakes to Canadian companies. See Adomaitis and Bousso (2017) and Jaremko (2017). Canadian fossil firms have also been increasing their investments in the United States and elsewhere. See, for instance, Bickis (2016) and Krugel (2016).

6. As with the analysis of the Top 50 (above), the data on the Top 200 and the ownership relations converging on them were downloaded from the business database ORBIS.

7. There are nuances in each of these control categories. For instance, in 2017, N. Murray Edwards, a Canadian, held a 16.61 percent stake in Ensign Energy Services, affording him minority control. As a profit-savvy capitalist, he chose in 2016 to move his official personal residence to the United Kingdom, to take advantage of lower tax rates on capital gains there. Ensign Energy is thus categorized here as British controlled, an accurate yet quite odd description since Edwards continues to be a central player in Canada's carbon-capital community. See Healing (2016).

8. This includes firms on the Oilweek "Top 100" list (used in the longitudinal analysis of ownership of the Top 50, in the previous section), available at https://www.jwnenergy.com/reports/oilweek-top-100/. As in that analysis, we have made substitutes to remove non-carbon-based energy companies (several hydroelectric firms). In their place, we added several large, privately held corporations, mostly under foreign control, namely, Apache Canada Ltd. (which was taken over by Canadian-owned Paramount Resources in the summer of 2017), Total E&P Canada Ltd., Chevron Canada Resources Ltd., Syncrude Canada Ltd., Korea National Oil, Murphy Oil, and Shell Canada.

9. In a few cases, firms in the Top 50 owned significant stakes in one another—for instance, Enbridge's shares in Union Gas, Westcoast Energy, and Enbridge Distribution.

10. The five subsidiaries are Shell Canada (owned by Royal Dutch Shell), Chevron Canada and Murphy Oil Canada (both owned by US-based companies), Total E & P Canada (a subsidiary of Total S.A., which is based in France), and Harvest Operations (owned by Korea National Oil). Together, these five plus their owners account for ten out of the sixteen isolates.

11. One of these is Lightstream Resources, in which CEO John D. Wright owns a 3.5 percent share. The other is Pacific Rubiales Energy, 19 percent of which is owned by the Alfa Group, a Moscow-based consortium of investors, 19 percent by the Spanish holding company Percacer, and 10 percent by O'Hara Administration, an asset management group based in Panama. These two Top 50 fossils plus the four owners make up the remaining six of the sixteen isolates.

12. The exception is Vancouver-based Teck Resources, whose major shareholder (owning 29 percent) is Norman Keevil (with additional financial participation by the government of China, Japan-based Sumitomo Metals, and a host of institutional investors).

13. The Bank of Nova Scotia's 0.93 percent holding in Teck Resources falls just short of our floor criterion for a significant holding. This pattern also holds for US-based Vanguard Group, which is invested in all eight Canadian-controlled carbon majors (as well as twenty-two other Top 50 carbon firms).

14. Notable victories include New York's Amalgamated Bank, which, in September 2016, became the first North American bank to divest its fossil fuel holdings in favour of a clean energy transition (Stewart 2016), and the French international banking conglomerate BNP Paribus, which, in October 2017, became the first global bank to announce divestment from tar sands and shale oil projects (Valentini and Ward 2017).

15. Moreover, ORBIS does not report all of a company's holdings every year. If a particular percentage holding was listed one year and then went unmentioned until a different ownership percentage was reported in a later year, we assumed that the holding had remained at the first percentage until the new one appeared. But if no new percentage was ever reported in the period under study, we assumed the holding had ceased to exist after the last year in which the holding was reported.

References

Adomaitis, Nerijus, and Ron Bousso. 2017. "Big Oil Abandoning Canada's Oilsands in Quest for Cleaner Crude." *Financial Post*, November 21, 2017. http://business. financialpost.com/commodities/energy/interview-statoil-plants-flag-in-big-oils-race-for-cleaner-crude.

Allan, Robyn. 2018. "What's Behind Kinder Morgan's May 31 Ultimatum? Follow the Money." *National Observer*, May 15, 2018. https://www.nationalobserver. com/2018/05/15/opinion/whats-behind-kinder-morgans-may-31-ultimatum-follow-money.

Berle, Adolf, and G. C. Means. 1932. *The Modern Corporation and Private Property*. New York: Macmillan.

Bickis, Ian. 2016. "Enbridge to Buy Spectra Energy in Stock Deal Worth $37 billion." *National Observer*, September 6, 2016. https://www.nationalobserver. com/2016/09/06/news/enbridge-buy-spectra-energy-stock-deal-worth-37-billion.

Brennan, Jordan. 2012. *A Shrinking Universe: How Concentrated Corporate Capital Is Shaping Income Inequality in Canada*. Ottawa: Canadian Centre for Policy Alternatives.

Burgess, Bill. 2002. "Canada's Location in the World System: Reworking the Debate in Canadian Political Economy." PhD diss., University of British Columbia.

Carroll, William K. 1986. *Corporate Power and Canadian Capitalism*. Vancouver: University of British Columbia Press.

———. 2004. *Corporate Power in a Globalizing World*. Don Mills, ON: Oxford University Press.

———. 2008. "The Corporate Elite and the Transformation of Finance Capital: A View from Canada." *Sociological Review* 56 (S1): 44–63.

———. 2012. "Capital Relations and Directorate Interlocking: The Global Network in 2007." In *Financial Elites and Transnational Business: Who Rules the World*, edited by Georgina Murray and John Scott, 54–75. Northampton, MA: Edward Elgar.

Carroll, William K., and Jerome Klassen. 2010. "Hollowing Out Corporate Canada? Changes in the Corporate Network Since the 1990s." *Canadian Journal of Sociology* 35, no. 1: 1–30.

Carroll, William K., and J. P. Sapinski. 2018. *Organizing the 1%: How Corporate Power Works*. Halifax: Fernwood.

Daub, Shannon, and William K. Carroll. 2016. "Why Is the CEO of a Big Canadian Bank Giving Speeches About Climate Change and Pipelines?" Corporate Mapping Project. October 6, 2016. http://www.corporatemapping.ca/rbc-ceo-speech-climate-pipelines/.

Dahrendorf, Rolf. 1959. *Class and Class Conflict in an Industrial Society*. London: Routledge and Kegan Paul.

Durand, Cedric. 2017. *Fictitious Capital: How Finance Is Appropriating Our Future*. London: Verso.

Gadhoum, Yoser. 2006. "Power of Ultimate Controlling Owners: A Survey of Canadian Landscape." *Journal of Management and Governance* 10, no. 2: 179–204.

Healing, Dan. 2016. "Billionaire Murray Edwards Changes Residency from Calgary to United Kingdom." *Calgary Herald*, March 24, 2016. http://calgaryherald.com/business/energy/billionaire-murray-edwards-changes-residency-from-calgary-to-united-kingdom.

Holgersen, Ståle, and Rikard Warlenius. 2016. "Destroy What Destroys the Planet: Steering Creative Destruction in the Dual Crisis." *Capital and Class* 40, no. 3: 511–32.

Huber, Matthew T. 2013. *Lifeblood: Oil, Freedom, and the Forces of Capital*. Minneapolis: University of Minnesota Press.

Jaremko, Deborah. 2017. "Charts: Canadian Companies About to Own 80 Percent of Oilsands Production." *JWN*. March 30, 2017. http://www.jwnenergy.com/article/2017/3/charts-canadian-companies-about-own-80-percent-oilsands-production/.

Kellogg, Paul. 2015. *Escape from the Staples Trap: Canadian Political Economy After Left Nationalism*. Toronto: University of Toronto Press.

Klassen, Jerome. 2014. *Joining Empire: The Political Economy of the New Canadian Foreign Policy*. Toronto: University of Toronto Press.

Klein, Seth, and Shannon Daub. 2016. "The New Climate Denialism: Time for an Intervention." Corporate Mapping Project. September 30, 2016. https://www. corporatemapping.ca/the-new-climate-denialism-time-for-an-intervention/.

Krugel, Lauren. 2016. "TransCanada to Buy Columbia Pipeline Group for $13 Billion." *National Observer,* March 17, 2016. http://www.nationalobserver. com/2016/03/17/news/transcanada-buy-columbia-pipeline-group-13-billion.

Leaton, James, and Andrew Grant. 2017. *2 Degrees of Separation: Transition Risk for Oil and Gas in a Low Carbon World*. London: Carbon Tracker Initiative and Principles for Responsible Investment. http://2degreeseparation.com/reports/2D-of-separation_PRI-CTI_Summary-report.pdf.

Lee, Marc. 2018. "Extracted Carbon and Canada's International Trade in Fossil Fuels." *Studies in Political Economy* 99, no. 2: 114–29.

Linnitt, Carol. 2016. "Suncor Opens Conversation About 'Stranded Assets' in Alberta's Oilsands." *The Narwhal,* August 2, 2016. https://thenarwhal.ca/suncor-opens-conversation-about-stranded-assets-alberta-s-oilsands.

Morck, Randall K., David A. Strangeland, and Bernard Yeung. 2000. "Inherited Wealth, Corporate Control, and Economic Growth: The Canadian Disease?" In *Concentrated Corporate Ownership*, edited by Randall K. Morck, 319–72. Chicago: University of Chicago Press.

Niosi, Jorge. 1978. *The Economy of Canada: Who Controls It?* Montréal: Black Rose Books.

———. 1981. *Canadian Capitalism: A Study of Power in the Canadian Business Establishment*. Toronto: Lorimer.

Porter, John. 1965. *The Vertical Mosaic: An Analysis of Social Class and Power in Canada*. Toronto: University of Toronto Press.

Scott, John. 1997. *Corporate Business and Capitalist Classes*. New York: Oxford University Press.

Shue, Henry. 2017. "Responsible for What? Carbon Producer CO2 Contributions and the Energy Transition." *Climate Change* 144, no. 4: 591–96.

Stewart, Hamish. 2016. "An American Bank Just Became the First in Continent to Pull Its Investments from Fossil Fuels." *National Observer*, September 21, 2016. https://www.nationalobserver.com/2016/09/21/analysis/american-bank-just-became-first-continent-pull-its-investments-fossil-fuels.

Valentini, Fabio Benedetti, and Russell Ward. 2017. "BNP to Halt Shale Oil Financing, Expand Funds for Renewables." *Bloomberg*, October 10, 2017. https://www.bloomberg.com/news/articles/2017-10-11/bnp-paribas-to-halt-shale-oil-financing-in-climate-change-pledge.

5   Canada's Fossil-Capital Elite
A Tangled Web of Corporate Power

William K. Carroll

Fossil capital—indeed, capitalism overall in the early twenty-first century—is heavily networked. Our network mapping in chapter 4 showed how ownership of substantial share blocs by major personal, corporate, and institutional investors further concentrates corporate power (in its strategic modality) in the hands of those investors, who include financial institutions. Complementing the network of corporate ownership is an elite network of interlocking directorates. This chapter maps the network of elites in and around Canada's fossil-capital sector.

Extensive research over the past decades has documented the tendency for large corporations to share the same directors (and sometimes the same executives: see Carroll and Sapinski 2018, chap. 5). These elite, extra-market relations among the largest companies create the basis for a "corporate community" (Domhoff 2006). The well-connected individuals at the network's centre form what Useem (1984) termed an "inner circle," further concentrating corporate power within the dominant stratum of the capitalist class. The elite social relations that underpin this community diverge sharply from the hegemonic "free enterprise" narrative of firms isolated from and in competition with one another. Directorate interlocks provide a structural basis for communication, coordination, and social cohesion, enabling the corporate

This chapter first appeared in the *Canadian Journal of Sociology* 42, no. 3 (2017): 225–60, under the title "Canada's Carbon-Capital Elite: A Tangled Web of Corporate Power." It is reprinted here, with minor revisions, by permission of the journal.

community to define and pursue its common interests in maintaining the status quo of concentrated corporate power (Brownlee 2005; Sapinski and Carroll 2018).

In Canada, a research program mapping the corporate elite was inaugurated in the 1950s by John Porter (1956) and later advanced by his student Wallace Clement (1975). More recent work has used social network analysis (SNA) to situate the Canadian corporate power structure within a transnational context (Carroll 2004; Carroll and Klassen 2010; Klassen and Carroll 2014). These studies have opened a window on the social organization of Canadian capitalism in an era of globalizing capitalism, but they have not considered how fossil capital is positioned within the power structure.

The Fossil-Capital Elite

Corporate community, corporate elite, inner circle, and dominant stratum are terms that flag the enormous concentration of power in a relatively small group of business leaders—the result of a combination of economic concentration, concentration of share ownership (see chapter 4), and elite social networking. If fossil capital has become a leading industrial sector, it is worthwhile to map the organization of corporate power within the *fossil-capital elite* that directs and manages those corporations. In turn, the fossil-capital sector is integrated with the broader national and transnational economy. Besides supply chains that link carbon extraction into other economic sectors, there is a strong codependency between fossil fuel corporations and the financial sector. In an era of extreme oil (see chapter 1), extractive megaprojects require massive financing; thus, corporate power over carbon extraction and processing is closely tied to corporate power in financing those activities (Albo and Yap 2016). These initial reflections lead to three research questions:

(1) What is the fossil-capital elite's *accumulation base* (Carroll 1986)? That is, what combination of carbon-extractive companies provides a basis for the streams of profit upon which the elite's power ultimately depends?

(2) How is the fossil-capital elite *internally structured* as a network of interlocking directorates, which operates simultaneously at two levels: that of the corporation and that of the individual (Carroll 1984)?

(3) How is the elite linked to the financial sector and other segments of corporate capital, national and transnational?

Answers to these questions illuminate our understanding of Canada's fossil-capital elite as a distinct grouping, or *fraction*, embedded within wider networks of corporate power.

Method

Many studies of the corporate elite begin by identifying the largest companies within a geographical space. My interest in the fossil-capital elite suggested a different sampling method. I began with the list of 114 carbon-extractive corporations with assets of at least $50 million, developed by Lee and Ellis (2013). To that I added 124 corporations involved in carbon extraction, transport, and processing, identified through searches of online databases, resulting in a "core sample" of 238 fossil-capital companies based in Canada, each with assets of at least $50 million at year end 2014. The selection process then snowballed to include several thousand companies, as I selected *direct* neighbours (defined as other firms directly linked to the core sample by interlocking directorates) and then *indirect* neighbours (firms linked indirectly to core-sample firms via interlocks with direct neighbours), using the online ORBIS database, which covers several million companies worldwide. I then gathered data on the directors and executives of all core and neighbour firms (direct and indirect) as well as company-level variables such as size, industry, and location of head office. Snowballing enables us to analyze carbon-sector firms as embedded nodes in wider interlocking networks: to locate the fossil-capital elite within the neighbourhoods of the Canadian and foreign-based corporations that form a global power structure.

The snowballing procedure identified an initial list of 15,569 corporations, 1,547 of which were direct neighbours to core-sample firms. Since my research interest lay in mapping Canada's fossil-capital sector within the network of the largest corporations, I introduced size criteria that excluded the smaller neighbours from the analysis. My sample thus comprises several *top strata*, which include the largest Canada-based neighbours (direct and indirect) to fossil-capital firms and the largest foreign-based neighbours (direct and indirect). The size criteria were geared to generating Canadian and foreign strata that would be analytically manageable. I selected Canadian-based direct and indirect neighbours with revenue of US$100 million or more (n = 155 and 244, respectively). This revenue floor is equal to that of the 130th ranked firm in my core sample; thus, the strata of Canada-based neighbours include very large firms as well as firms similar in size to mid-sized fossil-capital firms. I selected foreign-based direct neighbours with revenue of $1 billion or more (n = 258) and foreign-based indirect neighbours with revenue of $27 billion or more (n = 363). This stratification procedure yielded a sample of 1,258 top strata corporations, including 637 Canada-based companies and 621 foreign-based companies. With it, we can map the Canada-based carbon sector as it is embedded within the national and global formation of the largest corporations, but we need to remain aware of the size differences between strata that are built into this methodology.

Overall, the elite network is carried by a relatively small segment of corporate directors and executives. The 22,917 directors and executives of the 1,258 corporations generate over nine thousand interlocks, but most individuals (79.1 percent) are affiliated with single corporations, and most corporate networkers are affiliated with two firms, creating a single interlock. Yet most of the interlocks—three out of five—are carried by networkers who have three or more corporate affiliations. The 481 "big linkers" (each with four or more affiliations), a mere 1.7 percent of all directors and executives, account for nearly two in five interlocks. The network is largely the domain of an elite within the elite, an "inner circle" of well-connected individuals.

The Fossil-Capital Elite's Accumulation Base

A fundamental structuring condition in corporate capitalism is extreme disparities in the distribution of capital. Generally, economic sectors, national economies, and the global economy are dominated by a relative few large companies, concentrating corporate power in the hands of their owners, directors, and executives. Within the carbon-extractive sector, this is the basis for distinguishing between the handful of "majors," which claim most of the revenue generated in the sector, and the many mid-sized firms (see also chapter 1). The top fifteen revenue-earners, hereafter the "majors," comprise only 6.3 percent of core-sample firms but claim 63.5 percent of total revenue. They include six of the eight integrated oil and gas companies based in Canada and five of eighteen pipeline companies. In these capital-intensive subsectors, value flows are extremely concentrated: among integrated fossil-capital companies, the majors account for 97.5 percent of revenue; among pipeline companies they account for 70.6 percent of revenue. Majors represent less than half of total revenue in other subsectors: non-integrated oil and gas extraction (30 percent), services to extraction (15.2 percent), and coal/bitumen mining (47.4 percent).[1]

The fossil-capital elite is shaped by a *geography of accumulation*. Fossil capital clusters spatially, in centres of strategic command. Four-fifths of companies are headquartered in Calgary, representing 87.3 percent of total sectoral revenue. Only Toronto (thirteen firms accounting for 4 percent of sectoral revenue) and Vancouver (fifteen firms accounting for 3.7 percent) host any substantial number of companies (five corporations based in Edmonton claim only 0.2 percent of revenue).

Complementing head office location is location of investments. I developed a typology that views this aspect of corporate geography from the standpoint of western Canada, noting whether firms have substantial investments in western Canada, in the rest of Canada (ROC), in the United States, or beyond. Two-fifths of companies are active solely in western Canada, including the four western provinces and the northern territories. Another 37.4 percent are active in western Canada but also elsewhere. Many of these are active in the United States (15.5 percent) or both in the US and beyond (16.8 percent). Very few firms that are not invested in western Canada are active elsewhere in Canada, and seven of these eleven are also invested in the United States (two firms) and beyond (five firms).

Clearly, many Canadian fossil-capital corporations centre their activities in western provinces, but some companies' investments span the globe. A sizable stratum conducts activities entirely outside Canada, in the United States (seven firms) or more internationally (thirty-six).[2] Yet in terms of the capital (revenue) they represent, firms active in western Canada dominate. Indeed, *firms invested in western Canada make up 76.9 percent of the entire fossil fuel sector but account for 92.5 percent of revenue*. The fifty-four firms not active in western Canada account for only 7.5 percent of total revenue. Among the majors, the western Canada base is especially evident. None restricts its activities to that region but all are squarely based there.[3] Clearly, the western provinces are the centre of gravity of investments, complementing and reinforcing the dominance of Calgary as the command centre for most corporate head offices.

Foreign control of corporations concentrates corporate power transnationally, in the hands of owners located elsewhere. Since the publication of Kari Levitt's *Silent Surrender* (1970), the significance and extent of foreign control of corporate Canada have been debated. Although at the time Levitt wrote, US-based transnational corporations seemed poised to conquer the world, ensuing decades witnessed a decline of American hegemony and a more multilateral pattern of international investment, leading to a cross-penetration of capital among the advanced capitalist countries (Klassen and Carroll 2014, 164; Kellogg 2015). It is therefore not surprising that core-sample firms are predominantly controlled by Canadian interests, accounting for 71 percent of firms and 67 percent of total revenue. Corporate interests based in the United States control 12 percent of firms and of revenue, followed by those based in China (including Hong Kong), which account for 4 percent of firms but 11 percent of revenue. Foreign control is concentrated within a few of the largest firms. Six of fifteen majors are foreign controlled: Imperial Oil (US), Gibson Energy (UK), Talisman Energy (Spain), Shell Canada (Netherlands), Husky Energy, and Nexen (China, including Hong Kong). These represent 75 percent of the total sectoral revenue under foreign control.[4]

To summarize, the accumulation base for Canada's fossil-capital elite is bifurcated between a few majors and many mid-sized corporations. The elite's centre of gravity is western Canada (specifically, Calgary) but the capital it manages is extensively transnationalized. Most of the sector's revenue flows through companies whose investments reach beyond Canada's borders. Although the fossil-capital elite directs and manages corporations controlled mainly in Canada, some firms (including several of the majors) are controlled by interests in the United States, China, and Europe. Although centred in western Canada and predominantly controlled by Canadian interests, Canada's fossil-capital elite directs outward-bound international business activities while being penetrated by foreign interests. It participates in the cross-penetration of investment that is integral both to capitalist globalization and to the formation of a transnational capitalist class (Carroll 2018).

Social Organization of the Fossil-Capital Elite

Central to my second research question is whether elite interlocking within the fossil-capital sector provides a basis for a corporate community—whether the network is *integrated* or *fragmented* into many disconnected pieces. In this section I present a network analysis of the interlocks created by the multiple affiliations of directors and executives of fossil-capital firms.

Results of snowball sampling already showed that the fossil-capital elite is embedded in a national and transnational network. Its members interlock directly or at one remove with more than 15,000 corporations, nearly 2,000 of which are based in Canada.[5] Yet the entire network could still be disjointed if companies formed *cliques*, interlocking with one another to the exclusion of outsiders. Here, the question is not simply whether firms interlock with other corporations but whether their *neighbours* interlock with each other—that is, whether the *neighbourhoods* of fossil-capital firms overlap. Focusing on the 1,258 top strata corporations, we find that 92.4 percent form a *connected component* in which all members are directly or indirectly linked. This means that the neighbourhoods of fossil-capital firms overlap, constituting a single network. Its *density* is 0.007; in other words, 0.7 percent of all pairs of companies are interlocked. Overall, the network is quite sparse (as large networks typically are), yet this does not preclude the possibility of relatively dense subnetworks, as we shall see.

Any network is composed of points (or nodes) and lines (or edges). The nodes are characteristically organized along a dimension of *centrality*: some are positioned at or near the network's core; others are on its margins. The most basic index of centrality is *degree*, which in this case is simply the number of companies with which a given corporation is interlocked. Within my sample, the mean degree is 7.74. As with the distribution of capital, the distribution of interlocking is skewed (though not as severely): the most central 10 percent of corporations (each with a degree of at least 17) accounts for 31 percent of all interlocking.

In addition to simple degree, a measure of centrality that takes into account the centrality of one's neighbours in the network is *2-step degree*: the number of firms to which a given company is tied either directly or at one remove. Among the top strata corporations, the mean 2-step degree is 32.39. Degree and 2-step degree can illuminate whether and how Canada's fossil-capital companies form a distinct corporate community. Considering only the interlocks that link the 238 fossil-capital firms to one another, we find that 193 companies participate in at least one interlock *within* the sector, the mean within-sector degree being 4.01. In addition, companies are linked at one remove to a mean of 7.34 other fossil-capital firms. All but six of the 193 firms form a connected component.

Concentration of Capital and Network Structure

Fossil capital is highly concentrated (see chapter 4), with the fifteen majors claiming nearly two-thirds of revenue. This bifurcation structures the elite network. As a metric, degree can be decomposed into internal and external components. *Internal degree* refers to the number of firms in the same sector with which a firm interlocks; *external degree* refers to the number of firms in other sectors with which the same firm interlocks. When we distinguish between "introverted" networking within Canada's fossil-capital sector (internal degree) and "extraverted" networking beyond it (external degree), what stands out is the difference between majors and others (table 5.1). On average, majors interlock with three other fossil-capital firms but with eleven non-fossil neighbours: their networking reaches extensively beyond the fossil-capital sector, linking them at one remove to a mean of eighty-five companies beyond the core sample. Mid-sized core-sample companies interlock mainly with other fossil-capital firms, and their interlocks do not generate very many indirect ties beyond the Canadian fossil-capital sector.[6] The E-I index, a measure of relative extraversion that has a theoretical maximum of 1 (complete extraversion) and minimum of –1 (complete introversion), summarizes the difference nicely: majors are extraverted (mean E-I = 0.522); smaller fossil-sector firms are introverted (E-I = –0.304).[7] The fossil-capital network appears as a two-tiered formation, divided between majors and mid-sized firms. The latter form the backbone of a cohesive, if introverted, local elite; the former play a mediating role between mid-sized local firms and extra-local corporate communities.

Table 5.1. Comparing degree of interlocking: Majors and mid-sized firms

Size of corporation	Degree in core sample	2-step degree in core sample	Degree in rest of network	2-step degree in rest of network
Mid-sized	4.07	7.52	1.80	8.45
Majors	3.13	4.71	11.27	84.69
Total	4.01	7.34	2.40	13.26

Within the fifteen majors, however, is a further division: four show no ties to the other Canadian fossil-capital firms, and three of those four have long been under foreign control (Husky Energy, Imperial Oil, Shell Canada, and coal giant Teck Resources, whose investments extend to non-carbon mining and smelting). On the other hand, majors invested in oil and gas and with deep roots in Canada's capitalist class do participate in the fossil-capital subnetwork, though not to the exclusion of their broader networking. This pattern is evident for Canadian Natural Resources Limited (CNRL; internal degree = 8, external degree = 10), Encana (6, 15), Talisman Energy (5, 19), TransCanada Corporation (5, 20), Enbridge (4, 11), Nexen (4, 12), and Suncor (4, 14), suggesting that these firms (including two that recently fell under foreign control: Talisman and Nexen) play a mediating role in networking both within the local, Calgary-based community and beyond it.

The Core of the Fossil-Capital Corporate Community

Looking more closely within the subnetwork of fossil-capital firms, differences in internal degree between majors and smaller firms point to broader variation in centrality. On the one hand, a quarter of fossil-capital firms do not participate in any interlocks within the subnetwork, while 21.0 percent interlock with one fossil-capital firm and another quarter interlock with two such firms. On the other hand, 17.6 percent interlock with four or more other fossil-capital firms. This suggests that the fossil-capital community is organized around a dense core.

To explore this hypothesis, I dissected the connected component of 193 fossil-capital firms into successive *k-cores*. A k-core is a connected subnetwork whose members are directly linked to at least *k* other members (Seidman 1983). As *k* increases, the criterion for membership is ratcheted up, leaving a smaller subnetwork of densely connected members. The Canadian fossil-capital network does indeed contain a dense centre. Thirteen firms form a 12-core—a completely connected network. Fifty-one firms form a dense 4-core: 40 percent of these firms directly interlock with one another. The 4-core includes only 21.4 percent of fossil-capital firms, but interlocks among its members account for 54.1 percent of all core-sample interlocking.

We can see in table 5.2 that the 4-core is comprised mostly of non-integrated oil and gas producers with access to land (and thus resource rents), based in Calgary, invested primarily in western Canada (with some capital in the rest of Canada or in the United States), and controlled by Canadian interests. At the same time, integrated producers and coal companies, and companies that provide services to extraction but do not control land, are largely absent from the network's core. On average, firms in the 4-core are smaller than other fossil-capital firms. Only one of the fifteen majors is located within the 4-core.

Table 5.2. Composition of the 4-core

Attribute	4-core	Non-core
Non-integrated oil and gas extraction	88.2%	51.3%
Carbon holdings in land	90.2%	62.0%
Headquartered in Calgary	98.0%	74.3%
Invested in western Canada (+ ROC/US)	84.2%	54.1%
Controlled by Canadian interests	92.2%	65.6%
Mean revenue (2014)	$954 million	$1.682 million

Unpacking the Fossil-Capital Elite

A key property of corporate-interlock networks is their *duality* (Carroll 1984): they are composed of both corporations and the persons who actually "carry" the interlocks via their multiple corporate affiliations. Properly speaking, the "fossil-capital elite" refers not to corporations but to the key directors and executives in charge of them. Structurally, the *networkers*, whose multiple affiliations create the corporate-interlock network, play key integrative roles in the fossil-capital elite. A total of 834 individuals (including 105 presidents/ CEOS and 79 board chairs of core-sample firms) create all the interlocks within Canada's carbon-extractive sector and between it and the national and international network in which it is embedded. Nearly a third of them hold one position in a fossil-capital firm and one position in a neighbour of some sort; another quarter hold one fossil-capital affiliation but multiple affiliations with other corporations. These 458 individuals, comprising 54.9 percent of all networkers, link Canada's carbon-extractive sector to the wider corporate elite, without themselves networking across fossil-capital firms. On the other hand, more than a quarter of all networkers (27.6 percent) are network specialists entirely within Canada's carbon-extractive sector: their corporate affiliations do not extend to other industries. Another 16.5 percent are networkers within Canada's carbon-extractive sector *and* have at least one corporate affiliation beyond it. Within that category, 63 individuals (7.6 percent of networkers) hold multiple affiliations with *both* Canadian fossil-capital companies and neighbouring companies.

Taking the 834 networkers as an operationalization of the fossil-capital elite, we find a sharp underrepresentation of women (87.8 percent are men), continuing a patriarchal tradition documented in the 1950s by Porter (1965) and modestly eroded in subsequent years (Carroll 2004). An important class distinction within corporate elites is between *functioning capitalists* in executive positions, who own or manage corporations, and *advisors*, or "organic intellectuals," who serve as outside directors of multiple firms (Carroll 1984, 250). If the corporate network were carried mostly by advisors, it might amount to little more than "window dressing" (Helland and Sykuta 2004)—a side effect of firms retaining the same advisors. Alternatively, a network of interlocking directorates carried mainly by those in positions of authority comprises a structure of corporate power. I assigned each networker to a class category by determining his or her principal affiliation, as indicated by business databases at my disposal (primarily FP Infomart, secondarily Bloomberg and ORBIS). Overall, advisors (including fifteen legal advisors, six consultants, one academic, one state official, and three other advisors) comprise 3.1 percent of the elite. Retired capitalists (éminences *grises*) serving as outside directors—also advisors but recruited from within the class of business owners and executives—make up another 10.2 percent. But most elite networkers are functioning capitalists of one sort or another. The most common position held is that of non-presidential executive (vice president, CFO/treasurer, secretary) in a firm within my sample (44.5 percent of networkers), followed by executive and/or owner of a firm outside my sample (20.7 percent). Other networkers hold top positions in sample corporations, as presidents/CEOs (6.1 percent), presidents/CEOs and chairs (5.5 percent), chairs (5.2 percent), or leading shareholders (4.6 percent, twelve of whom are also presidents).

Although the entire elite is unwieldy to map as a network, we can depict as its inner circle the individuals and corporations that form the 4-core I have identified as the dense centre of the fossil-capital network. Figure 5.1 shows both the individuals and the corporations they direct or manage.[8] If the 4-core provides a backbone for Calgary's oil elite, who is doing the interlocking? The sixty-three individuals in the 4-core tend to be network specialists *within* the core sample—only 34.9 percent have any extraverted corporate affiliations. They tend to be functioning capitalists—only four are advisors or éminences *grises*. And they are overwhelmingly male—only four are women. The biggest linker in the network is J. A. Brussa, a corporate lawyer who chairs Crew Energy and directs eight other fossil-capital firms (all members of the 12-core). Besides Brussa, R. J. Zakresky, D. Shwed, D. R. Drall, M. D. Sandrelli, and E. Chwyl are the key individuals who co-constitute the 12-core through their multiple affiliations with its member firms. And of course, the 12-core is itself linked to other capitalist groups. In particular, Daryl H. Gilbert, managing director of JOG Capital and a key networker in a 6-core composed of eleven firms, sits on the board of Leucrotta Exploration, along with Brussa and Zakresky. It is through such cross-cutting affiliations that networkers like Gilbert, Zakresky, and Brussa knit the corporations into a fossil-capital community.

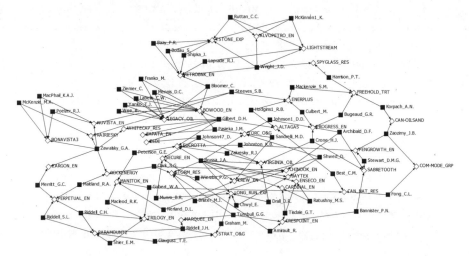

Figure 5.1. The 4-core as a two-mode network. Key: black squares = people; white diamonds = firms

This subnetwork at the heart of the fossil elite is heavily linked to the less central corporations that surround it, which include most of the fossil-capital majors. Although only CNRL participates in the 4-core, eleven of the fifteen majors participate in the connected component, and seven are within its 3-core.

The Fossil-Capital Elite and Its Neighbours

Mapping the Fossil-Capital Subnetwork and Its Canadian Neighbours

In this section I turn to my third research question. How is fossil capital embedded within the national network? In particular, how is it linked to the financial sector, a key source of investment capital and hence a key site of allocative power? Previous research showed that the Canadian corporate network became centred in Toronto during the long postwar boom (from the late 1940s to early 1970s), but that in the later decades of the twentieth century Calgary and Vancouver emerged as corporate command centres, even aspiring to the status of beta-global cities (Carroll 2004). Calgary is the epicentre of fossil capital, but, as table 5.3 shows, it hosts rather few direct and indirect corporate neighbours to that sector. Instead, Canadian neighbours tend to be based in Toronto, Montréal, and Vancouver.

Table 5.3. Percentage distribution of Canadian network members by city of head office

	Core sample	Direct neighbours	Indirect neighbours
Vancouver	6.3	15.5	11.5
Calgary	79.4	13.5	3.3
Edmonton	2.1	4.5	2.9
Winnipeg	0	3.9	2.5
Toronto	5.5	40.6	42.2
Ottawa	0	0.6	2.9
Montréal	0.4	12.3	18.4
Other cities	6.3	8.9	16.3

The national corporate network is structured by this geography. The sociogram in figure 5.2 comprises 525 corporations based in these seven key cities—core-sample firms, their neighbours, and neighbours of neighbours—all linked into a connected component. Once we cluster this corporate social space around Canada's major cities, as in the sociogram, the differences become clear: *Calgary's highly integrated network is specialized in the fossil-capital sector* (in black), with very few other industries represented. Vancouver hosts the second-largest complement of core-sample firms and also a variety of companies in other sectors, as direct and indirect neighbours to the carbon sector. Edmonton's network is much smaller but resembles Vancouver's as a centre for both core-sample firms and their neighbours. Toronto and Montréal show the obverse of Calgary's mono-sectoral profile. Montréal hosts only one core-sample company but many neighbours. Local networks in Calgary, Vancouver, Montréal, and Toronto are internally well integrated, but other cities host firms whose interlocks are extraverted toward companies based in the four main metropoli. The elite traffic among those four is extensive and tends to converge upon Toronto, while elite relations between corporations based in Vancouver and those based in Montréal are quite sparse.

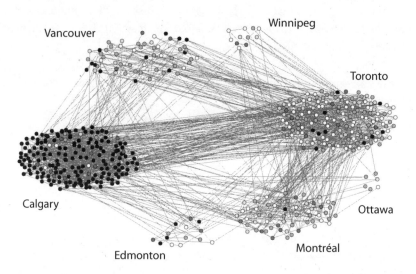

Figure 5.2. The Canadian corporate network, clustered by seven cities, showing five economic sectors. Key: black = carbon; dark grey = carbon-related industrial; grey = other industrial; light grey = commerce; white = finance.

Figure 5.2 also codes corporations in terms of their main economic activity, mapping the distribution of economic sectors across the landscape of the network. I have adopted a fivefold carbon-centred categorization scheme here, consistent with an interest in how that sector links to others. Alongside the fossil-capital sector (black points) is a carbon-related sector, composed of industrial firms closely implicated in the fossil-capital sector, including petrochemicals, electricity, steel, transport, and the automobile industry—what Urry (2013) includes within his broad conception of "carbon capital" (dark grey points). Other industries, whose connections to carbon extraction are more mediated (including non-carbon resource extraction, pharmaceuticals, food and beverage production, equipment manufacture, software, communication, and media), make up a third category (grey). The other two categories distinguish commerce (light grey) from finance (white). I recognize that within fossil capitalism virtually all economic activities depend on carbon directly or indirectly.

In the Toronto-based segment, financial capital is strikingly predominant, but we also see a substantial complement of more mediated production activities. Montréal's network likewise contains numerous financial institutions and a variety of industrial corporations, and to some extent this holds for Vancouver as well. Again, the mono-industrial character of Calgary's network stands out.

Symbiotic ties between industry and finance, abundant in our mapping of the ownership network in chapter 4, have been integral in the organization of corporate power ever since corporations emerged and grew in tandem with the modern credit system (Harvey 2006). One way of exploring this relation as it pertains to fossil capital is by analyzing the neighbourhoods of corporations. Considering first the 238 fossil-capital firms, we find that sixty-five of them include at least one financial company in their neighbourhoods; twenty-six have two or more, and ten have three or more. Interestingly, seven of those ten are majors, and the other three are not based in Calgary. Moreover, seven of the sixteen firms linked to two financials are either majors (three) or based in the east (four). The Calgary-based backbone of the fossil-capital network has comparatively less-extensive elite ties to financial capital.

Given their enormous financing needs, it stands to reason that the majors tend to interlock with multiple financial institutions and to participate more profusely in the national network. Looked at from the other side, among the 126 Canadian financial, investment, and real estate corporations in my sample, forty-five are tied to at least one fossil-capital company; twenty-one have two or more such interlocks, while twelve have three or more. Thirteen of the twenty-one with links to multiple fossil-capital firms are based in Toronto; one is based in Calgary.

If we focus on the seam between these two key sectors, and the firms whose boards interlock extensively across that seam, we arrive at the connected component in figure 5.3, which consists of thirty-six firms: twenty fossil-capital companies (in blue) and sixteen financials (in pink).[9] Here we see an intermingling of fossil capital predominantly based in Calgary (blue circles) and financial capital predominantly based in Toronto (pink diamonds). Ten of the fifteen fossil-capital majors participate; Imperial Oil, Teck Resources, CNRL, Enbridge, and TransCanada interlock with multiple financials—clarifying that their ties to major eastern-based financial corporations are a key aspect of the mediating role they play between Calgary's corporate community and the broader national formation. Along this seam between fossil capital and finance, the most central financial institutions are the Royal Bank of Canada, Toronto-Dominion Bank, Sun Life, Manulife, Brookfield Asset Management, and Great-West Life. Such profuse ties are to be expected, in view of the extensive financing needs of the majors as they pursue megaprojects requiring massive fixed-capital investment.

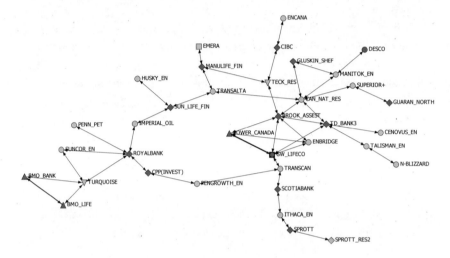

Figure 5.3. Key interlocks between Canadian carbon and financial sectors. Key: blue = carbon-sector firms; pink = financial firms. The city in which each firm is based is indicated by the shape of the symbol: down triangle = Vancouver; circle = Calgary; circle inside square = Winnipeg; diamond = Toronto; up triangle = Montréal; square = Halifax.

Linking into the Transnational Corporate Network

Earlier we observed how corporate concentration shapes the fossil-capital elite, as the largest companies mediate between the local and the extra-local. This mediating role also appears in the composition of neighbourhoods around the fifteen majors. In figure 5.4, the neighbourhoods interpenetrate extensively, forming a connected network of the fifteen majors and 174 neighbours. Most of the majors (and particularly CNRL, Enbridge, Encana, TransCanada, and Nexen) link extensively to both the core network (in red) and the network of Canadian and foreign neighbours (in pink and green, respectively). Husky

Energy (located in the lower right corner of the sociogram) is a noteworthy exception. Its neighbourhood reaches into the Canadian corporate network via a single interlock with Sun Life. Otherwise, Husky belongs to a corporate group organized around its Hong Kong–based controlling shareholder, Hutchison Holdings (and the family of mega-billionaire Li Ka-shing, who owns Hutchison).

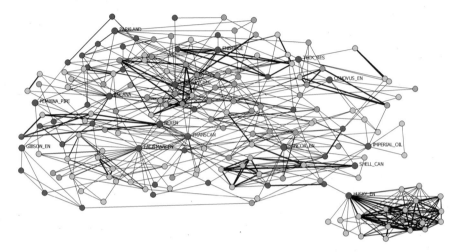

Figure 5.4. Overlapping neighbourhoods of fifteen core-sample majors. Key: red = core sample; dark pink = Canadian neighbours; light green = foreign neighbours.

Again, we find the majors playing a mediating role between the local scene and the extra-local formations of corporate power—distinct from the mid-sized fossil-capital companies that interlock with one another as a local corporate community. The *demography* of the fossil-capital sector weights the fossil-capital elite in a localist direction: most of the active carbon-sector capitalists are centred in Calgary and connected into a highly cohesive, somewhat introverted local network. But the largest *concentrations of capital*, and of corporate power, pull the network toward national and transnational scale.

However, transnationality is not simply a matter of scale. As argued elsewhere (Carroll 2018), the transnational corporate network is itself highly regionalized: most interlocking occurs in the same region, and the global network is organized around a North Atlantic core. When we consider the domicile of the foreign corporate neighbours to Canada's fossil-capital elite, we find that 58.8 percent of direct foreign neighbours are based in North America (including the United States plus the three tax havens of Bermuda, Cayman Islands, and Curacao), 23.1 percent are based in western Europe, and 9.2 percent are based in the Asia-Pacific core of Japan, South Korea, Hong Kong, Australia, and New Zealand. That is, most of the foreign corporations whose directors and executives interlock with Canada's fossil-capital community are based in the United States and the other core zones of the world economy. The same holds for foreign firms indirectly linked to Canada's fossil-capital elite: 61.4 percent are based in the rest of North America, 22 percent are based in the core states of Europe, and 9.4 percent are based in the core Asia-Pacific region. Thus, foreign neighbours are based in the world economy's core zones: the United States, Europe, and the affluent countries of the Asia-Pacific. Of the thirty-one direct and indirect neighbours based on the Asian semi-periphery, twenty-two are headquartered in mainland China, six in India, and three in Malaysia. Overwhelmingly, Canada's fossil-capital elite is nested within the triad of North America, western Europe, and Japan/ Australia, reflecting the well-established contours of the transnational capitalist class (Carroll 2018).

Table 5.4. Percentage distribution of interlocks by company domicile in the world system

Region / country	Canada: core sample	Canada: neighbours	Rest of North America
Canada: core sample	32.48	8.58	5.62
Canada: neighbours	8.58	15.05	3
Rest of North America	5.62	3	18.93
Core Europe	2.49	1.19	2.08
Core Asia-Pacific	0.89	0.1	0.85
S-P Latin America	0.03	0	0
S-P Eastern Europe/Middle East	0.17	0	0
S-P Asia	0.51	0	0
Africa	0.03	0	0

Note: S-P = semi-peripheral; "Rest of North America" = United States, Bermuda, Cayman Islands, and Curaçao.

The actual elite relations among Canadian fossil-capital firms and the national and transnational corporate network are strongly shaped by this pattern of participation. My snowball sampling identifies the complete network of interlocks among Canada's fossil-capital sector and all immediate neighbours. The percentages in table 5.4 break down the total volume of directorate interlocking in that transnational network, by each region of the world system. We see that firms based in Canada link predominantly to other Canada-based firms, whether core sample or neighbours. Interlocks among core-sample firms and their Canadian neighbours make up 56.11 percent of interlocks in the entire network, which is strongly clustered on a regional basis (only 18.96 percent of all interlocks link across the region/country categories in the table). The Canadian network is highly introverted—strongly integrated but more sparsely linked to the transnational network in which it is embedded. Indeed, its E-I score (−0.600) indicates far more introversion than found in the fossil-capital subnetwork it contains, thereby confirming the continuing cohesiveness of Canada's corporate community. It also points to that community's focal role vis-à-vis the fossil-capital elite nested within it. Beyond domestic interlocks, Canada's fossil-capital sector links primarily to the core regions of the North Atlantic; indeed, 93.17 percent of the total

Core Europe	Core Asia-Pacific	S-P Latin America	S-P Eastern Europe / Middle East	S-P Asia	Africa
2.49	0.89	0.03	0.17	0.51	0.03
1.19	0.1	0	0	0	0
2.08	0.85	0	0	0	0
3.75	1.43	0	0.1	0.1	0
1.43	1.5	0	0	0.37	0
0	0	0.07	0	0	0
0.1	0	0	0.07	0	0
0.1	0.37	0	0	0.61	0
0	0	0	0	0	0

volume of interlocking in the transnational network connects corporations based in the North Atlantic. Outside that zone, nearly all interlocks involve firms based in the core (5.14 percent) and semi-peripheral (1.59 percent) zones of south and east Asia. The elite connections of Canadian fossil capital do not as a rule extend to the Middle East, eastern Europe, Latin America, and Africa.

In figure 5.5, a view of the entire transnational network conveys another sense of the mediating role that the majors play, in this case between foreign and Canadian corporations. Nearly all top strata corporations I identified through snowball sampling form a connected component of 1,162 firms. In this sociogram, nodes are colour-coded according to sample stratum: red for the core sample, pink for direct neighbours based in Canada, light pink for indirect neighbours based in Canada, light green for foreign-based direct neighbours, and dark green for foreign-based indirect neighbours. As with the other sociograms in this chapter (with the exception of figure 5.2), nodes are positioned in concordance with their relative proximity to each other in the actual network (see note 8). The network's topography has of course been conditioned by the snowball sampling: indirect neighbours connect with core-sample members at only one remove; thus, core-sample firms tend to be at one end of the network, with indirect neighbours at the other.

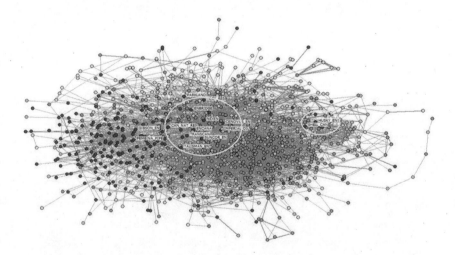

Figure 5.5. Core sample as embedded in the entire transnational network. Key: red = core sample; dark pink = Canadian neighbours; light pink = Canadian neighbours of neighbours; light green = foreign neighbours; dark green = foreign neighbours of neighbours.

Where do the fifteen Canadian fossil-capital majors fit into this space? With some partial exceptions—four of the smaller majors: Gibson Energy and Pembina Pipeline, Parkland Fuel and Teck Corporation—they are positioned more on the side of the neighbouring strata, both Canadian and foreign. Suncor, Talisman, Imperial Oil, and Cenovus occupy a liminal zone between the predominantly Canadian network to the left and the predominantly foreign-based network to the right. In contrast, Husky and Shell, both controlled by foreign owners, are ensconced in the foreign-based network. The majors either are distant from the fossil-capital network (Shell and Husky) or tend to mediate between it and the wider world of transnational capital.

Conclusion

This chapter began with three research questions regarding the fossil-capital elite's accumulation base, its internal relations, and its links to other fractions of capital. What has our mapping of its social organization revealed regarding those questions?

Regarding the elite's accumulation base, pronounced economic concentration shapes the landscape of corporate power, lodging it in four major urban centres: pre-eminently (for fossil capital) Calgary, then Toronto, Vancouver, and Montréal. The majors dominate particularly in the capital-intensive sectors: integrated oil and gas production and pipelines. While majors claim the lion's share of the sector's revenue, most fossil-capital firms are mid-sized, and although western Canada is the primary production site, many companies are invested in other locales, national and international. Most firms—whether majors or mid-sized—are controlled by interests based in Canada, and this tendency has strengthened recently as global majors such as Shell and ConocoPhillips have sold their tar sands assets to Canadian majors (Pineault and Hussey 2017).

Economic concentration is amplified by the social organization of corporate power. A relatively few directors and executives are corporate networkers, and a small proportion of them account for most interlocking, both among fossil-capital firms and in the wider network of their neighbours. Most corporate interlocking among carbon-extractive firms occurs within a single city and among one-fifth of the companies. But despite the high level of cohesion among the boards of Calgary-based companies, the fossil-capital elite is not an entity unto itself; it is a fraction nested within the national corporate elite, with additional ties to the transnational network. The individuals who comprise the elite are overwhelmingly male and engaged in top-level management—not simply corporate window dressing. Corporate power's spatial organization concentrates command over carbon resources largely in Calgary, while financial and other corporations are based in Toronto and, to a lesser extent, Montréal and Vancouver. Directorate interlocks stitch corporations into a cohesive national elite network. In its transnational connections (where the carbon majors are especially active), the network is concentrated largely within the North Atlantic zone of the global economy, the heartland for a transnational capitalist class.

The majors, several of which are controlled by foreign interests, link into the local network but are not at its centre. Instead, they play a multifaceted mediating role:

- between the tightly integrated, somewhat introverted Calgary-based network and corporations based elsewhere

- more specifically, between eastern-based financial capital (with which the majors have profuse ties) and western-based fossil capital

- between the Canadian corporate community and the wider world of transnational capital.

The top tier of Canada's carbon-extractive sector, while somewhat marginal to the Calgary-centred network, integrates the fossil-capital elite with other segments of corporate power, both nationally and transnationally. But ancillary organizations also provide such integrative capacity. Notably, the sharply stratified character of fossil capital is recognized by its primary representative body, the Canadian Association of Petroleum Producers (CAPP). At the time the data for this chapter were gathered, CAPP's board of governors was "balanced," with ten governors selected from the twelve largest member firms, ten from the next twenty members, and ten from smaller companies. Subsequently, CAPP's board was expanded to include "up to 78 volunteer governors," each representing member companies at the chief executive level—effectively guaranteeing that smaller firms will be strongly represented.[10] In presenting a single voice for the oil and gas sector, CAPP also mediates possible fractional divisions between big and mid-sized capital.

These mediating relations are important, both economically and politically. Although the local Calgary network is highly integrated, it is also highly specialized: the fossil-capital elite is spatially concentrated, setting up a symbiosis with sources of finance located elsewhere, but also the potential for political conflict between regionally inflected fossil-capital interests and other fractions within Canadian capitalism, such as eastern-based manufacturing—a dynamic evident since the National Energy Program of the early 1980s (Laxer 2015, 46–49). The sector over which the fossil-capital elite presides has been a strong motor of regional accumulation, with spread effects via commodity chains and fiscal/financial skim-off. Yet sharpening ecological concerns, both global and site-specific (as in local risks of carbon transport by land and water), portend intensified regional conflict over energy futures.

The architecture of corporate power in and around the fossil-capital sector reveals an organized minority of capitalists and their close advisors. Its oligarchic form embodies a key aspect of what is sometimes called "business-as-usual." In corporate boardrooms, decisions affecting communities, workers, and ecologies are made by small, often interlocked groups of men, according to a criterion that privileges short-term private profit over public and ecological concerns. At least since Britain's 2006 Stern Review (Stern 2006) business-as-usual has also referred to a climate scenario in which the current regime of largely unregulated corporate power is simply extended into the future. In the Stern Review and elsewhere, the projection is ecological *and* economic decline, in the current century, as catastrophic climate change erodes the basis for living systems, and thus for economic life.

In both senses of the term, business-as-usual—the oligarchic organization of corporate power within an energy sector increasingly recognized as ecologically disastrous—forms the core of Canada's regime of obstruction.

Notes

1. Services to extraction mainly involve services to production (drilling, transport). Coal/bitumen includes primarily coal mining but also five firms that mine bitumen exclusively. Three coal firms also mine bitumen. Five of the seven integrated producers extract bitumen, along with nine of the 130 non-integrated oil and gas producers.

2. The locations of these Canadian-based foreign direct investments include Africa (Tunisia, Morocco, Libya, Nigeria, Madagascar, Ethiopia, Kenya, Somalia, South Africa), Latin America (Mexico, the Caribbean, including Cuba, Guatemala, Brazil, Argentina, Peru, Colombia, Ecuador, Guyana, Belize, Venezuela, Chile,

Uruguay), Asia (Kazakhstan, Jordan, Syria, United Arab Emirates, Iraq, Oman, Bahrain, Dubai, Yemen, Saudi Arabia, Indonesia, Brunei, Malaysia, Thailand, Indonesia, Singapore, Bangladesh, Pakistan, India, China, Mongolia, Papua New Guinea), Europe (UK offshore, Greenland offshore, Iceland, Norway offshore, Ireland, Germany, Denmark, Sweden, the Netherlands, France, Spain, Italy, Cyprus, Poland, Albania, Romania, Hungary, Russia, Georgia, Ukraine, Turkey) and Australia and New Zealand.

3. Two (Imperial Oil and Shell Canada) have major refining operations in central Canada but not beyond, six are active in the United States, and seven are invested more internationally (four of which are also active in the US).

4. Data for the analysis of foreign control (as of late 2015) are from FP Infomart and ORBIS. We classified each fossil-capital corporation as to the country in which the owning interest is based. Revenue was not available for nine private corporations, including three controlled in Canada (Sprott Resource Corporation, Canada Energy Partners Inc., and Altex Energy Ltd.), four controlled in the United States (Murphy Oil Co. Ltd., Chevron Canada Resources, ExxonMobil Canada, and Prairie Mines and Royalty Ltd.), one controlled in France (Total E & P Canada), and one controlled in Japan (Grande Cache Coal Corporation). My estimates of revenue under foreign control are probably slightly conservative.

5. Note that my methodology constructs a view of the corporate power structure from a specific starting point in Canada's fossil-capital sector. This purposefully highlights the prominence of that sector.

6. The simple contrast between fifteen majors and the rest accounts for 14.7 percent of the variance in overall degree and 21.3 percent of the variance in overall 2-step degree.

7. For present purposes, the E-I index subtracts the proportion of each firm's total degree that is internal to the core sample from the proportion that is external. See Krackhardt and Stern (1988). Among the 238 core-sample members, the proportion of variance in E-I attributable to the distinction between majors and other firms (Eta^2) is 0.081.

8. To simplify the diagram, we have excluded nine companies that are linked into the 4-core by means of a single individual; thus, the sociogram displays 42 corporations and 63 individuals. A spring-embedded algorithm was used to map the points in concordance with their relative proximity to each other in the actual network (Hanneman and Riddle 2005).

9. The sociogram excludes isolates from the connected component: six fossil-capital companies interlocked with multiple financials and five financials interlocked with multiple fossil-capital companies.

10. See "Board of Governors," CAPP, 2020, https://www.capp.ca/about-us/our-organization/board-of-governors.

References

Albo, Greg, and Lilian Yap. 2016. "From the Tar Sands to 'Green Jobs'? Work and Ecological Justice." *The Bullet*, July 12, 2016. https://socialistproject.ca/bullet/1280.php.

Brownlee, Jamie. 2005. *Ruling Canada: Corporate Cohesion and Democracy*. Halifax: Fernwood.

Carroll, William K. 1984. "The Individual, Class, and Corporate Power in Canada." *Canadian Journal of Sociology* 9, no. 3: 245–68.

———. 1986. *Corporate Power and Canadian Capitalism*. Vancouver: University of British Columbia Press.

———. 2004. *Corporate Power in a Globalizing World*. Toronto: Oxford University Press.

———. 2018. "Rethinking the Transnational Capitalist Class." *Alternate Routes* 29: 188–206.

Carroll, William K., and Jerome Klassen. 2010. "Hollowing Out Corporate Canada? Changes in the Corporate Network Since the 1990s." *Canadian Journal of Sociology* 35, no. 1: 1–30.

Carroll, William K., and J. P. Sapinski. 2018. *Organizing the 1%: How Corporate Power Works*. Halifax: Fernwood.

Clement, Wallace. 1975. *The Canadian Corporate Elite: An Analysis of Economic Power*. Toronto: McClelland and Stewart.

Domhoff, G. William. 2006. *Who Rules America? The Triumph of the Corporate Rich*. New York: McGraw-Hill.

Hanneman, Robert A., and Mark Riddle. 2005. "Working with NetDraw to Visualize Graphs." Chap. 4 in *Introduction to Social Network Methods*. Riverside: University of California, Riverside. http://faculty.ucr.edu/~hanneman/nettext/C4_netdraw.html#location.

Harvey, David. 2006. *The Limits to Capital*. London: Verso.

Helland, Eric, and Michael Sykuta. 2004. "Regulation and the Evolution of Corporate Boards: Monitoring, Advising, or Window Dressing?" *Journal of Law and Economics* 47, no. 1: 167–93.

Kellogg, Paul. 2015. *Escape from the Staples Trap: Canadian Political Economy After Left Nationalism*. Toronto: University of Toronto Press.

Klassen, Jerome, and William K. Carroll. 2014. "Transnational Class Formation: Globalization and the Canadian Corporate Network." In Jerome Klassen, *Joining

Empire: *The Political Economy of the New Canadian Foreign Policy*, 154–79. Toronto: University of Toronto Press.

Krackhardt, David, and Robert N. Stern. 1988. "Informal Networks and Organizational Crisis: An Experimental Simulation." *Social Psychology Quarterly* 51, no. 2: 123–40.

Laxer, Gordon. 2015. *After the Sands: Energy and Ecological Security for Canadians.* Madeira Park, BC: Douglas and McIntyre.

Lee, Marc, and Brock Ellis. 2013. *Canada's Carbon Liabilities: The Implications of Stranded Fossil Fuel Assets for Financial Markets and Pension Funds.* Ottawa: Canadian Centre for Policy Alternatives. http://www.policyalternatives.ca/publications/reports/canadas-carbon-liabilities.

Levitt, Kari. 1970. *Silent Surrender: The Multinational Corporation in Canada.* Toronto: Macmillan of Canada.

Pineault, Éric, and Ian Hussey. 2017. "Restructuring in Alberta's Oil Industry: Internationals Pull Out, Domestic Majors Double Down." *Corporate Mapping Project.* April 18, 2017. http://www.corporatemapping.ca/restructuring-in-albertas-oil-industry-internationals-pull-out-domestic-majors-double-down/.

Porter, John. 1956. "Concentration of Economic Power and the Economic Elite in Canada." *Canadian Journal of Economics and Political Science* 22, no. 2: 199–220.

———. 1965. *The Vertical Mosaic: An Analysis of Social Class and Power in Canada.* Toronto: University of Toronto Press.

Sapinski, J. P., and William K. Carroll. 2018. "Interlocking Directorates and Corporate Networks." In *Handbook of the International Political Economy of the Corporation,* edited by Andreas Nölke and Christian May, 45–60. Cheltenham, UK: Edward Elgar.

Seidman, Stephen B. 1983. "Network Structure and Minimum Degree." *Social Networks* 5, no. 3: 269–87.

Stern, Nicholas. 2006. *Stern Review: Report on the Economics of Climate Change.* London: Her Majesty's Treasury. http://webarchive.nationalarchives.gov.uk/+/http:/www.hm-treasury.gov.uk/independent_reviews/stern_review_economics_climate_change/stern_review_report.cfm.

Urry, John. 2013. *Societies Beyond Oil: Oil Dregs and Social Futures.* London: Zed Books.

Useem, Michael. 1984. *The Inner Circle: Large Corporations and the Rise of Business Political Activity in the U.S. and U.K.* New York: Oxford University Press.

Part II
The Struggle for Hearts and Minds

6   Fossil Capital's Reach into Civil Society
The Architecture of Climate Change Denialism

William K. Carroll, Nicolas Graham, Michael Lang,
Kevin McCartney, and Zoë Yunker

As chapters 4 and 5 of this volume document, the interlocking networks of fossil-capital elite concentrate an enormous amount of economic power in the hands of an integrated corporate community that includes major shareholders, CEOs, and financial institutions. This elite is linked to wider national and transnational corporate networks through interlocking directorates and inter-corporate ownership. Yet these networks do not end at the border between economy and society. A raft of Canadian investigations, many inspired by the work of John Porter (1965), has mapped the intricate ties that bring business leadership into other domains (Brownlee 2005; Carroll 2004; Clement 1975; Fox and Ornstein 1986). Corporate power reaches into civil and political society with generally debilitating implications for democracy. At the centre of a robust democracy is an ongoing public conversation in which everyone with a stake in an issue has a say. As it reaches into the public sphere, concentrated corporate power distorts this conversation, privileging the interests and perspectives of those who own and control capital.

Corporate influence is, at its core, geared toward protecting investments and profit streams, opening new fields for investment, and minimizing intrusions into profit, such as taxes, regulations, and unions. This entails different initiatives in different contexts, from tactical manoeuvres designed to secure a specific objective (such as the green light for a new pipeline project) to the long game of cultivating a pro-business political and popular culture.

Our focus is on the fossil-capital sector of corporate capital and its interlocks with governance boards of civil society organizations (CSOs). Civil society constitutes a diverse but distinct sphere of action situated between economy and state (Urry 1981), comprising think tanks, lobby groups, political parties, charitable organizations, community and voluntary associations, families and households, and educational and religious institutions, among other groups. The CSOs of interest here produce and mobilize knowledge relevant in some way to the fossil-capital sector. Interlocking between company directorates and these CSOs creates pathways through which corporate perspectives, priorities, and strategies penetrate into civic life. The network enables the fossil-capital elite, a fraction of the broader corporate community, to exert influence by participating in the governance of institutions that are often assumed to be independent of big business.

As the climate crisis deepens, fossil capital's accumulation strategy demands deft ideological legitimation. With major stakes in continuing carbon extraction, fossil-capital corporations form part of a "denial regime," along with political allies that promote and implement convivial policies, and an ideological apparatus of think tanks, funded to some extent by the fossil-capital sector itself (Derber 2010, 75). As the scientific consensus on global warming has become uncontestable, climate-change denial on the part of fossil-capital corporations has evolved from the hard denialism of "stage 1" to a more insidious "stage 2," signalling "a basic change in the ideology and tactics of the denial regime, though not in its ultimate goals" (Derber 2010, 80), namely, the continued flow of profit to fossil-fuel and related companies. The key to stage 2 is to propose policies that appear as credible responses to the scientific consensus but do not harm big carbon—the three most typical being greater efficiency in carbon extraction and consumption, new technology, and incremental change inadequate to the scale and urgency of the problem (Derber 2010, 82–83). In tracing fossil-capital's reach into civil society, we aim to reveal the architecture of a stage 2 denial regime.

Sample and Data

Our research maps the network composed of fossil-capital corporations whose boards interlock with those of key civil society groups—thus, two samples of organizations. The corporate sample consists of the largest 238 Canada-based corporations whose activities are centred in fossil fuel production and/or transport. Data were gathered in the fall of 2015, at which time financial statements for year-end 2014 showed each firm to have at least $50 million in assets.[1] With respect to the CSOs, no one quantitative criterion summarizes an organization's importance in civil society. Moreover, the range of groups comprising civil society is truly vast, necessitating a highly focused sampling strategy. In selecting 112 organizations for this category, we compiled a judgment sample of key agencies within three sectors of civil society that have strategic value for carbon-extractive corporate business. Each sector produces and circulates ideas that inform public discourse and policy, from distinct social locations and in distinct ways. Our judgment sample enables us to hone in on key interfaces between the fossil-capital elite and select civil society sectors, but this comes at the expense of a more comprehensive mapping of corporate capital's footprint within civil society. In decreasing order of their direct alignment with corporate capital, the sectors are shown in table 6.1.

Table 6.1. The sample of organizations and their network participation

Sample Stratum	Overall sample (A)	Network participant (B)	B/A	In dominant component
1. Fossil-capital firms	238	81	0.340	76
2a. Industry associations	21	11	0.524	10
2b. Advocacy organizations	17	10	0.588	9
3. Think tanks	12	11	0.917	9
4a. Universities and other post-secondary institutions	46	27	0.587	20
4b. Research institutes	16	13	0.813	11
Total	350	153	0.437	135

First in order of alignment are organizations that define and advance corporate interests, including policies commensurate with those interests. These are often business-sponsored, and their governance boards typically include leading lights of the corporate elite. There are two kinds of such organizations: *industry associations*, which seek to further the interests of specific industries, and business *advocacy organizations*, which construct and advocate broad corporate perspectives, regardless of sector (Brownlee 2005). Both develop policy proposals and perspectives and promote them through reports, media releases and social media initiatives, advertising, lobbying, and so on.

No single industry association represents the entire fossil-capital sector, although the Canadian Association of Petroleum Producers (CAPP, whose remit includes natural gas) comes closest. In all, our sample includes twenty-one such groups (see table 6.1). Sectoral industry associations provide space for fractional interests within the broad fossil-capital sector to define issues of shared importance and to organize strategies for advancing the interests of the sector as a whole. On specific issues, however, the immediate interests of one fraction (coal, for example) may conflict with those of another (such as LNG, which is typically promoted as a transition fuel in the sun-setting of coal).

In contrast, intersectoral business advocacy groups such as chambers of commerce and business councils represent broader class interests. These are sites where wider strata of business leaders (including, for example, bankers or manufacturers) might rub shoulders with the fossil-capital elite. Such contacts provide opportunities for blending the specific, fractional interests of fossil capital within a broader corporate agenda. Most influential in this regard has been the Business Council of Canada, which since the 1980s has significantly shaped neoliberal policy at the federal level (Dobbin 1998; Langille 1987). Indeed, as Jamie Brownlee (2005, 81) rightly observes, the Business Council of Canada "may be unique in the developed world in terms of its capacity to dominate political life."

In all, seventeen business advocacy groups were selected. They may be further divided into ten elite advocacy groups (councils and chambers of commerce directed by top business leaders) and seven "grassroots" business advocacy groups. The former can be expected to link into the wider corporate-elite network, facilitating a consensus that enables big business to speak with one voice. The latter, initiated and led by pro-business activists, may lack elite ties to the corporate network but may be funded by corporate capital, as sympathetic voices apparently situated at arm's length.[2] Advocacy groups such as the Canadian Taxpayers Federation, Ethical Oil, and the Alberta Prosperity Fund are less about creating an elite consensus and more about promulgating to popular audiences what has been called the "corporate agenda" of neoliberal capitalism (Beder 2006), particularly as it applies to the fossil-capital sector. More astroturf than grassroots, these groups present themselves as citizens' initiatives from below, circumventing business-council elitism yet delivering similar messages to general publics and to a pro-business popular base.

A second kind of civil society organization consists of the *think tank*. Although formally autonomous from the corporate sector, these groups are often funded by large corporations and governed by their CEOs (Brownlee 2005). In contrast to industry associations and business advocacy organizations, think tanks are staffed chiefly by professional researchers and analysts and are generally more outward facing, aiming to reach a broader public audience. Rather than focus explicitly on defining and defending business interests, they seek instead to produce evidence-based commentary and analysis from a standpoint compatible with business interests. Think tanks are typically non-profit organizations, and, as Brownlee (2005, 95) notes, present themselves as "educational organizations, committed to increased public awareness about policy issues." The policy-planning process leads them to mobilize academics committed to business-friendly policy and to connect with governmental and media personnel through workshops, conferences, and other forums.

We selected twelve think tanks for this segment of the CSO sample. Since our interest is in mapping the interface between fossil capital and civil society, we chose groups in the centre or on the right of the political spectrum and excluded organizations critical of big business, such as the Canadian Centre for Policy Alternatives. Five of the groups—the C. D. Howe Institute, the Conference Board of Canada, the Fraser Institute, the Macdonald-Laurier Institute, and the Manning Centre for Building Democracy—have a high profile as commentators on national issues, while others have a regional focus. With the exception of the Atlantic Institute for Market Studies, we selected groups oriented toward western Canada (for example, the Frontier Centre for Public Policy, the Canada West Foundation, and the Clear Seas Centre for Responsible Marine Shipping). Eight of the twelve groups are members of the Atlas Network of nearly five hundred neoliberal think tanks worldwide.

Finally, *universities and research institutes* (with most of the latter hosted within universities) constitute a key sector in civil society. They produce both knowledge and knowledgeable people. They help to maintain and renew a liberal political culture and produce a technically proficient workforce while contributing scientific and technical advances relevant to corporations and government. These organizations operate as non-profits at arm's length from government and, in that sense, form part of civil society. In principle, universities and research institutes are autonomous from business, and their public-service mission may conflict with corporate priorities. In practice, however, they have become increasingly aligned with business interests, through processes of corporatization in which "the public interest—once defined as shielding public entities from the market—is assumed to be enhanced by embracing commercial values and practices" (Brownlee 2015, 27). Paralleling this shift has been a dramatic decline in government funding to universities, whose status as autonomous public institutions increasingly seems more nominal than real.[3] Our sample includes forty-six post-secondary institutions and nineteen research institutes.

Since the fossil-capital sector is centred in Canada's three westernmost provinces, we weighted our sample accordingly, selecting ten universities and four polytechnical schools located in those provinces. As corporate interests are particularly engaged with sectors of post-secondary education that contribute directly to the world of business, we also included seven business schools based in western Canada, as well as two engineering schools and the University of Calgary's School of Public Policy. Each of these has its own advisory board, potentially linking its governance practices to the corporate elite.[4] The other twenty-six post-secondary institutions in our sample include all the research and comprehensive universities based elsewhere in the country that appeared in the latest *Maclean's* magazine rankings (Schwartz 2015). As for research institutes, our concern with the fossil-capital sector directed us to fourteen institutes whose mandates focus on scientific and technological issues surrounding carbon extraction and processing, plus the Canadian Foundation for Innovation and the Saskatchewan Research Council.[5] Most of these institutes are based in Calgary (n = 5), Edmonton (n = 5), or other western Canadian cities (n = 4), but two are in Ottawa.

We gathered data on the names of the directors or governors of the 112 CSOs and the directors and top executives of the 238 fossil-capital corporations.[6] Sources for the latter included online business databases (ORBIS and FP Infomart) and company websites. Sources for the former were mainly organization websites and annual reports. Wherever there was ambiguity as to whether two name entries referred to the same person, the situation was investigated further to confirm the multiple affiliation.

Overall Findings

Table 6.1 indicates how many organizations participate in the network formed by fossil capital and civil society. As the table shows, approximately one-third (81) of the 238 fossil-capital corporations interlock with one or more of the civil society organizations, whereas two-thirds of the CSOs participate in the network. Rates of participation (column "B/A") are particularly high among think tanks. Within the advocacy groups, the business councils tend to participate in the network (seven of ten) while the astroturf groups are less likely to have elite-level ties to fossil-capital firms (three of seven). Among the fossil-capital firms, directors of the fifteen largest tend to serve on civil society boards (eleven of fifteen), whereas relatively few boards of smaller companies interlock with CSOs (70 of 223).

Our network analysis is restricted to the 153 organizations and 173 individual "networkers" whose multiple affiliations create the fossil-capital/civil society network. Since we are particularly interested in mapping the CSO network, we include the 108 directors/executives of fossil-capital firms with any CSO affiliations, plus 65 individuals who do not direct fossil-capital corporations but do direct multiple CSOs. The latter (most of whom have affiliations with corporations in other economic sectors) further integrate the CSO network.

Figure 6.1 offers a summary picture of interlocking across the sectors. Each point represents all organizations in a given sector; line thickness indicates how much interlocking occurs between a pair of sectors. The size of each point is proportionate to the total number of interlocks with other sectors. Considerable variation exists in the volume of interlocking within and across sectors. As shown in chapter 5, the fossil-capital sector is tightly integrated (in this instance, its eighty-one companies are linked via 112 interlocking directorates), yet advocacy groups do not share directors. Cross-sectorally, the corporations are especially closely linked to the think tanks (40 ties). The think tanks also interlock extensively with advocacy groups and universities and with one another. Interlocking between corporate directorates and universities (28 ties), advocacy groups (22 ties), and industry associations (20 ties) is also noteworthy, as are the twelve interlocks between universities and think tanks and the fourteen corporate representatives on the boards of research institutes.

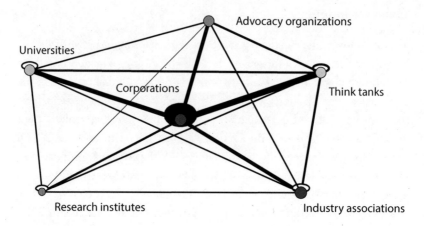

Figure 6.1. Levels of interlocking within and between fossil-capital and civil society sectors

The traffic in interlocking reveals an elite network in which directors of fossil-capital corporations participate in governance of key knowledge-producing organizations. It is not surprising that the industry associations and advocacy organizations have such ties, as they are strategic sites in civil society for defining and advancing business interests; however, the extensive reach into policy planning and higher education/research shows that directors of fossil-capital corporations participate heavily in governance of ostensibly independent knowledge-producing organizations.

Looking more closely, a basic issue is whether the organizations form a connected network or whether relations are segmented into disjointed networks. In the rightmost column of table 6.1, we indicate membership in the dominant component—the largest connected network. All but eighteen of the 153 organizations belong to the component. However, some are especially well connected. For instance, the four most interlocked organizations—the C. D. Howe Institute (with 22 interlocks), the Business Council of British Columbia (BC_BUSINESSC, with 19), CAPP (with 19), and the Business Council of Canada (BUSINESSC_C, with 16) comprise only 3 percent of the dominant component but account for 17 percent of interlocking within it. In contrast, thirty-one organizations each interlock with only one component member.

The Influence Network's Soft Core

This variation in centrality suggests that the network may fit a core-periphery pattern, with peripheral organizations linking into an integrated core but not with one another. A coreness partitioning of the dominant component identifies a core of 25 and periphery of 110.[7] With 150 interlocks, the core has a density of 0.250. The periphery contains 198 interlocks (density = 0.017). Core and periphery are linked by 109 interlocks, at a density of 0.040. Relative to all interlocking, the core claims 32.82 percent; its links to the periphery claim 23.85 percent; and relations among the 110 peripheral organizations (81.5 percent of the dominant component) claim 43.32 percent. However, the Pearson correlation between the input adjacency matrix and the output partitioned matrix (0.303) indicates only 9.18 percent shared variance. The core-periphery model's fit is poor, as many interlocks occur within the large periphery surrounding the core. The "core," though dense, is also soft.

In figure 6.2 we glimpse some of the architecture of fossil-capital influence, as corporate directorates interlock with CSOs that produce business-friendly knowledge mobilized across the public sphere. The core includes seven fossil-capital corporations, two industry groups, three advocacy groups, four think tanks, five post-secondary institutions, and four research institutes. Canada's biggest corporate-funded think tank, C. D. Howe, is most prominent, interlocked with twelve core organizations, including all but one of the fossil-capital firms. The Canadian Energy Pipeline Association (CEPA), an industry group, interlocks with nine organizations, most of which are not linked to Howe. On the right-hand side of the figure, one can see an intermingling of the academic and research sector and fossil-capital directors. Two research institutes—the Climate Change and Emissions Management Corporation (CCEMC) and Sustainable Development Technology Canada (SDTC)—and the University of Calgary's Board of Governors (UOFC) interlock with one another and with CEPA. Alberta Innovates—Energy and Environment Solutions (AI_EES) interlocks with CCEMC and SDTC as well as with Enbridge. For their part, the Fraser and Howe Institutes also interlock with two key schools at the University of Calgary (the School of Public Policy [UOFC_SPP] and the Haskayne School of Business [HASKAYNE_SB], respectively), and they share multiple directors with the main business councils (of BC and Canada, respectively). In some cases the interlocking is intense; for instance, the Fraser Institute and Business Council of British

Columbia (BCBC) share three directors. Major corporations also bridge civil society sectors. The Enbridge group, for example, interlocks not only with three university boards and AI_EES but also with three industry associations, two think tanks, and one business council. This mapping of the network core reveals a small world of corporate influence within which major fossil-capital players collaborate with one another and with other elites in the governance of CSOs.

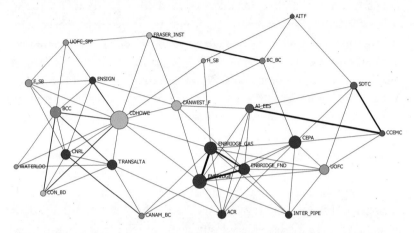

Figure 6.2. The core of 25 organizations. Key: brown = corporations; blue = industry associations; violet = advocacy organizations; light blue = think tanks; light green = post-secondary institutions; dark green = research institutes.

Social Circles and Elite Cohesion

Figure 6.2 shows that the network core is integrated through ties cutting *across* different kinds of organizations. In this, organizations with diverse social circles are key. Blau's (1977) index of heterogeneity measures such diversity as the probability that two randomly chosen members of a social circle belong to different categories (a corporation and an industry group, for instance).

Table 6.2 reveals that, among the 153 organizations that participate in board interlocks, industry groups and post-secondary institutions maintain relatively homogeneous social circles while elite advocacy groups, think tanks, and research institutes have relatively diverse contacts.[8] Further analysis shows that fifty-eight organizations, including eighteen universities and five industry groups, have completely homogeneous social circles. The eighteen universities are quite marginal to the network (mean degree = 1.11). Their social circles contain only one member and are by default homogeneous.

Table 6.2. Mean social-circle heterogeneity for all interlocking organizations

Organization type	Mean	Standard deviation
Corporation	0.38510	0.28881
Industry group	0.26848	0.27068
Advocacy organization	0.49727	0.34821
University	0.17825	0.26287
Research institute	0.45300	0.27986
Think tank	0.47388	0.25587
Total	**0.35970**	**0.29654**

In contrast, the five industry groups with completely homogeneous social circles tend to be relatively central in the network (mean degree = 7.00). Most significantly, CAPP, whose eighteen interlocks all link to fossil-capital firms, is the second most central organization in the entire network yet is excluded from the core because it does not interlock extensively with core members. This shows a degree of complexity in the architecture of elite cohesion. Industry groups fulfill an integrative function, within specific subsectors. Their mission to represent functional segments of fossil capital pulls companies of various sizes into the network, many of which would otherwise be isolated. At CAPP, this mission is institutionalized, as its board is mandated to include large, mid-sized, and smaller firms. In contrast, advocacy groups such as cross-sectoral business councils define and advance business interests more widely and tend to recruit well-connected business leaders to their boards (as do the think tanks). The combination of inter- and intra-sectoral integration is evident in the group differences in social-circle heterogeneity.[9]

Subgroups in the Network

Given that the core-periphery distinction is only one means of analyzing a network's structure, we explored the possibility of distinguishing other subgroups in the network's dominant component. Girvan and Newman (2002) present an elegant algorithm designed to identify relatively cohesive communities "in which network nodes are joined together in tightly knit groups, between which there are only looser connections" (7821). Applied iteratively, their approach successively partitions a network into mutually exclusive groups. When the dominant component of the network is decomposed in this step-wise way, the first three rounds of partitioning identify sociometric "stars" that cohere around leading industry associations: (1) the Explorers and Producers Association of Canada (the EPAC subgroup), (2) the Canadian Association of Oilwell Drilling Contractors and the Petroleum Services Association of Canada (the CAODC/PSAC subgroup), and (3) the CAPP subgroup (see table 6.3, rows 1–3). Each of these otherwise sparsely linked "star" formations is held together by the central industry association, which serves as the point of connection for the other members of the subgroup: executives from various fossil fuel companies all sit on the association's board, but they do not sit on one another's boards. These initial rounds of partitioning underline the sector-specific function of industry groups and cleave thirty organizations from the component.

Subsequent partitioning of the remaining 105 organizations yields four subgroups (see table 6.3, rows 4–7). With the exception of group 5, each subgroup is organized to some extent around one highly central organization and is named accordingly. All seven clusters are highly regionalized. The latter four subgroups, which consist of relatively densely connected organizations, are concentrated in three provinces, with a strong bias toward Alberta, while the three industry-group stars (rows 1–3), which are least integrated into the dominant component, are entirely Alberta-based.[10] This seven-group configuration reflects the overall network structure well: 83 percent of all interlocks occur within the subgroups, yielding an E-I score of −0.661.[11] The three industry-group stars are especially introverted; in these subgroups, the mean degree of interlocking (that is, the number of interlocks) approaches 1, signalling that without the central node they would not exist.

It is illuminating to profile each of the relatively central subgroups (numbered 4–7 in table 6.3), which are mapped in figure 6.3 (with members of the soft core of 25 organizations represented as circles).[12]

Table 6.3. The dominant component partitioned into seven subgroups

	N in sub-group	N based in BC/AB/ON	Mean degree[a]	E-I	N of members in core
1. EPAC star	7	0 / 7 / 0	1.00	−0.867	0
2. CAODC/PSAC star	6	0 / 6 / 0	1.00	−0.750	0
3. CAPP star	17	0 / 17 / 0	1.29	−0.692	0
4. Fraser Institute subgroup	14	1 / 9 / 2	1.14	−0.391	1
5. Alberta subgroup	41	2 / 31 / 5	2.17	−0.728	14
6. C. D. Howe Institute subgroup	31	0 / 22[b] / 8	2.10	−0.656	9
7. Business Council of BC subgroup	19	11 / 2 / 5	1.53	−0.568	1
Total	135	14 / 94[c] / 20	1.74	−0.661	25

[a] Among members of the subgroup.

[b] Includes four organizations based in Saskatchewan.

[c] Calculated on the basis of all possible relations within the seven groups.

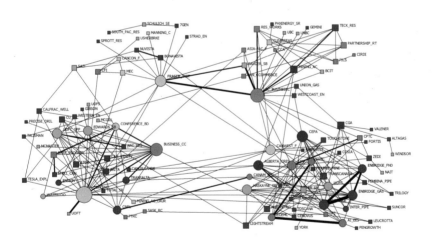

Figure 6.3. Four relatively central subgroups in the network. Key: brown = corporations; blue = industry associations; violet = advocacy organizations; light blue = think tanks; light green = post-secondary institutions; dark green = research institutes.

- The fourteen-member Fraser Institute cluster (upper left in figure 6.3) is least integrated and most extraverted of the four central subgroups. With nine of its fourteen members based in Alberta, it includes six fossil-capital firms (five of them interlocked with Fraser), three other think tanks (two of them interlocked with Fraser), three post-secondary institutions, and the Ottawa-based Canadian Foundation for Innovation. The Fraser Institute figures prominently not only in the ties that bind this subgroup together but in the extraverted ties to other subgroups. It participates in seven of the twelve out-group interlocks and shares multiple directors with two BC-based organizations in subgroup 7. Fraser is the only member of this subgroup that participates in the soft core of 25 (see figure 6.2), underlining again the institute's importance to elite cohesion.

- In contrast, organizations in the forty-one-member Alberta-centred subgroup (lower right), the most introverted of the four central subgroups, are extensively interlocked with one another, and no one node pulls the configuration together. Compared with other relatively central subgroups, this one is built less around business councils and think tanks: the network consists of twenty-two fossil-capital firms (nineteen of them based in Alberta), five industry associations, six research institutes, and six post-secondary institutions. Although the Calgary-based Canada West Foundation interlocks with other think tanks and with corporate-advocacy groups in the other subgroups. Eastern-based organizations—two corporate firms (Valener and Fortis), two universities (York and Windsor), and a research institute (Sustainable Development Technology Canada)—are marginal within this subgroup, three-quarters of whose members are based in Alberta. The close links between industry (and industry groups), research institutes, and three key academic institutions (the University of Calgary and the schools of business at Calgary and at the University of Alberta) point to what we have elsewhere termed a *carbon-centred scientific-industrial complex*, embodying a close alignment of interests between fossil capital and academic/research communities that enables big carbon "to draw on the veneer of academic prestige provided by its ties to higher education, polishing its reputation by employing the language of scientific validation, while cultivating a policy environment favourable to extractive interests" (Carroll, Graham, and Yunker 2018, 59).

- With thirteen of thirty-one members based outside Alberta, subgroup 6 (lower left) is the least provincially centred and more hooked into the national corporate community by virtue of two Ontario-based hegemonic organizations—the C. D. Howe Institute and the Business Council of Canada—and, secondarily, by two Ottawa-based think tanks, the Conference Board of Canada and the Smart Prosperity Institute. This subgroup is also highly cohesive (with a mean degree of 2.10) and relatively introverted, but within it we find the most extensive basis for cross-regional elite integration. Its members include fifteen corporations, some of them among the largest in the carbon-extractive sector (for example, Shell Canada, CNRL, Talisman Energy). As with the Alberta subgroup, members tend to participate in the network's soft core. Although research institutes have a minor presence, two post-secondary organizations are quite central: University of Calgary's School of Public Policy, which doubles as a neoliberal think tank (Gutstein 2014), and University of Saskatchewan's Edwards School of Business, whose namesake, N. Murray Edwards, sits on its Dean's Advisory Council and on the boards of two major fossil-capital firms he controls (CNRL and Ensign Energy) and was, at the time our data were gathered, also on the boards of the C. D. Howe Institute and the Business Council of Canada.

- Finally, with thirteen of nineteen members based in British Columbia, subgroup 7 (upper right) is organized primarily around the Business Council of British Columbia, which interlocks with twelve subgroup members and accounts for half of this subgroup's interlocks with the other three relatively central subgroups. This configuration is less cohesive and less introverted than the Alberta and the C. D. Howe formations. Like the Fraser Institute subgroup, only its most central node participates in the soft core of twenty-five. Composed predominantly of CSOs, including six corporate-advocacy groups and the Vancouver-based Mining Association of Canada (MAC), the subgroup's central firm is mining giant Teck Resources (a major coal producer also invested in bitumen), two of whose directors also direct the MAC.

As an expression of fossil capital's reach into civil society, the network is organized through both the distinct functions of different kinds of CSOs and cross-regional interlocking. Industry groups advance corporate interests and integrate the network on a sectoral basis, largely within fossil capital's Albertan heartland. Key research institutes and post-secondary institutions form a carbon-centred scientific-industrial complex within which technical knowledge can be put into the service of accumulation, often under the cover of "greening" carbon extraction. Business councils and think tanks are crucial sites for the elite, and their many affiliations often cut across the regions and subgroups, cementing a national influence network.

A Note on the Role of Financial Companies

Our focus in this chapter is on the network of elite influence extending from Canada's carbon-extractive sector. Yet within the broader economy, fossil capital comprises a fraction linked to others through commodity chains and elite relations. A full investigation would require another chapter, but the role of one sector is worth exploring here. Through its control of capital flows, the financial sector serves as a crucial enabler of fossil-capital accumulation and has become a lightning rod for the divestment movement (Alexander, Nicholson, and Wiseman 2014). A study of the Royal Bank of Canada's directorate and financial relations with the carbon sector documented that Canada's self-identified "leading energy bank" has "a very close relationship with the fossil fuel industry and a strong vested interest in its expansion" (Daub and Carroll 2016).

The question we explore here is whether and how leading financial companies interlock with key organizations in the fossil-capital influence network. We selected the fifteen largest Canada-based financial companies (financial intermediaries and investment companies) according to 2014 revenue, and we found that twelve of them participate in the fossil-capital influence network. Combining these twelve leading financial companies with the twelve largest fossil-capital firms that participate in the network's dominant component and the nineteen most central CSOs in the component (each with least seven interlocks with component members), we also found that all but two financials form a connected component with nine of the big fossil-capital firms and all nineteen of the CSOs, involving seventy-two interlocking directors (see figure 6.4).

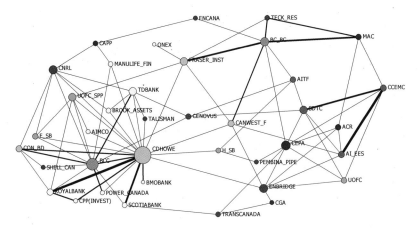

Figure 6.4. Interlocks among leading financial companies, fossil-capital firms, and CSOs . See Figure 6.3 for key. Financial institutions are shown in yellow.

Within this select grouping, eastern-based hegemonic institutions are prominent. At the time we conducted our analysis, the Howe board brought together directors of nine out of ten financial institutions (including four directors of the Royal Bank of Canada, three Scotiabank directors, two Bank of Montreal directors, and two directors of the Canada Pension Plan)—five of which also interlocked with the Business Council of Canada. Concurrently, four major fossil-capital corporations interlocked with the C. D. Howe Institute and/or the Business Council of Canada. The gravitational attraction of the Howe board cannot be overstated: twenty-one of the seventy-two individuals in this core elite of top fossil-capital, financial, and CSO directors were C. D. Howe directors. Similarly, top executives from Cenovus, Shell Canada, and CNRL were all on the Business Council of Canada. In the governance of these hegemonic institutions of Canada's capitalist class, bankers, financiers, and fossil capitalists collaborate, developing consensus positions on strategy and policy.

Besides these relations, mediated as they are by the hegemonic institutions, figure 6.4 also depicts direct relationships between high finance and big carbon. At the time, former Nova Scotia premier Frank McKenna directed CNRL as well as Toronto-Dominion Bank and Brookfield Asset Management. Brian M. Levitt, chair of Toronto-Dominion's board, also directed Talisman Energy, and Cenovus CEO Brian C. Ferguson joined Levitt on the TD board. In addition, former Scotiabank CEO Richard E. Waugh sat on the board of

TransCanada. Of course, in focusing on only the top dozen financials and carbons, we leave aside many other such relations, such as the RBC's interlocks with numerous smaller fossil-capital firms (see Daub and Carroll 2016).

Intriguingly, however, many organizations (positioned on the right-hand side of the sociogram) have no elite ties to the country's largest financial corporations, nor to the hegemonic think tanks and advocacy organizations. Indeed, the regional dimension is clear: much of the network is a western Canadian configuration of industry groups, research and post-secondary institutions (comprising the scientific-industrial complex), and carbon companies.[13] For instance, as figure 6.4 shows, Teck Resources interlocks with MAC, BCBC, and the Fraser Institute, while Encana interlocks with BCBC and CAPP (these two firms being the largest donors to BC Liberal Party; Graham, Daub, and Carroll 2017). Enbridge links into the eastern community via CEO Al Monaco's seat at the C. D. Howe Institute, but other Enbridge directors are affiliated with the Canada West Foundation, the Alberta Chamber of Resources, CEPA, AI_EES, and the U of C's board of governors. This suggests a continuing structural basis for regional elite formation, even as an industrial-financial nexus integrates carbon majors with eastern-based finance (nine of the ten financials being based in Toronto or Montréal) and national-level policy planning. From the Fraser Institute rightward in the sociogram, seventeen of the nineteen organizations are based in western Canada.

Conclusion

In this chapter we have mapped one vector of corporate influence based in the interlocking of their directorates with the boards of CSOs. Other vectors, such as lobbying, funding relationships, and media messaging, are no less important, but our analysis offers one essential vantage point on the architecture of stage 2 denialism—that of elite leadership. Unlike many of the chapters to follow, our mapping of network architecture does not trace the actual flow of discourse in the network and into civil and political society. However, our findings reveal a pervasive pattern of corporate influence, spanning across domains of civil society to form a single, connected network. The largest fossil fuel firms are particularly engaged, as are key CSOs that produce and disseminate various kinds of knowledge—from the strategic communications of industry groups and advocacy organizations through the policy analyses and prescriptions offered by think tanks to the academic knowledge produced within universities and research institutes. The network offers hegemonic pathways into the production of knowledge, culture, and identity and opportunities to align fossil-capitalist interests with discourses of national interest.

Knowledge is power, as Francis Bacon observed. Fossil capital's reach into civil society and its knowledge-producing organizations project corporate power from the economic realm into the public sphere. Different kinds of CSOs accomplish this in distinct ways, with implications for how they are positioned in the elite network. Industry groups convene representatives from ostensibly competing firms within specific sectors, to construct a common sectoral interest and to promote that interest through lobbying, advertising, and other persuasive communications, as well as through funding other organizations, including political parties (see Graham, Daub, and Carroll 2017). Among the organizations we studied, the most central industry group, CAPP, was also the most active federal lobbyist, with 1,015 meetings registered between 2011 and 2015. The Canadian Gas Association was also fairly active, with 477 meetings in that period, as was CEPA (with 319 meetings), while yet other industry associations registered more than 250 meetings.[14] However, industry groups, including CAPP, tend not to interlock with other CSOs: they integrate and mobilize the fossil-capital elite within, not between, sectors.

Interlocks with other kinds of CSOs create pathways of influence across sectors. Among corporate-advocacy organizations, business councils (of Canada and of British Columbia) stand out as places where business leaders, often active in other CSOs, collaborate in crafting a shared agenda for big business.[15] Their extensive affiliations convey the corporate world view to think tanks, universities, and research institutes, but they also enable knowledge from the latter sectors to be brought back to the business councils and related advocacy platforms. The absence from the elite network (with the exception of Resource Works) of the more popular, grassroots advocacy groups is not surprising, given our focus on elite interlocking. This is not to say that Ethical Oil, Canada Action, and similar astroturf groups are without importance in winning hearts and minds for big carbon (see chapter 7). They speak to different publics, in their own populist register.

It is no surprise that fossil-capital leaders participate extensively in governing these CSOs. Industry associations and business-advocacy CSOs are effectively *part of* the corporate sector; they form its political arm, reaching immediately into civil society and beyond—into the sites and spaces where state governance occurs. As they create and circulate policy briefs, media releases, and research reports, and as they lobby different levels of government and fund initiatives such as astroturf "citizen groups," these organizations shore up the case for "business-as-usual" in very unusual times that beg for a robust policy response to the climate crisis.

Strikingly, major think tanks such as the C. D. Howe Institute, Fraser Institute, and Canada West Foundation are profusely interlocked with fossil capital but also with one another. Moreover, as the triple interlock linking Fraser and the BCBC illustrates, think tanks also connect across civil society sectors. In the architecture of new denialism, think tanks play a pivotal role. Beneath the veneer of objectivity, these groups are in close communication with big carbon at the level of governance but also through committees (such as C. D. Howe's Energy Policy Council) that bring corporate representatives directly into agenda setting. These think tanks advocate greater efficiency in carbon extraction and consumption, new technologies such as carbon capture and storage, and a rate of decarbonization so slow that it makes a mockery of the scale and urgency of the problem. These are indeed the elements of new denialism.

In this new denialism, "the fossil fuel industry and our political leaders assure us that they understand and accept the scientific warnings about climate change—but they are in denial about what this scientific reality means for policy and/or continue to block progress in less visible ways" (Klein and Daub 2016). Thus, even as CAPP (2019) proclaims that "climate change is a global issue, requiring action from individuals, governments, organizations and industries around the world," it continues, on behalf of its members, to advocate expanded bitumen production and pipeline infrastructure. In effect, stage 2 denial involves talking one way and walking in the opposite direction, by obstructing the kinds of changes that could decarbonize our ecological footprint in a timely manner but that also threaten corporate profits and control of economic decisions.

Our focus has been on architecture, not discourse. We find a pattern of *elite cohesion paired with exclusion of voices from other social sectors*. Even the nonpartisan and ostensibly neutral think tanks that claim to have the public interest at heart generally lack any representation from civil society groups whose values and priorities do not align with those of the relatively privileged. Perhaps unsurprisingly, a review of the primary positions held by members of the boards of directors at the C. D. Howe Institute, the Fraser Institute, and the Canada West Foundation found no one from unions, environmental groups, or grassroots Indigenous organizations. Voices urging caution or alternatives to business-as-usual would disrupt the pro-business consensus that is a taken-for-granted element in the policy work of these think tanks.

The same pattern of elite cohesion and closure holds even in areas seemingly remote from the interests of fossil capital: the academic and research sectors. Corporate reach into these sectors is both diffused across many institutions and concentrated within an Alberta-based carbon-centred scientific-industrial complex. This complex embodies the close alignment of interests between fossil capital and academic and research communities. Framed as benign initiatives to maintain an "edge" in an increasingly competitive business environment, these ties blur the distinction between public and private interest, enabling big carbon to reap both symbolic and material advantage.

Finally, elite links to finance and investment companies construct a cross-regional bridge between western-based carbon extraction and eastern-based finance. The directors of both fractions share space on the boards of the major hegemonic institutions of the Canadian capitalist class.

In the architecture of stage 2 denialism, elite cohesion and closure combine with a rich organizational ecology of corporate influence: industry groups, think tanks, advocacy organizations, post-secondary institutions, and research institutes occupy distinct niches in a field of fossil-capital influence that also encompasses aligned sources of finance. As a hegemonic structure, the varied practices and forms of knowledge comprising such an organizational ecology offer the strategic advantage of diversity (Carroll and Shaw 2001). Fossil capital speaks not through a megaphone but through many voices and from many sites beyond its base in capital accumulation.

Our mapping of the new denialism's architecture helps explain the yawning chasm between scientific knowledge and political action. The many threads of communication and collaboration via interlocking governance boards enable the fossil-capital elite to define, defend, and advance its profit-driven concerns as "common sense," in the "public interest." What obstructs serious action are corporate interests, expressed in part through the intricate elite network that reaches from fossil-capital boardrooms to civil society. Central to the new denialism is promotion of policies and practices, convivial to profitable corporate revenue streams, which appear to be credible responses to the scientific consensus—as in the promise to phase out coal production by 2030 (while ramping up infrastructure and carbon extraction overall).

Missing from the picture are voices championing the long-term interests of most Canadians, among them advocates for a healthy environment, Indigenous and labour rights, and other values integral to our collective well-being.

Notes

1. See chapter 5 for more details on how the sample of 238 fossil-capital firms was compiled.

2. For instance, Resource Works—an organization that claims to promote "responsible resource development" in British Columbia (see https://www.resourceworks.com/)—was initially funded by the Business Council of British Columbia and has the council's CEO on its board, although most board members are lower-level managers and former politicians. The Partnership for Resource Trade, launched in 2014 by the Canadian Chamber of Commerce, has used local chambers of commerce to mobilize its campaigns. The Alberta Prosperity Fund was initiated in 2015 by business consultant Barry McNamar, who has held leadership positions at the Manning Foundation, the Fraser Institute, and the University of Calgary's School of Public Policy (DeSmog n.d.). Ethical Oil, funded in part by the corporate sector, with close ties to the Conservative Party of Canada (Pullman 2012), is the project of right-wing activist Ezra Levant. Similarly, Canada Action, initiated and led by Calgary realtor Cody Battershill, has close ties to the oil industry and to the Conservative Party of Canada (Linnitt and Gutstein 2015). Some groups, like CAPP-sponsored Canada's Energy Citizens, do not release any information on their leadership, precluding analysis of their network ties.

3. Although as recently as 1979 public funds made up 84 percent of the operating revenues of Canadian universities (Brownlee 2015, 41), by 2015 only 49 percent of funding came from public sources, with Canada ranking twenty-seventh among the thirty-three OECD countries reporting (CAUT 2019).

4. Our sample echoes emerging research indicating that business schools housed within major Canadian universities are leading the charge of academic corporatization (Alajoutsijärvi, Juusola, and Siltaoja 2015).

5. We identified these institutes through a review of existing literature (Adkin and Stares 2016; CAUT 2013) and by searching university websites. We included research centres that have their own advisory boards on which corporate directors and state managers are included (implying some level of university-industry-state research collaboration). Research parks, now a corporatizing

feature of many universities, were not included, although future research could beneficially trace the linkages between these research parks and corporate capital.

6. A list of sample organizations and the abbreviations used in the sociograms is available from the first author upon request.

7. Network analyses were executed within UCINET (Borgatti 2002).

8. Analysis of variance shows that type of organization accounts for 11.1 percent of the variance in social-circle heterogeneity.

9. Interestingly, CEPA, an industry group, *is* in the core. Its past president and CEO Brenda Kenny, who earlier served with the National Energy Board, currently sits on the boards of directors at the Canada West Foundation and at SDTC and recently completed a six-year term on the University of Calgary Board of Governors. Another former board member, Ian Anderson, is president and CEO of the Trans Mountains Corporation (and past president of Kinder Morgan Canada) and serves on the board of the BCBC.

10. The contingency coefficient of 0.624 indicates a strong relationship between region and subgroup membership.

11. Krackhardt and Stern's (1988) E-I index subtracts the proportion of "introverted" lines (linking members of subgroups with each other) from the proportion of "extraverted" lines that occur across subgroups. It varies from 1 (complete extraversion) to –1 (complete introversion).

12. Points in the sociogram are positioned in part on the basis of their subgroup membership, using the "scrunching" algorithm in NetDraw (Borgatti 2002).

13. Our findings are consistent with research pointing to the *regionalized* character of "fossil knowledge," which tends to cluster in post-secondary institutions based in areas with high levels of carbon extractive development (Gustafson 2012). At the same time, the regionalism observed may also reflect our decision to weight our sample in favour of western-based post-secondary institutions. More comprehensive research of this sort could reveal the full scope of the interlocks between fossil capital with post-secondary education. See also chapter 10 in this volume for an analysis of the infiltration of fossil-capital into Alberta's two major research universities and its influence on university priorities.

14. Figures for number of meetings were calculated from information found on the federal Registry of Lobbyists (https://lobbycanada.gc.ca).

15. This is not to say that all corporate interests are smoothly integrated into a homogeneous hegemonic project. Indeed, as Carroll and Shaw (2001, 211) have shown, *diversity* in the organizational ecology of corporate influence yields a richer discursive field than would a monocultural configuration—offering possibilities for "nuanced debate and diverse action repertoires, all within the perimeters of permissible neoliberal discourse."

References

Adkin, Laurie E., and Brittany J. Stares. 2016. "Turning Up the Heat: Hegemonic Politics in a First World Petro-State." In *First World Petro-Politics: The Political Ecology and Governance of Alberta*, edited by Laurie E. Adkin, 190–240. Toronto: University of Toronto Press.

Alexander, Samuel, Kara Nicholson, and John Wiseman. 2014. *Fossil Free: The Development and Significance of the Fossil Fuel Divestment Movement*. MSSI Issues Papers No. 4. Melbourne: Melbourne Sustainable Society Institute, University of Melbourne.

Alajoutsijärvi, Kimmo, Katarina Juusola, and Marjo Siltaoja. 2015. "The Legitimacy Paradox of Business Schools: Losing by Gaining?" *Academy of Management Learning and Education* 14, no. 2: 277–91. https://doi.org/10.5465/amle.2013.0106.

Beder, Sharon. 2006. *Suiting Themselves: How Corporations Drive the Global Agenda*. London and New York: Earthscan.

Blau, Peter M. 1977. *Inequality and Heterogeneity: A Primitive Theory of Social Structure*. New York: Free Press.

Borgatti, Stephen P. 2002. *NetDraw: Software for Network Visualization*. Analytic Technologies, Lexington, KY. https://sites.google.com/site/netdrawsoftware/home.

Brownlee, Jamie. 2005. *Ruling Canada: Corporate Cohesion and Democracy*. Halifax: Fernwood.

———. 2015. *Academia, Inc.: How Corporatization Is Transforming Canadian Universities*. Halifax: Fernwood.

CAPP (Canadian Association of Petroleum Producers). 2019. "Climate Change." Canadian Association of Petroleum Producers. https://www.capp.ca/environment/climate-change/.

Carroll, William K. 2004. *Corporate Power in a Globalizing World*. Toronto: Oxford University Press.

Carroll, William K., Nicolas Graham, and Zoë Yunker. 2018. "Carbon Capital and Corporate Influence: Mapping Elite Networks of Corporations, Universities and Research Institutes." In *Corporatizing Canada: Making Business Out of Public Service*, edited by Jamie Brownlee, Chris Hurl, and Kevin Walby, 58–73. Toronto: Between the Lines.

Carroll, William K., and Murray Shaw. 2001. "Consolidating a Neoliberal Policy Bloc in Canada, 1976 to 1996." *Canadian Public Policy* 27, no. 2: 195–216.

CAUT (Canadian Association of University Teachers). 2013. *Open for Business on What Terms?* Ottawa: Canadian Association of University Teachers. Retrieved November 21, 2017. https://www.caut.ca/sites/default/files/open-for-business-nov-2013.pdf.

———. 2019. "Table 1.5: Proportion of Public and Private Funding in Tertiary Education, Selected OECD Countries, 2015." Updated March 1, 2019. *Almanac of Post-Secondary Education 2019*. Table 1.5. Retrieved October 5, 2017. https://www.caut.ca/resources/almanac/1-canada-worldfinance.Clement, Wallace. 1975. *The Canadian Corporate Elite: An Analysis of Economic Power*. Toronto: McClelland and Stewart.

Daub, Shannon, and William K. Carroll. 2016. "Why Is the CEO of a Big Canadian Bank Giving Speeches About Climate Change and Pipelines?" *Policy Note* (blog). Canadian Centre for Policy Alternatives, BC Office. October 7, 2016. http://www.policynote.ca/rbc-ceo-on-climate-and-pipelines/.

Derber, Charles. 2010. *Greed to Green: Solving Climate Change and Remaking the Economy*. Boulder, CO: Paradigm.

DeSmog. n.d. "Alberta Prosperity Fund." *DeSmog* (blog). Accessed March 24, 2017. https://www.desmogblog.com/alberta-prosperity-fund.

Dobbin, Murray. 1998. *The Myth of the Good Corporate Citizen: Democracy Under the Rule of Big Business*. Toronto: Stoddart.

Fox, John, and Michael Ornstein. 1986. "The Canadian State and Corporate Elites in the Post-War Period." *Canadian Review of Sociology* 23, no. 4: 481–506.

Girvan, M., and M. E. J. Newman. 2002. "Community Structure in Social and Biological Networks." *Proceedings of the National Academy of Sciences* 99, no. 12: 7821–26. https://doi.org/10.1073/pnas.122653799.

Graham, Nicolas, Shannon Daub, and William K. Carroll. 2017. *Mapping Political Influence: Political Donations and Lobbying by the Fossil Fuel Industry in BC*. Vancouver: Canadian Centre for Policy Alternatives. https://www.policyalternatives.ca/bc-influence.

Gustafson, Bret. 2012. "Fossil Knowledge Networks: Industry Strategy, Public Culture, and the Challenge for Critical Research." In *Flammable Societies: Studies on the Socio-economics of Oil and Gas*, edited by John-Andrew Neish and Owen Logan, 311–34. London: Pluto.

Gutstein, Donald. 2014. *Harperism: How Stephen Harper and His Think Tank Colleagues Have Transformed Canada*. Toronto: James Lorimer.

Klein, Seth, and Shannon Daub. 2016. "The New Climate Denialism: Time for an Intervention." *Policy Note* (blog). Canadian Centre for Policy Alternatives, BC Office. September 22, 2016. http://www.policynote.ca/the-new-climate-denialism-time-for-an-intervention/.

Krackhardt, David, and Robert N. Stern. 1988. "Informal Networks and Organizational Crises: An Experimental Simulation." *Social Psychology Quarterly* 51, no. 2: 123–40. https://doi.org/10.2307/2786835.

Langille, David. 1987. "The Business Council on National Issues and the Canadian State." *Studies in Political Economy* 24, no. 1: 41–85.

Linnitt, Carol, and Donald Gutstein. 2015. "'Grassroots' Canada Action Carries Deep Ties to Conservative Party, Oil and Gas Industry." *The Narwhal*, July 22, 2015. https://thenarwhal.ca/grassroots-canada-action-carries-deep-ties-conservative-party-oil-gas-industry.

Porter, John. 1965. *The Vertical Mosaic: An Analysis of Social Class and Power in Canada*. Toronto: University of Toronto Press.

Pullman, Emma. 2012. "Cozy Ties: Astroturf 'Ethical Oil' and Conservative Alliance to Promote Tar Sands Expansion." *DeSmog*, January 13, 2012. https://www.desmogblog.com/cozy-ties-astroturf-ethical-oil-and-conservative-alliance-promote-tar-sands-expansion.

Schwartz, Zane. 2015. "Best of the Best: Introducing the 2016 Maclean's University Rankings." *Maclean's*, October 29, 2015. http://www.macleans.ca/education/best-of-the-best-introducing-the-2016-macleans-university-rankings/.

Urry, John. 1981. *The Anatomy of Capitalist Societies: The Economy, Civil Society and the State*. London: Macmillan.

7 "Our Oil"

Extractive Populism in Canadian Social Media

Shane Gunster, Robert Neubauer, John Bermingham,
and Alicia Massie

"Think of this like a football game and we're not putting enough players in the field. They've got people in every local community trying to create delay and create obstruction." So said Cody Battershill, a Calgary realtor, founder of the social media campaigns Oil Sands Action and Canada Action, and a vocal supporter of Canada's oil and gas industry. In an interview with radio personality and former right-wing provincial politician Danielle Smith, Battershill (2018) described a beleaguered industry under attack from a "very sophisticated, well-organized public relations campaign" intent on destroying the Albertan economy. But rather than simply decry the conspiracies of what former federal natural resources minister Joe Oliver (2012) famously described as foreign-funded "radical groups," Battershill spent the lion's share of the interview urging listeners to mobilize in response:

> Call your MP today. It doesn't matter what party they're with. [. . .] On
> our website, we have an email we sent out today asking everyone to call
> the Prime Minister's office. Call [then natural resources minister] Jim
> Carr's office. Go on social media. We have to apply the pressure: [. . .]
> I would encourage people to be vocal. Email the mayor of Burnaby.
> Email [BC premier] John Horgan's office. Call their offices. Let's flood
> the phonelines. Let's flood their inboxes. Let's stand up.

Listeners were invited to participate in a *Vancouver Sun* public-opinion poll regarding a proposal by the BC government to study and possibly restrict bitumen exports given the risk. Above all, he implored the audience to become active in communicating about this issue within their social networks: "We all have an opportunity to call friends and family. Use social media. Share Oil Sands Action, Canada Action. [. . .] We are all on the same team. We all need to be working together to make sure that Canada, Alberta, we are all getting the best price for our oil."

"Our oil." Battershill's interview—and the success of his campaigns in attracting social media support—exemplify what we describe as extractive populism, an emerging effort to position extractivism as under attack from elites, as an economic and political project that demands popular mobilization to defend, and as a democratic expression of the public will to fight for an industry that serves the common good. The term "extractive populist" has been invoked to characterize the political economy of Latin American states that rely upon extractive royalties to fund public services (Eisenstadt, Leon, and Wong 2017). Our application of the term pursues a markedly different ideological endeavour: to recruit and mobilize supporters of the (primarily North American) fossil fuel industry to counter what Naomi Klein (2014) has dubbed "Blockadia"—that is, growing regional resistance from environmental organizations, Indigenous groups, and local communities to the expansion of extractivism and associated infrastructure, such as pipelines. We situate this extractive populist discourse as both derivative of and complementary to contemporary forms of conservative populism that position "ordinary people" as the victims of a powerful minority of liberal elites who use their control over political and cultural institutions to impose their values upon society at large (Frank 2004; Gunster and Saurette 2014; Saurette and Gunster 2011).

Such discourse is frequently dubbed "astroturf," a pejorative moniker implying top-down corporate public relations campaigns that simulate "grass-roots" advocacy but with minimal linkages to real communities. Corporations do engage in such campaigns, and it is essential to explore their use of this strategy. Yet we believe that simply dismissing all industry-driven populist initiatives as "astroturf" underestimates the extent to which extractive populism genuinely resonates with (and amplifies) selective aspects of the world views and experiences of particular communities, especially those with significant ties to extractive industries. Such dismissals not only risk reinforcing populist narratives that accuse liberal elites of refusing to acknowledge the legitimacy of perspectives other than their own but also fail to recognize the potential of such campaigns to affirm, reinforce, and combine with more political forms of populism. Analyzing the authoritarian populism of Thatcherism, Stuart Hall (1988, 46) once cautioned that "the first thing to ask about an 'organic' ideology that, however unexpectedly, succeeds in organizing substantial sections of the masses and mobilizing them for political action, is not what is *false* about it but what about it is *true*. By 'true' I do not mean universally correct . . . but 'makes good sense.'" We believe that extractive populism deserves equally serious treatment.

Instead of characterizing these campaigns as astroturf, we find Edward Walker's (2014) conception of *subsidized publics* a more useful framework for analyzing such corporate-led civic engagement. Subsidized publics arise from the use of industry resources to catalyze and refine the participation of particular groups within the public sphere, thereby giving them a coherence, focus, and elevated profile that they would not have on their own. Walker traces the origin of such practices to the growth of business/trade associations that work on behalf of an entire sector: "As business became more aware of its political interests—especially in response to the crisis of corporate legitimacy starting in the late 1960s—industry groups utilized the services of grassroots firms in order to connect with the broader public and activate their stakeholders" (74). Such publics frequently serve as a form of elite legitimation, exacerbating existing political inequalities between those groups favoured with such subsidies and those who lack such political sponsorship. But such legitimation proceeds via active efforts to articulate corporate and popular interests rather than through the orchestration of democratic simulacra that conjure mass sentiments out of thin air.

The discourse of extractive populism is an ideal fit for the explosive growth of social media platforms as increasingly dominant venues for news consumption and public communication. An August 2016 survey conducted by Abacus Data found that the number of Canadians who rely on social media as a primary source of news and information had more than doubled since 2015, and Facebook had become the leading source for those under forty-five years of age. A report on the findings characterized Facebook as "a dynamic platform that many Canadians use to consume content, share their thoughts and comment on other people's posts. It's an interactive ecosystem ripe for political discussion and persuasion. A place where public affairs professionals can speak to a broad group of citizens or to a very specific argument" (Blevis and Coletto 2017). Unlike traditional corporate public relations, over which a company exercises control, speaking directly to its audience, extractive populism depends upon the active mediation, curation, and circulation of material through social networks. The hermeneutic labour signified through posting, sharing, liking, and commenting on specific pieces of media occludes the institutional origins and authority of extractivist discourse, dynamically repositioning it as a form of "common sense" emerging organically from the collective wisdom of communities of like-minded people. In this process, pro-industry ideas and arguments originally produced by elite sources (such as public relations firms, think tanks, and the editorial boards of newspapers and magazines) are rechristened as populist—that is, reflective of and emerging from "the people"—as they pass through social media circuits.

In what follows, we trace the contours of extractive populism as it is increasingly expressed in Canadian social media. First, we explore the genesis of Canadian extractive populism in industry's efforts to target and "activate" key constituencies of supporters to emulate the successes of their opponents' communication and engagement strategies. Following a description of our research, we dig deeper into the strategies of several Facebook groups that represent key nodes in the promotional infrastructure for extractive populism, focusing on the material they are sharing and how they are (re)framing extractivism.

The Shift: Subsidizing Canadian "Energy Citizens"

In "Energy's Citizens: The Making of a Canadian Petro-Public," Tim Wood notes that CAPP first explored the idea of civic engagement in the wake of internal-opinion surveys about a decade ago that found industry employees were reluctant to participate in public debates around the oil and gas sector. He quotes Jeff Gaulin, vice-president of communications at CAPP, as saying that people who might otherwise support the fossil fuel industry "felt it was like smoking. You were socially stigmatized to stand up and defend the oil sands or natural gas or pipelines" (quoted in Wood 2018, 11). The rapid expansion of production in the Alberta oil sands, combined with high-profile "accidents" such as the death of sixteen hundred migratory birds in Syncrude tailings ponds in 2008, had significantly elevated the industry's profile in Canadian media. Faced with increasing public scrutiny of its environmental and social impacts, industry sought to make its employees more active partners in championing the virtues of oil and gas development.

Cenovus, among the most aggressive firms in using advertising campaigns to shape public opinion (Turner 2012), was the first to engage its workforce, in October 2013, with the distribution of "wearable pride in the form of 'I ♥ Oil' T-shirts, toques, and ear-warming headbands; a 'Speak Up' package with tips, examples and industry facts all designed to encourage (or support) conversations with friends and family; and an update to the company's social media guidelines designed to encourage greater participation in online discussions and debates" (Stanfield 2015, 9). The following year, CAPP launched Canada's Energy Citizens, a hybrid marketing and engagement strategy designed to showcase public support for the sector and encourage ordinary Canadians—especially employees and their families—to become vocal industry advocates. In April 2015, this new emphasis on targeted engagement was profiled in a special issue of *Context*, CAPP's member magazine: "CAPP is building toward a full-blown grassroots outreach program that will begin to take shape in the coming months. The goal will be to shift industry supporters from a mode of passive endorsement to active engagement" (Stanfield 2015, 10). "We know the support is out there," explained Christina Pilarski, CAPP's campaign manager. "We've made some good progress in identifying that support. The next step is to build relationships with our supporters, and inspire them to become visible and vocal champions for industry" (quoted in Stanfield 2015, 10). Industry polling suggested that while strong supporters of industry outnumbered strong opponents two to one, supporters felt too uncomfortable and embarrassed to speak out in favour of an industry that had allegedly been so effectively demonized by a vocal minority (Hislop 2015). The Canada's Energy Citizens campaign aimed to embolden supporters, assuring them that their views were valid, broadly shared, and essential to express.

Anxiety about the power, skill, and determination of environmentalist opposition looms large in industry accounts explaining the shift from conventional public relations—prioritizing mass-market ad campaigns and information subsidies to corporate media—to a movement-based model of advocacy. Environmental organizations were perceived as far more effective campaigners in using social media to deliver values-driven, emotional appeals aimed at mobilizing small but motivated constituencies to become active participants in public debates. In an October 2014 speech, for example, CAPP's then president, David Collyer, observed that "high-priced advertising could nudge the needle of public opinion in the industry's favor, but a well-timed counterpunch from opponents on social media would almost always push it right back. In the new age of handheld-to-handheld combat, oil and gas was getting badly outflanked" (quoted in Coyne 2015). Industry therefore had little choice but to adopt its opponents' tactics, reconceptualizing social media as a space where supporters could envision themselves as part of a broader political movement.

While CAPP primarily describes its Canada's Energy Citizens initiative as stimulating more balanced conversations about energy in everyday life, assembling a network of impassioned supporters schooled in the necessity of political action (for example, participating in public consultations, pressuring politicians) has been a core program objective. In April 2015, CAPP invited Deryck Spooner, senior director of external mobilization for the American Petroleum Institute (API), to come to Calgary to discuss API's own "Energy Citizens" campaign. Titled "Harnessing Passion Through Grassroots," Spooner's presentation opened with a frank acknowledgement of industry's desire to drive its supporters to "take to the streets" in the same way as its opponents (Spooner 2015, 4). Building such support, he explained, involved a three-stage process—"recruit," "educate and train," and "motivate and activate"—to be implemented through various online and offline venues including town halls and rallies, social media, letters to the editor, petitions, and lobbying of elected officials. The program aimed to build "key, long-term ally relationships" based upon "the principle that *conditioned allies are likely to be better advocates*" (19; emphasis in the original). Three different constituencies were identified as priorities: "local influentials" (small business owners, community leaders, media), "industry voices" (companies, pro-industry think tanks), and "energy voters" (rank-and-file constituents, industry employees) (19). Subsequent slides described the millions of supporters cultivated by API who could duly be "activated" to pressure politicians and local and state governments to support industry objectives. The presentation concluded with three examples in which such mobilization produced tangible results: first, generating over 120,000 comments in support of an LNG export facility in Maryland, which helped to win an uphill battle to secure regulatory approval; second, defeating a "Community Bill of Rights" in Youngstown, Ohio, that would have constrained local oil and gas development; and third, defeating a "Waterfront Protection Ordinance" in South Portland, Maine, that would have banned bitumen exports from the harbour.

Advocates and supporters have also developed their own social media campaigns to defend the Canadian oil and gas industry. Officially, these supporter groups claim to operate at arm's length from industry, although the extent to which they receive support is an ongoing question (Linnitt and Gutstein 2015). Over the past several years, Cody Battershill's Oil Sands Action and Canada Action have attracted hundreds of thousands of followers on Facebook, Twitter, and other platforms. Battershill—a regular contributor to the *Huffington Post* who occasionally pens op-eds in the *Calgary Herald*— has indicated that his activism emerged out of frustration with the anti–oil sands messaging of environmental groups as well as the ineffectiveness of the oil industry's response. In his perception, wrote *National Post* commentator Claudia Cattaneo (2015), "industry's own efforts have been hampered by too little co-ordination, too many unchallenged claims, and industry leaders censoring themselves from what needed to be said." More recently, similar groups have appeared on the scene: Oil Sands Strong, Oilfield Dads, Albertans Against the NDP, and Alberta Proud combine a relentless advocacy of extractivism as a Canadian public good with caustic attacks on industry critics. They are playing a key role in building a more robust and differentiated promotional field around the fossil fuel sector that is especially well suited to the compartmentalized echo chambers of social media.

The Seven Groups in Our Sample

On the basis of an initial review of pro-industry social media, we selected seven Canadian Facebook groups that are broadly representative of four different types of organizations—corporations, industry engagement groups, supporter/activist groups, and elite advocacy groups—involved in social media extractivist advocacy. First, we identified Cenovus and Enbridge as two of the most active corporations on social media; both companies have also spearheaded significant advertising and public relations campaigns to build public support for the sector. Second, we selected CAPP's Canada's Energy Citizens (CEC), as well as Oil Respect (OR), the engagement initiative of the Canadian Association of Oilwell Drilling Contractors, an Alberta-based industry organization representing small and medium enterprises. Third, we identified Oil Sands Action (OSA), headed by Battershill, and Oil Sands Strong (OSS), founded and run by Robbie Picard—an oil and gas worker from Fort McMurray—as two of the most popular industry-oriented supporter groups on Facebook. Finally, Resource Works (RW), a BC-based policy and advocacy organization promoting resource development, was selected as a more traditional lobby group that is active on social media.

Table 7.1 compares the level and growth in group likes for these seven pages with the profiles of some of the most popular Canadian and BC environmental organizations to illustrate the relative size and reach of industry-friendly social media communications. As the table illustrates, both CEC and OSA have attracted a sizable number of followers, comparable to Greenpeace Canada, though still many fewer than the David Suzuki Foundation, the largest Canadian environmental organization on Facebook. OR and OSS possess a smaller but still significant social media footprint, with RW and the two corporations attracting less attention. With the exception of RW, the growth in group likes has been very strong for all of the industry advocacy groups and is generally much higher than those for many environmental groups.

Table 7.1. Group likes, 2017 and 2018

	2017	2018	Growth
Cenovus	5,839	8,645	48.1%
Enbridge	10,714	30,529	184.9%
CEC	153,810	216,055	40.5%
OR	50,180	57,895	15.4%
OSA	112,843	134,835	19.5%
OSS	30,226	38,927	28.8%
RW	7,174	7,369	2.7%
David Suzuki Foundation	477,614	492,440	3.1%
Greenpeace Canada	197,330	213,034	8.0%
Dogwood BC	28,563	32,140	12.5%
Sierra Club BC	9,286	11,249	21.1%

Note: In 2018, group likes were all collected on the same day (February 23). In 2017, the collections for the various groups were made on several different days spanning roughly a two-week period (January 30 to February 15).

Using NVivo, we scraped data about our seven groups' 2016 posts to explore the volume of content they were generating as well as their level of engagement with Facebook users. This generated a total sample of 3,725 posts. As table 7.2 illustrates, uneven patterns of posting and audience engagement were visible among the groups.

Table 7.2. Facebook engagement metrics, 2016

	2016 posts		Likes per post		Shares per post		Comments per post	
	Total	Per day	Average	Max	Average	Max	Average	Max
Cenovus	171	0.47	46	1,743	13	967	3	114
Enbridge	155	0.42	148	1,393	10	467	10	245
CEC	693	1.90	1,621	25,298	841	48,870	187	5,416
OR[a]	551	1.69	305	13,401	191	5,812	56	2,635
OSA	631	1.73	1,369	44,865	1,271	76,841	88	4,181
OSS	290	0.79	317	7,505	702	28,064	25	345
RW	1,232	3.38	8	153	3	126	2	67

[a] Oil Respect launched on February 11, 2016; thus, the sample does not include a full year of posts.

During 2016, the seven groups generated a total of 3,723 posts. Cenovus and Enbridge were the least active, with less than one post every two days, and they attracted comparatively few likes, shares, and comments. RW had a much higher volume of posts, but, like the corporations, it struggled to attract audience engagement. Conversely, the two industry engagement groups, CEC and OR, and the two supporter/activist groups, OSA and OSS, were much more successful in generating engagement. We incorporate these different levels of engagement in our analysis through a measure called the *composite engagement metric* (CEM), which adds together likes, shares, and comments to provide a quantitative weighting for each post based on the engagement it generated. A post with one like, one share, and one comment has a CEM of 3, while a post with ten likes, ten shares, and ten comments has a CEM of 30; the second post would be assigned a weighting ten times larger than the first.

We then calculated each group's share of the total number of posts (prior to weighting) and of the total CEM score for the seven groups (see table 7.3). Once engagement metrics are taken into account, CEC and OSA emerge as clearly dominant, accounting for over 80 percent of total engagement, while OR and OSS attracted much smaller but still significant levels of interest from Facebook users. However, posts from RW and the two corporations generated only minimal engagement.

Table 7.3. Group shares of total volume of posts and of total engagement with posts

	Proportion (%) of total post volume	Proportion (%) of total post engagement
Cenovus	4.6	0.2
Enbridge	4.2	0.7
CEC	18.6	43.5
OR	14.8	7.2
OSA	16.9	40.8
OSS	7.8	7.2
RW	33.1	0.4

Accordingly, we focused our analysis on a smaller sample of items consisting of all 2016 posts (a total of 2,165) from the top four groups—CEC, OR, OSA, and OSS—which accounted for 98.7 percent of engagement in the total sample. We coded each post for two variables: the *type* of content and its *primary frame*, that is, the dominant theme of the post.[1] In the case of posts that contained links to external content (such as an article in the *National Post*), we included the source of the content and its author in our analysis, but we did not code the linked material itself.

Types of Posts and an Analysis of Frames

Types and Sources of Posts

Social media platforms such as Facebook are primarily used to circulate and share content among social networks, but the content itself is naturally diverse. We coded posts (including the source and author of linked content, if any) for fourteen different types of content, as described in table 7.4.

The distribution of types for each of the four groups is shown in table 7.5. Sharing favourable content from mainstream media and the trade press was a clear priority for both industry association groups: 42.2 percent of CEC posts and 46.8 percent of OR posts consisted of material produced by news organizations. In contrast, the two supporter/activist groups emphasized the circulation of memes, which occupied close to half of CEC's posts and almost 80 percent for OSS. Memes were especially effective in generating user engagement, accounting for close to 40 percent of engagement across the four groups.

Table 7.4. Types of content

	Description
MSM news	Mainstream news items
MSM opinion	Mainstream media commentary and opinion (including journalists' blogs)
Trade press	Specialized industry and business media (including journalists' blogs)
Alt. media	Alternative media
Corporate PR	Promotional material produced by a corporation
Group PR	Material produced by CEC, OR, OSA, or OSS to promote itself
Meme	A combination of visuals/text designed to convey/support an argument
Infographic	A combination of visuals/text designed to convey impartial information
Government content	Material produced by a government ministry or agency
Industry content	Material produced by a company, business association, or industry-friendly think tank
Other social media	Links to social media content of other groups or individuals (including personal blogs)
Other photo	Photos not accounted for in the above categories
Other video	Video not accounted for in the above categories
Other content	Material not accounted for in the above categories

Virtually all memes circulated by these groups were self-produced, prominently branded with group names and logos, and served to communicate industry-friendly arguments and claims in a simplistic, highly accessible, and often memorable style. Indeed, we argue that one of the core functions of these groups is *meme labour*, that is, the ideological and rhetorical work of mining news media, trade publications, industry public relations, and think-tank research for ideas, images, and soundbites that can be circulated quickly and easily, inviting audiences to actively confirm pro-industry world views by liking and sharing memes. One of the most popular memes in the sample, for example, asserted, "I'm a Canadian. I have the right to choose! So why can't I choose Canadian oil over Saudi Arabia oil!" (OSS, January 30). (All posts date to 2016.) Produced by OSS—with a graphic that urges readers to "help us reach our goal of 100,000 likes!"—the meme received 7,500 likes and nearly 30,000 shares. While one might justifiably criticize such a blatant misrepresentation of how individual consumers intersect with global energy markets, it offers the stark and compelling proposition of celebrating Canadian values by choosing "our oil" over imports from authoritarian regimes.

Table 7.5. Percentage of post types per group, by volume and level of engagement

	CEC		OR		OSA		OSS		Total	
	Posts	CEM	Posts	CEM	Posts	CEM	Posts	CEM	Posts	CEM
MSM news	20.2	17.1	26.9	24.0	3.2	2.0	1.0	0.3	**14.4**	**10.4**
MSM opinion	15.2	14.1	16.0	15.5	9.7	12.3	0	0	**11.7**	**12.7**
Trade	5.6	5.8	2.4	1.9	3.2	1.9	0	0	**3.3**	**3.6**
Alt. media	1.2	0.6	1.5	1.5	0.6	0.4	0	0	**0.9**	**0.5**
Corporate PR	3.2	3.2	0.2	0	0.5	5.8	0.3	0.3	**1.2**	**3.9**
Group PR	15.6	13.3	14.7	5.8	1.3	0.6	3.1	0.5	**9.5**	**6.7**
Meme	10.8	27.4	17.4	33.4	48.7	47.9	79.7	86.1	**32.7**	**39.6**
Infographic	2.7	2.1	1.3	0.8	10.5	5.7	1.0	1.5	**4.4**	**3.5**
Government	2.9	2.7	1.6	1.3	0.5	0.3	0.7	0.1	**1.6**	**1.4**
Industry	1.6	0.5	0.9	0.2	1.9	1.2	0	0	**1.3**	**0.8**
Other social media	7.6	2.9	3.3	1.0	0.2	0	1.0	0.1	**3.5**	**1.4**
Other photo	8.9	6.3	11.1	12.3	11.6	12.3	3.1	1.9	**9.5**	**9.1**
Other video	2.5	1.1	2.4	2.3	3.5	5.9	6.9	8.6	**3.3**	**3.6**
Other content	2.0	2.9	0.5	0.1	4.9	3.6	3.1	0.8	**2.6**	**2.8**

Memes offer a condensation of core factoids, arguments, and values that enable audiences to easily understand the world and their relation to it: "Another foreign oil tanker on the East Coast. Where are the protesters?" (OSA, September 1, 16K shares); "Canada is oil rich, and imports 736,000 barrels of oil every day. Energy East can fix that" (CEC, March 3, 10K shares); "Share if you think Leo [DiCaprio] should stop lecturing you about your carbon footprint" (OSA, November 1, 6K shares); "77% of Canadians surveyed support the Trans Mountain pipeline" (CEC, November 4, 4K shares). In 2016, OSA posted over three hundred memes, close to one per day (often adding additional memes in the comments section), providing Battershill with not only a constant supply of feedback about the comparative efficacy of different arguments but also a steady accumulation of extractivist agitprop that can easily be recycled as required depending upon circumstances and events. Such memes furnish the core ingredients of an extractivist-oriented world view that is simple, self-evident, and appealing to many, helping inoculate readers against countervailing arguments and evidence, and hardening views about energy politics.

Self-generated content was the largest source of material for all four groups: 33.2 percent for CEC, 41.7 percent for OR, 72.9 percent for OSA, and 92.8 percent for OSS. Overall, 57.6 percent of the posts in the total sample were produced by one of the four groups or parent organizations.

The most significant external sources of content shared by these groups were news and commentary from corporate media and the trade press, accounting for over 70 percent of all such external links. Given the well-documented tendency of Postmedia to offer sympathetic coverage of the industry (see, for example, Gunster and Neubauer 2018; Gunster and Saurette 2014), as well as the conglomerate's dominance of English-language Canadian print media, it was unsurprising to find that articles, columns, and op-eds from Postmedia papers constituted almost one-half of all links to mainstream, trade, and alternative media items. Figure 7.1 illustrates the top fifteen sources of links to news sources in the sample. The *National Post* and the *Calgary Herald* lead the list, with Postmedia papers constituting seven of the top fifteen sources. Also noteworthy, however, was the high volume of links to the CBC, an organization often maligned by conservatives as possessing a left-wing, anti–fossil fuel bias (for example, Cross 2014) yet one that supplied a range of news and commentary that clearly fit with these groups' pro-extractivist bias. Indeed, when posts are weighted according to audience engagement, the CBC constituted the top source in the sample. A January 2016 Rick Mercer "rant" railing against Canadians who accept equalization payments but are not willing to support the Energy East pipeline was the highest weighted post in the entire sample—shared by OSA, it generated nearly 45,000 likes and over 62,000 shares (the video was also posted by CEC, attracting over 5,000 likes and almost 5,000 shares).

Another surprising finding was the prominence of news media that have little profile in the broader public sphere but loom large in pro-industry social media. The online *BOE Report*, for instance, was founded in 2013 by

Josh Groberman, a former traffic helicopter pilot from Calgary. It primarily serves up industry-oriented business news, yet it also regularly publishes pro-extractivism commentary. It claimed that over 1.4 million users visited the site in 2016, including a core user base of fifty thousand oil and gas sector employees from Calgary (*BOE Report* Staff 2017).

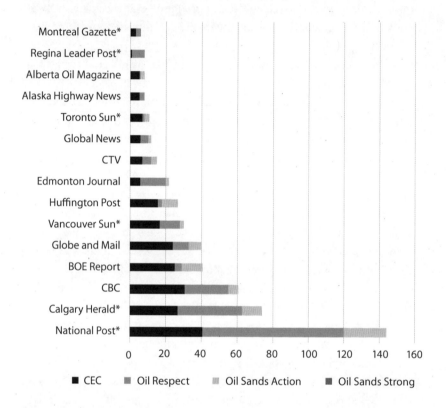

Figure 7.1. Top fifteen news sources (unweighted). Postmedia newspapers appear with an asterisk.

One of the *BOE Report*'s proudest accomplishments was a piece by Terry Etam, a Calgary-based oil and gas consultant, which it published on January 25, 2016. Titled "Saudi Oil Filling a New Brunswick Refinery—What Kind of Domestic Energy Policy Is That?" (Etam 2016), the piece made the case for Energy East by decrying the seeming absurdity of importing oil from Saudi Arabia to service a Canadian refinery that could be processing Alberta oil. Both CEC and OSA promoted the piece on the day it was posted, generating close to 6,000 shares that drove traffic to the site and attracted attention to the argument. Two weeks later, columnist Claudia Cattaneo (2016) wrote a piece that recycled Etam's arguments, probably hoping to capitalize on the social media buzz that CEC and OSA had helped to create. Both OSA and CEC then immediately shared Cattaneo's column (OSA, February 9; CEC, February 10), generating over 4,000 likes and 3,500 shares between them. A week later, OSA posted a meme referring to both the Etam piece and a second *National Post* story on the same theme, which generated a further 1,200 likes and almost 1,300 shares (OSA, February 18). At the end of the year, OSA pitched Etam's piece a final time, attracting 4,000 likes and almost 5,000 shares (OSA, December 29). The *BOE Report* described Etam's piece as its most widely read and circulated story of 2016, boasting that it had been shared over 50,000 times (*BOE Report* Staff 2017). Together, CEC and OSA posts and memes about the Etam article in 2016 generated 12,800 shares and were likely responsible for a significant proportion of the attention it ultimately received.

Frames

We also coded for the presence of seventeen primary frames, described in table 7.6. As mentioned earlier, a single primary frame was coded for each post. Given that posts often contained more than one frame, we used a sequence of coding based upon four tiers of priority. In posts containing memes, info-graphics, photos, and videos, coding priority was assigned to the embedded image or visual (with the first thirty seconds used for videos). In the case of posts that contained embedded links, coding priority was assigned to the text preceding the embedded link. If such text contained multiple frames, the most prominent frame, as defined by the number of sentences, was selected. If multiple frames had equivalent amounts of text, the frame in the highest tier (see table 7.6) was selected. If multiple frames in the same tier were equally present, the frame appearing first was selected. In posts without prefatory text, the embedded visual was coded.

Table 7.6. Primary frame values

Tier 1 frames

Canadian/public interest	Representations of extractivism as serving the Canadian public good and/or national interest
Public opinion/support	Expressions of public support for extractivism
Attack on opponents	Criticism of individuals/organizations that oppose extractivism
Energy lifeworld	Assertions of the necessity of fossil fuels in everyday life
Ethical oil	Positioning of Canada's fossil fuel sector as ethically superior to that of other countries
Indigenous nations	References to the support of Indigenous communities for fossil fuel development

Tier 2 frames

Mobilizing support	Requests to supporters to engage in specific actions
Government sustainability	Assertions that government regulation of environmental impacts ensures the long-term sustainability of the fossil fuel industry
Tech/corporate sustainability	Assertions that the long-term sustainability of the fossil fuel industry is ensured by ongoing technological innovations and/or other industry-driven initiatives
Petro-civilization	Assertions of continuing global demand for fossil fuels

Tier 3 frames

CSR (corporate social responsibility)	References to CSR in contexts other than sustainability (e.g., charitable gifts)
Industry news	News about policy and market trends and their impact on industry
Resource history	Historical accounts of fossil fuel industry
Low-carbon transition	Positioning of fossil fuel industry as essential in a low-carbon future
Non-FF nationalism	Expressions of nationalism not connected to the fossil fuel industry
Self-promotion	Promotion of a group's identity/brand, objectives, and/or achievements.

Tier 4 frame

Other	Any post that does not include the above frames

Two dominant frames in the sample—the representation of extractivism as a Canadian public good and attacking fossil fuel industry opponents—accounted for close to 40 percent of all posts (see table 7.7). Additional prominent frames included public support, ethical oil, mobilizing support, technologically-driven/corporate sustainability, and self-promotion. Comparing the proportion of posts ("Posts") to the proportion of engagement ("CEM") illustrates how different frames generated varying levels of engagement both in the overall sample and within particular groups: overall, Canadian public interest, attacks on opponents, energy lifeworld, ethical oil, and efforts to mobilize supporters produced strong levels of engagement, while public support and especially self-promotion were less successful (with some notable differences between groups).

Table 7.7. Percentage of weighted and unweighted frames

Primary frame	CEC		OR		OSA		OSS		Total	
	Posts	CEM	Posts	CEM	Posts	CEM	Posts	CEM	Posts	CEM
Canadian public interest	22.2	25.3	23.0	20.0	20.0	24.2	14.8	8.8	20.8	23.6
Public opinion/support	13.3	8.6	12.7	22.1	4.6	2.8	10.7	7.9	10.3	7.1
Attack on opponents	12.7	15.5	19.6	19.8	24.9	25.5	15.2	11.0	18.3	19.8
Energy lifeworld	2.7	1.4	4.0	3.5	2.7	7.4	0.0	0.0	2.7	4.0
Ethical oil	5.2	7.9	3.4	6.8	12.7	10.6	11.4	25.3	7.8	9.9
Indigenous peoples	0.9	1.0	0.4	0.2	4.0	2.3	4.8	2.2	2.2	1.5
Mobilizing supporters	14.9	21.0	6.2	8.8	0.2	0.1	6.9	12.7	7.3	10.8
Government sustainability	1.2	1.2	2.0	1.9	3.0	4.3	1.4	1.2	1.9	2.5
Tech/corporate sustainability	5.9	5.2	4.4	3.7	8.2	7.3	6.9	11.1	6.3	6.3
Petro-civilization	2.7	2.3	2.4	3.1	5.4	3.8	2.1	1.3	3.3	3.0
CSR	0.6	1.1	0.2	0.2	0.2	0.1	0.7	0.2	0.4	0.5
Industry news	4.2	2.9	2.9	2.3	0.3	0.1	1.4	1.9	2.4	1.6
Resource history	0.0	0.0	0.4	0.4	1.3	1.4	0.0	0.0	0.5	0.6
Low-carbon transition	0.1	0.0	0.2	0.1	0.3	0.1	0.3	0.1	0.2	0.1
Non-FF nationalism	0.1	0.1	0.2	0.0	3.2	1.9	2.8	3.5	1.4	1.0
Self-promotion	5.2	1.1	10.0	2.6	2.9	1.8	8.3	4.3	6.1	1.7
Other	8.1	5.7	8.2	4.6	6.3	6.4	12.4	8.6	8.2	6.0

Figures 7.2 and 7.3 provide a visual representation of the relative prominence of the significant frames in the sample. (CSR, resource history, and low-carbon transition are not included owing to their low frequency), the comparative significance of each group in mobilizing different frames, and differences between these groups' posting and engagement patterns. In the remainder of this section, we explore the most prominent frames in more detail to flesh out the vision of extractive populism developed in these groups.

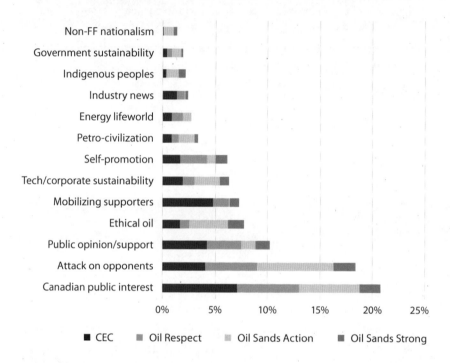

Figure 7.2. Frequency of frames (unweighted)

The *Canadian public interest* frame primarily emphasized the economic benefits of the fossil fuel industry to the country, including economic growth, employment, and taxation revenue. These benefits were described both abstractly, through statistics, and concretely, through allusions to the many Canadian families who depend upon the sector. In the latter case, the interactivity of social media was often leveraged to reinforce perceptions of collective dependence upon the sector while positioning this dependence as a source of national pride. For example, one meme featured an image of an oil pump set against an iconic backdrop of snow-capped mountains and invited readers, "Share if Canadian oil put food on your table" (CEC, July 11). The post was shared over fifteen thousand times.

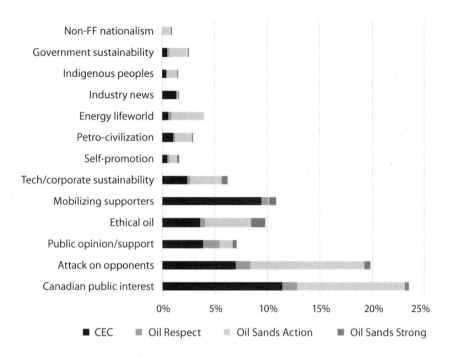

Figure 7.3. Frequency of frames (weighted)

Elsewhere, this process has been described as a form of *symbolic nationalization* (Gunster and Saurette 2014) in which a thoroughly capitalist enterprise organized to profit private corporations and shareholders is depicted as if it were a public endeavour that had been nationalized, oriented around serving the interests of citizens and the common good. Such a rhetorical strategy is profoundly hypocritical given the bitter and strenuous opposition of industry (and many of its supporters) to any attempt by federal and provincial governments to increase the public's share of revenues from the sector or reduce the negative ecological and health impacts of bitumen extraction and processing (Gunster and Saurette 2014).

These groups filled their social media with signifiers of Canadian national identity to make the case that oil and gas development is intrinsically Canadian.

Posts referenced iconic events, places, people, activities, and objects designed to invoke national pride and then graft these sentiments on to the fossil fuel sector. A strong performance by Team Canada at the Olympics, a national holiday, Vimy Ridge Day—these groups used any and all opportunities to fuse pride in Canada with pride in extractivism. This is symbolic and emotional terrain that these groups worked hard to claim as their own, advancing the case that a healthy oil and gas sector is itself part of what makes "us" Canadian (Barney 2017).

While this frame was generally celebratory and upbeat, it was at its most emotionally resonant when conveying stories of loss and hardship. OR's feed, in particular, was filled with posts emphasizing the lived experiences of unemployed workers harmed by a sectoral downtown that was framed as having predominantly political origins, namely, excessive regulation and the government's failure to facilitate pipeline expansion rather than the boom-and-bust cycle of global commodity markets and layoffs imposed by corporations. "More and more Canadians losing their jobs, homes and businesses," lamented one OR post, "while shovel ready projects sit waiting, and carbon levies and corporate taxes chase investment away" (OR, July 30). Pitting employment against environmental protection has long been a staple of pro-industry communication (Beder 2002), but the populist trope of standing up for embattled working-class families was a striking characteristic of this communication.

The *public opinion/support* frame recalls a key claim underlying CAPP's engagement initiatives: that most Canadians support oil and gas development but have been effectively silenced by a small but vocal minority of opponents. These groups advance this claim by highlighting sympathetic media stories that give play to the "silent majority" argument (for instance, "Chilliwack farmer says he's among silent majority in favour of oil pipelines," CEC, February 25) and trumpeting polls showing support for projects. Such posts not only aspire to legitimate oil and gas advocacy as representative of what most "ordinary" Canadians desire but also set the stage for a populist David and Goliath narrative, in which a naïve and helpless industry (and its employees) are victims of biased media that largely showcases opposition to extractivism.

One of the most distinctive elements of this frame are photos of people—both celebrities and non-celebrities—proudly wearing "I ♥ oil sands" merchandise. OSA and OSS showcased athletes from the Calgary Flames and the Calgary Stampeders displaying their apparent love for pipelines, oil sands, and Canadian energy (for example, OSA, January 22, February 25, and May

23). Several posts showed NDP MLAs from Alberta wearing OSA merchandise, including a well-travelled photo of then Alberta premier Rachel Notley posing with OSS founder Picard (OSA, March 4), implying that supporting industry ought to be viewed as a bipartisan cause.

Groups also sought to *mobilize supporters* to take specific actions: this was the third most engaging frame in the sample and especially prevalent in CEC posts. Readers were asked to contact elected officials to express support for projects, write letters to the editor, call in to talk shows, and participate in public hearings. The spectre of industry opponents dominating public reviews was invoked regularly. "You only have two days left!" warned an OR post linking to a survey from Natural Resources Canada. "So don't let radical environmentalists monopolize the TransMountain Expansion pipeline questionnaire. Have your say on Canadian jobs and natural resources" (OR, September 28).

Alongside calls to action were stories about "ordinary" Canadians engaged in the movement, helping to give supporters a sense of their collective power and responsibility to intervene in public debates around industry. Supporters were addressed not simply as individuals who benefit from or support resource development but as members of a collective movement whose actions (or inaction) would determine their community's future. At one level, this rhetoric serves the instrumental goal of getting people to do things. But it also aims to redefine extractivism as itself emerging from the democratic will of a social movement (and not corporate power and special interests). If enough supporters mobilized, the payoff would be government decisions such as the federal approval of the Trans Mountain Expansion project, portrayed as emanating from the activism of Canadian "energy citizens."

Failure to mobilize would abandon public and policy-making spheres to liberal elites and radical activists devoted to ending Canadian resource development. Measured in terms of both frequency and engagement, the *attack on opponents* frame was the second most prominent in the sample, accounting for just under 20 percent of overall posts and engagement. Fear-mongering about environmental groups and demonizing of industry opponents were pervasive in all four groups but especially dominant (and often intensely personalized and caustic) in OR and OSA. Actor and environmental advocate Leonardo DiCaprio was a favourite target because he enabled the symbolic condensation of all the negative attributes of industry critics into a single figure. Such criticism, the argument goes, is invariably rooted in wealthy, foreign, fear-mongering celebrities and elite organizations that attack Canada's industry while ignoring other producers or the role of consumer demand. Industry opponents were ridiculed as being ill informed about Canadian operations and hostile to the fate of Canadian workers. The storyline of Canada—or, more particularly, Alberta—as under attack from outside interests played extremely well for these groups and resonates with long-standing Alberta tropes of western alienation.

Canadian environmental organizations and activists generally received less attention than foreign celebrities and groups, presumably to avoid drawing attention to the fact that there are many within the country (even within Alberta) critical of how industry operates and is (or is not) regulated. Canadian environmentalists were consistently denigrated as "paid protesters," with posts framing domestic environmental NGOs as little more than the lackeys of wealthy US foundations, thereby positioning criticism itself as a foreign import. The arguments of commentator Vivian Krause that "the anti-pipeline machine is a 'directed, network campaign,' a new breed of professional, staged activism" (OSA, October 4) received much attention. Environmentalists were unequivocally presented as objects of ridicule and outrage who are either naïve and ill informed or as misanthropic, dangerous hypocrites who care little about workers, their families, and the broader Canadian economy. One post, a photo of smiling staff members from Greenpeace Canada, was prefaced with the assertion "Getting paid good money spreading misinformation while hurting Canadian family's [sic]!" (OSS, March 4). Industry critics appeared not as political opponents with whom one negotiates but instead as devious political enemies whose ideas and actions represent an existential threat to Canadian prosperity.

Both the *ethical oil* and *energy lifeworld* frames reinforced the argument that criticism of Canada's fossil fuel industry is unfair and irrational. The ethical oil frame—originally popularized by conservative activist and Rebel · Media founder Ezra Levant—defined global energy markets as offering a stark choice between authoritarian oil-producing regimes and a democratic Canada that respects human rights, the rule of law, and strong environmental regulation. "I want to know that the oil used in my car was not generated using slave labour in a country without a free press," one pro-industry blogger declared. "I want my oil being produced by well-paid Canadians in a country with a demonstrably free press, strong government oversight and a strong tradition of NGOs to watch over the regulator's shoulder" (OSA, January 30).

The ubiquity of oil in everyday life was the focus of the *energy lifeworld* frame. Although it played a comparatively small role in the sample as a primary frame, the theme was often present in posts that attacked opponents as hypocrites for condemning an industry that enabled their quality of life. A cartoon from the American Energy Alliance caricaturing a nude divestment protester's alarm once stripped of his oil-based clothing and accessories—presented as "an oldie but a goodie" by CEC—was shared over six thousand times (CEC, October 6). The most widely circulated item in the entire sample was a 2010 ad from Occidental Petroleum that likewise dramatized the shock of a suburban man experiencing the sudden disappearance of petroleum-based products from his life: it was shared nearly 77,000 times (OSA, December 12). Beyond the invocation of hypocrisy, such stark "life with oil" versus "life without oil" binaries helped shift discussion of extractivism out of the realm of politics and policy (where industry is vulnerable) and into the sphere of everyday life and personal consumption, in which it becomes so much harder to envision individually reducing one's fossil fuel dependence.

A final frame worth discussing given its emerging public significance is *Indigenous nations*. In contrast to their relentless denunciation of environmentalist opponents of the industry, these groups were almost entirely silent about Indigenous resistance to extractivism. CEC and OR, closely connected to key industry lobby groups and probably concerned about accusations of racism, were especially quiet on this topic, with fewer than ten posts between them (out of a total of more than twelve hundred). Recognition of Indigenous criticism would also have posed a serious narrative threat to storylines that emphasize the benefits to all of fossil fuel development, an unmitigated celebration of Canadian nationalism, and the demonization of opposition as foreign. Perhaps exploiting their greater rhetorical autonomy, OSA and OSS challenged conventional associations of Indigenous groups (especially First Nations) with opposition, instead arguing that most Indigenous people were themselves part of a silent majority of industry supporters and beneficiaries. The views of pro-industry Indigenous spokespeople such as Fort McKay Chief Jim Boucher and Métis Nation BC president Bruce Dumont were showcased, as were the sentiments of "ordinary" Indigenous supporters. Relevant memes celebrated the revenues from oil sands operations accruing to Indigenous businesses and suggested that Indigenous support for oil and gas development was much more widespread than opposition.

Conclusion

Given ongoing debates surrounding social media, populist discourse, and the polarization of Canadian energy politics, it is tempting to brush off extractive populism as "astroturf" or deride it as "fake news." Such dismissals, we argue, should be resisted insofar as they misrecognize the cultural and ideological force of these groups' political communications and strategy. A more urgent task is to understand how the skillful but partial assemblage of factual raw material by these groups constructs a world view that is simultaneously compelling and pernicious. The selective mining, framing, circulation, and amplification of decontextualized factoids has subsidized the formation of online and offline publics encouraged to (re)conceptualize extractivism not only as serving the public good but also as a fragile project that depends on political mobilization to save it from the insidious efforts of powerful, well-funded industry opponents.

Canadian extractive populism rests upon the presumption that all Canadians—as workers, as taxpayers, as consumers—benefit extensively, and equally, from fossil fuel development. The relentless circulation, via social media, of exaggerated claims and decontextualized statistics about royalties, equalization payments, and employment obscures the rationale for widespread regional opposition to projects such as Northern Gateway, Kinder Morgan, and Energy East. The groups who indulge in pro-industry rhetoric fail to mention, for example, that the vast majority of economic benefits from these projects would accrue to predominantly corporate actors outside the provinces where they would be built. Such narratives also belie how Indigenous and coastal communities, taxpayers, and workers would be forced to absorb the majority of ecological and economic risk from a spill or leak (Hoberg 2013). The inequities baked into these projects mirror the much deeper inequality that structures the oil sands industry in toto, in which low royalty and taxation rates, high capital intensity, and low employment intensity generate large corporate profits, comparatively modest (and unpredictable) state revenues, and a boom-and-bust cycle that provides little employment security to workers (Campanella 2012). Such a disproportionate allocation of benefits is hardly surprising within a regional political economy that has become subservient to the international oil industry (Adkin and Miller 2016), a condition that former Alberta provincial Liberal leader Kevin Taft (2017) has described as oil's "deep state."

In a similar vein, the conspiratorial depiction of industry criticism as emanating from a small number of foreign-funded and -controlled elite organizations both ignores and delegitimizes the broad popularity and grassroots organization of resistance to new pipeline and tanker projects in British Columbia, Québec, and other regions across Canada (Hoberg 2013). While some Indigenous leaders and communities are partners in resource extraction on their territories, such arguments willfully obscure the long history of Alberta First Nations opposing oil sands development in their traditional territories (Audette-Longo 2018). And they neglect the fierce opposition of many West Coast Indigenous communities to pipeline and tanker projects such as Northern Gateway or the Trans Mountain expansion.

Identifying and challenging the inaccuracies and omissions that constitute the monochromatic portrait of the fossil fuel industry offered by extractive populism is an essential task. We argue, however, that such critical work depends upon a substantive engagement with how and why extractive populism has begun to empower and motivate what industry sees as its natural constituency, transforming alienated workers and other pro-industry individuals into an engaged petro-public that can forcefully advocate for the sector in social media, everyday life, and the public sphere. Taking such groups seriously requires moving beyond simply dismissing them as astroturf or peddlers of fake news. The strength of these groups lies predominantly in their capacity to strategically cull and repurpose information from a wide variety of sources so as to generate compelling narratives that distort and misrepresent the structure of, degree of public support for, and negative externalities of the industry. Those seeking to build the political will for a rapid transition away from an extractivist economy would do well to think seriously about what makes these narratives attractive and how to develop compelling alternative visions organized around democracy, social justice, and sustainability.

Note

1. Intercoder reliability was measured through Krippendorff's alpha coefficient, based on coding a random selection of one hundred items from the sample. It was assessed at 0.894 for the post type variable and 0.877 for the primary frame variable, well above the 0.8 threshold normally required for consistency in content analysis (Krippendorff 2004). All posts in the smaller sample were also qualitatively analyzed by the first author to identify dominant themes, rhetorical strategies, and patterns of representation.

References

Adkin, Laurie E., and Byron Miller. 2016. "Alberta, Fossil Capitalism, and the Political Ecology of Change." In *First World Petro-Politics: The Political Ecology and Governance of Alberta*, edited by Laurie E. Adkin, 527–60. Toronto: University of Toronto Press.

Audette-Longo, Patricia H. 2018. "'Fighting the Same Old Battle': Obscured Oil Sands Entanglements in Press Coverage of Indigenous Resistance in the Winter of 1983." *Canadian Journal of Communication* 43, no. 1: 127–46.

Barney, Darin. 2017. "Who We Are and What We Do: Canada as a Pipeline Nation." In *Petrocultures: Oil, Politics, Culture*, edited by Sheena Wilson, Adam Carlson, and Imre Szeman, 78–119. Montréal and Kingston: McGill-Queen's University Press.

Battershill, Cody. 2018. Radio interview by Danielle Smith. *Danielle Smith Show*. CHQR. February 2, 2018. https://omny.fm/shows/danielle-smith/cody-battershill.

Beder, Sharon. 2002. *Global Spin: The Corporate Assault on Environmentalism*. White River Junction, VT: Chelsea Green Publishing.

Blevis, Mark, and David Coletto. 2017. "Matters of Opinion 2017: 8 Things We Learned About Politics, the News and the Internet." Abacus Data. February 7, 2017. http://abacusdata.ca/matters-of-opinion-2017-8-things-we-learned-about-politics-the-news-and-the-internet/.

BOE Report Staff. 2017. "Over 1,400,000 Users Visited the *BOE Report* in 2016." BOE Report. January 3, 2017. https://boereport.com/2017/01/03/over-1400000-users-visited-the-boe-report-in-2016/.

Campanella, David. 2012. *Misplaced Generosity: Update 2012—Extraordinary Profits in Alberta's Oil and Gas Industry*. Edmonton: Parkland Institute.

Cattaneo, Claudia. 2015. "Oilsands at a Crossroads: How the Next Chapter of Alberta's Oil Future—and Canada's Workhorse—Is a Big Unknown." *Financial Post*, September 24, 2015. https://business.financialpost.com/commodities/energy/oilsands-at-a-crossroad-how-the-next-chapter-of-albertas-oil-future-and-canadas-workhorse-is-a-big-unknown.

———. 2016. "As Oilsands Punished, Tanker Loads of Cheap Saudi Oil Sail into Canadian Ports Daily." *Financial Post*, February 9, 2016. http://business.financialpost.com/commodities/energy/as-politicians-gloat-about-climate-leadership-saudi-arabias-oil-is-dumped-in-canada.

Coyne, Todd. 2015. "How Social Media Is Changing the Debate on Energy Infrastructure Projects." *Alberta Oil*, February 2, 2015.

Cross, Philip. 2014. "CBC: Not the Public's Broadcaster After All." *Financial Post*, December 11, 2014. http://business.financialpost.com/opinion/cbc-not-the-publics-broadcaster-after-all.

Eisenstadt, Todd, Daniela Stevens Leon, and Marcela Torres Wong. 2017. "Does Prior Consultation Diminish Extractive Conflict or Just Channel It to New Venues? Evidence from a Survey and Cases in Latin America." Paper presented at the annual meeting of the Latin American Studies Association, Lima, Peru, May 1, 2017. https://www.academia.edu/33702778/Does_Prior_Consultation_Diminish_Extractive_Conflict_or_Just_Channel_It_to_New_Venues_Evidence_from_a_Survey_and_Cases_in_Latin_America.

Etam, Terry. 2016. "Saudi Oil Filling a New Brunswick Refinery—What Kind of Domestic Energy Policy Is That?" *BOE Report*, January 25, 2016. https://boereport.com/2016/01/25/saudi-oil-filling-a-new-brunswick-refinery-what-kind-of-an-energy-policy-is-that/.

Frank, Thomas. 2004. *What's the Matter with Kansas? How Conservatives Won the Heart of America*. New York: Henry Holt.

Gunster, Shane, and Robert Neubauer. 2018. "From Public Relations to Mob Rule: Media Framing of Social Licence in Canada." *Canadian Journal of Communication* 43, no. 1: 11–32.

Gunster, Shane, and Paul Saurette. 2014. "Storylines in the Sands: News, Narrative and Ideology in the Calgary Herald." *Canadian Journal of Communication* 39, no. 3: 333–59.

Hall, Stuart. 1988. "The Toad in the Garden: Thatcherism Among the Theorists." In *Marxism and the Interpretation of Culture*, edited by Cary Nelson and Lawrence Grossberg, 35–73. Champaign: University of Illinois Press.

Hislop, Markham. 2015. "Canada's Energy Citizens: Big Oil Fights Back vs. Big Green." *Oilfield Pulse*, May 21, 2015. http://www.oilfieldpulse.com/canadas-energy-citizens/#sthash.yBPEEUVP.dpbs.

Hoberg, George. 2013. "The Battle over Oil Sands Access to Tidewater: A Political Risk Analysis of Pipeline Alternatives." *Canadian Public Policy* 39, no. 3: 371–92.

Klein, Naomi. 2014. *This Changes Everything: Capitalism vs. the Climate*. Toronto: Knopf Canada.

Krippendorff, Klaus. 2004. "Reliability in Content Analysis: Some Common Misconceptions and Recommendations." *Human Communication Research* 30, no. 3: 411–33.

Linnitt, Carol, and Donald Gutstein. 2015. "'Grassroots' Canada Action Carries Deep Ties to Conservative Party, Oil and Gas Industry." *The Narwhal*, July 22, 2015. https://thenarwhal.ca/grassroots-canada-action-carries-deep-ties-conservative-party-oil-gas-industry.

Oliver, Joe. 2012. "An Open Letter from Natural Resources Minister Joe Oliver." *Globe and Mail*, January 9, 2012.

Saurette, Paul, and Shane Gunster. 2011. "Ears Wide Shut: Epistemological Populism, Argutainment and Canadian Conservative Talk Radio." *Canadian Journal of Political Science* 44, no. 1: 195–218.

Stanfield, Clara. 2015. "From Passive Endorsement to Active Engagement." *Context: CAPP's Member Magazine*, April 2015, 8–11.

Spooner, Deryck. 2015. "Harnessing Passion Through Grassroots." Presentation to the Canadian Association of Petroleum Producers, April 2015. https://www. slideshare.net/OilGasCanada/capp-presentation-draft-2.

Taft, Kevin. 2017. *Oil's Deep State: How the Petroleum Industry Undermines Democracy and Stops Action on Global Warming—in Alberta, and in Ottawa.* Toronto: James Lorimer.

Turner, Chris. 2012. "The Oil Sands PR War." *Marketing Magazine*, July 30, 2012. http://marketingmag.ca/advertising/the-oil-sands-pr-war-58235/.

Walker, Edward. 2014. *Grassroots for Hire: Public Affairs Consultants in American Democracy.* Cambridge: Cambridge University Press.

Wood, Tim. 2018. "Energy's Citizens: The Making of a Canadian Petro-Public." *Canadian Journal of Communication* 43, no. 1: 75–92.

8   Episodes in the New Climate Denialism

Shannon Daub, Gwendolyn Blue, Lise Rajewicz, and Zoë Yunker

Canada looks forward to playing a constructive role at COP 21. . . .
We have an opportunity to make history in Paris—an agreement
that supports a transition to a low-carbon economy that is necessary
for our collective health, security, and prosperity. Canada is back,
my good friends.

> Prime Minister Justin Trudeau, speaking on November
> 30, 2015 at the UN Climate Change Conference in Paris

No country would find 173 billion barrels of oil in the ground and
just leave them there. The resource will be developed.

> Prime Minister Justin Trudeau, speaking at the
> CERAWeek Global Energy and Environment Leader-
> ship Award Dinner in Houston, Texas, on March 9, 2017

Justin Trudeau and the Liberal Party swept to power in the October 2015 federal election amid much optimism about the prospects for renewed environmental leadership. Climate action was a centrepiece of Trudeau's campaign, which promised to rehabilitate Canada's international role during the Paris climate talks, bring in a national price on carbon, phase out fossil fuel subsidies, overhaul the National Energy Board (the country's national energy regulator), invest millions in clean technologies, and put a moratorium on oil tanker traffic on British Columbia's north coast.[1] While cagey on the issues of oil sands development and highly contentious proposed new pipelines to export Alberta bitumen, Trudeau's campaign nevertheless provided a stark contrast to the approach taken by incumbent Stephen Harper. Harper's Conservative government earned an international reputation for climate obstruction, aggressively pursued fossil fuel extraction with the aim of making Canada an "energy superpower" (Taber 2006), and labelled environmental groups a "threat" to "Canada's national economic interest" (Oliver 2012).

Within a year, however, the new Trudeau government approved a major liquefied natural gas (LNG) facility on British Columbia's north coast, green-lighted two major new oil sands pipelines, and directly acknowledged its intention to continue supporting expanded fossil fuel production. What explains this apparent contradiction? Is it a simple matter of crass political strategy—campaigning to win, with no intention to deliver? Or a case of corporate intervention behind the scenes to moderate the ambitions of a government committed to environmental protection? A closer look at the Trudeau government's policies and rhetoric suggests that both explanations miss the mark. Rather, the deployment of energetic talk of climate leadership and the adoption of greenhouse gas (GHG) reduction policies alongside an expansionary stance on fossil fuel production is, paradoxically, entirely consistent with an approach to climate change we call the "new denialism."[2]

Trudeau's ongoing commitment to climate policies and expanded oil and natural gas production is but one example of what we argue is a more nuanced and increasingly dominant approach to climate change by national governments and industry that profit from fossil fuel extraction. The new denialism is distinct from "traditional" denialism in that it eschews skepticism about anthropogenic climate change in favour of acceptance of climate science, while refusing to acknowledge the full implications of the science in terms of the public policies and societal changes required to prevent global temperature rise from producing catastrophic effects. The new denialism can be understood as both a discursive strategy and a substantive policy agenda that together sow confusion about the nature and scale of the policy transformations required to meet international climate targets, while normalizing market-based "solutions" and the inevitability of continued fossil fuel production.

What we refer to here as "traditional" climate denial has received significant attention in the scholarly literature. This scholarship, along with important work by investigative journalists and environmental NGOs, continues to expose the full scale of a concerted effort by the fossil fuel industry over the past four decades to "manufacture" uncertainty and controversy about climate science—that is, scientific evidence about the existence, severity, causes, and consequences of climate change—and the need to transition away from dependence on fossil fuels (see Dunlap and McCright 2015, 305–9). Thus far, however, the literature on climate change denialism has devoted relatively scant attention to organizations and institutions that embrace the scientific consensus on climate change, while continuing to support fossil fuel extractive practices or status quo policy approaches. A notable exception is an important study of the climate rhetoric and policies of conservative governments in Australia and Canada by Nathan Young and Aline Coutinho (2013) (see also Blue 2018; Bonds 2016; Levy and Spicer 2013; Methmann 2010). While the discourse of climate denial provides a useful approach for examining institutional resistance to implementing climate policy, one of our objectives in this chapter is to broaden the scope of climate denial and its dynamics. We do so in relation to Canadian responses to climate change where the populist-conservative ideology and movement driving the traditional denial industry in the United States have historically been relatively less powerful.

We begin by examining three recent "episodes" of the new denialism, all of which took place leading up to and following the Paris climate negotiations in December 2015. The first was the emergence of the Oil and Gas Climate Initiative (OGCI), which saw major fossil fuel corporations join together to advocate for an ambitious global climate agreement and the adoption of GHG reduction measures. The second was the development of provincial "climate leadership" plans in British Columbia and Alberta, during which the fossil fuel industry commented extensively about its policy preferences. And the third was the Trudeau government's decision to approve new oil sands pipelines, which coincided with the negotiation of the country's first national climate framework. We assess the implications of the policy stances adopted by industry and government actors in these episodes, compared with the outright rejection of policy action associated with traditional denial, and dig deeper into the similarities and differences between these two forms of denial.

Although what we call the "new denialism" is not a brand-new phenomenon, it has become an important mode of obstructing progress on climate action, particularly in Canada. As the ongoing push to expand production grows ever more indefensible in a period now widely recognized as a climate emergency, the fossil fuel industry and its political allies have increasingly turned to this strategy in an effort to preserve the status quo.

Episode 1: Oil and Gas Majors Call for Global Climate Action—More Than "Blah, Blah, Blah"?

The lead-up to the UN climate talks in Paris (otherwise known as COP21) in December 2015 was characterized by widespread optimism that a new international climate accord to limit GHG emissions could be reached. After the collapse of the 2009 climate negotiations in Copenhagen and the failure in subsequent rounds to reach a new deal, key global players were positioning themselves for a successful agreement (Darby 2015). Into this mix stepped six of the world's largest oil and gas corporations, with a May 2015 joint letter avowing their commitment to GHG reduction and calling on national governments to adopt carbon pricing systems in order to provide greater policy certainty to the fossil fuel industry and encourage the use of less carbon-intensive energy sources.[3] A few months later, an expanded group of ten majors issued a declaration through the OGCI supporting a global climate agreement and recognizing "the general ambition to limit global average temperature rise to 2 degrees centigrade" (OGCI 2015, 1).[4] Notably, the declaration dropped the call for carbon pricing, instead focusing on a carefully crafted list of other climate measures.

The options favoured by these oil and gas giants—including the initial inclusion of carbon pricing—are instructive, constituting an action plan that is typical of the new climate denial. These corporations' advocacy is anchored in a commitment to "reducing the GHG intensity of the global energy mix" (OGCI 2015, 1), meaning fewer GHGs emitted per unit of energy produced. A reduction in emissions intensity is not the same as an absolute reduction in emissions, however, the latter being the most basic and widely recognized policy implication of climate science. The OCGI declaration asserted that more energy is needed to support population and economic growth, while also noting that this energy "has to be provided in a sustainable and afford-able manner" (1). To this end, the signatory corporations planned to improve efficiency in their own oil and gas production, increase investment in natural gas (implicitly positioned as a relatively clean fossil fuel), invest in "R&D and technology innovation," and engage in partnerships with governments and civil society agencies (2). One of the signatories, Repsol CEO Josu Jon Imaz, argued that the commitments were meaningful: "This is not all blah, blah, blah. We are fully convinced that we can reduce CO2 emissions. We could be part of the problem, but we are convinced we are part of the solution" (quoted in Willsher 2015). Such optimism, expressed as belief or even faith in the power of market-based solutions to overcome the climate crisis, is typical of the new climate denialism.

The contradictions inherent in the OGCI member companies' efforts did not go unnoticed. A Greenpeace representative pointed out that "each and every one of them has a business plan that would lead to dangerous global temperature rises," adding that "arsonists don't make good firefighters" (quoted in Willsher 2015). A study by the UK watchdog group InfluenceMap supported Greenpeace's skepticism, finding that key OGCI members were "systematically obstructing" climate action through their active participation in trade associations that aggressively oppose efforts in the United States and European Union to bring in carbon pricing and GHG emissions regulations. (InfluenceMap 2015, 2). A senior executive with Total, for example, was found to be on the board of the American Petroleum Institute, among the most notoriously aggressive opponents of both climate science and policy (8). Similarly, BP and Shell were found to have close ties to numerous trade associations in the United States and Europe that have advocated against various climate initiatives.

The cases of BP and Shell are especially interesting, given their long-standing public acceptance of the imperative to act on climate change. In the lead-up to the 1997 Kyoto Protocol negotiations, both companies broke with their industry counterparts to proclaim support for a global climate agreement and announced a commitment to reduce their own GHG emissions (for detailed accounts of this history, see Levy and Spicer 2013; McCright and Dunlap 2003; Pulver 2007). Prior to the 2009 Copenhagen talks, as policy discussions about climate change once again intensified, a similar dynamic unfolded with the creation of the US Climate Action Partnership (USCAP), a coalition of large environmental NGOs and multinational corporations from a number of sectors including fossil fuels (BP, Shell, Duke Energy, and ConocoPhillips were among its members). USCAP advocated the adoption of a cap-and-trade system in the United States (Whittingham 2008). Given this pattern, the creation of the OGCI can be understood as part of a trajectory of pragmatic accommodation by a growing number of key industry players. This accommodation takes place amid a continuation of more direct obstructionism by the fossil fuel industry through their continued support for industry associations and right-wing think tanks that question the existence of anthropogenic climate change.

Episode 2: Climate Policy Development in British Columbia and Alberta—"Leadership" or "Social Licence" to Extract?

In 2015, with the Paris negotiations on the horizon, the provincial governments of British Columbia and Alberta each embarked on new "climate leadership" plans. The development of these policy frameworks offers a window into the dynamics of the new climate denialism in Canada. Both provinces are producer jurisdictions—with BC's fossil fuel industry driven by natural gas and coal extraction, and Alberta's by the exploitation of oil and gas (in addition to a declining coal sector). Climate policy featured prominently in the BC Liberal government's agenda from 2007 to 2009, most notably through the introduction of a widely lauded carbon tax.[5] By 2015, however, the government's enthusiasm for climate action had been eclipsed by the aggressive pursuit of an LNG industry as its primary economic development strategy, along with support for an expanded fracked gas sector. Alberta's approach to climate change has also varied considerably. Earlier Conservative provincial governments had vehemently opposed Canadian ratification of the Kyoto Accord and then adopted limited climate policies that proved largely ineffectual. The election of Alberta's first-ever New Democratic Party (NDP) government in 2015, however, put climate policy at the top of the province's agenda.

Each province appointed a multi-sector advisory panel tasked with making recommendations to government and established public-consultation processes in which fossil fuel corporations participated actively. We analyzed corporate submissions to these consultations to better understand the narrative strategies they used to frame climate change and shape policy responses.[6] While there were some differences between the submissions made in each province and within subsectors of industry, several dominant themes emerged.

All the submissions implicitly or explicitly acknowledged the reality of anthropogenic climate change, and all generally expressed a willingness to support some form of climate policy. Many submissions urged the provincial government in question to be a climate leader. However, the submissions also cautioned that a particular form of leadership was needed, one that "balanced" environmental and economic concerns. While couched in win-win terms, the notion that environmental protection and economic well-being must be balanced presumes that these imperatives are in tension and therefore represent trade-offs. Maintaining industry "competitiveness" was prescribed over and over as the key to good climate leadership, particularly for those sectors that rely on global export markets. Policies harmful to competitiveness were defined as imposing additional costs on industry (whether through regulatory measures or the imposition of direct costs such as higher taxes or royalties). Favoured means of ensuring competitiveness were reduced regulation or enhanced industry subsidies, particularly through support for "technology innovation" (such as the subsidization of hydroelectricity to power natural gas fracking and liquefaction in British Columbia and public spending for research and development on less-emissions-intensive bitumen extraction techniques in Alberta).

"Climate leadership" was also expressly positioned as essential to securing international exports for the two provinces' unconventional fossil fuels. Many of the submissions explicitly linked a desire to brand Alberta as a climate leader to industry's perceived need to rehabilitate the reputation of the oil sands in order to secure "social licence" for new pipelines and to expand international markets for bitumen exports.[7] In British Columbia, increased fossil fuel production was positioned as a climate solution, with LNG proponents and business associations positioning natural gas as a clean(er) energy source that should be subsidized and marketed as a transition fuel to help reduce coal consumption in Asia (a claim that does not stand up to scrutiny).[8]

Both provinces ultimately adopted plans that framed climate action in very similar terms. Substantively, Alberta's plan departed from the policy preferences expressed in many industry submissions by introducing an economy-wide carbon tax of $20 per tonne, a 100-megatonne (Mt) cap on total annual GHG emissions from oil sands production (which would allow production to grow by 45 percent over 2014 levels), and a phase-out of coal-fired electricity generation by 2030. These moves were nevertheless endorsed by four of the five largest oil sands producers in Alberta at the time, as well as by several prominent environmental and Indigenous leaders. Shell Canada's then-president called the plan "a turning point" that marked "the end of a chapter for Alberta, and for Canada, where the economy and the environment were at odds" (Mitchelmore 2015). In British Columbia, the provincial government opted to proceed with a plan that was couched in bold claims about climate leadership but that contained little by way of credible climate measures. The plan effectively abandoned the province's existing legislated GHG reduction targets, while promising to subsidize use of hydroelectricity in natural gas production and processing "to ensure that BC has the cleanest LNG in the world" (British Columbia 2016, 17).

Episode 3: New Pipelines and a National Climate Framework—"Like Paddles and Canoes"?

At the Paris climate talks in December 2015, Canada pledged to reduce emissions by 30 percent (below 2005 levels) by 2030 to help meet the goal of keeping global temperature rise below 2°C. On the eve of the Paris Accord's one-year anniversary, Prime Minister Trudeau announced his government's approval of two new oil pipelines: the Enbridge Line 3 and Kinder Morgan Trans Mountain expansion projects. Together, these two projects would increase net oil sands pipeline capacity by nearly one million barrels per day and add approximately 137 Mt of carbon to the atmosphere annually (Lee 2017b, 25, table 3). Nine days later, Trudeau announced the Pan-Canadian Framework on Clean Growth and Climate Change (Canada 2016), a plan negotiated with the provinces and territories that represents the means by which Canada intends to meet its Paris commitment. The plan established a national carbon price "floor" (leaving it to provinces to implement their preferred pricing system) along with a series of measures related to renewable energy, buildings, transportation, industrial emissions, and forestry and agriculture.

The contradiction between approving new pipelines and developing climate-mitigation policies is resolved discursively within the particular version of the new denialism espoused by the current federal government. Consider the following statements from Trudeau's pipeline announcement in November 2016:

> Voters rejected the old thinking that what is good for the economy is bad for the environment. They embraced the idea that we need strong environmental policies if we expect to develop our natural resources and get them to international markets.
>
> Canadians know that strong action on the environment is good for the economy. It makes us more competitive, by fostering innovation and reducing pollution. . . .

But we also know that this transition will take investment, and it won't happen in a day. We need to create good jobs and strong growth to pay for it. . . .

Our challenge is to use today's wealth to create tomorrow's opportunity. . . .

We said that major pipelines could only get built if we had a price on carbon, and strong environmental protections in place.

We said that Indigenous peoples must be respected, and be a part of the process. (Trudeau 2016)

The above statements highlight three key interrelated arguments that knit together Trudeau's (and his government's) particular brand of new climate denialism.

First is the explicit linking of environmental and economic performance. Trudeau's rhetoric contrasts with that of the fossil fuel industry in their submissions to the BC and Alberta government consultations (discussed in the previous section). Those submissions largely professed support for action on climate change in principle but positioned environmental and economic imperatives as trade-offs that must be balanced. In contrast, the environmentalism espoused by Trudeau presents economic and environmental concerns as inseparable, positioning climate policy as an "opportunity" to lead economies into a clean growth-driven future (Gaouette 2017). Or, as the prime minister put it in a pre-election speech, "The environment and the economy . . . go together like paddles and canoes" (quoted in Do 2015). (See chapter 17 in this volume for an in-depth examination of clean growth policy discourse.) Indeed, Trudeau and his colleagues argue that expanded fossil fuel production is essential to finance the transition to a low-carbon economy—meaning the royalty and tax revenues from growing production are needed to pay the costs of climate mitigation policies and infrastructure. Éric Pineault (2016) characterizes this logic as a northern version of the progressive extractivism seen in Latin American countries, where governments in recent decades have embraced extractive industries as a means to fund social services and poverty reduction. As he goes on to point out, it is a logic that sits comfortably with the fossil fuel industry and wider corporate elite because "even if it implies limits on carbon emissions, it forgoes adequate limits on hydrocarbon extraction. Which means the asset value of unconventional reserves is largely protected from climate policy."

Second, Trudeau explicitly positions climate policy as a means to make Canadian oil exports more viable by securing "social license." In Trudeau's eyes, the adoption of a national carbon price offers a means by which to neutralize opposition to oil sands pipelines by the environmental movement. The federal government's adoption of a leadership stance on climate change also aims to rehabilitate the international reputation of Alberta oil sands—which the campaigns of numerous environmental and Indigenous groups succeeded in tarnishing over the last decade—in order to secure export markets for Canadian heavy crude. This rationale is baldly captured in his November 2016 pipeline speech:

> And let me say this definitively: We could not have approved this project without the leadership of Premier Notley, and Alberta's *Climate Leadership Plan*—a plan that commits to pricing carbon and capping oilsands emissions at 100 megatonnes per year.
> . . . Alberta's climate plan is a vital contributor to our national strategy. It has been rightly celebrated as a major step forward by industry and the environmental community. (Trudeau 2016)

Finally, Trudeau's speech highlights the importance of "respecting" Indigenous peoples in the development of oil sands pipelines. Commitments to Indigenous rights featured prominently in the federal Liberal Party's 2015 election platform, which promised a "renewed, nation-to-nation relationship" and the implementation of the United Nations Declaration on the Rights of Indigenous Peoples (UNDRIP) (Liberal Party of Canada 2015, 46, 48). Article 32 of UNDRIP establishes the right of Indigenous peoples "to determine and develop priorities and strategies for the development or use of their lands or territories and other resources" and further that governments must "obtain their free and informed consent prior to the approval of any project affecting their lands or territories and other resources" (United Nations 2008, 12). As with climate policy, it appears the federal government hoped its adoption of a leadership stance on Indigenous rights would enable it to advance new pipeline projects. At the time of Trudeau's pipeline approval speech, more than one hundred First Nations and tribes had declared their opposition to any further expansion of oil sands development, including both the Trans Mountain and Line 3 pipeline projects.[9]

The government's claim to respect the legal and historic basis of Indigenous rights and title while refusing to accept what those rights mean in concrete policy terms represents a related form of denial. This variant of Indigenous rights denial goes hand in hand with the new climate denialism. While there is, sadly, an abundance of examples of governments failing to act on stated commitments to respect Indigenous rights in a wide range of policy areas, these rights seem to be most expendable when they run up against the interests of the fossil fuel corporate sector. Not to be outdone in the empty-endorsement sweepstakes, the industry has increasingly embraced Indigenous rights, in its own fashion. The Canadian Association of Petroleum Producers (CAPP 2016, 1), for example, purports to "endorse" UNDRIP "as a framework for reconciliation in Canada," yet it continues to vigorously advocate in favour of new oil sands development and pipelines.

The federal government's commitment to expanded oil sands production is so strong that in May 2018 it announced plans to buy the existing Trans Mountain pipeline from Kinder Morgan for $4.5 billion and take over the financing and building of the expansion project.

Discussion: Traditional Versus New Denialism—Potato/ Potato?

The episodes reviewed above describe a mode of denial that we contend is as problematic and dangerous as the outright rejection of climate science. Notwithstanding the accolades Canada received for its role in the Paris climate negotiations, the country's commitment under the Paris Agreement to reducing GHG emissions by 30 percent below 2005 levels by 2030 is the same target adopted by the blatantly obstructionist Harper government. The target itself has long been viewed as inadequate, and the measures contained in the Pan-Canadian climate framework are insufficient to meet even this target. The 2017 UN emissions gap report warned that, under current its policies, Canada would miss its nationally determined contribution (NDC) target "by a large margin" (UNEP 2017, 24).[10] As the report also points out, the collective pledges made by Paris signatories account for only one-third of the GHG reductions needed to avert catastrophic warming (xiv). Similarly, the 2019 emissions gap report lists Canada as one of six G20 countries that are likely to miss their 2020 reduction targets and as one of seven that "require further action" in order to meet their 2030 NDCs (UNEP 2019, 7, 8).

Despite ongoing proclamations by the prime minister and his cabinet colleagues about the importance of climate action, the notion that Canada can be a climate leader while expanding fossil fuel production is simply not tenable. David Hughes (2016) calculates that if Alberta oil sands production grows to the level allowed under the province's 100 Mt emissions cap and just one major LNG export terminal is built on British Columbia's coast to export fracked gas, fossil fuel sector emissions will balloon to nearly half of Canada's total allowable emissions by 2030 (as limited by the Paris target).

Traditional and new denialism thus have the same ultimate outcome, namely, to delay societal responses that are commensurate with the scale and urgency of the climate crisis. Nevertheless, the origins and operation of these two modes of denial differ significantly (see table 8.1). The organized effort to deny and/or cast doubt on the scientific certainty of human-caused climate change began in the late 1980s, as the issue initially captured the attention of policy makers and the public (Dunlap and McCright 2015; Oreskes and Conway 2011). Peter Jacques, Riley Dunlap, and Mark Freeman (2008) trace the origins of this effort back further, to the resurgence of the conservative movement in the United States in the 1970s in response to the societal changes and progressive social movements of the 1960s. They document the rise of an "anti-environmental counter-movement" (356), catalyzed by the emergence of environmentalism along with the associated problematization of industrial capitalism's ecological impacts and the adoption of environmental protection policies by governments. This countermovement promoted what Jacques, Dunlap, and Freeman call "environmental skepticism": an epistemological stance that rejects scientific knowledge about environmental problems and therefore their seriousness; challenges the need for environmental policies; eschews corporate responsibility for environmental problems via regulation or legal liability; and portrays environmental policies "as threatening Western progress" (354).

The driving force behind the climate denial movement in the United States has been a cadre of conservative think tanks—allied with fossil fuel corporations and industry groups (along with swaths of the wider corporate sector) and working in tandem with a vast network of conservative front groups, media pundits, bloggers, politicians, and contrarian scientists (Dunlap and McCright 2015; Jacques, Dunlap, and Freeman 2008; McCright and Dunlap 2003). Powered by funding from conservative foundations and wealthy right-wing elites (Brulle 2014; Mayer 2016), the denial counter-movement systematically undermines climate science by manufacturing uncertainty (attacking the validity of climate science and the credibility of climate scientists) and manufacturing controversy (promoting the myth of significant "debate and dissent within the scientific community") (Dunlap and McCright 2015, 308). Even though climate science naturally entails a measure of uncertainty, especially with regard to interpretation and prediction, climate denier groups make strategic use of this uncertainty in order to obstruct policy efforts to regulate industry. Jacques (2012, 11) argues that the denial movement's efforts have created a "science trap," in which "elites and masses cannot differentiate between authentic controversy in scientific literature and manufactured controversy outside of the literature."

Table 8.1. Traditional and new denialism compared.

Traditional climate denialism	New climate denialism
Rejects or casts doubt on the science of climate change	Accepts the science of climate change
Manufactures uncertainty and controversy about climate science (Dunlap and McCright 2015)	Manufactures confusion about the nature and extent of the policy and societal response needed to address climate change, allowing for the illusion of action
Fights mandatory GHG reductions and other climate policies	Accepts and advocates for mandatory or voluntary GHG reductions together with market-driven and demand-side policy measures such as carbon pricing, provided these don't impinge upon industry profits and assets (with exception of coal phase-out policies)
Reassures people in the face of threat to "ontological security" (Jacques 2012, 15)	Reassures people in the face of transformative societal changes that feel uncertain, unimaginable, or threatening
Is promoted especially by right-wing think tanks, along with other conservative-movement actors	Is promoted directly by fossil fuel corporations and governments, along with actors from a variety of ideological positions
Equates climate-change science with "an immanent critique of industrial power, Western modernity and the ideals of Western progress" and an "ontological threat to Western modernity" (Jacques 2012, 11)	Equates adequate climate-change action with a challenge to Western modernity and carboniferous capitalism *and* accepts Indigenous world views, rights, and title in principle but denies them in practice if they hinder business-as-usual
Adheres to the "exemptionalist paradigm" (Dunlap and McCright 2015; Foster 2012)	Adheres to the "new exemptionalism" and ecological modernization theory (Foster 2012)

Proponents of the new denialism diverge sharply by accepting the science of climate change and advocating an active policy response. Whereas the traditional climate denial movement seeks to camouflage its "true ideological and material objectives" by confusing the public about climate science (Jacques 2012, 11), proponents of the new denialism camouflage their objectives by promoting a limited agenda for action that does not threaten capital accumulation by the fossil fuel industry. The championing of modest climate-mitigation strategies by institutions and elites is a process that Chris Methmann (2010, 346) dubs the "mainstreaming of climate protection," one that leads to "paradoxical results": while references to the need for climate protection become widespread, "climate protection itself changes its meaning and becomes ambiguous." In making the meaning of climate action ambiguous, the new denialism allows industry and governments to create the illusion of action—whether through the adoption of voluntary emissions reduction measures or incremental policy action. Traditional and new denialism thus achieve similar results by limiting the scope of climate policy.

Drawing on the work of Kari Norgaard (2006; 2011), who has studied how everyday people participate in the "social organization" of climate denial, Jacques (2012, 15) notes that denial can function as a psychological strategy of self-protection in the face of the existential threat of climate change. In a similar vein, the comforting illusion of action may function to neutralize demand for more ambitious climate mitigation requiring deeper social transformations. In other words, the new denialism creates a policy trap, in which the public struggles to differentiate between effective policy responses that match the scale and severity of climate change and inadequate solutions that sound good but do little to address the problem.

The new denialism also diverges from the traditional mode in both degree of organization and ideological orientation. The traditional climate denial movement is an "extension" of the American conservative movement (Brulle 2014), though it reaches into and has counterparts in other 'developed' fossil-fuel producing countries like Canada and Australia (Dunlap and McCright 2015). Whereas "political conservatism is the hegemonic glue that binds" the climate denial movement together (Dunlap and McCright 2010), new denialism is more disparate and cannot really be characterized as a movement per se, though it is more generally aligned with liberal ideology and its proponents. Traditional denialism espouses the "exemptionalist paradigm"—the belief that human ingenuity and technology exempt capitalist industrial society from ecological constraints (Catton and Dunlap 1980; Dunlap and McCright 2015). New denialism is instead rooted in the "new exemptionalism" of policy discourses founded on ecological modernization theory (Blue et al. 2018; Foster 2012), which attempt to reconcile contradictions between industrial capitalist economies and the environmental damage they cause. In this paradigm, climate change is understood as a serious problem that must be addressed, but primarily via technological and market-based fixes (for example, carbon capture and storage, carbon pricing), while leaving corporate power largely intact. Adherence to ecological modernization is typical of contemporary liberal political movements, as well as more progressive strains of conservativism, particularly in Canada.

Given Canada's similar-yet-different political culture vis-à-vis the United States, it is not surprising that new denialism has played a particularly strong role in the country's history of engagement with climate change. As Young and Coutinho (2013) remind us, it was Brian Mulroney's government that made Canada one of the first countries to commit to GHG reductions. Even so, the negotiation of the UNFCCC in the early 1990s and subsequent Kyoto Protocol in 1997 triggered a backlash from the corporate elite, building to a crescendo of opposition as the federal government moved slowly toward formal ratification of the Kyoto Accord. The opposition movement was led by an informal coalition of powerful business groups: the Business Council on National Issues (now the Business Council of Canada), the Canadian Manufacturers and Exporters Association, the Canadian Chamber of Commerce, and the Canadian Association of Petroleum Producers (Macdonald 2007). Together they challenged the need for action and the scale of the GHG reductions that Canada's Kyoto commitment entailed, relying especially on exaggerated claims about "catastrophic consequences" and casting doubt on the "certainty" of climate science (Canadian Manufacturers and Exporters 2002; Chase 2002; Marshall 2002). The federal Liberal government of Jean Chrétien ultimately ratified the accord in 2002 but proceeded to do little else. Indeed, given decades of lip service to targets but little concrete action by both Liberal and Conservative governments (Lee 2017a; Simpson, Jaccard, and Rivers 2008), one could argue that Canada has pioneered the new denialism.[11]

An Era of New Denialism?

The new denialism has emerged as a strategic effort to proactively define the solutions to climate change in a manner that mitigates the threat of action, to protect not only the interests of producer industries and governments but also the larger economic regime. As we have discussed, the new denialism's roots stretch back to the 1990s, but we suggest that as the impacts of climate change worsen and become more visible to larger numbers of people, it is becoming an increasingly dominant mode of obstruction. In this sense, we may be entering an "era" of new denialism—within Canada and in other Western producer jurisdictions.[12]

Even within the conservative movement in the United States, where adherence to traditional climate denial has long been a "litmus test" for Republican political hopefuls (Dunlap and McCright 2015, 300), the new denialism is gaining ground. In 2017, for example, a group of corporations, NGOs, political leaders, and prominent thinkers launched the Climate Leadership Council, whose founding members included ExxonMobil, Shell, BP, and the Nature Conservancy.[13] One of its first publications, authored by a team of prominent Republicans, was titled *The Conservative Case for Carbon Dividends: How a New Climate Strategy Can Strengthen Our Economy, Reduce Regulation, Help Working-Class Americans, Shrink Government, and Promote National Security.* The document proposed a gradually increasing national carbon tax, whose revenues would be returned to Americans as dividend cheques, ostensibly justifying, in turn, the elimination of wide swaths of regulation, including "much of the EPA's regulatory authority over carbon dioxide emissions" (Baker et al. 2017, 3). While such policy would not be taken up by the Trump administration, its emergence is nevertheless notable.

It is important to clarify that, while we may be in an era of new denialism, the "new" and "traditional" modes of climate denial are not fundamentally at odds, nor do we see evidence to suggest that traditional denial efforts will disappear. Instead, these modes reinforce each other and structure climate politics around an apparent divide between the reactionary conservative-populist forces of outright denial, on one side, and a more progressive-leaning incremental agenda for action, on the other.

David Levy and André Spicer (2013) identify three key periods of struggle over responses to climate change: the "carbon wars" (1990s), a "carbon compromise" (1998–2008), and a "climate impasse" (2009–13). We propose a fourth period of "climate contradiction." This current period is increasingly dominated by the new denialism, while also characterized by sharpening contestation over fossil fuel extraction. We see these dynamics reflected in movements for fossil fuel corporate accountability in Western producer countries. These movements are supported by a mounting body of research that focuses on the urgent need to curtail fossil fuel production (see, for example, Heede 2014; Lee 2017b; McGlade and Ekins 2015; Muttitt 2016), and they explicitly call out the fundamental illogic of the new climate denialism. As Bill McKibben (2017), of the climate action group 350.org, points out, "Trudeau says all the right things, over and over. . . . But those words are meaningless if you keep digging up more carbon and selling it to people to burn."

Notes

1. For Trudeau's "Clean Environment" platform, see Liberal Party of Canada (2015, 39–44); see also Hayward (2015). Canada had first pledged to phase out fossil fuel subsidies in 2009, at the G20 summit in Pittsburgh.

2. The idea of the new climate denialism was first outlined by Seth Klein and Shannon Daub (2016). Our colleague Marc Lee (2015) had earlier called the approach "all of the above" policy making.

3. The letter—dated May 29, 2015, and signed by representatives of the BG Group, BP, Eni, Royal Dutch Shell, Statoil, and Total—is available at https://www.shell.com/media/news-and-media-releases/2015/oil-and-gas-majors-call-for-carbon-pricing/_jcr_content/par/textimage_1.stream/1441316901849/0faacac1359323824 43c58c83c1d575dc85ff382/letter-to-unfccc.pdf.

4. The ten corporations were BG Group, Eni, Pemex (Petróleos Mexicanos), Reliance Industries, Repsol, Royal Dutch Shell, Saudi Aramco, Statoil, and Total.

5. Chapter 9 in this volume offers an in-depth look at the evolution of British Columbia's climate policies under the BC Liberal Party, including the involvement of industry in their development. The BC Liberal Party is a coalition of conservatives and liberals and is more aggressively neoliberal in its policy stances than the federal Liberal Party of Canada, with which the provincial party is not affiliated.

6. The sample of submissions (BC n = 17, AB n = 37) from fossil fuel corporations, other GHG-intensive industrial corporations, and general business groups was analyzed using an iterative coding scheme to identify key themes. For a more detailed discussion of methodology and findings, see Blue et al. (2018).

7. On social licence, see Prno and Slocombe (2012). The term refers to the need to secure local community acceptance for extractive projects.

8. J. David Hughes (2015, 7) found that, in view of the substantial methane emissions associated with the production and transport of LNG, "BC LNG exports to China would increase GHG emissions over at least the next fifty years, compared to building state-of-the-art coal plants." Further, there is no guarantee that BC LNG would displace coal-powered electricity generation, rather than simply adding to total energy consumption (see Lee 2017b).

9. Indigenous peoples have expressed their opposition through the Treaty Alliance Against Tar Sands Expansion: http://www.treatyalliance.org/. As of April 30, 2018, the number of signatories had grown to 150. "Signatory Nations," Treaty Alliance Against Tar Sands, April 30, 2018, http://www.treatyalliance.org/wp-content/uploads/2018/04/TAATSE-SignatoryNations-EN-R12-20180430-OL.pdf.

10. On the inadequacy of Canada's targets, both current and historical, see also "Canada," Climate Action Tracker, n.d., accessed December 5, 2018, https://climateactiontracker.org/countries/canada/.

11. For a detailed discussion of the factors that led to Canada's early divergence from the United States on climate policy, see Harrison (2007), Macdonald (2007), and Young and Coutinho (2013).

12. On the concept of climate "eras," see Dunlap and McCright (2015).

13. The Climate Leadership Council announced its formation by taking out a full-page advertisement in the *Wall Street Journal*: see https://www.clcouncil.org/founding-members/. The ad listed the initial members, although, since then, "founding" members have continued to be added.

References

Anderson, Kevin, and Alice Bows. 2012. "A New Paradigm for Climate Change." *Nature Climate Change* 2, no. 9: 639–40. https://doi.org/10.1038/nclimate1646.

Baker, James A., III, Martin Feldstein, Ted Halstead, Gregory N. Mankiw, Henry M. Paulson Jr., George P. Shultz, Thomas Stephenson, and Rob Walton. 2017. *The Conservative Case for Carbon Dividends*. Washington, DC: Climate Leadership Council. https://www.clcouncil.org/wp-content/uploads/2017/02/TheConservativeCaseforCarbonDividends.pdf.

Blue, Gwendolyn. 2018. "Scientism: A Problem at the Heart of Formal Public Engagement with Climate Change." *ACME: An International Journal for Critical Geographies* 17, no. 2: 544–60.

Blue, Gwendolyn, Shannon Daub, Zoë Yunker, and Lise Rajewicz. 2018. "In the Corporate Interest: Fossil Fuel Industry Input into Alberta and British Columbia's

Climate Leadership Plans." *Canadian Journal of Communication* 43, no. 1: 93–110. https://doi.org/10.22230/cjc.2018v43n1a3309.

Bonds, Eric. 2016. "Beyond Denialism: Think Tank Approaches to Climate Change." *Sociology Compass* 10, no. 4: 306–17.

British Columbia. 2016. *Climate Leadership Plan*. Victoria: Province of British Columbia. https://www2.gov.bc.ca/assets/gov/environment/climate-change/action/clp/clp_booklet_web.pdf.

Brulle, Robert J. 2014. "Institutionalizing Delay: Foundation Funding and the Creation of U.S. Climate Change Counter-Movement Organizations." *Climatic Change* 122, no. 4: 681–94. https://doi.org/10.1007/s10584-013-1018-7.

Canada. 2016. *Pan-Canadian Framework on Clean Growth and Climate Change*. Ottawa: Government of Canada. http://publications.gc.ca/collections/collection_2017/eccc/En4-294-2016-eng.pdf.

Canadian Manufacturers and Exporters. 2002. *Pain Without Gain: Canada and the Kyoto Accord*. Ottawa: Canadian Manufacturers and Exporters.

CAPP (Canadian Association of Petroleum Producers). 2016. *Discussion Paper on Implementing the United Nations Declaration on the Rights of Indigenous Peoples in Canada*. April 26, 2016. Calgary: Canadian Association of Petroleum Producers. https://www.capp.ca/wp-content/uploads/2020/01/CAPP-Discussion-Paper-on-Implementing-the-United-Declaration-on-the-Rights-of-Indigenous-Peoples-in-Canada_354411.pdf.

Catton, William R., and Riley E. Dunlap. 1980. "A New Ecological Paradigm for Post-Exuberant Sociology." *American Behavioral Scientist* 24, no. 1: 15–47.

Chase, Steven. 2002. "Ratifying Kyoto Estimated to Cost up to 450,000 Jobs." *Globe and Mail*, February 27, 2002. https://www.theglobeandmail.com/report-on-business/ratifying-kyoto-estimated-to-cost-up-to-450000-jobs/article18286832/.

Coulthard, Glen Sean. 2014. *Red Skin, White Masks: Rejecting the Colonial Politics of Recognition*. Minneapolis: University of Minnesota Press.

Darby, Megan. 2015. "'I'm Pretty Optimistic'—Lead US Climate Lawyer on Paris Talks." *Climate Home News*, January 26, 2015. http://www.climatechangenews.com/2015/01/26/us-top-climate-lawyer-overcoming-the-firewall/.

Do, Trinh Theresa. 2015. "Justin Trudeau's Environment Plan: End Fossil Fuel Subsidies, Invest in Clean Tech." *CBC News*, June 29, 2015. http://www.cbc.ca/news/politics/justin-trudeau-s-environment-plan-end-fossil-fuel-subsidies-invest-in-clean-tech-1.3131607.

Dunlap, Riley E., and Aaron M. McCright. 2010. "Climate Change Denial: Sources, Actors and Strategies." In *Routledge Handbook of Climate Change and Society*, edited by Constance Lever-Tracey, 240–59. Abingdon, UK: Routledge.

————. "Challenging Climate Change: The Denial Countermovement." In *Climate Change and Society: Sociological Perspectives*, edited by Robert Brulle and Riley E. Dunlap, 300–32. New York: Oxford University Press.

Foster, John Bellamy. 2012. "The Planetary Rift and the New Human Exemptionalism: A Political-Economic Critique of Ecological Modernization Theory." *Organization and Environment* 25, no. 3: 211–37. https://doi.org/10.1177/1086026612459964.

Gaouette, Nicole. 2017. "Trudeau Issues Rallying Cry for Climate Fight." *CNN*. September 21, 2017. https://www.cnn.com/2017/09/21/politics/trudeau-canada-unga-remarks/index.html.

Harrison, Kathryn. 2007. "The Road Not Taken: Climate Change Policy in Canada and the United States." *Global Environmental Politics* 7, no. 4: 92–117. https://doi.org/10.1162/glep.2007.7.4.92.

Hayward, Jonathan. 2015. "Trudeau Promises to Safeguard Northern B.C. Coast from Pipelines." *Globe and Mail*, September 10, 2015. https://www.theglobeandmail.com/news/politics/trudeau-promises-to-safeguard-northern-bc-coast-from-pipelines/article26317327/.

Heede, Richard. 2014. "Tracing Anthropogenic Carbon Dioxide and Methane Emissions to Fossil Fuel and Cement Producers, 1854–2010." *Climatic Change* 122, no. 1–2: 229–41. https://doi.org/10.1007/s10584-013-0986-y.

Hughes, J. David. 2015. *A Clear Look at BC LNG: Energy Security, Environmental Implications and Economic Potential.* Vancouver: Canadian Centre for Policy Alternatives, BC Office. https://www.policyalternatives.ca/publications/reports/clear-look-bc-lng.

————. 2016. *Can Canada Expand Oil and Gas Production, Build Pipelines and Keep Its Climate Change Commitments?* Ottawa: Canadian Centre for Policy Alternatives; Edmonton: Parkland Institute. http://www.corporatemapping.ca/can-canada-expand-oil-and-gas-production-build-pipelines-and-keep-its-climate-change-commitments/.

InfluenceMap. 2015. *Big Oil and the Obstruction of Climate Regulations.* London: InfluenceMap. https://influencemap.org/site/data/000/103/InfluenceMap_Oil_Sector_October_2015.pdf.

Jacques, Peter J. 2012. "A General Theory of Climate Denial." *Global Environmental Politics* 12, no. 2: 9–17. https://doi.org/10.1162/GLEP_a_00105.

Jacques, Peter J., Riley E. Dunlap, and Mark Freeman. 2008. "The Organisation of Denial: Conservative Think Tanks and Environmental Scepticism." *Environmental Politics* 17, no. 3: 349–85. https://doi.org/10.1080/09644010802055576.

Klein, Seth, and Shannon Daub. 2016. "The New Climate Denialism: Time for an Intervention." *Policy Note* (blog). Canadian Centre for Policy Alternatives, BC

Office. September 22, 2016. http://www.policynote.ca/the-new-climate-denialism-time-for-an-intervention/.

Lee, Marc. 2015. "Real Test of Paris Climate Agreement Will Be How Markets and Regulators React." *Policy Note* (blog). Canadian Centre for Policy Alternatives, BC Office. December 13, 2015. https://www.policynote.ca/real-test-of-paris-climate-agreement-will-be-how-markets-and-regulators-react/.

———. 2017a. "Canada Is Still a Rogue State on Climate Change." *Behind the Numbers* (blog), December 11, 2017. http://behindthenumbers.ca/2017/12/11/canada-still-rogue-state-climate-change/.

———. 2017b. *Extracted Carbon: Re-examining Canada's Contribution to Climate Change Through Fossil Fuel Exports*. Ottawa: Canadian Centre for Policy Alternatives; Edmonton: Parkland Institute. https://www.policyalternatives.ca/publications/reports/extracted-carbon.

Levy, David L., and André Spicer. 2013. "Contested Imaginaries and the Cultural Political Economy of Climate Change." *Organization* 20, no. 5: 659–78. https://doi.org/10.1177/1350508413489816.

Liberal Party of Canada. 2015. *Real Change: A New Plan for a Strong Middle Class.* https://www.liberal.ca/wp-content/uploads/2015/10/New-plan-for-a-strong-middle-class.pdf.

Macdonald, Douglas. 2007. *Business and Environmental Politics in Canada.* Toronto: University of Toronto Press.

Marshall, Dale. 2002. *Making Kyoto Work: A Transition Strategy for Canadian Energy Workers.* Ottawa: Canadian Centre for Policy Alternatives. https://www.policyalternatives.ca/publications/reports/making-kyoto-work.

Mayer, Jane. 2016. *Dark Money: The Hidden History of the Billionaires Behind the Rise of the Radical Right.* New York: Penguin Random House.

McCright, Aaron M., and Riley E. Dunlap. 2003. "Defeating Kyoto: The Conservative Movement's Impact on U.S. Climate Change Policy." *Social Problems* 50, no. 3: 348–73. https://doi.org/10.1525/sp.2003.50.3.348.

McGlade, Christophe, and Paul Ekins. 2015. "The Geographical Distribution of Fossil Fuels Unused When Limiting Global Warming to 2°C." *Nature* 517, no. 7533: 187. https://doi.org/10.1038/nature14016.

McKibben, Bill. 2017. "Stop Swooning over Justin Trudeau: The Man Is a Disaster for the Planet." *Guardian*, April 17, 2017. http://www.theguardian.com/commentisfree/2017/apr/17/stop-swooning-justin-trudeau-man-disaster-planet.

Methmann, Chris Paul. 2010. "'Climate Protection' as Empty Signifier: A Discourse Theoretical Perspective on Climate Mainstreaming in World Politics." *Millennium* 39, no. 2: 345–72. https://doi.org/10.1177/0305829810383606.

Mitchelmore, Lorraine. 2015. "Shell Canada President: Why Our Industry Got Behind Alberta's Carbon Plan." *Globe and Mail*, November 25, 2015. https://

www.theglobeandmail.com/report-on-business/rob-commentary/shell-canada-president-why-our-industry-got-behind-albertas-carbon-plan/article27465831/.

Muttitt, Greg. 2016. *The Sky's Limit: Why the Paris Climate Goals Require a Managed Decline of Fossil Fuel Production*. Washington, DC: Oil Change International. http://priceofoil.org/2016/09/22/the-skys-limit-report/.

Norgaard, Kari Marie. 2006. "'We Don't Really Want to Know': Environmental Justice and Socially Organized Denial of Global Warming in Norway." *Organization and Environment* 19, no. 3: 347–70.

———. 2011. *Living in Denial: Climate Change, Emotions, and Everyday Life*. Cambridge, MA: MIT Press.

OGCI (Oil and Gas Climate Initiative). 2015. "OGCI Joint Collaborative Declaration." February 16, 2015. http://oilandgasclimateinitiative.com/wp-content/uploads/2017/10/ogci-ceo-Declaration-2015.pdf.

Oliver, Joe. 2012. "An Open Letter from Natural Resources Minister Joe Oliver." *Globe and Mail*, January 9, 2012. https://www.theglobeandmail.com/news/politics/an-open-letter-from-natural-resources-minister-joe-oliver/article4085663/.

Oreskes, Naomi, and Erik M. Conway. 2011. *Merchants of Doubt: How a Handful of Scientists Obscured the Truth on Issues from Tobacco Smoke to Global Warming*. New York: Bloomsbury.

Pineault, Éric. 2016. "Welcome to the Age of Extractivism and Extreme Oil." *National Observer*, May 18, 2016. https://www.nationalobserver.com/2016/05/18/opinion/welcome-age-extractivism-and-extreme-oil-%C3%A9ric-pineault.

Prno, Jason, and D. Scott Slocombe. 2012. "Exploring the Origins of 'Social License to Operate' in the Mining Sector: Perspectives from Governance and Sustainability Theories." *Resources Policy* 37, no. 3: 346–57. https://doi.org/10.1016/j.resourpol.2012.04.002.

Pulver, Simone. 2007. "Making Sense of Corporate Environmentalism: An Environmental Contestation Approach to Analyzing the Causes and Consequences of the Climate Change Policy Split in the Oil Industry." *Organization and Environment* 20, no. 1: 44–83. https://doi.org/10.1177/1086026607300246.

Simpson, Jeffrey, Mark Kenneth Jaccard, and Nic Rivers. 2008. *Hot Air: Meeting Canada's Climate Change Challenge*. Toronto: Emblem.

Taber, Jane. 2006. "PM Brands Canada an 'Energy Superpower.'" *Globe and Mail*, July 15, 2006. https://www.theglobeandmail.com/news/world/pm-brands-canada-an-energy-superpower/article1105875/.

Trudeau, Justin. 2016. "Prime Minister Justin Trudeau's Pipeline Announcement." November 29, 2016. http://pm.gc.ca/eng/news/2016/11/30/prime-minister-justin-trudeaus-pipeline-announcement.

UNEP (United Nations Environment Programme). 2017. *Emissions Gap Report 2017*. Nairobi: United Nations Environment Programme. http://wedocs.unep.org/bitstream/handle/20.500.11822/22070/EGR_2017.pdf?sequence=1&isAllowed=y.

———. 2019. *Emissions Gap Report 2019*. Nairobi: United Nations Environment Programme. https://wedocs.unep.org/bitstream/handle/20.500.11822/30797/EGR2019.pdf?sequence=1&isAllowed=y.

United Nations. 2008. *United Nations Declaration on the Rights of Indigenous Peoples*. New York: United Nations. http://www.un.org/esa/socdev/unpfii/documents/DRIPS_en.pdf.

Whittingham, Ed. 2008. *The US Climate Action Partnership: A Novel, Pragmatic Alliance for Promoting Legislative Action on Climate Change*. Drayton Valley, AB: Pembina Institute. http://www.pembina.org/reports/US_Climate_Action_Partnership.pdf.

Willsher, Kim. 2015. "Oil Companies Deny That Joint Climate Pledge Is Lip Service." *Guardian*, October 16, 2015. https://www.theguardian.com/environment/2015/oct/16/oil-companies-deny-that-joint-climate-pledge-is-lip-service.

Young, Nathan, and Aline Coutinho. 2013. "Government, Anti-Reflexivity, and the Construction of Public Ignorance About Climate Change: Australia and Canada Compared." *Global Environmental Politics* 13, no. 2: 89–108.

9   "Doing Things Better Together"

Industry Capture of Climate Policy in British Columbia

Shannon Daub, Chuka Ejeckam, Nicolas Graham, and Zoë Yunker

In the Canadian political imaginary, British Columbia is often thought of as the country's "Left Coast" or "Lotus Land." Indeed, BC's political culture has a long-standing progressive bent, and the province has a rich history of activism and resistance driven especially by Indigenous, labour, environmental, and other movements. British Columbia is arguably the heartland of environmentalism in Canada, home to many high-profile leaders and organizations. Opposition to oil sands pipelines is fierce, particularly in coastal regions, with mass mobilizations and civil disobedience organized by Indigenous, environmental, and local citizen-driven groups underway against the Trans Mountain Expansion (TMX), along with legal challenges by First Nations. But the province is also the country's second-largest producer of fossil fuels, primarily natural gas and coal (Natural Resources Canada 2019, 5). Natural gas production has soared in BC since the mid-2000s, driven largely by unconventional gas extraction using hydraulic fracturing (fracking) in the province's northeast region, and industry aspires to establish a liquefied natural gas (LNG) export sector in the coastal regions. Moreover, industry and the provincial government have aggressively pursued the construction of natural gas extraction sites, pipelines, and other infrastructure on the traditional territories of Indigenous peoples without gaining their free, prior, and informed consent. As a result, the province has a complicated relationship with respect to both climate policy and Indigenous rights and title that belies its progressive image.

The tension between curbing greenhouse gas (GHG) emissions, on the one hand, and a growing and politically powerful fossil fuel industry, on the other, can be readily seen in British Columbia's engagement with climate policy. The province enjoys an international reputation as a climate leader, thanks largely to its introduction of North America's first carbon tax in 2008.[1] The carbon tax was the centrepiece in a suite of policies developed at that time by the BC Liberal government under then-Premier Gordon Campbell.[2] In the years following, however, the BC Liberal government's enthusiasm for meaningful climate policy waned, overtaken by enthusiasm for developing an LNG industry, particularly under Premier Christy Clark (who took over from Campbell in 2011 and held the office until 2017).

This chapter examines industry capture as a key factor in British Columbia's turn away from substantive climate action. We briefly review different concepts of capture and provide an overview of the province's climate-policy trajectory from the late 2000s to 2017. We then focus on two interrelated arenas of capture—political donations and lobbying by the fossil fuel industry and closed-door joint policy making by industry and government officials—and conclude with reflections on the prospects for democratizing energy politics in British Columbia.[3]

Conceptualizing Capture

"Capture" is a simple and powerful concept that refers to the subversion of the public interest in democratic processes or institutions by vested private interests. A wide range of scholarship deals with issues of capture, notably theories of regulatory capture developed primarily by American political scientists and economists beginning in the mid-twentieth century. These scholars grappled with the tendency of regulatory agencies (and often legislators) to become unduly influenced by the very interests that are subject to regulation.[4] More recently, the global financial crisis in 2008–9 and the Deepwater Horizon oil spill in 2010 contributed to a resurgence of interest in regulatory capture and related ideas such as institutional corruption. Lawrence Lessig (2013, 553) defines institutional corruption as a "systemic and strategic influence which is legal, or even currently ethical, that undermines the institution's effectiveness by diverting it from its purpose or weakening its ability to achieve its purpose, including . . . weakening either the public's trust in that institution or the institution's inherent trustworthiness." Developed within the fields of ethics and law, the concept of institutional corruption reminds us that all varieties of capture ultimately represent problems of political corruption and, further, that many forms of political corruption are not illegal.

In discussing the enduring utility of the idea of capture, Daniel Carpenter and David Moss (2014, 8–9) note that research in this field nevertheless lacks a clear standard for "detecting and measuring" capture. Carpenter (2014, 63) argues that in order to diagnose capture, empirical study "needs (a) to posit a defensible model of public interest, (b) to show action and intent by the regulated industry, and (c) to demonstrate that ultimate policy is shifted away from the public interest and toward industry interest." The current chapter utilizes these tests in assessing the trajectory of BC climate policy.

A further limitation of regulatory capture theory is that it often fails to deal critically with larger questions of how political institutions and practices are shaped by the economic system in which regulation is created. Much of this literature originates within neoclassical economics, which has, perversely, viewed capture as an argument for deregulation rather than more robust intervention by government in the public interest (see, for example, Stigler 1971).[5] Particularly with respect to the governance of natural resources, left perspectives, such as analyses of staples-based economies and theories about rentier and petro-states, instead treat capture as a systemic problem in historically resource-dependent capitalist economies. Kevin Taft (2017, 117) argues, for example, that in fossil fuel producer jurisdictions, multiple democratic institutions may be captured by one interest over a prolonged period, leading to the development of a deep state—that is, an "unofficial system of government that arises separately from, but is closely connected to, the official system." These more critical approaches shift our attention from relatively isolated examples of capture toward the broader problem of state capture (see, for example, Adkin 2016; Carter 2018; Drache 2014; Haley 2011; MacNeil 2014).

Climate Policy in British Columbia: A Brief History

BC's Climate Moment, 2007–9

British Columbia's engagement with climate policy is relatively recent. In the early 2000s, the BC Liberal government under Premier Gordon Campbell resisted federal efforts to implement the Kyoto Protocol and had no climate framework or other significant measures aimed at reducing GHG emissions. That started to change in 2007, when Campbell led his government through an about-face and made climate action a central focus of its agenda. The Greenhouse Gas Reduction Targets Act, passed in November 2007, legislated ambitious GHG emissions reduction targets (33 percent below 2005 levels by 2020 and 80 percent below by 2050). A few months later, the 2008 BC budget announced a new carbon tax, starting at $10 per tonne of GHGs and rising to $30 per tonne by 2012, applied to the burning of fossil fuels (British Columbia, Ministry of Finance 2008, 1). A flurry of activity followed, including the development of the full 2008 Climate Action Plan (British Columbia 2008) and the establishment of a Climate Action Secretariat to coordinate policy implementation across ministries and public agencies.

The introduction of a carbon tax launched British Columbia into the international spotlight ahead of the 2009 Copenhagen climate talks. There were significant problems in its design, however, and the overall policy agenda was limited. The principle of "revenue neutrality" built into the carbon tax meant its revenues were completely offset by personal and corporate income tax cuts, making corporations and upper-income earners net beneficiaries despite having the largest ecological footprints (Lee and Sanger 2008). Moreover, this approach meant carbon tax revenues could not be invested into related green initiatives such as expanded transit or transition plans for rural regions. Notably, the carbon tax did not cover emissions from natural gas production (emissions from agriculture and cement making were also exempt). In addition, much of the government's progress toward its interim GHG reduction target was to be achieved through the purchase of offsets, rather than by actual reductions in emissions (Lee 2017).

Reactions within British Columbia to the new climate plan varied widely and mostly focused on the carbon tax. Environmentalists were thrilled to see a long-sought policy measure realized, and most voiced enthusiastic support. The opposition New Democratic Party (NDP) was initially vehemently opposed on the grounds that the carbon tax would ostensibly penalize rural and northern residents while favouring business. The corporate sector itself responded in generally positive, if cautious, terms (with some exceptions, such as the trucking industry). That a significant advance in climate policy would be greeted without any real fuss by business elites was a reflection of the plan's substantive limitations, summarized above. Reaction to the plan also reflected the long-standing political alignment between the corporate sector and the BC Liberal Party, which describes itself as a "free enterprise coalition."

BC's Climate Retreat, 2011–16

No significant further actions were taken in the years following the 2008 Climate Action Plan, and when Christy Clark took over as premier in 2011, she showed little interest in her predecessor's legacy. Under her watch, the provincial government froze the carbon tax at $30 per tonne, claiming that it negatively impacted BC businesses and taxpayers. The government also created a highly favourable tax and regulatory regime geared to establishing an LNG industry on British Columbia's coast that would liquefy gas piped from the northeast extraction region for shipment overseas. In 2012, the government introduced both its Natural Gas Strategy and its Liquefied Natural Gas Strategy. These policy frameworks were refined and expanded in 2013 when the government also created a new Ministry of Natural Gas Development. In an effort to entice LNG developers despite poor global market conditions, in 2014 the province lowered and then locked in a near-negligible LNG tax rate for twenty-five years and introduced a corporate income tax credit for LNG producers and other industry subsidies. Also in 2014, the government introduced the Greenhouse Gas Industrial Reporting and Control Act, which replaced BC's cap-and-trade system for regulated emitters with emissions intensity targets (GHGs per unit of production)—effectively enabling the industry's total emissions to rise substantially. Developed and released through the Ministry of Environment, the new GHG regulations were branded as a climate initiative (British Columbia, Ministry of Environment 2016).

Facing criticism for its backslide on climate policy, and with the Paris climate talks approaching, the provincial government announced in May 2015 that it would develop a new climate plan. A "Climate Leadership Team" (CLT) was struck, composed of representatives from First Nations, local government, industry, the provincial government, and environmental organizations. The CLT was tasked with developing recommendations on how British Columbia could meet its existing legislated GHG reduction targets for 2020 and 2050. The CLT was, however, required to ensure that its recommendations could accommodate the province's LNG strategy and Jobs Plan—two policy frameworks that implied significant increases in industrial emissions—signalling a limited desire for substantial new measures from the outset.

In the summer of 2015, the provincial government released a Climate Leadership Plan discussion paper and launched a public consultation process. That fall, the CLT's thirty-two recommendations were released, which the CLT noted should be taken together as a cohesive package (BC Climate Leadership Team 2015, 7). The most significant recommendation was to increase the carbon tax by $10 per tonne every year starting in 2018 and expand it to cover all GHG emissions after five years (with the exception of methane from natural gas production, provided industry reached a 40% voluntary reduction target in the meantime). The CLT also called for targeted support for "emissions intensive trade exposed industries"; changes to the low-income and rural/northern tax credits; measures to improve the energy efficiency of buildings and reduce vehicle emissions; and for the public hydro utility (BC Hydro) to provide "clean electricity" to the natural gas sector for both upstream production and LNG. This last policy, also called "electrification," is a means to reduce the emissions intensity of both fracking and liquefaction, which are extremely energy-intensive and otherwise rely on burning natural gas for power.

Overall the recommendations represented a very modest package (not surprisingly, given the constraints imposed on the CLT by the provincial government). Nevertheless, a broad range of environmental and other groups urged the provincial government to adopt the recommendations. Instead, however, the province embarked on further consulation while delaying the release of its draft new climate plan, saying little in the meantime about its intentions with respect to the CLT recommendations. The new plan (British Columbia 2016) was eventually released in August 2016, many months later than promised. The plan did not fully take up any of the CLT's recommendations, with the partial exception of electrification of natural gas production—effectively a major industry subsidy geared to facilitating increased production and to supporting the government's dubious claim that British Columbia was poised to become "one of the world's cleanest producers and distributors" of natural gas (15).

British Columbia's failure to adopt a meaningful climate policy along with its enthusiastic support for fracking and LNG were significant issues in the 2017 provincial election, which the long-governing BC Liberal Party lost. The close relationship between the provincial government and its corporate donors (in particular the fossil fuel industry) and the absence of any limits on political contributions figured centrally during the election campaign.

Political Capture

Two of the most obvious ways that corporations pursue capture is through donations to political parties and lobbying of public officials. Political contributions can be thought of as "interested gifts" for which corporations expect general policy returns (Ansolabehere, de Figueiredo, and Snyder 2003; Brownlee 2005, 137). At worst, such contributions represent "a form of legal bribery" (Etzioni 2009, 323) or sanctioned corruption. Until 2017, there were no limits on political donations by corporations, unions, or individuals in British Columbia, including foreign contributions. Political donations help secure access to key decision makers and therefore function in tandem with or may be considered as part of the lobbying process (McMenamin 2012), the fundamental purpose of which is policy capture (Miller and Harkins 2010).

Lobbying in British Columbia is governed by the Lobbyists Registration Act. The act places modest restrictions on who may lobby but does not limit the volume of lobbying an organization or individual may conduct. As of 2010, the act requires lobbyists to register and to report whenever they communicate with (or intend to communicate with) a public official in a lobbying effort—information that is publicly reported via the Office of the Registrar of Lobbyists—but the amount of detail that must be disclosed about meetings with officials is fairly minimal (date, public official targeted, public body they are associated with, and a brief summary of the nature of the issues discussed).[6]

Fossil Fuel Industry Political Donations, 2008–16

Using Elections BC's Financial Reports and Political Contributions System, we examined fossil fuel industry donations to the provincial Liberals and NDP between 2008 and 2016. This eight-year period covers the three election cycles that occurred during the climate policy period reviewed above and also corresponds to the rapid increase in natural gas production that began in 2008–9. Forty-eight fossil fuel companies and industry groups donated a total of $5,789,141 to the two parties over this period, 90 percent of which ($5,279,906) went to the BC Liberals. Ten fossil fuel industry donors (see table 9.1) accounted for more than three-quarters (77 percent) of total donations, with the two top firms—mining giant Teck Resources and natural gas major Encana—contributing more than half of this amount.

Among these top ten donors, there is a distinct geography of giving, with the majority of firms headquartered in Calgary, Alberta. Notably, the Canadian Association of Petroleum Producers (CAPP)—the country's most powerful oil and gas lobby group—gave over $128,100. Only two of the companies—Teck Resources and FortisBC—are headquartered in BC, and one company—Spectra Energy—was headquartered in the United States (Spectra was purchased by Enbridge in the fall of 2016). Chevron Canada and Imperial Oil are, however, foreign-controlled subsidiaries of US-based parent companies.

Table 9.1. Top ten fossil fuel industry political donors, 2008–16

	BC Liberals	BC NDP	Total	Head-quarters	Primary activity
Teck Resources	$1,646,794	$61,440	$1,708,234	Vancouver	Mining (diversified)
Encana	$976,716	$72,565	$1,049,281	Calgary	Oil and gas production
CNRL	$254,200	$5,500	$259,700	Calgary	Oil and gas production
Spectra Energy[a]	$252,005	$53,620	$305,625	Houston	Oil and gas production
Terasen / FortisBC[b]	$249,812	$79,090	$328,902	Surrey	Gas distribution
Enbridge	$213,115	$11,550	$224,665	Calgary	Oil and gas transport
Chevron Canada	$170,443	$11,315	$181,758	Calgary and Vancouver	Oil and gas production and retail
Pristine Power / Veresen[c]	$137,475	—	$137,475	Calgary	Gas transport and distribution
Imperial Oil	$134,790	$4,000	$138,790	Calgary	Oil and gas production and retail
CAPP	$113,175	$14,925	$128,100	Calgary	Oil and gas lobby group
Total political donations	$4,148,525	$314,005	$4,462,530		

Source: Financial Reports and Political Contributions System, BC Elections, https://contributions.electionsbc.gov.bc.ca/pcs/Welcome.aspx. Figures do not include donations made by individuals (such as executives, board members, and paid lobbyists) associated with these companies or with CAPP.

[a] Donations from Spectra Energy in 2016 predate its merger with Enbridge.

[b] FortisBC supplies both electricity and gas. The gas distribution arm of the company was known as Terasen Gas until 2011, when it was renamed FortisBC Energy Inc.

[c] In November 2010, Pristine Power was acquired by Fort Chicago Energy Partners LP, which changed its name to Veresen at the start of 2011. Veresen is now owned by Pembina Pipeline, another Calgary-based corporation.

Looking beyond these top ten, we see that newly formed LNG operators made significant donations starting in the early 2010s. Pacific NorthWest LNG (a consortium of foreign energy corporations, led by Malaysian state-owned Petronas, that until 2017 was seeking to build a massive LNG export plant on BC's north coast), Prince Rupert Gas Transmission (owned by Calgary-based TransCanada and created to build a pipeline to transport gas from northeast British Columbia to the Pacific NorthWest LNG terminal), Woodfibre LNG (owned by the Singapore-based RGE group of companies, which is controlled by Indonesian tycoon Sukanto Tanoto), and Steelhead LNG gave combined contributions of $160,400 to the BC Liberals and $55,350 to the BC NDP between 2014 and 2016. Progress Energy, a wholly owned subsidiary of Petronas and one of the top fracking operators in northeast British Columbia, gave $100,250 to the BC Liberals between 2010 and 2013. TransCanada gave $105,400 to the BC Liberals between 2008 and 2016 (over 70 percent of which was contributed since 2012).

Fossil Fuel Industry Lobbying, 2010–16

We conducted an exhaustive search of the Lobbyists Registry and found forty-three fossil fuel corporations and industry groups with registered lobbying efforts between April 2010 and October 2016.[7] Of these forty-three, the ten most active accounted for more than three-quarters of the lobbying by the fossil fuel sector. Together, they reported a total of 19,517 lobbying contacts with BC public office holders between 2010 and 2016, an average of fourteen lobbying contacts per business day.

Substantial overlap was uncovered between giving and lobbying, with seven of the top ten political donors also ranking among the ten most active lobbyists (see table 9.2). The amount of lobbying by environmental NGOs pales in comparison: only eight such organizations were registered as active lobbyists, reporting a total of 1,324 contacts over the same period.

Almost half (48 percent) of lobbying contacts were with staff at ministries (such as deputy ministers) and government agencies. The central lobbying targets were the Ministry of Energy and Mines, the Ministry of Natural Gas Development, and the Ministry of Environment. The BC Oil and Gas Commission also figured prominently: the registry data show 984 contacts by the ten most active firms. The Ministry of Aboriginal Relations and Reconciliation, the Ministry of Finance, and the Ministry of Forests, Lands and Natural Resources also attracted considerable attention. It is striking how many lobbying ties led to the Ministry of Environment, whose responsibilities ought to be quite distinct from those of industry-focused ministries (like Energy and Mines), which typically facilitate business investment.[8]

Table 9.2. Ten most active fossil fuel industry lobbyists, 2010–16

Organization	Contacts with ministries or agencies	Contacts with cabinet ministers	Contacts with MLAs	Total
Spectra Energy	936	1,176	2,230	4,342
Enbridge	1,318	1,006	186	2,510
FortisBC	1,234	438	705	2,377
Encana	1,405	784	76	2,265
Chevron Canada	1,348	834	74	2,256
CAPP	1,546	127	175	1,848
Teck Resources	267	318	953	1,538
TransCanada	457	355	190	1,002
Cenovus	547	240	27	814
CEPA	393	151	21	565
Total	9,451	5,429	4,637	19,517

Source: Active and terminated lobbyists, Lobbyists Registry, Office of the Registrar of Lobbyists for BC, April 2010–October 2016.

Note: Figures include both actual and planned contacts.

Cabinet ministers were also frequently targeted, accounting for 28 percent of contacts by the ten most active lobbyists. Rich Coleman, minister of Natural Gas Development, was the most frequently targeted, with the ten firms reporting a total of 733 contacts—an average of nearly three contacts per week for Coleman alone. The next most often contacted were Premier Christy Clark (618 contacts), Minister of Energy and Mines Bill Bennett (437), Minister of Environment Mary Polak (354), and Minister of Finance Mike de Jong (330).

The remaining 24 percent of contacts were with members of the Legislative Assembly (MLAs). Spectra Energy and Teck Resources were particularly active at this level: in contrast to the rest of the top ten, the majority of their total lobbying contacts were with MLAs. This focus on elected representatives may reflect the nature of their business operations, which are spread throughout the province. Both NDP and Liberal MLAs were heavily targeted. This was especially the case for two leaders of the BC NDP, Adrian Dix and

John Horgan (the latter is now premier), who were among those most often contacted.

Oil and gas industry associations play an important role in lobbying efforts. Associations like CAPP and the Canadian Energy Pipeline Association (CEPA) are central to the network of lobbyists and are far more active than other resource and manufacturing associations in the province. Of particular note, CAPP reported 201 expected lobbying contacts with government ministers and agencies in relation to development of the provincial government's Climate Leadership Plan between October 2015 and August 2016. Alex Ferguson, former commissioner and CEO of the BC Oil and Gas Commission (whose tenure ended in 2011), reported lobbying his former organization nineteen times on behalf of CAPP.

As noted earlier, Carpenter (2014, 63) argues that to diagnose capture, researchers must demonstrate both "action and intent by the regulated industry." The massive political donations and lobbying documented above do so unequivocally. Further, even the limited reporting on lobbying activities required under British Columbia's Lobbyists Registration Act reveals the explicit intentions of fossil fuel corporations and industry groups—for example, to "promote the establishment of a new LNG export industry in BC" (CAPP) and to "advocate for provincial climate change and greenhouse-gas reduction policies and strategies that fully recognize the cost implications for industry" (Chevron Canada). Of course, intentions are not the same as outcomes, given that they do not guarantee favourable results. However, as we detail in the following section, an unparalleled level of direct industry influence in the policy-making process served to weaken the already relatively modest climate action options under consideration.

Institutional Capture

As we have seen, when the provincial government embarked on the creation a new climate plan in 2015, it established a process that began with the appointment of a Climate Leadership Team and included two phases of public consultation. The first phase took place following the July 2015 release of a discussion paper that outlined the full process (see figure 9.1), along with the goals and action areas on which the government wished to focus (British Columbia 2015). The discussion paper was prepared by the Climate Action Secretariat, which was housed within the Ministry of Environment and responsible for developing and monitoring provincial climate policy. The discussion paper made no mention any special role for the corporate sector—though after releasing the CLT recommendations in the fall of 2015, the government stated that it would carry out further consultation with the public and industry before releasing its draft climate plan.

To ascertain how the fossil fuel industry sought to influence the new climate plan (beyond participation in the formal public consultations), we submitted a series of seventeen requests under BC's Freedom of Information and Protection of Privacy Act. The requests, made over a fourteen-month period, were directed to a number of agencies, primarily the Ministries of Environment, Natural Gas Development, and Energy and Mines. Our initial requests focused specifically on the development of the climate plan in 2015 and 2016, while several subsequent requests broadened the scope in an effort to learn how industry and government interacted more generally on policy and regulation related to the energy sector over that period of time and beyond. The requests yielded 2,055 pages of records (more than a hundred additional pages were withheld under various exemptions in BC's FOI act). Here we highlight two key findings from our review of the records.

First, the records reveal that the provincial government undertook an elaborate closed-door policy development process with the fossil fuel industry alongside the second phase of its official public consultations. A January 2016 document from the Ministry of Natural Gas Development titled *Climate Leadership Team Recommendations: Consultation with Oil and Gas Industry* provides an overview of the structure and aims of this parallel process.[9] As the document reveals, this was much more than a "consultation" exercise. Rather, oil and gas corporations were invited to participate in a series of meetings over several months to directly shape the provincial Climate Leadership Plan (see figure 9.2). The meetings were structured around three working groups, each focused on a key policy concern of industry: the carbon tax, methane and fugitive emissions, and electrification (that is, the provision of hydroelectricity for natural gas extraction and liquefaction). The document outlined the "tangible deliverables" each working group was to achieve. Regarding the carbon tax, these included "Determine 'the art of the possible' (how much and how fast)." For the groups working on methane and other emissions and on electrification, deliverables included "Add detail and policy direction (timing / voluntary vs. regulatory tools)" and "Refine language in CLT recommendation."

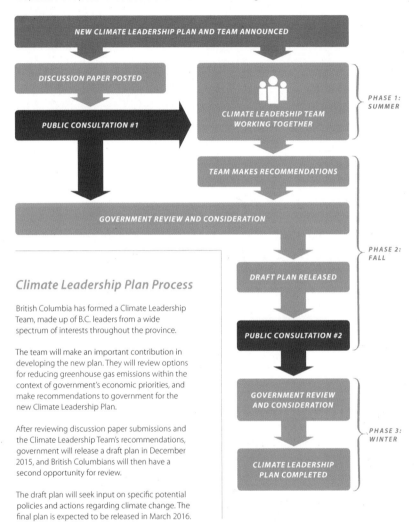

THE CLIMATE LEADERSHIP PLAN PROCESS
This process will help determine the actions needed to reach our climate goals.

NEW CLIMATE LEADERSHIP PLAN AND TEAM ANNOUNCED

DISCUSSION PAPER POSTED

PUBLIC CONSULTATION #1

CLIMATE LEADERSHIP TEAM WORKING TOGETHER

PHASE 1: SUMMER

TEAM MAKES RECOMMENDATIONS

GOVERNMENT REVIEW AND CONSIDERATION

PHASE 2: FALL

DRAFT PLAN RELEASED

PUBLIC CONSULTATION #2

GOVERNMENT REVIEW AND CONSIDERATION

PHASE 3: WINTER

CLIMATE LEADERSHIP PLAN COMPLETED

Climate Leadership Plan Process

British Columbia has formed a Climate Leadership Team, made up of B.C. leaders from a wide spectrum of interests throughout the province.

The team will make an important contribution in developing the new plan. They will review options for reducing greenhouse gas emissions within the context of government's economic priorities, and make recommendations to government for the new Climate Leadership Plan.

After reviewing discussion paper submissions and the Climate Leadership Team's recommendations, government will release a draft plan in December 2015, and British Columbians will then have a second opportunity for review.

The draft plan will seek input on specific potential policies and actions regarding climate change. The final plan is expected to be released in March 2016.

Figure 9.1. BC's official climate policy process. Source: British Columbia (2015, 4)

Consultation with Upstream Oil and Gas Industry on B.C.'s Climate Leadership Plan (CLP)

Phase 1: CLP Framework
Timeline: December 2015 – February 2016

- Working Groups
  - WG 1: Carbon Tax/Trade-expose
    - Chair:
    - Members:
  - WG 2: Fugitives/Offsets
    - Chair:
    - Members:
  - WG 3: Electrification
    - Chair:
    - Members:

- Meetings:
  - December 8, 2015: Launch – Meeting in Calgary with DM & ADM MNGD and CAS
  - Week of December 14: CAPP to determine membership of WGs
  - December 14 – January 11: CAPP and members work internally to provide feedback and start modelling as needed
  - Week of January 11: First batch of meetings
    - WG 1: starts deliberations / modelling needs
    - WG 2: fugitives language / start offsets conversation
    - WG 3: electrification language
  - Week of January 25th:
    - WG 1: continue discussions / modelling results / start language
    - WG 2: finalize language / continue offsets conversation
    - WG 3: finalize language
  - Week of February 8th:
    - WG 1: finalize language
    - WG 2 + WG 3: join to work on offsets
    - Plenary: DM meeting in Calgary
  - Week of February 22nd:
    - Wrap up

Phase 2: CLP Tools Design
Timeline: Spring 2016 – Spring 2017

Figure 9.2. BC's unofficial climate policy process

With tangible Deliverables
Working Group 1: Carbon Tax

- Competitiveness analysis
- Explore EI-TE* approaches
- Ensure consistency with other jurisdictions
- Determine "the art of the possible" (how much and how fast)

*EI – TE: Energy Intensive – Trade Exposed sectors

With tangible Deliverables
Working Group 2: Methane and Fugitives

- Refine language in CLT recommendation
- Add detail and process direction (timing / voluntary vs. regulatory tools)
- Make tangible commitments

With tangible Deliverables
Working Group 3: Electrification

- Work collaboratively with BC Hydro
- Refine language in CLT recommendation
- Add detail and process direction (timing / voluntary vs. regulatory tools)

The meetings themselves were co-organized by the BC government and the Canadian Association of Petroleum Producers, and all took place in CAPP's boardroom in Calgary. Participants included deputy ministers and other senior BC government officials from the Ministry of Environment and the Ministry of Natural Gas Development and representatives from oil and gas corporations and industry groups. To date, we have obtained the list of industry participants for only one of the meetings, on January 13, 2016, which included at least sixteen different fossil fuel corporations and industry groups, including the BC LNG Alliance (which also had a seat on the official Climate Leadership Team), Canadian Natural Resources Limited (CNRL), Chevron Canada, ConocoPhillips, Encana, Imperial Oil, Nexen Energy, Progress Energy, Shell Canada, Suncor, Teck Resources, Woodfibre LNG, and, of course, CAPP. Of the sixteen industry organizations present at that one meeting, only four had *not* made political donations to the BC Liberal Party in recent years.

This closed-door joint policy development process, carried out with the industry most directly implicated by climate policy, represents a clear case of the variety of capture that ethicists call institutional corruption. Handwritten notes made by the executive director of the Climate Action Secretariat during the January meeting include several troubling comments that reinforce this diagnosis:

> "CLT recommendations just that—government can take or leave"
> "Doing things better together"
> "Deliverables: wording that could go into a climate plan"
> "Overall competitiveness is the Big Picture that comes even before carbon tax and climate change."

No other sector was afforded this kind of direct hand in the policy-making process, and, in personal communications with the authors, two CLT members indicated that they were unaware it had taken place.

When these documents were made available to the public and media, industry and government representatives professed surprise at the outcry that resulted. With regard to the location of the meeting, Rich Coleman, the minister of Natural Gas Development at the time, argued there was nothing to be concerned about. "Our folks responsible for climate action were sent to consult with everybody," he stated, and the meetings took place in Calgary "because that's where all their head offices are" (quoted in Woodward 2017).

A vice-president with CAPP similarly characterized the meetings as a typical approach to consulting with a key stakeholder, describing the choice of meeting location as "as simple logistics thing" (Uechi 2017). Extensive follow-up FOI requests show that the government carried out proactive consultations with a variety of other corporate sectors, such as the mining, automotive, trucking, renewable energy, and energy technology industries, as well as with municipal governments, but nothing equivalent with environmental groups, First Nations, or scientists.

Taft (2017, 118) observes that, in a deep state, "captivity becomes normal," meaning that it becomes an inherent part of the state's institutional culture. Our FOI requests illustrate the extent to which capture had become commonplace within the Ministries of Natural Gas Development, Energy and Mines, and Environment. These requests revealed, for example, that senior BC government officials routinely travelled to Calgary to meet with fossil fuel corporations and industry organizations. More than a hundred such meetings took place between January 1, 2015, and September 18, 2017, ranging from meetings with a single company regarding matters of particular concern to sectoral meetings on issues such as the development of a new caribou habitat plan and ongoing "working group" sessions on methane emissions and electrification of natural gas. During his tenure as minister of Natural Gas Development, even Coleman travelled to Calgary to "meet with CAPP members" on July 12, 2016—little more than a month before the government's Climate Leadership Plan was released.

Email communication records also show that powerful industry groups like CAPP, the Mining Association of British Columbia, and the BC LNG Alliance enjoyed routine, casual access to government officials, including deputy ministers. In 2016, for example, two emails from the Mining Association of British Columbia communicated displeasure with the province's carbon tax regulations, prompting a flurry of emails from two officials in different ministries rushing to arrange a meeting with the association. Such meetings frequently entailed coordination across multiple ministries, usually including five to ten different staff members, along with the development of background materials or briefing notes, hinting at the massive amount of publicly funded resources that government expends liaising and working with industry.

In other correspondence, public officials communicated how strongly they valued industry's close relationship with government. An internal Ministry of

Environment document pertaining to a half-day meeting in June 2015 between CAPP and a number of deputy ministers included a recommended response to CAPP's concern about "how upstream industry participates in Climate 2.0": "The Ministry and CAS [the Climate Action Secretariat] are prepared to meet with the sector as and wherever necessary." In a similar vein, a meeting note prepared for a September 2015 meeting between the environment minister and CAPP suggests that the minister should convey the message that "the province values the ongoing partnership with CAPP, and the individual companies in the oil and gas sector, on climate change policy development."

CAPP is among the ten most active fossil fuel industry lobbyists in British Columbia (see table 9.2). While a handful of specific oil and gas corporations report a larger volume of lobbying contacts than CAPP, it is clear from the records we obtained that CAPP is the single most active voice in government's ear when it comes to matters of industry regulation and oversight, including climate and energy policy. In its communications with government, the organization speaks authoritatively on behalf of industry overall and is engaged in a much more complex process than the term "lobbying" conveys. For example, CAPP routinely prepares and submits sophisticated technical briefings on range of matters of concern to industry, such as regulations governing the detection and control of methane emissions. Often taking the form of slide decks, these documents typically exceed fifty pages in length and include substantial, original research. CAPP thus plays an especially pivotal role: one of host, facilitator, technical advisor, and lobbyist all rolled up in one.

Conclusion

"Capture" is a useful and powerful concept—but it also implies a movement from a state of independence to one of capture, from an ideal state to a compromised one. In a resource-based jurisdiction like British Columbia, where extractive corporations have long played a central role in economic development and politics, it may be more appropriate to view the period of relatively ambitious climate action from 2007 to 2009 as an aberration, followed as it was by a reassertion of corporate economic interests as the province's natural gas industry went through major expansion, including both rapid increases in production and the shift from conventional wells to shale gas fracking. But does this mean a deep state exists in British Columbia? That the provincial government is entirely captured by the oil and gas industry?

We have presented troubling evidence that this may be so. Yet the challenge is not so much one of "reclaiming" the state as of recognizing the state as a long-standing terrain of struggle.

The election of a minority NDP government in 2017 highlighted the contested nature of British Columbia's status as a petro-state. The NDP minority was supported by the BC Green Party on the basis of a confidence-and-supply agreement negotiated by the two parties shortly after the election. That agreement included commitments to implement the United Nations Declaration on the Rights of Indigenous Peoples—which in turn requires that resource development and infrastructure projects proceed only with the free, prior, and informed consent of impacted First Nations—and to implement a climate strategy capable of meeting the province's GHG reduction targets. While the agreement was silent on the specific question of the future of British Columbia's natural gas industry, the NDP-Green relationship has been strained by the government's enthusiasm for LNG, which grew steadily after the election. In March 2018, for example, Premier John Horgan announced major new tax exemptions for the LNG industry, in hopes of advancing the proposed LNG Canada export terminal in Kitimat (Linnitt 2018).[10]

The NDP government has also sent mixed messages with respect to climate policy. It has, as promised, brought in modest increases to the carbon tax and has attempted, through a court challenge, to restrict the flow of heavy oil through the expanded Trans Mountain Pipeline. In addition, the government has banned political donations from corporations and unions and has taken steps to reform the province's lobbying rules. At the same time, the government's new Climate Solutions and Clean Growth Advisory Council is co-chaired by a senior executive from Teck Resources, and the province has yet to explain how it will meet existing GHG reduction targets if plans for new LNG facilities come to fruition.

As movements for Indigenous rights and energy democracy grow, and as the climate crisis becomes more extreme, industry's grip on public institutions and policy making processes will be increasingly subject to challenge. In turn, we can expect fossil fuel companies and industry groups to double-down on their efforts to control the trajectory of climate policy in order to protect their bottom line. How this struggle will unfold, both in British Columbia and elsewhere in Canada, remains to be seen.

Notes

1. Alberta has had a limited carbon price for large industrial emitters since 2007, initially in the form of its Specified General Emitters Regulation, but this was not an "economy-wide" carbon tax.

2. The BC Liberal Party is entirely separate from the federal Liberal Party of Canada and is a more right-leaning coalition of both ideologically liberal and conservative forces.

3. A third arena of the capture process, the discursive realm, is discussed in chapter 8 in this volume.

4. See Novak (2013) and Spence (2013) for a detailed history of this work.

5. For a critical analysis of this literature, see Novak (2013). Novak notes some key exceptions, pointing to early left scholars of regulatory capture such as Gabriel Kolko, who viewed capture as an inherent and systemic problem in a capitalist economy. See also the discussion of capture theory in Spence (2013, 466–68), specifically in the context of rationales for regulation at the federal level, rather than at the state (or provincial) level.

6. The discussion in this section is based on research published in greater detail in *Mapping Political Influence: Political Donations and Lobbying by the Fossil Fuel Industry in BC* (Graham, Daub, and Carroll 2017) and "State-Capital Nexus and the Making of BC Shale and Liquefied Natural Gas" (Graham 2017).

7. The Lobbyists Registry can be searched through BC's Office of the Registrar of Lobbyists, at https://justice.gov.bc.ca/lra/reporting/public/registrySearch.do?method=init.

8. Several of these ministries have been restructured and/or renamed since 2016.

9. A scan of the pages from the document that our request yielded is available at https://www.corporatemapping.ca/wp-content/uploads/2017/09/NGD-2017-72320.pdf. See also Daub and Yunker (2017).

10. In October 2020, the NDP won a majority government, bringing the NDP-Green agreement to an end.

References

Adkin, Laurie E., ed. 2016. *First World Petro-Politics: The Political Ecology and Governance of Alberta*. Toronto: University of Toronto Press.

Ansolabehere, Stephen, John M. de Figueiredo, and James M. Snyder Jr. 2003. "Why Is There So Little Money in U.S. Politics?" *Journal of Economic Perspectives* 17, no. 1: 105–30.

BC Climate Leadership Team. 2015. *Recommendations to Government.* October 31, 2015. https://www2.gov.bc.ca/assets/gov/environment/climate-change/action/clp/clt-recommendations-to-government_final.pdf.

British Columbia. 2008. *Climate Action Plan.* Victoria: Province of British Columbia. https://www2.gov.bc.ca/assets/gov/environment/climate-change/action/cap/climateaction_plan_web.pdf.

———. 2015. *Discussion Paper: Climate Leadership Plan.* July 2015. https://engage.gov.bc.ca/app/uploads/sites/121/2018/07/ClimateLeadershipPlanDiscussionPaper.pdf.

———. 2016. *Climate Leadership Plan.* Victoria: Province of British Columbia. https://www2.gov.bc.ca/assets/gov/environment/climate-change/action/clp/clp_booklet_web.pdf.

British Columbia. Ministry of Environment. 2015. "Climate Leadership Team Report Released." News release. BC Gov News, November 27, 2015. https://archive.news.gov.bc.ca/releases/news_releases_2013-2017/2015ENV0074-001983.htm.

———. 2016. "New GHG Reporting and Compliance Act Comes into Force." News release. BC Gov News, January 1, 2016. https://news.gov.bc.ca/releases/2015ENV0087-002158.

British Columbia. Ministry of Finance. 2008. *Budget and Fiscal Plan, 2008/09–2010/11.* Victoria: Ministry of Finance and Corporate Relations. https://www.bcbudget.gov.bc.ca/2008/bfp/2008_Budget_Fiscal_Plan.pdf.

Brownlee, Jamie. 2005. *Ruling Canada: Corporate Cohesion and Democracy.* Black Point, NS: Fernwood.

Carpenter, Daniel. 2014. "Detecting and Measuring Capture." In *Preventing Regulatory Capture: Special Interest Influence and How to Limit It,* edited by Daniel Carpenter and David A. Moss, 57–68. Cambridge: Cambridge University Press.

Carpenter, Daniel, and David A. Moss. 2014. "Introduction." In *Preventing Regulatory Capture: Special Interest Influence and How to Limit It,* edited by Daniel Carpenter and David A. Moss, 1–22. Cambridge: Cambridge University Press.

Carter, Angela. 2018. "Policy Pathways to Carbon Entrenchment: Responses to the Climate Crisis in Canada's Petro-Provinces." *Studies in Political Economy* 99, no. 2: 151–74.

Daub, Shannon, and Zoë Yunker. 2017. "B.C. Climate Leadership Team Recommendations Were Revised, Re-written in a Big Oil Boardroom." *Rabble.ca,* September 19, 2017. https://rabble.ca/blogs/bloggers/policy-note/2017/09/bc-climate-leadership-team-recommendations-were-revised-re.

Doyle, John. 2013. *An Audit of Carbon-Neutral Government.* Victoria: Office of the Auditor General of British Columbia. https://www.bcauditor.com/sites/default/files/publications/2013/report_14/report/OAG%20Carbon%20Neutral.pdf.

Drache, Daniel. 2014. "'Rowing and Steering' Our Way Out of the Modern Staples Trap." In *The Staple Theory @ 50*, edited by Jim Stanford, 58–64. Ottawa: Canadian Centre for Policy Alternatives.

Etzioni, Amitai. 2009. "The Capture Theory of Regulations—Revisited." *Society* 46, no. 4: 319–23. https://doi.org/10.1007/s12115-009-9228-3.

Graham, Nicolas. 2017. "State-Capital Nexus and the Making of BC Shale and Liquefied Natural Gas." *BC Studies*, no. 194 (Summer): 11–38. https://doi.org/10.14288/bcs.v0i194.188618.

Graham, Nicolas, Shannon Daub, and William K. Carroll. 2017. *Mapping Political Influence: Political Donations and Lobbying by the Fossil Fuel Industry in BC*. Vancouver: Canadian Centre for Policy Alternatives, BC Office. http://www.corporatemapping.ca/bc-influence/.

Haley, Brendan. 2011. "From Staples Trap to Carbon Trap: Canada's Peculiar Form of Carbon Lock-In." *Studies in Political Economy* 88, no. 1: 97–132. https://doi.org/10.1080/19187033.2011.11675011.

Lee, Marc. 2017. "The Rise and Fall of Climate Action in BC." *Policy Note* (blog). Canadian Centre for Policy Alternatives, BC Office. February 13, 2017. http://www.policynote.ca/the-rise-and-fall-of-climate-action-in-bc/.

Lee, Marc, and Toby Sanger. 2008. *Is BC's Carbon Tax Fair? An Impact Analysis for Different Income Levels*. Vancouver: Canadian Centre for Policy Alternatives, BC Office. https://www.policyalternatives.ca/publications/reports/bcs-carbon-tax-fair.

Lessig, Lawrence. 2013. "Institutional Corruption Defined." *Journal of Law, Medicine and Ethics* 41, no. 3: 553–55.

Linnitt, Carol. 2018. "NDP Offers Tax Breaks, Subsidies to Attract B.C.'s Single Largest Carbon Polluter: LNG Canada." *The Narwhal*, March 22, 2018. https://thenarwhal.ca/ndp-offers-tax-breaks-subsidies-attract-b-c-s-single-largest-carbon-polluter-lng-canada/.

MacNeil, Robert. 2014. "The Decline of Canadian Environmental Regulation: Neoliberalism and the Staples Bias." *Studies in Political Economy* 93, no. 1: 81–106. https://doi.org/10.1080/19187033.2014.11674965.

McMenamin, Ian. 2012. "If Money Talks, What Does It Say? Varieties of Capitalism and Business Financing of Parties." *World Politics* 64, no. 1: 1–38.

Miller, David, and Claire Harkins. 2010. "Corporate Strategy, Corporate Capture: Food and Alcohol Industry Lobbying and Public Health." *Critical Social Policy* 30, no. 4: 564–89.

Natural Resources Canada. 2019. *Energy Fact Book, 2019–2020*. Ottawa: Minister of Natural Resources. https://www.nrcan.gc.ca/sites/www.nrcan.gc.ca/files/energy/pdf/Energy%20Fact%20Book_2019_2020_web-resolution.pdf.

Novak, William J. 2013. "A Revisionist History of Regulatory Capture." In *Preventing Regulatory Capture: Special Interest Influence and How to Limit It*, edited by

Daniel Carpenter and David A. Moss, 25–48. Cambridge: Cambridge University Press.

Spence, David B. 2013. "Federalism, Regulatory Lags, and the Political Economy of Energy Production." *University of Pennsylvania Law Review* 161, no. 2: 431–508.

Stigler, George J. 1971. "The Theory of Economic Regulation." *Bell Journal of Economics and Management Science* 2, no. 1: 3–21. https://doi.org/10.2307/3003160.

Taft, Kevin. 2017. *Oil's Deep State: How the Petroleum Industry Undermines Democracy and Stops Action on Global Warming—in Alberta, and in Ottawa.* Toronto: James Lorimer.

Uechi, Jenny. 2017. "Canadian Oilpatch Says Critics Exaggerated Its Influence on Christy Clark Government." *National Observer*, September 25, 2017. https://www.nationalobserver.com/2017/09/25/news/canadian-oilpatch-says-critics-exaggerated-its-influence-christy-clark-government.

Woodward, Jon. 2017. "B.C.'s Climate Plan Written in Oil Industry Boardroom: Documents." *CTV News*. September 18, 2017. https://bc.ctvnews.ca/b-c-s-climate-plan-written-in-oil-industry-boardroom-documents-1.3594811.

10   **Petro-Universities and the Production of Knowledge for the Post-carbon Future**

Laurie Adkin

For more than six decades, the University of Alberta has been instrumental in developing Alberta's renowned oil and gas industry, from the education of its workforce and leaders to geological discovery to technological innovation.

University of Alberta media release, 19 March 2008

The oilsands industry would not exist without this university.

Doug Goss, former chair, University of Alberta Board of Governors, October 2014

Universities have great potential to provide the ethical leadership and diverse forms of knowledge needed to help our societies transition to ecologically sustainable paths of development. Yet the capacity of universities to fulfill these roles is obstructed in multiple ways.

First, universities are embedded in regional, national, and global political economies whose dominant logics and actors exert pressures on universities to serve their ends. Publicly funded post-secondary institutions are, to a substantial degree, policy *takers*, subject to the ideological discourses and developmental priorities of governments. Governments, in turn, typically set goals related to university-based research and development (R&D), as well as to programs of education, in accordance with the interests of the economic actors who have the most structural power and political influence. When little light exists between governmental vision and corporate interests, as in neoliberal regimes, the mandate of the university to serve the public good is squeezed from every side. This happens through processes that have been labelled the "corporatization of universities," a phenomenon characterized by:

- the alignment of university research and teaching priorities with the current priorities of market actors

- the marginalization of non-commodifiable knowledge

- the shift from self-government by academics to an executive style of management by professional(ized) administrators

- the involvement of corporate representatives in university governance bodies (boards of governors, boards of centres or institutes)

- the privatization of knowledge (through intellectual property agreements and funder agreements)

- the shrinking share of public funding in university budgets.

While these general structural trends have affected universities everywhere, differences among regional and national political economies help us to understand the conflicts and tensions operating within particular universities as well as the opportunities open to them to push for greater autonomy in serving the public good. In this chapter, I examine the implications of Alberta's (and Canada's) carbon-extractive political economy for the production of knowledge in Alberta's leading research universities.

Universities situated in the extractive nodal points of fossil-capitalist networks are expected to perform functions that correspond to specific industry needs. A handful of reports have documented industry influence in universities located in the carbon-extractive jurisdictions of Canada (CAUT 2013), the United Kingdom (Lander 2013; Muttitt 2003), and the United States (Gustafson 2012; Lockwood 2015; Washburn 2010). These authors have noted how these universities act as training centres for graduates who go to work for the fossil fuel companies. They have described the awarding of honorary degrees to senior executives from fossil fuel companies as a form of "greenwashing." In addition, they have begun to document the research collaboration agreements made between university researchers and fossil fuel corporations, asking questions about academic freedom and intellectual property rights. These relationships are important, and all may be observed in Alberta's post-secondary education institutions. However, some aspects of fossil capital's shaping of knowledge production have received little attention.

First, the influence of fossil fuel companies over what universities do has been associated with corporate donations or endowments to universities. These ties are very important, but in the case of Alberta, at least, an equally important means of influence is the determination of government research-funding priorities. In this sense, influence is less visible, or more indirect: it is mediated by governments through discourses of "innovation" and funding decisions. Governments, corporations, and university administrators collaborate in constructing the public interest in ways that conform to the short- and medium-term interests of fossil capital. This collaboration is facilitated by these actors' close and frequent interactions (and employment mobility) within industry-government-university networks.

Second, "external" pressures and incentives restructure universities internally. The resulting changes in stratification and power relations within the university have important consequences for how (and by whom) the university's mission is defined and for its capacity to serve the public good.

Third, while a number of studies have identified negative consequences for public health of a "too close" relationship between university scientists and private corporations (for example, in the areas of medical research, pharmaceuticals, and agrochemicals), very few studies of corporatization touch on the consequences of research-funding priorities for universities' production of knowledge that is critical to ecological transition—knowledge related, for example, to renewable energy, energy efficiency, water conservation, sustainable agriculture, forestry, fisheries, and urban design, low-carbon transportation, democratic planning processes, institutional reform, economic regulation to achieve sustainability targets, or the media and cultural practices that shape public opinion about such things as the feasibility of post-carbon transition.

As the analysis in this chapter reveals, Alberta's major research universities have not taken a leadership role in producing the knowledge needed to advance our transition to a post-carbon, ecologically sustainable economy. While other universities in Canada and elsewhere have begun to play important roles in leading sustainable development initiatives, Alberta's major universities have missed out on opportunities to do so and are, in fact, obstructed by the extractive-industry interests that have become entrenched within state innovation agencies and the universities themselves. To support these claims, I present evidence from research that reconstructs the universities' priorities in relation to energy and environmental knowledge production and technology development. The importance attached to different types of research was measured in multiple ways: the numbers of researchers associated with these areas; the amounts of provincial and federal government research funding they receive; the establishment of research chairs, centres, and networks; corporate endowments; and the discourse of senior university administrators, corporate executives, and government policy makers.

Government Funding of R&D at Alberta Universities: A Fossil-Fuelled Future, or Green Transition?

To map any changes in funding priorities against developments in provincial or federal policy or in the economics of fossil fuel extraction in Alberta, funding flows to the Universities of Alberta and Calgary were tracked over a period of nearly two decades, from the late 1990s (when investment in the oil sands began to take off) through to 2016–17. Setting aside the very large portions of government funding, both federal and provincial, directed to these universities' medical faculties, as well as the comparatively small amount of federal funding directed to the social sciences and humanities, the study zeroed in on financial support for science and technology. This support took the form of:

- awards from the Natural Sciences and Engineering Research Council of Canada (NSERC) in all program areas except for graduate student scholarships, as well as funding for Canada Research Chairs and Industrial Research Chairs

- awards from the Canada Foundation for Innovation (CFI) in all areas related to energy research and development and environmental sciences

- grants made by federal ministries and by Sustainable Development Technology Canada

- funding from the Alberta Science and Research Investments Program (ASRIP)

- disbursements from the Climate Change Emissions Management Fund (CCEMF) since its establishment in 2009–10

- funding from the Alberta Innovates corporations (2010–16) for university-based research, research chairs, and research centres
- numerous royalty credit or other funds administered by provincial ministries for investment in R&D.

It is impossible to present all the findings of this research here, but some highlights will help to explain my conclusions.[1]

Essentially, the goal was to see what kinds of R&D had been funded, and in what amounts, over roughly the past two decades and whether significant changes had occurred in the priorities of funding agencies. Projects that received funding were initially classified according to whether their primary orientation was toward the production of energy or toward some aspect of environmental science. They were then sorted into subcategories. An energy project could be coded "fossil fuel–related" (FFR) or as "renewable energy," "biofuel," "fuel cell," "energy efficiency/conservation," "nuclear," "fusion," or "uranium." Within the FFR subcategory, energy projects were then further coded on the basis of specific areas of fossil fuel R&D. These subcategories were carbon capture and storage, coal, reservoir exploration, extraction, hydraulic fracturing, processing (upgrading and refining), petrochemical production, and transportation (including pipelines), plus two others that are discussed further below: remediation and greenhouse gas (GHG) mitigation. Projects in the second main category, environmental science, were likewise sorted into categories: agriculture-related, forestry-related, ecosystems/conservation biology, climate change science, and "other environmental" (for example, toxicology, soil and plant science, air quality, municipal water treatment). Finally, for the relatively rare project funded by these sources that focused on sustainability (such as the development of sustainability indicators or of sustainable agricultural or forestry practices), we used the label "sustainable development."

Much of what governments characterize as "environmental" or "clean technology" R&D falls into the category of FFR research. Some of this research is directed toward the development of technologies intended to reduce GHG emissions. One example is carbon capture and storage, which aims to sequester emissions from coal-fired power plants or oil sands upgraders—although such technologies are now widely regarded as too costly to be implemented on the scale needed to stop global warming. Others are the use of CO_2 injection as a method of enhanced oil recovery (EOR) and the addition of solvents (natural gas liquids) to the steam used in steam-assisted gravity drainage (SAGD) extraction, which reduces the amount of both water and energy required to thin and extract the bitumen. Also in the FFR category is R&D related to the remediation of the environmental harms caused by fossil fuel extraction. Examples of research in this area are projects that concern the reclamation of contaminated soil, the detoxification of tailings ponds, and the restoration of land to usable condition.

Mitigation and remediation technologies are, of course, necessary and important. Yet those related to fossil fuels exist to offset the effects of an extractive model of development that needs, ultimately, to be replaced. In this sense, they are not "future energy system" technologies. Moreover, in the context of government commitments to maintaining oil sands operations for as long as possible, and in the absence of a green transition plan that phases out the extraction and consumption of fossil fuels apart from essential uses, the "clean energy technology" focus of funding has primarily served the purpose of legitimation. That is, governments routinely point to their investments in these areas to support claims that the fossil fuel–based economy can be made "sustainable." Such claims have become central to government and corporate efforts to obtain "social licence" for their continuing investments in fossil fuel extraction and exports.

Meanwhile, the alternatives to dependence on fossil fuels are typically left out or downplayed in the framing of policy choices. Little attention is given to the comparative lack of government investment in areas of research such as renewable, low-carbon energy technologies (wind, solar, geothermal), passive heating and cooling, energy conservation, low-carbon public transportation, ecological urban design, sustainable agriculture, water conservation, ecological economics, and integrated transition planning—research needed to put us on a path to ecologically sustainable development.

NSERC-Funded Research

In Canada, federal funding for university-based research is disbursed via three agencies collectively known as the Tri-Council: the Social Sciences and Humanities Research Council of Canada (SSHRC), the Canadian Institutes of Health Research (CIHR), and Natural Sciences and Engineering Research Council of Canada (NSERC). Our research focused solely on funding distributed through NSERC. Multiple searches of the NSERC awards database using different keywords and names of researchers gleaned from other sources eventually yielded a total of 356 faculty researchers at the University of Alberta (UAlberta) and the University of Calgary (UCalgary) working in the energy production or the environmental science domain over the period from 1999–2000 to 2015–16. Associated with these researchers were 4,567 projects that were coded and analyzed. Of the 356 researchers, 60 percent (210) worked primarily on energy projects, and, of these, 76 percent (159 of 210) worked on FFR projects.

Given its larger size, UAlberta had more researchers working on projects in the energy domain (134) than did UCalgary (83).[2] However, UCalgary had a slightly higher percentage of researchers working in the energy domain (61 percent, compared with UAlberta's 58 percent) and a substantially higher percentage of researchers working on FFR projects (60 percent, compared with UAlberta's 49 percent). Of the 356 researchers in total, 52 percent (185) were engaged in projects related to fossil fuels. Only 15 percent of energy researchers at the two universities worked in the non-FFR areas of renewable energy, biofuels, or energy efficiency/conservation combined. FFR research was also significant for researchers in the environment category, with 18 percent of these researchers (26 out of 146) participating in projects related to some aspect of FFR remediation.

Over the entire period, we found only thirty-one researchers (8.7 percent of the total) whose research pertained to sustainable agriculture, sustainable forestry, waste management, municipal water treatment, or water conservation. Most strikingly, only a single project (on integrated pest management) satisfied our criteria for research on sustainable agriculture. A snapshot of the distribution of researchers by research category taken in 2015–16 also found a huge imbalance between the number of researchers at the two universities who were engaged in some kind of FFR R&D (151) and the number working on projects related to sustainable agriculture, sustainable forestry, waste management, municipal water treatment, or water conservation research (19). In a province where sustainable food production may become a key part of a future low-carbon economy and where both climate change and other factors increasingly put water supply and quality at risk, the absence—as late as 2015–16—of NSERC-funded research in the areas of sustainable agriculture and water management is remarkable.

To shed light on the question of changes in energy research priorities *over time*, we assessed of the distribution of researchers at three different points: in 1999–2000, in 2009–10, and in 2015–16. Overall, the number of researchers in the *energy* domain has more than tripled since 1999 (from 56 to 174). Figure 10.1 shows the percentage of each category of energy researchers as a share of the total number of NSERC-funded researchers in our study at each point in time. We see that while modest increases have occurred since 1999–2000 (and especially since 2009–10) in the percentages of researchers working on FFR remediation and GHG mitigation and on renewable energy, these researchers are at all points greatly outnumbered by those working in other FFR areas of R&D (56 percent of researchers in 2015–16).

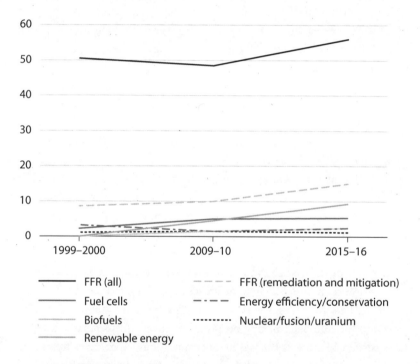

Figure 10.1. Percentage of NSERC-funded researchers in each sub-category of energy research. Source: NSERC Awards Database, https://www.nserc-crsng.gc.ca/ase-oro/index_eng.asp.

The number of NSERC-funded *environmental* researchers more than doubled from 47 in 1999–2000 to 105 in 2009–10, before finally levelling off at 113 in 2015–16 (74 of them at UAlberta and 39 at UCalgary). In proportional terms, however, the opposite trend was observed: whereas environmental researchers constituted 37 percent of all NSERC-funded researchers at the two universities in 1999–2000 and 39 percent in 2009–10, the figure *declined* to 30 percent in 2015–16.

Over this period, an increasing share of NSERC funding went to environmental researchers working on projects related to fossil fuels, with the percentage growing from 9 percent in 1999–2000 to 14 percent in 2015–16. After researchers working on various environmental science questions, fossil-fuel researchers became the second-largest group in 2015–16. In contrast, the proportion of environmental researchers working on some aspect of climate change *declined* from 10 percent in 1999–2000 to 6.5 percent in 2015–16 (their number dropping from twenty to sixteen).

The number of researchers working on questions related to forestry, agriculture, water, and waste management was comparatively small. Although those conducting forestry-related research grew in number from seven in 1999–2000 to sixteen in 2015–16, the number working on agriculture-related projects stood at five in both 1999–2000 and 2015–16. Similarly, in 2015–16, we found only five NSERC-funded scientists working on water quality and conservation problems.

We then examined research priorities within the two universities by calculating the amounts of *funding* awarded within the different categories. With regard to energy-related research, our data showed that, over the period under study, NSERC awarded a total of $165.8 million to UAlberta and UCalgary for research related to fossil fuels, whether the research concerned the exploration phase or the extraction, processing, or transportation of these fuels. This figure amounts to 67 percent of all funding for energy-related research (which totalled $207.7 million). If we add research related to remediation and GHG mitigation to the FFR category, NSERC funding for this category amounted to 84 percent of all energy-related research funding over this period. The cumulative amounts for each category are shown in figure 10.2.

In figure 10.3, we see that funding for FFR research other than that related to remediation or GHG mitigation increased steeply from 1999–2000 to 2015–16, with NSERC awards growing from an initial $4.9 million to a height of $16.2 million in 2014–15, before falling slightly to $15.7 million the next year. FFR funding for research into remediation and GHG mitigation remained comparatively minor for roughly the first decade of this period, averaging $886,493 per year until 2009, when it rose abruptly, reaching a peak of $8.3 million in 2012–13. This spike in funding (also visible in figure 10.4), which lasted through 2012, aligned with a provincial investment in carbon capture and storage and with efforts by the government of Premier Edward Stelmach to legitimize the oil sands as a source of "clean energy" (see Adkin and Stares 2016, esp. 201–8). Thereafter, funding for remediation and GHG mitigation plummeted to $2.9 million in 2013–14 and has not exceeded $2.7 million since then. Funding for renewable-energy research has seen only a modest increase and has remained below $2 million per year, while funding for research into fuel cells had a boost in 2007–9 but then declined. The major beneficiary of NSERC funding has been R&D related to bitumen processing—concentrated in the UAlberta engineering faculty—followed by R&D on unconventional oil and gas extraction (EOR, SAGD, fracking), an area in which UCalgary seeks to be a leader.

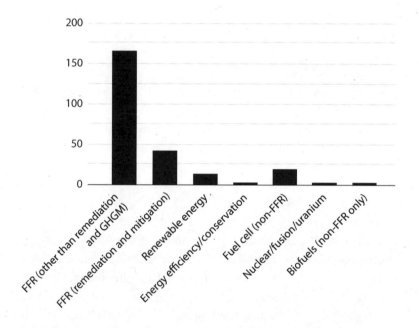

Figure 10.2. Cumulative amounts in millions disbursed by NSERC for different energy-related research categories at UAlberta and UCalgary from 1999–2000 to 2015–16. Source: NSERC Awards Database, https://www.nserc-crsng.gc.ca/ase-oro/index_eng.asp.

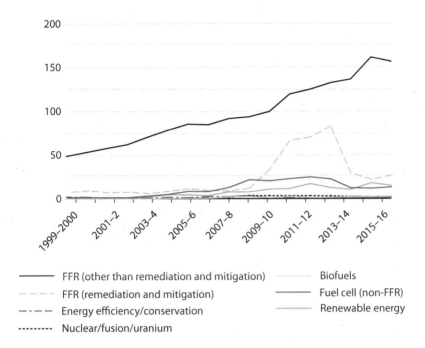

200

150

100

50

0

1999–2000 2001–2 2003–4 2005–6 2007–8 2009–10 2011–12 2013–14 2015–16

――――― FFR (other than remediation and mitigation)   ··········· Biofuels
― ― ― ― FFR (remediation and mitigation)   ――――― Fuel cell (non-FFR)
― · ― · ― Energy efficiency/conservation   ――――― Renewable energy
·········· Nuclear/fusion/uranium

Figure 10.3. Amounts in millions disbursed by NSERC for different types of energy research conducted at the Universities of Alberta and Calgary from 1999–2000 to 2015–16. Source: NSERC Awards Database, https://www.nserc-crsng. gc.ca/ase-oro/index_eng.asp.

NSERC funding of *environmental* research over the same period totalled $74.4 million, or just over a third of the amount spent on energy research. The percentage of NSERC funding awarded to the environmental sciences reached its peak in the period from 2002–3 to 2006–7; this percentage has since declined, from a high of about 28 percent in 2006–7 to about 22 percent in 2015–16. We further examined the allocation of funding to non-energy technology research projects that we grouped under the label of "sustainable development." These included: sustainable agriculture, sustainable forestry, waste management, municipal water treatment, water conservation, and "other sustainable development" projects such as those that related to land use or indicators of well-being. Over the entire period, the awards to such projects totalled $8.4 million (in 2015 constant dollars). As a percentage of all NSERC funding to the two universities for energy or environment-related research, funding for (non-energy-related) "sustainability" research accounted for between 1 and 5 percent, depending on the funding year.

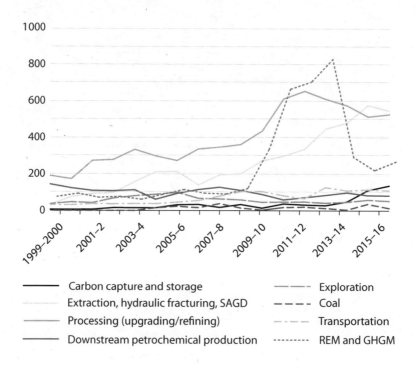

Carbon capture and storage ——— Exploration ——— Extraction, hydraulic fracturing, SAGD — — — Coal ——— Processing (upgrading/refining) — · — Transportation ——— Downstream petrochemical production ········· REM and GHGM

Figure 10.4. Breakdown of NSERC funding in millions of fossil fuel–related research at the Universities of Alberta and Calgary from 1999–2000 to 2015–16. Source: NSERC Awards Database, https://www.nserc-crsng.gc.ca/ase-oro/index_eng.asp.

Canada Foundation for Innovation

The Canada Foundation for Innovation was created in 1997 to fund infrastructure for R&D conducted in post-secondary education institutions and research hospitals. Its mandate was amended by the Conservative government in 2010 to place more emphasis on R&D with potential commercial value and on the development of "industrial clusters," in partnership with provincial governments and other funding agencies (CFI 2012, 8). Over the first two decades of its existence, the CFI invested more than $7 billion in research infrastructure (CFI 2017, 6).

From the CFI awards database, we selected and coded all awards made from 1998–99 to 2016–17 to the Universities of Alberta, Calgary, and Lethbridge. Health and medical funding takes the largest share (55 percent) of all CFI funding to the three universities, while energy-related research accounts for only 9.2 percent. Within this relatively small share, however, fossil fuel–related R&D again predominates in terms of the number of awards as a percentage of all energy awards: 61 percent at UCalgary and 84 percent at UAlberta. Fossil-fuel-related research also accounted for the largest shares of CFI funding for energy research at the two universities: 77 percent at the University of Alberta and 85 percent at the University of Calgary. In comparison, funding for R&D related to renewables amounted to only 22 percent of energy-domain funding at UAlberta and 6.3 percent at UCalgary.

Over the entire period, awards for environmental initiatives accounted for 8.3 percent of UCalgary's CFI funding and 7.1 percent of UAlberta's (as well as 6.2 percent of CFI funding at the University of Lethbridge). At UAlberta, environment-related research did better than energy-related research, which garnered 6.3 percent of CFI funding over this period. The same is not true for UCalgary, however, where energy projects secured 15.3 percent of CFI funding compared with environment's 8.3 percent.

Of the 833 CFI-funded projects that we coded, only eight (0.9 percent) fell into the "sustainable development" category. Together, these accounted for $1.2 million, or 2.7 percent of CFI spending.

Alberta Science and Research Investments Program

Excluding projects in areas of research other than energy, environmental sciences, agriculture, forestry, or social sciences, we found a total of 159 projects funded from 1997–98, when ASRIP was founded, to 2014–15.[3] Of the $95 million (in constant 2015 dollars) disbursed in these five areas over the period, more than half (52 percent) went to energy-related projects, followed by environment (28 percent) and agriculture (19 percent)—although only two of these projects met our criteria for sustainable agriculture. The single largest recipient of energy-related funding was fossil fuel extraction (56 percent), followed by GHG mitigation and remediation (16 percent). In third place was funding for renewable energies (15 percent). The total expenditure for environment-related research was only about $26 million, compared with $49 million for energy-related research. Only 1 percent of ASRIP funding went to forestry, and we found only one project in the social sciences.[4]

In terms of *trends* in ASRIP funding to these five areas over this period, four findings stand out. First, from 1997–98 through to 2009–10, environment-related projects gained in importance, receiving their largest share of funding in the period from 2005–6 to 2009–10. After that, however, their share of ASRIP funding shrank drastically, from 48 to 20 percent. Second, funding for agriculture-related research plummeted from $13.2 million in the three years from 1997–98 to 1999–2000 to a mere $300,000 in the five years from 2010–11 to 2014–15. This decline was equivalent to a fall from 61 percent of total funding (for our five domains) to a minuscule 1 percent. Third, the share of energy-related projects increased, by contrast, from 28 percent to 79 percent. Fourth, within the domain of energy research, ASRIP funding for both renewables and fuel cells research increased substantially after 2010, accounting for 30 percent and 26 percent, respectively, of all energy-area spending between 2010 and 2015. Still, FFR-related research took the largest share of funding in this period, at 43 percent.

Alberta Innovates

In 2009–10, the Alberta government established four Alberta Innovates (AI) Crown corporations, which replaced the Alberta Ingenuity Fund system of research institutes, the Alberta Research Council, and other bodies. Of these four, AI–Technology Futures (AITF) received 42 percent of all government budget allocations between 2010 and 2016 and was the most important funder of energy-related R&D, followed by AI–Energy and Environment Solutions (AI-EES). Over this period, AITF—now InnoTech Alberta, in the wake of government restructuring in 2016—funded six research centres, two "accelerator" programs (one in nanotechnology, at UAlberta, and the other in energy, at UCalgary), and multiple university-based research chairs, with expenditures for research chairs alone totalling over $71 million. Although detailed information about the projects funded by AI is not presently available from the Alberta government, it appears that most of this AITF funding was directed toward R&D related in some way to fossil fuels. Similarly, it appears that only a small portion of AI-EES grants to universities went to environmental research that was not related to the oil sands or to other FFR areas. Agricultural research received about $4 million from AI–Bio-Solutions over this period, or 3.7 percent of the agency's funding to universities.[5]

Research Centres and Institutes

Over the past two decades, the Government of Alberta has provided funding to only two institutes conducting environment-related research. From 2002–6, the Alberta Ingenuity Fund provided $5.3 million to the Alberta Ingenuity Centre for Water Research (Alberta Ingenuity 2006, 27). The centre had university-based "scientific directors" and secured funding from 11 other sources—most importantly, the CFI. In 2007, this centre was replaced by the Alberta Water Research Institute (AWRI), also funded from the Alberta Ingenuity Fund, with an initial funding base of $30 million over seven years. Its Management Advisory Board was chaired by Lorne Taylor, who served as minister of Alberta Environment in the Conservative government of Ralph Klein. While the AWRI had a wide scope of concerns, at least two of the projects it funded were related to research on the oil sands tailings ponds.[6] In 2010, when the Stelmach government replaced the Alberta Ingenuity Fund institutes with the Alberta Innovates corporations, AWRI became part of AI-EES.

The second environmental institute that received funding from the Government of Alberta is the Alberta Biodiversity Monitoring Institute, created in 2010 as part of the Joint Canada-Alberta Implementation Plan for Oil Sands Monitoring. It is supported by InnoTech and its partners over the years have included Alberta-Pacific Forest Industries, oil companies, Canada's Oil Sands Innovation Alliance (COSIA), the Petroleum Technology Alliance of Canada, as well as both UAlberta and UCalgary.[7] For the most part, the relatively few environmental institutes at Alberta's universities have generally relied on their own institutions and on private endowments for their operating funding.[8]

In contrast, *twelve* research centres or institutes in the energy domain have been established at UAlberta, benefitting from varying combinations of federal government, provincial government, and energy industry funding. *Seven* energy-related centres have been based at UCalgary, although two of these date to the 1970s. *Seven more* government-operated R&D centres that host university-government-industry research partnerships operate in the province.[9] Of these twenty-six energy research centres, one—the Alberta Carbon Conversion Technology Centre—was created in 2018 to advance the commercialization of technologies that make use of captured CO_2, while seven others have been engaged in energy economics or energy systems research (rather than in technology R&D). None, however, has been known for producing research that supports phasing out the oil sands and/or a rapid transition to carbon-neutral economy. The remaining eighteen centres have been dedicated primarily to fossil fuel R&D—particularly R&D related to the oil sands.

Consortia, Networks, and Research Initiatives

Like research centres and institutes, research consortia and networks play an important role in the integration of graduate students and post-doctoral fellows into research groups with close relationships to fossil capital. Most of the research carried out in the twenty-five energy research consortia we identified is related to the fossil fuel industry. Consortia and networks include government departments or innovation agencies, corporations, and university researchers in varying combinations, with funding or support in kind coming from any of these sources. In-situ heavy oil research, for example, has been a core research program of the Alberta Research Council and its successors since 1984, involving collaboration between company and government-employed researchers. Other consortia are based in the universities of Alberta or Calgary and are supported by corporate and government funders. The partners in the Reservoir Simulation Research Group and the Tight Oil Consortium at the University of Calgary, for example, have included Alberta Innovates, Alberta Advanced Education and Technology, the CFI, NSERC, and individual corporations. Industry associations, like the Canadian Association of Petroleum Producers (CAPP) and the Canadian Energy Pipeline Association (CEPA), also participate in these networks and consortia.

UCalgary's Global Research Initiative (initially named the Unconventional Hydrocarbon Resources GRI, now renamed the Sustainable Low Carbon Unconventional Resources GRI), was established in 2016 with $75 million from the Tri-Council's Canada First Research Excellence Fund (CFREF) and has partners in China, Israel, and Mexico.[10] The University of Alberta received a CFREF award in the same year for its Future Energy Systems Research Initiative (FESRI). Since the applications for these multi-million-dollar projects have not been made public, we do not have access to their budgets or details of the kinds of R&D they proposed to prioritize. The primary research areas of the Calgary GRI have been described, on university websites, as being heavy oil and bitumen, tight oil and gas, and CO_2 conversion. The FESRI was initially described as having a focus on making unconventional hydrocarbon resource extraction more energy-efficient, on pipelines, and on remediation of tailings ponds and reclamation of mined lands. It also aimed to "build on U of A strengths in advanced materials, smart electrical grids and bioprocessing to help move Canada to a low-carbon energy economy" (Folio Staff 2016). As a Tri-Council-funded initiative, FESRI was to allocate a portion of its budget to research in the social sciences and humanities.[11] In 2018, following the successful CFREF bid, senior administrators at the University of Alberta approved the creation of a "signature area of research and teaching excellence" in "Energy Systems."[12] The largest component of this signature area is the FESRI, which has been disbursing funding to projects ranging from engineering and science R&D on in situ extraction and upgrading of bitumen to Arts-based research on economic or cultural questions related to energy.[13]

As was the case with research centres and institutes, we found that *environment*-related research consortia or networks were typically small in scale and reliant upon *internal* funds. Several proposals to create a Signature Area of interdisciplinary research and teaching in the area of social and eco-logical sustainability were submitted to the Signature Areas Selection Panel at the University of Alberta in January 2017 and November 2018, but these were rejected.[14] While it is clear that both universities are home to faculty members who are concerned with environmental issues, at neither university is there a sustainable development initiative with external funding on the scale routinely provided to energy-area initiatives.

Research Chairs

Research chairs, like centres and consortia, are funded by multiple governmental and private sources and play a large part in defining the profile of faculties, schools, and universities. They typically come with considerable resources for operating laboratories or other research facilities, hosting conferences, and paying salaries to post-doctoral fellows and graduate student research assistants. Our study reconstructed the appointment of research chairs at the two universities since 2000 in the areas of either energy or environmental studies. These chairs can be grouped into three categories: positions for which the federal government provides funding, a category comprising Canada Excellence Research Chairs (CERCs) and NSERC-funded Canada Research Chairs (CRCs) and Industrial Research Chairs (IRCs); the provincially funded Campus Alberta Innovates Program chairs; and chairs or professorships endowed by private corporations.

Federally funded chairs. Federal funding for research chairs in energy-related areas and in environmental studies flows to universities through the three channels mentioned above. The CERC program, initiated by Stephen Harper's Conservative government in 2008, provides funding for major research initiatives that typically involve a team of researchers, whereas CRCs and IRCs are intended to support the work of individual researchers. The CRC program, in which all three Tri-Council agencies (including NSERC) participate, aims to draw particularly prominent or promising researchers to Canadian universities. NSERC's IRC program seeks to "support the establishment of applied research leaders and promote their role as catalysts in the advancement of business-focused applied research programs."[15] IRCs are jointly funded by NSERC and one or more partners.

- The CERC program provides universities with up to $10 million over a period of seven years to pay not only the chair holder's salary but also the salaries of other members of the research team and to fund the direct costs of the research program. In the first round of CERC awards, made in May 2010, UAlberta secured one CERC in the energy field—the Chair in Oil Sands Molecular Engineering—while UCalgary secured a CERC Chair in Materials Engineering for Unconventional Oil Reservoirs.

- From 2000 to 2016, thirteen CRCs were appointed at UAlberta in the energy domain and six in the environmental domain. Ten of the thirteen energy CRCs worked on fossil fuels. Of the approximately $17 million awarded to these nineteen CRCs, 63 percent went to the chairs in FFR R&D, whereas only 6 percent went to renewable-energy-related research, and a mere 3 percent to fuel cell research.

- Over the same period, UCalgary secured twelve energy CRCs and five environment CRCs. Of the twelve energy CRCs, six were in FFR R&D, three in renewable energy, one in fuel cell research, and two in other areas. FFR R&D captured 40 percent of the funding for these seventeen CRCs, while renewables got 7 percent, and fuel cell research 15 percent.

- Of the twenty-two IRCs awarded to UAlberta in the energy and environment domains, twenty were in energy and *all of these* were FFR, accounting for approximately $28 million in funding. The two environment IRCs were in land reclamation and wildlife protection in the oil sands region.[16]

- At UCalgary, there was a total of seventeen IRCs in energy- or environment-related areas over the same period. A full sixteen of these were in the energy domain, and *all but one* were in FFR R&D. These fifteen FFR IRCs captured approximately $18.8 million in NSERC funding, or 96 percent of NSERC's funding for these seventeen IRCs. The sole environment IRC was in municipal water engineering.

In short, thirty-five of the thirty-six energy-domain IRCs established at these two universities since 2000 have been in areas related to fossil fuels. To illustrate the extent of industry-university relationships involving engineering faculties, table 10.1 lists the industry partners for these IRCs.

Table 10.1. IRC industry partners at the Universities of Alberta and Calgary, by economic sector

Oil, gas, coal, petro-chemicals	Alberta Sulphur Research Ltd., Albian Sands Energy Inc., Angstrom Power Inc., Aramco Services, Athabasca Oil Sands Corporation, Baker Hughes, Baker Petrolite Canada, Barrick Energy Inc., BP Americas, Brion, Canadian Association of Oilwell Drilling Contractors, Canada's Oil Sands Innovation Alliance, Cenovus Energy Inc., Champion Technologies Ltd., Chevron Canada Resources Ltd., CMG Reservoir Simulation Foundation, CNOOC Ltd., CNRL, ConocoPhillips Canada Resources Corporation, Devon Canada Corporation, Dow Chemical, Enbridge Pipelines Inc., Encana, Enerplus Corporation, Enmax Corporation, EPCOR Utilities, ExxonMobil Upstream Research Company, Husky Energy Inc., Husky Oil Operations Ltd., Imperial Oil, Intertek Commercial Microbiology, Japan Canada Oil Sands Ltd., Laricina Energy Ltd., MacKay Operating Corporation, Maersk Oil, Matrikon Inc., Nalco, Nalco Canada Company, Nexen Inc., Nova Chemicals, Oil Search Ltd., Pason Systems, PEMEX Exploración y Producción, Penn West Petroleum Ltd., Petrobank Energy and Resources Ltd., Petro-Canada, Petroleum Technology Alliance Canada, Schlumberger Canada Ltd., Shell Canada Ltd., Shell Global Solutions, Statoil Hydro Canada Ltd., Suncor Energy Inc., Syncrude Canada Ltd., Talisman Energy Inc., Teck Metals, Total E&P Canada Ltd., TransCanada Pipelines Ltd., WSP Canada Inc., Yara International ASA
Forestry, pulp	West Fraser Mills Ltd., Weyerhaeuser Canada Ltd.

Construction	AECOM, Alberco Construction Ltd., Clark Builders, Colt Engineering Corporation, Construction Owners Association of Alberta, Falcon Fabricators and Modular Builders Ltd., Finning Canada Ltd., Flint Energy Services Ltd. Graham Industrial Services Ltd., InSituForm Technologies Ltd., JV Driver Projects Ltd., Kellogg Brown & Root, Landmark Master Builder, Ledcor Group of Companies, Ledcor Industrial Ltd., Licerbie & Hole Contracting Ltd., North American Construction Group Inc., PCL Constructors Inc., PME Inc., Standard General Construction, Waiward Steel Fabricators Ltd.
Other	Apex Engineering, Atomic Energy of Canada Ltd., IOWC Technologies, Outotec Canada Ltd., QuestAir Technologies Inc., Sherritt International Corporation, Virtual Materials Group Inc.

Source: NSERC Awards Database, https://www.nserc-crsng.gc.ca/ase-oro/index_eng.asp.

The CAIP chairs. In 2011, the Alberta government launched a research chair program in support of four "strategic priority areas" for the province's economy: *energy and the environment, food and nutrition, neuroscience/prions,* and *water.* The chairs were to be awarded to the four "comprehensive" post-secondary institutions—the Universities of Alberta, Calgary, and Lethbridge, and Athabasca University—and to be funded for seven years in the amount of $300,000 to $650,000 per year. As of May 2017, eighteen CAIP chairs had been appointed at the four universities. All appointments were made in the science and technology fields, with the exception of one award to the School of Business at UAlberta. Three of the four CAIP chairs appointed in the "energy and environment" category have applications for the oil industry. The designation of a "water" category may indicate a renewed governmental interest in water issues; of the eighteen chairs appointed between 2012 and 2015, nine were in this area.

Endowed research chairs. We identified sixteen chairs at UAlberta and UCalgary in energy or environment domains that were endowed during the period under study. The engineering schools have been the main beneficiaries of these endowments. In the UAlberta Faculty of Engineering alone, ten chairs or professorships have been endowed in the area of energy research, all of them related to fossil fuels extraction and processing. The corporations or industry associations that fund the energy chairs include Suncor, Encana, Petroleum Society, Husky Energy, ConocoPhillips, Dow Chemical, Nexen, Alberta Chamber of Resources, Xstrata Canada (now Glencore Canada),

Teck, Cominco Ltd., Syncrude, Hatch, Canada's Oil Sands Innovation Alliance (COSIA), Cenovus Energy, and Enbridge. Government partners include Alberta Innovates and Natural Resources Canada. In the domain of environmental research, we identified five chairs at UAlberta; none were found at UCalgary.

Endowments for facilities, student programs, scholarships, and lecture series. In addition to funding chairs and professorships, corporations in the energy sector and closely allied firms in the construction, manufacturing, and petrochemicals sectors have made endowments to university faculties for buildings, lecture halls, laboratories, and scholarships. University faculties have internship programs with the companies, bring in company executives and scientists to give lectures, and host career fairs. ConocoPhillips, for example, finances geoscience field schools at UAlberta, as well as the Engineering Safety and Risk Management Program. In recognition of its ongoing support, the Faculty of Engineering has named a science laboratory, a conference room, and a lecture theatre after the company (Graham 2014).

In 2014, Shell Canada gave $600,000 in support of the Shell Enhanced Learning Fund at UAlberta, which enables students interested in sustainable energy and the environment to take field trips, attend conferences, and pursue special projects (Williamson 2016). Shell's donation also supported the programs of WISEST (Women in Science, Engineering and Technology). Commenting on Shell's relationship with the engineering school in 2016, the company's university and college relations advisor noted that "the programs UAlberta offers have direct relevance to Shell Canada's core business in Alberta's oil sands" (Williamson 2016). Also in 2014, Enbridge was identified as the single largest employer of engineering co-op students, providing about a hundred four-month work terms per year as well as scholarships (Cairney 2014, 10). Other corporations, including Encana, Cenovus, and Syncrude, have provided funding for scholarships, while Syncrude is also a sponsor of the WISEST programs.[17]

In the Department of Chemical and Materials Engineering, lecture series have been sponsored by the Institute for Oil Sands Innovation, ICI Canada, and Schlumberger. Faculty of Engineering alumni often maintain connections with the school, giving lectures, taking up posts after retiring from their corporate jobs, or becoming benefactors. Energy corporation executives have received honorary doctorates from both universities and are often the bridges to corporate donations.[18]

Involvement of Fossil Capital in University Governance

Names on buildings are the most visible signs of industry influence within the universities. However, corporations exercise direct influence through representation on the management boards of centres and research consortia, and in these venues universities guard information carefully. In its 2013 report on collaborations between Canadian universities and corporations, the Canadian Association of University Teachers (CAUT) examined the constitution of four research collaborations at Alberta universities that have been co-funded by companies operating in the oil sands: the Alberta Ingenuity Centre for In Situ Energy, the Consortium for Heavy Oil Research by University Scientists (CHORUS), and the Enbridge Centre for Corporate Sustainability (now simply the Centre for Corporate Sustainability), all based at UCalgary, and the Centre (later Institute) for Oil Sands Innovation at UAlberta. CAUT identified a series of problems, including corporate dominance on management boards, the absence of provisions for the protection of academic freedom, the unavailability of information regarding funding arrangements and the selection criteria for projects, agreements that allowed corporate funders to withdraw support on short notice, and conflicts of interest on the part of university administrators (with regard to the Enbridge centre).[19]

More visible roles for the industry in university governance take the form of appointments of corporate executives to university boards of governors, senates, or chancellorships. At UAlberta, for example, appointees to the board of governors since 1996 have included Eric Newell, chair and CEO of Syncrude Canada from 1989 to 2003 and previously an executive with Imperial Oil and Esso Petroleum Canada; Gerard Protti, executive VP of corporate relations at Encana from 1995 to 2009, "executive advisor" to Cenovus Energy, and founding president of the Canadian Association of Petroleum Producers; and Gordon Winkel, a vice-president at Syncrude who retired in 2010 to join the university's Faculty of Engineering, where he became the chair of the Engineering Safety and Risk Management Program. Also on the list are Ken Chapman, formerly executive director of the Oil Sands Developers Group; David Ferro, who served as health and safety supervisor at Suncor from 2002 to 2004; and Martin Kennedy, director of public and government affairs at Epcor and the former vice president of external affairs at Capital Power Corporation.

At UCalgary, Bonnie DuPont—a vice-president at Enbridge until 2010— served on the board of governors from 2006 to 2016 and as its chair from 2012 to 2016. Enbridge's CEO, Al Monaco, also served on the board, as well as on the Dean's Advisory Board to the Faculty of Medicine. Other board members with employment connections to fossil fuel companies have been Rob Allen (Oil and Gas Canada), Kris Frederickson (Suncor; MEG Energy), Lawna Hurl (Chevron Canada), Alison Taylor Love (Enbridge), and Firoz Talakshi (Canadian Petroleum Tax Society).

Two former Syncrude executives have been credited with fusing the mission of the UAlberta Faculty of Engineering with the heroic project of developing the oil sands. One is Eric Newell, who not only served on the board of governors from 1996 to 2002 but was appointed university chancellor in 2004. According to an article in the university's *Folio* newsletter, Newell recognized that developing the oil sands would require not only skilled trades workers but also a supply of engineers and scientists. Upon becoming CEO of Syncrude in 1989, Newell thus "embarked on a mission of education that would rock every post-secondary school in the province—none more so than the University of Alberta" (Brown 2014). The other is Jim Carter, Syncrude's president from 1997 to 2007. Carter also served for twenty-five years at the Alberta Chamber of Resources, where, as chair of its mining industry advisory committee, he worked closely with UAlberta's Faculty of Engineering to build both its enrolment and a global reputation. When Carter stepped down from that position in April 2016, he was praised by the organization's executive director, Brad Anderson, for his determination to build "the best mining engineering department in the world right here" and by the dean of engineering at the time, Fraser Forbes, who commented, "He was instrumental in the rescue of our program in the early 1990s, when it was slated to be canceled. Jim brought the mining industry together to build a support community for our program, which has only strengthened over the last three decades" (both quoted in Lamphier 2016). According to the Canadian Petroleum Hall of Fame, during his time with the Alberta Chamber of Resources, Carter "created the *Oil Sands Technology Roadmap*, which envisions a third wave of oilsands development."[20]

A View from the Inside

The findings reviewed above indicate the enormous influence of fossil fuel industry interests in shaping the priorities of government research funding (and hence the nature of the knowledge and technologies produced) and in blurring the lines between the public/academic and private/corporate spheres regarding the goals of knowledge production. There is, however, an additional consequence for the university as an institution with a leading role to play in advancing sustainable development. The flow of external resources to the sectors of the university that carry out FFR R&D and "employee training" fuels their growth—in faculty numbers, research chairs, student enrolments, new buildings, and new research facilities. At the same time, the sectors that are home to critics of fossil capitalism, advocates of post-carbon transition, or simply defenders of the value of liberal arts education are constrained by limited access to external funding and reliance upon provincial government grants and student tuition for their revenue. With a Progressive Conservative provincial government in power for the entire period of our study and a federal Conservative government in office from 2006 to 2015—both committed to expansion of bitumen exports—one announcement of new funding for FFR R&D followed another. And with each new centre, consortium, research chair, or capital endowment, the faculties of engineering, in particular, expanded in size and influence.

On his LinkedIn page, David Lynch claims that during his tenure from 1994 to 2015 as dean of engineering at UAlberta,

> the total engineering undergraduate and graduate student enrolments doubled and quadrupled, respectively, to a total of over 6,000 students with over 18,000 engineering graduates, over 270 new engineering professors were hired, over 50 Chair positions (endowed, industrial and government funded) were established, and five new buildings were constructed containing over 130,000 sq.m. of space for engineering education and research along with the major renewal of an existing building. I was directly involved in securing over $900 million through donations and grants to support these developments and a further $700 million in incremental research funding was obtained as a result of these expansions of faculty, graduate students and facilities.[21]

According to its website, the Faculty of Engineering is presently home to roughly two hundred professors and fifteen hundred graduate students and attracts more than $65 million in external research funding annually, with $1.5 million in scholarships available to students.[22] The expansion of corporate investment in the oil sands over the same period accounts for a substantial portion of the growth in the number of professors and students in the Faculty of Engineering. In May 2016, the faculty's website reported that more than eighty faculty members and some eight hundred graduate students and other researchers were employed in R&D related to the oil sands. The Faculty's international profile was linked to its specialization in heavy oil extraction and processing, with the website highlighting its top ranking in the world in oil sands research publications.[23] Meanwhile, other faculties (the Faculty of Arts, in particular) have undergone repeated rounds of funding cuts, despite their large and increasing undergraduate enrolments.

In the sustainable development discourse of government ministers, corporate CEOs, and university administrators (see, for example, Cannon 2015), the university is among the titans whose technological knowledge will make never-ending extraction and consumption of fossil fuels possible in a carbon-constrained world. In this story, those with the requisite knowledge are the engineers, with other sectors of the university trailing along in descending order, sometimes offered bit parts—such as the 6 percent of UAlberta's Future Energy Systems research initiative's $75 million budget that was to be set aside for social sciences and humanities research on energy futures.[24] A broad interdisciplinary approach to the complexities of planning and building an ecologically sustainable society in Alberta has never been on the table.

What has this shift of power to the Private Prometheans meant for the university's sustainable development roles? I can offer some observations from "the inside" of the University of Alberta, where I have been employed since 1991. During this time, efforts to secure university support for the now-defunct Environmental Studies and Research Centre, a leading role for the university in interdisciplinary water research, a CAIP Chair in Food Security, and a Signature Area in ecological and social sustainability have all failed. An interdisciplinary Bachelor of Arts degree in environmental studies was implemented in 2011, but has never secured funding to hire teaching faculty; its future is in question due to a lack of support among senior administrators and a new budget model that intensifies competition for students among faculties. UAlberta has never been home to a major initiative or institute with a mandate to advance post-carbon transition in Alberta and Canada. Indeed, the existence of such a centre or area of "global excellence" at the university would be antithetical to its commitment to perpetuating fossil fuels extraction.

Events at UAlberta in the spring of 2018 reveal the institutional schisms that reflect the larger conflicts in which the province's universities are embedded. A decision to offer an honorary doctorate of science to David Suzuki, world-renowned ecologist and proponent of phasing out oil sands production, was met by Dean Forbes, of the Faculty of Engineering, with a vocal public protest. He described the honour as an "alarming threat" to and "betrayal" of his faculty—an action that called into question the "fundamental values" of the "engineering community." Forbes further expressed his solidarity with "aggrieved Albertans," stating that the university had become "disconnected from the people that we are meant to serve." He demanded that the offer of the honorary doctorate be rescinded and that, in the future, "the Engineering voice, the voice of Alberta's industrial sectors, including energy and natural resources" be "given a place at the table of the key decision-making bodies of our university." He also called upon his colleagues to "intensify our advocacy for Alberta's industrial sectors" and to ensure that "everyone, our youth in particular, understand the crucial role that our energy and resource industries play in powering our life, protecting our environment, and building fair and equitable societies."[25]

In light of the evidence that engineering has been one of the faculties most privileged by the governmental innovation agenda that has predominated in Alberta and Canada for decades, that fossil fuels–related R&D has received the lion's share of energy research investment, and that UAlberta's national and international profile has been built upon its energy research, the dean's representation of his faculty (and of "industrial sectors") as having no voice in university decision making may seem incomprehensible. This paradox is better grasped when we consider that Forbes's reaction occurred in the context of a much larger campaign, led by Rebel Media, Postmedia Corporation, CAPP and its astroturf social media groups, and the United Conservative Party to discredit not merely Suzuki but climate science and the Indigenous-led climate justice movement. One element of this campaign consisted of public statements from businessmen associated with the oil and gas industry that they were cancelling planned donations to the university. Another element painted the university as having been taken over by the "left-wing thinking" associated in particular with the humanities and social sciences—a claim offered by way of explaining why the university would do something as "tone-deaf" and as allegedly unrepresentative of "the political views of the general population" as to award Suzuki an honorary degree (Staples 2018).[26]

Dean Forbes was joined the following day by Dean Joseph Doucet, of the School of Business. Doucet is an energy economist and former director of the Centre for Applied Business Research in Energy and the Environment, whose corporate sponsors include Cenovus, AltaLink, Enbridge, Encana, Suncor, and Capital Power. The School of Business is also one of the partners in the Network for Business Sustainability—co-funded by SSHRC (to the tune of $2.5 million)—that includes CNRL, Suncor, and Cenovus, along with Alberta Innovates and Natural Resources Canada (JWN Staff 2017). Doucet apologized to "friends of the Alberta School of Business" for the "distress and anger" that the Suzuki doctorate had caused "many Albertans."[27]

UAlberta president David Turpin, a former biology professor, issued a statement that the university would stand by its decision to offer the degree to Suzuki because "our reputation as a university—an institution founded on the principles of freedom of inquiry, academic integrity, and independence—depends on it." The role of the university, he said, was to be the "champion" of "controversy."[28] More than one hundred other UAlberta academics, mostly based in the Faculty of Arts, signed a letter published in the *Edmonton Journal* denouncing what they called a campaign by the oil and gas industry to "bend a public institution to the will of a private interest" and arguing that the industry's financial clout "does not entitle it to threaten and bully the universities or Albertans" (Adkin et al. 2018).[29]

The Suzuki episode illustrates how the strong alliances between fossil capital (and their business clients) and certain faculties within the university have deepened internal divisions. University resources have been devoted to securing multimillion-dollar government grants, corporate sponsorships, and collaboration agreements with other institutions in the areas of R&D related to fossil fuels. The deans of the professional schools that benefit most from external sources of funding often have, or expect to have, a bigger say in university strategic directions than those in the traditional core faculties. Senior administrators are expected to promote partnerships with the private sector, court wealthy donors, and "work with" the priorities set out in provincial innovation policy. These priorities do not include the production of knowledge and technology aimed at phasing out the use of fossil fuels.

Yet corporate power and the institutional incentive structures created by captured governments (often with the active collaboration of university administrators) do meet resistance. Universities also have traditions rooted in democratic and humanist values. Some sectors of the university continue to strongly defend the ideals of university autonomy, of a community of scholars who grow in knowledge when their knowledge is shared, and of the production of knowledge for the public good. As we also see in the case of the Suzuki honorary doctorate, actors can—and do—push back against the external pressures exerted by the political economy of fossil capitalism on programs of research, teaching curricula, institutional citizenship, and academic freedom. There is room to manoeuvre in setting research priorities, but it requires vocal, principled leadership on the part of academics and administrators. University leaders can choose to "follow the money," trying to position their institutions to profit from the latest shift in government funding. Alternatively, they can try to mobilize public and political support for an independent vision, generated from the bottom up, through consultation with academics, students, and our surrounding communities about how the university can best serve the public interest.

Acknowledgements

The author would like to acknowledge the contributions of four research assistants to the project of which this chapter presents one part. Eric Abrahams, Lauren Muusse, and Elinor Bajraktari worked with me over successive summers, thanks to funding support from the Department of Political Science and a University of Alberta VP Research Small Operating Grant (2014). Funding provided by the SSHRC-funded grant Mapping the Power of the Carbon-Extractive Corporate Resource Sector and by the Confederation of Alberta Faculty Associations (2016) permitted me to hire the indispensable Laura Cabral in 2017–18.

Notes

1. For a full review of the project's findings see Adkin 2020. See Adkin 2019 for research into the CCEMC's disbursements.
2. These numbers do not total 210 because some researchers worked in more than one area of energy research and so were counted in more than one sub-category.
3. We recorded all projects that were not clearly situated in the fields of medicine, information and communication technologies, or nanotechnology, and that were connected to energy, environmental, agricultural, forestry, or sustainability areas of research. Included in this group was one project conducted by a social scientist at the University of Alberta. We coded the ASRIP projects by broad

area of research (5 areas) and then by sub-categories of energy, environmental, and sustainability research.

4. This one project, "Core Facility for Spatial Applications of Social Ecology," was based in the Department of Resource Economics and Rural Sociology at the University of Alberta and was funded in 2001–2.

5. The figures in this paragraph are based on information provided by the FOIP officer for Alberta Innovates, 17 July 2017.

6. In a 2009 blog, Taylor referred to a $15 million "public/private partnership" between the AWRI and GE Water & Process Technologies to improve the treatment of water used in oil sands operations, and to a AWRI-funded project involving researchers at the University of Alberta that was studying the potential of micro-organisms to break down chemical compounds in the tailings ponds and convert them to methane gas. Lorne Taylor, "Water Challenges in Oil Sands Country: Alberta's Water for Life Strategy," *The Bog: Alberta WaterPortal Blog*, Alberta WaterPortal Society, Guest Blog on the Alberta Water Government Portal, September 12, 2009, https://albertawater.com/alberta-water-blog/12-guest-columnist-lorne-taylor.

7. Annual reports going back to 2003 can be found on ABMI's website, https://www.abmi.ca/home/publications/551-600/562.

8. We found only six centres with some connection to environmental studies for the period 1990–2015 at the University of Alberta, four of which were still operating in 2017. The Alberta Centre for Sustainable Rural Communities receives operating support from Augustana Campus and the Faculty of Agriculture, Life and Environmental Sciences. At the University of Calgary, we found only two centres conducting environmental research: the Arctic Institute of North America and the Canadian Institute of Resources Law. A Centre for Environmental Engineering Research and Fabrication is located in the engineering school. Since 2016, the UCCities—Global Urban Research Group has been supported by the VP Research. See "UCCities—Global Urban Research Group at UCalgary: About," University of Calgary, 2020, https://arts.ucalgary.ca/labs/global-urban-research/about.

9. This list does not include the Edmonton-based Advanced Energy Research Facility, which is dedicated to research into biofuels and is supported by the City of Edmonton, Alberta Innovates, and Enerkem.

10. See "Global Research Initiative in Sustainable Low Carbon Unconventional Resources," University of Calgary, 2020, https://research.ucalgary.ca/energy/energy-research/global-research-initiative, and "Global Impact," University of Calgary, 2020, https://research.ucalgary.ca/energy/energy-research/global-research-initiative/global-impact.

11. Larry Kostiuk, the FESRI director at the time, said that the portion allocated to the social sciences and humanities would be six percent. Actual expenditures or awards for FESRI-funded projects have not been published. Author's notes from an information meeting about the initiative, November 7, 2016, University of Alberta.

12. See "Energy Systems: A University of Alberta Signature Area," accessed January 11, 2020 https://www.ualberta.ca/energy-systems/index.html.

13. For a breakdown of projects see "Future Energy Systems," https://www.futureenergysystems.ca/. Since there are no public annual reports, we do not know how the budget has been allocated among areas of energy research.

14. The author was co-author of two of these proposals and sole author of a third. All of the proposals drew on extensive data-gathering about faculty areas of teaching and research across the campus as well as existing degree programs, research clusters, or centres related to ecological and social sustainability.

15. "Chairs and Faculty Support Overview," Natural Sciences and Engineering Research Council of Canada, last modified April 24, 2019, https://www.nserc-crsng.gc.ca/Professors-Professeurs/CFS-PCP/index_eng.asp.

16. A former CEO of Syncrude and President of the Alberta Chamber of Resources, Jim Carter, is credited with securing several IRCs for the energy sector in Alberta. See "James Edward Clarke Carter," Canadian Petroleum Hall of Fame, n.d., accessed September 30, 2019, http://www.canadianpetroleumhalloffame.ca/james-carter.html.

17. University of Alberta, "Women in Scholarship, Engineering, Science, and Technology: Donors," https://www.ualberta.ca/services/wisest/donors.html.

18. Lander (2013, 35) notes that the practice of bestowing honorary degrees upon corporate patrons from fossil fuel corporations is common in the United Kingdom as well. He counted twenty such awards between 2003 and 2013 for senior executives from BP and Shell alone.

19. On the controversy surrounding UCalgary's relationship with Enbridge, see Bakx and Haavardsrud (2015). The Enbridge Centre for Corporate Sustainability (now the Centre for Corporate Sustainability) at the university's Haskayne School of Business was founded in 2012 with an initial pledge of $2.25 million from Enbridge. Notably, Elizabeth Cannon, UCalgary president from 2010 to 2018, became an "independent director" of Enbridge Income Fund Holdings late in 2010, a position for which she was receiving $130,500 in compensation in 2014. Bonnie DuPont, former vice president at Enbridge, sat on the board of the Enbridge centre at the university.

20. "James Edward Clarke Carter," Canadian Petroleum Hall of Fame, n.d., accessed September 30, 2019, http://www.canadianpetroleumhalloffame.ca/james-carter.html.

21. "David Thomas Lynch," LinkedIn, n.d., accessed September 30, 2019, https://www.linkedin.com/in/david-thomas-lynch-79b09022/.

22. "About Us," Faculty of Engineering, University of Alberta, 2020, https://www.ualberta.ca/engineering/about-us. For staff numbers, see under "Faculty and Staff Information."

23. These figures were published on the UAlberta Faculty of Engineering website in May 2016, however the url is no longer active: http://research.engineering.ualberta.ca/research-specializations/research-leaders/WorldsTopOilSandsResearch.aspx (accessed May 9, 2016).

24. Author's notes from an information meeting about the initiative, November 7, 2016, University of Alberta. See also the Future Energy Systems website, https://futureenergysystems.ca/, especially the "About" page.

25. "Message from Fraser Forbes," University of Alberta, Faculty of Engineering, April 23, 2018, https://www.ualberta.ca/engineering/news/2018/april/message-from-fraser-forbes.

26. David Staples (2018) quotes NDP premier Rachel Notley, who described the university's decision as "a bit tone-deaf."

27. "Message from Dean Doucet Regarding UAlberta Honorary Degrees," University of Alberta, Alberta School of Business, April 24, 2018, https://www.ualberta.ca/business/about/news/articles-and-press-releases/2018/april/message-from-dean-doucet-regarding-ualberta-honorary-degrees.

28. David Turpin, "Why Should the University Stand Up for an Unpopular Honorary Degree?" University of Alberta, April 24, 2018, https://www.ualberta.ca/news-and-events/mediarelations/media-statements-2017-current/2018/april/why-should-the-university-stand-up-for-an-unpopular-honorary-degree.

29. The letter had a total of 109 signatories, including four from universities other than UAlberta. Although most taught in the humanities and social sciences, some were from the Faculties of Education, Nursing, Medicine and Dentistry, and Science.

References

Adkin, Laurie E. with Laura Cabral. 2020. *Knowledge for an Ecologically Sustainable Future? Innovation Policy and Alberta Universities.* Edmonton, AB: Parkland Institute and the Corporate Mapping Project.

Adkin, Laurie E. 2019. "Technology Innovation as a Response to Climate Change: The Case of the Climate Change Emissions Management Corporation of Alberta." *Review of Policy Research* vol. 36, no. 5 [10.1111/ropr.12357].

Adkin, Laurie E., and Brittany J. Stares. 2016. "Turning up the Heat: Hegemonic Politics in a First World Petro-State." In *First World Petro-Politics: The Political Ecology and Governance of Alberta*, edited by Laurie E. Adkin, 190–240. Toronto: University of Toronto Press.

Adkin, Laurie E., et al. 2018. "Energy Industry Must Not Be Allowed to Bully Universities." *Edmonton Journal*, May 3, 2018. http://edmontonjournal.com/opinion/columnists/opinion-energy-industry-must-not-be-allowed-to-bully-universities.

Alberta Ingenuity. c2006. Alberta Ingenuity Centres Program Highlights 2002–2006. Government of Alberta, n.d.

Bakx, Kyle, and Paul Haavardsrud. 2015. "How the University of Calgary's Enbridge Relationship Became Controversial." *CBC News*, November 2, 2015. http://www.cbc.ca/news/canada/calgary/university-calgary-enbridge-sponsorship-1.3286369.

Brown, Michael. 2014. "Eric Newell Receives Double Honours for Advancing Education." *Folio* (newsletter). University of Alberta. May 21, 2014. https://www.folio.ca/eric-newell-receives-double-honours-for-advancing-education/.

Cairney, Richard. 2014. "Stepping Up to the Plate." *U of A Engineer*, Spring 2014, 8–10.

Cannon, Elizabeth. 2015. "University Research Funding Key to Cutting Canada's Carbon Footprint." *Globe and Mail*, July 7, 2015. https://www.theglobeandmail.com/report-on-business/rob-commentary/university-research-funding-key-to-cutting-canadas-carbon-footprint/article25325058/.

CAUT (Canadian Association of University Teachers). 2013. *Open for Business on What Terms?* Ottawa: Canadian Association of University Teachers. http://www.caut.ca/docs/default-source/academic-freedom/open-for-business-%28nov-2013%29.pdf?sfvrsn=4.

CFI (Canada Foundation for Innovation). 2012. *CFI Strategic Roadmap 2012–17.* April 2012. https://www.innovation.ca/sites/default/files/pdf/2011%20CFI%20Strategic%20Roadmap%20final%20English%202012-04-04.pdf.

———. 2017. *Research Builds Our Communities: Annual Report, 2016–17.* Ottawa: Canada Foundation for Innovation. https://www.innovation.ca/sites/default/files/pdf/annual-report/cfi-annual-working-eng-web.pdf.

Folio. 2016. "UAlberta awarded $75 million for energy research." University of Alberta. September 6, 2016. https://www.folio.ca/ualberta-awarded-75-million-for-energy-research/.

Graham, Sheila. 2014. "ConocoPhillips Rocks UAlberta Science and Engineering Students." *Folio* (newsletter). University of Alberta. November 21, 2014. https://www.folio.ca/conocophillips-canada-rocks-ualberta-science-and-engineering-students/.

Gustafson, Bret. 2012. "Fossil Knowledge Networks: Industry Strategy, Public Culture and the Challenge for Critical Research." In *Flammable Societies: Studies* on the *Socio-economics of Oil and Gas*, edited by John-Andrew McNeish and Owen Logan, 311–34. London: Pluto Press.

JWN Staff. 2017. "COSIA Joins with Government, Universities to Accelerate Sustainability-Focused Oilsands Innovation." JWN.com, September 19, 2017. http://www.jwnenergy.com/article/2017/9/cosia-just-joined-ottawa-and-quebec-alberta-universities-accelerate-sustainability-focused-innovation/.

Lamphier, Gary. 2016. "Former Syncrude Boss Bids Farewell to U of A Mining School." *Edmonton Journal*, April 21, 2016. http://edmontonjournal.com/business/local-business/former-syncrude-boss-bids-farewell-to-u-of-a-mining-school.

Lander, Ric. 2013. *Knowledge and Power: Fossil Fuel Universities*. London: Platform, People & Planet, and 350.org. October. www.platformlondon.org/p-publications/unis.

Lockwood, Jeffrey A. 2015. *Behind the Carbon Curtain: The Energy Industry, Political Censorship, and Free Speech*. Albuquerque: University of New Mexico Press.

Muttitt, Greg. 2003. *Degrees of Capture: Universities, the Oil Industry, and Climate Change*. London: New Economics Foundation, Corporate Watch, and Platform. February 18. http://neweconomics.org/2003/02/degrees-of-capture/.

Staples, David. 2018. "University of Alberta Reveals Blind Spot in Deciding to Honour David Suzuki." *Edmonton Journal*, April 26, 2018. http://edmontonjournal.com/opinion/columnists/david-staples-8.

Washburn, Jennifer. 2010. *Big Oil Goes to College: An Analysis of 10 Research Collaboration Contracts Between Leading Companies and Major U.S. Universities*. Washington, DC: Center for American Progress. October 14. https://www.americanprogress.org/issues/green/reports/2010/10/14/8484/big-oil-goes-to-college/.

Williamson, Shelley. 2016. "Shell Canada Supports UAlberta Efforts to Attract a Variety of Qualified Engineers to the Field." University of Alberta (website). October 6, 2016. https://www.ualberta.ca/giving/giving-news/2016/october/women-in-engineering.html.

11 The Oil Industry Is Us

Hegemonic Community Economic Identity in Saskatchewan's Oil Patch

Emily Eaton and Simon Enoch

It is no secret that, in the face of public attack, the fossil fuel industry is on the defensive. As the realities of global climate change become ever more apparent, environmental campaigners have turned to "supply-side" activism (Mooney 2015), challenging the very legitimacy of the construction of new fossil fuel infrastructure in a world that must transition to a post-carbon future. How fossil fuel companies attempt to legitimize their operations in an atmosphere of critical scrutiny and growing doubt has been the subject of considerable academic study, much of it focused on industry's efforts to market itself through the creation of positive images that seek to displace negative associations in the public mind (see, for example, Krashinsky 2015; Matz and Renfrew 2015; Schneider et al. 2016; Wall 2015). As the politics of transition intensify, and as climate change activists target the issue of production, local sites of extraction increasingly become arenas of struggle. For that reason, it is imperative that we understand the mechanisms whereby oil companies garner grassroots support among those who live and work in oil-producing communities.

Portions of this chapter were previously published in "Oil's Rural Reach: Social Licence in Saskatchewan's Oil-Producing Communities," *Canadian Journal of Communication* 43, no. 1 (2018): 53–74. They are reprinted here by permission of the journal.

In the discursive wars between jobs and the environment, the fossil fuel industry regularly relies on the authenticity of workers' voices. In chapter 7, for example, Shane Gunster and his colleagues explore industry's use of "engagement" campaigns that encourage workers to defend their industry against environmental critics and climate change policies and to amplify their emotion-laden messages through social media. The emergence of anti-industry sentiment at local sites of extraction—that is, the potential growth of a countervailing movement that emphasizes the possibility of building alternative green economies at a local or regional level—clearly poses a significant threat to industry's efforts to maintain its legitimacy. Fossil fuel companies thus have a major stake in preventing people who live in extractive communities from questioning the ecological, economic, and moral viability of the industry on which their livelihoods depend.

In this chapter, we examine how the fossil fuel industry produces hegemonic community identities tied to oil and gas extraction in rural Saskatchewan. Our research indicates that residents of oil-producing communities do more than merely consent to the operations of industry: they actively identify with the oil industry and perceive their interests and the industry's interests as one and the same. This intense identification is further manifest in community members' vocal defence of the industry and in their adoption of industry-propagated frames of reference for understanding wider energy-related issues. We argue that industry practices of direct community engagement and strategic philanthropy are key to securing this thoroughgoing identification of "us" with "them." Our focus is not merely on the discursive strategies that industry uses to gain consent but also on the material benefits that industry delivers in regions that are economically dependent on oil and on the ideological dimensions latent in industry attempts to secure legitimacy in areas where oil is part of everyday life.

Saskatchewan's Oil Boom

The oil industry is not new to Saskatchewan: commercial production dates back to the late 1940s and intensified during the 1950s. Over roughly the past two decades, however, new extraction technologies—notably horizontal drilling and hydraulic fracturing (fracking), as well as thermal recovery, miscible gas injection, and chemical flooding—have enabled the recovery of oil trapped in shale and sandstone. These techniques have, in turn, expanded the scope of oil recovery, leading to increases in both the pace and scale of drilling in many parts of the world, including Saskatchewan. In the mid-2000s, at a time when many rural areas were undergoing economic decline and depopulation associated with agricultural consolidation and corporatization, oil-producing communities in the province were instead catapulted into a period of frenzied economic growth that slowed only when oil prices crashed in late 2014. For the better part of a decade, these communities found themselves in the midst of an oil boom characterized by high rates of employment, along with explosive population growth that strained social services and sent rental markets soaring as vacancy rates plunged. In addition to influxes of oilfield workers, the boom in production also fed the development of secondary businesses to service both drilling sites and the workers themselves. These, too, required staff, and new arrivals included a large number of temporary foreign workers destined for the restaurant and accommodation industries.[1]

Shale oil development has been met with significant social opposition in many areas, largely in connection with the fracking technologies used to recover the oil (see, for example, Smith and Richards 2015, 82–83). In 2011, public opposition prompted France to ban fracking, and, in 2015, more than twelve hundred groups from sixty-four countries participated in anti-fracking actions coordinated by Global Frackdown (Fusco and Carter 2017, 276). Several US states have outlawed fracking, while, in Canada, Nova Scotia and, more recently, Québec have banned the practice. In New Brunswick, a moratorium has been in place since 2014, and opposition is also intense in Newfoundland and Labrador (see Carter and Fusco 2017).[2] Saskatchewan has, however, seen little organized opposition to oil extraction, whether from members of rural oil-producing communities or from urban-based environmental movements (Olive and Valentine 2018)—despite the very real grievances that people living in the province's oil-producing communities have voiced about environmental contamination from oil-related activities (Eaton and Kinchy 2016; see also Jackson et al. 2014; Steinzor, Subra, and Sumi 2013).

Our research focused on three oil-producing communities in Saskatchewan, each comprising a city or town and the surrounding rural municipality (see figure 11.1). Two of these communities—Weyburn and Oxbow—lie in the southeastern corner of the province, atop the shale of the Bakken Formation (which stretches south into Montana and North Dakota). The third, Kindersley, is located in west-central Saskatchewan in an area rich in petroleum reserves and, to a lesser extent, natural gas. For each community, we identified philanthropic contributions from the oil industry and from oil advocacy organizations via a content analysis of local newspapers from 2007 to 2016, as well as company websites, annual reports on corporate social responsibility (CSR) initiatives, and newsletters. Donations made by oil production and oil-well-servicing companies primarily came from the regional or local offices of firms headquartered either in Calgary, Alberta, or from more locally based firms headquartered in Saskatchewan. The oil advocacy organizations included two service clubs (the Oxbow Oilmen's Club and the Weyburn Oilfield Technical Society Oilwomen), as well as the Canadian Association of Petroleum Producers.

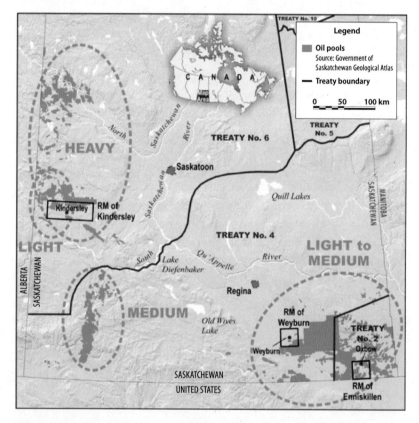

Figure 11.1. Oil pools and study areas. RM = rural municipality. *Source*: Map drawn by Weldon Hiebert. Contains information licensed under the Open Government Licence—Canada. Base map courtesy NASA/JPL-Caltech.

In addition to collecting publicly available information about the three communities, we conducted twenty-five semi-structured interviews in the summer of 2016 with municipal and town councillors and administrators, farmers, representatives of landowner associations, members of conservation groups, representatives from community organizations, human services staff, schoolteachers, local business owners, and representatives of oil companies. Interviewees were chosen on the basis of their experiences with the oil industry and with a view to ensuring a diversity of perspectives and geographic locations. To protect privacy, we have omitted any reference to organizational affiliation and/or community of residence.

The Construction of Hegemonic Community Identities

Originating in discussions of the mining sector, the concept of a "social licence" to operate is perhaps the most common academic approach to understanding the role of communities in sanctioning the activities of business. The notion of a social "licence" reflects the recognition that a company (or an entire industry) requires broad and sustained approval from society in order to conduct its activities successfully. Don Smith and Jessica Richards (2015, 89) describe social licence as "an ongoing social contract with society," one that "derives from communities' perception of a company and its operations" and allows companies to "manage socio-political risk by conforming to a set of implicit rules imposed by their stakeholders." Jason Prno and Scott Slocombe (2012, 347) further observe that, while social licence may be "issued by society as a whole (e.g., governments, communities, the general public and media), local communities are often a key arbiter in the process by virtue of their proximity to projects, sensitivity to effects, and ability to affect project outcomes."

As Smith and Richards (2015, 93) explain, Ian Thomson and Robert Boutilier (2011) argue that, in order secure full social licence, a company must establish its legitimacy and credibility as a business, and it must also gain the community's trust. Thomson and Boutilier accordingly identify four levels of social licence: withdrawal, acceptance (that is, the recognition of a company as a legitimate operation), approval (the level at which both legitimacy and credibility are established), and psychological identification—the highest level of social licence that a company can achieve. At this level, which companies rarely attain, a community demonstrates "full trust" in a company, to the extent that a sense of partnership emerges and the community actively defends the company against criticism (Smith and Richards 2015, 95, citing Thomson and Boutilier 2011, 1786).

A key means of building social licence is the adoption of CSR initiatives, an umbrella term for a host of practices in which businesses voluntarily engage in an effort to demonstrate that they operate "in a manner that meets or exceeds the ethical, legal, commercial, and public expectations that society has of business" (UNCTAD 2004, 22).[3] In attempting to gain social licence, companies operating in extractive communities commonly rely on two CSR practices in particular: strategic philanthropy and community engagement (see, for example, Ellis et al. 2015; Smith and Richards 2015, 126–27). Unlike ordinary altruism, strategic philanthropy is designed to be "synergistic with a firm's missions, goals and objectives" (Foster et al. 2005, 3). Such philanthropy deploys funds in the community with a view to achieving certain business-related goals, whether material or discursive. For instance, oil industry support for fire and emergency services is pervasive in North American oil-producing communities because it ensures that these local services will have the equipment and personnel needed to respond adequately to oil-site accidents or emergencies (Ellis et al. 2015, 14–15). Industry may also dispense philanthropy to garner community goodwill and positive publicity (see Foster et al. 2005; Logsdon, Reiner, and Burke 1990).

Community engagement strategies focus on building relationships with key stakeholders in the communities in which businesses operate. These encompass a wide range of initiatives, such as company-sponsored open houses, employee-volunteer programs, community consultations, public tours of company facilities, school field trips, and awards events. Community engagement enables firms not only to showcase their contributions to the community but also to proactively manage risk and respond to community concerns (Kytle and Ruggie 2005), while these initiatives also enhance the overall legitimacy of their operations (Bowen, Newenham-Kahindi, and Herremans 2010).

While the social licence and CSR literature demonstrates how firms can build and maintain consent for local operations, it has less to say about the potential ideological dimension of these strategies. As we hope to demonstrate, the practices used to build social licence assist in the production of what we term a "hegemonic community economic identity," in which the interests of industry and community are so tightly bound up that community members actively police criticisms of the industry and adopt ideological perspectives on wider energy issues that align with those of industry. While this phenomenon can be described as psychological identification, we find that Gramscian conceptions of hegemony offer a more theoretically useful means of understanding how the material and discursive practices of industry work to produce this degree of identification.

Antonio Gramsci used the term "hegemony" to connote a "congruence of material and ideological forces that enables a coalition of interests to maintain a dominant position in society" (Levy 1997, 129). This dominant position is primarily maintained not through force—although the power to compel through coercion is always readily available—but through an ideological and cultural dominance that is capable of securing popular consent. The ability to mobilize and maintain hegemony requires not only certain material concessions to subordinate groups—such as an industry's provision of jobs, revenue, essential services, and infrastructure—but also "discursive frameworks that actively constitute perceptions of mutual interests" (Levy and Egan 2003, 807). In other words, a hegemonic social structure must make the interests of the dominant group appear as the general interest. As we will see, the goal of creating a perception of mutuality is particularly well realized in communities where the "community interest" and the interests of industry are so thoroughly blurred as to become almost indistinguishable. Gramsci suggested that insofar as the views of the dominant group are internalized by subordinate groups, they become "common sense," a taken-for-granted conception of the world, rarely challenged, that equates the status quo with the "natural order of things" (Boggs 1999, 161; see also Enoch 2009, 18–20).

Although Gramsci's insights into hegemony have rarely been applied in studies of communities that are home to extractive industries, they dovetail well with research that examines how, in seeking to secure ongoing community support, companies engaged in natural resource extraction adopt a variety of coercive measures that ultimately serve to promote and maintain a sense of "community economic identity." In an analysis of West Virginia coal-mining communities, Shannon Bell and Richard York (2010) show how, in the face of both economic decline and environmental challenges, the coal industry draws on culturally iconic images of masculinity and works to maintain a high level of visibility in an effort to establish itself as integral to the economic and cultural identity of the community. These efforts at "economic identity maintenance" (112) function to bind the community to the industry even as employment wanes, as well as to thwart environmental opposition by framing it as a threat to economic security.[4]

Importantly, in Bell and York's analysis, economic dependence is positioned not only as material fact but also as an active ideological construction in the service of power. As Gramsci's theorizing of hegemony suggests, discursive power is essential to the ability of elites to construct and maintain their domination. Following Steven Lukes's (2005) description of the third dimension of power, where power is used to shape people's perceptions, thoughts, and preferences, Thomas Shriver, Alison Adams, and Chris Messer (2014) investigate the tactics employed by corporations, government officials, and regulators to shape the way that grievances surrounding environmental contamination are perceived (or not) by local populations. By controlling information and intervening in environmental assessments, as well as by pursuing community engagement practices and mounting public relations campaigns, industry is able to mute complaints and produce a state of community quiescence. Similarly, in a study of a public relations initiative undertaken by the oil and gas industry, Jacob Matz and Daniel Renfrew (2015) examine industry's efforts to "sell" fracking to local communities by mobilizing discursive frames of patriotism, environmental imagery, and technological and scientific innovation designed to emphasize the benefits of shale development to the community, while casting those who opposed the extraction of shale gas as "irrational obstructionists." Indeed, fossil fuel industries regularly pursue a series of rhetorical strategies, including "astroturf" campaigns, that portray critics as naïve, reckless, and dangerous, while representing industry as moderate, rational, and even progressive (see, for example, Schneider et al. 2016). At times, the vilification of opponents provokes open confrontations, and, as Amaranta Herrero Cabrejas (2012) demonstrates, can conspire to produce a "culture of silence" that serves to stifle dissent.

In short, through a variety of rhetorical tactics and interventions, the fossil fuel industry builds the ideological foundations of a community identity founded on the perception of shared economic interests, such that industry is woven into the very fabric of community life. The hegemonic nature of such constructions of community economic identity is evident in two convictions that pervaded the communities we studied. First, people overwhelmingly understand their community as having a singular economic identity, rather than as home to competing economic interests. Second, people assume that the general interests of the community are indistinguishable from the particular interests of the oil and gas industry. So embedded are these two notions that they have come to seem like a matter of common sense. In other words, they have become hegemonic.

Evidence of Psychological Identification

Residents of the communities we studied demonstrated a high degree of trust in and identification with the oil industry. As we noted earlier, "psychological identification" is the highest level of social licence that a firm or industry can achieve. At this level, "rather than 'us and them,' the relationship between community and company represents a 'we' marked by co-ownership" (Smith and Richards 2015, 95). We observed this level of identification in our interviews, where community residents regularly represented industry not as an intruder or outsider to be tolerated but as a valued member of the community itself. Indeed, the notion of "industry as community" was widespread among the people to whom we spoke, regardless of their relationship to the industry—this despite the fact that some also gave voice to serious grievances.

The local roots put down by many of the companies that make up what people understand to be "the oil industry" help to entrench the image of industry as part of the community. One woman—a former administrator at a local oil company and now an active community volunteer—commented, "Big oil—there's no such thing as 'big oil.' It's all of our friends and neighbours and people running our towns and supporting us." The multiple direct relationships that people in oil-producing communities have with the oil industry further erode any sense of division between the two. An employee at an oilfield service firm noted that "pretty much everyone" in the area is tied in some way to the oil industry: "Either their husband works in the oilfield or they work in the oilfield somewhere along the line. [. . .] Usually everyone has some sort of a connection."

A production superintendent at a local oil firm highlighted the tight connection that has developed between community and industry:

> Years ago, there were no donations; there was no nothing. I think there was a "we and they." But now, through donations and a lot of people that I know that are in the oil patch—they volunteer either for the fire department or a lot of volunteer hours coaching for kids' sports and stuff like that. So that helps as well, right? It's no more a "we and they": it's really come together.

As his remarks suggest, this sense of support and connection is grounded in industry's local philanthropic and community engagement initiatives.

Philanthropy and Community Engagement

The oil firms operating in Saskatchewan regularly engage in strategic philanthropy and community engagement efforts that provide material benefits to communities while reinforcing discursive frameworks that contribute to the prevailing conviction that industry is simply part of the community. Both activities reinforce the perception of a mutuality of interests that is required to forge a hegemonic community identity. They also serve to present the industry as virtually indispensable to the prosperity, if not the very economic viability, of the community.

While firms in these communities regularly engage in the types of corporate philanthropy that one would expect—such as sponsoring sports teams, contributing to food banks, and making charitable donations to local hospital foundations—we found that oil-producing communities also rely on industry for the provision of public services and infrastructure that many would consider to be the sole purview of government. Indeed, oil-producing communities rely extensively on oil industry money for the maintenance of a host of crucial public services, including fire and emergency response, health, education, and human services, as well as for recreational facilities and other community infrastructure. That many of these necessities are perceived as being supplied—or at least supplemented—by industry rather than by government is another reason why communities view their interests as inextricably tied to those of the oil industry.

It is no exaggeration to say that many public services in oil-producing communities simply could not be provided at current levels without direct funding from the oil industry. For example, local fire departments rely on industry for an extensive array of vital equipment, including fire trucks, ambulances, rescue airbags, hydraulic rescue tools, automated external defibrillators, self-contained breathing apparatuses, and hydrogen sulphide gas monitors. Similarly, industry funding enables rural communities to purchase expensive medical equipment needed for diagnostic services such as digital X-rays, ultrasounds, and electrocardiograms. Industry philanthropy is equally important to critical infrastructure in both health and education, with donations from the oil industry supplying the majority of private funding for local hospital construction and school improvements in the three communities we studied. Human services—often taxed to their limit by the economic and social crises inherent in a boom-and-bust commodity cycle—also rely to a large extent on industry, with programming and expanded service provision frequently contingent on industry largesse (see the examples in table 11.1).

Table 11.1. Selected industry contributions.

Donation	Company	Recipient
$4,500,000	Crescent Point Energy	Weyburn and District Hospital Foundation
$250,000	Penn West	Penn West Diagnostic Wing at the Kindersley Hospital (digital X-ray and ultra-sound equipment and hospital renovations)
$250,000	Cenovus Energy	Weyburn Triple C (Community, Culture, and Convention) Centre
$150,000	Cenovus Energy	Weyburn Fire Department (safety training trailer)
$100,000	CNRL	Oxbow New School Fundraising Committee (construction of Oxbow Prairie Horizons School)
$100,000	Encana	Weyburn Leisure Centre (outdoor pool)
$100,000	Red Hawk Well Servicing	Oxbow New School Fundraising Committee (construction of Oxbow Prairie Horizons School)
$50,000	MayCo Well Servicing	Oxbow New School Fundraising Committee (construction of Oxbow Prairie Horizons School)
$25,000	Valleyview Petroleum	Weyburn Wor-Kin Shop (support services for intellectually disabled)
$20,000	CNRL	Sun Country Health Region, Weyburn (ambulance)
$20,000	Cenovus Energy	Weyburn Care-A-Van Society (wheelchair-accessible van)
$10,000	Enbridge	Oxbow/Enniskillen Fire Department (fire truck and other equipment)
$10,000	ARC Resources	Sun Country Health Region (electrocardiogram monitors)
$10,000	Longhorn Oil and Gas	West Central Crisis and Family Support, Kindersley

Local residents were keenly aware that many of the things they enjoy in their communities are the direct result of oil industry philanthropy. One of the teachers we interviewed attributed the success of efforts to raise funds for a new school to the presence of oil wealth in the community, commenting that "we raised about a million dollars, and, had it not been in oilfield country, that million dollars likely would not have been raised." Similarly, a local fire chief discussed the difficulties experienced by non-oil-producing jurisdictions, where the oil industry cannot be relied on for funding and equipment:

> I know if you get north of #1 highway, the oil revenue runs out, and it's very hard for them to fund the fire department and to buy good graders for the roads, and to pay the maintenance crew decent money. And so I can see that being a challenge, to fund a fire department or to get them the equipment that they need.

The community volunteer formerly employed at an oil company echoed the same theme: "We had a giant flood that wiped out the ball diamonds, and they got rebuilt—and that didn't happen because of the teachers at the school, because the teachers wouldn't be here if the industry wasn't here. No one would be here."

As these comments demonstrate, community members are acutely conscious of how much they rely on the oil industry, to the point that some cannot imagine their communities existing without it. Oil industry philanthropy quite literally allows people in these communities access to health, education, recreation, and other services that they might not otherwise enjoy. One can easily see how industry philanthropy encourages a community economic identity that equates community welfare with the oil industry.

Most of the larger oil firms also regularly host a variety of community engagement efforts. As a production superintendent at a local oil firm explained,

> One thing that we used to do—and [name of company] has done it a couple of times—is have open houses. We open it up to the public, so if you have some questions or concerns, bring it up, and we'll provide you with the answers and stuff like that. So that's helped kind of bring the local people together and understand what the oil patch is all about.

As the literature on community engagement suggests, industry typically characterizes such efforts as a means to build relationships with the community and other key stakeholders (see Bowen, Newenham-Kahindi, and Herremans 2010, for example). In addition to allowing firms to highlight their contributions to the community, these events provide an opportunity to disseminate information about operations and performance, as well as to reinforce industry viewpoints.

For the oil industry, schools are a particularly attractive site for community engagement efforts that can enhance social licence for the industry overall. Working in partnership with both major oil companies and local oilfield companies, the Canadian Association of Petroleum Producers (CAPP) began bringing its "Energy in Action" program to schools across Saskatchewan in the mid-2000s (see Eaton and Enoch 2017). Described as "an energy and environmental literacy program for students primarily in grades four to six in under-serviced schools in rural communities, where there are oil and natural gas operations" (CAPP 2012a, 2), the program consisted of classroom presentations that provided industry perspectives on topics such as the use of natural resources, both renewable and non-renewable, to meet energy needs, energy development, and environmental stewardship, coupled with an outdoor project such as building bird boxes or planting trees. As CAPP explained in a promotional video: "Energy in Action is community engagement in action. Building understanding, growing roots in the community, reinforcing reputations, ensuring our social licence to operate. Skilled educators and a curriculum linked to energy realities opens eyes and opens minds. Energy in Action works" (CAPP 2012b, 0:30–1:00). Given that the program was clearly designed to present the oil industry in a sympathetic light, it amounted to a powerful tool of advocacy—an intervention in the daily lives of children that, under the guise of educational curriculum, sought to instill a industry-friendly ideological orientation and further cement the relationship between industry and the community.

In a more ad hoc form of community engagement, oil companies also make representatives available to meet with local groups that might have questions or concerns about a company's operations. Members of a local conservation group, for example, explained that they had invited a representative from Cenovus Energy to make a presentation to the group about the environmental regulation of the oil and gas industry. At a time when Saskatchewan's regulations were, in fact, the least stringent in the country (Carter and Eaton 2016), members of the nature group praised what they characterized as increased stringency in environmental oversight. Reporting on their meeting with Cenovus, one member of the group explained that the application for a licence to drill is now "quite involved" and that the company's applications are "a lot thicker now than they ever used to be, on every project. So, yeah, it's quite good, I think." Overall, another said, the group felt that "the oil companies are doing an adequate job. We're not sure how much they do because we don't know enough about their work areas, but certainly we've been quite impressed with their abilities." Indeed, community engagement initiatives often target specific community stakeholders, with a view to managing grievances and/or reinforcing industry perspectives. Insofar as such efforts are successful, they broaden industry's base of support within the community, thereby strengthening the sense of partnership and an alignment of interests.

Defending the Oil and Gas Industry

The policing of internal criticism is crucial to the maintenance of community economic identities tied to oil extraction. Like Cabrejas (2012) and Bell and York (2010), we found a pervasive culture of silence in oil-producing communities in Saskatchewan. For example, when those we interviewed shared complaints about the oil industry operating in their backyards, they often mentioned that they were reluctant to talk openly about their grievances for fear of censure, which some had experienced in the past. One interviewee, the owner of an oilfield-related company, offered the following example:

> A woman I know [. . .] she lives kind of on the edge of [name of the town], and there's a couple of wells over here. She posted on Facebook, "Is anybody smelling the rotten eggs? I can smell it in my yard, and I had to go in the house." So a few other people said, "Yeah, I thought that was the sewer." I said, "No, there's a well," and [. . .] I said, "Just call the Ministry of the Economy"—I put his number. That's all I said, but holy crap you would have thought I committed murder. The oil field guys came at me with a vengeance. [. . .] When you talk about keyboard warriors and online bullies and—well, just horrible.

In another case, a farmer recounted his long struggle to have an oil company acknowledge and address the contamination of his well water with natural gas. As he explained, there was so much gas in the water coming out of his kitchen tap that he had been able light a fire. His daughter, whose bedroom was in the basement next to the main water tank, plumbing, had also been suffering severe health problems, which he attributed to the gas. It took seven years for the company to do tests and admit to the problem in the first place, and then it was another four years before a permanent solution was implemented. When we asked him whether he talks about this experience to others in the community, he replied, "We're very careful—well, we don't really talk about it," adding that what he had just told us was "the most I've talked about it." In order to have the well water remediated, he said, he had to sign a non-disclosure agreement that forbids him to talk about his experience.

In addition to the "keyboard warriors" and non-disclosure agreements that help to maintain silence, nearly everyone is financially dependent on the industry in some way. Two of the farmers we interviewed explained that landowners who have experienced problems caused by industrial activity are reluctant to speak because they also derive income from small contracts with the industry. "A lot of them have companies that support the industry," one said. "They push snow; they do lots of work for the industry." Another agreed: "They don't want to rock the boat, and it's a difficult personal decision, because to have that extra revenue on your farm is phenomenal [. . .] especially when there's drought and grasshoppers."

When things do go wrong, money is spent to keep people from speaking out. One person we interviewed, an economic development officer, remembered a situation in which local rancher lost a number of his calves to what he believed was sour gas poisoning from nearby oil wells and infrastructure. The rancher took the dead calves to a veterinarian to have them examined and then complained to the oil company after the veterinarian was unable to identify a clear cause of death and opined that the rancher's suspicion about sour gas poisoning was reasonable. As the development officer commented:

> He lost all these calves, and they sent him a cheque for whatever the cattle would have been worth as adults and [that] made him happy. They've got little kids. They have grandkids out there. I'm thinking I would not have shot my mouth over repaying that. It's very difficult here, because people are very well aware of who pays the bills.

This reluctance to "rock the boat" or make public space for frank discussion means that residents self-police the airing and addressing of their grievances. When residents do act, they tend to engage in individual, rather than collective, action by, for example, confronting industry on their property or phoning the police (see Eaton and Kinchy 2016). Because such individual acts of resistance can easily be dismissed as isolated occurrences or chalked up to a grumpy personality, they fail to disrupt the hegemonic quality of a community economic identity.

Community Adoption of Industry Framings

Although, within the communities we studied, criticisms of the industry were generally suppressed, they were also, at times, acknowledged but actively challenged, especially when they were deemed to emanate from sources outside of the community. We were repeatedly struck by the degree to which community members talked about energy and energy-related issues through industry-sanctioned frames of reference. This phenomenon illustrates a dimension of social licence that has thus far received relatively little attention: an identification so thorough that individuals internalize an industry's ideological position on issues of concern to society as a whole.

The ideological alignment of community with industry was especially evident when those we interviewed were asked about specific criticisms of the oil industry. In discussing such criticisms, community residents adopted many of the frames of reference and rhetorical tactics that have been associated with industry discourse (see, especially, Bell and York 2010; Matz and Renfrew 2015; Schneider et al. 2016). Regardless of their relationship to the oil industry, for example, community members often expressed significant skepticism about the validity of the notion of anthropogenic climate change—a pattern that also emerged in another study of the Weyburn region (Boyd 2014). Regarding climate change, a municipal councillor commented, "I'm not the best climate change person to talk to because I don't necessarily buy into all of that, and I struggle with [. . .] I struggle with the fact that Canada is taking responsibility for so much of an issue that we are actually a very small emitter in the grand scheme of things." The idea that Canada—despite having among the highest per capita greenhouse gas emissions in the world—is a "small emitter" relative to other countries has been a favourite talking point of both industry advocacy groups and the Saskatchewan government (Morrow 2015; Oil Respect 2017).

The doubts about climate change voiced by community members also contained elements of what Jen Schneider, Steve Schwarze, Peter Bsumek, and Jennifer Peeples (2016, 27) identify as the "industrial apocalyptic" strategy: a set of rhetorical appeals that herald the impending demise of an industry assumed to be vital. According to this scenario, powerful but fundamentally misinformed outsiders use the spectre of climate change to justify imposing onerous regulations or taxation on the oil industry, while failing to recognize the catastrophic economic and social consequences of such constraints. Adopting this line of argument, the community volunteer previously employed in the industry cast ignorant policy makers as a threat to the economic welfare of rural communities:

> I would say the prevailing opinion is those who are making decisions about things like climate change are making them on broad-brush-stroke generalities, and I think it's—the opinion is they don't know what they are talking about, the opinion is they've got the data wrong. [. . .] It's fear-based, because someone like Justin Trudeau who didn't get any votes this side of the Manitoba border is talking about making broad sweeping changes that are literally going to put our entire communities in financial jeopardy.

Similarly, an employee at an oilfield service company not only expressed doubt about the existence of climate change but also argued that rural communities have been unjustly singled out for blame:

> Well, no one really knows what the weather was like how many years ago. I think us being in the rural area see the cities and all the pollution they're creating, right? We feel like we get hounded on for what we're doing, more so than what goes on in industrial areas in other cities. There's lots of pollution there. I think we're fairly regulated, and we abide by the rules. I know I'm environmentally conscious.

Community members drew on other elements of the "industrial apocalyptic" strategy as well, such as the notion that modern life depends on fossil fuels, and that, in the absence of a viable alternative, those who advocate the winding down of fossil fuel use would have us court catastrophe. When asked about the possibility of a post-carbon world, the municipal councillor remarked, "You can't just turn the tap off oil and say, 'There's no more oil, find a different way to power your car. Find a different way to get some of your plastics. Find a different way to run some of the generating plants that you need to produce hydro.'"

We also regularly witnessed the use of elements of what Schneider et al. (2016, 107) identify as the "hypocrite's trap," a rhetorical strategy that seeks to disarm opponents of the fossil fuel industry by pointing out that these critics rely on fossil fuels themselves. Declaring that "the world runs on oil," the community volunteer explained:

> So it's this sense of, how would you get from here to a place where there was no oil? And just that whole sense of betrayal where [. . .] for somebody who is using what we're producing to actively—to rally, to protest, enact changes against it. David Suzuki with his diesel-burning bus driving across the country telling everybody that fossil fuels are bad. And you go, "That's the problem." It's that hypocriticalness.

The owner of a local oil company made a similar comment about environmentalists:

> So there's lots of these groups that are kind of lobbying or they're sort of lobbyists, but I think they're totally missing the point. I always kind of chuckle—even if it's on Twitter—when you see everybody is in some bay in Vancouver and just up the coast, and there's oil tankers going past them—because it's happening right now as we speak—and everybody is sitting in a kayak that's made from petroleum.

This strategy works by pinpointing what is presented as a fatal logical contradiction: the failure of actions to align with words. Yet the strategy rests on the false assumption that individuals can align their actions to a fossil-free world that does not yet exist or that ceased to exist several hundred years ago. In fact, contemporary economies and lives are thoroughly structured around fossil fuels, but this does not negate the need to transition off them.

Finally, we often encountered the belief that technological advances, particularly those initiated by the oil industry, will render current environmental concerns moot. This conviction illustrates what Schneider et al. (2016, 4) call the "technological shell game"—a "rhetorical process of misdirection that relies on strategic ambiguity about the feasibility, costs, and successful implementation of technologies in order to deflect attention from environmental pollution and health concerns." As they note, this strategy emphasizes the notion that fossil fuel corporations already stand at the "frontier" of technological innovation and environmental responsibility, making further regulation unnecessary and even detrimental to future innovation (95). The owner of a small business (not one related to the oil industry) offered an ironic description of this technological optimism:

The culture is so married to our ability through technology to master nature. Everybody thinks we'll have no problem—we'll geo-engineer our way out of this climate change issue through efficient fracking technology. We'll be able to extract for years and years without really thinking about the fact that we're burning this shit.

As he observes, and as our research confirmed, a fairly uniform consensus exists in these communities that the oil industry is only getting better and better at reducing its environmental impact. Likewise capturing the idea that technological improvement will automatically improve environmental outcomes, a volunteer with the local conservation group used the example of agricultural practices in the region: "Our machinery is getting better, and our farming practices, with the no-till and what not. So we're getting better. Like the oil companies are getting better, we're getting better." Another member of the group then chimed in, adding that "we're doing it on our own, not because we're mandated to." Here, with respect to safeguarding the environment, regulations are cast as inferior to the self-motivated adoption of new and improved technologies.

Conclusion

In the case of most industries, gaining social licence to operate primarily entails securing consent from communities at sites where a company plans to set up business. Efforts to obtain social licence are thus typically concerned with the operations of individual firms rather than with defending the legitimacy of an entire industry. Over the past two decades, however, the future of fossil fuel extraction has been called into question by global climate change, coupled with the work of climate justice movements and the development of green-energy alternatives. In such circumstances, the focus shifts from specific companies to the industry as a whole: an individual firm cannot gain social licence if it is part of an industry that has lost the trust of the public at large. As we mentioned at the outset, in the ongoing public debate about the future of fossil fuels, local extractive communities have become key voices of support for industry. It is not surprising, then, that the psychological identification we observed in interviews also manifested itself in a vigorous defence of the industry in the face of criticism, whether from local community members or from those perceived as outsiders.

The frequency with which those we interviewed adopted discursive frameworks disseminated by the fossil fuel industry points to a phenomenon that extends beyond merely generating consent for industry operations. What we witnessed was the adoption of industry's world view, a form of psychological identification so complete that community members internalize the discourse and come to regard it as their own. Central to this phenomenon is the creation and curation of a hegemonic community identity forged through continuous but subtle reminders of a community's economic dependence on industry for the provision of jobs, revenues, public services, and critical infrastructure. The result is the collapse of boundaries between community and industry, such that the interests of fossil fuel producers coalesce with the general interest of the "oil-producing" community.

In this context, oil-producing communities come to understand their fate as inextricably tied to that of industry. Residents of the three communities we studied routinely reproduced industry discourses on energy that envisage no alternatives to oil and that position the industry and, by extension, the community, as under siege. The active defence of industry, the identification of threats to industry as threats to the community, and the creation of a culture of silence about the negative consequences of fossil fuel production are the predictable responses of communities who see their existential survival as contingent on the survival of the industry. The hegemonic character of this community identity cannot be overstated. The concept of social licence rests on the assumption that communities have agency: a community can grant its consent, or it can choose to withdraw it. Once a hegemonic identity is in place, however, a community is, for all practical purposes, deprived of much of its ideological and moral autonomy. In the hands of industry, such a totalizing form of identity could be used to mobilize resistance in local oil-producing communities and thus pose as a serious obstacle to a post-carbon transition.

Notes

1. For an in-depth look at this boom and its impact on the social and economic fabric of rural Saskatchewan, see Zink and Eaton (2016).
2. In May 2019, the Progressive Conservative government of Premier Blaine Higgs enacted regulatory changes that would allow fracking to resume in the area

around Sussex, but plans are now on hold as the province failed its in duty to consult with local Mi'kmaq nations (see Magee 2019).

3. The quotation is from a widely adopted definition of CSR originally proposed by Business for Social Responsibility. For a critical evaluation of CSR approaches, especially as applied by Western development experts in countries of the Global South, see Blowfield and Frynas (2005).

4. Along similar lines, in a study of two cities in eastern Spain where formerly dominant industries (textiles, in one case, and shoe manufacture in the other) were in a state of decline, Francisco José Tovar and his colleagues (2011) explore the ways in which industry sought to sustain its importance by positioning itself as an essential partner in a shared cultural heritage around which community identity could cohere.

References

Bell, Shannon Elizabeth, and Richard York. 2010. "Community Economic Identity: The Coal Industry and Ideology Construction in West Virginia." *Rural Sociology* 75, no. 1: 111–43.

Blowfield, Michael, and Jedrzej George Frynas. 2005. "Setting New Agendas: Critical Perspectives on Corporate Social Responsibility in the Developing World." *International Affairs* 81, no. 3: 499–513.

Boggs, Carl. 1999. *The Two Revolutions: Gramsci and the Dilemmas of Western Marxism.* Boston: South End Press.

Bowen, Frances, Aloysius Newenham-Kahindi, and Irene Herremans. 2010. "When Suits Meet Roots: The Antecedents and Consequences of Community Engagement Strategy." *Journal of Business Ethics* 95, no. 2: 297–318.

Boyd, Amanda D. 2015. "Connections Between Community and Emerging Technology: Support for Enhanced Oil Recovery in the Weyburn, Saskatchewan Area." *International Journal of Greenhouse Gas Control* 32 (January): 81–89.

Cabrejas, Amaranta Herrero. 2012. "'Laciana Is Black. Greens Go Away!' Environmentalists as Scapegoats in a Mountaintop Removal Conflict in Laciana Valley, Spain." *Organization and Environment* 25, no. 4: 419–36.

CAPP (Canadian Association of Petroleum Producers). 2009. "Planting Long-Term Relationships." *Upstream Dialogue* (CAPP newsletter), July/August 2009.

———. 2012a. *Energy in Action: Final Report, 2012.* Calgary: Canadian Association of Petroleum Producers.

———. 2012b. *Energy in Action: What a Difference a Day Makes.* Video. https://www.youtube.com/watch?v=iEiPEO5iBkc.

Carter, Angela V., and Emily Eaton. 2016. "Subnational Responses to Fracking in Canada: Explaining Saskatchewan's 'Wild West' Regulatory Approach." *Review of Policy Research* 33, no. 4: 393–419.

Carter, Angela V., and Leah M. Fusco. 2017. "Western Newfoundland's Anti-Fracking Campaign: Exploring the Rise of Unexpected Community Mobilization." *Journal of Rural and Community Development* 12, no. 1: 98–120.

Eaton, Emily, and Simon Enoch. 2017. "Petro-Partners: Energy and Education in Saskatchewan's Rural Communities." *Monitor*, March/April 2017, 33–35. Ottawa: Canadian Centre for Policy Alternatives.

———. 2018. "Oil's Rural Reach: Social Licence in Saskatchewan's Oil-Producing Communities." *Canadian Journal of Communication* 43, no. 1: 53–74.

Eaton, Emily, and Abby Kinchy. 2016. "Quiet Voices in the Fracking Debate: Ambivalence, Nonmobilization, and Individual Action in Two Extractive Communities (Saskatchewan and Pennsylvania)." *Energy Research and Social Science* 20 (October): 22–30.

Ellis, Colter, Gene L. Theodori, Peggy Petrzelka, and Douglas Jackson-Smith. 2015. *Socially Responsible Drilling: Perspectives of Industry Representatives in the Eagle Ford Shale.* Huntsville, TX: Center for Rural Studies, Sam Houston State University. http://www.shsu.edu/dotAsset/170a5b8f-6554-46a1-b41b-fcab3f5be2f3.pdf.

Enoch, Simon. 2009. "The Potemkin Corporation: Corporate Social Responsibility, Public Relations and Crises of Democracy and Ecology." PhD diss., Ryerson University.

Enoch, Simon, and Emily Eaton. 2018. *A Prairie Patchwork: Reliance on Oil Industry Philanthropy in Saskatchewan Boomtowns.* Regina: Canadian Centre for Policy Alternatives, Saskatchewan Office.

Foster, Mary, Agnes Meinhard, Ida Berger, and Pike Wright. 2005. *From Philanthropic Strategy to Strategic Philanthropy: Selected Canadian Case Studies.* Toronto: Centre for Voluntary Sector Studies, Ryerson University.

Fusco, Leah M., and Angela V. Carter. 2017. "Toward an Anti-fracking Mobilization Toolkit: Ten Practices from Western Newfoundland's Campaign." *Interface* 9, no. 2: 276–99.

Jackson, Robert B., Avner Vengosh, J. William Carey, Richard J. Davies, Thomas H. Darrah, Francis O'Sullivan, and Gabrielle Pétron. 2014. "The Environmental Costs and Benefits of Fracking." *Annual Review of Environment and Resources* 39: 327–62.

Krashinsky, Susan. 2015. "Oil Companies Seek to Rebrand with Friendly Campaigns." *Globe and Mail*, July 16, 2015.

Kytle, Beth, and John Gerard Ruggie. 2005. "Corporate Social Responsibility as Risk Management: A Model for Multinationals." Corporate Social Responsibility

Initiative Working Paper No. 10. Cambridge, MA: John F. Kennedy School of Government, Harvard University.

Levy, David L. 1997. "Environmental Management as Political Sustainability." *Organization and Environment* 10, no. 2: 126–47.

Levy, David L., and Daniel Egan. 2003. "A Neo-Gramscian Approach to Corporate Political Strategy: Conflict and Accommodation in the Climate Change Negotiations." *Journal of Management Studies* 40, no. 4: 803–29.

Logsdon, Jeanne M., Martha Reiner, and Lee Burke. 1990. "Corporate Philanthropy: Strategic Responses to the Firm's Stakeholders." *Nonprofit and Voluntary Sector Quarterly* 19, no. 2: 93–109.

Lukes, Steven. 2005. *Power: A Radical View.* 2nd ed. Basingstoke, UK: Palgrave Macmillan.

Magee, Shane. 2019. "Sussex-Area Fracking Plans Shelved over 'Regulatory Uncertainty.'" *CBC News*, August 13, 2019. https://www.cbc.ca/news/canada/new-brunswick/corridor-fracking-sussex-regulatory-uncertainty-1.5245024.

Matz, Jacob, and Daniel Renfrew. 2015. "Selling Fracking: Energy in Depth and the Marcellus Shale." *Environmental Communication* 9, no. 3: 288–306.

Mooney, Chris. 2015. "Why Activists Are Pushing a 'Supply Side' Strategy for Fighting Climate Change." *Washington Post*, September 15, 2015.

Morrow, Adrian. 2015. "Interprovincial Climate Summit Reveals Rifts in Canada's Carbon Strategy." *Globe and Mail*, April 14, 2015.

Oil Respect. 2017. "Get the Facts: How Much Does Canada Contribute?" Oil Respect Infographic. July 7, 2017. https://oilrespect.ca/get-the-facts-how-much-does-canada-contribute/.

Olive, Andrea, and Katie Valentine. 2018. "Is Anyone Out There? Exploring Saskatchewan's Civil Society Involvement in Hydraulic Fracturing." *Energy Research and Social Science* 39 (May): 192–97.

Prno, Jason, and D. Scott Slocombe. 2012. "Exploring the Origins of 'Social License to Operate' in the Mining Sector: Perspectives from Governance and Sustainability Theories." *Resources Policy* 37, no. 3: 346–57.

Schneider, Jen, Steve Schwarze, Peter Bsumek, and Jennifer Peeples. 2016. *Under Pressure: Coal Industry Rhetoric and Neoliberalism.* London: Palgrave Macmillan.

Shriver, Thomas E., Alison E. Adams, and Chris M. Messer. 2014. "Power, Quiescence, and Pollution: The Suppression of Environmental Grievances." *Social Currents* 1, no. 3: 275–92.

Smith, Don C., and Jessica M. Richards. 2015. "Social License to Operate: Hydraulic Fracturing-Related Challenges Facing the Oil and Gas Industry." *Oil and Gas, Natural Resources, and Energy Journal* 1, no. 2: 81–163.

Steinzor, Nadia, Wilma Subra, and Lisa Sumi. 2013. "Investigating Links Between Shale Gas Development and Health Impacts Through a Community Survey Project in Pennsylvania." *New Solutions* 23, no. 1: 55–83.

Thomson, Ian, and Robert G. Boutilier. 2011. "Social License to Operate." In *SME Mining Engineering Handbook*, 3rd ed., edited by Peter Darling, 1:1779–96. Littleton, CO: Society for Mining, Metallurgy, and Exploration.

Tovar, Francisco José, María Arnal, Carlos de Castro, Arturo Lahera-Sánchez, and Juan Carlos Revillo. 2011. "A Tale of Two Cities: Working Class Identity, Industrial Relations and Community in Declining Textile and Shoe Industries in Spain." *International Journal of Heritage Studies* 17, no. 4: 331–43.

UNCTAD (United Nations Conference on Trade and Development). 2004. *Disclosure of the Impact of Corporations on Society: Current Trends and Issues.* New York and Geneva: United Nations.

Wall, Karen. 2015. "'The Sharpest Knives in the Drawer': Visual Culture at the Intersection of Oil and State." In *Alberta Oil and the Decline of Democracy in Canada*, edited by Meenal Shrivastava and Lorna Stefanick, 333–61. Edmonton: Athabasca University Press.

Zink, Valerie, and Emily Eaton. 2016. *Fault Lines: Life and Landscape in Saskatchewan's Oil Economy.* Winnipeg: University of Manitoba Press.

12 Indigenous Gendered Experiences of Work in an Oil-Dependent, Rural Alberta Community

Angele Alook, Ian Hussey, and Nicole Hill

The development of Alberta's oil sands is often touted not merely as essential to the province's economy but as key to the prosperity of Canada as a whole. Yet the Indigenous residents of the oil sands region do not necessarily reap the benefits of this immensely profitable industry. Quite apart from ongoing efforts to restrict their land rights, Indigenous people have only a limited opportunity to participate in decisions surrounding economic development or to rise to positions of influence within the oil industry itself. Researchers have documented the educational and training barriers that exist for Indigenous individuals in the oil sands region, as well as the sidelining of both First Nations and Métis in the public-private "partnerships" promoted by a neoliberal regime (see Taylor and Friedel 2011; Taylor, Friedel, and Edge 2009). Research in the Fort McMurray area has also shed valuable light on how gender and race shape experiences of work in the region (see Dorow 2015; Foster and Barnetson 2015; O'Shaughnessy and Doğu 2016), although these studies do not focus specifically on Indigenous workers.

Moreover, despite the studies that have been done, little is known about the impact of involvement with the oil industry on the day-to-day life of Indigenous families and communities. As Tara Joly and Clinton Westman

This chapter was originally published as a Corporate Mapping Project report (Edmonton: Parkland Institute, 2019). It is reprinted here, in somewhat revised form, by permission of the publisher.

(2017, v) point out in a recent review of social science research in the oil sands region, "there has been virtually no monitoring of economic or employment benefits" that allegedly accrue to Indigenous communities as a result of development, a neglect evident in "a lack of information about labour market participation and experiences." In particular, the implications of employment in a highly masculinized industry have yet to be explored. This chapter aims to help address these knowledge gaps through a case study of Wabasca, an oil-dependent community located about 135 kilometres northeast of Slave Lake, to the southwest of Fort McMurray. Specifically, by examining the lived experiences of Indigenous people employed in the oil industry, we seek to provide an in-depth understanding of how working conditions impact gender relations within Indigenous families and communities.

Wabasca is headquarters to the Bigstone Cree Nation (BCN), whose lands in the area are divided among five separate reserves, the largest only about 8,500 hectares, that cluster around the hamlet of Wabasca-Desmarais and together cover just a little over 21,000 hectares.[1] These "checkerboard" reserves are surrounded by Municipal District of Opportunity No. 17—which describes itself as the "land of opportunity" to emphasize its abundant natural resources and large land base. It is, indeed, the third-largest municipality in Alberta, stretching across more than 2.91 million hectares. Overall, the district is very sparsely populated. At the time of the 2016 census, the off-reserve population of the municipal district stood at only 3,181, with almost half of these individuals (1,406)—the majority of whom identified as Indigenous—living in the Wabasca-Desmarais community. At that time, the population of the five Wabasca reserves totalled 2,157, for a total resident population of 3,563 in the Wabasca area.[2]

In addition to the resident population, the Wabasca area is home to a temporary oil industry workforce housed in work camps—a "shadow population" that, in 2015/16, was forecast to number 2,200.[3] These work camps exist because Wabasca is also home to the Wabasca oil field. Now considered a southwestern extension of the vast Athabasca oil sands area, the Wabasca deposits are the source of a thick crude known as Pelican Lake heavy oil, which is recovered by horizontal drilling in combination with a process called polymer flooding. Operations at Wabasca are dominated by Canadian Natural Resources Limited, which, in 2017, acquired assets previously owned by Cenovus, for a price of $975 million. At the time of the sale, production stood at roughly 19,600 barrels per day (Hislop 2017).

Gender, Race, and the Oil Industry

Jobs in the oil, gas, and mining industry accounted for 6.1% of total employment in Alberta in 2017 (Alberta 2018, 2). Unsurprisingly, these industries were, and continue to be, dominated by men. Only 21.5 percent of the workers in this sector were women, whereas women made up 45.5 percent of Alberta's overall labour force at the time (5). At $40.40 per hour, the median wage of workers in these industries considerably exceeded the median wage of $26.40 for the province as a whole (6). But these statistics give us only part of the story.

One persistent, and widespread, problem is pay equity. As law professor Kathleen Lahey (2016) points out, at an average of 33 percent, Canada's gender income gap is already enormous, typically ranked as the third largest among the thirty-four OECD countries. In 2016, however, the income gap in Alberta stood at 41 percent—the highest in the country. On average, women working full time, all year, were earning $31,000 less than their male counterparts. The gender pay gap is even more troublesome when we consider that most women are working a "double day." In Alberta, women perform approximately 35 hours of unpaid work per week, more than twice the average of 17 hours for men (Lahey 2016, 1).

These inequities carry over to oil industry workers. Social science research on Alberta's oil sands industry—most of it conducted in Fort McMurray, with no particular focus on Indigenous workers—reveals that disparities grounded in gender and in race and ethnicity are built into the division of labour in the industry. Describing the frenzied work environment of Fort McMurray as a "pressure cooker," sociologist Sara Dorow (2015) argues that this pressure is especially felt by women and racialized people. Through their paid and unpaid work, these marginalized populations support men's work in a highly masculinized industry, not only to the benefit of male workers themselves but also to the profit of (mostly male) oil executives and the shareholders in oil corporations. Some women stay home with children to free up earning time for their partners, but many are employed themselves, and Dorow finds that both women and racialized workers "are overrepresented in the feminized, precarious, and invisible work of service, retail, and care in Fort McMurray" (2015, 277). This gendered inequality of access to high-paying jobs means that men's incomes in the region are more than double those of women (280).

In homes in which both parents work, nannies—often Filipina temporary foreign workers (TFWs)—pick up the slack in child care, as well as performing some housework. Outside the home, other TFWs do much of the care and cleaning work that supports the retail, service, and hospitality sectors in the Fort McMurray region (see Hill, Alook, and Hussey 2017). By servicing the needs of oil industry workers, both in Fort McMurray and in the surrounding work camps, these TFWs fill a critical role in the social reproductive processes on which capitalist accumulation depends. Yet this type of employment is highly precarious. TFWs have only limited access to citizenship rights and to the labour market, given that their work permits are tied to a specific employer, while their jobs typically come with low wages and few benefits and sometimes with a heightened risk of injury or ill health. Labour researchers Jason Foster and Bob Barnetson (2015, 264) point to the creation of a "two-tiered labour market, populated by citizen workers and noncitizen workers," in which the fundamental distinction is one of skin colour, with the latter group made up mostly of individuals from the Global South.

In addition to TFWs, Fort McMurray has a significant Somali refugee population. Sara O'Shaughnessy and Göze Doğu (2016) find that Somali women in Fort McMurray experience discrimination based on their gender, race, religion, and culture. Given that some employers are reluctant to hire them at all, many of these women end up in janitorial jobs. In one case, several Somali women who were employed by a cleaning service were fired, as a group, for wearing long skirts to work, on the grounds that company safety policy required them to wear pants (280). As O'Shaughnessy and Doğu further point out, women in general have a hard time in the masculine culture of the oil industry. They describe how women who attempted to downplay their femininity in an effort to fit in were ostracized by other women as "bitches" or as "mannish," while women who insisted on maintaining their femininity were ostracized for being too "giggly-girly" or were perceived as "not tough enough" to succeed in their job (288). Add to this the industry's bias toward male workers, a significant pay gap between men and women, and the normalization of verbal, physical and sexual harassment, and the challenges faced by women are readily apparent.

In the case of Indigenous women, these challenges are compounded, and not only in Alberta's oil industry. In the context of the rapidly escalating development of the fossil fuel industry in northeastern British Columbia's Peace River region, a study by Amnesty International (2016, 40) identified patterns of inequality and discrimination against Indigenous workers in general and Indigenous women in particular. First Nations and Métis workers reported that, at some worksites, co-workers made them feel "unwelcome and even unsafe," while others spoke of employers who took a "last hired, first fired" approach to Indigenous workers. "There's an old boys' club that controls hiring," explained Marvin Yahey, chief of the Blueberry River First Nations. "After everything is in play, they invite the First Nations in for the shovel jobs, the grunt jobs." In this highly masculine environment, women "work twice as hard to get half the recognition," said one female worker.

The Amnesty International report (2016, 40) also called attention to "the conflict between jobs that require long, multi-day and multi-week shifts often far from home, and cultural traditions of being out on the land with extended family." Perhaps its key finding, however, is that violence against Indigenous women is a routine part of life for those involved in BC's extractive sector. Many women indicated that they would refuse a job if it required them to live in a work camp, where, as the report noted, a "highly stressful environment, physical isolation, and the drug and alcohol abuse at some camps" combine to create a dangerous environment for women (42). Women described daily sexual harassment on some worksites, much of which goes unreported. Echoing Chief Yahey's comment about hiring, one Indigenous woman explained, "It's a boys' club, so if something happens you don't say anything" (42). Others described the sexual expectations of some of their male co-workers, and even cases of sexual assault. As a social worker observed, the risk to Indigenous women is exacerbated "by the large numbers of men who come to the region to work in industry and the way that their economic power emboldens them to express racist and sexist attitudes they might suppress elsewhere" (51).

In regions such as northeastern British Columbia, where resource extraction takes place on a huge scale, Indigenous peoples bear the brunt of the socioeconomic and environmental burdens, yet they benefit the least from the massive profits generated by these industries. Likewise in Alberta, workers in the extractive industries are afforded a different worth based on their race and gender. White men are significantly advantaged in employment in the province, earning significantly higher incomes in nearly every occupational field in comparison both to women and to visible minority and Indigenous men (see Lahey 2016, 21, table 4). Similarly, white women typically earn more than non-white women. Although roughly one in five white women work in relatively low-paying sales and service jobs, visible minority and Indigenous women are even more likely to be employed in such positions, yet their median incomes are lower (particularly in the case of Indigenous women, who earn about a quarter less than white women). In much the same way, while a third of white men are employed in trades, transport, and equipment operation, among Indigenous men the figure rises to nearly half, but their median income is about 20 percent less than that of their white counterparts.

In short, Albertans are living in a petro-province in which fossil fuel corporations wield enormous power, a province located in a settler-colonial country whose economy relies an intersectional hierarchy of labour value characterized by the hyperexploitation of women and racialized people. In a corporate-capitalist economy, even well-paid white workers have little job security, but racialized people—especially non-white women—tend to be confined to precarious, marginal positions in which their low wages contribute to high profits. In short, Alberta's ongoing commitment to the fossil fuel sector is obviously leaving some people behind. Although women, Indigenous, and racialized people are finding their way into these jobs, they are still the exception, and they face enormous challenges of discrimination when they get there.

Researching Indigenous Gender Relations in Wabasca

As of the 2016 census, Indigenous people accounted for roughly 6.5 percent of Alberta's total population—a proportion considerably higher than the figure of 4.8 percent for Canada overall. Just over half of the province's Indigenous people—52.8 percent—were First Nations, while 44.2 percent were Métis.[4] At the time, the oil sands region was home to approximately 23,000 Indigenous people, from eighteen First Nations and six Métis settlements (Natural Resources Canada 2016, 1).

In Alberta, as in Canada as a whole, the relationship between Indigenous people and the state has been deeply shaped by colonialism, past and present. The systemic racism that Indigenous peoples still face throughout the country is rooted in the process of colonization. This bitter legacy is manifested today in intergenerational trauma related to the breakdown of Indigenous families, as Indigenous children continue to be taken into foster care in disproportionate numbers and poverty takes its toll on family life. Indigenous people are beset by chronic underemployment and denied equal access to basic human and citizenship rights, including education, health care, safe drinking water, and decent housing. They are overrepresented in the prison system, while the country is witnessing an epidemic of missing and murdered Indigenous women and girls.

The present chapter builds on research conducted by Angele Alook in 2011 and 2012 (Alook 2016). Alook interviewed young Indigenous men and women living in Edmonton and in the Wabasca area, both on and off reserve, with a view to exploring the formation of cultural identity and the influence of gender on experiences of family, school, and work. She found that extended family networks and the building of healthy family relations not only promote resilience but also offer a form of resistance to the colonial and gendered structures encountered in school and at work. At the same time, her research revealed that involvement with the resource extraction industry encourages a highly gendered division of labour, which is reflected in gendered life scripts. Indigenous men often end up in traditionally masculine oil industry occupations, working as tradesmen, general labourers, or heavy equipment operators. In interviews, men talked about leaving school early to take jobs in the oilfield and about how they felt steered into this life course by both the school system and the oil industry. Indigenous women were less likely to work directly in the industry but tended to be streamed into female-dominated professions, serving, for example, as administrative assistants, teachers, or social workers. The women with whom Alook spoke indicated that they needed to get an education if they hoped to avoid the fate of early childbearing and a life of poverty.

Although these men and women clearly valued traditional extended family networks, Alook discovered that, within families, gender relations varied from the egalitarian patterns traditional in Indigenous cultures, in which neither sex is regarded as inherently superior to the other, through to Western-style patriarchal relations that impose a clear gender hierarchy. These findings raised a number of key questions that provided the impetus for further research. What impact does oil industry employment have on Indigenous family relationships? What are the implications of the oil industry for Indigenous family and community health? How does the streaming of Indigenous men and women into gendered occupations that reflect Western values affect family and community well-being?

In approaching these questions, we have been guided by the Cree and Anishinaabe concept of *miyo-pimatisiwin* (or, in Anishinaabemowin, *mino-bimaadiziwin*), often translated as the "good life," and the emphasis it places on extended families and on mutually respectful gender relations in which power is evenly distributed. To live a good life is, among other things, to understand health in a holistic way, in which individual well-being is connected to overall family health, which is in turn integral to community health (see Hart 2002). Within this communal understanding of health, all aspects of self and community—spiritual, emotional, physical, and mental—are viewed as essential to well-being.

In our ongoing research with the BCN community, we employ a decolonizing methodology, one that generates knowledge grounded in local Indigenous world views and insists that research must give back to communities. Such a methodology avoids Western colonial practices in which Indigenous peoples are treated as objects of study who furnish information for the benefit of the researcher (Smith 1999). Our research is accordingly done *with* and *for* the BCN community (Menzies 2001). As a member of that community, Alook secured permission to undertake the study from the chief and council in the form of a band council resolution, and she also conducted all of the interviews, carefully observing Cree protocol. As was the case in her earlier research, Alook modelled the interviews on the Cree practice of *âcimowin*, or storytelling, inviting participants to tell her stories about their lives.[5]

The following analysis draws in part on eight interviews that Alook conducted in 2011 and 2012, three with women and five with men. All eight were married, with one to three children each, and their average age was thirty-two at the time. Two of the women were public sector workers; the third was a skilled tradeswoman. Of the five men, two were managers in oilfield service companies, and the other three worked in the oilfield, two as power system engineers and one is a truck driver. These interviews were then supplemented by eight new ones, which took place in the spring of 2018. This group consisted of six men and two women, with an average age of thirty-five. Four were married, with two or three children each, and four were single, with no children. Three of the men were managers or assistant managers at oilfield service companies, and the other three were skilled tradesmen. Of the two women, one was an administrator at an oilfield service company, and the other had a job in the public sector in the community of Wabasca. Those who were employed in the oil industry all worked for Indigenous companies, owned either by BCN or by an Indigenous person or family. One of the sixteen people interviewed was Métis; the rest were Cree.

A variety of themes emerge from the interviews, which can be grouped into three overarching categories. One has to do with nature of the oil industry and, in particular, with the impact of systemic racism on Indigenous workers, as well as the gender discrimination that women often encounter. A second theme revolves around the differential impact of oil industry employment on men and women, as well as the effects of this employment on family life and on employees themselves. A final theme concerns Indigenous understandings of community and the challenges posed to traditional community values by the presence of the oil industry.

The Impact of Discrimination on Indigenous Workers

In Wabasca, as in any oil-producing community, the oil industry is the main source of job opportunities for men. But finding a job is only the first step in building a career. In discussing oil industry employment, the men we interviewed often spoke about the discrimination they encountered in attempting to rise up the ladder. Workers frequently pointed out that labourer jobs are the standard entry point into the industry for local men. As one explained, "A lot of people here in this town, they'll start basically coming in as a labourer if they have no experience running equipment previously." At the same time, many commented on how difficult it is to advance from these low-level jobs, despite a desire to do more than just physical labour. One worker reflected that he "should have went the education way and got some kind of degree or diploma" because he "was in the mud for a long time." Another explained that "it's hard to move up as a labourer . . . you're in maintenance, like, there's nothing higher." This streaming of Indigenous workers into jobs as labourers is a form of systemic discrimination in the industry.

The Enduring Force of Racial Stereotypes

"If a person puts all their effort into it," said one participant, "there's no reason why they shouldn't advance, right?" Yet the idea that only certain individuals possess the "drive" needed to climb the labour ladder frequently came up. As the manager of an oil service company put it, "You can pick up on the people that are able to move up." The suggestion was that adequate opportunities to advance do exist but that "some people like to stay back." In the opinion of a senior worker, "only some" Indigenous people take work "seriously enough that they're willing to move up" and who "find the drive and determination." He went on to say, "You see that in a lot of kids here. They're so happy that they got *a* job; they don't want that job that's one step up." While perhaps not intentionally, such attitudes perpetuate stereotypes of Indigenous workers as unmotivated—as deficient in energy and ambition.

Adding to this racist image of Indigenous people as fundamentally lazy is the assumption that workers employed by oilfield companies owned by First Nations simply get "work handed to them" because they are Indigenous. Some of those interviewed raised the notion of "handouts," often in a disparaging way or to distance themselves from them. One worker explained, "Nothing I got has been handed to me." Such comments reflect negative stereotypes according to which Indigenous people feel a sense of entitlement—that, rather than viewing success as something one earns through hard work and a willingness to seize on opportunities, they rely on handouts from the state and other forms of favouritism. This formulation, which attributes the failure to "move up" to a refusal to exercise personal agency, ignores the educational barriers and the racism and colonial trauma that make it hard for some Indigenous people to participate successfully in the waged economy.

Another stereotype that emerged in interviews was the idea that Indigenous workers are only good enough for unskilled work. As one service company manager noted, "The conception that Natives will only be a labourer is something that we've had years and years and we have to try and break that norm. . . . We don't just operate shovels." This normalization of the racist notion that Indigenous workers are best suited to labourer jobs has the effect of stalling them in unskilled, lower-paying work. A number of people pointed out that Indigenous workers are not treated in the same way as other oilfield workers: they miss out on wage raises, and they are also more likely to be laid off.

One worker who had previously been employed with a non-Indigenous company explained that "it was harder to move up" in such companies. "Even if I was better than someone else," he said, "they would move up quicker than I would . . . usually just white guys." Another commented, "Because I was First Nations, not because I had less experience . . . it's taken me longer to get up the ladder." Both individuals were skilled workers who were able to advance once they moved to Indigenous companies. One senior oilfield official was convinced that a major oil company operating nearby would simply not hire Indigenous workers. "They're all in cahoots," he said, noting that nobody living on reserve was employed at this company. "That impacts a lot of people 'cause there's a lot of work there, but we're not allowed to work there. It's only *môniyaw* [white people] that are allowed there."

Alluding to another commonplace stereotype, one oilfield worker described an incident that had occurred while he was in another town. He and fellow Indigenous workers were being harassed by local white guys and were even assaulted at one point, yet they were the ones ultimately questioned by the police, who warned them that they would be "keeping an eye" on them. After this incident, he said, "It was so bad I never did go back there again to work." Another skilled worker remarked that people in the surrounding community often make derogatory comments about those living on reserve, "as if we're all criminals and such, alcoholics or drug abusers." In view of such stereotypes, several of those we interviewed mentioned the need to work harder than white workers. As one put it, "It's almost like you're trying to prove yourself a little bit as well that, you know what? we're just as good as anybody else."

For similar reasons, it is not easy for an Indigenous company to compete in an industry dominated by non-Indigenous corporations. As one person explained, "We really have to sell our people and say, 'No, we're not the typical Native.' There's a typical Native that people assume is out there: lazy, late, and never there the next day." At a time when First Nations are being encouraged to set up their own companies and thus create jobs, such attitudes clearly place them at disadvantage—nor does the existence of flourishing companies owned and operated by First Nations seem to have seriously dislodged the stereotype that Indigenous people lack drive and ambition. Moreover, workers who are prevented by systemic discrimination from getting ahead in non-Indigenous companies but who subsequently do well in Indigenous companies are denied their success by the racist assumption that opportunities must have been handed to them that they didn't actually deserve.

After breaking through racist barriers and winning contracts in the oil industry, Indigenous-owned companies and their employees feel a sense of genuine accomplishment, and workers often expressed a sense of relief to be employed at such a company. Being part of an Indigenous company, one said, "is probably the most I ever felt comfortable at the workplace." As he explained, "before I felt like, don't matter how hard I work here, I was still like, the brown boy." In contrast, the environment at his current company seemed friendly and welcoming—more like a family, he said.

The racism embedded in the industry has one other serious consequence for Indigenous workers, however, which stems from the boom-and-bust commodity cycle to which the oil industry is subject. In such an unstable environment, even a relatively modest downturn in oil prices can lead to layoffs. As one man put it, "with the industry, you got to work when there's work or, because you never know when—you know what I mean—it could get slow again and not be any work." During a downturn, production drops, and unskilled workers are generally the ones to be let go first, a pattern that places Indigenous labourers at a disadvantage. In the meanwhile, workers who continue to be employed face the stress of watching co-workers lose their jobs and the constant fear that the axe may swing in their direction, even as their own workloads increase. As one commented. when someone is laid off, "we kind of just take on everything for that role."

Although, in a male-dominated industry, downturns clearly take their heaviest toll on men in terms of numbers, one male worker suggested that it is "maybe a little harder for the women to get work" at such a time. Downturns also have a ripple effect, such that oil service companies suffer when the rate of production drops. One skilled worker said that he felt "fortunate to just be working" during the three-year bust period that followed the sharp decline in oil prices in the fall of 2014. Another grimly observed, "Everybody's replaceable, right?" During that period, one Indigenous company in Wabasca shrank from two hundred employees to as few as seventy. In a community of thirty-five hundred people, the loss of those high-paying jobs matters a lot.

Gender Discrimination

The men with whom we spoke expressed differing views about the extent to which the oil industry is male dominated. One service company manager commented that "it's pretty rare to see women doing labour-type work in the oilfield. I have come across one or two female workers, but they generally don't seem to last as long maybe as a male worker." When asked whether women have equal opportunity for advancement, male workers could only speculate. "Yeah, I guess—I've never really seen the issue before," one said, while another suggested that, as an industry minority, women actually get special treatment: "I think girls actually get treated better when they do get jobs . . . like everyone's just nice to them all the time." Yet the lack of women in upper-level positions made some aware that a disparity exists. One male worker observed that, despite his company's claim that women are given equal opportunities, "I haven't really seen any females in higher positions like that."

Some men argued that, even though the industry is male dominated, no bias exists against women, whom they felt were treated equally. By way of explaining the imbalance, they pointed instead to "family commitments" and especially to the role of women as mothers. In the opinion of one, "Women have a tougher time with having to commit to the work schedule. Basically they're not able to have the daycare or the care for their children at home, especially single mothers or mothers in general."

Several of the men called attention to a few Indigenous women in the community who had learned a trade and were certified as journeymen, pointing to these women as evidence that, with enough initiative and drive, women can succeed. Speaking of one such woman "down the road," a male journeyman acknowledged that "for a woman to try and break through, it's not easy," noting that "we're not a rig company, but you hear of that 'rig pig' mentality." He went on to say that "it's gotten better over the years, but it definitely wouldn't be an easy place for a woman to work."

According to a woman who had certified as a pipefitter, working in the oil industry can be "a bit tough at times," partly because "guys with all their testosterone" think that they are better than women. She recognized the male tendency to regard women as sexual objects, noting that, in terms of their appearance, women in the industry need to downplay their femininity and try to avoid making themselves "attractive to the opposite sex." She also observed that women must do their best not to be "so high maintenance" or otherwise call attention to themselves as women. "You definitely have to be comfortable with yourself," she said. In her view, when it came to sexual remarks or physical advances, "you just deal with it and do something about it if you feel [you need to], you know."

A manager at an Indigenous-owned service company also raised the issue of harassment. "We're trying to promote equality out in the field," he said, "yet female workers do get harassed by other workers, and they're out there working just like anybody else." As he explained, "We're here to protect them if they come up and ask us for assistance," but he acknowledged that the source of the problem was old-fashioned patriarchal attitudes that flourish within the oil industry itself. "It's a different industry," he said, and "a lot of old-fashioned Aboriginal men are probably the most old-fashioned people out there. As an Aboriginal company, that's the tough part." Part of the old-fashioned way of thinking is that a woman's place is in the home. Unfortunately, the oil industry still generally subscribes to the masculinist idea that physical labour is a job for men.

Working Families

Conversations with both male and female participants revealed an unequal sharing of social reproductive labour—a pattern that is in no way unique to Indigenous families. As a general rule, women who were employed outside the home were also responsible for most or all of the child care, cooking, and cleaning. A woman explained that her husband "was raised by old-school parents that think that the wife should be the cook and the cleaner—so that's my role." One working mother who was also in school struggled to balance three major commitments. "It's tough," she said, "and then having a family, it's overwhelming.... Just managing the kids and coming to work and then going home and cooking supper and then take care of your kids, make sure they get fed and to bed—and that's when you [have] time for school." Women's unpaid work is often invisible: it is taken for granted and thus goes unacknowledged. Yet one senior manager did openly recognize his wife's contribution to the household: "If I didn't have a wife that stayed home and she was a full-time mom," he noted, "I think we'd have difficulty doing my job and trying to do that at the same time."

Women's responsibilities for reproductive labour were reflected in their daily schedules: women typically worked a standard nine-to-five day. In contrast, men in oilfield jobs often put in long shifts or worked standard hours plus overtime as needed (and it was often needed). "There's days where I feel like I lose time with my kids because I work," one male worker commented, adding that because he works long shifts he tries to be with them when he is not at work. Others pointed out that they do make an effort to help with laundry, cooking, extracurricular activities with children, and yard work, trying to maintain an equitable division of labour as far as their work schedules permit.

Beyond assigning women to the domestic sphere, such that outside employment becomes an add-on, patriarchal family structures are also deeply bounded up with notions of masculinity. Although the idea that the man should be the primary breadwinner in the family has slowly begun to erode, it is still very much the ruling assumption among men who work in resource extraction. One man described his emotional struggles after the 2014 crash in oil prices. He lost his job during the downturn, and his female partner became the breadwinner in their home—a change that "definitely affected self-esteem," he said, "as in not being able to provide." He went on to explain that he did not feel that a man necessarily had to be the main provider, but "you talk to peers, right? And there's jokes that are made." Embracing the caregiver role in the household required him to confront problematic notions about masculinity, including ideas like "men don't cry" and "men don't talk about feelings."

Men who do not have to grapple with the emotional consequences of unemployment face a different problem: work-related stress. The pressures of oil industry work, with its frenetic pace and long hours, often find an outlet in alcohol or drug abuse. A number of men described their efforts to make healthier choices in dealing with stress. They talked about surrounding themselves with people that do not use, about spending time with family and friends, and about engaging in various forms of physical recreation to burn off steam. Several workers mentioned taking part in outdoor activities such as hunting, fishing, camping, and sledding, as well as heading out into backcountry on all-terrain vehicles or skidoos.

On the whole, those we interviewed saw oil industry employment as a double-edged sword. Some pointed to the high incomes earned by industry workers as an asset, providing families with a good overall quality of life, enabling parents to enrol their kids in organized sports such as hockey, and allowing their children to pursue post-secondary education. Yet many recognized the negative impact that oil industry employment can have on family life. One worker summed up his life: "long hours away from home, always on the phone, too tired to do anything in the evenings." He added that "you're always in a conflict one way or another with somebody when it comes to the family." Another admitted that he sometimes brings job stress home, although he recognized that his family was also a source of strength and support. A number of those we interviewed likewise pointed to the important role of extended family in providing child care and emotional support, particularly when women were in school and/or worked outside the home.

Community

The Indigenous men and women whom we interviewed felt a strong bond to the Bigstone Cree community, from which they derived much of their sense of self-identity. Central to this perception of community was a shared awareness of "which family you belong to," as one person put it: "everybody knows who your mom is, who your dad is, who your grandparents are." Another defined community as "knowing where your roots are." This prioritization of family relationships, together with a sense of belonging to a particular place, is key to Indigenous understandings of personal identity as emerging from and situated within the collective.

Community was also perceived in terms of mutual support, founded on the conviction that each person is responsible for the welfare of the whole. One person pointed to the way in which the community comes together "when needed at a time of crisis or celebration," and many spoke of the importance of supporting other community members who had fallen on hard times, through donations and fundraisers, for example. "The community is so willing to give—it's amazing to see that," one said. She saw this sense of reciprocity as "more of an Aboriginal thing. People taking care of their own." Similarly, describing her extended kin network, another woman commented, "We help each other . . . we're not alone, we have each other all the time." Others emphasized their efforts to reach out to those in difficulty, including people with addictions and youth who seem to need help. "There was people when I was young that took the time out to stop and talk to me," one man said. "I feel that I owe the younger generation the same."

The sense of membership in a community carried over to the workplace, which became a site for solidarity among Indigenous workers. "We talk a lot in Cree and joke around, yeah, so—it's fun," one explained, adding that "the majority of us are all First Nations." Those working in Indigenous companies often described a sense of loyalty to the company and to their co-workers. As one manager put it, "We kind of pride ourselves here . . . there's not too many oilfield companies that are 100 percent Native owned and operated." It was through his work community that one man discovered his connection to the land. Others at the company where he worked used to "go out hunting," he recalled, "and I started hanging out with them out in the bush, and it became something I liked doing." He went on to say that he eventually started going out into the bush on his own, which enabled him to reconnect his family to the land as well.

As many of those to whom we spoke acknowledged, the Bigstone Cree community has benefitted materially from the presence of the oil industry. In addition to providing needed employment, companies donate to local sports teams and provide financial support for community projects (a pattern discussed in the previous chapter). At the same time, the industry has in many ways destabilized the community. As one person put it, "The industry brought in jobs, and it has brought in a ton of money, but when you bring in jobs and you bring in money, you also bring in drugs and you bring in alcohol. Now you can afford those things." Moreover, community residents do not have equal access to this newfound prosperity.

As the chief source of work, the oil industry has also been a source of tensions, with multiple local service companies competing for a finite number of oilfield contracts. These tensions were especially evident in the period following the 2014 crash, when production slowed and with it the demand for external services. As the manager of a service company noted, a downturn "makes it a little harder to get work," explaining that his company would bid on a job only to find that another company had come in under its bid. "And we're all working against each other," he said, competing for whatever work can be had. Another manager noted that their Indigenous-owned, private business was sometimes in the position of competing for contracts with a BCN-owned company, commenting ironically that the "biggest people we have to compete with are our own nation." Others described tensions in the community between people who were working for different Indigenous-owned companies, as well as between those who were in a position to do hiring and workers in the community who had been laid off and needed jobs but were not being hired.

In short, the spirit of competition essential to capitalist economies, along with the willingness to exploit others and to be exploited oneself, runs counter to Indigenous understandings of community, in which the welfare of the whole takes precedence over individual material gain. Although members of the Bigstone Cree community had been exposed to capitalist waged labour long before the oil industry arrived, the sheer scale of that industry and the "ton of money" associated with it are unprecedented. This influx of wealth has provided new opportunities, but it has also served to unsettle traditional values and the sense of community integrity and balance that these values provide.

Conclusion: Seeking the "Good Life" in the Oilfields of Capitalism

For Cree peoples, a life founded on *miyo-pimatisiwin* is a life of health and balance, within individuals, families, and the community as whole. *Miyo-pimatisiwin* is a state in which all aspects of life stand in their proper relation to all other aspects and people give equal attention to all parts of the whole, in accordance with traditional values such as respect and reciprocity. Indigenous people lost *miyo-pimatisiwin* in their lives when colonialism severed their relationship with the land and traditional modes of subsistence were lost. This way of life entailed spiritual, emotional, physical, mental, and material balance with the earth, as well as between genders. As Indigenous lands were appropriated, Indigenous peoples were drawn into the colonial capitalist economy, with its hierarchical division of labour. Today, workers and families in Wabasca must struggle to restore *miyo-pimatisiwin* in their day-to-day lives.

The oil industry's boom-and-bust cycle and the competitive pressures of capitalism have brought significant imbalance and disruption to oil-dependent Indigenous communities. Individuals working in the oil industry have experienced discrimination related to both race and gender, and some of those we interviewed had internalized hegemonic racist stereotypes according to which Indigenous workers lack the drive needed to move up the labour ladder. Others were conscious of these stereotypes and resisted them. At the same time, Indigenous companies have been able to carve out space in an industry dominated by non-Indigenous corporations. In so doing, these companies have created family-like communities where Indigenous workers are no longer held back or excluded and can take pride in who they are.

The oil industry's boom-and-bust cycle and the pressures of capitalism can bring significant imbalance and disruption to communities, as described here. However, through relationality in the community—specifically, paid and unpaid caring work performed largely by women—the community works to establish balance.

The male-dominated oil industry has itself contributed to this imbalance. In a community where a single industry is the primary source of employment, the patriarchal attitudes embedded in the oil industry create barriers and deterrents for women that not only reduce their access to relatively high-paying oilfield jobs but ultimately limit their opportunities for employment of any sort, given that few alternatives are available. Work-related stress has thus become a significant issue for community members. Whether the product of immediate pressures at work or of the loss of a job or the fear of losing one, stress can create family tensions, as well as contributing to social issues such as drug and alcohol addiction and interpersonal violence.

Also of concern are the class divisions created by the industry. Many Indigenous workers end up stuck in unskilled labourer positions, but a few manage to learn a trade and move into better-paying jobs as skilled journeymen. These men sometimes start their own contracting companies and so wind up becoming relatively prosperous business owners. The result is the emergence of small-scale Indigenous capitalists. Although they may view themselves, and perhaps are to some degree seen by others, simply as members of the community, these local business owners are in a position to provide jobs. In terms of capitalist class structure, they are employers, not workers, and this distinction is a source of division within the community.

At the same time, in the wake of the 2014 downturn, local Indigenous oilfield service companies struggled to stay afloat, given that they depend for their survival on oil production companies—which are, for the most part, large multinational corporations. A number of Indigenous business managers complained about the unfairness of a situation in which large corporations own the rights to the oil, while First Nations are not even shareholders in these corporations. These massive multinational corporations exploit the oil, and local Indigenous workers end up being racialized and exploited in the process. Glen Coulthard (2014) is strongly critical of the encroachment of capitalism onto reserves, in the form of Indigenous-owned business enterprises, as well as of "partnerships" between Indigenous communities and large extractivist corporations. As he points out, the economic power of capital is also a form of social power, although it is not necessarily recognized as such. As Indigenous peoples become enmeshed in capitalist relations, they absorb the values essential to these relations, displacing the traditional values that lie at the heart of *miyo-pimatisiwin*.

Through their participation in massive, multinational industries, Indigenous communities are hooked into the extra-local relationships integral to corporate power, which require that they relinquish their autonomy.

Community members who profit from the oil industry often become strong supporters of continued fossil fuel development, on which their revenue streams rely, while resenting their own exclusion from the corridors of corporate power. In the meanwhile, others are exploited, and still others engage in efforts to stop such development and assert their rights to the land and its minerals. The community is thus divided against itself. From the perspective of *miyo-pimatisiwin*, how can Indigenous holistic understandings of being as a web of relationships ("all my relations") and of the importance of caring for the collective good be maintained when capitalist class structures and the privileging of the individual fragment the community?

What emerged from the interviews we conducted was a sense that individuals and families are working hard to adapt to the fluctuations of the oil industry and to preserve the health and happiness of their communities, families, and selves. At the same time, they are part of a far broader process of decolonization that is constantly challenged by efforts on the part of the dominant society to reinforce and sustain colonial structures—and, in this, capitalism has proved to be a powerful tool. As climate change progresses, the wisdom of Indigenous values of respect and reciprocity is becoming ever more apparent, and the oil industry is already attempting to co-opt those values by invoking them as its own. In the meanwhile, members of the Bigstone Cree Nation are, like Indigenous peoples everywhere, left seeking ways to recentre traditional values and restore health to themselves and their community in the face of relentless countervailing forces.

Notes

1. Of the five Wabasca reserves, four (Wabasca 166A, 166B, 166C, and 166D) are immediately adjacent to Wabasca-Desmarais, while the fifth (Wabasca 166) lies a little to the southeast, at nearby Sandy Lake. A sixth reserve, Jean Baptiste Gambler 183, is located at Calling Lake, about 115 kilometres southeast of Wabasca, but it is very tiny: only about 190 hectares. In December 2010, when BCN's Treaty Land Entitlement claim was finally settled, the nation was promised an additional 77,000 acres of land (roughly 31,160 hectares) for its three communities—those at Wabasca and at Calling Lake, plus a third at Chipewyan Lake, about 140 kilometres north of Wabasca. But the boundaries of these new reserves have yet to be surveyed. On February 20, 2017 Chief Gordon T. Auger and Lands Manager Troy Stuart wrote a letter to the Minister

of Indigenous Affairs, informing him that the nation was preparing to install gates near the entrances into our traditional territory and reserve lands. The "lack of contract opportunities for local companies; unfulfilled impact benefit agreements; lack of meaningful consultation by both multinational corporations and the Aboriginal Consultation office; protection of surface and groundwater; delayed transfer of treaty entitlement lands; and neglect of a referendum in the transfer of administration and control of highways" made the move necessary. The First Nation did not go ahead with a blockade in 2017, once the Minister of Indigenous Affairs met with the Chief and Council. As far as Alook is aware, the lands from the TLE have not yet been transferred. See the following for more: https://www.parklandinstitute.ca/letter_of_concern_on_the_land_rights_and_water_rights_of_bigstone_cree_nation

2. Figures for population and land area can be found at "Census Profile, 2016 Census," Statistics Canada, https://www12.statcan.gc.ca/census-recensement/2016/dp-pd/prof/index.cfm?Lang=E, February 8, 2017; last updated June 18, 2019. For the municipal district, search "Opportunity No. 17." The figure for the on-reserve population at Wabasca is the total of figures for the individual reserves: Wabasca 166, 166A, 166B, 166C, and 166D. For the off-reserve population, see "Wabasca, unincorporated place [UNP]" (which the census lists as a "designated place").

3. "Quick Facts and Figures," Municipal District of Opportunity No. 17, accessed March 9, 2021, http://www.mdopportunity.ab.ca/quick-facts-figures-industry.

4. See the 2016 census profile for Alberta available at https://www12.statcan.gc.ca/census-recensement/2016/dp-pd/prof/index.cfm?Lang=E (search "Alberta"). See also "Focus on Geography Series, 2016 Census: Aboriginal Peoples, Province of Alberta," Statistics Canada, 2016, https://www12.statcan.gc.ca/census-recensement/2016/as-sa/fogs-spg/Facts-PR-Eng.cfm?TOPIC=9&LANG=Eng&GK=PR&GC=48. (Note that the census profile now shows a slightly higher figure for Alberta's total population, which in turn reduces the proportion of Indigenous people just a little, to 6.36 percent.)

5. All participants voluntarily granted informed consent, and the interviews were subsequently transcribed and thematically coded. We have taken steps to safeguard the anonymity of the participants.

References

Alberta. 2018. *Industry Profiles 2018: Mining and Oil and Gas Extraction Industry.* Edmonton: Government of Alberta.

Alook, Angele. 2016. "Indigenous Life Courses, Racialized Gendered Life Scripts, and Cultural Identities of Resistance and Resilience." PhD diss., York University, Toronto.

Alook, Angele, Nicole Hill, and Ian Hussey. 2017. "Seeking 'Good Jobs' in the Oil Patch: How Gender and Race Shape Experiences of Work in Alberta's Extractive Industries." *Monitor*, November/December 2017, 28–32. Ottawa: Canadian Centre for Policy Alternatives.

Amnesty International. 2016. *Out of Sight, Out of Mind: Gender, Indigenous Rights, and Energy Development in Northeast British Columbia, Canada.* London: Amnesty International.

Coulthard, Glen Sean. 2014. *Red Skin, White Masks: Rejecting the Colonial Politics of Recognition.* Minneapolis: University of Minnesota Press.

Dorow, Sara. 2015. "Gendering Energy Extraction in Fort McMurray." In *Alberta Oil and the Decline of Democracy in Canada*, edited by Meenal Shrivastava and Lorna Stefanick, 275–92. Edmonton: Athabasca University Press.

Foster, Jason, and Bob Barnetson. 2015. "Exporting Oil, Importing Labour, and Weakening Democracy: The Use of Foreign Migrant Workers in Alberta." In *Alberta Oil and the Decline of Democracy in Canada*, edited by Meenal Shrivastava and Lorna Stefanick, 249–73. Edmonton: Athabasca University Press.

Hart, Michael Anthony. 2002. *Seeking Mino-Pimatisiwin: An Aboriginal Approach to Helping.* Halifax: Fernwood.

Hill, Nicole, Angele Alook, and Ian Hussey. 2017. "How Gender and Race Shape Experiences of Work in Alberta's Oil Industry." *Parkland Blog*, Parkland Institute, June 27, 2017. https://www.parklandinstitute.ca/how_gender_and_race_shape_experiences_of_work_in_albertas_oil_industry.

Hislop, Jude. 2017. "Cenovus Sells Pelican Lake Oil Sands Assets to CNRL for Nearly $1 Billion." *North American Energy News.* September 6, 2017. http://theamericanenergynews.com/canada/cenovus-sells-pelican-lake-cnrl-06sep17.

Joly, Tara L., and Clinton N. Westman. 2017. *Taking Research Off the Shelf: Impacts, Benefits, and Participatory Processes Around the Oil Sands Industry in Northern Alberta.* Saskatoon: University of Saskatchewan.

Lahey, Kathleen A. 2016. *Equal Worth: Designing Effective Pay Equity Laws for Alberta.* Edmonton: Parkland Institute.

Menzies, Charles R. 2001. "Reflections on Research With, For, and Among Indigenous Peoples." *Canadian Journal of Native Education* 25, no. 1: 19–36.

Natural Resources Canada. 2016. *Oil Sands: Indigenous Peoples.* Ottawa: Minister of Natural Resources. https://www.nrcan.gc.ca/energy/publications/18736.

O'Shaughnessy, Sara, and Göze Doğu. 2016. "The Gendered and Racialized Subjects of Alberta's Oil Boomtown." In *First World Petro-Politics: The Political Ecology and*

Governance of Alberta, edited by Laurie Adkin, 263–96. Toronto: University of Toronto Press.

Slowey, Gabrielle, and Lorna Stefanick. 2015. "Development at What Cost? First Nations, Ecological Integrity, and Democracy." In *Alberta Oil and the Decline of Democracy in Canada*, edited by Meenal Shrivastava and Lorna Stefanick, 195–224. Edmonton: Athabasca University Press.

Smith, Linda Tuhiwai. 1999. *Decolonizing Methodologies: Research and Indigenous Peoples*. London: Zed Books.

Taylor, Alison, and Tracy L. Friedel. 2011. "Enduring Neoliberalism in Alberta's Oil Sands: The Troubling Effects of Private-Public Partnerships for First Nations and Métis Communities." *Citizenship Studies* 15, no. 6–7: 815–35.

Taylor, Alison, Tracy L. Friedel, and Lois Edge. 2009. *Pathways for First Nations and Métis Youth in the Oil Sands*. Ottawa: Canadian Policy Research Networks.

13   Between a Rock and a Hard Place

Canada's Carbon Economy and Indigenous Ambivalence

Clifford Atleo

Indigenous peoples have a long and complicated history with settler colonialism and resource extraction in Canada. While there has certainly been a lot of opposition to some of the more egregious forms of resource extraction, some Indigenous communities have also tried to work with corporations and settler governments for a myriad of reasons—not only because of dire socioeconomic circumstances but also as a way of asserting their right to self-determination and of influencing management decisions regarding environmental sustainability. These efforts have been contentious, both within Indigenous communities and among some Canadians, particularly environmentalists. In this chapter I look at Indigenous opposition to, and participation in, energy extraction and transportation projects. My intent is not to set up a simple binary of those for and those against development, or those who have "sold out" and those who have "remained true" to their Indigenous values. Contemporary Indigenous resource management is more complicated and warrants a critical examination and nuanced analysis that places the dilemmas of leaders within the contexts of settler colonialism, neoliberal capitalism, environmental politics, and the ongoing struggles for Indigenous self-determination. I argue that these contexts in particular are critical to understanding Indigenous ambivalence with respect to oil and gas extraction and management in North America.

Settler Colonialism

Māori scholar Linda Tuhiwai Smith (2005, 19) writes, "Imperialism frames the indigenous experience. It is part of our story, our version of modernity." Indigenous peoples all over the world have struggled with various iterations of imperialism and colonialism for centuries. Of particular interest here is Canadian settler colonialism. A number of scholars, including Patrick Wolfe (1999, 2006), Carol Elkins and Susan Pedersen (2005), and Lorenzo Veracini (2010, 2011), have greatly expanded our understanding of settler colonialism as a distinct structure and not merely a historical event. Put simply, settler colonialism arose when European colonists did not leave or relinquish power and instead continued to occupy Indigenous lands, setting up Euro-Canadian political and economic institutions. Although, like Australia and New Zealand, the United States of America and Canada transitioned from British colonies into independent states, albeit in very different ways, these newly formed states maintained asymmetrical colonial relations with the continent's Indigenous peoples. As Zapotec scholar Isabel Altamirano-Jiménez (2011, 107) points out, "Settler colonialism . . . focuses on claiming land and on creating permanent settlements that replicate social, political, economic, legal and cultural structures of settlers' homeland over the new territories and the colonized." With regard to Canada, James Tully (2000), Emma Battell Lowman and Adam Barker (2015), and Taiaiake Alfred (2005) concur with this description. They all stress that colonialism in Canada is not simply a legacy but a persistent reality that Indigenous peoples still endure.

The ramifications of settler colonialism do not, however, emanate only from the occupation of Indigenous lands and waters, the alienation of Indigenous peoples from their territories, and the pillaging of resources. The negation and suppression of unique cultures, ways of being, governance, and economies has also had profound and ongoing impacts on Indigenous people today. Nuu-chah-nulth legal scholar Johnny Mack (2011, 293) writes of his peoples' experience: "For 150 years efforts have been taken to change the way we related to each other and the territory to which we belong. We would be wise to acknowledge that these efforts have been somewhat successful in their aims." This statement might seem controversial, especially in Indigenous communities, but Mack and I believe that our experiences with settler colonialism warrant critical honesty to better understand our present predicaments. In Canada, the structure of settler colonialism that specifically oppresses

Indigenous peoples includes the legacy of Indian residential schools, religious indoctrination, the Indian Act, and other government legislation and policies, as well as neoliberal capitalism. Settler colonialism in Canada frames our experiences and constrains our options.

Neoliberal Capitalism

There are literally hundreds of thousands of articles and books about capitalism, engaging in countless debates about its definition, origins, stages, or presumptive demise. I am most interested in what Geoff Mann (2013) describes as "actually existing capitalism," which is distinguished to a certain extent from its theoretical foundations. I am interested in how capitalism plays out on Indigenous lands and waters and in the lives of Indigenous peoples. It is impossible to know with certainty if capitalism will remain as resilient as it seems in the present moment, but, as the work of the Russian economist Nikolai Kondratieff demonstrated, "capitalism's tendency is not to collapse, but rather, to mutate" (Mason 2015, 34). Here, I focus on the present era of neoliberal capitalism that is so hegemonic that some people no longer even refer to it as capitalism. Canadian-born economist John Kenneth Galbraith (2004, 3) felt that the term had lost favour among proponents, coming instead to be known by the rather benign sounding "market system." And while more people are talking about the growing inequities and precariousness of our capitalist market system (see, for example, Piketty 2014), its core tenets of private property, competition, and endless economic growth roll easily off the tongues of politicians, Indigenous and settler alike. Collectively, we experience capitalism as ubiquitous and everlasting.

There are specific concerns about neoliberal capitalism that I want to address. The neoliberal era began roughly during the tenures of Ronald Reagan and Margaret Thatcher in the late 1970s and early 1980s, and neoliberalism continues to spread around the globe. It is marked by government austerity, deregulation, enhanced market penetration into more and more spaces, and a hyperdeveloped focus on individualism. But, as scholars have recognized, neoliberalism as a governing paradigm is more than simply economic policies meant to favour corporations. Neoliberalism alters individual and communal subjectivity in profound ways. Jeff Shantz and José Brendan Macdonald (2013, xvi) warn of "the creation of neoliberal subjects for whom neoliberalism is regarded simply as a 'way of life,' the only possible world," echoing Margaret Thatcher's infamous summation: "There is no alternative." It is this sense of inevitability that is disconcerting—that the march of neoliberal capitalist progress has necessarily led us here, with no other options. Altamirano-Jiménez (2004) suggests that this neoliberal subject transformation grants Indigenous peoples only "market citizenship." While neoliberal discourse allows for a certain shallow recognition of Indigenous cultures, it conceives of Indigenous citizenship purely in terms of participation in the mainstream market economy rather than viewing citizenship as flowing from the legal and territorial autonomy of Indigenous nations.

Not only does neoliberal capitalism reframe our (settler and Indigenous) conceptions of citizenship; it tells us that if we fail, we have only ourselves to blame. As African American scholar Lester Spence (2016, xxiv) observes, "The neoliberal turn, the gradual embrace of the general idea that society (and every institution within it) works best when it works according to the principles of the market," produces "a society that increasingly shirks its responsibilities to those perceived to be losers in an increasingly stark competition over material, social, and psychic resources." Under neoliberalism, social problems are individualized and pathologized. David Harvey (2006, xiv) writes, "If conditions among the lower classes deteriorated it was because, it is said, they failed, usually for personal or cultural reasons, to enhance their own human capital through dedication to education, the Protestant work ethic, submission to labour discipline." Wendy Brown goes further, stating that neoliberalism renders people "*as* human capital, not simply having it to deploy or to invest or to enhance." Consequently, some people are "credit-worthy," while others are "disposable" (Cruz and Brown 2016, 80). Elsewhere, Brown (2016, 3) adds that the effects of neoliberalism "generate intensely isolated and unprotected individuals, persistently in peril of deracination and deprivation of basic life support, wholly vulnerable to capital's vicissitudes." To clarify, Brown is speaking primarily of people in democratic societies. I argue that Indigenous people and peoples are especially vulnerable to the effects of neoliberal capitalism because of historical trauma and the contemporary dynamics of settler colonialism.

Environmental Politics

Having laid out the contexts of settler colonialism and neoliberal capitalism, I want to shift to the realm of environmental politics, on which much of the debate over resource extraction focuses, especially with respect to Indigenous peoples. Indigenous people in Canada are often confined to stereotypical caricatures that obscure the totality of their diversity and depth. These stereotypes include the drunkard, the princess, the noble savage, and their multiple iterations. Included in the noble savage stereotype is "the ecologically noble Indian," which Paul Nadasdy (2005) has already deftly critiqued and complicated. He writes of Indigenous peoples,

> They are simply people with a complex set of beliefs, practices, and values that defy standard Euro–North American schemes of categorization. To be sure, they sometimes make use of environmentalist rhetoric, because it confers on them a degree of legitimacy and power in certain political contexts. But in my experience, they seldom do so cynically; more often they genuinely believe that their own practices are more environmentally benign than those of the dominant Euro–North American society. Their claims to this effect must be considered on their own merits, rather than as part of a larger general debate over their ecological nobility. (322)

I would argue that these matters are not straightforward and that we must use caution when applying dominant Western conceptions of the environment, economy, or governance when seeking to understand Indigenous communities.

While some might readily accept the simplistic narrative of Indigenous peoples as "natural" environmentalists, the political-economic contexts introduced here must be considered to develop a more accurate and nuanced understanding. In critiquing the environmental movement of the 1990s, Bruce Braun (2002, 2) challenges the binary logic that pits "pristine nature" against "destructive humanity." The reality is that Indigenous peoples have had contentious relationships with environmental activists and corporate and government representatives alike. Braun reminds us that in 1994, in the aftermath of the "War in the Woods" in Clayoquot Sound, Nuu-chah-nulth Tribal Council chairman George Watts accused the environmental movement of "neocolonialism," and in 1996, the tribal council "banned" Greenpeace (107–8). As Nadasdy has pointed out, Indigenous people have made use of environmentalist rhetoric and have even genuinely allied with environmental NGOs to fight the more destructive forms of resource extraction, but these actions primarily take place, I argue, within the context of Indigenous self-determination.

Indigenous Self-Determination

As Chippewa scholar Duane Champagne (2007, 2) observes, "The indigenous self-determination movement is about maintaining land, culture, institutional relations, government, and self-sufficiency under terms compatible with indigenous cultures and beliefs." Champagne writes mostly about Native American tribes, and in this case he is also referring to Indigenous community survival via "tribal capitalism" within the contexts of American settler colonialism and capitalism. Indigenous self-determination is widely discussed and debated in academic and political circles with common terms such as sovereignty, nationhood, self-government, and autonomy. Here, I am referring to the persistent belief in, and struggle for, the right of Indigenous peoples to exercise the authority of self-determining nations with clear corresponding rights, entitlements, jurisdictions, and responsibilities. Article 3 of the United Nations Declaration on the Rights of Indigenous Peoples states, "Indigenous peoples have the right to self-determination. By virtue of that right they freely determine their political status and freely pursue their economic, social and cultural development" (UN General Assembly 2007, 8). Although the declaration has been adopted by all UN member states, it has yet to resonate in the daily lives of most Indigenous people.[1] Of particular interest to Indigenous peoples is the principle of free, prior, and informed consent with respect to laws, lands, cultures, and economic development including resource extraction and environmental hazards outlined in articles 10, 11, 19, 28, 29, and 32. I will expand on this below in the examples of oil sands and pipeline development in Canada.

The struggle for Indigenous self-determination in Canada is older than the country and remains ongoing. I do not have the space here to present the entire history of Indigenous-colonial settler relations, but I do want to make a few key points regarding the matter of land. Altamirano-Jiménez (2011, 107) writes, "Settler colonialism presupposes that the annexation and colonization of new territories is based on *terra nullius* or unoccupied, empty lands." The concept of *terra nullius* has provided a theoretical foundation for the theft of Indigenous lands and resources under settler colonialism, but it was based on a false premise. Indigenous peoples with their own complex languages, cultures, and political and economic systems already inhabited North America. Indigenous peoples also had their own land tenure systems and relationships with land and non-human life forms that were distinct from, and often befuddling to, European understandings (Stark 2012). Even those who did not ignore Indigenous presence in what would later become North America argued that Indigenous societies were not advanced enough to maintain legitimate claims to the lands that would be devoured by European colonialism. Here, I am thinking of John Locke and his labour-based theory of land ownership ([1689] 2003, 288): "Whatsoever then he removes out of the State that Nature hath Provided, and left in, he hath mixed his *Labour* with, and joined to it something that is his own, and thereby makes it his *Property*." Settler colonialists believed that Indigenous peoples did not *improve* the land through their labour and therefore could not be said to truly own it. Many still believe this to be true. They cannot comprehend why some people would want to leave resources in the ground. We will now look at some background and examples of Indigenous resistance, before also considering examples of cooperation that defy stereotypes but nonetheless represent Indigenous efforts to assert agency.

Indigenous Resistance and Adaptation

"Resistance is futile," Onondaga scholar David Newhouse (2000) once proclaimed. Employing a *Star Trek* analogy, Newhouse likened the hegemony and power of capitalism to that of the Borg—the cybernetic collective that seeks to assimilate all sentient beings and all knowledge into its hive mind. In Newhouse's analysis, Indigenous cultures will eventually be absorbed and assimilated into the liberal-democratic-capitalist mainstream. "We have participated at the edges of capitalism, as labourers, as small business people, as debtors," he writes. "Now we seek to enter its heart. We will be transformed by it. Just as the Borg absorbs cultures, capitalism will absorb Aboriginal cultures. And the moral order of Aboriginal societies will be changed" (153–54). Admittedly, I was angered the first time I encountered Newhouse's take on capitalism and Indigenous societies, but over time I have, with some sadness, come to understand the astuteness of his position. I still disagree with the conclusion that Indigenous peoples should wholeheartedly embrace capitalism, but I certainly acknowledge the power of capitalism and the way it persists and invades every corner of both the earth *and* our imaginations. It is a force that Indigenous peoples cannot afford to underestimate or ignore.

Indigenous peoples have had diverse experiences with settler colonialism, yet with respect to timing and pace, we witnessed an alarming decline in traditional and adaptive livelihoods on Indigenous lands and waters at the end of the twentieth century. This was especially pronounced in the more remote and sparsely populated areas that have relatively recently come to the attention of voracious resource-extraction companies. As Indigenous peoples have had their traditional and adaptive livelihoods, we have become increasingly dependent on the mainstream economy for survival. Perhaps more contentiously, I also argue that alienation from traditional territories can have the effect of desensitizing Indigenous people to the adverse environmental impacts that often come with intensive resource extraction.

More than half of Indigenous people in Canada live in urban centres. In the case of my father's people, the Nuu-chah-nulth, the majority now "live away from home." Additionally, changes to our main adaptive livelihood—commercial fishing—have been swift and dramatic. The Nuu-chah-nulth commercial fishing fleet dropped from a peak of two hundred boats in the mid- to late twentieth century to only six by 2002. We now find ourselves in the unenviable position of struggling with high rates of poverty (by any standard), a loss of connection to our home waters, including many traditional Indigenous foods, and the ongoing pressure of industrial economic development in our territories. The dominance of neoliberal capitalism, settler colonialism, and rampant resource extraction in Canada truly places Indigenous communities between the proverbial rock and hard place.

The forces of neoliberal capitalism and settler colonialism have left us with very few choices, yet I do not want to completely ignore the ongoing efforts of Indigenous leaders to assert agency in the political-economic decisions in their territories. Since the first days of Captain James Cook's arrival in Nuu-chah-nulth waters, Ha'wiih (hereditary chiefs) have worked consistently to assert their jurisdiction and authority in their respective Ha'houlthlii (chiefly territories). As the relationships with imperial actors shifted from trade to settler colonialism in the nineteenth century, the agency of Nuu-chah-nulth Ha'wiih became greatly diminished. The story is long and complex, but it begins with the assertion of Crown sovereignty, the endangerment of whale populations by commercial whaling fleets, and the multi-layered and interconnected components of settler colonialism in Canada, which include Indian residential schools, religious indoctrination, the persistent undermining of traditional Indigenous cultures, ways of living, economics, and governance. Even in the current era of reconciliation, Canadian governments refuse to acknowledge or respect traditional Indigenous governing institutions. I argue that all of this has worked to discredit Indigenous ways of knowing and live-lihoods generally and traditional Indigenous political-economic governance specifically. This is not only true in the territories I am most familiar with, but a common experience of Indigenous peoples across the country. Over-shadowing Indigenous political economies are the paradigms of neoliberal democracy and capitalism.

Despite Newhouse's Borg-like assessment that Indigenous resistance to capitalism is futile, I believe that Indigenous resistance is both fertile and necessary but also complicated and certainly not inevitable. First, I want to address Indigenous resistance and the ways it is often criticized as being reactionary or unprogressive. The rhetoric surrounding Indigenous economic development in Canada is laced with notions of liberal teleological progress and modernity. Much as in Francis Fukiyama's (1992) notion of the "end of history," Canada is often thought to have achieved the pinnacle of human political and economic progress. Ergo, anything that stands in the way of "Canadian progress" must be backward, and many Indigenous people, espe-cially political leaders, have internalized this logic. Here I am thinking of people like long-time Osoyoos Indian Band chief Clarence Louie and Tsim-shian lawyer and author Calvin Helin. Louie is known for his inflammatory rhetoric, such as "If your life sucks, it's because *you* suck" and "Quit your sniffling" (quoted in MacGregor 2006). Louie has also advised, "If you call yourself a leader, give all your people the chance at the dignity of a job, equal opportunity and the individual responsibility to earn a living" (quoted in Helin 2006, 235). Helin (2006, 30) writes optimistically, "Aboriginals are likely in the best position ever to integrate economically with the mainstream, to partner with industry, and create wealth and opportunities for all." Notably, Louie and Helin are not really outliers. It is safe to say that many Indigenous leaders in Canada support some form of economic development that inevit-ably plugs into mainstream neoliberal capitalism.

This is not to suggest that even the most economically minded Indigenous leaders are not concerned about negative environmental, social, and cultural impacts of capitalism, but, as is the case with their settler counterparts, the rhetoric tends to ring hollow in the face of billion-dollar industrial projects and profits. Those who oppose destructive projects are often criticized as being fringe radicals. But Dene scholar Glen Coulthard (2014) reminds us that resistance is not simply a negative reaction within the context of Canadian political, legal, and economic orders; it is also an affirmative action in the context of *Indigenous political, legal, and economic orders*. When Indigenous people resist and say no, "they also have ingrained within them a resounding 'yes': they are the affirmative *enactment* of another modality of being, a different way of relating to and with the world" (169). This position is often incomprehensible when we prioritize neoliberal Canadian political and economic values or take them for granted as being universal. Some Indigenous people still remind us that there are other, older ways of organizing politically and economically that are divergent from Canadian norms but equally valid. What happens when these older, but equally valid, Indigenous world views come into contact with big oil?

Indigenous Peoples and Big Oil

The issue of Indigenous peoples and big oil in Canada first appeared on my radar with the stirring footage from the Mackenzie Valley Pipeline Inquiry, led by Justice Thomas Berger, between 1974 and 1976. I was particularly moved by the testimony of Frank T'Seleie, then chief of the Fort Good Hope Dene Band, a K'asho Got'įnę community located on the eastern shore of the Mackenzie River in the Sahtu Region of the Northwest Territories. Chief T'Seleie stated,

> Let me tell your nation that this is Dene land and we the Dene people
> intend to decide what happens on our land. Mr. Berger, there will be
> no pipeline. There will be no pipeline because we have our plans for
> our lands. There will be no pipeline because we no longer intend to
> allow our land and our future to be taken away from us and that we are
> destroyed to make someone else rich. There will be no pipeline because
> we, the Dene people, are awakening to see the truth of the system
> of genocide that has been imposed on us and we will not go back to
> sleep. We do not say we are better or worse than the white man. We
> are proud of who we are, proud to be Dene and loyal to our nation,
> but we are not saying that we do not respect you and your ways. We
> are only asking now, as we asked you then, to let us live our own lives,
> in our own way, on our own land, without forever being threatened by
> invasion and extinction. We do not want to have to fight and struggle
> forever just to survive as a people.[2]

Chief T'Seleie, and the position he articulated on behalf of his community, inspired generations of Indigenous activists. The 1970s Mackenzie Valley pipeline proposal did not succeed, and neither did the recently revived project proposed by Imperial Oil, ConocoPhillips, and ExxonMobile, but the positionality of many Indigenous communities was markedly different this time around. T'Seleie was also involved in the recent incarnation, but this time as a proponent and as a director of the Aboriginal Pipeline Group, which proposed a 33.3 percent Indigenous ownership stake. He says, simply and unapologetically, "Times have changed" (quoted in Laird 2003). When Imperial Oil announced that it would not go forward with the pipeline (citing low natural gas prices), many Indigenous community leaders were disappointed. Duane Smith, chair of the Inuvialuit Regional Corporation, stated, "I just hope that Canada as a government recognizes the valuable resources that we are sitting on in this region and the potential it provides for the economy of this country as well as to the people of the region" (in Strong 2017). The apparent about-face of T'Seleie and others is partially responsible for my interest in this area of research. Such reactions have become more common. My question is simple: What has changed?

Actually, I have two questions. The second one is this: What has stayed the same? I am interested in both change *and continuity* in Indigenous-settler relations generally and in Indigenous community governance and political economies specifically. Not only are Indigenous peoples diverse, but their experiences of settler colonialism have been diverse. Native American legal scholar Robert Williams Jr. (1997) has written about what he calls "the Encounter era," a period during which Indigenous-settler relations were more reflective of mutual dependence and cooperation than they would later come to be. The Kaswentha, or Two-Row Wampum, a treaty originally negotiated between the Dutch and Haudenosaunee in the seventeenth century, was meant to symbolize not only mutual respect and interdependence but also, importantly, non-interference (Parmenter 2013, 97). Others, particularly in the north and the west, experienced colonialism and development in different ways. Diverse origins and experiences are bound to lead to a diversity of responses to colonialism and contemporary capitalism. How different Indigenous nations navigate settler colonialism varies from place to place, despite many similarities in our collective treatment by federal, provincial, and territorial governments. If some continuity exists within and across Indigenous nations, it is that they have almost always attempted to act in ways that would preserve and perpetuate their political and economic autonomy. How this is manifested looks different depending on the nation, treaties (or their absence), and options and strategies for survival and resilience. There is no template.

Oil and gas pipelines and Indigenous peoples are back in the headlines in both Canada and the United States. Opposition to the Dakota Access Pipeline erupted in 2016 and 2017, particularly in the territories of the Standing Rock Sioux Tribe in North Dakota. Regarding the resonance and significance of the protests, Eric Steinman (2019, 1070–71) writes, "With grassroots participation by members of other American Indian tribal nations, formal encouragement by many tribal governments, support from Indigenous people from elsewhere in the Americas and allies of all kinds from American society, the historic effort was the most broad-base grassroots social movement campaign that featured or centrally included American Indians." Opposition leadership to the pipeline originated among Indigenous women and youth, who emerged as "water protectors" to stand in the way of the "black snake" (1081).

Reflecting on the protests, Standing Rock Elder LaDonna Brave Bull Allard commented, "When people want to say, 'Who started this?' Nobody. Everybody. There was no one leader. There was no one person. It was everybody. Each with their own journey. In the middle of all of this was the youth, who continued to stand up. Who continued to bring that power, that healing" (quoted in Halpin 2017). US president Barack Obama's outgoing administration responded to the protests in December 2016 by denying the Army Corps of Engineers a permit required to build the pipeline under the Missouri River, but newly elected president Donald Trump promptly issued an executive order reversing that decision, and the pipeline was completed in April 2017. Even though the pipeline did go through (at a cost of $3.8 billion), Dave Archambault II, the tribal chairman of the Standing Rock Sioux at the #NoDAPL protests, felt that the protests were important expressions of tribal sovereignty and calls for environmental justice. As he stated, "What tribes are doing is saying, we have value, we have worth, we're still here, and that is exercising your sovereignty" (quoted in McKenna 2017).

Yet not all Native American tribes or citizens oppose oil and gas projects, although this fact receives less media attention. According to a CNN report from November 2016, not all Standing Rock Sioux citizens opposed the Dakota Access Pipeline, and some found the invasion of protesters from all over the world to be a nuisance rather than a help (Ravitz 2016). In this regard, I want to stress two points. First, diversity of opinion in Indigenous communities should be a surprise to no one; however, stereotypical caricatures tend not to allow for an acceptance of this diversity. Second, supporting economic development initiatives, even controversial ones, *is also an expression of tribal sovereignty*. After seventy years of American oil and gas companies operating on tribal lands, the Diné people formed the Navajo Nation Oil and Gas Company. Headquartered in Arizona, with operations in New Mexico and Utah as well, the company currently employs more than fifty people and generates millions of dollars in income for the Navajo Nation.[3] This does not mean I agree with those who support oil and gas projects, but I understand their dilemma, and I certainly think that all political and economic decisions should be debated and critiqued by Indigenous people. Moreover, as illustrated in the Clayoquot Sound example raised by Braun (2002), it is also possible for environmental NGOs to act in neocolonial ways with respect to Indigenous peoples and priorities, especially when the latter do not conform to the preconceived notions of authentic indigeneity by the former. These issues are far from straightforward.

This complexity is also apparent in the current dispute over the expansion of the Trans Mountain Pipeline, which is intended to triple the amount of diluted bitumen being transported from Alberta's oil sands to Greater Vancouver. The pipeline expansion was originally proposed by Kinder Morgan, a Texas-based company, but amid legal objections and extensive protests, the Canadian government announced in May 2018 that it would buy the existing pipeline for $4.5 billion and commit to the project's completion, estimated at an additional cost of $7.4 billion (Harris 2018).

Much as in the case of the defeated Northern Gateway pipeline proposal, Indigenous people find themselves on both sides of the Trans Mountain fight. Both the Sḵwx̱wú7mesh and Tsleil-Waututh Nations (and the City of Vancouver) have opposed the pipeline expansion in court, and the Tsleil-Waututh led a diverse group of protesters on Burnaby Mountain, where Kinder Morgan had been working to expand their tank farm to accommodate the increase in diluted bitumen. Tsleil-Waututh leader Rueben George stated at a 2015 Kinder Morgan AGM, "I am here to let you know that the Tsleil-Waututh will never consent to the Trans Mountain project—because it will destroy our culture, our way of life and our spirituality" (quoted in Kresnyak 2015). The issue is even more complicated because Indigenous communities are not dealing with the open hostility of former Conservative prime minister Stephen Harper but with Justin Trudeau, a Liberal who campaigned on support for Indigenous rights and renewed nation-to-nation relationships. Regarding the federal government's purchase of the Trans Mountain Pipeline, Sḵwx̱wú7mesh Nation councillor Khelsilem stated, "This is a continued betrayal of promises made to us by Prime Minister Justin Trudeau." He went on to clarify the Sḵwx̱wú-7mesh Nation's position: "We have a right to practice our culture, our way of life, and to continue our right to self-determination in our territories. This is a right that we have never surrendered, and it is a right we will continue to defend" (quoted in Ritchie 2018). And yet others claim to be asserting their self-determination rights by supporting the pipeline.

Kinder Morgan signed "mutual benefit agreements" with forty-three Indigenous groups along the pipeline route, including thirty-three in British Columbia (Bailey 2018). And since Canada has purchased the pipeline, some people, including Suncor Energy's CEO and several First Nation leaders, have talked about the possibility of a percentage of Indigenous ownership in the pipeline (Lewis 2018). Suncor previously partnered with the Fort McKay and Mikisew Cree First Nations, in 2017, on an oil-storage facility, with the local Indigenous people owning 49 percent of the project. Athabasca Chipewyan First Nation Chief Allan Adam has stated, "We want to be owners of a pipeline," which is a noteworthy change from 2014, when he toured with Neil Young and David Suzuki to raise money to legally oppose oil sands expansion (Lewis 2018).

In British Columbia, Chief Ernie Crey of the Cheam First Nation has led discussions about support for and an ownership stake in the Trans Mountain Pipeline. Chief Crey is a long-time advocate for Indigenous fishing rights and has been a key figure in raising awareness about the issue of missing and murdered Indigenous women. He believes that the pipeline is inevitable and that Cheam will be better positioned to accrue benefit and have a say about environmental oversight if they are involved. As Crey puts it, "The pipeline goes through our territories. Our job is to look after our territories and make sure things of value in those territories are taken care of. To do that, we need to be more than advisers" (quoted in Bailey 2018).

Chief Crey is part of the Indigenous Advisory and Monitoring Committee, whose members include representatives of First Nations that object to the pipeline but do not want to be sidelined should it go ahead. While some First Nation leaders appear to be enthusiastic supporters of the oil and gas industry, others do so while holding their noses. Chief Ken Hansen of the Yale First Nation, who felt obligated to sign a mutual benefit agreement with Kinder Morgan because his nation had run out of money, later commented,

"When I signed this deal, I felt a lot of shame." Chief Robert Joseph of Dit-idaht, a Vancouver Island First Nation, is another one of those leaders. "At the end of the day, we are not really in favour of any pipeline, but we believe it's going to go through anyway," he stated. "They will not listen to anybody and that's the history of consultation with First Nations people. . . . They consult and go ahead and do what they were going to do anyways" (both quoted in Paling 2018).

At the heart of this conundrum are several key factors: loss of Indigenous ways of living and subsequent community poverty, relentless industrial development pressures, and hollow relationships with settler governments. In April 2018, Prime Minister Trudeau declared, "We are going to get the pipeline built. It is a project in the national interest. . . . This project will go ahead" (quoted in Snyder 2018). Despite the fact that the Government of Canada finally adopted the UN Declaration on the Rights of Indigenous Peoples, it clearly has a different interpretation of both the principle of free, prior, and informed consent and its duty to meaningfully consult First Nation communities. As Chief Joseph stated rather glumly, "Even if it's the best consultation on the face of the earth, if they do what they were going to do anyhow, what's the point?" Despite his feelings of shame, Chief Hansen says, "I'm about the people. . . . Our people needed help and this is one way of getting it" (both quoted in Paling 2018).

Conclusion

In 2016, when the Northern Gateway pipeline proposal was still being considered in British Columbia, the rifts within First Nation communities were shockingly exemplified when one of the Haida Nation's twenty-two clans held a traditional feast to strip two of its hereditary chiefs of their titles because they had signed a letter to the National Energy Board in support of the pipeline (Lee 2016). Other nations are similarly divided, and while this is certainly cause for concern, I do not want to focus on those divisions themselves as much as I want readers to consider the contexts within which those divisions manifest themselves. And while we may be rightfully critical of any politician's decisions, I would argue that most Indigenous leaders want to do what they truly believe is best for their communities. Within the constraints of settler colonialism, environmental politics, and neoliberal capitalism, options for Indigenous communities are tremendously limited. Colonialism and capitalism have at times been devastating for Indigenous peoples and lands. That being said, we cannot ignore the current socioeconomic conditions in Indigenous communities or the right to self-determination. If well-meaning Canadians truly seek environmental justice *and* reconciliation with Indigenous peoples, they must better understand the socio-political-economic realities faced by those communities as well as their rightful assertions for self-determination.

Notes

1. Notably, in 2016, Canada became the last country to remove its objector status to the declaration, almost a decade after the UN first adopted it, in 2007. And, not surprisingly, the last four countries to adopt the declaration were Canada, the United States, Australia, and New Zealand—arguably the most prominent English-speaking settler states in the world.
2. "Dene Chief Frank T'Seleie—MacKenzie Valley Pipeline/Gas Project in 1975," CBC News video, posted April 5, 2013, available at https://www.youtube.com/watch?v=pohp-gYL1Io. The passage quoted runs from 2:35 to 4:18.
3. "What We Do," n.d., Navajo Nation Oil and Gas Company, https://www.nnogc.com/what-we-do/ (accessed December 9, 2019).

References

Alfred, Taiaiake. 2005. *Wasáse: Indigenous Pathways of Action and Freedom.* Peterborough, ON: Broadview Press.

Altamirano-Jiménez, Isabel. 2004. "North American First Peoples: Slipping Up into Market Citizenship?" *Citizenship Studies* 8, no. 4: 349–65.

———. 2011. "Settler Colonialism, Human Rights and Indigenous Women." *Prairie Forum* 36, no. 2: 105–25.

Bailey, Ian. 2018. "Some First Nations Seek Inclusion in Trans Mountain Talks." *Globe and Mail*, June 6, 2018.

Battell Lowman, Emma, and Adam J. Barker. 2015. *Settler: Identity and Colonialism in the 21st Century.* Halifax: Fernwood.

Braun, Bruce. 2002. *The Intemperate Rainforest: Nature, Culture, and Power on Canada's West Coast.* Minneapolis: University of Minnesota Press.

Brown, Wendy. 2016. "Sacrificial Citizenship: Neoliberalism, Human Capital, and Austerity Politics." *Constellations* 23, no. 1: 3–14.

Champagne, Duane. 2007. *Social Change and Cultural Continuity Among Native Nations*. Lanham, MD: Altamira Press.

Coulthard, Glen Sean. 2014. *Red Skin, White Masks: Rejecting the Colonial Politics of Recognition*. Minneapolis: University of Minnesota Press.

Cruz, Katie, and Wendy Brown. 2016. "Feminism, Law, and Neoliberalism: An Interview and Discussion with Wendy Brown." *Feminist Legal Studies* 24, no. 1: 69–89.

Elkins, Carol, and Susan Pedersen, eds. 2005. *Settler Colonialism in the Twentieth Century: Projects, Practices, Legacies*. New York: Routledge.

Fukiyama, Francis. 1992. *The End of History and the Last Man*. New York: Avon Books.

Galbraith, John Kenneth. 2004. *The Economics of Innocent Fraud: Truth for Our Time*. New York: Houghton Mifflin.

Halpin, Mikki. 2017. "Standing Rock Sioux Tribe Historian LaDonna Brave Bull Allard on DAPL Protests and Seventh Generation Activists." *Teen Vogue*, April 26, 2017. https://www.teenvogue.com/story/standing-rock-sioux-tribe-ladonna-brave-bull-allard-interview-dapl-protests.

Harris, Kathleen. 2018. "Liberals to Buy Trans Mountain Pipeline for $4.5B to Ensure Expansion Is Built." *CBC News*. May 29, 2018. http://www.cbc.ca/news/politics/liberals-trans-mountain-pipeline-kinder-morgan-1.4681911.

Harvey, David. 2006. *The Limits of Capital*. New and fully updated ed. London: Verso.

Helin, Calvin. 2006. *Dances with Dependency: Indigenous Success Through Self Reliance*. Vancouver: Orca Spirit.

Kresnyak, Danny. 2015. "Rueben George Blasts Pipeline Expansion Project at Kinder Morgan AGM." *National Observer*, May 7, 2015. https://www.nationalobserver.com/2015/05/07/news/rueben-george-blasts-pipeline-expansion-project-kinder-morgan-agm.

Laird, Gordon. 2003. "The Big Thaw: The Mackenzie Pipeline, Once Spurned, Promises Energy Security for North America and a Reckoning for Northern Natives." *Report on Business Magazine* 20, no. 4 (October): 74–82.

Lee, Jeff. 2016. "Northern Gateway Pipeline Project Exposes Divides in First Nations Governance." *Vancouver Sun*, August 18, 2016. http://vancouversun.com/news/politics/northern-gateway-pipeline-project-exposes-divides-in-first-nations-governance.

Lewis, Jeff. 2018. "Suncor CEO Touts Indigenous States in Trans Mountain." *Globe and Mail*, June 7, 2018.

Locke, John. (1689) 2003. *Two Treatises of Government*. New York: Cambridge University Press.

MacGregor, Roy. 2006. "'Indian Time Doesn't Cut It' for Innovative Chief with On-the-Edge Humour." *Globe and Mail*, September 21, 2006.

Mack, Johnny. 2011. "*Hoquotist*: Reorienting Through Storied Practice." In *Storied Communities: Narratives of Contact and Arrival in Constituting Political Community*, edited by Hester Lessard, Rebecca Johnson, and Jeremy Webber, 287–307. Vancouver: University of British Columbia Press.

Mann, Geoff. 2013. *Disassembly Required: A Field Guide to Actually Existing Capitalism*. Edinburgh and Oakland, CA: AK Press.

Mason, Paul. 2015. *Postcapitalism: A Guide to Our Future*. New York: Farrar, Straus and Giroux.

McKenna, Phil. 2017. "Ousted Standing Rock Leader on the Pipeline Protest That Almost Succeeded." *Inside Climate News*, November 13, 2017. https://insideclimatenews.org/news/13112017/dakota-access-pipeline-protests-standing-rock-chairman-dave-archambault-interview.

Nadasdy, Paul. 2005. "Transcending the Debate over the Ecologically Noble Indian: Indigenous Peoples and Environmentalism," *Ethnohistory* 52, no. 2: 291–331.

Newhouse, David R. 2000. "Resistance Is Futile: Aboriginal Peoples Meet the Borg of Capitalism." In *Ethics and Capitalism*, edited by John Douglas Bishop, 141–55. Toronto: University of Toronto Press.

Paling, Emma. 2018. "B.C. Chiefs Say They Don't Support Trans Mountain Pipeline Despite Signing Agreements." *Huffington Post*, June 10, 2018. https://huffingtonpost.ca/2018/06/10/b-c-chiefs-say-they-don't-support-trans-mountain-pipeline-despite-signing-agreements_a_23455419.

Parmenter, Jon. 2013. "The Meaning of *Kaswentha* and the Two Row Wampum Belt in Haudenosaunee (Iroquois) History: Can Indigenous Oral Tradition Be Reconciled with the Documentary Record?" *Journal of Early American History* 3, no. 1: 82–109.

Piketty, Thomas. 2014. *Capital in the Twenty-First Century*. Cambridge, MA: The Belknap Press of Harvard University Press.

Ravitz, Jessica. 2016. "Not All the Standing Rock Sioux Are Protesting the Pipeline." *CNN*. November 3, 2016. https://www.cnn.com/2016/10/29/us/dakota-pipeline-standing-rock-sioux/index.html.

Ritchie, Haley. 2018. "Squamish Nation Reacts to Federal Government Kinder Morgan Purchase." *Squamish Chief*, May 30, 2018. https://www.squamishchief.com/news/local-news/squamish-nation-reacts-to-federal-government-kinder-morgan-purchase-1.23318785.

Shantz, Jeff, and José Brendan McDonald, eds. 2013. *Beyond Capitalism: Building Democratic Alternatives for Today and the Future*. New York: Bloomsbury Academic.

Smith, Linda Tuhiwai. 2005. *Decolonizing Methodologies: Research and Indigenous Peoples*. New York: Zed Books.

Snyder, Jesse. 2018. "'We Are Going to Get the Pipeline Built': Trudeau Begins Federal Talks with Kinder Morgan to Guarantee Trans Mountain." *National Post*, April 15, 2018. http://nationalpost.com/news/we-are-going-to-get-the-pipeline-built-trudeau-begins-federal-talks-with-kinder-morgan-to-guarantee-trans-mountain.

Spence, Lester K. 2016. *Knocking the Hustle: Against the Neoliberal Turn in Black Politics*. Brooklyn: Punctum Books.

Stark, Heidi Kiiwetinepinesiik. 2012. "Marked by Fire: Anishinaabe Articulations of Nationhood in Treaty Making with the United States and Canada." *American Indian Quarterly* 36, no. 2: 119–49.

Steinman, Erich. 2019. "Why Was Standing Rock and the #NoDAPL Campaign So Historic? Factors Affecting American Indian Participation in Social Movement Collaborations and Coalitions." *Ethnic and Racial Studies* 42, no. 7: 1070–90. https://doi.org/10.1080/01419870.2018.1471215.

Tully, James. 2000. "The Struggles of Indigenous Peoples for and of Freedom." In *Political Theory and the Rights of Indigenous People*, edited by Duncan Ivison, Paul Patton, and Will Sanders, 36–59. Cambridge: Cambridge University Press.

UN General Assembly. 2007. "United Nations Declaration on the Rights of Indigenous Peoples." Resolution Adopted by the General Assembly on 13 September 2007. A/RES/61/295. https://www.un.org/development/desa/indigenouspeoples/wp-content/uploads/sites/19/2018/11/UNDRIP_E_web.pdf.

Veracini, Lorenzo. 2010. *Settler Colonialism: A Theoretical Overview*. New York: Palgrave Macmillan.

———. 2011. "Isopolitics, Deep Colonizing, Settler Colonialism." *Interventions* 13, no. 2: 171–89.

Williams, Robert. 1997. *Linking Arms Together: American Indian Treaty Visions of Law and Peace, 1600–1800*. New York: Oxford University Press.

Wolfe, Patrick. 1999. *Settler Colonialism and the Transformation of Anthropology: The Politics and Poetics of an Ethnographic Event*. London: Cassell.

———. 2006. "Settler Colonialism and the Elimination of the Native." *Journal of Genocide Research* 8, no. 4 (December): 387–409.

Part III
Resistance and Beyond

14 From Clean Growth to Climate Justice

Marc Lee

In the wake of Prime Minister Justin Trudeau's remarks at the opening of the Paris climate change conference in December 2015, the term "clean growth" has become a popular mantra in Canadian climate policy. Canada's federal-provincial climate policy framework, released a year later, is titled the Pan-Canadian Framework on Clean Growth and Climate Change (Canada 2016). The BC government also adopted this language in naming its Climate Solutions and Clean Growth Advisory Council, appointed in October 2017. Outside government, prominent NGOs, such as the Pembina Institute, have made "clean growth" a prominent feature of their recent news releases and reports.[1]

Given that "clean growth" is a relatively new expression, it is worthwhile asking what it means and why climate policy is being framed this way. The term was first formally used in the March 2016 Vancouver Declaration on Clean Growth and Climate Change, a work plan for federal, provincial, and territorial governments that emerged from a meeting of Canada's first ministers. The declaration opens with a bold claim:

> Canada stands at the threshold of building our clean growth economy. This transition will create a strong and diverse economy, create new jobs and improve our quality of life, as innovations in steam power, electricity and computing have done before. We will grow our economy while reducing emissions. We will capitalize on the opportunity of a low-carbon and climate-resilient economy to create good-paying and long-term jobs. (Canada, First Ministers 2016, 1)

In November 2017, in announcing the creation of his department's "Clean Growth Program," natural resources minister James Carr took the opportunity to reiterate the federal rhetoric:

> Clean growth is good for our planet and our economy. It also plays to Canada's competitive advantage with the clean technology innovation that will make our country a global leader in the transition to a low-carbon economy. Strategically developing and using clean technologies in our natural resource sectors is one more way we can make Canada stronger and more sustainable, future-proof our economy and create new opportunities for generations to come. (Quoted in Natural Resources Canada 2017)

In this chapter, I argue that "clean growth" is, at best, a reassuring but conveniently elastic and vague term that functions as a means of providing green cover for a business-as-usual expansion of fossil fuel production and exports. In unpacking the term, I review debates about economic growth in the context of environmental protection and examine the dubious usage of the adjective "clean." I also review past efforts by governments, notably in British Columbia and Alberta, to persuade citizens of their "action" and "leadership" on climate change under the banner of clean growth. I then examine clean growth in practice and, in particular, the components of the federal Pan-Canadian Framework on Clean Growth and Climate Change.

In place of clean growth, I propose an alternative framework of *climate justice*, based on the research findings of the Canadian Centre for Policy Alternative's Climate Justice Project (CJP), a project that I have led since its inception in 2007. This research has emphasized structural changes and collective action to equitably meet aggressive carbon emission reduction targets. A range of research findings from the CJP—spanning carbon pricing, transportation, household energy use and energy poverty, and green jobs and industrial strategies—is considered as a counterpoint to the corporate-friendly climate denialism of clean growth.[2]

The Rhetoric of Climate Policy in Canada

Canadian climate policy is full of terminology coined by governments to communicate that the government in question is in charge and is getting things done. The term "climate action" came to prominence in British Columbia in 2007 as part of a whole-of-government exercise that spawned a Climate Action Secretariat and a 2008 Climate Action Plan. With a carbon tax as its centrepiece, the BC government claimed the plan would achieve 73 percent of the province's legislated target of a 33 percent reduction in emissions by 2020 relative to 2007 levels. Unfortunately, within a few years the BC government lost its zeal for climate action (see Lee 2017a).

The more self-congratulatory term "climate leadership" emerged in British Columbia and Alberta in 2015, in the lead-up to the Paris climate conference. The BC government launched an expert panel, the Climate Leadership Team (CLT), to provide policy advice. The CLT recognized that the province would not be able to meet its 2020 target largely because of government plans to develop a large liquefied natural gas (LNG) export industry. The CLT proposed a replacement target (40 percent below 2007 levels by 2030), but its recommendations for reducing emissions were left out of the subsequent Climate Leadership Plan, released by the government in August 2016. As Shannon Daub and Zoë Yunker (2017) discovered, BC government officials consulted extensively with industry leaders in Calgary and essentially gutted the CLT's recommendations.[3]

Alberta's claim to climate leadership is somewhat different, although equally dubious. In the summer of 2015, the province's then-NDP government convened a Climate Change Advisory Panel, which submitted its final report, *Climate Leadership*, that November, following which its recommendations were essentially adopted by the Alberta government as its Climate Leadership Plan. The plan contains some bona fide climate policies, including a carbon tax and a commitment to reduce leakages of methane gas, and a commitment to phase out coal-fired electricity (Alberta Climate Change Advisory Panel 2015, 5–8).

However, the Alberta plan contained no emission reduction targets. The government's own modelling showed that, at best, emissions would be flat over the coming decades. This is because emission reductions from the above policies are set against growing emissions from the oil and gas industry. While the plan included a cap on oil sands emissions, the cap was sufficiently high that it allowed emissions to grow 40 percent above current levels. In short, under this vision of climate leadership, Alberta's emissions would have gone down only if other countries had simply stopped buying Alberta fossil fuels.

The Emergence of Clean Growth

In the face of climate policy that is full of jargon—from the underlying climate science to technical issues of regulation and carbon pricing—it is too easy for governments to pat themselves on the back for setting targets and making rhetorical calls to action. Meanwhile, the status quo of growing fossil fuel production and exports remains unchallenged, with the result that stated emission reduction targets are rarely met.

Clean growth follows in this tradition of promising change without fundamentally disrupting the existing economic and social order. "Clean growth" is a purely political term that frames mitigation policy in terms of opportunities for business and away from the need for individual and collective sacrifice to avert future horrors (that is, the harsh reality painted by climate science). The rhetoric of clean growth evokes decarbonization, the replacement of fossil fuel energy with renewables.

The practice of clean growth, however, includes paradoxical claims that also accommodate expansion of oil sands and fracked gas production, accompanied by new bitumen pipelines and LNG terminals. While the Pan-Canadian Framework on Clean Growth and Climate Change includes some positive steps, it lacks the urgency that climate science calls for and fails to confront the entrenched power of the fossil fuel industry. The federal government has gone so far as to nationalize the Alberta-to-BC Trans Mountain Pipeline in order to ensure that a new pipeline along the same corridor (opposed by the BC government) takes place.

It is telling that economic growth gets first billing in the Pan-Canadian Framework. Since at least the middle of the twentieth century, the federal government has been obsessed with growth as its top policy priority, and growth is viewed as synonymous with progress and prosperity. Such calls mask ideological disagreements about the determinants of economic growth in advanced capitalist economies. The common neoliberal prescription for growth by means of tax cuts, deregulation, and free trade is, however, but one perspective. Progressives have often made the case for increased public infrastructure and services within the framework of growth.

There is a long-standing critique of economic growth from the standpoint of ecological limits. A thorough review is beyond the scope of this chapter, but a central point is that economic growth—through both increased population and increased consumption per capita—has been directly correlated with the use of fossil fuel energy and thus growing carbon emissions. In addition, a narrow focus on carbon emissions neglects other serious ecological challenges, including waste, environmental degradation, and a loss of biodiversity and the extinction of entire species (Jackson 2009).

From an economic perspective, the critique of growth extends to the use of gross domestic product (GDP) as the measured entity that must be grown. As Peter Victor (2008, 9) notes, GDP captures the growth of expenditures for items such as pollution control devices and home security systems that indicate a worsening of external circumstances, while leaving out the growth of such things as unpaid household work, voluntary labour, and environmental degradation. These shortcomings of GDP have prompted scholars to develop alternative and more comprehensive economic indicators, including the Index of Sustainable Economic Welfare (Daly and Cobb 1989) and the Genuine Progress Indicator (developed in 1995 by Redefining Progress, an organization dedicated to economic sustainability). Moreover, a relatively new branch of economics studies the determinants of well-being and happiness to promote a broader conception of what policies seeking progress and prosperity should entail (more on this below).

The focus on growth also glosses over extreme and growing inequality—the other "inconvenient truth." For example, in 2016 the top 20 percent of households controlled 67 percent of total wealth (assets less debts), while the bottom 40 percent held a mere 2 percent.[4] Inequality also shows up in terms of who benefits from consuming fossil fuels. The carbon footprint of the richest 20 percent of Canadians is almost double that of the poorest 20 percent, thanks to bigger houses, additional cars, greater frequency of travel, and higher levels of general consumption (Lee and Card 2011).

Thus, while "clean growth" is a convenient rhetorical shortcut, it is ultimately deceptive in light of the energy transition that is needed. That the power of the fossil fuel industry is unchecked in Canada's climate change program speaks to the limitations of the current approach. As Blue (2016, 76) comments,

> An underpinning assumption is that the same logic that precipitated
> the climate crisis can be used to fix it. . . . While proposed solutions
> demand that people undergo changes in lifestyle, behaviour and
> expectations, this is only to be accomplished within the existing
> system of economic and political relations in which technological
> and market-based solutions reign large. The problems associated with
> climate change are not perceived to be the result of existing political

and economic systems as such but of excessive behaviours within these systems.

In other words, in the absence of systemic changes in the political and economic relations that underlie the ideology of growth, it is unlikely that climate change will be brought under control.

What's Clean?

The adjective "clean" has repeatedly been used to rebrand dirty activities. Among the most popular is "clean coal," an industry-led renaming of the most polluting fossil fuel in terms of carbon dioxide emissions as well as other air pollution harmful to human health. Clean coal is predicated on carbon sequestration and storage: the idea that smokestack emissions can be captured and piped into underground reservoirs where they will stay forever. In practice, however, such technology has been used to re-pressurize wells so that more oil and gas can be extracted. Moreover, the costs of carbon sequestration have proven to be extremely high, and storage methods unreliable.

"Clean LNG" is another term that greenwashes a fundamentally carbon-intensive activity. The proposed Woodfibre LNG plant near Squamish, BC, is one example. The plant will use grid electricity from BC Hydro rather than natural gas to power the energy-intensive liquefaction process. In this case, "clean" does not apply to the extraction and processing of natural gas, nor does it apply to the downstream emissions when that gas is combusted. Instead, it refers narrowly to electrification at one stage of the supply chain, where gas is chilled to liquid form. This is an extremely energy-intensive process, even if powered by renewables. This narrow focus also ignores fugitive methane emissions, a principal component of natural gas and a greenhouse gas (GHG) much more potent than carbon dioxide. According to the Intergovernmental Panel on Climate Change, over a twenty-year time horizon, methane has a global warming potential eighty-six times that of carbon dioxide (cited in Vaidyanathan 2015). As a result, even very small amounts of methane leakage from a wellhead or during the transportation of natural gas have significant climate impacts.

Even the term "clean energy" is deceptive. While one might assume that "clean" energy means renewables such as wind and solar power, both governments and industry advocates often use the term to refer to a fossil fuel, namely, natural gas. For example, in the *Canada-China Joint Statement on*

Climate Change and Clean Growth (Trudeau and Li 2017), "clean energy" includes natural gas, which is discussed as if it were not a fossil fuel at all. While gas is a cleaner-burning fossil fuel than coal in terms of GHG emissions, the process of fracking for gas has huge environmental implications for water supplies, while also resulting in leakages of methane.

Putting a Price on Carbon

No policy has been as closely linked to climate policy as carbon pricing. A central component of the Pan-Canadian Framework on Clean Growth and Climate Change is a commitment to a federally mandated carbon-pricing system, which obliges provincial and territorial governments to put in place their own carbon tax or cap-and-trade system or else face a decrease in federal climate-related funding and the imposition of a federal carbon tax (which would return revenues in full to the province). The framework calls for a national minimum carbon tax of $10 per tonne in 2018, rising by $10 each year to $50 per tonne in 2022, with no further increases specified (Canada 2016, 50).

The intuition behind a steadily rising carbon tax is that carbon emissions represent an external cost (or externality) imposed on third parties to a market transaction. That is, people in the future, including those living in other parts of the world, will have to pay for some of the damage caused by fossil fuels, in the form of climate-related impacts, used by Canadians today. Carbon taxes have a long pedigree in economics as a market-based tool such that prices would reflect the costs of carbon emissions on third parties outside the market transaction. Simply put, a rising carbon tax aims to alter behaviour over time by making emissions steadily more expensive. Consumers and businesses respond by changing the decisions they make, and so we achieve emission reductions.

How high would a carbon tax need to be in order to cover the cost of ongoing emissions? Calculating the "social cost of carbon"—that is, attempting to quantify the long-term economic cost to society of emitting a single additional tonne of CO_2—is fraught with uncertainties. A number of models exist, each encompassing certain scenarios, and none is regarded as wholly reliable. In 2010, the US government placed the social cost of carbon at $21 (in 2007 US dollars) per ton of CO_2 emissions. On the basis of the US analysis, Environment Canada then followed suit, pegging the social cost of carbon at $25.60 per tonne of CO_2 of in 2011 (in 2009 Canadian dollars), rising to

$31.50 per tonne by 2020 and then to $53.70 by 2050 (Heyes, Morgan, and Rivers 2013, S70).[5] In a critical analysis of the methodology used in the US, Frank Ackerman and Elizabeth Stanton (2012) argued that the figure of $21 per tonne was far too low: the cost in 2010 could be as high as nearly $900 per tonne, with the high-end estimate rising to $1,550 in 2050 (14, figures 4 and 5; costs are in 2007 US dollars). As they point out, "a review of scenarios that reach zero or negative net global emissions within this century finds that they often imply carbon prices, and marginal abatement costs, of $150 to $500/tCO2 by 2050" (2).

In view of the uncertainties built into such modelling, these estimates are bound to be imperfect. As Ackerman and Stanton (2012, 20) point out, "we cannot know in advance how large climate damages, or climate sensitivity, will turn out to be." No consensus exists regarding projections of future growth, the appropriate discount rate to use in translating future costs into present-day values, how best to accommodate the possibility of catastrophic impacts resulting from the crossing of climate tipping points, and so on. Nor can such calculations capture long-term, large-scale consequences of climate change such as the effects of a loss of biodiversity on food cycles or the increased displacement of both human populations. Such estimates are, however, inherently flawed in a more fundamental way. They quantify environmental damage purely in terms of *human* use value, "implying that climate damages can be perfectly compensated for by increased economic productivity" (Heyes, Morgan, and Rivers 2013, S71). In a sense, then, social cost of carbon estimates attempt to assign a dollar value to nature.

Putting a price on carbon is, moreover, not the same as putting a *sufficient* price on carbon, or at least to developing a future trajectory of prices consistent with meeting stated emission reduction targets. This has led to excessive praise for pricing at levels that are more symbolic than effective. British Columbia's carbon tax, for example, was introduced at $10 per tonne in July 2008, rose to $30 per tonne in July 2012. In April 2018, and then again in 2019, the tax was increased by $5 per tonne. The current rate of $40 per tonne, equivalent to 8.89 cents per litre of gasoline, will rise to a maximum of $50 per tonne by April 2021. As Mark Jaccard, Mikela Hein, and Tiffany Vass (2016) comment, moreover, while carbon pricing may be the most efficient way to meet an emissions reduction target, the size of the tax needed to accomplish this will be politically unpalatable (and they thus recommend a package of flexible regulations that would be a better political option).

A deeper concern is that taxes on carbon emissions are endorsed as a market-driven solution to the problem of climate change, a matter of "getting the prices right." Yet carbon emissions are but one of many environmental hazards associated with fossil fuels. Moreover, an obsession with market solutions distracts attention away from other well-known market imperfections, including inequities in bargaining power between workers and employers, asymmetries in access to information, and the disproportionate market power exercised by large corporations. Each of these issues points to a more complicated reality that merits public-sector interventions in the form of infrastructure, public services, taxes, and regulation.

In the case of British Columbia, the market-friendly nature of the carbon tax was amplified by adherence to the principle of "revenue neutrality," according to which all revenues should be returned to taxpayers in the from of tax cuts or credits, that was fashionable in academic and policy circles at the time. The theory was that revenue neutrality would yield a "double dividend": the carbon tax would reduce emissions, while the tax cuts would stimulate growth. The newly elected government removed the revenue neutrality provision in the fall of 2017, recognizing the need for public investments as complementary climate policies.

Letting Industry Off the Hook

With most of the attention on the need for households to reduce their emissions, industry, the largest source of emissions in Canada, was largely spared direct regulations intended to reduce emissions. Indeed, in the name of "competitiveness," fossil fuel lobbyists are pressing for exemptions from climate policies that affect so-called "trade-exposed emissions-intensive industries." Any meaningful climate plan would push up strongly against entrenched interests in the fossil fuel industries, and yet this renewed call for climate action in the wake of the Paris Agreement and the release of the Pan-Canadian Framework provoked no scathing op-eds or oppositional campaigns from corporate Canada.

The most notable federal commitment on industrial emissions is a promise, made in June 2016, to reduce methane emissions by 40 percent to 45 percent by 2025 (Canada 2016, 51). This target has been endorsed by the BC and Alberta governments. The subsequent BC and Alberta plans include a narrow focus on preventing leaks in oil and gas facilities and equipment. While such efforts hold promise, there is no accurate baseline: governments do not monitor or measure methane emissions but instead rely on data reported by industry and modelling to develop the numbers reported in the national GHG inventory. Recent scientific studies have found significant underreporting by industry of methane emissions from fracking operations in British Columbia (Werring 2018) and oil sands mining Alberta (Johnson et al. 2017).

The most significant policy in the Pan-Canadian Framework is the phase-out of coal-fired electricity in Alberta by 2030. If all this power were to be replaced by renewables, it would represent a major leap toward the target. But much of the shift will be to natural gas, which will have a much more modest impact on emissions than would a shift directly to renewable energy sources. And in the case of fracked gas, leakages of methane would undermine any benefit relative to coal.

Special treatment for fossil fuels, chemical production, and other carbon-intensive sectors is wrapped in calls for innovation and technology, which seem founded more than anything on wishful thinking. Especially concerning are government efforts to subsidize the very industries causing the problem. Of the $200 million in funding promised in the 2017 federal budget to support the research and development of "clean technology" in the resource sectors, just over three-quarters—$155 million—subsequently went to Natural Resources Canada's Clean Growth Program, launched in November 2017. Hailed by Environment Minister Catherine McKenna as one of Canada's "smart and strategic investments," the program aims to fund "clean technology" projects in the areas of energy, mining, and forestry, thereby "helping to reduce greenhouse gas emissions and improve environmental outcomes" (Natural Resources Canada 2017).

Finally, in accordance with the Western Climate Initiative cap-and-trade system, the Pan-Canadian Framework counts as emission reductions planned purchases of carbon credits by Ontario and Québec from California. Notwithstanding the dubious environmental credibility of offsets, and the withdrawal of Ontario from the initiative in June 2018, this assumes that California will have excess credits to sell. It is also an implicit admission that provinces may not be willing to do the hard work of reducing industrial emissions within their own borders.

Growing Fossil Fuel Production and Exports

While the above actions to reduce emissions are inadequate, even worse has been the federal decision to double down on fossil fuel production. More than one-quarter of Canada's GHG emissions come from the oil and gas sector, but plans for a major expansion of the sector continue unabated. Emissions from the oil and gas sector are anticipated to grow by 21 percent up to 2030 (National Energy Board 2016), an increase that would counter most of the benefit from phasing out coal-fired electricity.

The Pan-Canadian Framework does not put reductions in fossil fuel production on the table. This is, unfortunately, consistent with the Paris Agreement, which places no limits or sanctions on the supply of fossil fuels being brought to market by producing countries. The Paris Agreement is thus a "good deal" for Canada because only half of the fossil fuels we extract get counted in our GHG inventory (Lee 2017b), with the remainder exported and the emissions counted in the place where the fuel is burned. Exported emissions might not be a problem if the commitments made by countries in the Paris Agreement were enough to keep global warming below 1.5°C to 2°C (above pre-industrial levels—about two hundred years ago). But this is not the case. Sinn (2012) calls this a "green paradox," in that producing countries have a powerful incentive to respond to the Paris Agreement by doubling down on fossil fuels now before their value evaporates. The problem with new fossil fuel infrastructure projects—in particular, LNG terminals and bitumen pipelines—is that they lock us in to a high-emissions trajectory for several decades to come, giving up on the 1.5°C to 2°C limit of the Paris Agreement.

A Climate Justice Framework

In contrast to clean growth, a framework of climate justice offers an alternative approach. The term originates from the international context of climate change and who wins and who loses from the production and consumption of fossil fuels. As Shane Gunster (2016, 62) notes,

> [A] climate justice frame insists that the most important thing to know about the problem is the highly unequal and grossly unfair distribution of risks, responsibility and benefits: simply put, those who are least responsible for causing climate change will suffer the most harm from its impacts, while those who bear the most responsibility will not only suffer the least but also are, in fact, the principal beneficiaries of fossil fuel use.

The Climate Justice Project, led by the BC Office of the Canadian Centre for Policy Alternatives, explored the concept of climate justice primarily in the context of British Columbia, with extensions to federal policies. A central premise was that if climate policies fail to take into account inequalities and differing resources, they will likely make things worse for vulnerable people—those who have done the least to contribute to the problem. Instead, the concept of climate justice integrates social justice principles into climate policy for an approach that seeks win-win outcomes spanning employment, health and well-being, and systemic changes that reduce emissions across society. Climate justice is thus an inclusive approach to overcoming political inertia and other barriers to change. It makes the case that effective and fair climate action is also good industrial and employment policy. The theme of rethinking the "good life," including additional co-benefits in terms of health and well-being, has been at the heart of the CJP since its inception. Done well, the shift away from fossil fuels can provide additional benefits in terms of health and well-being, economic security, and reduced inequality.

Fair and Effective Carbon Pricing

In place of a market-based preoccupation with "getting the prices right," a climate justice approach recognizes that a well-designed carbon tax perhaps more importantly provides the revenues needed to make public investments that reinforce climate action. A challenge in moving away from fossil fuels is that companies are putting billions of dollars on the table for their investments. While the carbon tax is an ideal source of revenue to support alternative investments in needed services and infrastructure, in order to alter marketplace behaviour, federal and provincial carbon prices would need to be much higher, eventually reaching $200 per tonne or more. For a carbon tax to be both fair and effective, however, some reforms to the revenue recycling regime are needed before the tax is increased.

First, the carbon tax is a regressive tax, applied uniformly across all income brackets, which means that the tax consumes a larger share of the income of low-income households than it does in high-income households. Although carbon-pricing systems (including that in British Columbia) generally attempt to offset this effect by means of low-income carbon credits, these credits typically represent only a small portion of the total revenue from the tax and are often too low to compensate for its regressive nature. In order to address this problem effectively, roughly one-third to one-half of carbon tax revenues should be used to fund a credit that would flow to a broad range of lower-income households. In an earlier publication (Lee 2011), I lay out a credit system based on the Canada Child Tax Benefit model that would provide a carbon credit to roughly 80 percent of all households, with the bottom half of all households receiving more in credits, on average, than they would pay in carbon tax. Under such an approach, the heavy lifting would be accomplished by households with higher incomes—those who already have the largest carbon footprints.

Second, the principle of revenue neutrality must be rejected, with what remains of carbon tax revenues after credits are paid out used to support complementary climate policies. These could include major new public investments that accelerate climate action in the form of public transit, retrofit programs for buildings, green jobs training and just transition programs, and forest conservation and stewardship. Using the revenues to build the infrastructure we need for the twenty-first century would also support green job creation.

Shifting to 100 Percent Renewable Energy

Conservation and energy efficiency are generally accepted as the least expensive, lowest-impact way to meet energy demands. Reductions in consumption through demand-side management, together with improvements in the energy efficiency of buildings, lighting, and appliances, are probably sufficient to offset additional demand arising from population increase and economic growth. The central planning challenge stems from two major sources of demand on the system: residential and commercial buildings that use fossil fuels for heating and hot water and the transportation of people and goods.

Like carbon taxes, electricity pricing must take into account the proportionally greater adverse impact of price hikes on lower-income groups. Low-income households already pay a greater share of their income in energy and electricity costs, and they are far more likely to rent their housing. Yet, as tenants, they typically are not in a position to choose to make improvements to their housing with respect to energy efficiency. Most home energy retrofit programs are geared toward homeowners and so benefit the relatively affluent. Although significant emission reductions could result from energy efficiency investments in multi-unit rental buildings and older housing stock (Lee, Kung, and Owen 2011), the challenge lies in persuading building owners to make such investments.

Complementary initiatives that can reduce the demand for electricity include neighbourhood-scale energy projects. District energy systems produce thermal energy (in the form of hot water) at a central plant, which is then distributed by a network of underground pipes to buildings and houses in a local area. While such systems have a long history in urban areas, they should have a greater profile in the transition. Such systems provide a green infrastructure that enables the reduction of carbon emissions from buildings. The City of Vancouver's Neighbourhood Energy Utility, which serves Southeast False Creek, is a leading example. By providing space heating and hot water to buildings through the recapture of waste heat from the sewage system, the utility has achieved more than a 60 percent reduction in GHG emissions.[6]

In addition, new models of public ownership, often described as "energy democracy," that aim to alter the locus of control over energy resources align well with a potential shift to 100 percent renewable energy. As James Angel (2016, 3) observes, the discourse of energy democracy contests the terrain of energy production by arguing for collective ownership and for systems that reflect the public interest and place social justice and environmental objectives ahead of profit.

Transportation and Complete Communities

In transportation, an area that represents another quarter of Canada's GHG emissions, the Pan-Canadian Framework (Canada 2016, 19) calls for "increasingly stringent standards for emissions from light-duty vehicles" and the swift development of a Canada-wide strategy for zero-emission vehicles. However, shifting from internal combustion engines to electric cars is only part of the picture for mitigating carbon emissions, and policy makers are arguably focusing too narrowly on decarbonizing tailpipe emissions rather than making investments in mobility through higher-efficiency modes like public transit. While the framework does mention public transit expansion and upgrades, federal funding commitments have thus far been more modest.

Yet with dedicated and sufficient funding for public transit expansion, faster and higher-capacity transit networks could be built within a decade. Investments could also be made in existing public transit infrastructure to improve its efficiency, especially if measures were undertaken to repurpose roadways and parking areas. Indeed, quite apart from carbon emissions, a heavy reliance on automobiles comes with other costs: air and noise pollution, the need for adequate parking space, time lost owing to congestion, and accidents that can cause injury or death. This suggests that well-designed transportation investments could not only reduce emissions but improve the quality of life in many ways.

A climate justice vision is one of "complete communities," in which people can meet their everyday needs without having to travel long distances (see Condon et al. 2010). Such communities emphasize walking, biking, and transit, supplemented by car-sharing, with homes located close to work, shops, entertainment, parks, and public services. Signs of such a shift are already beginning to appear in some Canadian cities. According to the 2016 census, for example, nearly half of all commuters in the City of Vancouver walk, bicycle, or take public transit to work.[7] Complete communities create an inclusive environment for seniors, youth, people with disabilities, and low-income families, one where they can live and move about easily even if they are not able to drive or cannot afford a car. However, affordable housing must be integrated into such communities, with the need for new housing in fact providing an opportunity for redevelopment plans that reinforce complete communities. Public-sector investments in libraries, child care facilities, and community health centres can also help to anchor redevelopment.

Closing the Loop

"Closing the loop" refers to the shift from a linear economic model, in which raw materials are extracted, transformed into consumer goods, and ultimately thrown out, toward a resource recovery model, sometimes called a "circular economy," in which materials are recycled. Upstream, proactive solutions include aggressive materials reduction, redesign, and reuse *before* recycling and composting. The goal is a dramatic reduction in the volume of materials that flow through the economy, with corresponding reductions in the amount of energy used and carbon emissions from resource extraction, processing, and transportation. Indeed, carbon dioxide is the single largest waste product by weight. The difference is that carbon pollution goes into the atmosphere, not into landfill.

A climate justice approach rejects incineration (typically rebranded as waste-to-energy), which creates the perception that waste has disappeared. However, incineration only transforms materials into other forms, releasing GHGs and other toxic compounds like dioxins and furans into the air, while still leaving solid waste (toxic ash) that must be landfilled. Incineration also wastes the embodied energy in products that result from resource extraction and processing, product manufacture, and transportation.

A wide range of innovative economic activity is possible with well-designed zero-waste policies, including dematerialization, support of sharing economies, and new leasing models for various services. In a study of reducing GHG emissions by eliminating waste, my colleagues and I estimated that, by 2040, aggressive zero-waste policies in British Columbia could result in 6.2 million tonnes of CO_2 savings by displacing organics from landfills and reducing the need for energy-intensive upstream extraction and processing activities (Lee et al. 2013, 37). Well-designed reuse policies can support local economic development and the creation of new green jobs by increasing local capacity to manage and add value to recovered materials. In the same study, we estimated that, if waste exports were reduced and domestic markets for recovered materials developed, approximately seven thousand new direct jobs that would result from 100 percent recycling of British Columbia's waste (34). Governments can help build this capacity through their procurement policies and by setting minimum recycled-content standards for the marketplace.

Shifting to Green Jobs

Importantly, in comparison to investments in fossil fuel infrastructure, green investments tend to require more labour power and therefore generate a greater number of jobs (see Lee and Card 2012, 38–39). Thus, a well-designed transition plan should have a net positive impact on employment. Investments in low-carbon services would have a similar effect. Key areas include early learning and child care, which would benefit children and families, and seniors' care, including home and residential care.

We will also need to ensure a "just transition" strategy for resource industry workers. The costs of adjustment should not be shouldered by those most impacted by them. In past resource busts, families have faced extreme instability because of lost incomes, manifest in drug and alcohol addiction, increased domestic violence, and divorce (Cooling et al. 2015). Stable management of fossil fuel industries over a two-to-three-decade wind-down period would better serve workers and communities. This should include averting the boom and bust of commodity markets, with strategic use of limited fossil fuels in the transition to a zero-carbon economy.

Conclusion: From Growth to Well-Being

CJP research has emphasized structural changes and collective action, rather than individual behavioural change, as means of lowering carbon footprints. It also makes the case that effective and fair climate action is good industrial and employment policy. The theme of rethinking the "good life," including additional co-benefits in terms of health and well-being, has been at the heart of the CJP since its inception.

A growing body of research into well-being and happiness tells us to look beyond money and consumption. While income matters a great deal at lower levels—when one is poor, a little money makes a big difference—once basic needs are met, higher income does not necessarily translate into gains in happiness. Research points to substantial benefits to be had from a more equitable distribution of wealth; inequality manifests in weaker performance on a range of social and health indicators (Wilkinson and Pickett 2009). Social fairness in terms of income and employment distribution may, in fact, be vital for achieving the changes required for a transition to a sustainable economy. Some key insights into well-being relevant to climate justice include the following:

- *Full employment and decent work.* Unemployment has been shown to have huge negative consequences for our well-being. The quality of the work we do also affects our well-being because it gives us purpose, a challenge, and opportunities to develop relationships with others. Work not only provides income but helps to sustain social relationships. A green jobs program that promotes work that has meaning and purpose fosters precisely the type of work that contributes to higher levels of well-being.

- *Time and work-life balance.* The amount and quality of leisure time is important for well-being, in view of the physical and mental health benefits associated with recreation, whereas long work hours may harm our health and increase stress. Time pressures from work can also reduce time available for family activities, for caring work, and for volunteering. Reducing long commutes can also liberate time and increase well-being.

- *Community and social cohesion.* The most important factors contributing to happiness seem to include having close relationships with family and friends, helping others, and being active in community, charitable, and political activities. In large urban areas, participation in community and thus the ability to psychologically flourish can be constrained by social isolation and loneliness.

These findings have led to a growing understanding that focusing on economic growth is a flawed approach to well-being. This expanding body of research is broadly consistent with the notion of climate justice. As the authors of the 2012 *World Happiness Report* comment,

> The environmental debate could be importantly recast by changing the fundamental objectives from economic growth to building and sustaining the quality of lives, as assessed by those whose lives they are. This will depend crucially on the human capacity for cooperation. . . . People gain in happiness by working together for a higher purpose. There can be no higher purpose than promoting the Earth's environmental balance, the well-being of future generations, and the survival and thriving of other species as well. Sustainability is an instrumental goal, because without it, our health and prosperity are bound to collapse. But environmental sustainability is also an end goal: we care about nature, we care about other species, and we care about future generations. (Helliwell, Layard, and Sachs 2012, 96)

Resistance begins when we recognize the damage done to us by those whose values prioritize self-interest over respect for nature and basic human needs. Canada is a wealthy nation with abundant geological, physical, and human assets that should enable it to make a fair and effective energy transition. Being a climate leader means developing a coherent program of green investment, job creation, and industrial policy and not indulging in vacuous rhetoric about "clean growth."

Notes

1. See, for example, Pembina Institute (2017), as well as the institute's comments on Budget 2019 (Turcotte 2019). Nor has Canada been alone in embracing the term: witness the United Kingdom's 2017 "Clean Growth Strategy."
2. Much of the CJP's key research has been conducted in partnership with academics, environmental NGOs, labour unions, and others through a multi-year SSHRC grant (2009–15).

3. Chapter 9 in this volume offers an in-depth discussion of British Columbia's evolving climate policy, including an account of these closed-door consultations.

4. Calculated from data in Statistics Canada, Table 11-10-0049-01 (formerly CANSIM 205-0004), "Survey of Financial Security (SFS), Assets and Debts by Net Worth Quintile, Canada, Provinces and Selected Census Metropolitan Areas (CMAs)," Statistics Canada, https://www150.statcan.gc.ca/t1/tbl1/en/tv.action?pid=1110004901. Here, I have expressed the figures for the second and for the highest net worth quintiles as percentages of the figure for total net worth.

5. Clearly, these dollar values are not directly comparable, owing to differences in both currency and unit of measurement (a ton is roughly nine-tenths of a tonne). The estimates are, however, closely similar. https://www.canada.ca/en/revenue-agency/services/forms-publications/previous-year-forms-publications/archived-rc4152/archived-average-exchange-rates-2007.html.

6. "Southeast False Creek Neighbourhood Energy Utility," City of Vancouver, n.d., accessed February 28, 2020, https://vancouver.ca/home-property-development/southeast-false-creek-neighbourhood-energy-utility.aspx. See also Lee (2015) for a detailed study of the system.

7. "Census Profile, 2016 Census: Vancouver, City [Census Subdivision], British Columbia and Greater Vancouver, Regional District [Census Division], British Columbia," Statistics Canada, last modified August 9, 2019, https://www12.statcan.gc.ca/census-recensement/2016/dp-pd/prof/details/page.cfm?Lang=E&Geo1=CSD&Code1=5915022&Geo2=CD&Code2=5915&SearchText=Vancouver&SearchType=Begins&SearchPR=01&B1=Journey%20to%20work&TABID=1&type=1 ("Journey to work," view by Rank). The breakdown is 29.7 percent by public transit, 13.7 percent by foot, and 6.1 percent by bicycle.

References

Ackerman, Frank, and Elizabeth A. Stanton. 2012. "Climate Risks and Carbon Prices: Revising the Social Cost of Carbon." *Economics* 6 (2012-10): 1–25. http://dx.doi.org/10.5018/economics-ejournal.ja.2012-10.

Alberta Climate Change Advisory Panel. 2015. *Climate Leadership: Report to Minister*. November. https://www.alberta.ca/documents/climate/climate-leadership-report-to-minister.pdf.

Angel, James. 2016. *Toward Energy Democracy: Discussions and Outcomes from an International Workshop, Amsterdam, 11–12 February*. Amsterdam: Transnational Institute. https://www.tni.org/files/publication-downloads/energy_democracy_workshop_report_for_web-2.pdf.

Blue, Gwendolyn. 2016. "Framing Climate Change for Public Deliberation: What Role for Interpretive Social Sciences and Humanities?" *Journal of Environmental Policy and Planning* 18, no. 1: 67–84. https://doi.org/10.1080/15239 08X.2015.1053107.

Canada. 2016. *Pan-Canadian Framework on Clean Growth and Climate Change.* Ottawa: Government of Canada. http://publications.gc.ca/collections/ collection_2017/eccc/En4-294-2016-eng.pdf.

Condon, Patrick, Eric Doherty, Kari Dow, Marc Lee, and Gordon Price. 2010. *Transportation Transformation: Building Complete Communities and a Zero-Emission Transportation System in BC.* Vancouver: Canadian Centre for Policy Alternatives, BC Office. https://www.policyalternatives.ca/ transportationtransformation.

Cooling, Karen, Marc Lee, Shannon Daub, and Jessie Singer. 2015. *Just Transition: Creating a Green Social Contract for BC's Resource Workers.* Vancouver: Canadian Centre for Policy Alternatives, BC Office. https://www.policyalternatives.ca/ publications/reports/just-transition.

Daly, Herman E., and John B. Cobb Jr. 1989. *For the Common Good: Redirecting the Economy Toward Community, the Environment, and a Sustainable Future.* Boston: Beacon Press.

Daub, Shannon, and Zoë Yunker. 2017. "BC's Last Climate 'Leadership' Plan Was Written in Big Oil's Boardroom (Literally)." *Policy Note* (blog). Canadian Centre for Policy Alternatives, BC Office. September 18, 2017. http://www.policynote.ca/ climate-leadership-plan-big-oils-boardroom/.

Canada. First Ministers. 2016. *Vancouver Declaration on Clean Growth and Climate Change.* March 3, 2016. Ottawa: Canadian Intergovernmental Conference Secretariat. http://www.scics.ca/en/product-produit/vancouver-declaration-on- clean-growth-and-climate-change/.

Gunster, Shane. 2017. "Engaging Climate Communication: Audiences, Frames, Values and Norms." In *Journalism and Climate Crisis: Public Engagement, Media Alternatives,* edited by Robert A. Hackett, Susan Forde, Shane Gunster, and Kerrie Foxwell-Norton, 49–76. London: Routledge.

Helliwell, John, Richard Layard, and Jeffrey Sachs, eds. 2012. *World Happiness Report.* New York: Earth Institute, Columbia University. https://worldhappiness. report/ed/2012/.

Heyes, Anthony, Dylan Morgan, and Nicholas Rivers. 2013. "The Use of a Social Cost of Carbon in Canadian Cost-Benefit Analysis." *Canadian Public Policy / Analyse de politiques* 39, suppl. 2 (August): S67–S79.

Jaccard, Mark, Mikela Hein, and Tiffany Vass. 2016. *Is Win-Win Possible? Can Canada's Government Achieve Its Paris Commitment . . . and Get Re-Elected?* Burnaby, BC: School of Resource and Environmental Management, Simon Fraser

University. http://rem-main.rem.sfu.ca/papers/jaccard/Jaccard-Hein-Vass%20
CdnClimatePol%20EMRG-REM-SFU%20Sep%2020%202016.pdf.

Jackson, Tim. 2009. *Prosperity Without Growth: Economics for a Finite Planet.*
London: Earthscan.

Johnson, Matthew R., David R. Tyner, Stephen Conley, Stefan Schwietzke, and
Daniel Zavala-Araiza. 2017. "Comparisons of Airborne Measurements and
Inventory Estimates of Methane Emissions in the Alberta Upstream Oil and Gas
Sector." *Environmental Science and Technology* 51, no. 21: 13008–17. https://pubs.
acs.org/doi/pdf/10.1021/acs.est.7b03525.

Lee, Marc. 2011. *Fair and Effective Carbon Pricing: Lessons from BC.* Vancouver:
Canadian Centre for Policy Alternatives, BC Office; Victoria: Sierra Club BC. https://
www.policyalternatives.ca/publications/reports/fair-and-effective-carbon-pricing.

———. 2015. *Innovative Approaches to Low-Carbon Urban Systems: A Case Study
of Vancouver's Neighbourhood Energy Utility.* Cambridge, MA: Future Economy
Project, Economics for Equity and Environment (E3) Network. https://
www.policyalternatives.ca/sites/default/files/uploads/publications/BC%20
Office/2015/02/CCPA-BC-NEU-Case-Study.pdf.

———. 2017a. "The Rise and Fall of Climate Action in BC." *Policy Note* (blog).
Canadian Centre for Policy Alternatives, BC Office. February 13, 2017. http://
www.policynote.ca/the-rise-and-fall-of-climate-action-in-bc/.

———. 2017b. *Extracted Carbon: Re-examining Canada's Contribution to Climate
Change Through Fossil Fuel Exports.* Ottawa: Canadian Centre for Policy
Alternatives; Edmonton: Parkland Institute. https://www.policyalternatives.ca/
publications/reports/extracted-carbon.

Lee, Marc, and Amanda Card. 2011. "Who Occupies the Sky? The Distribution
of GHGs in Canada." *Behind the Numbers,* November 2011. Ottawa: Canadian
Centre for Policy Alternatives. https://www.policyalternatives.ca/publications/
reports/who-occupies-sky.

———. 2012. *A Green Industrial Revolution: Climate Justice, Green Jobs and
Sustainable Production in Canada.* Ottawa: Canadian Centre for Policy
Alternatives. https://www.policyalternatives.ca/publications/reports/green-
industrial-revolution.

Lee, Marc, Eugene Kung, and Jason Owen. 2010. *Fighting Energy Poverty in the
Transition to Zero-Emission Housing: A Framework for BC.* Vancouver: Canadian
Centre for Policy Alternatives, BC Office. http://www.policyalternatives.ca/
energy-poverty.

Lee, Marc, Ruth Legg, Sue Maxwell, and William Rees. 2013. *Closing the Loop:
Reducing Greenhouse Gas Emissions Through Zero Waste in BC.* Vancouver:
Canadian Centre for Policy Alternatives, BC Office, and the Wilderness
Committee. http://www.policyalternatives.ca/publications/reports/closing-loop.

Litman, Todd. 2010. *Evaluating Transportation Economic Development Impacts Understanding How Transport Policy and Planning Decisions Affect Employment, Incomes, Productivity, Competitiveness, Property Values and Tax Revenues.* Victoria: Victoria Transport Policy Institute. https://www.vtpi.org/econ_dev.pdf.

National Energy Board. 2016. *Canada's Energy Future 2016: Update—Energy Supply and Demand Projections to 2040.* Ottawa: National Energy Board. https://www.neb-one.gc.ca/nrg/ntgrtd/ftr/2016updt/index-eng.html.

Natural Resources Canada. 2017. "New $155-Million Clean Growth Program Launched to Address Climate Change." News release. November 20, 2017. https://www.canada.ca/en/natural-resources-canada/news/2017/11/new_155-million_cleangrowthprogramlaunchedtoaddressclimatechange.html.

Pembina Institute. 2017. *Vision for Clean Growth in B.C.* Calgary: Pembina Institute. https://www.pembina.org/pub/cleangrowthbc.

Sinn, Hans-Werner. 2012. *The Green Paradox: A Supply-Side Approach to Global Warming.* Cambridge, MA: MIT Press.

Stiglitz, Joseph E., Amartya Sen, and Jean-Paul Fitoussi. 2009. *Report by the Commission on the Measurement of Economic Performance and Social Progress.* Submitted to the Government of France. http://ec.europa.eu/eurostat/documents/118025/118123/Fitoussi+Commission+report.

Trudeau, Justin, and Li Keqiang. 2017. *Canada-China Joint Statement on Climate Change and Clean Growth.* December 4, 2017. https://pm.gc.ca/eng/news/2017/12/04/canada-china-joint-statement-climate-change-and-clean-growth.

Turcotte, Isabelle. 2019. "The Ongoing Journey Towards Canada's Clean Growth Economy: Budget 2019 Highlights." *Pembina Institute* (blog), March 20, 2019. https://www.pembina.org/blog/ongoing-journey-towards-canadas-clean-growth-economy.

Vaidyanathan, Gayathri. 2015. "How Bad of a Greenhouse Gas Is Methane?" *Scientific American: E&E News*, December 22, 2015. https://www.scientificamerican.com/article/how-bad-of-a-greenhouse-gas-is-methane/.

Victor, Peter. 2008. *Managing Without Growth: Slower by Design, Not Disaster.* Northampton, MA: Edward Elgar.

Werring, John. 2018. *Fugitives in Our Midst: Investigating Fugitive Emissions from Abandoned, Suspended and Active Oil and Gas Wells in the Montney Basin in Northeastern British Columbia.* Vancouver: David Suzuki Foundation. https://davidsuzuki.org/science-learning-centre-article/fugitives-midst-investigating-fugitive-emissions-abandoned-suspended-active-oil-gas-wells-montney-basin-northeastern-british-columbia/.

Wilkinson, Richard, and Kate Pickett. 2009. *The Spirit Level: Why Equality Is Better for Everyone.* London: Penguin.

15 Flashpoints of Possibility
What Resistance Reveals About Pathways Toward Energy Transition

Karena Shaw

The influence of fossil fuels on our contemporary world, and on our potential futures, is difficult to overstate: our built infrastructure, political institutions, economies, ideologies, and collective aspirations have all been profoundly shaped by the exploitation of fossil fuels (Huber 2013; Malm 2016; Mitchell 2011; Paterson 2007). Imagining and building futures beyond fossil fuels thus poses a range of challenges. Perhaps first among these is the need to expose and denaturalize the influence of the fossil fuel industry, an influence that—as detailed elsewhere in this volume—obstructs our collective efforts to develop the infrastructures, institutions, and aspirations that will allow us to thrive in a climate-constrained world. This chapter seeks to illustrate how flashpoints of resistance challenge the industry's influence and, in the process, offer crucial resources that can help build a future without fossil fuels. In the details of the intensely critical work of resistance reside essential resources for thinking and acting differently. These resources emerge from the critical process itself: by revealing and redescribing what *is* with attentiveness to its contingency, the potential for being otherwise can be articulated. This chapter attempts to illustrate this general point about the work of resistance by examining a specific flashpoint: the proposal to expand the Trans Mountain Pipeline between Edmonton, Alberta, and Burnaby, British Columbia, to facilitate the export of bitumen and thus the expansion of tar sands development in Alberta.

Many potential conceptual and methodological starting points exist for an analysis of the work being done at particular sites of resistance. I use "flashpoints" here to refer to sites at which resistance—often long-standing but not widely recognized or understood—becomes visible in ways that have the potential to reshape public understanding and relations of power. The term "flashpoints" has been used more narrowly to refer to sites at which violence—or the potential for violence—has flared up in the context of demonstrations or other policing interactions (see, for example, Borrows 2005; Russell 2010; Waddington 2010). My use is somewhat more expansive, although still grounded in acts of resistance and the points at which these become "unmanageable" or uncontained, as well as in how these acts are apprehended by other forces in society, including the media. As Peter Russell (2010) emphasizes, although these flashpoints often seem to appear suddenly, they are usually the expression of long-standing grievances and/or sustained organizing work. My focus here is less on the actual dynamics of the resistance and more on what this resistance—whether expressed through demonstrations, civil disobedience, critical commentary, or other disruption of expectations—brings to light: how it is understood within, and reshapes, public dialogue and the landscape of political possibility. Through an exploration of the public conversation about whether the Trans Mountain Pipeline Expansion will be built, this chapter asks, What does this flashpoint reveal about how the political landscape has been shaped by the fossil fuel industry and thus must be reshaped to facilitate a transition beyond fossil fuels?

Asking such a question in the heat of the moment might seem foolhardy: What clarity can possibly emerge from the midst of the battlefield? Winners and losers are unclear, the spoils not yet divided up: patience will surely lead to greater clarity. It's a sensible point. However, such moments of intensity can also bring into sharp focus structural configurations of power that shape political possibility and thus help to reshape political strategies. Embedded in such moments are insights and resources that must be exploited in the moment in order to reshape trajectories long into the future (Chaloupka 2003), even if that endgame is far from clear.

Some Background

The proposal to expand (by twinning) the Trans Mountain Pipeline became public in February 2012, when Kinder Morgan—the Texas-based owner of the pipeline—indicated that it had received support from oil shippers for additional capacity. The existing pipeline, opened in 1953, linked loading facilities east of Edmonton to refining and distribution points in British Columbia, including an export terminal in Burnaby on the province's south coast—a roughly 1,150-kilometre route. In December 2013, Kinder Morgan initiated an application to expand the pipeline to the National Energy Board (NEB), proposing to begin construction in 2017 with the aim of having oil flowing by December 2019. This timeline corresponded in general terms to a number of other major—and contentious—pipeline proposals focused on transporting Alberta's bitumen to tidewater. Notably, Enbridge's proposed Northern Gateway pipeline (from the tar sands region to Kitimat, on the northern BC coast) provoked intense resistance in British Columbia, which ended only in late 2016, when the federal government rejected Enbridge's proposal. But other Canadian pipeline projects—the Energy East pipeline proposed by TransCanada (now TC Energy) in 2013 and cancelled in 2017, the Keystone XL (also a TC Energy project), and Enbridge's plans to expand its Line 3 and Line 9 pipelines—have also generated widespread opposition.

Opposition to the proposed Trans Mountain Expansion (TMX) emerged quickly, with more than one hundred people arrested in November 2014 for acts of civil disobedience when they interfered with preliminary drilling and survey work conducted on Burnaby Mountain. This opposition was not confined to civil disobedience but included active engagement with the NEB, where concerns were raised about the scope and process of the NEB's review, particularly in relation to the opportunities provided for public input and Indigenous consultation (Ball 2018a; McSheffrey and Uechi 2016). Nonetheless, the NEB concluded that the project was in the public interest and, on May 29, 2016, recommended approval of the pipeline, subject to 157 conditions. Federal government approval followed on November 30, 2016.

Christy Clark, then premier of British Columbia, endorsed the project in January 2017. Her government was defeated in a provincial election a few months later, however, and replaced by a minority government led by the BC NDP, to which the BC Green Party then formally pledged its support. This de facto coalition shifted the context somewhat. Both the NDP and Greens had actively campaigned against the TMX, with future premier John Horgan declaring on the campaign trail that an NDP government would use "every tool in the box" to prevent the project from being built (Kane 2017). Perhaps emboldened by the new government's stance, as well as the initiation of pre-construction activities, opposition to the project began to ramp up. Again, this opposition took a variety of forms, from a large number of legal cases brought forward by a variety of First Nations and the City of Burnaby to the vow of the "Tiny House Warriors" to construct a series of tiny homes on Secwepemc Territory in the path of the pipeline, as well as substantial mobilization in the form of letter writing, petitions, and demonstrations. By late 2017, it was clear that the project faced a potential morass of resistance, just as the company wished to move toward "shovels in the ground." This is when the protest really began to heat up.

Sparked by the BC government's proposal to pass legislation that would allow it to restrict any increase in diluted bitumen shipments until spill response could be better studied, Alberta premier Rachel Notley went on the offensive against what she described as British Columbia's obstructionism, announcing that the Alberta Gaming and Liquor Commission would stop importing BC wines. Faced with a looming interprovincial trade war and under pressure to take a leadership role, Prime Minister Justin Trudeau insisted the pipeline would be built and was in the public interest (McSheffrey 2016; Snowdon 2018). His rejection of the concerns raised within British Columbia—with the exception of ocean protection, which he countered with an Oceans Protection Plan—clarified the political landscape for protesters, who on March 10, 2018, coordinated an anti-pipeline rally on Burnaby Mountain that attracted thousands of supporters, built a Coast Salish watch house that still stands on the pipeline route, and settled in for an on-the-ground battle. Over the next several weeks, over two hundred individuals were arrested for acts of civil disobedience.

Faced with this intensification of resistance, Kinder Morgan issued an extraordinary ultimatum on April 8, citing the "unquantifiable risk" associated primarily with the Province of British Columbia's opposition to the project. The company indicated that it had stopped all non-essential spending on pipeline construction and would consider walking away unless risk to shareholders could be reduced and certainty on the project timeline offered by May 31 (Cryderman and Bailey 2018). The ultimatum immediately had the desired effect. Aggression toward British Columbia intensified, with Notley introducing a bill on April 16 that would allow Alberta to restrict oil exports to BC, and the federal government publicly reassuring Kinder Morgan that the desired certainty would be provided. After intensive backroom negotiations, the federal government announced on May 29 that it would purchase the existing Trans Mountain Pipeline outright for $4.5 billion and take over the expansion project from Kinder Morgan Canada (Meyer and Sharp 2018). Although the federal government no doubt hoped this would be the conclusion of the flashpoint, there is no indication that resistance has abated—on the contrary, in fact (Ball 2018b; Khelsilem 2018; Vomiero 2018). It does, however, mark the end of the flashpoint period covered in this chapter. This bare-bones narrative omits many twists and turns, some of which will emerge through the more sustained analysis below.

Reading a Flashpoint

There are, of course, many different ways to "read" a flashpoint and many different stories that can be built from one. What I do here is examine the busy and somewhat disjointed public record of the evolution of the flashpoint, as it has been expressed in the media. To establish the timeline of events and identify key themes for further investigation, we used Google News and the search term "trans mountain pipeline" to search the daily record beginning on March 6, just before the 2018 protests began to ramp up, and concluding on June 7, shortly after the federal government's decision to purchase the pipeline outright.[1] For this search, we limited the news outlets to CBC, Global News, CTV News, the *Globe and Mail*, the *National Observer*, the *National Post*, the *Financial Post*, the *Georgia Straight* (Vancouver), the *Calgary Herald*, the *Edmonton Journal*, the *Vancouver Sun*, the *Toronto Star*, and the *Star Vancouver*. Our choices were intended to offer perspective from different scales and regions, although with a western Canadian bias. From this initial search we established the timeline of events and a representative sample of the media-structured conversation during that period. In particular, we sought to identify the arguments being made for and against the pipeline, and the key voices in the conversation.

We used this initial data set to identify key themes, on which we did a deeper dive drawing on a wider range of media sources. For this deeper dive we sought out more reflective and analytical sources—here we were not seeking to be comprehensive but attempting to identify the arguments and analysis being deployed. We were, in other words, more after the "why" than the "what." Many longer articles and opinion pieces identified in the first search remained, but new sources came much more to the fore, including *The Tyee, DeSmog, Yes!* magazine, iPolitics, Policy Options, and Ricochet

Media. The following analysis is organized according to several of the themes we identified, although these were reshaped through the analytical process itself.

Importantly, then, this is not primarily a media analysis and the conclusions do not speak in any comprehensive way to how the media reported the issue. There is material here to speculate on what narrative about the Trans Mountain Pipeline struggle will prevail over time and through history, to assess how the media itself has shaped the jostling conversation about what is important in this moment, or to critically assess the media representation itself. That, however, is not what I have done. Rather, the analysis here draws from a very diverse conversation themes and issues that may be important to ongoing efforts to build realistic and just pathways toward climate stabilization.

A Fractured Public Sphere?

Perhaps the most crucial insight arising from our examination of the media record is that there is not one conversation about the TMX; there are many. Further, these conversations are happening in virtually entirely separate contexts. Media coverage of any flashpoint such as this would typically be characterized by substantial jostling among different efforts to define or frame the key issues at stake, to determine the narrative. This is no different, but the parameters of that jostling—what narratives are considered "legitimate" enough to report on—vary widely among different outlets. Yet the debate is lively and rich enough internal to these outlets that it is possible to have the impression that those parameters are adequate, that particular issues are resolved, despite them having extensive play elsewhere.

A key example of this is offered by the in-depth investigative journalism published in the group of BC-based, largely reader-supported, online outlets such as *The Tyee*, *DeSmog* (renamed *The Narwhal* mid-flashpoint), and the *National Observer*. Through consistent, in-depth investigative reporting (including, in the *National Observer*'s case, an extensive series of special reports on the TMX), as well as regular and sympathetic coverage of the protests themselves, these outlets collectively established a rich conversation—about the failures of the energy governance and regulatory system, about the influence of corporate power on governance, and about the dubious economics of the pipeline itself—that offers a robust and powerful set of arguments against the project. Although widely read and praised in "progressive" media circuits (Green Majority 2018), these arguments have had fairly modest uptake in the wider mainstream print-based media and are virtually never represented as "game-changing" issues. For example, despite repeated critical analyses of the economic case for the pipeline (Allan 2018; M. Anderson 2018; Hughes 2018; Kilian 2018), overstated claims about its economic benefits—including the assertion that Canada is losing $40 million a day in the absence of a pipeline to tidewater—were widely reproduced across the print media (Ljunggren and Schnurr 2018; Schmidt 2018) with barely a mention that these had been questioned robustly elsewhere.[2] Too frequently, whether as the result of a lack of reporting capacity or of editorial pressures, the mainstream print media reliably picked up and disseminated industry and government talking points, yet failed to pay attention to the substantive critical engagement with these talking points that appeared in alternative media sources. As a consequence, important conversations remained siloed.

There were occasional breakthroughs, of course, when issues broken by alternative sources were picked up more widely (De Souza 2018b), although such breakthroughs tended to occur when these investigations began to directly influence decision-making processes (McCarthy 2018). Similarly, issues raised by these alternative outlets would find their way into mainstream print media through articles in "Opinion" sections. However, the majority of the core themes covered by this extensive reporting—flaws in the approval process, corporate influence in decision making, the risky economics of the pipeline, the implications of the pipeline with respect to climate change, and so on—generally occupied a marginal position in mainstream print sources, which preferred to characterize opposition in very vague or limited terms. The overarching narratives—the importance of the fossil fuel industry to the health of the Canadian economy and the necessity of getting Alberta's oil to tidewater to ensure our continued prosperity—remained entirely dominant in some media bubbles, to the exclusion of other concerns (CBC 2018b; Cryderman and Bailey 2018; McKay 2018). The struggle over the TMX was thus not conducted anywhere as a wide-ranging, collective conversation. Although concern about media "echo chambers" and their influence on collective decision making is neither new nor surprising, this fracturing of the public sphere remains an important consideration that must be navigated in developing pathways toward change (Hoggan and Litwin 2016; Sunstein 2017).

The Power of the Fossil Fuel Industry

One of the most important characteristics of the political landscape to emerge through this flashpoint is the sustained power of the fossil fuel industry to shape the parameters of political possibility in Canada. In light of apparent setbacks to efforts to build pipelines recently—the rejected Northern Gateway pipeline, delay of Keystone XL, cancellation of the Energy East proposal, as well as Premier Notley's advances toward a "carbon cap" for tar sands emissions and Prime Minister Trudeau's efforts to advance a nationwide climate change strategy—it might have been possible to imagine that Canada was beginning to confront the challenge of transitioning away from its reliance on fossil fuel exploitation. This flashpoint put any such imagination to rest. Indeed, this may have been most centrally what was at stake for industry, the federal government, and some provincial governments in this flashpoint.

The power of the fossil fuel industry was perhaps most evident in how little the industry had to participate directly in the media conversation: the governments of Canada, Alberta, and Saskatchewan were doing an effective job of speaking on its behalf (Global News 2018; Hall 2018; Notley 2018), and in all possible forums, including paid advertising (Meyer 2018).[3] That the voices of industry were relatively silent in the public realm, however, in no way suggests that they were not very active behind the scenes, both in the decision-making process (De Souza 2018a) and in lobbying efforts (Lang and Daub 2016; Nikiforuk 2018). Trudeau's repeated assertion that "it will be built" and Notley's sabre-rattling with British Columbia were clearly designed not only to reassure industry but to quell any notion that stopping the pipeline merited public discussion, let alone serious consideration—all this, again, despite reporting that repeatedly raised a range of substantial concerns about the project and its proponent (Nikiforuk 2018). When industry did speak, however—in the form of Kinder Morgan's extraordinary ultimatum that certainty had to be provided by May 31—it completely commanded not only the public narrative but the government's attention, leading to the yet more extraordinary decision on the part of the federal government to purchase the pipeline itself. In the process, Kinder Morgan managed to unload what was looking like a potentially substantial liability (Allan 2018), a success hailed by Kinder Morgan's CEO, who celebrated "a great day, not only for our company but for Canada" and rewarded executives (with substantial bonuses) and those who devised the strategy (with promotions) inside Kinder Morgan

(Ljunggren, Hampton, and McWilliams 2018). Little ambiguity exists here: the fossil fuel industry came away as the winner, with the risk posed by the pipeline transferred entirely to the public and assurances offered to industry that the planned infrastructure would be built.

Crucially, the discursive strategy through which this closure of public dialogue was effected was the creation of a crisis narrative, most notably expressed through the statements and strategic responses of Alberta's then premier, Rachel Notley, but quickly taken up and expanded on by others. "Sky is falling" narratives included the claims that, should resistance to this pipeline be given any leeway, Canada would no longer be seen as a safe place for investment (Healing 2018); that democracy and the rule of law would be overturned by a rabble-rousing minority (Murphy 2018a); that this could mark the beginning of the end of the Canadian confederation (Gerson 2018); that troops should be brought in to ensure the pipeline could be built (Johnston 2018); and indeed that "people are going to die" protesting the Trans Mountain Pipeline (Kent 2018). Less dramatic, but likely more plausible, was the narrative that failing to build the TMX would spell the end of Trudeau's federal climate change strategy (Hunter 2018), on the grounds that Alberta's support for the national climate framework is contingent on getting a bitumen pipeline to tidewater. The frenzy generated by this crisis narrative was astonishing, as one fairly extreme statement or strategy after another was trotted out—including Trudeau's unconditional assertion that the pipeline would be built (Snyder 2018), Notley's ban on BC wine (Parish 2018), and subsequent legislation to turn off the oil taps to British Columbia (Romero 2018)—as if their very extremity offered evidence of the crisis.[4] The overwhelming narrative was one of crisis and of the need for closure, although only one possible form of closure was envisaged: building the pipeline. The message was clear: no further discussion or dialogue, no further process of engagement, was possible at this moment. Those opposing the pipeline had to be stopped, with force if necessary.

Following the media pattern described above, efforts were made to resist or challenge this narrative, again primarily in the alternative press (Gilchrist 2018; Goulet 2018; Moscrop 2018). The federal commitment to purchase the pipeline, however, offered evidence of the narrative's success. Here was an opportunity to open up a meaningful, and long overdue, public conversation about the future of fossil fuels in Canada (Rand 2018). Instead, the federal government, along with its provincial allies, bent over backward to shut down the possibility of such a conversation. This foreclosure, perhaps more than anything, offers an indication of the ongoing power of the fossil fuel industry in Canada.

How Will Canada Navigate Climate Change?

The ways in which climate change has—and has not—been part of the story of this flashpoint are complex. The flashpoint brought into sharp relief the potential fracture points that must be navigated in any effort to move Canada toward real action to mitigate climate change. At one level these are obvious: some provincial and territorial economies are deeply intertwined with fossil fuel production, others less so; some are more immediately threatened by climate change itself, and so on. What has perhaps been less evident to the casual observer of Canadian politics are the governance challenges this poses, at virtually all scales. Events around the TMX have not only exposed these challenges but reignited old grievances and potentially laid the groundwork for new configurations of conflict.

Perhaps most obvious in this regard was the extraordinary upsurge of tension between Alberta and British Columbia, which ignited and then advanced very quickly from expressions of frustration to a nearly full-on trade war, with corresponding inflammation of public opinion (Morgan 2018). Although the case can be made that with more cool-headed leadership, on the part of either Alberta's premier or the prime minister, these tensions could have been navigated with substantially less heat (Cryderman 2018), the underlying historical, economic, and cultural differences between the two provinces, and how these intersect with the requirements for climate action, will not be easily resolved (Proctor 2018b).

Most extraordinary, however, was Trudeau's handling of the situation. At least from the BC perspective, he exacerbated the tensions by clearly taking a side on the issue at precisely the moment when mediation was needed (Guly 2018b). The Trudeau government's absolute unwillingness to recognize or engage with the concerns raised in British Columbia, with the exception of oil spill response preparation (McKenna 2018), left residents of the province feeling angry and alienated (Bains 2018). These feelings were validated when Québec weighed in on Trudeau's rejection of the concerns raised by BC Premier Horgan, raising serious and substantive concerns about the precedents potentially set by asserting federal jurisdiction unilaterally in an area where jurisdiction is shared with the provinces, if in a somewhat murky way (Guly 2018a). That Trudeau justified his position in part by reference to his (tenuous) federal climate change strategy brought the longer-term challenges of action on climate change into stark relief (Leach 2018; *Star* Editorial Board 2018).

But, of course, the complexity does not end there. Although it was not particularly evident during the period considered here, municipal resistance to the TMX on the part of both Burnaby—where the pipeline would terminate—and Vancouver is long-standing and fierce (Boothby 2018; Lye 2018; Pearson 2018). In both jurisdictions, the TMX became an issue in the provincial elections, although the extent to which it definitively shaped the outcome is far from clear. Some polling indicated that overall support in British Columbia for the TMX had grown during the flashpoint (Zussman 2018), while other polling suggested that over 12 percent of citizens in the region would contemplate civil disobedience to express their opposition to the pipeline (Cruickshank 2018). The cross-scale resistance to the TMX remains unresolved, ranging as it does across many different areas of concern. However, dismissal of it does not seem likely to be an effective long-term strategy for building governance coalitions strong enough to navigate the challenges of climate action.

One reading of Trudeau's actions in this regard could be that he prioritized appearing to be a strong and decisive leader capable of creating a stable and welcoming investment climate in Canada over ensuring equitable, responsive, and robust governance of decision making about large-scale infrastructure projects (Ball 2018a; McMillan 2018). Given how closely the effectiveness of decision making is connected with social support for those decisions (and thus with a stable and welcoming investment climate), the long game here seems strategically myopic (Shaw et al. 2015). However, it is consistent with both the short- and medium-term priorities of corporate Canada—especially the financial sector, which is, of course, heavily invested in fossil fuel production—and this could go a long distance toward explaining Trudeau's fierceness on this point (Lang and Daub 2016).

The aggravation of these political tensions generated a fair amount of light and heat in the media (Climenhaga 2018; Connolly 2018; Gerson 2018; Graney 2018; Homer-Dixon and Strauch 2018). Although some of this commentary appears hyperbolic, there are a few issues that will likely persist and will influence history's judgment of the broader implications of this flashpoint. Not least, as discussed above, Trudeau's tactic of dismissing opposition to the pipeline in British Columbia has exacerbated rather than effectively navigating regional tensions exposed by the TMX proposal. The opportunity to develop a shared national conversation about what is required to address climate change has been ignored, in favour of an approach of forcing a trade off of one region's interests against another. This approach alters the prospects for sustaining a federal climate policy across electoral cycles. In the absence of a shared conversation about what the energy transition should look like it is difficult to imagine how to sustain the regional political will given the required compromises. In addition, it is not at all clear that Trudeau's choice to purchase the pipeline will facilitate actually getting it built. Substantial on-the-ground and municipal resistance remain, with the change of ownership failing to daunt resolve (Campbell 2018; Horter 2018) and simultaneously creating new layers of legal and political awkwardness around forcing the pipeline through against this resistance (Harper 2018; McKibben 2018b). The business case for the pipeline remains problematic (Allan 2018). Although the pipeline purchase eliminated the risks to Kinder Morgan shareholders, it has exposed the public to these risks in ways that could exacerbate the political tensions described above. The federal government is fully exposed as a self-interested proponent; there is not even a façade that it can act as a neutral arbiter to help navigate the situation. Finally, there is the most sustained, uncertain, and potentially explosive element of the flashpoint going forward: the rights of First Nations.

Who Will Decide? First Nations, Pipelines, and the Meaning of Reconciliation

The necessity of recognizing Indigenous peoples' rights to and central role in governing their lands has now been apparent for decades, with slow, incremental advances. A significant promise of the Liberal campaign in the 2015 federal election was to implement the United Nations Declaration on the Rights of Indigenous Peoples (UNDRIP), with Trudeau promising a new relationship between Indigenous peoples and settlers in Canada. Unfortunately for Trudeau, the TMX has become a potent site through which the seriousness of these commitments will be judged (Khelsilem 2018; Palmater 2018a). It is possible that this is a slowly dawning realization for many—although the role of First Nations in resisting the TMX has been evident on the ground from the outset, the mainstream press has tended to ignore or marginalize their leadership (Ditchburn 2018; Lukacs 2018). Specifically, as mentioned above, it is largely through opinion pieces—rather than systematic reporting—that the role of First Nations has broken into the mainstream press (Hyland 2018; Phillip and Simon 2018).

As coverage of the flashpoint has evolved, however, the central role of First Nations resistance in—as well as their involvement with and support of—the TMX has begun to surface in the media. Unfortunately, much of this coverage has repeated variations on the theme that "First Nations are divided" on TMX (CBC 2018a; Hopper 2018; McKinley 2018; Paling 2018), with journalists seeking out "for" and "against" spokespeople from First Nations groups (Braid 2018; Cattaneo 2018; McNeill 2018). Although they were generally able to find both, those quoted were often careful to undermine this theme in their comments. Even the strongest proponents of the project tended to emphasize a shared experience of colonization and the constraints that economic circumstances place on communities (with support thus reflecting a lack of other viable options), as well as their recognition that the consultation and approval process has been inadequate and must be improved and that other communities may have entirely legitimate reasons to oppose the project (CBC 2018a; Markusoff 2018; McKinley 2018). In this way, despite the media's apparent determination to promote themes of discord, public statements made by representatives of First Nations frequently offered a model of respectful, rather than divisive, discussion of the issues. The stress repeatedly fell on the need for government to act in good faith and do more to ensure that affected First Nations genuinely consent to proposed development (Gilmore 2018).

The tone and substance of the media's coverage of the TMX proposal offers important insights into the longer-term implications of this flashpoint, as well as into immediate strategic considerations. The emphasis placed by the media on the theme of division might suggest a "divide and conquer" approach to dealings with First Nations, in which the support of some is used to override the objections of others. Given the resistance that rapidly emerged to the federal government's proposed framework for the recognition and implementation of Indigenous rights, with its promised "new relationship" with Indigenous peoples (King and Pasternak 2018), such a response raises the prospect of a new flashpoint, one with historical resonances. The 1969 White Paper, proposed by the government of Pierre Trudeau, also proposed a new relationship between Indigenous peoples and the state of Canada. That proposal galvanized a wave of resistance on the part of Indigenous peoples, leading to a new era of Indigenous-state relations that bore very little resemblance to the vision of assimilation laid out in the White Paper. The younger Trudeau might be well advised to consider the potential of the TMX flashpoint to frame the "new relationship" in similar terms: as a front for a continuing assertion of the priorities of settler society over the specific—and diverse—interests of Indigenous peoples.

In the meantime, the landscape of resistance posed by First Nations is both nuanced and complex (Brake 2018; Lukacs 2018; Manuel 2018). Expressed within it are both local, immediate concerns and the growing strength of international movements for Indigenous rights (Beaumont 2018; Morin 2017). Strategies of resistance include court cases, an area in which Indigenous peoples have consistently asserted their voices in relation to specific, concrete issues and have often won greater recognition of their rights (Ditchburn 2018; Gilchrist 2018; Kassam 2018; Paling 2018; Proctor 2018a). Such strategies build momentum, not only with regard to particular issues but also in terms of altering the trajectory of settler-Indigenous politics in Canada.

Put differently, many things are in motion that intersect with this flashpoint in potentially potent ways: the implementation of UNDRIP, the development of the "new relationship," the building of a climate change strategy that does not reinforce existing forms of marginalization in Canada, and, not least, the future of Indigenous rights and jurisdiction. In short, the TMX flashpoint—what is revealed here and how it reshapes the political landscape of "reconciliation"—will likely have far-reaching implications.

Whither Environmentalism?

One of the most striking things about the TMX flashpoint is how the environment and environmentalism figured into the public discussion. For many commentators, especially those writing from outside British Columbia, resistance to the pipeline has been assumed to hinge on the climate change implications of expanding tar sands production, which the pipeline would facilitate (Brown 2018; Gillis 2018; Homer-Dixon and Strauch 2018; McKibben 2018a), and indeed would require in order to be profitable (Kilian 2018). However, on the ground in British Columbia, and particularly in the Lower Mainland where the pipeline will terminate, the environmental concerns are much more focused on the prospect of oil spills and increased tanker traffic (Genovali, MacDuffee, and Paquet 2018). Insofar as these have a species focus, it is the endangered Southern Resident killer whales (orcas), whose population numbers have reached a critical low. However, when people who have been arrested at protests are asked why they chose to be arrested, they are as likely to identify the failure to gain Indigenous consent to the pipeline as the crucial reason (Pawson 2018). On placards and in chants at marches and protests, a broad range of issues are raised, and, for many, these issues are intimately, and logically, intertwined.

People's concerns about the pipeline proposal are rarely explored in any depth in the mainstream media coverage of the flashpoint. On the contrary, there is frequently a fairly superficial gesture toward either climate change or oil spill concerns as motivation, without any sustained consideration of the diversity of the environmental movement or the complexities it represents. This lack of curiosity is amplified among those criticizing the resistance, who, like conservative columnist Rex Murphy (2018a), tend to dismiss environmental crusaders out of hand, misrepresenting them as foreign-funded radicals ("green fanatics") out to destroy the Canadian economy—or, in the case of Chief Ernie Crey's oft-quoted complaint about environmentalists "red-washing" their opposition to the TMX, out to sabotage Indigenous opportunities for prosperity (McKinley 2018; Shore 2018; see also Cattaneo 2018). These representations have multiple desired effects: of marginalizing and undermining the supposed authority these groups have but also of erasing First Nations' leadership role in the resistance and—perhaps most worrisome—implicitly sanctioning aggression toward those who resist. In some ways, "environmentalists" have become equal-opportunity whipping boys, an easy target for everyone to bash. The caricatures are not surprising and their purpose is fairly transparent (if by no means benign). Troubling as they are, though, the extent to which they—deliberately or not—misunderstand how "environmentalism" is evolving and how resistance in this case is coming to expression is telling.

Pinpointing the role and impact of "environmentalism" in this flashpoint is not straightforward. Without the resistance that environmental organizations have helped—alongside First Nations, municipalities, and others—to articulate, organize, and coordinate, the construction of the TMX might have proceeded smoothly and silently (Kheraj 2018). However, it is far too simplistic to either credit or blame environmentalists for the resistance. What some environmental organizations have done is to work diligently to understand the concerns of diverse groups, to research and expose the stakes of the proposal along a range of axes (if it goes ahead, to climate change; if it spills, to wildlife and biodiversity; if it is a stranded asset, to the forgone investments that could have been pursued in its place, and so on), and to build coalitions that allow these concerns to be expressed in ways that support and are amplified through these relationships.

Frustrating as this might be to pipeline proponents, environmental organizations are not "pulling the strings" of the protests or manipulating First Nations to become the front for their agenda. Nor do these organizations have a shared secret agenda they are foisting on a naïve public. The resistance—whether expressed in demonstrations, protests, arrests, critical media commentary, electoral campaigns, legal cases, or through other forms—is making visible and giving voice to concerns that have come to be understood as shared. This understanding did not happen automatically: it has taken years of work for organizations to build this understanding, to communicate about the stakes of the proposal in ways that are responsive to a wide range of audiences. The resistance is rooted in those audiences, not controlled by the organizations. Nor is it exclusive to narrowly defined "environmental" issues. The interrelations among environmental risks, Indigenous rights, climate justice, electoral reform, and many other "progressive" issues are not only intricate but constantly in a state of flux.

Once this is understood, it changes everything, or at least it should. Insofar as the resistance expresses new forms of political identity and alliance, including but not limited to environmental ones, its trajectory will be unpredictable, because there is a chemistry that resides in this complex web of alliances that exceeds the logic or priorities of any single component of it (D. Anderson 2018; Lazaruk 2018).[5] This flashpoint thus reveals an environmentalism that is evolving beyond a single-issue movement, as narrowly environmental concerns are coming to be understood as interrelated with broader, system-level forces. How this will translate to strategic or tactical changes is intriguing, with some hints offered by the transformation of the media landscape itself to include digital media platforms. These new media outlets both express and support the emergence of new political identities and relationships, in what could be a potent synergy.

Concluding Thoughts About the Not Yet Concluded

Although the federal government no doubt hoped to write the concluding chapter of this story by purchasing the Trans Mountain pipeline, initial indications are that the tale is far from over. The resistance has been rapidly recalibrating itself to respond to this new configuration of political and economic forces (Bains 2018; Cox 2018), leaving the conclusion still very much open.

However, the analysis above does reveal some preliminary insights about the political terrain facing those attempting to develop pathways toward rapid and just climate stabilization. The media landscape has been transformed by the rise of new digital media platforms, simultaneously facilitating more diverse and in many ways more satisfying conversations but also reflecting a more fractured public sphere. This new landscape is exciting in many ways: resources exist now for research and storytelling that are deeply critical, exposing the operations of power, discursive manipulations, and deep capture of political institutions. These conversations in turn help readers to "connect the dots" and build a more sophisticated movement, one able to connect diverse and previously divisive issues together into a shared narrative. As such, the new digital media platforms have helped reflect and build the basis for the diverse alliances that characterize the resistance. Resistance to the pipeline is not solely "environmental" but is embedded in concerns about social justice, public health, Indigenous rights, climate change, endangered species, and democracy itself. The resistance is stronger and more effective as a result.

Crucially, because of the complexity and wide-ranging social and political changes required by energy transitions (Shaw 2011), diversity of this kind is essential to building effective pathways toward climate stabilization. The challenge, of course, is in expanding not only the depth of these conversations, so that more diverse concerns are expressed and navigated within these outlets, but also their reach, so that these concerns are taken up and engaged substantially across different media. The flashpoint has likely helped to advance each of these goals, but they both require sustained strategic focus.

The need for these expanded conversations is nowhere more apparent than in relation to the other challenges exposed by the flashpoint, especially the grip of corporate influence on both politics and collective imaginaries. Although related, these two kinds of influence likely need to be tackled separately and on a variety of fronts. Yet no major political party is yet committed to the scale of change required to shift economies away from fossil fuels. In this context, the importance of electoral reform becomes clearer. By no means a silver bullet, electoral reform might nonetheless offer potential to disrupt the structural stranglehold on political power that provides the fossil fuel industry such a friendly landscape for influence. Enhancing the capacity for voters to express desires for change without risking dividing the vote could help ensure that the diverse and complex coalitions for change that are building in civil society might also begin to find expression in politics. Although pressures in this direction are mounting, electoral reform can feel like a long game at a time when more urgent action is needed; this flashpoint reveals that it is nonetheless likely a game worth playing.

The flashpoint has also revealed that the struggle for a collective public imagination of a transition beyond a fossil fuel–based economy is underway but nascent (Abreu 2018). That the resistance has flourished as much as it has, and where it has, indicates that, for some, a future beyond fossil fuels is becoming imaginable. For others—many of whose lives are deeply intertwined with the fossil fuel economy (whether directly, as workers in extraction and production activities, or indirectly, as, for example, investors or pension fund members)—it remains unimaginable. The work of making a transition not only possible but desirable requires building this imagination at a community, regional, and national level. This in turn requires both the kind of critical work developed elsewhere in this volume and work on the ground at all levels to create the alternatives we need.

Expanding people's capacity to imagine what is possible is not separate from what is happening at this flashpoint, however. On the contrary, in some ways this may be the most important work of the flashpoint. Resistance to the TMX has offered a focal point for what are otherwise divergent conversations at times, revealing how land occupation and the building of tiny houses are part of a solution to climate change, expressing as they do the resurgence of Indigenous visions and practices for their futures; revealing that public health and safety require a healthy environment and offer a basis for collective solutions; uncovering common causes—and critical focal points—among a plurality of interests and values. Debate provoked by this flashpoint has expanded many people's sense of what is possible, and what is desirable, as well as pointing to some of the blockages obstructing the needed transition. Embedded in these emerging understandings are the key resources needed to build momentum toward a just and healthy climate. Importantly, the end game here is not the construction, or not, of the pipeline but rather the reshaping of the political landscape that this emergent configuration of political identity and alliance must achieve.

Notes

1. I say "we" because I was assisted in this process by two excellent research assistants, Dana Cook and Claire O'Manique. Several readers also offered vital feedback on earlier drafts: Paul Bowles, Bill Carroll, Shannon Daub, Shane Gunster, Matthew Paterson, and James Rowe. I owe thanks to each of them, and especially to Dana.

2. Note that citations are representative examples of the media's coverage of an issue: they are by no means an exhaustive list.

3. Worryingly for the progressive press, polling data allegedly demonstrating the BC public's support for the pipeline further suggested that the arguments forwarded in the mainstream media had exerted the greater influence (Zussman 2018).

4. Some would add to this list BC premier John Horgan's pledge to use "every tool in the toolbox" to prevent the pipeline from being built. Although certainly a forceful expression of robust commitment, Horgan's comment does not, in my view, necessarily buy into the crisis narrative, in that it resists an appeal to impending disaster. Trying as hard as possible to stop something does not necessarily imply that the sky will fall if it proceeds.

5. As just one example, for LeadNow's National Day of Action on June 4, 2018, to "stop the Kinder Morgan buyout" (https://act.leadnow.ca/stop-km-buyout/), the organization aligned with 350.org, the Council of Canadians, the Leap, the Sierra Club of BC, Greenpeace, Coast Protectors, and SumofUs.org. Other organizations involved in the TMX protests include Stand, BROKE, Pipe Up, the Dogwood Initiative, the Georgia Straight Alliance, and the Union of BC Indian Chiefs.

References

Abreu, Catherine. 2018. "Working on Climate Change Is an Act of Love." *National Observer*, May 28, 2018. https://www.nationalobserver.com/2018/05/28/opinion/working-climate-change-act-love.

Allan, Robyn. 2018. "What's Behind Kinder Morgan's May 31 Ultimatum? Follow the Money." *National Observer*, May 15, 2018. https://www.nationalobserver.com/2018/05/15/opinion/whats-behind-kinder-morgans-may-31-ultimatum-follow-money.

Anderson, Duncan. 2018. "Arrests to Continue as Kinder Morgan Protests Heat Up." *The Tyee*, April 4, 2018. https://thetyee.ca/News/2018/04/04/Kinder-Morgan-Protest-Arrests/.

Anderson, Mitchell. 2018. "Pipeline Expansion: US Refineries Win, Canadians Lose." *The Tyee*, April 19, 2018. https://thetyee.ca/Opinion/2018/04/19/Pipeline-Expansion-Refineries-Win-Canadians-Lose/.

Bains, Camille. 2018. "Pipeline 'Betrayal' Could Trigger Unprecedented Protests: Activist." *CTV News*. May 30, 2018. https://bc.ctvnews.ca/pipeline-betrayal-could-trigger-unprecedented-protests-activist-1.3951639.

Ball, David. 2018a. "'Flawed from the Get-Go': In Pipeline Feud, National Energy Board Process Questioned." *Star Vancouver*, April 18, 2018. https://www.thestar.com/vancouver/2018/04/17/flawed-from-the-get-go-in-pipeline-feud-national-energy-board-process-questioned.html.

———. 2018b. "Protests Target Liberal MPs Countrywide over Feds' Trans Mountain Buyout." *Star Vancouver*, June 4, 2018. https://www.thestar.com/vancouver/2018/06/04/protests-target-liberal-mps-countrywide-over-feds-trans-mountain-buyout.html.

Beaumont, Hilary. 2018. "Is This the Next Standing Rock?" *Vice News*, June 13, 2018. https://news.vice.com/en_ca/article/3k44vk/is-this-the-next-standing-rock-trans-mountain-justin-trudeau-kinder-morgan.

Boothby, Lauren. 2018. "Burnaby Mayor Predicts 'Chaos' If Kinder Morgan Pipeline Proceeds." *Burnaby Now*, April 16, 2018. http://www.burnabynow.com/news/burnaby-mayor-predicts-chaos-if-kinder-morgan-pipeline-proceeds-1.23269571.

Borrows, John. 2005. "Crown and Aboriginal Occupations of Land: A History and Comparison." Ipperwash Inquiry, Toronto, October 15, 2005. https://www.attorneygeneral.jus.gov.on.ca/inquiries/ipperwash/policy_part/research/pdf/History_of_Occupations_Borrows.pdf.

Braid, Don. 2018. "Braid: The Myth of First Nations Unity Against Kinder Morgan." *Calgary Herald*, May 16, 2018. https://calgaryherald.com/news/politics/braid-the-myth-of-first-nations-unity-against-kinder-morgan.

Brake, Justin. 2018. "Indigenous Resistance, Title Make Trans Mountain Pipeline Extension 'Untenable,' Says Economist." *APTN National News*. June 8, 2018. http://aptnnews.ca/2018/06/08/indigenous-resistance-title-make-trans-mountain-pipeline-extension-untenable-says-economist-2/.

Brown, Martyn. 2018. "What's Really Criminal in Canada's Kinder Morgan Pipeline Debacle." *Georgia Straight*, April 14, 2018. https://www.straight.com/news/1058116/martyn-brown-whats-really-criminal-canadas-kinder-morgan-pipeline-debacle.

Campbell, Meagan. 2018. "Can Protesters Still Stop the Trans Mountain Pipeline?" *Macleans*, May 29, 2018. https://www.macleans.ca/politics/ottawa/can-protestors-still-stop-the-kinder-morgan-pipeline/.

Cattaneo, Claudia. 2018. "'Eco-Colonialism': Rift Grows Between Indigenous Leaders and Green Activists." *Financial Post*, January 4, 2018. https://business.

financialpost.com/feature/eco-colonialism-rift-grows-between-indigenous-leaders-and-green-activists.

CBC (Canadian Broadcasting Corporation). 2018a. "Kinder Morgan Trans Mountain Pipeline Expansion Divides Indigenous Communities." *The Current*, CBC Radio. April 17, 2018. https://www.cbc.ca/radio/thecurrent/the-current-for-april-17-2018-1.4622103/kinder-morgan-trans-mountain-pipeline-expansion-divides-indigenous-communities-1.4622170.

———. 2018b. "Notley Demands 'Concrete Action' from Ottawa to Get Trans Mountain Pipeline Moving." *CBC News*. April 8, 2018. http://www.cbc.ca/news/canada/edmonton/kinder-morgan-puts-brakes-on-trans-mountain-pipeline-activities-1.4610626.

Chaloupka, William. 2003. "There Must Be Some Way Out of Here: Strategy, Ethics, and Environmental Politics." In *A Political Space: Reading the Global Through Clayoquot Sound*, edited by Warren Magnusson and Karena Shaw, 67–90. Minneapolis: University of Minnesota Press.

Climenhaga, David J. 2018. "The Claim That Canada's Facing a Constitutional Crisis Is Just Politics." *Rabble.ca*, April 16, 2018. http://rabble.ca/blogs/bloggers/alberta-diary/2018/04/claim-canadas-facing-constitutional-crisis-just-politics.

Connolly, Amanda. 2018. "Kinder Morgan Pipeline Battle 'a Complete Violation' of Canadian Economic Union: Jason Kenney." *Global News*. April 22, 2018. https://globalnews.ca/news/4157850/kinder-morgan-pipeline-jason-kenney-confederation/.

Cox, Ethan. 2018. "Kinder Morgan Will Be Trudeau's Waterloo." *Ricochet*, May 29, 2018. https://ricochet.media/en/2221/kinder-morgan-will-be-trudeaus-waterloo.

Cruickshank, Ainslie. 2018. "MP-Commissioned Poll Finds 12 Per Cent of British Columbians Would Engage in Civil Disobedience." *Star Vancouver*, April 28, 2018. https://www.thestar.com/vancouver/2018/04/27/mp-commissioned-poll-finds-12-per-cent-of-british-columbians-would-engage-in-civil-disobedience.html.

Cryderman, Kelly. 2018. "We Should Not Fight Among Ourselves." *Globe and Mail*, February 9, 2018. https://www.theglobeandmail.com/news/alberta/will-a-trade-war-threaten-the-ties-that-bind-alberta-andbc/article37928615/.

Cryderman, Kelly, and Ian Bailey. 2018. "Kinder Morgan Issues Ultimatum, Suspends 'Non-essential' Spending on Trans Mountain Pipeline." *Globe and Mail*, April 8, 2018. https://www.theglobeandmail.com/canada/alberta/article-kinder-morgan-cites-bc-opposition-as-it-suspends-non-essential/.

De Souza, Mike. 2018a. "High-Ranking Federal Officials Sped Up Trans Mountain Review After Phone Call from Kinder Morgan's Ian Anderson." *National Observer*, April 18, 2018. https://www.nationalobserver.com/2018/04/18/news/

high-ranking-federal-officials-sped-trans-mountain-review-after-phone-call-kinder.

———. 2018b. "National Observer Releases Its Trans Mountain Files." *National Observer*, April 30, 2018. https://www.nationalobserver.com/2018/04/30/analysis/national-observer-releases-its-trans-mountain-files.

Ditchburn, Jennifer. 2018. "Indigenous Rights Aren't a Subplot of Pipeline Debate." *Policy Options*, April 11, 2018. http://policyoptions.irpp.org/magazines/april-2018/indigenous-rights-arent-subplot-pipeline-debate/.

Genovali, Chris, Misty MacDuffee, and Paul C. Paquet. 2018. "Genovali: Kinder Morgan Case Ignores Fragility of the B.C. Coast." *Ottawa Citizen*, April 16, 2018. http://ottawacitizen.com/opinion/columnists/genovali-kinder-morgan-case-ignores-fragility-of-the-b-c-coast.

Gerson, Jen. 2018. "Trans Mountain and the Slow Western Break from Confederation." *CBC News*. April 11, 2018. http://www.cbc.ca/news/canada/calgary/road-ahead-jen-gerson-opinion-trans-mountain-pipeline-confederation-1.4613796.

Gilchrist, Emma. 2018. "'They're Not Getting How the Constitution Works': Why Trudeau, Notley Can't Steamroll B.C. on Kinder Morgan Pipeline." *The Narwhal*, April 13, 2018. https://thenarwhal.ca/they-re-not-getting-how-constitution-works-why-trudeau-notley-can-t-steamroll-b-c-kinder-morgan-pipeline.

Gillis, Damien. 2018. "Justin Trudeau's Two-Faced Climate Game." *New York Times*, May 2, 2018. https://www.nytimes.com/2018/05/02/opinion/trudeau-climate-kinder-morgan-pipeline.html.

Gilmore, Rachel. 2018. "First Nations Being 'Left Out' on Kinder Morgan: Bellegarde." *iPolitics*, April 12, 2018. https://ipolitics.ca/2018/04/12/first-nations-being-left-out-on-kinder-morgan-bellegarde/.

Global News. 2018. "Full Transcript: Trudeau Defends Trans Mountain, Criticizes Trump Tariffs in Exclusive Interview." *Global News*. June 6, 2018. https://globalnews.ca/news/4256498/justin-trudeau-interview-pipelines-tariffs/.

Goulet, André. 2018. "Kinder Morgan Surprise: Trudeau, Notley, Horgan and the Politics of Pipelines." *Ricochet*, April 25, 2018. https://ricochet.media/en/2187/kinder-morgan-surprise-trudeau-notley-horgan-and-the-politics-of-pipelines.

Graney, Emma. 2018. "Trans Mountain Pipeline Battle Not 'Too Far Off' from Constitutional Crisis: Rachel Notley." *Edmonton Journal*, April 9, 2018. http://edmontonjournal.com/news/local-news/premier-rachel-notley-to-address-cabinet-day-after-kinder-morgan-announcement.

Green Majority. 2018. "Kinder Morgan Pipeline Comprehensive." Episode 602, *Green Majority Radio Show and Podcast*. April 13, 2018. http://www.greenmajority.ca/the-podcast/2018/4/13/kinder-morgan-pipeline-comprehensive-602.

Guly, Christopher. 2018a. "Deadlock at Pipeline Summit." *The Tyee*, April 16, 2018. https://thetyee.ca/News/2018/04/16/Pipeline-Summit-Deadlock/.

———. 2018b. "Liberals' 'Collective Insanity' over Trans Mountain Creating New Western Alienation, Say BC Politicians." *The Tyee*, May 10, 2018. https://thetyee. ca/News/2018/05/10/Liberals-Collective-Insanity-Trans-Mountain-Alienation/.

Hall, Chris. 2018. "Bill Morneau's Kinder Morgan Surprise Comes with Huge Price Tag, Lots of Political Risk." *CBC News*. May 29, 2018. http://www.cbc.ca/news/ politics/pipeline-morneau-nationalize-1.4682199.

Harper, Tim. 2018. "Justin Trudeau Becomes the Pipeline Prime Minister." *Toronto Star*, May 29, 2018. https://www.thestar.com/opinion/star-columnists/2018/05/29/ justin-trudeau-becomes-the-pipeline-prime-minister.html.

Healing, Dan. 2018. "Kinder Morgan Canada's Pipeline Woes Hurting Investment in Canada: Observers." *CTV News*. June 4, 2018. https://www.ctvnews.ca/ business/kinder-morgan-canada-s-pipeline-woes-hurting-investment-in-canada-observers-1.3877328.

Hoggan, James, and Grania Litwin. 2016. *I'm Right and You're an Idiot: The Toxic State of Public Discourse and How to Clean It Up*. Gabriola Island, BC: New Society Publishers.

Homer-Dixon, Thomas, and Yonatan Strauch. 2018. "The Great Canadian Climate Delusion." *Globe and Mail*, June 1, 2018. https://www.theglobeandmail.com/ opinion/article-is-canada-going-to-be-the-first-country-to-break-apart-over-climate/.

Hopper, Tristin. 2018. "What Do First Nations Really Think About Trans Mountain?" *National Post*, April 19, 2018. https://nationalpost.com/news/canada/ what-do-first-nations-really-think-about-trans-mountain.

Horter, Will. 2018. "Kinder Morgan and the Power of Civil Resistance." *The Tyee*, May 25, 2018. https://thetyee.ca/Opinion/2018/05/25/Kinder-Morgan-Civil-Resistance/.

Huber, Matthew T. 2013. *Lifeblood: Oil, Freedom, and the Forces of Capital*. Minneapolis: University of Minnesota Press.

Hughes, David. 2018. "The Faulty Math Behind Trudeau's Reasoning for Buying Trans Mountain from Kinder Morgan." *Macleans*, May 29, 2018. https://www. macleans.ca/opinion/the-faulty-math-behind-trudeaus-reasoning-for-buying-trans-mountain-from-kinder-morgan/.

Hunter, Justine. 2018. "Environment Minister Catherine McKenna Says Pipeline Fight Puts National Climate Plan in Peril." *Globe and Mail*, March 18, 2018. https://www.theglobeandmail.com/politics/article-environment-minister-catherine-mckenna-says-pipeline-fight-puts/.

Hyland, Ocean. 2018. "10,000 People Protested a Proposed Kinder Morgan Pipeline." *Teen Vogue*, March 20, 2018. https://www.teenvogue.com/story/10000-people-protested-this-proposed-kinder-morgan-pipeline.

Johnston, Patrick. 2018. "Send In the Troops,' Former Alberta Politicians Mulls About Kinder Morgan Protests." *Vancouver Sun*, April 16, 2018. http://vancouversun.com/business/energy/send-in-the-troops-former-alberta-politician-mulls-about-kinder-morgan-protests.

Kane, Laura. 2017. "B.C. NDP Vows to Fight Kinder Morgan Pipeline Expansion, but Won't Say How." *Global News BC*. May 4, 2017. https://globalnews.ca/news/3426234/b-c-ndp-vows-to-fight-kinder-morgan-pipeline-expansion-but-wont-say-how/.

Kassam, Ashifa. 2018. "Our Land Is Our Home': Canadians Build Tiny Homes in Bid to Thwart Pipeline." *The Guardian*, May 8, 2018. https://www.theguardian.com/world/2018/may/08/canadian-activists-pipeline-tiny-homes-british-columbia.

Kent, Gordon. 2018. "People 'Are Going to Die' Protesting Trans Mountain Pipeline: Former Bank of Canada Governor." *Edmonton Journal*, June 13, 2018. http://edmontonjournal.com/business/energy/people-are-going-to-die-protesting-trans-mountain-pipeline-former-bank-of-canada-governor.

Khelsilem. 2018. "Justin Trudeau Promised to Protect Indigenous Rights. He Lied, Again." *The Guardian*, June 19, 2018. https://www.theguardian.com/world/commentisfree/2018/jun/19/salish-sea-pipeline-indigenous-salish-sea-canada-trans-mountain.

Kheraj, Sean. 2018. "The Complicated History of Building Pipelines in Canada." *Macleans*, May 31, 2018. https://www.macleans.ca/news/canada/the-complicated-history-of-building-pipelines-in-canada/.

Kilian, Crawford. 2018. "Why Kinder Morgan's Pipeline Is DOA." *The Tyee*, April 17, 2018. https://thetyee.ca/Opinion/2018/04/17/Why-Kinder-Morgan-Pipeline-DOA/.

King, Hayden, and Shiri Pasternak. 2018. "Canada's Emerging Indigenous Rights Framework: A Critical Analysis." Yellowhead Institute, Ryerson University, Toronto, June 5, 2018. https://yellowheadinstitute.org/wp-content/uploads/2018/06/yi-rights-report-june-2018-final-5.4.pdf.

Lang, Mike, and Shannon Daub. 2016. "826 Reasons Kinder Morgan Got a Green Light for Its Trans Mountain Pipeline Expansion." Corporate Mapping Project. November 30, 2016. https://www.corporatemapping.ca/826-reasons.

Lazaruk, Susan. 2018. "Mayors, First Nation Leaders Vow to Keep Opposing Kinder Morgan Pipeline." *Vancouver Sun*, April 16, 2018. https://vancouversun.com/news/local-news/mayors-first-nation-leaders-vow-to-continue-opposition-to-kinder-morgan-pipeline.

Leach, Andrew. 2018. "The B.C.-Alberta Pipeline Fight Could Undo Our National Climate Plan." *Macleans*, February 19, 2018. https://www.macleans.ca/economy/economicanalysis/the-b-c-alberta-pipeline-fight-could-undo-our-national-climate-plan/.

Ljunggren, David, Liz Hampton, and Gary McWilliams. 2018. "How Kinder Morgan Won a Billion-Dollar Bailout on Canada Pipeline." *Reuters*. May 30, 2018. https://www.reuters.com/article/us-kinder-morgan-cn-strategy-insight/how-kinder-morgan-won-a-billion-dollar-bailout-on-canada-pipeline-idUSKCN1IV1B5?il=0.

Ljunggren, David, and Leah Schnurr. 2018. "Canada Ready to Cover Kinder Morgan Loss, Sees Outside Interest." *Reuters*. May 16, 2018. https://www.reuters.com/article/us-kinder-morgan-cn-pipeline/canada-ready-to-cover-kinder-morgan-loss-sees-outside-interest-idUSKCN1IH1PU.

Lukacs, Martin. 2018. "Who's Defending Canada's National Interest? First Nations Facing Down a Pipeline." *The Guardian*, April 16, 2018. https://www.theguardian.com/environment/true-north/2018/apr/16/whos-defending-canadas-national-interest-first-nations-facing-down-a-pipeline.

Lye, Jeremy. 2018. "City of Burnaby Doubles Down on Anti-Pipeline Stance After NEB Hearing Announcement." *Global News*. January 18, 2018. https://globalnews.ca/news/3974015/burnaby-anti-pipeline-route-hearing/.

Malm, Andreas. 2016. *Fossil Capital: The Rise of Steam Power and the Roots of Global Warming*. London: Verso.

Manuel, Kanahus. 2018. "This Is More than a Renaissance. It's a Revolution." *Huffington Post*, February 23, 2018. https://www.huffingtonpost.ca/kanahus-manuel/kinder-morgan-indigenous-resistance_a_23349533/.

Markusoff, Jason. 2018. "Trans Mountain and First Nations Along the Pipeline Route: It's Not a Dichotomy of 'For' or 'Against.'" *Macleans*, May 8, 2018. https://www.macleans.ca/news/canada/trans-mountain-politics-and-first-nations/.

McCarthy, Shawn. 2018. "First Nations Leaders Claim Ottawa Did Not Properly Consult B.C. Communities on Trans Mountain Project." *Globe and Mail*, May 2, 2018. https://www.theglobeandmail.com/business/article-first-nations-leaders-claim-ottawa-did-not-properly-consult-bc/.

McKay, Paul. 2018. "Media Malpractice and the Bitumen Bubble." *National Observer*, April 26, 2018. https://www.nationalobserver.com/2018/04/26/opinion/media-malpractice-and-bitumen-bubble.

McKenna, Catherine. 2018. "Dear Minister George Heyman." Statement. Environment and Climate Change Canada. April 26, 2018. https://www.canada.ca/en/environment-climate-change/news/2018/04/dear-minister-george-heyman.html.

McKibben, Bill. 2018a. "The Globe and Mail Didn't Want to Publish This About Kinder Morgan." *National Observer*, March 3, 2018. https://www.nationalobserver.

com/2018/03/13/opinion/globe-and-mail-didnt-want-publish-about-kinder-morgan.

———. 2018b. "Say Hello to Justin Trudeau, the World's Newest Oil Executive." *The Guardian*, May 30, 2018. https://www.theguardian.com/commentisfree/2018/may/29/justin-trudeau-world-newest-oil-executive-kinder-morgan.

McKinley, John. 2018. "Trans Mountain Pipeline: First Nations Remain Divided." *Columbia Valley Pioneer*, May 28, 2018. https://www.columbiavalleypioneer.com/news/first-nations-question-looms-over-pipeline/.

McMillan, Tim. 2018. "Kinder Morgan Controversy Signals a Bigger Problem for Canada's Economy." *Globe and Mail*, April 11, 2018. https://www.theglobeandmail.com/opinion/article-kinder-morgan-controversy-signals-a-bigger-problem-for-canadas/.

McNeill, Keith. 2018. "Another B.C. First Nation Voices Support for Kinder Morgan Pipeline." *Terrace Standard*, April 23, 2018. https://www.terracestandard.com/news/another-b-c-first-nation-voices-support-for-kinder-morgan-pipeline/.

McSheffrey, Elizabeth. 2016. "Trudeau Government Finished Its Math Homework on Climate, Says Transport Minister." *National Observer*, November 30, 2018. https://www.nationalobserver.com/2016/11/30/news/trudeau-government-finished-its-math-homework-climate-says-transport-minister.

McSheffrey, Elizabeth, and Jenny Uechi. 2016. "NEB Sides with Texas-Based Pipeline Company Against B.C. Citizens, First Nations." *National Observer*, May 19, 2016. https://www.nationalobserver.com/2016/05/19/news/neb-expected-approve-kinder-morgan-trans-mountain-expansion-today.

Meyer, Carl. 2018. "Alberta Rolls Out $1.2 Million Pro-Pipeline Ad Campaign." *National Observer*, May 10, 2018. https://www.nationalobserver.com/2018/05/10/news/alberta-rolls-out-12-million-pro-pipeline-ad-campaign.

Meyer, Carl, and Alastair Sharp. 2018. "Trudeau Says He Planned Pipeline Takeover After Kinder Morgan Told Government It Was 'Risky' Investment." *National Observer*, May 29, 2018. https://www.nationalobserver.com/2018/05/29/news/trudeau-says-he-planned-pipeline-takeover-after-kinder-morgan-told-government-it-was.

Mitchell, Timothy. 2011. *Carbon Democracy: Political Power in the Age of Oil.* London: Verso.

Morgan, Geoffrey. 2018. "Filling Up in B.C. Could Cost $120 If Alberta Cuts Off Oil Supplies amid Trans Mountain Fallout." *Vancouver Sun*, April 12, 2018. http://vancouversun.com/news/economy/filling-up-in-b-c-could-cost-120-if-alberta-cuts-off-oil-supplies-amid-trans-mountain-fallout/wcm/360c0283-4d0a-4ad6-860d-6ea990226c72.

Morin, Brandi. 2017. "Activists in B.C. Gear Up for 'the Next Standing Rock' with Tiny House Protest." *CBC News*. September 7, 2017. https://www.cbc.ca/news/indigenous/kinder-morgan-pipeline-activists-tiny-houses-1.4279740.

Moscrop, David. 2018. "The Kinder Morgan Spat Is an Intractable Slog—but It's Also Democracy in Action." *Macleans*, April 11, 2018. https://www.macleans.ca/opinion/the-kinder-morgan-spat-is-an-intractable-slog-but-its-also-democracy-in-action/.

Murphy, Rex. 2018a. "Trudeau Still Gives Green Fanatics Cover as They Strangle Trans Mountain." *National Post*, April 10, 2018. http://nationalpost.com/opinion/rex-murphy-our-economy-is-at-stake-confederation-strained-and-whose-fault-it-is.

———. 2018b. "Why Trudeau and His Liberals Are Now the Targets That Kinder Morgan Once Was." *CBC News*. June 6, 2018. https://www.cbc.ca/news/canada/calgary/road-ahead-opinion-rex-murphy-trans-mountain-buyout-1.4692446.

Nikiforuk, Andrew. 2018. "Facts About Kinder Morgan Canadian Taxpayers Need to Know." *The Tyee*, April 20, 2018. https://thetyee.ca/Opinion/2018/04/20/Facts-About-Kinder-Morgan/.

Notley, Rachel. 2018. "The Trans Mountain Pipeline Must Be Built." *Vancouver Sun*, May 22, 2018. http://vancouversun.com/opinion/op-ed/rachel-notley-the-trans-mountain-pipeline-expansion-must-be-built.

Paling, Emma. 2018. "Kinder Morgan Pipeline Won't Be Allowed Through First Nations Territories, Leaders Say." *Huffington Post*, April 15, 2018. https://www.huffingtonpost.ca/2018/04/15/kinder-morgan-pipeline-first-nations-block-trans-mountain-indigenous_a_23411828/.

Palmater, Pamela. 2018a. "By Buying Trans Mountain, the Trudeau Government Breaks an Array of Promises." *Macleans*, May 30, 2018. https://www.macleans.ca/opinion/by-buying-trans-mountain-the-trudeau-government-breaks-an-array-of-promises/.

———. 2018b. "Trans Mountain Pipeline Crisis Is a Watershed Moment for Trudeau-First Nations Relations." *Toronto Now*, April 26, 2018. https://nowtoronto.com/news/trans-mountain-trudeau-first-nations/.

Parish, Julia. 2018. "AGLC to Halt Imports of B.C. Wine Following Proposals from B.C. Gov't." *CTV News*, February 6, 2018. https://edmonton.ctvnews.ca/aglc-to-halt-imports-of-b-c-wine-following-proposals-from-b-c-gov-t-1.3792254.

Paterson, Matthew. 2007. *Automobile Politics: Ecology and Cultural Political Economy*. Cambridge: Cambridge University Press.

Pawson, Chad. 2018. "7 Arrested as Faith Leaders Protest Trans Mountain Pipeline Expansion in Burnaby." *CBC News*, April 28, 2018. http://www.cbc.ca/news/canada/british-columbia/faith-leaders-trans-mountain-protest-burnaby-1.4640502.

Pearson, Natalie Obiko. 2018. "Vancouver Mayor Says Kinder Morgan Pipeline Won't Get Built 'Based on the Resistance on the Ground.'" *Vancouver Sun*, May 9, 2018. https://vancouversun.com/business/energy/vancouver-mayor-says-kinder-morgan-pipeline-wont-get-built-based-on-the-resistance-on-the-ground/wcm/41fa72c8-d09c-4294-85cc-0716bc6472f1.

Phillip, Stewart, and Serge Simon. 2018. "If Ottawa Rams Through Trans Mountain, It Could Set Up an Oka-Like Crisis." *Globe and Mail*, April 12, 2018. https://www.theglobeandmail.com/opinion/article-if-ottawa-rams-through-trans-mountain-it-could-set-up-an-oka-like/.

Platt, Brian. 2018. "These Are the Court Challenges the Trans Mountain Pipeline Expansion Is Facing." *National Post*, May 16, 2018. https://nationalpost.com/news/politics/these-are-the-court-challenges-the-trans-mountain-pipeline-expansion-is-facing.

Proctor, Jason. 2018a. "'A Tough Lesson': Do First Nations Hold Trump Card on Trans Mountain Debate?" *CBC News*. April 12, 2018. https://www.cbc.ca/news/canada/british-columbia/first-nations-kinder-morgan-transmountain-1.4615263.

———. 2018b. "Trans Mountain Pipeline Fight: Can We Ever Be Friends Again?" *CBC News*. May 27, 2018. https://www.cbc.ca/news/canada/british-columbia/kinder-morgan-transmountain-pipeline-politics-1.4678739.

Rand, Tom. 2018. "A Sound Debate About Canada's Emissions, Brought On by Fury over Trans Mountain." *Globe and Mail*, May 2, 2018. https://www.theglobeandmail.com/business/commentary/article-a-sound-debate-about-canadas-emissions-brought-on-by-fury-over-trans/.

Romero, Diego. 2018. "Alberta Proposes Bill to Control Oil, Gas Exports." *CTV News*. April 16, 2018. https://edmonton.ctvnews.ca/alberta-proposes-bill-to-control-oil-gas-exports-1.3887505.

Russell, Peter H. 2010. "Oka to Ipperwash: The Necessity of Flashpoint Events." In *This Is an Honour Song: Twenty Years Since the Blockades*, edited by Leanne Betasamosake Simpson and Kiera L. Ladner, 29–46. Winnipeg: ARP.

Schmidt, Colleen. 2018. "Morneau Says Ottawa Willing to Provide Indemnity to Ensure Expansion of Trans Mountain Pipeline." *CTV News*. May 16, 2018. https://calgary.ctvnews.ca/morneau-says-ottawa-willing-to-provide-indemnity-to-ensure-expansion-of-trans-mountain-pipeline-1.3931989.

Schmunk, Rhianna. 2018. "B.C. Going to Province's Highest Court in Attempt to Fight Trans Mountain Pipeline." *CBC News*. April 18, 2018. https://www.cbc.ca/news/canada/british-columbia/bc-reference-case-pipeline-1.4624848.

Shaw, Karena. 2011. "Climate Deadlocks: The Environmental Politics of Energy Systems." *Environmental Politics* 20, no. 5: 743–63. https://doi.org/10.1080/09644016.2011.608538.

Shaw, Karena, Stephen D. Hill, Amanda D. Boyd, Lindsay Monk, Joanna Reid, and Edna F. Einsiedel. 2015. "Conflicted or Constructive? Exploring Community Responses to New Energy Developments in Canada." *Energy Research and Social Science* 8 (July): 41–51. https://doi.org/10.1016/j.erss.2015.04.003.

Shore, Randy. 2018. "Environmentalists 'Red-Wash' Their Fight Against Pipeline, First Nation Chief Says." *Vancouver Sun*, April 13, 2018. http://vancouversun.com/news/local-news/environmentalists-red-wash-their-fight-against-pipeline-first-nation-chief-says.

Snowdon, Wallis. 2018. "Trans Mountain Pipeline Project Will Be Built, Prime Minister Vows." *CBC News*. February 1, 2018. https://www.cbc.ca/news/canada/edmonton/alberta-b-c-bitumen-restrictions-trans-mountain-trudeau-1.4514015.

Snyder, Jesse. 2018. "'We Are Going to Get the Pipeline Built': Trudeau Begins Federal Talks with Kinder Morgan to Guarantee Trans Mountain." *National Post*, April 15, 2018. https://nationalpost.com/news/we-are-going-to-get-the-pipeline-built-trudeau-begins-federal-talks-with-kinder-morgan-to-guarantee-trans-mountain.

Star Editorial Board. 2018. "Trudeau Must Lead on Both Pipeline and Climate Change." *Toronto Star*, April 12, 2018. https://www.thestar.com/opinion/editorials/2018/04/12/trudeau-must-lead-on-both-pipeline-and-climate-change.html.

Sunstein, Cass R. 2017. *#Republic: Divided Democracy in the Age of Social Media.* Princeton: Princeton University Press.

Tindall, David. 2018. "Justin Trudeau's Risky Gamble on the Trans Mountain Pipeline." *iPolitics*, May 30, 2018. https://ipolitics.ca/2018/05/30/justin-trudeaus-risky-gamble-on-the-trans-mountain-pipeline/.

Vomiero, Jessica. 2018. "Over 800 Businesses Slam Trudeau Government's Purchase of Trans Mountain Pipeline." *Global News*. May 30, 2018. https://globalnews.ca/news/4243861/businesses-slam-trudeau-government-purchase-trans-mountain-pipeline/.

Waddington, David P. 2010. "Applying the Flashpoints Model of Public Disorder to the 2001 Bradford Riot." *British Journal of Criminology* 50, no. 2: 342–59. https://doi.org/10.1093/bjc/azp082.

Zussman, Richard. 2018. "Support for the Trans Mountain Expansion Grows Amidst Pipeline Dispute." *Global News*. April 18, 2018. https://globalnews.ca/news/4151592/support-for-the-trans-mountain-expansion-grows-amidst-pipeline-dispute.

16 Toward a Typology of Fossil Fuel Flashpoints

The Potential for Coalition Building

Fiona MacPhail and Paul Bowles

Fossil fuel projects—coal, natural gas, and oil—have met with resistance around the world challenging the power and logic of capitalist fossil fuel companies. The analytical lenses through which fossil fuel resistance have been viewed include those of justice (principally environmental justice, energy justice, climate justice, and social justice) and of sovereignty (notably Indigenous sovereignty and food sovereignty), with contestation arising from one or more class-based organizations, social movements, NGOs, and civil society organizations. In other words, theoretical and empirical analyses of fossil fuel resistance have been broad-ranging and varied.

This chapter examines the roots of resistance at the local level, with a view to enhancing possibilities for activism. We build on existing frameworks from the literature on energy justice (see, for example, Finley-Brook and Holloman 2016; Jenkins et al. 2016; Sovacool and Dworkin 2015), and apply them to advance a typology of fossil fuel flashpoints, with illustrations from northern British Columbia. Efforts to bring about change typically require the building of coalitions. By offering a systematic analysis of where and why flashpoints occur, this typological approach highlights and illustrates the circumstances under which coalition building is both necessary and possible.

The term "flashpoint" has been applied to many issues and across various time periods and economic and political spaces. For example, the word has been used in the environmental context to denote long-standing policy controversies that inhibit the goal of sustainability (Vos 1997), in the socio-logical analysis of public disorder, including riots (Waddington 2010), and in the geopolitical literature to denote areas in which conflicts, whether active or latent, produce instability (Anderson 2000).

"Flashpoint" is used here to capture many of these same dimensions: long-term controversies that can suddenly intensify around specific projects and that may be (though are not necessarily) accompanied by forms of public disorder or other forms of protest. The term therefore signifies a sense of urgency, intensity, and contestation, while also implying the existence of con-cerns that are more enduring and deeply rooted and that may lie dormant for a period before intensifying again. The term therefore seems particularly apt in the context of natural resource projects in which long-running concerns over the costs and benefits of such projects often lead to intense periods of scrutiny and forms of public contestation. Indeed, the term has entered pol-itical discourse in much the same way. We concentrate here on the persistent, underlying causes of flashpoints and use these to motivate our typology, rather than focusing on short-term strategies, such as media campaigns, that invoke these long-standing concerns to intensify immediate political action.

Our flashpoint typology is based on three axes (drawn from the energy justice literature noted above) and commodity chain nodes. We then illus-trate the application of the typology using examples predominantly from northern British Columbia and briefly discuss some of the implications of this analysis for building the broader coalitions needed to challenge fossil fuel projects.

A Fossil Fuel Flashpoint Typology

The proposed typology locates the roots of flashpoints along three axes. Each represents a complex of interrelated factors, but, taken together, they provide us with a description of fossil fuel contestations and a basis for strategic action.

Along the economic and distributive axis, hereafter the *distributive axis*, causes of resistance relate to both the total economic benefits to be generated by proposed fossil fuel projects, as well as their distribution. With regard to the level of employment, the key issue is whether a project will generate what community members regard as an acceptable number of jobs, both direct and indirect. In addition, a project may be contested if it appears to pose a threat to existing capitalist industries, such as tourism, and thus to established sources of employment. At the same time, concerns may be voiced regarding the number of new jobs promised versus the number actually delivered and/or the projected number of new jobs versus the potential increase in employment if further value-added linkages were created within the country. As we argue elsewhere, opposition framed in terms of concerns about the lack of domestic linkages reflects the persistence of the staples approach in Canada, with its emphasis on the need to foster a robust domestic economy rather than relying too heavily on exports (see Bowles and MacPhail 2018, esp. 169–70).

Resistance may also emerge in connection with the distribution of employment—for example, with whether local Indigenous residents will have adequate access to jobs and the barriers to women's employment. Moreover, issues surrounding the terms of employment and the use of non-unionized labour and temporary workers may provoke conflict between capital and labour. Finally, the organization of employment may be viewed negatively if a project entails the construction of "man camps" in which to house on-site workers. Such camps may exacerbate social problems associated with rapid demographic change within the community, including pressure on local health and social services and housing, and may also lead to increased rates of violence against women and rising levels of crime (Jenkins 2014).

Conflicts may also arise along the distributive axis with regard to the distribution of the energy generated by the fossil fuel project. Will local communities, especially Indigenous ones, benefit from it? That is, will "energy justice" be achieved (Sovacool and Dworkin 2015)? The W. A. C. Bennett Dam, in north-central British Columbia, offers an instructive example of this problem. During the dam's construction, which was completed in 1967, both the Tsay Keh Dene and Kwadacha First Nations were caught without forewarning when their lands were flooded in order to provide hydroelectric energy for the province. Yet, as of June 2016, the Kwadacha First Nation was still relying on a diesel generator for its electricity (Cox 2016).

Moving from the community to levels of government, both the amount and the distribution of the tax revenue generated by fossil fuel projects may prove to be sources of contention. One concern is the appropriate level of taxation—that is, the rate at which companies should be taxed (or charged royalties) such that the flow of revenue is commensurate with the profits earned from a project. Another is whether lower levels of government and local communities will receive revenues adequate to compensate for the costs imposed upon them by the fossil fuel project. That such issues may become flashpoints for conflict between different levels of government allows us to expand the concept of a flashpoint to include not just public protest but also rivalry between levels of public authority that could likewise derail fossil fuel projects.

The second axis is the procedural and consultative axis, hereafter the *procedural axis*. Procedural justice, as Benjamin Sovacool and Michael Dworkin (2015, 437) describe it, is "concerned with how decisions are made in the pursuit of social goals." Flashpoints may arise in connection with the form of the consultation and/or the subject on which decisions must be made, but they may also be grounded in inequitable relations of power. In practice, then, beyond opposition relating primarily to violations of established procedure, conflict along this axis may extend to the instrumental use of procedural failings to challenge projects that are opposed for reasons pertaining to the other two axes.

With regard to the form of the consultation, issues of contention typically involve which groups are included in (or excluded from) consultative processes and the manner in which their voice is recognized. For example, how is a "stakeholder" defined (and by whom), and are members of civil society allowed to participate in these processes only if they are deemed to be stakeholders? Does the process acknowledge the treaty and other rights of Indigenous peoples, and is the consultation that flows from the "duty to consult" with Indigenous groups substantive or purely pro forma? The subject of decision making may be of concern if consultation is carried out only on certain aspects of a project. For example, the terms of reference of the body responsible for conducting a review may be constrained so as to rule out certain areas of consideration, or the views of those who hold specialized knowledge about a topic may not be adequately sought out.

While power relations underlie the above sources of contestation, an asymmetric balance of power and resources may also be built into the processes of project review. In most instances, local actors are at a disadvantage relative to corporations and governments in terms of their access to information and overall capacity to prepare an effective formal response to projects. With respect to the representation of minority opinion, decision-making processes tend to replicate and reinforce existing power inequities in ways that reflect "white privilege" and as Laura Pulido (2010, 15) argues, the "hegemonic structures, practices and ideologies reproduce whites' privileged status" (also referred to by Jenkins et al. 2016, 178). Thus, white privilege undermines the equal representation necessary for procedural justice.

The *ecological and recognition axis* captures potential conflicts of fossil fuel projects with ecological sustainability and cultural values. This axis includes resistance arising from the environmental and ecological risks associated with a project, whether local, regional, or global. The axis also includes issues surrounding the recognition of non-capitalist world views and alternative sets of priorities founded on principles such as sustainability, equity, and reciprocity. Contestation here might be concerned with the impact of a project on non-capitalist uses of land and water and the production of non-market goods, as well as with whether the project will entail capitalist accumulation by means of dispossession, including the transfer of public assets into private hands (Harvey 2004). Opposition may reflect Indigenous world views, or it may emanate from environmentalist and eco-socialist activists responding to what Marx described as a rift in the "universal metabolism of nature" (Foster 2013). While it might seem more appropriate to view ecological and cultural sources of contestation as two separate axes, we prefer to consider them as a single axis to emphasize their interrelatedness. Although conflict may focus on the impact of a fossil fuel project on specific uses of land or water, these uses are culturally embedded and are often inseparably bound up with place and ceremony. Conflict may also arise from a broader understanding of the capacity of fossil fuel development to threaten entire ways of living and being, whether by undermining traditional means of livelihood grounded in reciprocity and non-market forms of exchange or by accelerating global climate change.

Concerns about the adverse cultural and ecological impacts of fossil fuel development resonates in some ways with the quest for what is often called "recognition justice," which exists when the values, world views, and lifeways of *all* peoples are acknowledged and respected (see, for instance, Finley-Brook and Holloman 2016, 1).[1] By including "recognition" in the name of this axis, we mean to indicate that opposition arising along it is not limited to ecological issues per se. Rather, this contestation also involves a struggle over the validity of the alternative perspectives and the conceptualizations of "sustainability" embodied in them.

While these axes capture the main reasons underlying the emergence of flashpoints, it is also clear that flashpoints may occur at different points in the production process, for example, during the extraction phase or the distribution phase. To arrive at a more complete understanding of flash-points, we therefore examine the three axes from the standpoint of the commodity chain. Commodity chains obviously differ from industry to industry, as they depend on the nature of the production process, and they may be further modified by technological innovations. While a "generic" commodity chain approach can be applied to many industries, from horti-culture to manufacturing, it is useful to proceed on the basis of a concrete example drawn from the fossil fuel sector. Gavin Bridge (2008) describes the oil commodity chain as consisting of six sequential processes: exploration, extraction/production, refining, distribution, consumption, and carbon capture. As he points out, it is a chain "the end points of which are rooted in the natural environment" (395).

A commodity chain approach contributes analytically to our understand-ing of flashpoints. First, the six processes identified above typically take place at different geographical locations and at different points in time. Exploration may, for example, occur many years or even decades prior to extraction, and extraction may occur in one location with refining in another. Second, while the connection between a flashpoint and a particular node in the commod-ity chain may be quite clear, the activities that take place at specific nodes often have different consequences for the environment, as well as different social, economic and/or cultural implications. Finally, the processes associated with individual nodes are licensed and regulated by agencies that operate at different levels of government, which may be particularly important for understanding the procedural axis.

Fossil Fuel Flashpoint Illustrations from Northern British Columbia

Especially since the start of this century, northern British Columbia has become the site not only of a rapidly growing natural gas industry but also of projects designed to transport liquefied natural gas (LNG) and tar sands oil to tidewater and then ready these fuels for shipment to Asian markets. Our interest lies with resistance to this development at the local level, from municipal governments, local NGOs, First Nations, and rural communities. These are the people who experience the impacts of fossil fuel projects most immediately, and their active resistance to these projects may be less familiar than the work of groups that operate more widely. To simplify the analysis, we organize the discussion around three components of the commodity chain: exploration and extraction, distribution, and refining or liquefaction.

Exploration and Extraction Nodes: Natural Gas Production in Northeastern BC

Exploration for and the extraction of fossil fuels in northern British Columbia centre on natural gas in the northeastern part of the province. As one might expect, flashpoints arise along all three axes.

Distributive axis. Projects related to the discovery and extraction of natural gas have become flashpoints in northeast British Columbia, with opposition arising in connection with the nature of the jobs themselves and with inequities in access to them. While natural gas extraction offers well-paid employment for some workers, job insecurity is considerable, with employment levels highly sensitive to fluctuations in natural gas prices. Furthermore, many workers live in camps set up by employers, and since workers often have little choice but to live in a camp, they also have little recourse when the living conditions are poor. In 2012, BC's Northern Health district counted a total of 1,567 camps associated with the oil and gas industry in the northern half of the province (Northern Health 2012, 4). Although conditions vary, these camps are, on the whole, associated with risks to both the physical and mental health of workers, stemming in part from the combination of long work hours and inadequate recreational outlets other than substance abuse (see Northern Health 2012, 8–10).

The lack of employment opportunities for First Nations people and women is evident. As a result of the usual barriers to women's employment in resource extraction, such as long shifts, it is primarily men who benefit from employment opportunities. Moreover, the fact that these jobs are tied to living in camps makes it harder for the women "left behind," who must attempt to balance possible paid employment with unpaid domestic labour and the work of child care (Eckford and Wagg 2014). While differential access to employment and wage gaps are clearly problems in themselves in terms of gender equity, the influx of male workers into a community has also been linked to an increase in violence against women (Amnesty International 2016; Eckford and Wagg 2014). Other negative social consequences that have been reported include a rise in crime, increased alcohol and drug abuse, and decreases in housing access and affordability (Amnesty International 2016).

In the realm of government, the expanding natural gas industry has heightened contentious fiscal issues which are of particular concern to local governments in Northeast British Columbia. The benefits and costs of expanding natural gas extraction in Northeastern British Columbia are accrued to different levels of government. In 2015, two local governments in Northeastern British Columbia raised the concern that the benefits of increased resource exploration and extraction in the area have accrued to the provincial government in the form of $20 billion in land sales and royalties, over the preceding decade (District of Taylor and City of Fort St. John 2015, 4). Yet, the increasing costs of providing services to support the expanding industrial sector fall on local governments; and as the North East BC Resource Municipalities Coalition notes, such services include the provision of "serviced land, transportation and utility systems, recreation and cultural facilities, policing and a host of other services" (NEBC Resource Municipalities Coalition 2015, 5). The constraints on funding these services from local government revenue is particularly challenging in Northeastern British Columbia because, as the NEBC Resource Municipalities Coalition notes, "approximately 90% of the industrial property tax base is located within unincorporated rural areas, and therefore beyond the direct taxing jurisdiction of municipalities" (NEBC Resource Municipalities Coalition 2015, 5). As one of their key initiatives, the North East BC Resource Municipalities Coalition (formed in 2014) indicated they would attempt to address the imbalances in provincial revenue sharing agreements and would propose a new agreement that would recognize the link between funding and rural industrial tax base (NEBC Resource Municipalities Coalition 2015, 10).[2]

Procedural axis. Regardless of other potential sources of conflict, some fossil fuel projects are opposed on procedural grounds. Several provincial government units are involved in the regulation of the oil and gas industry in British Columbia, including the BC Oil and Gas Commission and, in connection with water licences, the Ministry of Forests, Lands, Natural Resource Operations and Rural Development. The contestation of projects on procedural grounds thus typically involves one or both of these two regulatory agencies. Three types of procedural issues can be identified at the exploration and extraction commodity chain nodes.

One of the main procedural issues giving rise to the contestation of natural gas projects is the lack of meaningful consultation. The large number of projects and the system of site-specific permits with short timelines for consultation deprive First Nations of the opportunity to provide thoughtful and informed comment, as Kathryn Garvie and Karena Shaw (2014) document in connection with the Fort Nelson First Nation (see also Parfitt 2017). Further, the consultations rarely, if ever, lead to substantial changes in how resources are managed. With respect to the construction of unlicensed dams to provide water for fracking operations, for example, Grand Chief Stewart Phillip, president of the Union of BC Indian Chiefs, commented that "First Nations were not fully consulted about the true size and extent of these dams" and noted that "our Indigenous Title, Rights and Treaty rights are still completely ignored or denied." Phillip stated that there have been "no substantive or meaningful opportunities to fully participate in decisions around how water resources are managed in our respective territories" (quoted in Johnston 2017).

The opposition to industrial water usage is illustrated by the Fort Nelson First Nation's 2015 successful court challenge of Nexen's five-year licence to extract water from North Tsea Lake, which was granted in May 2012 by the assistant water manager for the province (British Columbia, Environmental Appeal Board 2015, 4). That the Fort Nelson First Nation had the support of the broader population was indicated by the 32,702 signatures on a petition it circulated urging Premier Christy Clark to revoke the water licence.[3]

A second issue giving rise to resistance on procedural terms is the failure to monitor and enforce existing regulations, particularly around dams and water usage. In 2017, for example, multiple groups, including the Canadian Centre for Policy Alternatives and West Coast Environmental Law, made submissions to the BC Environmental Assessment Office expressing outrage over a retrospective application by Progress Energy for a regulatory exemption in connection with two very large dams. In a submission on behalf of the Blueberry River First Nations, Norma Pyle (2017, 1) noted that the dams, which had been constructed "without regulatory oversight or approval," would have the effect of impounding vast quantities of water drawn from her nation's lands. The Blueberry River First Nations, she wrote, are "very concerned that the Environmental Assessment Office is entertaining 'exemption' requests for these dams, rather than taking enforcement action against the illegal construction and operation of the dams, and rather than undertaking a full environmental review of the risks and impacts of the dams going forward" (1).

Pyle also raised questions about the impact of the dams and then stated, "All of these questions should, under proper conditions, be asked and answered to the satisfaction of an independent regulator who is acting in the public interest and in the interest of ensuring the protection of the lands and waters upon which our treaty rights depend. Instead, the Crown agencies have worked in the interest of industry and have obscured information from us and the public" (3).

Third, concerns have been voiced about the narrow frame of the environmental assessment process and, in particular, about whether the process can adequately assess the negative impacts of the fracking technology used to extract natural gas. Fracking risks causing earthquakes, uses massive amounts of water, as well as contaminating it, and is associated with methane leaks from well sites. Chief Marvin Yahey, of the Blueberry River First Nations, has pointed out the limitations of the scientific methodology used in environmental assessments, specifically with respect to methane leaks at the extraction sites, incremental greenhouse gas (GHG) emissions, and cumulative impacts (Yahey and Blueberry River First Nations 2016). Numerous groups—including local organizations such as the Friends of Wild Salmon Coalition, provincial non-profit organizations such as BC Tap Water Alliance, and national organizations such as the Council of Canadians—have questioned the scientific basis of granting permits for fracked gas, while the Canadian Centre for Policy Alternatives has called for a public inquiry into fracking.[4]

Ecological and recognition axis. Natural gas extraction projects have become a flashpoint in northeast British Columbia on ecological and cultural grounds. For example, the Blueberry River First Nations have argued that the multiple natural gas extraction projects underway and their cumulative impacts are affecting their treaty rights, which include traditional activities of fishing and hunting. In March 2015, the Blueberry River First Nations filed notice of a civil claim in the Supreme Court of British Columbia, seeking to prohibit the province from breaching its obligations under Treaty 8 and infringing against their treaty rights. Decisions of the Crown, they argued, have resulted in "land alienation, resource extraction and industrial activities in the traditional territories upon which the Nations' culture, economy and Treaty rights depend"—activities that "have damaged the forests, lands, waters, fish and wildlife that are integral to the Nations' mode of life, and upon which the Nations rely" (Yahey and Blueberry River First Nations 2015, 2).

A study conducted in the aftermath of this claim and based on BC government data found that 73 percent of the traditional territory of the Blueberry River First Nations lay within 250 metres of an industrial disturbance and 84 percent within 500 metres of one (Macdonald 2016, 6). Speaking in June 2016, when the study was released, Chief Marvin Yahey observed:

> Fracking, forestry, roads and other development is pushing us further and further to the edges of our territory and we are no longer able to practice our treaty rights in the places we've always known. . . . Instead, the province continues to approve major industrial undertakings in our territory, including major fracking operations and the Site C dam, willfully ignoring that each new approval brings our unique culture closer to extinction.

In a press release, the Blueberry River First Nations underscored their desire "to ensure that generations to come are able to meaningfully exercise their treaty rights to live off the land" (both quoted in Carter 2016).

Distribution Node: Pipelines for Oil and Natural Gas Across Northern BC

The distribution node of the commodity chain is applicable to pipelines for both oil and natural gas. The (cancelled) Enbridge Northern Gateway oil pipeline and the multiple proposals for natural gas pipelines from the northeast to the coastal northwest of British Columbia offer numerous examples across our three axes.

Distributive axis. The Enbridge Northern Gateway oil pipeline became a flashpoint in northwestern British Columbia (see Bowles and Veltmeyer, 2015). On April 12, 2014, the municipality of Kitimat held a plebiscite on the pipeline in which 3,071 people voted, 58.4 percent of them against the project (CBC 2014; see also Bowles and MacPhail 2017). Douglas Channel Watch (DCW), a small NGO based in Kitimat, opposed the pipeline on five main grounds, three of which spoke directly to the employment linkage effects (or lack thereof). A DCW leaflet prepared as part of the plebiscite campaign drew upon explicit statements in the federal Joint Review Panel report to make its case against the Enbridge Northern Gateway pipeline. The campaign leaflet stated that the pipeline (1) would "allow *temporary foreign workers* to build pipelines in Canada"; (2) is "a diluted bitumen *export only* pipeline"; and (3) "does *not* mandate upgrading or any other job-creating projects" (emphasis in the original).[5]

The first argument points to the lack of employment benefits for local workers; the second points to the absence of local or national outlets for the commodity under production and the dependence instead on external markets, while the third highlights the absence of forward (that is, downstream) linkages for the project, such as job opportunities associated with refining oil into higher-value products. While this flashpoint occurred at the distribution node in a community that was slated to receive the majority of the permanent jobs from the project, it is interesting to note that labour unions opposed the pipeline proposal as well, on the grounds that the project lacked sufficient forward employment linkages and would result in the export of potential processing jobs. The opposition included the Alberta Federation of Labour (AFL), which represents labour at the extraction and production node in Alberta. The AFL campaigned against the pipeline on the grounds that it involved not only the export of unprocessed crude but also no refining in Alberta. The AFL (2013) estimated that the pipeline would generate only 228 permanent jobs and 1,500 short-term construction jobs, while the lack of linkages to a refinery would mean that "more than 26,000 long-term high-value upgrading jobs will be farmed out to low-wage jurisdiction overseas."[6]

Procedural axis. At the distribution node, as with the extraction node, some pipelines are opposed on the procedural grounds of the lack of consultation and flawed scientific methods used in the assessment process. In terms of consultation, one example is the decision of the Carrier Sekani Tribal Council, which represents seven BC First Nations, to boycott the federal Joint Review Panel hearings on the Enbridge Northern Gateway pipeline proposal because its member nations believed that their participation in the hearings would have provided the Joint Review Panel process with an appearance of legitimacy that it did not warrant(see Sharp 2014). Instead, the members of the council organized protest marches and joined with other First Nations in engaging in anti-pipeline activism, as well as lending support to various legal actions.

The Enbridge Northern Gateway oil pipeline was further contested by many northern (and other) organizations on the grounds that the Joint Review Panel's interpretation of its terms of reference was biased and that the state was not supporting equitable representation. For instance, the panel was willing to consider only those GHG emissions generated directly by the pipeline, rather than examining the project's wider role in global warming—partly because it refused to consider either the upstream implications, in terms of accelerated tar sands production, or the downstream implications, in terms of increased fossil fuel consumption, while also overlooking a series of other concerns raised by First Nations (West Coast Environmental Law 2011, 2). The Carrier Sekani Tribal Council (2007, 2) further noted argued that, as a result of amendments in 2002, BC's Environmental Assessment Act "does not require that an environmental assessment consider impacts on Aboriginal rights and title or cultural heritage" and that, even when an environmental assessment does take such impacts into consideration, "they are not considered from an *Aboriginal* perspective." These arguments also exemplify how conflicts in the procedural axis may have an underlying root motivation in one of the other axes.

Ecological and recognition axis. Numerous flashpoints have arisen at the distribution node because of underlying concern that pipelines threaten ecological and cultural vitality. For example, the Luutkudziiwus—a *wilp*, or house, of the Gitxsan First Nation—state that TransCanada's Prince Rupert Gas Transmission pipeline project "will fragment our ancestral cultural infrastructure, fish and wildlife habitat and diminish the exercising of our fishing, hunting and gathering rights," pointing out that "TransCanada has already shown disregard for wildlife habitat and local traditional knowledge by carrying our test drilling directly within moose habitat during calving season."[7] In the words of Hereditary Chief Xsim Wits'iin (Lester Moore), "The province has been stealing from our territory and culture for 150 years, and this needs to end. The proposed pipeline and LNG project is in deep conflict with core Luutkudziiwus interests and values."[8]

Other groups and coalitions, both Indigenous and non-Indigenous, have actively opposed oil and natural gas pipelines. In December 2010, the Indigenous Nations of the Fraser Valley Watershed released the Save the Fraser Declaration, resolving not to allow the Northern Gateway pipeline and other such projects "to cross our lands, territories and watersheds, or the ocean migration routes of Fraser River salmon." Issued in accordance with Indigenous laws and authority, the declaration unequivocally states that "our inherent Title and Rights and legal authority over these lands and waters have never been relinquished through treaty or war" and issues a reminder that "water is life, for our peoples and for all living things that depend on it." In support of the declaration, the Yinka Dene Alliance issued the Save the Fraser Solidarity Accord in December 2013, inviting people everywhere to pledge to stand with the Fraser Valley First Nations in their fight to save their lands and waters.[9] The following summer, residents of a small community in northwestern British Columbia's Skeena River watershed released the Kispiox Valley Declaration, which 161 people had signed. Acknowledging their acceptance of "a shared regional and global responsibility to protect our water and air," the signatories declared that "we cannot stand by and allow any industrial presence, including oil and gas development, that would threaten or harm our values and responsibilities."[10] In addition, in conjunction with anti-Enbridge protests, various organizations fought a "No Tankers" campaign, seeking to outlaw oil tanker traffic in British Columbia's coastal waters—a campaign that was, in the long run, at least partly successful. In June 2019, federal Bill C-48 (the Oil Tanker Moratorium Act) finally received royal assent, thereby placing restrictions on such traffic.

Refining/Liquefaction Node: Natural Gas Terminals in Northwestern BC

The refining process appears as a flashpoint primarily for the natural gas industry, although it should be noted that the *absence* of a refinery played a role in opposition to the Northern Gateway pipeline project within the distributional axis. In terms of the commodity chain, a natural gas terminal is required to liquefy the natural gas so that it can be loaded onto tankers and transported to markets, primarily in Asia. There have been at least 15 LNG terminals proposed in British Columbia since the early 2010s (see Mihlar 2015), although many of these proposals have now been cancelled citing industry conditions; we focus here on opposition to two specific projects, the Pacific NorthWest LNG and the Aurora LNG.[11]

The Pacific NorthWest LNG project—proposed by the Malaysian state oil company, Petronas, along with four minority partners (China's Sinopec, Japan's JAPEX, Indian Oil Corporation, and PetroleumBRUNEI)—sought to build a liquefaction and export terminal on Lelu Island, near Port Edward. By late January 2017, the project had received both federal and provincial environmental approval, but only six months later, Petronas announced that plans for the project had been cancelled. The chair of Pacific NorthWest LNG's board of directors pointed to "prolonged depressed prices and shifts in the energy industry" (quoted in Gilchrist 2017). Shortly thereafter, the Aurora LNG project met a similar fate. The facility, proposed by Nexen Energy (a Calgary-based subsidiary of CNOOC, the China National Offshore Oil Corporation), along with several Japanese partners, was slated for construction on Digby Island, southwest of Prince Rupert and not far north of the site chosen for the Pacific NorthWest LNG terminal. In September 2017, however, CNOOC decided to abandon the project, citing "the current macro-economic environment" (Jang 2017).[12]

Distributive axis. LNG terminals, such as those proposed by Petronas and Nexen, provoked resistance because of the threat they pose to existing employment and livelihoods. Along this axis, opposition to Petronas's proposed Pacific NorthWest LNG terminal arose from concerns that the project's probable impact on the Skeena River estuary would devastate the salmon stock. The resistance, which was spearheaded by First Nations (notably the Gitwilgyoots, one of the allied tribes of the Lax Kw'alaams Band), was supported by a number of other groups who rely on wild salmon for their livelihoods. For example, the United Fisherman and Allied Workers' Union–Unifor, representing organized commercial salmon and herring fishermen in British Columbia, opposed the terminal because of its predicted impact on commercial fishing (UFAWU-Unifor 2016). For similar reasons, the project also met with opposition from a group of guides, lodge owners, and others involved in the sport-fishing business in the Skeena region, who argued that "our way of life depends on healthy fish populations" (Skeena Sport Fishing Group 2016).

Procedural axis. Multiple groups have opposed the proposed LNG terminals on two procedural grounds discussed above in connection with other flashpoints, namely, flawed consultation and biased assessments in scientific terms. Both of these factors are well illustrated by the Lelu Island flashpoint sparked by Petronas's proposed LNG terminal. In February 2016, the Canadian Environmental Assessment Agency (CEAA) released the *Pacific NorthWest LNG Draft Environmental Assessment Report* (CEAA 2016), approving the Petronas project, and as part of the process, the public was invited to comment on the report.[13] Some of the resulting submissions shed light on the nature of the opposition.

In addition to detailing numerous environmental shortcomings, the Gitxaala Nation argued that the CEAA report was based on an inadequate approach to consultation. "Gitxaala objects to public open houses being classified as Aboriginal consultation," the submission stated, noting that "even if Nation members were invited and attended, that consultation is not with the Nation as a collective but rather with individuals" (Gitxaala Nation 2016, 4).

The Pacific NorthWest LNG project was also challenged procedurally on the grounds that the scientific methodology used in CEAA report was fundamentally flawed. A letter submitted by 135 scientists identified five major failings of the draft assessment report: it misrepresented the importance of the project site to fish populations (especially salmon); it assumed that a lack of information was equivalent to an absence of risks; it disregarded scientific research other than that funded by the proponent; it gave inadequate consideration to cumulative effects; and it exhibited an "unsubstantiated reliance" on various forms of mitigation (Colquhoun et al. 2016, 1–2). When, despite the raft of criticisms, the federal government approved the project some six months later, legal actions were simultaneously brought by representatives of the Gitwilgyoots Tribe, the Gitanyow Band, and the SkeenaWild Conservation Trust, seeking a judicial review of the government's decision. "Once again," said Gitwilgyoots Chief Yahaan, "we are forced to ask the courts to do what our politicians seem unable to do—to honor Canada's obligations to its Indigenous communities and to protect our environment from catastrophic harm" (quoted in SkeenaWild Conservation Trust 2016).

Ecological and recognition axis. LNG projects have, of course, also met with resistance for ecological reasons. As we have seen, opposition to Petronas's proposed Pacific NorthWest LNG terminal stemmed in part from the project's potential to devastate the salmon stock by destroying the eel grass in Flora Bank region of the Skeena River estuary, a habitat crucial to juvenile salmon. Similarly, Nexen's proposed Aurora LNG terminal generated over a thousand submissions to the BC Environmental Assessment Office, the majority of which opposed the project on ecological and/or environmental grounds.

Along these lines, a group known as Friends of Digby Island argued that, in addition to damaging watersheds and destroying natural habitats, the LNG terminal would contribute to the growth of the fracking industry in northeastern British Columbia and thus of the environmental problems associated with it, while it would also increase atmospheric levels of carbon dioxide, thereby accelerating global climate change. At the same time, the group pointed to the danger posed to both workers and the local community by the potential leakage of natural gas, which could cause explosions, and to the project's "irreversible" impact on the "commercial fishing industry, sportsfishing industry, foodfishing and tourism."[14] Their argument thus connects different nodes along the commodity chain (from extraction to refining), as well as linking considerations located on different axes. Such linkages are critical to building coalitions of the sort that can lead to successful challenges not just to particular projects but to carbon capitalism in general.

Conclusion: Potentials and Challenges for Coalitions

As Roger Hayter (2004) observes, the late twentieth century witnessed a "war in the woods" in British Columbia that pitted logging industry workers against environmentalists and Indigenous groups. Since then, alignments have shifted somewhat, creating greater scope for coalition building in this contemporary period of fossil fuel resource development. By enabling us to analyze the factors that give rise to resistance, the typology presented in this chapter helps us to understand when, and under what conditions, such coalitions might be possible.

The case of Enbridge's Northern Gateway pipeline proposal illustrates the possibility of forming a coalition grounded in opposition across multiple axes. From the standpoint of distribution, the argument centred on insufficient local employment benefits from the project; groups voicing opposition included the Alberta Federation of Labour. The failure of the BC government to consult adequately with Indigenous groups prompted various organizations, including unions, to sign the Solidarity Accord in support of the Save the Fraser Declaration, thereby consolidating opposition along the procedural axis. But the declaration also articulated a myriad of local environmental concerns, in addition to providing an alternative vision of planetary governance, thereby demonstrating that issues arising along the ecological and recognition axis were also key to building the broad coalition that opposed the pipeline.

Coalitions can also be formed within a single axis by establishing links among sources of resistance positioned at various points along the commodity chain. In the case of natural gas projects, for example, groups concerned about the ecological and environmental hazards associated with fracking (at the extraction node), with natural gas pipelines (at the distribution node), and with LNG terminals (at the refining node) can join forces in opposition.

As we saw, the Friends of Digby Island, a group situated at the refining node, included upstream concerns about fracking in its reasons for opposing Nexen's Aurora LNG project as well as concerns about global climate change, a problem that encompasses activities even further downstream, at the point of consumption.

Of course, no coalition-building tactic is foolproof. In the case of the Trans Mountain Pipeline, the AFL has expressed its opposition to the export of unprocessed bitumen in the same way that it did in connection with the Northern Gateway pipeline. Yet other labour organizations favour the project for the jobs that it will create at other points on the commodity chain. For example, the director of the United Steelworkers' western district, Stephen Hunt, urged support for the pipeline on the grounds that it will use Canadian steel (an upstream employment linkage) and will "offer family-supporting employment to thousands of working people" at the distribution node of the chain.[15]

Such challenges can be particularly damaging to the opposition when combined with appeals to "the national interest" on the part of governments seeking to approve fossil fuel projects. When resistance is mounted in multiple communities and along many points of the commodity chain, however, as it was in the Northern Gateway case, then it becomes considerably more difficult to defend a project using "national interest" rhetoric. Building coalitions across the axes and along the chains is therefore critical. But it is important to recognize that resistance is context specific. Even along a single axis, sources of opposition will vary from project to project, owing to differences in, for example, employment volumes and locations, specific environmental impacts and threats, and the technologies used, all of which further depend on the particular commodity chain. By providing us with a flexible analytical model that can be used to "map" particular projects, the typology presented here can aid us in the task of creating effective coalitions while enhancing our understanding of fossil fuel flashpoints in general.

Notes

1. Recognition justice is also pertinent for the procedural axis in the sense that who gets to speak and whose voices are heard and are considered important may mean that certain views will not be formally "recognized" in the consultative process. This situation also speaks to the question of "expertise":

who is recognized as an "expert" in providing testimony and how "local" or Indigenous peoples' knowledge and expertise is incorporated (or not) in consultative and review processes.

2. At the time, the North East BC Resource Municipalities Coalition—now simply the Resource Municipalities Coalition—was made up of three municipal governments, but a fourth joined in 2018. Another coalition of communities, the Northwest BC Resource Benefits Alliance, similarly aims to negotiate an equitable share of the revenues received at the provincial level in order fund necessary infrastructure and services required by the economic expansion currently underway.

3. "Premier Clark, Don't Give Away Our Fresh Water for Fracking," Change.org, n.d., https://www.change.org/p/premier-clark-don-t-give-away-our-fresh-water-for-fracking (accessed December 12, 2019).

4. For more information, including a letter template, see "Add Your Voice to the Call for a Public Inquiry into Fracking," Canadian Centre for Policy Alternatives, n.d., https://www.policyalternatives.ca/fracking-inquiry (accessed December 14, 2019).

5. These statements appeared on a DCW leaflet, a copy of which is in the authors' possession. The first factor—concerns about temporary foreign workers taking jobs away from locals—also led the Construction and Specialized Workers' Union and the International Union of Operating Engineers to challenge in court the permits obtained by HD Mining International to bring in 201 temporary foreign workers from China to work in a coal mine in northeastern BC. The federal court ruled in favour of the company (see Drews 2013).

6. Similarly, the Unist'ot'en clan of the Wet'suwet'en people, who set up a camp in opposition to pipelines running through their traditional territory, identified the limited number of jobs as one reason (of many) for their opposition. See "Background of the Campaign," Unist'ot'en Camp, 2017, https://unistoten.camp/no-pipelines/background-of-the-campaign/.

7. "Why We Oppose LNG Pipelines and Terminals," Madii 'Lii, n.d., http://www.madiilii.com/lng (accessed December 16, 2019). Madii 'Lii is the traditional territory of the Luutkudziiwus.

8. Richard Wright, "Luutkudziiwus to Launch Court Challenge to Prince Rupert Gas Transmission Pipeline That Would Supply Petronas LNG," Luutkudziiwus news release, October 14, 2015, https://www.madiilii.com/press.

9. Save the Fraser Gathering of Nations, "Save the Fraser Declaration," https://savethefraser.ca/Fraser-Declaration-May2013.pdf; Yinka Dene Alliance, "Save the Fraser Solidarity Accord," https://savethefraser.ca/SolidarityAccord-nov2013.pdf. A year after the Solidarity Accord was issued, it had gathered some 26,000 signatures (Hughes 2014).

10. The Kispiox Valley Declaration, https://kispioxvalley.files.wordpress. com/2014/06/the-kispiox-valley-declaration.pdf.

11. Fazil Mihlar, assistant deputy minister of the Oil and Strategic Initiatives Division in the Ministry of Natural Gas Development, refers to 18 proposed terminals, https://www.emaofbc.com/wp-content/uploads/2015/03/Mihlar-LNG-in-BC-An-Update.pdf. The BC Oil and Gas Commission website currently lists 7 LNG terminals, https://www.bcogc.ca/public-zone/major-projects-centre/list.

12. For additional information, see "Pacific NorthWest LNG," BC Oil and Gas Commission, 2017, https://www.bcogc.ca/public-zone/major-projects-centre/pacific-northwest-lng; and "Aurora LNG–Digby Island," BC Oil and Gas Commission, 2017, https://www.bcogc.ca/public-zone/major-projects-centre/aurora-lng-digby-island.

13. Public comments on the draft report can be accessed at "Pacific NorthWest LNG Project," Government of Canada, https://iaac-aeic.gc.ca/050/evaluations/proj/80032?culture=en-CA, last modified March 28, 2018. (Click on "View comments" and search the contributor's name.) In the case of Nexen's Aurora LNG project, no such report was ever prepared: on October 24, 2017, the CEAA terminated the assessment process at the proponent's request. See "Aurora LNG Project," Government of Canada, https://iaac-aeic.gc.ca/050/evaluations/proj/80075?culture=en-CA (last modified December 13, 2017). Note also that on August 28, 2019, when the new Impact Assessment Act came into force, the CEAA was replaced by the Impact Assessment Agency of Canada.

14. "Impacts," Friends of Digby Island, n.d., https://friendsofdigby.wordpress.com/impacts/ (accessed 18 December 2019).

15. Stephen Hunt, director, USW District 3: Western Provinces and Territories, to George Heyman, BC Minister of Environment and Climate Change Strategy, February 1, 2018, https://www.usw1-2017.ca/uploads/Pipeline%20Letter.pdf.

References

AFL (Alberta Federation of Labour). 2013. "AFL Blasts Northern Gateway Decision." Media release. December 19, 2013. http://www.afl.org/tags/environment.

Amnesty International. 2016. *Out of Sight, Out of Mind: Gender, Indigenous Rights, and Energy Development in Northeast British Columbia, Canada*. London: Amnesty International.

Anderson, Ewan W. 2000. *Global Geopolitical Flashpoints: An Atlas of Conflict*. Chicago: Fitzroy Dearborn.

Bowles, Paul, and Fiona MacPhail. 2017. "The Town That Said 'No' to the Enbridge Northern Gateway Pipeline: The Kitimat Plebiscite of 2014." *Extractive Industries and Society* 4, no. 1: 15–23.

———. 2018. "Contesting Natural Resource Development in Canada: The Legacies and Limits of the Staples Approach." *British Journal of Canadian Studies* 31, no. 2: 167–79.

Bowles, Paul, and Henry Veltmeyer. 2015. "Pipelines and Protest: Enbridge and After." In *Resource Communities in a Globalizing Region: Development, Agency and Contestation in Northern British Columbia*, edited by Paul Bowles and Gary Wilson, 254–79. Vancouver: University of British Columbia Press.

Bridge, Gavin. 2008. "Global Production Networks and the Extractive Sector: Governing Resource-Based Development." *Journal of Economic Geography* 8, no. 3: 389–419.

British Columbia. Environmental Appeal Board. 2015. Chief Sharleen Gale and Members of the Fort Nelson First Nation v. Assistant Regional Water Manager and Nexen Inc. Decision No. 2012-WAT-013(c). September 3, 2015. http://www. eab.gov.bc.ca/water/2012wat013c.pdf.

Carter, Mike. 2016. "B.C. Not Doing Enough to Uphold Treaty Rights: Blueberry River FN." *Dawson Creek Mirror*, June 28, 2016. https://www.dawsoncreekmirror. ca/regional-news/lng/b-c-not-doing-enough-to-uphold-treaty-rights-blueberry-river-fn-1.2289299.

CBC (Canadian Broadcasting Corporation). 2014. "Kitimat, B.C., Votes 'No' to Northern Gateway in Plebiscite." *CBC News*. April 12, 2014. https://www.cbc.ca/news/canada/british-columbia/kitimat-b-c-votes-no-to-northern-gateway-in-plebiscite-1.2607877.

CEAA (Canadian Environmental Assessment Agency). 2016. *Pacific NorthWest LNG Draft Environmental Assessment Report*. Ottawa: Government of Canada. https://www.ceaa-acee.gc.ca/050/evaluations/document/104785.

Colquhoun, Ian C., et al. 2016. "Re: Scientific Flaws in Assessment of Environmental Risks from the Proposed Pacific NorthWest Liquefied Natural Gas Facility at Lelu Island, Skeena River Estuary." Submission to the Canadian Environmental Assessment Agency. March 9, 2016. http://www.ceaa-acee.gc.ca/050/documents/p80032/108936E.pdf.

Cox, Sarah. 2016. "BC Hydro Apologizes for Bennett Dam's 'Profound and Painful' Impact on First Nations at Gallery Opening." *The Narwhal*, June 20, 2016. https://thenarwhal.ca/bc-hydro-apologizes-bennett-dam-s-profound-and-painful-impact-first-nations-gallery-opening/.

CSTC (Carrier Sekani Tribal Council). 2007. "First Nations Perspectives on the B.C. Environmental Assessment Process." http://www.carriersekani.ca/images/docs/lup/EAO%20Critique%20-%20CSTC.pdf.

District of Taylor and City of Fort St. John. 2015. "Appendix G: NEBC Resource Municipalities Coalition Position Paper." In NEBC Resource Municipalities Coalition, *Municipalities Role in Oil, Gas and Resource Development in Northeastern BC*.

Drews, Keven. 2013. "Federal Court Dismisses Union Challenge Against B.C. Foreign Workers." *Global News*. May 21, 2013. https://globalnews.ca/news/580367/federal-court-dismisses-union-challenge-against-b-c-foreign-workers/.

Eckford, Clarice, and Jillian Wagg. 2014. *The Peace Project: Gender Based Analysis of Violence Against Women and Girls in Fort St. John*. Report prepared for the Fort St. John Women's Resource Society. https://thepeaceprojectfsj.files.wordpress.com/2014/03/the_peace_project_gender_based_analysis_amended.pdf.

Finley-Brook, Mary, and Erica L. Holloman. 2016. "Empowering Energy Justice." *International Journal of Environmental Research and Public Health* 13, no. 9: 1–19.

Foster, John Bellamy. 2013. "Marx and the Rift in the Universal Metabolism of Nature." *Monthly Review* 65, no. 7: 1–19. https://monthlyreview.org/2013/12/01/marx-rift-universal-metabolism-nature/.

Garvie, Kathryn H., and Karena Shaw. 2014. "Oil and Gas Consultation and Shale Gas Development in British Columbia." *BC Studies*, no. 184: 73–102.

Gilchrist, Emma. 2017. "Pacific NorthWest LNG Is Dead: 5 Things You Need to Know." *The Narwhal*, July 25, 2017. https://thenarwhal.ca/pacific-northwest-lng-dead-5-things-you-need-know/.

Gitxaala Nation. 2016. "Re: Gitxaala Nations Comments on CEAA's Draft Environmental Assessment Report and Proposed Conditions for the Proposed Pacific NorthWest LNG Project." Submission to the Canadian Environmental Assessment Agency. March 11, 2016. http://ceaa.gc.ca/050/documents/p80032/108469E.pdf.

Grossman, Zoltan. 2017. *Unlikely Alliances: Native Nations and White Communities Join to Defend Rural Lands*. Seattle: University of Washington Press.

Harvey, David. 2004. "The 'New' Imperialism: Accumulation by Dispossession." *Socialist Register* 40: 63–87.

Hayter, Roger. 2004. "'The War in the Woods': Post-Fordist Restructuring, Globalization, and the Contested Remapping of British Columbia's Forest Economy." *Annals of the Association of American Geographers* 93, no. 3: 706–29.

Hughes, Bradley. 2014. "First Nations Winning Against Tar Sands Pipelines." *Socialist.ca*, December 16, 2014. http://www.socialist.ca/node/2575.

Jang, Brent. 2017. "China's CNOOC Cancels Aurora LNG Project in B.C." *Globe and Mail*, September 14, 2017. https://www.theglobeandmail.com/report-on-business/industry-news/energy-and-resources/chinas-cnooc-cancels-aurora-lng-project-in-bc/article36259169/.

Jenkins, Katy. 2014. "Women, Mining and Development: An Emerging Research Agenda." *Extractive Industries and Society* 1, no. 2: 329–39.

Jenkins, Kirsten E. H., Darren McCauley, Raphael Heffron, Hannes R. Stephan, and Robert W. M. Rehner. 2016. "Energy Justice: A Conceptual Review." *Energy Research and Social Science* 11: 174–82.

Johnston, Patrick. 2017. "More than Two Dozen Groups Join Call for Fracking Inquiry in B.C." *Vancouver Sun*, November 6, 2017. https://vancouversun.com/news/local-news/embargoed-to-midnight-more-than-two-dozen-groups-join-call-for-fracking-inquiry-in-b-c.

Macdonald, Eliana. 2016. *Atlas of Cumulative Landscape Disturbance in the Traditional Territory of Blueberry River First Nations, 2016*. Vancouver: David Suzuki Foundation and Ecotrust Canada.

Mihlar, Fazil. 2015. "LNG in British Columbia: An Update" (PowerPoint presentation, 2015 Environmental Managers Association Workshop, February 19, 2015), https://emaofbc.com/wp-content/uploads/2015/03/Mihlar-LNG-in-BC-An-Update.pdf.

NEBC Resource Municipalities Coalition. 2015. *Municipalities Role in Oil, Gas and Resource Development in Northeastern BC*. http://rmcoalition.com/reports/coalition-publications/.

Northern Health. 2012. *Understanding the State of Industrial Camps in Northern BC: A Background Paper*. Version 1. October 17, 2012. Prince George, BC: Northern Health.

Parfitt, Ben. 2017. *Fracking, First Nations and Water: Respecting Indigenous Rights and Better Protecting Our Shared Resources*. Vancouver: Canadian Centre for Policy Alternatives, BC Office.

Pulido, Laura. 2010. "Rethinking Environmental Racism: White Privilege and Urban Development in Southern California." *Annals of the Association of American Geographers* 90, no. 1: 12–40.

Pyle, Norma. 2017. "Re: Blueberry River First Nations Public Comments on Town and Lily Dam Exemption Applications." Submission to the Environmental Assessment Office, Ministry of Environment and Climate Change Strategy, Government of British Columbia. September 21, 2017. https://projects.eao.gov.bc.ca/api/document/59c4361cf97b16001803081l/fetch.

Sharp, Karyn. 2014. "Karyn Sharp, Prince George." In *The Answer Is Still No: Voices of Pipeline Resistance*, edited by Paul Bowles and Henry Veltmeyer, 15–25. Halifax: Fernwood.

Skeena Sport Fishing Community. 2016. "Re: Skeena Sport Fishing Community Opposed to PNW LNG Terminal in Flora Bank Region of Skeena River Estuary." Submission to the Canadian Environmental Assessment Agency. March 9, 2016. http://www.ceaa.gc.ca/050/documents/p80032/110873E.pdf.

SkeenaWild Conservation Trust. 2016. "PNW LNG Legal Action: Canadian Courts Asked to Block Approval of Massive Petronas LNG Project." News release. October 27, 2016. https://skeenawild.org/news/press-release-pnw-lng-legal-action.

Sovacool, Benjamin, and Michael H. Dworkin. 2015. "Energy Justice: Conceptual Insights and Practical Applications." *Applied Energy* 142: 435–44.

UBCM (Union of British Columbia Municipalities). Select Committee on Local Government Finance. 2013. *Strong Fiscal Futures: A Blueprint for Strengthening BC Local Governments' Finance System.* Richmond, BC: Union of British Columbia Municipalities.

United Fishermen and Allied Workers' Union–Unifor. 2016. "Re: Impacts of the [Proposed Pacific NorthWest] LNG Terminal on Commercial Fishing." Submission to the Canadian Environmental Assessment Agency. March 11, 2016. http://www.ceaa.gc.ca/050/documents/p80032/113556E.pdf.

Vos, Robert O. 1997. "Introduction: Competing Approaches to Sustainability: Dimensions of Controversy." In *Flashpoints in Environmental Policymaking: Controversies in Achieving Sustainability*, edited by Sheldon Kamieniecki, George A. Gonzalez, and Robert O. Vos, 1–30. Albany: State University of New York Press.

Waddington, David P. 2010. "Applying the Flashpoints Model of Public Disorder to the 2011 Bradford Riot." *British Journal of Criminology* 50, no. 2: 342–59.

West Coast Environmental Law. 2011. "The Joint Review Panel's Decision on the Scope of the Environmental Assessment for Enbridge Northern Gateway Pipelines." Vancouver: West Coast Environmental Law. https://www.wcel.org/publication/west-coast-backgrounder-joint-review-panels-decision-scope-environmental-assessment.

Yahey, Marvin, and Blueberry River First Nations. 2015. "Notice of Civil Claim." Claim S-151727, Victoria Registry, filed March 3, 2015, in the Supreme Court of British Columbia. http://www.ratcliff.com/sites/default/files/news_articles/2015-03-03%20Notice%20of%20Civil%20Claim.PDF.

———. 2016. "Re: Pacific NorthWest LNG Project, Canadian Environmental Assessment Agency Draft Report." Submission to the Canadian Environmental Assessment Agency. March 11, 2016. http://www.ceaa.gc.ca/050/documents/p80032/113550E.pdf.

17 Fossil Fuel Divestment, Non-reformist Reforms, and Anti-capitalist Strategy

Emilia Belliveau, James K. Rowe, and Jessica Dempsey

In the spring of 2013, students from the University of Victoria approached two of us (Rowe and Dempsey) to ask whether we would be willing to organize fellow faculty in favour of fossil fuel divestment. We were wary of the campaign. Both of us had done critical research on market-based sustainability strategies (Collard, Dempsey, and Rowe 2016; Dempsey 2016; Rowe 2005). And, at first glance, divestment appeared to be a market mechanism relatively narrow in scope, encouraging large investors simply to withdraw their assets from one industry and invest them in some other, hopefully more sustainable, enterprise. Assets are moved around, but the endless and ecologically harmful compound growth that results from capitalist patterns of production and consumption is largely left unchallenged. Because fossil fuel divestment appears to be a "green capitalist" reform with limited potential for system transformation, it has been met with both skepticism and outright dismissal by eco-socialists. Writing about the "fossil fuels war," John Bellamy Foster (2013) communicates an openness to the tactic of divestment but raises important questions about the climate movement's trajectory, asking, "Will the current struggle metamorphose into the necessary full-scale revolt against capitalist environmental destruction? Or will it be confined to very limited, short-term gains of the kind compatible with the system? Will the movement radicalize, leading to the full mobilization of its popular base? Or will the more elite-technocratic and pro-capitalist elements within the movement leadership in the United States ultimately determine its direction, betraying the grassroots resistance?" As yet, the answers to Foster's questions remain unwritten. The ideological direction of fossil fuel divestment is still up for grabs.

Despite the open-endedness of divestment's political trajectory, other eco-socialists, such as economic historian Richard Smith, have been sharply critical. For Smith, the divestment movement has thus far failed to seriously reduce emissions and should therefore be abandoned. In an online public debate on the strategic value of divestment, hosted on the climate movement website System Change, Not Climate Change, Smith argues that, "given the failure to date of all 'green' capitalist efforts to suppress fossil fuel emissions—cap & trade, carbon taxes, and fossil fuel divestment, the time has come (actually it's long overdue) for the environmental movement to call for directly suppressing fossil fuel production/consumption."[1] In his view, this suppression can best be achieved by state action.

The highest-profile eco-socialist critic of divestment has been Christian Parenti. He has questioned the tactic's effectiveness in the *Huffington Post* (2012), the *New York Times* (2013), and *The Nation* (Nathanson 2013), as well as on the radio programs *Democracy Now* (Goodman 2013) and *Against the Grain*. Among other things, Parenti sees divestment as a market-based strategy that unwittingly plays into neoliberalism's suspicion of the state. According to Parenti (2012), "regulation is the only thing that will actually check the industries—oil, gas, coal—that are destroying the planet." Deploying tactics that fail to centre the state is therefore foolish, he argues, because only states have sufficient powers of enforcement to ensure that emissions are kept in check. For him, as for Smith, divestment is an ineffective strategy with minimal system-transforming potential.

We (Rowe and Dempsey) had similar concerns when our students invited us to become involved in the campaign. We teach about the challenges of "market environmentalism," but we also emphasize to students the central role of social movements in achieving more socially and ecologically just societies. The fledgling divestment movement had captured our students' attention, and we wanted to support them. Despite our reservations, we were also aware that a tendency toward political perfectionism can be counterproductive, given the fundamental messiness and unpredictability of the political terrain. In the face of this instability, waiting for the ideal tactic, campaign, organization, or movement that perfectly reflects one's principles can result in inaction, disconnection, and even resentment. Maybe the divestment movement had possibilities that were not evident to us from the standpoint of outsiders. So we decided to get into the mix and find out.

Upon joining the campaign in 2013, we were heartened to discover that a great number of the student organizers we encountered were similarly interested in system transformation and saw divestment as one pathway in that direction. In 2014, we started working with one such organizer, our co-author Emilia Belliveau. She had recently graduated from Dalhousie University, where she was active with their divestment campaign, and had moved from Nova Scotia to British Columbia to begin a master's degree at the University of Victoria. All three of us were intrigued by how the divestment movement appeared to aim merely at reforming the existing capitalist system and yet magnetized organizers who had more transformational agendas. We set out to explore this tension within the movement itself, to examine divestment as a site of both system modification and system transformation. Was our initial impression about the pervasiveness of anti-capitalist perspectives among student organizers in Canada accurate? Did more transformative potential exist in the tactic of fossil fuel divestment than was immediately apparent? Or, as Foster (2013) wondered, would the "more elite-technocratic and pro-capitalist elements" within the movement ultimately prevail?

To answer our research questions, we pursued interviews with student divestment organizers at three Canadian universities: the University of British Columbia (UBC), the University of Toronto (U of T), and Dalhousie University (Dal), located in western, central, and eastern Canada, respectively. Our goal was to capture multiple perspectives within a shared campaign experience, as well as an overarching picture of the national divestment movement. All three universities had well-established divestment campaigns, and the organizers of these campaigns represent some of the early leaders in the Canadian divestment movement. The three campaigns face different institutional challenges, and their organizational structure varies. All campaigns must contend with high-pressure strategy discussions, however, as well as with internal group dynamics and varying priorities around issues of solidarity and escalation. At the time of our interviews, all three university administrations had rejected divestment proposals. This has since changed. UBC has signalled that it will fully divest from fossil fuel divestment in the near future (UBC 2020).

Interviews were conducted (by Belliveau) with five leaders from each campaign. We supplemented these interviews with perspectives offered by national divestment coordinators from the Canadian Youth Climate Coalition and 350.org Canada, along with additional reflections from divestment organizers at Mount Allison University, McGill University, the University of Victoria, and the University of Winnipeg. Expanding our sample beyond the three major university campaigns helped us to identify nationally relevant themes.

Writing about divestment, Naomi Klein (2015, 354) observes that "no tactic in the climate wars has resonated so powerfully." As organizers graduate from university and hence leave their respective divestment campaigns behind, their analytical and ideological perspectives point to potential trends in the next generation of environmental leaders in Canada. Campus divestment campaigns are thus a helpful site at which to learn where environmentalism may be heading. Earlier environmental movements have, in particular, been criticized for failing to target the systemic drivers of ecological decline and pursue a more transformative agenda (Dale, Mathai, and Oliveira 2016; Magdoff and Foster 2011). The question is whether the upcoming generation of organizers is prepared to engage with these critiques, act in accordance with them, and mobilize alternatives.

André Gorz and Non-reformist Reforms

The divestment movement is premised on the theory that if enough reputable institutions divest from fossil fuel companies, the industry will lose its credibility, making it harder for companies to use their economic muscle to obstruct climate legislation. The industry has an unenviable record of stalling climate action by funding climate denialism and lobbying against needed legislation (Daub and Yunker 2017; Oreskes and Conway 2011). According to movement leaders such as Bill McKibben, the fossil fuel industry's obstructionism is the primary reason for the political deadlock on climate action. As McKibben (2012) wrote in his now famous essay in *Rolling Stone*, "We have met the enemy and they is Shell."

McKibben's analysis helped to kick-start the fossil fuel divestment movement, which has since grown rapidly, faster than earlier movements to discourage investments in the tobacco industry and in the South African economy (see Ansar, Caldecott, and Tilbury 2013, 49–50). At the time we write, roughly 1,180 institutions with assets worth more than $14 trillion have divested from fossil fuel companies. The Rockefeller Brothers Fund has fully divested, as have a number of major world cities (including San Francisco, Stockholm, Sydney, and Montréal) and numerous universities; in late 2019, Norway's Government Pension Fund Global—which manages assets valued at roughly $1.1 trillion—announced a partial divestment from oil and gas exploration.[2] In Canada, the divestment movement has garnered extensive support from faith-based organizations, but universities have been slower to respond. In Québec, Concordia University and Université du Québec à Montréal have fully divested. In November 2019, the University of British Columbia board of governors voted for a partial divestment (CBC 2019) and have since signalled plans for full divestment (Vice-President Finance and Operations, UBC 2020). Despite considerable uptake, however, the question remains whether the fossil fuel divestment movement holds the potential for systemic change.

Articulating the relationship between reforms and the ultimate goal of revolution, that is, the overthrow of the capitalist system, has been a long-standing challenge for socialist theories of transition. In 1964, in *Stratégie ouvrière et néocapitalisme* (translated in 1967 as *Strategy for Labor*), New Left theorist André Gorz introduced the concept of "non-reformist reforms" to help fellow anti-capitalists think through the process of transition. In so doing, Gorz was following in the footsteps of his socialist predecessors, such as Rosa Luxemburg and Leon Trotsky, who also took up the question of how interim reforms can best serve longer-term revolutionary goals. What sets Gorz's work apart is that the historical circumstances of his writing are closer to our own than those of earlier socialist thinkers.

As Gorz notes near the outset of *Strategy for Labor*, the objective need for revolution is less obvious today than it was in previous generations. "As long as misery, the lack of basic necessities, was the condition of the majority," he writes, "the need for a revolution could be regarded as obvious." He continues, "But conditions have changed since then. Nowadays, in the richer societies, it is not so clear that the status quo represents the greatest possible evil" (1967, 3). With the insurrectionary path to revolution blocked by both the coercive force of the modern state and late capitalism's relative popularity, socialists needed a path to revolution that began from *within* the capitalist order. Hence the strategic importance of non-reformist reforms—reforms that, rather than serving to maintain the system, create the conditions for deeper transformations.

What exactly distinguishes non-reformist reforms from ordinary reforms, or what Gorz sometimes calls "neo-capitalist reforms"? As Gorz himself acknowledges, the dividing line between the two is "not always very clear" (1967, 7), noting elsewhere that many non-reformist reforms will not "reveal their anti-capitalist logic *directly*" (1968, 118). Just because a tactic has (or seems to have) neoliberal or green capitalist features or adherents (as is the case for divestment), that does not immediately disqualify it from socialist consideration. It is worth quoting Gorz at length in this regard:

> The error is to postulate that any struggle must now be entered into only with a clearly stated socialist intention and for aims which imply the destruction of the system. . . . For in reality, the socialist intention of the masses never emerges *ex nihilo*, nor is it formed by political propaganda or scientific proof. A socialist intention is constructed in and through the struggle for plausible objectives corresponding to the experience, needs, and aspirations of the workers. (1968, 121–22)

Although the people with whom we engaged in the course of our research identified more as students than as workers, Gorz's point about how reform struggles can grow socialist consciousness is applicable to multiple sites of struggle, including the university.

For Gorz, non-reformist reforms have three features that distinguish them from neo-capitalist reforms. First, non-reformist reforms should disrupt the capitalist status quo in ways that can work to the benefit of socialist forces. As Gorz (1968, 119) observes, "A socialist strategy of reforms must aim at disturbing the balance of the system, and profit by this disturbance to prepare the (revolutionary) process of the transition to socialism." Second, socialist reforms should prefigure the new system by building popular power in the process of fighting for the reform. According to Gorz (1967, 8), "Whether it be at the level of companies, schools, municipalities, regions, or of the national Plan, etc., structural reform always requires decentralization of the decision-making power, a restriction on the powers of State or Capital, an extension of popular power, that is to say, a victory of democracy over the dictatorship of profit." This criterion includes the importance of self-transformation through participation in collective struggle, a participation that develops political and organizing abilities while also instilling a belief in the possibility of systemic change—counteracting what Dieter Klein called the "TINA" ("there is no alternative") syndrome with

"TAMARA" ("there are many and realistic alternatives") (quoted in Brie 2010, 3). Finally, the reform cannot be the end goal in itself but instead needs to be part of a larger transformative plan. Non-reformist reforms need to be deployed as "dynamic phases in a process of struggle, not as resting stages" (Gorz 1968, 118).

As Gorz recognizes, drawing distinctions between reformist and non-reformist reforms is challenging given the contingencies of the political terrain. Under the right conditions, a seemingly system-maintaining reform could develop radical potential. Our own research suggests that fossil fuel divestment is a site where critiques of the dominant liberal society, including capitalism and white supremacy, are being worked on and out. We locate three transformative potentials in the movement that align with Gorz's criteria for non-reformist reforms. With regard to Gorz's first criterion, the movement sparks an awareness of how far the fossil fuel industry has captured public institutions, including universities. Given the fossil fuel industry's integral position in global capitalism, divestment's efforts to undermine its power has the potential to disturb the balance of the system. Second, the movement challenges individualistic approaches to social change (change a light bulb, plant a tree) that are all too common in mainstream environmentalism and builds concrete, transferable skills in collective organizing, with an explicit focus on anti-oppressive approaches—a shift that aligns with Gorz's emphasis on the building of popular power in the course of struggle. Finally, by providing an educational space where people (often students) are introduced to and engage in anti-capitalist and anti-colonial analysis, the movement's reach extends beyond the immediate goal of divestment, becoming part of a broader process of struggle.

Despite eco-socialist criticisms, then, we would argue that divestment is part of a wider shift in environmentalism toward a more transformative political orientation. The divestment movement underscores the importance of collective challenge, in this case to the concentrated economic power of an industry central to the contemporary capitalist economy. As we will see, many of its participants hold anti-capitalist values that predispose them to move beyond the targeting of one industry and to challenge the coercive effects of concentrated economic power more generally. None of the organizers we interviewed saw divestment as a "resting stage," to use Gorz's expression. Rather, they were more apt to stress the need for transformative change.

Anti-capitalism in the Fossil Fuel Divestment Movement

Although we did not attempt to survey the entire divestment movement, our research suggests that anti-capitalism is widespread among Canadian student organizers. We asked participants whether their campaigns incorporate critiques of capitalism. In almost every case, organizers used the question as a springboard to comment on the ideological orientation of their campaign *and* to offer their personal perspective on capitalism. Nearly three-quarters (73 percent) of those we interviewed thought that critiques of capitalism were ideologically important to their campaigns. The same percentage of participants—although not an identical group of people—articulated anti-capitalist views of their own. Their primary grievances included the system's drive for infinite growth on a finite planet, as well as the ecological and social exploitation that results, and the system's tendency to promote individual and consumerist solutions to structural problems. As Joanna, from the Dal campaign, commented,

> Capitalism, colonialism, racism, patriarchy, and many other -isms
> are causes of climate change. Our economic system that exploits
> people and our planet is not working. Or it's doing exactly what it is
> programmed to do, but that is not [to] look out for the people or the
> land that we all live on. I think the idea and the understanding that
> capitalism is at the heart of this is quite prominent. That idea is quite
> prominent within our group.

Even those participants whose own views were not anti-capitalist recognized the influence of anti-capitalist politics in the wider movement. For example, an organizer from U of T reflected, "It's been very interesting that the movement has accrued so many anti-capitalist members, because it is a movement that is inherently about shifting where institutions hold their equities, using the stock market to try and influence public opinion on climate change, which is the epitome of capitalist tools."

The organizers with whom we spoke, whether invested in system reform or focused more on system transformation, did not conceive of divestment as an inherently anti-capitalist tactic. Although the tactic can resonate with a green capitalist approach to climate action, none of the Canadian campaigns we engaged saw their work as part of a system-maintaining project. According to Divest Dal organizer Simon,

We could just do this as a "green capitalism" thing, whereby we're going to save the university some money, we're going to avoid the carbon bubble, and our stock portfolio is going to be healthier. But I've never met a divestment organizer who thinks that way. . . . Certainly no one in Divest Dal has really focused on that. It's always been seen as a cog in the long-term promotion of climate justice.

Most organizers located their work under the banner of "climate justice." And, indeed, it is this climate justice approach that informs the anti-capitalist politics of many divestment campaigners.

The term *climate justice* became popular in international climate politics around the turn of this century, particularly as a way to conceive of differential national responsibility based on historical emissions (Schlosberg and Collins 2014). The climate justice politics that have since emerged foreground the intersectional impacts of climate change, particularly the ways in which race, class, gender, and nationality interact to determine which individuals suffer most from these impacts. Climate justice perspectives also emphasize how the injustices of climate change are connected to broader systems of colonialism, white supremacy, patriarchy, and neoliberal capitalism (Bond 2012; Mohai, Pellow, and Roberts 2009; Schlosberg and Collins 2014). By implicating structural inequality in the problem of climate change, the concept of climate justice implies the need for transformative system change (Satgar 2018). Much as we did, researchers have found climate justice perspectives to be predominant among divestment organizers on US campuses (Bratman et al. 2016; Grady-Benson and Sarathy 2015). Working under the banner of climate justice does not immediately make an organizer anti-capitalist, but it does situate them within the milieu of a movement that prioritizes system transformation, even if the precise shape of that transformation remains somewhat indefinite. The anti-capitalist perspectives that organizers communicated to us did not regularly cohere into a firm political identity such as "Marxist" or "socialist." And yet deep frustration with capitalism's systemic effects, such as climate change and the uneven distribution of its dangers, was common ground for a majority of the organizers with whom we spoke.

Critical analysis being developed in the movement is consistent with key themes in anti-capitalist scholarship, and yet divestment organizers are articulating their critiques of capitalism without identifying with traditional anti-capitalist theorists. For example, no one we interviewed referenced Marx. When asked about what resources they use to develop their critical thinking around divestment and theories of change, the majority of participants did not mention academic texts but preferred resources developed from within the movement, such as organizer training guides and activist-produced materials, or online articles and think pieces. Organizers often indicated that their perspectives had evolved in casual social settings with other campaign members, through conversation and experiential learning.

Naomi Klein's 2014 book, *This Changes Everything: Capitalism vs. the Climate*, was also mentioned regularly by organizers, and one referenced David Harvey's 2005 work *The New Imperialism*. Although academic and canonical anti-capitalist theory has undoubtedly informed the thinking of movement organizers, it is not a primary resource, and the movement would undoubtedly benefit from more engagement with socialist and eco-socialist analysis—a point to which we will return. But while eco-socialist observers express skepticism about divestment, even viewing it as a neoliberal distraction, the gap between an apparently green capitalist tactic and the overtly anti-capitalist viewpoints of movement organizers seems to us worth exploring.[3]

Transformational Values and Reformist Messaging: Why the Gap?

Organizers at each of the case-study campaigns communicated concern that expressing an explicit anti-capitalist message would be a barrier for people who might otherwise support their efforts. Sydney, from the U of T, spoke directly to the limited scope for explicit anti-capitalist messages in the media: "In trying to get the media to pick up our stories, we frame it in a certain way. If we're doing this big anti-capitalist critique, no one is going to pick up on it in the news." As she went on to say, "I think our campaign purposefully framed it in a way that would get media attention—that would get us published in newspapers. In trying to make the movement accessible to lots of people, we purposefully do that." Similarly, Stephanie, from UBC, talked about divestment as an approach that encourages investors to think about more than just profit, while not deterring people who have yet to confront capitalism's systemic challenges. She noted that "divestment opens that conversation without immediately jumping to 'Shut down capitalism!'"

A number of those we interviewed used the word "layered" to describe the various arguments in favour of divestment. Organizers reported how they strategically modify their arguments, according to the audience they are addressing, and suggested that the broad appeal of the movement is partly due to this ideological flexibility. This finding corresponds with the account offered by Rupinder Mangat, Simon Dalby, and Matthew Paterson (2018) of how divestment activists use a multitude of narratives in their public messaging, some focused on economics and others on justice and morality. In the strategic calculus of divestment organizers, blatant anti-capitalism does not always serve anti-capitalist goals. One UBC organizer, Julie, was ambivalent about the movement's tendency to shy away from explicit anti-capitalist framing, while acknowledging the strategic value of the approach: "The less radical the solution is the more likely it is to be accepted—which isn't necessarily helpful, because we need radical solutions. But it's easier to have the conversations around small steps, rather than big transformational changes."

There are signs that the ideological hegemony of capitalism is growing brittle. For example, a 2019 Pew poll found that 50 percent of adults under thirty—the same age group from which divestment organizers emerge—held positive views of socialism but that older adults are more likely to favour capitalism (Hartig 2019). Similarly, another poll, conducted in 2016, found 60 percent popular support for capitalism across all age groups but noted that millennials tend to be more critical than others (Steverman 2017). The widespread anti-capitalist sentiment we encountered in the divestment movement thus seems to align with "millennial" ideological preferences writ large. Given the system's continued support from a solid majority, however, it makes sense to engage the public in such a way that capitalism's proponents are not immediately repelled.

Integrating practical organizer knowledge and canonical socialist and social movement theory, John Matthew Smucker's *Hegemony How-To: A Roadmap for Radicals* (2017) offers useful insights into the asymmetry that can exist between internal movement values and public messaging. "Movements always have a propagandistic face—or at least they had better if they hope to mobilize people—so it is just silly for scholars or strategists to take movements' self-presentations at face value," he writes (129). Smucker's book helpfully diagnoses and challenges the ideological purism and perfectionism common on the left, a purism that regularly gets in the way of reaching publics "beyond the choir" (25). For Smucker, building genuine hegemony means growing the ranks of the left. If stridently impugning capitalism were enough to achieve this goal, we would all be sipping socialist champagne right now. Instead, building hegemony requires a willingness to engage with those whose values differ from our own, using language that is inviting instead of overwhelming. "Organizing entails starting with what already is and engaging with people as they are," writes Smucker, "not trying to build something pure from scratch. . . . Organizing is a mess, not a refuge" (161). He goes on to say, "It is not a matter of 'compromising our politics.' It's about speaking in a language that people can hear" (226).

In Smucker's analysis, the left's tendency toward political perfectionism is partly a product of ongoing defeat. With so little experience with wielding real power, leftists can easily confuse righteous critique with political efficacy. Might may not make right, but neither does right amount to might. Yet, in the absence of access to political power, righteousness can seem like the next best thing. As Smucker argues, (2017, 142), "if a political goal is too big to believably accomplish anytime soon—e.g., ending capitalism—then winnable interim victories have to be articulated, if we don't want our core dedicated folks to gravitate toward the self-righteous over the political." Divestment organizers recognize this tension. As one participant wisely observed,

> We've spent so much time as activists arguing with other activists, who on the scale of Canadian public opinion are such a small fraction of the population, that we have left behind the discussion of how do we actually sell these ideas to the other 95 percent of the population. And I think that the inclusion of climate justice and those ideas is import-ant, is incredibly beneficial, but it's not beneficial if it's just us patting ourselves on the back and feeling good about having agreed on this—it needs to be about changing people's minds outside of our movement who don't currently agree with us.

The danger of co-optation exists in any movement, but one of our core claims is that, even with its more reform-oriented public messaging, divestment still builds important system-transforming potential for the left.

Divestment Campaigns and the Transformation of Political Consciousness

According to Gorz, non-reformist reforms should disrupt the capitalist status quo in ways that benefit socialist forces and broader system change. Given the fossil fuel industry's integral position in global capitalism, divestment's efforts to undermine its power have the potential to disturb the balance of the system. Our interviews reveal how the movement develops a critical assessment of the extent to which the fossil fuel industry has captured public institutions, including universities. Interviewees described how their campaigns had exposed the lack of democratic transparency and responsiveness in university decision-making processes and had demonstrated that administrative bodies are often more beholden to external donors than to university constituents. In July 2015, for example, members of Divest Dal began filing freedom of information requests to investigate Dalhousie's relationship with major oil and gas companies. Their probe revealed that during the period when the administration was deciding on the motion to divest its endowment, it was also negotiating a new donor agreement with Shell Canada (Cousins 2015). A report in the *National Observer* the following spring revealed that Shell had donated $1.9 million to Dalhousie over the past decade and quoted the university's dean of science as saying that he had been informed by a senior executive at Shell that the company was monitoring the divestment movement and "would look unfavorably on any university that divested" when it came to future donations (Mandel 2016).

Organizers reported that this experience alerted them to the power that corporations, and fossil fuel companies in particular, exert in the public realm. This knowledge heightened their commitment to divestment, but it also taught them how influence is wielded in the world beyond the university. As Stephen, a Divest Dal organizer who helped to file the freedom of information requests and launch the story about Dalhousie's relationship with Shell, pointed out,

> Many of the battles that we're fighting in our communities, in our municipalities, in our provinces or states, and with our federal governments are pretty analogous to the fights we have with our universities' administrations. So, when we find ourselves in the "real world" after our university experiences, we have a toolkit for how to work with one another.

Campaigns to change investment practices at public universities serve to illustrate the disproportionate influence of concentrated economic power at universities and in the broader society. Beyond that, however, such learning can transform the world views of campaign participants and deepen their understanding of why such power is arguably the biggest barrier to addressing both social injustices and the problem of climate change.

Gorz also argues that non-reformist reforms should prefigure the new system by building popular power in the process of fighting for the reform. Divestment challenges individualistic approaches to social change and builds concrete, transferable skills in collective organizing—thus aligning with Gorz's emphasis on building popular power in the course of struggle. As Mangat, Dalby, and Paterson (2018, 190) point out, the discourse surrounding divestment contributes to "a distinct repoliticisation of climate change" through the emphasis it places on "questions of power, legitimacy and conflict, that is, properly political questions." The connection they draw between divestment campaigns and a politicized perspective on environmentalism was borne out in our interviews. Organizers from several different campaigns discussed the role that the divestment movement plays in countering the tendency of mainstream environmentalism to promote individual actions as solutions to collective problems. As Sinead, from the U of T, argued,

> One of the things neoliberal ideology has accomplished is individual-
> izing climate change solutions to very consumer-based actions. And I
> think that's made it very easy for people to feel complacent and feel like
> they're doing their part. Like recognizing that climate change is bad
> but feeling like they're doing their part by buying recycled clothing. So
> I think divestment makes it a collective response, and makes it so that
> institutions need to respond and do something, not just as individuals
> changing their lifestyle. I think that's valuable.

Another organizer, Kate, from UBC, echoed this point, commenting that "the kind of environmental work that so many people are doing I find tends not to be subversive in that it encourages small-scale changes, like behavioural change and planting gardens and encouraging people to recycle, over the kind of systemic large-scale changes that we need to see if we are going to actually challenge climate change." Similarly, Laura, from Divest Dal, shared her view that divestment "shifts the conversation away from just environmentalism, or more individual actions, to bigger issues and more system change." Engaging in collective action that targets concentrations of economic power thus provokes a broader challenge to individualized and entrepreneurial approaches to addressing climate change and other environmental problems.

Given that the prominence of climate justice perspectives and anti-capitalist analysis in the divestment movement has attuned participants to the need for structural change, the movement has served as a training ground for more radical forms of critique. Gorz's third defining feature of non-reformist reforms is that they need to lay the groundwork for deeper transformations in the future. The training in radical politics provided by the divestment movement matches this criteria. For U of T organizer Ben, divestment changed his politics. "My priorities are definitely more about challenging white supremacy and challenging capitalism and building across movements," he said. "We need a cross-sectoral movement that uses a new economy approach. We have to be working with people who are affected by carding and police violence and linking that in a common fight to change the economy." Like Ben, many student organizers talked about how participating in the divestment movement helped them to recognize and confront white, heteropatriarchal dominance in the environmental movement and how these struggles are integral to transforming capitalism. Kate summarized these intersections well. "Environmentalism tends to be a very exclusive and classed movement," she noted, and then went on to say,

> Climate justice has forced me to think about the privilege that I hold as an organizer, and the ways that I act out that privilege in the work that I do. And within the movement itself, it's opened my eyes to the fact that we need to be better at standing in solidarity, at being allies to marginalized communities, and at breaking down the structures of colonialism, and patriarchy, and capitalism, that underlie climate change.

The movement provided a space in which students came to recognize their own positions of privilege and began to work on building inclusive and genuinely transformative movements.

Many of the students to whom we spoke specifically reflected on how the movement strengthens the ability of participants to engage in collective action. Joanna, for example, commented that "there's a culture of training and mentoring—we don't always do it well, but it's definitely there." She continued,

> I look at the amount of campaigners and organizers that have come out of the Divest Dal group, and look at the cool, insane powerful things that people are doing, whether it's here or across the country. And I think a lot of people, myself included, gained this power and understanding that we have the tools within us and the power to act. So I think Divest Dal, and divestment campaigns more widely, have done that better than any other thing I've seen in this place, in this city.

Her perspective affirms that the movement-building practices employed are integral to divestment's political value. The sense of self-transformation and self-empowerment that organizers expressed resonates with an insight from Stuart Hall, who insists that we think more about the mobilization of popular forces. Hall (1987, 21) argues that "people become empowered by doing something: first of all about their immediate troubles; then, the power expands their political capacities and ambitions, so that they begin to think again about what it might be like to rule the world." In this way, divestment is a kind of "entry project" (see Brie 2010) that provides space for self-transformation, where participants constantly refine their political values and organizing skills.

At least some of the many hundreds of young people engaged in divestment organizing across Canada, as well as the many thousands in the global movement, will bring the transformative world views developed in the campaign to other careers, political activity, volunteer work, or future organizing. Katie, who organizes in support of divestment at the national level, calls the movement a "gateway drug." According to her, divestment organizing is the "first of many things that people will get involved with once they take that pill and their minds are open to the reality of what climate justice means." The North American environmental movement appears poised to shift left, thanks to the influx of a new generation of organizers trained in the importance of challenging concentrations of power with collective action.

Fossil Fuel Divestment as a Non-reformist Reform?

We have been arguing that the fossil fuel divestment movement has considerable transformative potential. As we noted earlier, Gorz offers three principal criteria for distinguishing a non-reformist reform from a neo-capitalist one. The first is that a non-reformist reform should disturb "the balance of the system, and profit by this disturbance to prepare the (revolutionary) process of the transition to socialism" (Gorz 1968, 119). By helping to speed the transition away from fossil fuels—capitalism's primary energy source—divestment could have greater impact than is first apparent. The growing body of literature on "fossil capitalism," to which the present volume contributes, helps to clarify how integral fossil fuels are to capitalist production, exchange, and profit-making (Altvater 2007, 2016; Huber 2013; Malm 2016). While it is possible that alternative energies can meet these needs without requiring a fundamental transformation in capitalism itself (Jacobson and Delucchi

2009), the need to radically shift energy systems will necessarily disturb "the balance of the system."

The divestment movement has not yet advocated for alternative forms of ownership with the same force with which it insists upon energy alternatives. The climate justice movement, including the campaign for divestment, needs to engage further with the ownership question. But we see the opposition to white supremacy and heteropatriarchy that exists within the divestment movement as equally important to ownership in the transition away from capitalism. As Sara Ahmed (2015) writes, "Capitalism is . . . identity politics," in which "the few become the universe/universal," a universal that is "handy" for accumulation because "it makes others into the hands, helping hands, those who have to help reproduce the very system that reproduces their own subordination, or risk becoming unhandy hands." By this definition, identity politics—often maligned as divisive—is a necessary, but insufficient, aspect of anti-capitalism, just as, in our view, questions of ownership are necessary but, on their own, insufficient.

Gorz's second criterion for non-reformist reforms is that they decentralize decision-making power away from economic elites. He encourages anti-capitalists to prefigure the socialist alternative by pursuing reforms that grow autonomous power for workers, students, and other popular constituencies. The campus-based divestment movement has helped students better to understand the elitist governance regimes that control endowment funds at public universities. Likewise, it has worked to highlight the limited say that public-sector workers have over the management of their own pension capital. And it continues to demand that investment capital be accountable to more than returns. Yet the movement has yet to take the next step and systematically advocate for greater student control over endowments and greater worker control over specific pension-fund investments. Again, such developments remain possible, however, especially if more voices internal to the movement are advocating for it.

Finally, the movement satisfies Gorz's third criterion by having ambitions beyond divestment itself: non-reformist reforms need to be undertaken as "dynamic phases in a process of struggle, not as resting stages" (Gorz 1968, 118). According to Simon, from Divest Dal,

> There are lots of people in divestment campaigns that are critical of capitalism, myself included, and that's embraced. . . . It's a motivating factor, but no one thinks that "once we divest, we'll have really stuck it

to capitalism." But, in the same breath, once we divest we won't have stuck it to colonialism, we won't have stuck it to oppression: we will have done something good in a way that has been good.

Divestment here is seen as a step on a path toward more systemic change. For Gorz, it is also important that movements use reform struggles to build momentum toward socialist transformation. Not all divestment organizers, even the anti-capitalists, identify as socialists. And yet there was an overriding sense among the majority of those we interviewed that capitalism needs to be fundamentally reworked and that divestment is only one small step in that direction.

Conclusion

Gorz emphasizes the processual nature of political struggle. While he does offer criteria for recognizing non-reformist reforms—criteria that the divestment movement partially meets at present—he acknowledges that distinguishing between neo-capitalist and non-reformist reforms is difficult and that what might appear merely reformist at one point could, under the right conditions, develop radical potential. His emphasis on struggle as an evolving process raises an age-old question that we on the left must constantly ask: "What is to be done?" That is, how do we get from where we are today to where we want to be? The divestment movement is one site where answers are being worked out. Participants are coming to understand the toxic effects of concentrated economic power and how, in a regime of obstruction, this power is wielded so as to block both university divestment decisions *and* climate legislation. Our research also suggests that the movement is honing the collective-organizing skills that participants need to confront concentrated power, while at the same time deepening their conviction that transformative social and political change is truly possible. As socialist thinkers such as Gorz, Hall, and Smucker remind us, the social forces necessary to confront entrenched power structures do not emerge overnight. And such social forces also do not easily dislodge the centuries of heteropatriarchal and racist social relations that still permeate society, including progressive movements. Determining what should be done requires diligent, thoughtful effort.

As our research revealed, while divestment organizers clearly saw a need for systemic changes to capitalist social relations, they also understood the pragmatic need for strategic manoeuvring, recognizing that one does not move from here to there overnight. Aiming to reach a broad audience, the divestment movement strategically toggles between financial and ethical arguments. This tightrope act is dangerous. Yet the risk of co-optation—of the liberal and possibly even neoliberal absorption of environmentalist-leftist tactics and demands—is ever present, especially if one is attempting to reach beyond the choir. All we can do is remain alert to where and when a strategy is being deflected or, alternatively, making real gains. In the present case, if the financial argument for divestment does achieve broad acceptance, becoming "mainstream," then this is not a sign of failure but rather a signal that the movement has served its purpose: it would mean that fossil fuels are now regarded as a bad investment, which would in turn mean that the energy transition has advanced considerably. It would also signal that the climate justice movement needs to find a new strategic target, a new approach. Sadly, we are not there yet. Still, it is worth reminding ourselves that divestment will not be a suitable tactic forever and that we should think about where the campus-based climate justice movement could go next.

This means thinking harder about where we want to end up. That is, what is the longer-term goal? While many student organizers were strongly critical of capitalism, their vision of what they hoped for remained blurry: they had not worked out what this anti-capitalist future might look like in terms of concrete social relations, including the shape and role of the state. Greater engagement with anti-colonial, socialist, and eco-socialist thinkers could help organizers to move beyond the ecological boundaries of climate change and to formulate demands grounded in more than just the need to remain under the 1.5°C limit. In the meantime, we see two promising directions for divestment campaigns, directions that reinforce the shift toward system transformation.

One lies in deepening existing solidarities with Indigenous resurgence movements that have been at the forefront of efforts to block new fossil fuel infrastructure in Canada, such as the Northern Gateway, Energy East, Trans Mountain, and Coastal GasLink pipelines. After the Standing Rock protest against the Dakota Access Pipeline was broken up by US authorities in 2017, Indigenous activists opened up a divestment front, encouraging people to remove their holdings from banks invested in the pipeline. This campaign is part of Mazaska Talks, a broader Indigenous effort to divest from banks financing pipeline proposals on Turtle Island.[4] In the wake of the Truth and Reconciliation Commission, universities in Canada are presently striving to

"Indigenize" their curricula and operations. Now is an opportune time for divestment organizers to broadcast the mismatch between these actions and university investments that finance neo-colonial incursions onto Indigenous lands (Rowe et al. 2019).

The second promising direction is the Green New Deal that was launched into mainstream political discourse in the United States in mid-November 2018, when youth activists from the Sunrise Movement held a sit-in in the office of Democratic Party leader Nancy Pelosi, in hopes of spurring immediate and definitive action on climate change. Their sit-in was joined by democratic socialist and newly elected congresswoman Alexandria Ocasio-Cortez. Three months later, Ocasio-Cortez, alongside Democratic Senator Ed Markey, tabled the Green New Deal Resolution in Congress, which drew on the vision advanced by the Sunrise Movement (Friedman 2019). The Sunrise activists describe the Green New Deal as a plan "to mobilize every aspect of American society to 100% clean and renewable energy" and to "guarantee living-wage jobs for anyone who needs one," as well as to build "a just transition for both workers and frontline communities—all in the next 10 years."[5] The resolution itself calls on the US government to transform the American economy and society through a massive ten-year government effort "to get to net-zero GHG emissions through a fair and just transition for communities and workers" and "to create millions of good, high-wage jobs and ensure security and economic prosperity for all people of the United States."[6]

In addition to disincentives such as a robust carbon tax, realizing such goals will require extensive public investments in infrastructure upgrades, public transportation, and clean energy development. Policies and programs designed to support the shift to clean energy would open up new opportunities for investors (including those responsible for managing university endowments, public-sector pension funds, and sovereign wealth funds). The divestment movement will be better positioned to make common cause with the labour movement if it is helping to articulate a concrete vision for a just transition, one that includes good jobs and secure retirement savings (see Brown et al. 2019).

One of the founders of the Sunrise Movement, Varshini Prakash, came out of the fossil fuel divestment movement at the University of Massachusetts Amherst (Klein 2019). Indeed, many of the organizers working toward a Green New Deal in Canada and the United States gained invaluable political experience through their work with divestment campaigns (Adler-Bell

2019). Beyond serving as training grounds, divestment campaigns can link their existing calls for private reinvestment in clean energy to the priorities of the Green New Deal, such as massive public investments that transform the energy system while also addressing poverty and unemployment. Both private and public capital need to be radically reallocated if we hope to tackle the climate challenge successfully. The divestment movement is ideally positioned to articulate how new private investment opportunities for endowment funds and pension funds can be opened up by new public spending under the auspices of a Green New Deal (Parenti 2019).

The assumption underlying the divestment movement is that if enough institutions of record—universities, churches, charitable trusts—withdraw their financial support for fossil fuels, this will reduce the social power of the industry and create space for the transformative system change needed to avoid climate catastrophe. The fact that the bold vision for a Green New Deal has quickly gained popular appeal suggests that the divestment movement has already changed the conversation around climate change. The fact remains, however, that the concentrated power of the fossil fuel industry is the single greatest impediment to achieving a just transition such as that envisioned by the Green New Deal. Continuing to push for divestment not only on university campuses but also with pension funds and other institutional investors thus remains a crucial front in collective bids for system change.

Notes

1. Post by Richard Smith, January 22, 2018, "Discussion on Divestment," System Change Not Climate Change (SCNCC) Community Forum, https://scncc.net/threads/discussion-on-divestment.260/.
2. "1000+ Divestment Commitments," Go Fossil Free, n.d., accessed March 10, 2020, https://gofossilfree.org/divestment/commitments/#.
3. For example, in 2017, Leigh Phillips, a socialist author who has written for the *Guardian* and *Jacobin*, visited Divest UVic's Facebook page in 2017. "Divestment campaigns," she wrote, "are neoliberal distractions at best: 'Don't invest in these corporations, invest in these other corporations instead!'" For Phillips, fighting for divestment "is a total waste of time."
4. In the Lakota language, *mazaska* means "silver"—that is, money. See "About," Mazaska Talks website, n.d., accessed 10 February 2020, https://mazaskatalks.org/about.

5. "What Is the Green New Deal?" Sunrise Movement, n.d, accessed September 14, 2020, https://www.sunrisemovement.org/green-new-deal/.

6. "Recognizing the Duty of the Federal Government to Create a Green New Deal," H. Res. 109, 116th Cong., 1st sess., February 7, 2019, https://www.congress.gov/116/bills/hres109/BILLS-116hres109ih.pdf, 5.

References

Adler-Bell, Sam. 2019. "The Story Behind the Green New Deal's Meteoric Rise." *New Republic*, February 6, 2019. https://newrepublic.com/article/153037/story-behind-green-new-deals-meteoric-rise.

Ahmed, Sara. 2015. "It Is Not the Time for a Party." *feministkilljoys* (blog), May 13, 2015. https://feministkilljoys.com/2015/05/13/it-is-not-the-time-for-a-party/.

Altvater, Elmar. 2007. "The Social and Natural Environment of Fossil Capitalism." *Socialist Register* 43, no. 1: 37–59.

———. 2016. "The Capitalocene, or, Geoengineering Against Capitalism's Planetary Boundaries." In *Anthropocene or Capitalocene? Nature, History, and the Crisis of Capitalism*, edited by Jason W. Moore, 138–52. Oakland, CA: PM Press.

Ansar, Atif, Ben Caldecott, and James Tilbury. 2013. "Stranded Assets and the Fossil Fuel Divestment Campaign: What Does Divestment Mean for the Valuation of Fossil Fuel Assets?" Stranded Asset Programme, Smith School of Enterprise and the Environment, University of Oxford. https://www.smithschool.ox.ac.uk/publications/reports/SAP-divestment-report-final.pdf.

Bond, Patrick. 2012. *Politics of Climate Justice: Paralysis Above, Movement Below*. Durban, SA: University of KwaZulu-Natal Press.

Bratman, Eve, Kate Brunette, Deirdre C. Shelly, and Simon Nicholson. 2016. "Justice Is the Goal: Divestment as Climate Change Resistance." *Journal of Environmental Studies Science* 6, no. 4: 667–90.

Brie, Michael. 2010. "Entry Projects to a Politics of Solidarity: A Radical Practice Test of Counter Hegemony in Times of the Crisis of Neo-liberal Financial Market Capitalism." Policy Paper, Rosa Luxemburg Foundation, Brussels. https://www.rosalux.eu/kontext/controllers/document.php/40.9/1/2e6e1a.pdf.

Brown, Keith Brower, Jeremy Gong, Matt Huber, and Jamie Munro. 2019. "A Real Green New Deal Means Class Struggle." *Jacobin*, March 21, 2019. https://jacobinmag.com/2019/03/green-new-deal-class-struggle-organizing.

CBC News. 2019. "UBC Votes to Divest $380M from Fossil Fuels, but Students Demand More." *CBC News*, November 24, 2019. https://www.cbc.ca/news/canada/british-columbia/ubc-divestment-vote-1.5371719.

Collard, Rosemary-Claire, Jessica Dempsey, and James Rowe. 2016. "Re-regulating Socioecologies Under Neoliberalism." In *The Handbook of Neoliberalism*, edited by Simon Springer, Kean Birch, and Julie MacLeavy, 469–80. New York: Routledge.

Cousins, Ben. 2015. "Dalhousie to Shell Out for Donation." *Chronicle Herald*, April 9, 2015.

Dale, Gareth, Manu V. Mathai, and Jose A. Puppim de Oliveira. 2016. *Green Growth: Ideology, Political Economy and the Alternatives.* London: Zed Books.

Daub, Shannon, and Zoë Yunker. 2017. "BC's Last Climate 'Leadership' Plan Was Written in Big Oil's Boardroom (Literally)." *Policy Note* (blog). Canadian Centre for Policy Alternatives, BC Office. September 18, 2017. http://www.policynote.ca/climate-leadership-plan-big-oils-boardroom/.

Dempsey, Jessica. 2016. *Enterprising Nature: Economics, Markets, and Finance in Global Biodiversity Politics.* New York: Wiley.

Foster, John Bellamy. 2013. "The Fossil Fuels War." *Monthly Review* 65, no. 4 (September 1, 2013). https://monthlyreview.org/2013/09/01/fossil-fuels-war/.

Friedman, Lisa. 2019. "What Is the Green New Deal? A Climate Proposal, Explained," *New York Times*, February 21, 2019. https://www.nytimes.com/2019/02/21/climate/green-new-deal-questions-answers.html.

Goodman, Amy. 2013. "Will 350.org Fossil Fuel Divestment Campaign Be Key Tactic in 2013 Battle over Climate Change?" *Democracy Now*, January 2, 2013. https://www.democracynow.org/2013/1/2/will_350org_fossil_fuel_divestment_campaign.

Gorz, André. 1967. *Strategy for Labor: A Radical Proposal.* Translated by Martin A. Nicolaus and Victoria Ortiz. Boston: Beacon Press.

———. 1968. "Reform and Revolution." *Socialist Register* 5: 111–43. http://www.socialistregister.com/index.php/srv/article/view/5272/2173.

Grady-Benson, Jessica, and Brinda Sarathy. 2015. "Fossil Fuel Divestment in US Higher Education: Student-Led Organising for Climate Justice." *Local Environment: The International Journal of Justice and Sustainability* 21, no. 6: 661–81.

Hall, Stuart. 1987. "Gramsci and Us." *Marxism Today*, June 1987, 16–21. http://www.banmarchive.org.uk/collections/mt/pdf/87_06_16.pdf.

Hartig, Hannah. 2019. "Stark Partisan Divisions in Americans' Views of Socialism, Capitalism." Pew Research Center. June 25, 2019. https://www.pewresearch.org/fact-tank/2019/06/25/stark-partisan-divisions-in-americans-views-of-socialism-capitalism/.

Harvey, David. *The New Imperialism.* Oxford: Oxford University Press, 2005.

Huber, Matthew T. 2013. *Lifeblood: Oil, Freedom, and the Forces of Capital.* Minneapolis: University of Minnesota Press.

Jacobson, Mark Z., and Mark A. Delucchi. 2009. "A Plan to Power 100 Percent of the Planet with Renewables." *Scientific American*, November 1, 2009. https://www.scientificamerican.com/article/a-path-to-sustainable-energy-by-2030/.

Klein, Naomi. 2014. *This Changes Everything: Capitalism vs. the Climate*. Toronto: Knopf Canada.

Klein, Ezra. 2019. "'No Permanent Friends, No Permanent Enemies': Inside the Sunrise Movement's Plan to Save Humanity." *Vox*, July 31, 2019. https://www.vox.com/ezra-klein-show-podcast/2019/7/31/20732041/varshini-prakash-sunrise-movement-green-new-deal.

Magdoff, Fred, and John Bellamy Foster. 2011. *What Every Environmentalist Needs to Know About Capitalism: A Citizen's Guide to Capitalism and the Environment*. New York: Monthly Review Press.

Malm, Andreas. 2016. *Fossil Capital: The Rise of Steam Power and the Roots of Global Warming*. London: Verso.

Mandel, Charles. 2016. "How Big Oil Seeps into Canadian Academia." *National Observer*, April 27, 2016. https://www.nationalobserver.com/2016/04/27/news/how-big-oil-seeps-canadian-academia.

Mangat, Rupinder, Simon Dalby, and Matthew Paterson. 2018. "Divestment Discourse: War, Justice, Morality and Money." *Environmental Politics* 27, no. 2: 187–208.

McKibben, Bill. 2012. "Global Warming's Terrifying New Math." *Rolling Stone*, July 19, 2012. www.rollingstone.com/politics/news/global-warmings-terrifying-new-math-20120719.

Mohai, Paul, David Pellow, and J. Timmons Roberts. 2009. "Environmental Justice." *Annual Review of Environment and Resources* 34: 405–30.

Nathanson, Rebecca. 2012. "Doing the Math Better: A Talk with Christian Parenti." *The Nation*, December 5, 2012. www.thenation.com/blog/171597/doing-math-better-talk-christian-parenti.

Oreskes, Naomi, and Erik M. Conway. 2011. *Merchants of Doubt: How a Handful of Scientists Obscured the Truth on Issues from Tobacco Smoke to Global Warming*. New York: Bloomsbury Press.

Parenti, Christian. 2012. "Problems with the Math: Is 350's Carbon Divestment Campaign Complete?" *Huffington Post*, November 29, 2012. www.huffingtonpost.com/christian-parenti/carbon-divestment-_b_2213124.html.

——. 2013. "A Worthy Goal, but a Suspect Method." *New York Times*, January 27, 2013. www.nytimes.com/roomfordebate/2013/01/27/is-divestment-an-effective-means-of-protest/a-worthy-goal-but-a-suspect-method.

——. 2019. "Make Corporations Pay for the Green New Deal." *Jacobin*, March 13, 2019. https://jacobinmag.com/2019/03/green-new-deal-private-investment-energy.

Rowe, James K. 2005. "Corporate Social Responsibility as Business Strategy." In *Globalization, Governmentality and Global Politics: Regulation for the Rest of Us?* edited by Ronnie D. Lipschutz and James K. Rowe, 130–71. New York: Routledge.

Rowe, James K., Lisa Chalykoff, Jeff Corntassel, and Colin Goldblatt. 2019. "Why UVic Faculty Voted Massively to Divest From Fossil Fuels." *The Tyee*, December 23, 2019. https://thetyee.ca/Opinion/2019/12/23/UVic-Faculty-Vote-Divest-Fossil-Fuels/.

Satgar, Vishwas. 2018. "The Climate Crisis and Systemic Alternatives." In *The Climate Crisis: South African and Global Democratic Eco-socialist Alternatives*, edited by Vishwas Satgar, 1–28. Johannesburg: Wits University Press.

Schlosberg, David, and Lisette Collins. 2014. "From Environmental to Climate Justice: Climate Change and the Discourse of Environmental Justice." *WIREs Climate Change* 5, no. 3: 359–74.

Smith, Richard. 2015. *Green Capitalism: The God That Failed*. Bristol: World Economics Association.

Smucker, Jonathan Matthew. 2017. *Hegemony How-To: A Roadmap for Radicals*. Chico, CA: AK Press.

Steverman, Ben. 2017. "Get Rid of Capitalism? Millennials Are Ready to Talk About It." *Bloomberg*, November 6, 2017. https://www.bloomberg.com/news/articles/2017-11-06/get-rid-of-capitalism-millennials-are-ready-to-talk-about-it.

Vice-President Finance and Operations, UBC (University of British Columbia). 2020. "Update: Next Steps Following Climate Emergency Declaration and Commitment to Divestment." January 10, 2020. https://vpfo.ubc.ca/2020/01/ubc-update-moving-toward-divestment/.

18 Conclusion

Prospects for Energy Democracy in the Face of Passive Revolution

William K. Carroll

This book has mapped the relations and contours of a powerful regime of obstruction within contemporary Canada. In conclusion, I take stock of what we have learned and reflect on the implications for crafting a socially just escape route from impending climate catastrophe.

Rooted in the political economy of fossil capitalism—and conjoined with a panoply of hegemonic practices that reach into civil and political society and into Indigenous communities whose land claims and world views challenge state-mandated property rights—the regime is driven by the quest for profit through the carbon extraction that continues to fuel capital accumulation globally. As this book has shown, the regime combines several modalities of power—economic, political, and cultural—that operate through a variety of channels (see figure I.1, in the introduction).

Antonio Gramsci's thinking on capitalism and hegemony can be helpful in coming to grips with these interrelated modalities. Capital accumulation is the source of corporate power, in that it appropriates wealth from labour and nature and lodges it in the hands of a tiny elite: leading investors and corporate executives. But, as Gramsci emphasized, economic power is itself

Portions of this chapter were previously published in "Fossil Capitalism, Climate Capitalism, Energy Democracy: The Struggle for Hegemony in an Era of Climate Crisis," in *Socialist Studies / Études socialistes* 14, no. 1 (2020): 1–26. They are reprinted here by permission of the journal.

underwritten and legitimated by power resident in political and cultural practices. To the extent that they cohere as a way of life, these economic, political, and cultural relations form the institutional and ideological foundations for what Gramsci called an *historical bloc*—the basis of a stable regime. Discussing Gramsci's concept, Ngai-Ling Sum and Bob Jessop point out that

> the historical bloc reflects 'the necessary reciprocity between structure and superstructure.' This reciprocity is realized through specific intellectual, moral and political practices. These translate narrow sectoral, professional, or local (in his terms, 'economic-corporate') interests into broader 'ethico-political' ones. Thus the ethico-political not only helps to co-constitute economic structures but also provides them with their rationale and legitimacy. (Sum and Jessop 2013, 199, quoting Gramsci 1971, 366)

The various studies collected herein have mapped the relations and practices that position fossil capital within "the decisive nucleus of economic activity" (Gramsci 1971, 161) while legitimating continued carbon extraction as business-as-usual. In the economic field, we have mapped the *operational* power of management, flowing through a chain of command within an "oligopolistic bloc" of a few large corporations (chapter 1) and wielded along commodity chains that are also "corridors of power" (chapter 2). Our mapping of who owns leading Canada-based fossil-capital corporations revealed a network of *strategic* power that is concentrated among major shareholders (corporate and personal) and institutional investors, amounting to a massive centralization of economic power in the hands of private investors accountable only to themselves (chapter 4). Complementing the power of ownership is the *allocative* power of finance. Canada's financial sector is dominated by five big banks. As lenders to and shareholders in fossil fuel companies, the banks enable the accumulation of fossil capital while appropriating a portion of the surplus, and some of them also share directors with the same firms (Daub and Carroll 2016). As financial capital "digests" the looming climate catastrophe, biospheric degeneration gets converted into risk factors that help steer accumulation without addressing the scale and scope of the ecological crisis itself (chapter 3). These economic power modalities are integrated within a complex circuitry in which capital metamorphoses across the productive, commercial, and financial forms initially identified by Marx (1967).

As for the *hegemonic* modalities of corporate power, my analysis of the fossil-capital elite in chapter 5 reveals a cohesive corporate community, embedded in a transnational elite network, that enables big business to reach a working consensus on long-term goals and vision and, on that basis, to speak politically with a single voice and lead. The fossil-capital elite is fully integrated with financial and other fractions of corporate capital in Canada, participating in what Nico Poulantzas (1973, 141) called a relatively integrated "power bloc."

Part of what makes the elite network a power bloc, and complementing this elite integration, is the *reach* of corporate power into the public sphere. The extensive elite network extending from fossil-capital boardrooms into key knowledge-producing sectors of civil society (mapped in chapter 6) offers many channels for corporate influence in constructing the public interest.

Fossil Capital Within the Hegemonic Bloc

As it organizes a consensus for business-as-usual, not only among corporate leaders but more widely through civil and political society, the power bloc obstructs democratic alternatives that jeopardize immediate capitalist interests in redeeming past investments and securing new revenue streams. But the hegemony of fossil capital and its allies extends well beyond the leading echelons—the power bloc itself—as we have seen in the cases of online pro-industry activism and small-town industry boosterism (chapters 7 and 11).

This raises the issue of how the regime of obstruction is organized not only through modalities of economic and political-cultural power but also on distinct *scales*—from households and families up to "the historic blocs underpinning particular states [that] become connected through the mutual interests and ideological perspectives of social classes in different countries—portending 'an incipient world society'" (Cox 1987, 7). Indeed, the regime operates on multiple scales, from the everyday to the global. Table 18.1 offers some key instances (discussed below) but is not intended as anything like a complete inventory.

Table 18.1. The regime of obstruction as expressed at different scales

	Key instances
Everyday life	Fossil-fuelled consumer capitalism as a way of life: the privatized geography of automobility and suburbanization
Local community	Civic privatism/boosterism and hegemonic community economic identity; Indigenous ambivalence
Institutions	Entrenchment of fossil interests in institutions of knowledge production, etc.: petro-universities and state-subsidized R&D
Subnational	Alberta as petro-state, industry boosterism in extractive and sacrifice zones
National	Defining the "national interest," through elite policy planning and online extractive populist networks
Transnational	Global governance and transnational policy planning to manage crisis and maintain fossil-capital predominance

Matthew Huber's (2013) study of postwar suburbanized consumerism remains a key work in revealing how fossil-capital hegemony is accomplished in everyday life. Without even getting behind the wheel, anyone who views an SUV commercial experiences automobility (vicariously) as empowering and liberating, and, although home ownership is out of reach for many, the single detached house continues to function as a symbolic representation of personal sovereignty. The hegemony of fossil capital is both deeply ingrained in everyday pleasures, identities, and aspirations and reinforced through media content that trumpets corporate social responsibility while often vilifying critics.

With regard to local communities, Emily Eaton and Simon Enoch's study of "hegemonic community economic identity" in small-town Saskatchewan (chapter 11) shows how the allocative power of corporate funders of local amenities combines with the discursive power of industry-propagated frames of reference to produce a hegemony deeply lodged in an acceptance of industry narratives and an othering of those who challenge the environmental viability of business-as-usual. In Canada, some local communities are Indigenous, and their strong claims to land and self-governance have always troubled a hegemonic bloc based in settler colonialism. Until relatively recently, individuals deemed to be members of First Nations under the Indian Act were considered wards of the state and were excluded from full citizenship rights. It was only in 1960, when Parliament passed the Canada Elections Act, that "registered Indians" were granted the right to vote and only in 2011 that

First Nations individuals finally received full access to Canada's human rights protection. Genocidal policies mandated by the Indian Act, which succeeded for many decades in marginalizing and silencing Indigenous voices, have bequeathed a legacy of injustice that in our era spurs resistance and demands reparation. Resurgent Indigenous politics speaks in an ethico-political voice, championing a holistic vision of the health and balance in which humanity recovers a harmonious relationship with the rest of nature.

Yet, as Angele Alook and her colleagues document in chapter 12, Indigenous workers in extractive zones often have little choice but to take lower-rung jobs in the industry, with women doubly marginalized. Moreover, as Cliff Atleo argues in chapter 13, Indigenous struggles for self-determination coexist with capitalism's powerful colonizing capacities, both economic and ideological. In these instances, hegemony is expressed as *Indigenous ambivalence*—a contradictory consciousness situated between the aspiration for Indigenous resurgence and the pragmatic lure of partnership as a means to secure a portion of the wealth that capital and state continue to extract from Indigenous lands. "Partnership" is now presented as a form of self-determination, through which Indigenous peoples can become sovereign subjects in a capitalist way of life in which they are already participants. "Partnership" forms a crucial aspect of the hegemonic project favoured by the Canadian state and capitalist class, as a means of winning effectively permanent consent to capitalist development on Indigenous land.

At a subnational scale, we encounter a diversity of scenarios, shaped by the uneven spatial distribution of carbon resources. In extractive and sacrifice zones, industry boosterism often prevails, with good-news narratives displacing dissent and critique. As Laurie Adkin and others argue (see Adkin 2016), Alberta in particular functions largely as a petro-state. At first blush, British Columbia, currently governed by a social-democratic party that has opposed the expansion of a bitumen pipeline from Alberta to Vancouver, might appear as just the opposite. Yet the ongoing extraction of massive reserves of methane in British Columbia's northeast—under the ideological cover of a mythical notion of liquefied natural gas as a "transition fuel" (Lee 2019)—suggests otherwise, as does the "captured" status of the BC Oil and Gas Commission, which, as Shannon Daub and her colleagues show in chapter 11, rubber-stamps new fossil-capital projects. In Alberta, where fossil capital reigns supreme, the same regulatory capture is evident, but capital's hegemonic reach extends to an industrial-scientific complex that subsidizes corporate profitability by lowering production costs as it also transfuses market values into the public sphere (Carroll, Graham, and Yunker 2018). This industrial-scientific complex exemplifies fossil capital's reach into knowledge-producing institutions, including the universities and research institutes examined in depth in chapter 10 (and, more broadly, in Gray and Carroll 2018).

At the national scale, the struggle for hearts and minds is condensed into contention around the "national interest." In the federal government's 2016 Pan-Canadian Framework on Clean Growth and Climate Change, for example, analyzed in chapter 8, the "national interest" in "clean growth" incorporates the interests of Alberta-centric fossil capital, as well as of financial institutions based in central Canada, while also promising jobs to workers and a healthy environment—in a compelling illustration of the new climate denialism. Yes, we must address a pressing climate crisis and, yes, we must build more pipelines to speed all extractable carbon to market, while also stoking accumulation in the renewable energy sector. This is the thinking that enabled the Trudeau government to reapprove the Trans Mountain Pipeline Expansion on June 18, 2019, the day after it declared a climate emergency (see Hughes 2019). This seemingly incoherent construction of the national interest continues a long tradition of brokerage politics for which the Liberal Party of Canada has been the leading agent. But with right-wing populist governments now installed in Alberta, Saskatchewan, and Ontario, the clean growth framework has been unravelling. The challenges facing the framework illustrate how entrenched fossil-capital interests are within the federated Canadian polity and how low-tax, light-regulation neoliberalism deepens those trenches.

Of course, the practices that maintain an historical bloc for fossil capitalism extend beyond the state-capital nexus (van Apeldoorn, de Graaff, and Overbeek 2017), in both elite and popular registers. The elite networks that reach into knowledge-producing domains of civil society are complemented, in everyday life, by emergent online networks of what Shane Gunster and his colleagues, in chapter 7, term *extractive populism*. In combination, such communities of discourse constitute a petro-bloc "oriented around neoliberal extractivism, ecoskepticism and transnational 'market fundamentalist' epistemic communities" (Neubauer 2017, iii). In contrast to the new climate denialism, extractive populism ignores the need for "climate leadership" altogether. It portrays "ordinary people" as victims of liberal elites who impose their environmental values upon everyone else (Gunster and Saurette 2014) and constructs within online echo chambers a pro-fossil "national interest" grounded in anti-elite resentment.

As political projects, the new climate denialism and extractive populism work in tandem within both policy discourse and popular discourse, the former closely hooked into ruling relations and the latter posing as "outsider" to power. Together, they delimit the boundaries of mainstream discussion, posing a choice between "climate action" inadequate to the scale of the crisis and no action at all—and, in the process, contributing to the maintenance of business-as-usual.

Climate Capitalism as Passive Revolution

Notwithstanding the various practices and modalities of power that obstruct meaningful climate action in Canada, changes are afoot, as China and Europe (as well as subnational jurisdictions such as California) open space in the energy mix for renewables and as transnational carbon majors like Shell, BP, and Total write down billions as stranded assets. In a June 2020 report titled *Decline and Fall: The Size and Vulnerability of the Fossil Fuel System*, researchers at the Carbon Tracker Initiative conclude that, as demand for fossil fuels continues its decline, companies "will face major asset write-downs as it becomes clear that high-cost fossil fuel supply and demand infrastructure has limited value" (Bond, Vaughan, and Benham 2020, 46). At the same time, major international financial institutions are choosing to divest from the dirtiest fossil fuels, including Alberta's tar sands (McSheffrey 2017).

This brings us to climate capitalism, an emergent accumulation strategy that "seeks to redirect investments from fossil energy to renewable energy generation so as to foster an ecological modernization of production and reduce greenhouse gas (GHG) emissions" (Sapinski 2015, 268; see also Adkin 2017). The promise of climate capitalism is to shepherd the world to a safe landing without disrupting its essential nucleus in capitalist relations of production. However, the presence of major fossil-capital companies at the heart of the "climate capitalist corporate-policy elite"—that is, those corporate directors who also sit on climate and environmental policy groups—suggests "a weak project of climate capitalism," one in which the transition to sustainable energy production takes place relatively slowly (Sapinski 2015, 273, 276). This gradual shift averts the threat of stranded assets while allowing fossil capital time to expand its control of replacement energy sources (Sapinski 2016, 106).

Climate capitalism faces two challenges, however. For one thing, its pace of change is too slow, compared to the realities of climate breakdown, and, for another, capital's growth imperative essentially precludes a shrinking footprint. In these senses, climate capitalism, closely akin to the "green economy" and "clean growth" thinking that Marc Lee critiques in chapter 14, is the strategic framework behind what we have termed the new climate denialism. Looking ahead, as measures such as carbon taxing and cap-and-trade prove ineffective, the climate-capitalist strategy seems poised to incorporate geoengineering—both carbon capture and storage (CCS) and stratospheric aerosol injection (SAI)—into its action repertoire, with potentially catastrophic ramifications.

SAI has been aptly described as "a mechanism that can relieve (for capital) some of the immediate pressures of the climate crisis and enable a passive revolution from fossil capitalism to green capitalism, blunting the more radical alternatives advanced by the climate justice movement" (Surprise 2018, 1230; see also Mookerjea 2017). Indeed, climate capitalism exemplifies the Gramscian notion of *passive revolution*. Deployed in an organic crisis, when bourgeois hegemony is weakened, passive revolution is "a strategy which allows the bourgeoisie to reorganize its dominance politically and economically" (Sassoon 1982, 134). As Thomas Wanner (2015, 31) suggests, climate capitalism "is the promise of a green capitalism without questioning the underlying dynamics and power relations and causes of unsustainability of this system. On the contrary, the green economy/growth discourse further intensifies the privatisation and marketisation of the fictitious commodity of 'nature,' and perpetuates the myth of limitless growth." Climate capitalism's system-friendly reforms are a formula for continuity in change, managed from above. They appeal to subjectivities already normalized within fossil-fuelled consumer capitalism and portend only minor shifts in capitalism's historical bloc.

Within climate-capitalist rhetoric, Prime Minister Justin Trudeau's mantra "grow the middle class" invokes the reassuringly familiar desire for more of the same (material goods and services), while "clean growth" provides the means to that regnant end. Given fossil capital's weight in both the Canadian economy and the country's power bloc, and as a concession to extractive populist elements, the 2016 Pan-Canadian Framework on Clean Growth and Climate Change melds fossil capitalism with climate capitalism, in the form of robust sales of bitumen while global demand still exists, combined with a gentle program of state support for renewables and other mitigation efforts.

But time is not on this venture's side, as the costs of renewables have already undercut those of carbon. Moreover, evidence strongly indicates that demand for fossil fuels overall reached a peak in 2019, in which case "it is clearly not necessary to build new supply or demand infrastructure" (Bond, Vaughan, and Benham 2020, 43). A recent study (Mercure et al. 2018) charts the likely outcome. As demand for carbon wanes, stranding the assets of high-cost producers, Canada's GDP is projected to plummet (in step with a milder US decline) while Europe and China grow as new centres of climate capitalism.

Meanwhile, efforts are underway to develop and co-opt the organizations and cadres needed in constructing a climate-capitalist historical bloc—whether in state-led climate leadership initiatives or in new state- and industry-supported groups in civil society, such as University of Ottawa–based Smart Prosperity (McCartney 2018; see also Graham 2019) and the McGill University–based Ecofiscal Commission. Concurrently, resurgent right-wing governments in Ontario and Alberta practice a more entrenched obstructionism grounded in extractive populism—complete, in the latter case, with a publicly funded "energy war room" based in Calgary set to crank out rapid responses to fossil capital's critics, with assistance from Postmedia (Bellefontaine 2019; Heydari 2019). Now the epicentre of a retrograde fossil capitalism, Alberta's strident obstructionism is echoed at the federal level by the Conservative Party of Canada, whose base in Alberta is foundational. Whereas the Liberals have pursued a hybrid project to valorize fossil capital while implementing climate-capitalist measures such as taxing carbon, the Conservatives defend fossil capitalism and pay only lip service to climate capitalism (see, for instance, Willcocks 2019). As fossil capital and its allies redouble their obstructive endeavours, prospects for a just transition seem grim, and resistance may face sharper repression.

As several Gramscian scholars have suggested, to counter a passive revolution one must conduct an "anti-passive revolution": a war of position that extends popular-democratic and class struggles "so as to mobilize ever-wider sections of the population for democratic reforms" (Simon 1982, 49; see also Buci-Glucksmann 1979; Sassoon 1982). In that spirit, I want to turn to an alternative, which is currently on the margins of public discourse but not without the prospect of securing practical grounding in the emerging era.

Energy Democracy as Non-reformist Reform

The four essays comprising part three of this volume offer many insights into policy measures that could move Canada toward climate justice (chapter 14), the revelatory role of resistance in illuminating pathways toward such a future (chapter 15), and the challenges of building popular coalitions to counter the power of fossil capital—at key points along the commodity chain (chapter 16) as well as extra-locally, as in the divestment movement (chapter 17). As I noted in this book's introduction, these various initiatives add up to a bundle of non-reformist reforms, not a full-blown project of system change. However, the former are precisely what can, in a process of countering a passive revolution, set the stage for deeper transformation. Clearly, such a process requires coordinated efforts at various sites and scales, converging on a shared vision/ strategy that informs effective public policy.

Energy democracy, a concept grounded in recent European struggles for a just energy transition (Szulecki 2018), offers a point of convergence, pointing us toward a twofold power shift: from fossil fuel power to renewables and from corporate oligarchy to democratic control of economic decisions. A feasible and just alternative to the oligarchic organization of fossil capitalism and climate capitalism, energy democracy has been endorsed by the international trade union movement through Trade Unions for Energy Democracy, an organization whose members include Canada's largest unions and the Canadian Labour Congress. Energy democracy's three overarching goals—"*resisting* the fossil-fuel-dominant energy agenda while *reclaiming* and democratically *restructuring* energy regimes"—inform a strategy that connects the dots between divestment initiatives, Indigenous activism, anti-fracking protests, community solar projects, and so on (Burke and Stephens 2017, 35, 45).

The three projects on offer might be hypothetically charted as follows, with fossil capitalism morphing in the organic crisis into climate capitalism, while an incipient bloc organized around energy democracy forms as an alternative:

Fossil capitalism	Climate capitalism	Energy democracy
organic crisis →	passive revolution	alternative strategy/project

There are signs that such an alternative bloc is emerging. In conjunction with an international workshop on energy democracy held in Amsterdam in

February 2016, participating NGOs formed an international alliance and have created a virtual meeting space, energy-democracy.net, for groups committed to the struggle. The alliance upholds the following core principles:

- *Universal access and social justice*: ending energy poverty while reducing energy consumption and prioritizing the needs of communities, households, and marginalized people
- *Renewable, sustainable, and local energy*: shifting to renewables by leaving fossil fuels in the ground, divesting from fossil fuels, and investing public funds in local renewable energy systems to create thriving communities
- *Public and social ownership*: bringing energy production under democratic control, within new forms of public ownership by municipalities, citizens' collectives, and workers
- *Fair play and creation of green jobs*: building renewable energy through fairly paid, unionized jobs
- *Democratic control and participation*: empowering citizens and workers to participate in energy policy by democratizing governance and instituting complete transparency.

We can recognize in this framing a project that is at once ethico-political, economic, and ecological, that addresses both the forces and relations of production, and that resonates with the concerns of several intersecting movements.

As Stuart Hall (1988) observed, struggles for an alternative hegemony occur on terrain already shaped by the existing hegemony. In this light we can revisit some of the key instances in fossil-capital hegemony, with an eye toward the forms that energy democracy might take at different scales (see table 18.2). In everyday life, politically inflected lifestyle changes and informal networks that reject fossil-fuelled consumerism can foster changes in "common sense" that pull people away from the doxa of oil as "lifeblood" (Huber 2013) and enlarge the popular base for energy democracy.

Within local communities, the decarbonization and decommodification of public transit can have a broader impact beyond individual lifestyles, as can practices such as community gardening that present alternatives to car-boniferous industrial agriculture. Although eco-localism has its limits (Albo 2008), bringing decision making down to local scale, where feasible (also known as the principle of subsidiarity), can open new possibilities for participatory democracy and citizen empowerment. Indigenous resistance to colonization, closely associated with Indigenous resurgence (Coburn and Atleo 2016), can propel Indigenous communities into positions of leadership, in alliance with environmental and other movements, in a principled politics of decolonization.

Table 18.2. Practices of fossil capitalism and energy democracy at different scales

	Instances of fossil-capital hegemony	Practices of energy democracy
Everyday life	Fossil-fuelled consumer capitalism as a way of life, automobility as freedom	Politically inflected lifestyle changes; informal discussion in local and online networks
Local community	Civic privatism/boosterism; Indigenous ambivalence	Free public transit, alliance politics of decolonization and democratization, subsidiarity
Institutions	Entrenchment of fossil interests in institutions of knowledge production, etc.	Reclaiming public institutions, divestment, knowledge, and culture for the people
Subnational	Industry boosterism in extractive and sacrifice zones	Reclaim Alberta, Iron and Earth
National	Contention over the "national interest," through elite policy planning and online extractive populist networks	The Leap, RAVEN (Respecting Aboriginal Values and Environmental Needs), Green New Deal
Transnational	Global governance and transnational policy planning	Trade Unions for Energy Democracy, Indigenous Environmental Network

Meanwhile, as public institutions such as universities begin to divest from fossil capital, they undermine its hegemony. To enhance prospects for energy democracy, institutional investments can be redirected toward post-carbon "solidarity economy" initiatives (Williams 2014), with facilitation from credit unions and (potentially) publicly owned green banks. More broadly, universities, media outlets, and other institutions that have been colonized by corporate power can be reclaimed as public services, as can science and technology, attuning knowledge and culture to the social and political needs of the times.

At subnational scale, the inevitable decline of the tar sands creates openings for contesting hegemony in fossil capital's heartland. Grassroots groups like Reclaim Alberta are calling for a just transition that heals the Earth from carbon extraction's notorious externalities. Reclaim Alberta envisages "a wide-scale, industry-funded reclamation of Alberta's aging and expired oil and gas infrastructure that puts thousands of workers back to work in every corner of the province," while Iron and Earth, led by tar sands workers, has created "a platform to engage in renewable energy development issues, and to empower us to advocate for an energy future we can be proud of creating."

Across Canada, both the Leap Manifesto and the movement it has spawned represent a significant intervention in redefining the national interest that explicitly uses an energy democracy frame. The Manifesto, in particular, is deeply reflective of Indigenous world views. RAVEN (Respecting Aboriginal Values and Environment Needs) provides financial support to assist Indigenous Nations "in lawfully forcing industrial development to be reconciled with their traditional ways of life, and in a manner that addresses global warming or other ecological sustainability challenges." As I write, another important initiative, the Pact for a Green New Deal, has been taking shape in Canada, involving community-based discussions that feed into a bottom-up process to define "what a Green New Deal should look like, to identify commonalities, and to start developing specific proposals." These mutually reinforcing struggles for energy justice contest the notion of a "'national interest' that prioritizes short-term economic gain from finite and polluting resources" (Berman 2018), advocating instead alternative conceptions that prioritize human and ecological well-being.

At transnational scale, hegemonic networks of global governance are countered by networks from below that include the Indigenous Environmental Network and Trade Unions for Energy Democracy. As I argue in greater depth elsewhere (Carroll 2016), such transnational formations are crucial in view of the scale and scope of fossil capitalism's organic crisis—a crisis that cannot be adequately addressed in the absence of a global vision and strategy.

The challenge is to articulate these progressive forces into a coherent bloc that includes energy-sector workers, for whom a just transition must foster "upward-leveling relationships" so that as fossil energy is decommissioned, displaced workers find comparable positions in a rapidly expanding renewable energy sector (Abramsky 2010, 657). As Sean Sweeney and John Treat (2018, 43) argue,

> A Just Transition is possible, but it will have to be *demanded and driven forward* by a broad, democratic movement, with unions playing a key role. There will be no Just Transition without social and political transformation, and such a transformation will be contingent on a successful challenge of existing ownership relations and the expansion of economic democracy at all levels. And there will be no such transformation until unions and their allies fully grasp the fact that such a transformation is both possible and absolutely necessary.

A broad vision of energy democracy can help pull together what might otherwise be siloed movements for green jobs, climate mitigation, moratoriums on fossil fuel development, and greater public and local control over energy decision making (Hess 2018). Because climate breakdown is occurring at global scale, adequate responses will require "some form of energy planning at regional, national, and transnational levels" (Thombs 2019, 165) to wind down the production and use of fossil fuels, complemented by decentralized systems offering direct democratic control. Yet, to encompass a deep transformation, the emerging historical bloc must extend beyond energy democracy per se. In view of the foundational relationship in Canada between colonialism and capitalism, decarbonization and democratization must be conjoined with decolonization, enhancing capacities for Indigenous self-determination. By the same token, the close symbiosis between energy and finance means that a robust energy democracy must bring the financial sector itself under democratic control. Much the same can be said about the need to undo hegemonic corporate power within communications media, to "remake media" by democratizing public communication (Hackett and Carroll 2006).

For André Gorz (1967), non-reformist reforms are steps toward system change that avoid co-optation by disturbing the capitalist status quo in ways that build popular power. Energy democracy is in this sense a bundle of targeted, non-reformist reforms, an "entry project" (Brie 2010) that can open space for democratization and decolonization of economic, political, and cultural life. In such a transformation, corporate power would give way to popular power and participatory planning in production and allocation, to environmental stewardship and authentic reconciliation, and to public communication and inclusive community development.

Toward Democratic Eco-socialism

This volume has mapped the various modalities of corporate power that constitute a regime of obstruction. To contest capitalist hegemony effectively, we will need to address the full spectrum of these modalities. Energy democracy will thus need to be developed in concert with other non-reformist reforms in the workplace, in finance and cultural production, and in the state, in a war of position that adds up to a project of democratic eco-socialism (see Baer 2019; Löwy 2018; Satgar 2018). The "just transition" we need is not simply from fossil fuels but from fossil *capitalism*. To achieve such wide-ranging change, corporate power in its various modalities must give way to democratic alternatives.

As J. P. Sapinski and I have argued, "Corporate power is power-over: over workers, over finance and investment (and thus the future), over communities and governments, over the marginalized and dispossessed, and over ecosystems, which get reduced to 'natural resources' to be extracted at the lowest cost" (2018, 122–23). Yet "power-over" is only one form of social power, predominant within class societies and distinct from both "power-to"—the exercise of one's own agency in shaping one's world and one's self in it—and "power-with," which grows as people gain collective strength through collaboration with peers (VeneKlasen and Miller 2007). Each of the modalities of corporate power mapped in this collection can be transformed from current arrangements, which give the owners and managers of capital power over workers, communities, and states, to democratic alternatives that empower subalterns and foster equitable collaboration, within an ecologically sustainable framework (Carroll and Sapinski 2018, 131).

These ideas resonate with Mario Candeias's notion of "green socialism"—a concept founded on a "transition to *a green-socialist reproductive economy beyond growth*" (2013, 15; emphasis added). Candeias lays out a program for transition that breaks not only from fossil capital but also from capitalism as a way of life by advocating:

the *decentralization* of public decision making and the *remunicipalization* of infrastructure (bringing energy, water, and other utilities under public control);

reclaiming the public sphere and commons by expanding public services and collective consumption;

a shift from top-down operational power and bureaucratic planning to *planning based in economic democracy* and decentralized participation; and

deglobalization, or the recentring of economic activity within domestic economies.

These shifts are convergent with aspirations for energy democracy, but they extend beyond the energy sector. Candeias's Green Socialism proposal also calls for:

the redistribution of wealth through the expansion of different *forms of socialization and social property*; and

the *socialization of investment* through participatory investment decisions.

These measures challenge capital's strategic and allocative power and reject the logic of capitalist accumulation. A just and ecologically sustainable world implies democratic control of investment, which can be initiated through "a network of public banks and the introduction of participatory budgeting at all levels of society" (Candeias 2013, 16).

The program of Green Socialism also has a strong bent toward ecological and feminist values, including:

a shift from production of endlessly accumulating things to enhanced provision of services in *a care economy geared to enriched socio-ecological relations*; and

a *new division of labour addressing gender equity* across four domains of paid employment, family, community, and self-development.

These eight components of the Green Socialism project could, in principle, be implemented in individual countries, rather than worldwide. To bring the transformation to a global scale, Candeias (2013, 19) identifies two key requirements:

> *Global planning regarding resource flows* will be needed to ensure a just distribution of wealth while limiting consumption, as some sectors associated with climate change and the depletion of raw materials shrink while others (particularly the care economy) evolve and expand.

> In a *just transition* that integrates the climate justice and labour movements, the needs of those most harmed by climate crisis must be prioritized.

In Canada, the regime of obstruction has bequeathed political conditions that are not well disposed to this plan. The plan is, in the Canadian context, aspirational. It specifies the necessary changes for moving beyond fossil capitalism into a democratic and ecologically sustainable way of life, but the challenge is to create the political conditions under which the transition becomes widely recognized as both desirable and possible. In our current circumstances, the Green Socialism program offers a yardstick against which we can appraise political projects that seem feasible in the here and now—in particular, initiatives in energy democracy and the Green New Deal. An early skeptic with regard to the transformative potential of the Green New Deal as it initially arose in Europe a decade ago, Candeias (2013, 13) observed that the Green New Deal's failure to address capitalism's relations of class power set it on a course to reproduce capitalism's contradictions, including endless growth and increasing economic disparities (see also Candeias 2011).

Although the European Green Deal (EGD), officially launched by the European Commission in December 2019, is a first step toward carbon neutrality, "the fingerprints of industry, and in particular the fossil fuel industry," are all over it, as the Corporate Europe Observatory (2020) points out. In October 2019, shortly before the official launch, Fossil Free Politics—an alliance in which the Corporate Europe Observatory is a leading member—reported that, over roughly the past decade, the five largest fossil fuel corporations (BP, Chevron, ExxonMobil, Shell, and Total) had together spent upwards of a quarter of a billion euros buying influence at the heart of European decision making (Fossil Free Politics 2019, 4). Moreover, in the first one hundred days after the EGD launch, European Commission members charged with overseeing its development met with industry lobbyists an average of eleven times per week, as opposed to only twice a week with representatives of the public interest (Corporate Europe Observatory 2020). Not surprisingly, the emerging EGD relies heavily on the same measures that are central to the Pan-Canadian Framework on Clean Growth and Climate Change: carbon trading, natural gas as a "transitional fuel," and emissions reductions targets that are "too modest and too slow" (Corporate Europe Observatory 2020).

The Green New Deal movement now emerging in Canada has been germinating along different lines, from the bottom up, emphasizing social justice and decolonization (see MacArthur et al. 2020). Yet the danger of passive revolution—of co-optation into the project of climate capitalism—remains. The Green New Deal resonates precisely because it calls for a new deal within the existing order, sidestepping controversial issues of transformation. To avoid co-optation, advocates of the Green New Deal and their allies will need to incorporate the struggle for energy democracy into their program. As part of that, yet reaching beyond it, the movement will need to devise strategies and policies that erode and replace corporate power over workplaces, finance, culture, and politics with democratic forms, building the conditions for Green Socialism.

Energy democracy and the Green New Deal thus need to be approached not as end goals but as non-reformist reforms impelling a transition to a democratic eco-socialism that incorporates, within an expansive historical bloc, those struggling for gender justice and against racism and ongoing colonization. As Vishwas Satgar (2018, 14) suggests, "A renewed democratic eco-socialism faces squarely the challenge to save human and non-human nature from capitalism's ecocidal logic through a radical practice and conception of democracy as people's power, mediated by an ethics to sustain life." As climate breakdown accelerates, "failure to construct alternatives rooted in new relations of production, exchange, consumption, and livelihoods is likely to have disastrous effects" (Abramsky 2010, 657). Unless we are able to replace corporate power with a participatory-democratic alternative that meets people's needs while healing the Earth, capitalism's ecocidal logic will continue to determine the contours of our lives. And the climate crisis will continue to spin out of control—to our common peril. The stakes are high; the time is short.

Notes

1. In a recent ranking of the world's banks, the five big Canadian banks—Bank of Montreal, Bank of Nova Scotia (Scotiabank), Canadian Imperial Bank of Commerce (CIBC), Royal Bank of Canada, and Toronto-Dominion Bank—numbered among the top twenty-five lenders to fossil-capital companies. The Royal Bank of Canada ranked fifth overall, having lent more than $110 billion to big carbon between 2017 and 2019. Along with JPMorgan Chase, all five big Canadian banks top the league table of lenders to major tar sands production and pipeline companies (Rainforest Action Network et al. 2020, 8–9, 28–29).

2. Until 2008, registered Indians were barred by the Canadian Human Rights Act (CHRA) from filing complaints about discrimination with the Canadian Human Rights Commission, given that section 67 of the CHRA stipulated that the act did not apply to provisions of or pursuant to the Indian Act. In 2008, Bill C-21 repealed section 67, at which point the Indian Act was no longer exempt from the CHRA, but the bill also imposed a three-year "transition period" before complaints could in fact be filed (see CHRC 2011, 3–4). As a result, First Nations were effectively unable to access the amended legislation until June 2011.

3. In June 2020, both BP and Shell slashed the book value of their oil and gas assets by tens of billions of dollars (Kusnetz 2020). Total followed suit at the end of July, writing off $9.3 billion (US$7 billion) in tar sands assets and also cancelling its membership in the Canadian Association of Petroleum Producers—the latter action prompted by "a 'misalignment' between the organization's public positions and those expressed in Total's climate ambition statement announced in May" (Canadian Press 2020).

4. As I write this, BankTrack's ongoing compilation lists twenty-two major financial institutions (none Canadian) that have ended financing for tar sands operations ("Banks and Tar Sands," BankTrack, n.d., accessed July 28, 2020, https://www.banktrack.org/campaign/banks_and_tar_sands_1). These include Deutsche Bank, which declared on July 27, 2020, that it will not finance new projects to explore, produce, transport, or process tar sands bitumen (see Varcoe 2020).

5. These geoengineering schemes have been in development for some time, but the large-scale feasibility of CCS remains unproven, for reasons both of financial costs and of energy consumption. SAI—a solar radiation management (SRM) technology that entails the injection of inorganic particles (notably sulphates) into the atmosphere in order to create a reflective shield against sunlight—has been deemed potentially dangerous on a global scale. Still, SAI is quickly moving from the margins (as a last-resort "Plan B") to the mainstream. As the

climate crisis deepens, it is increasingly likely that SAI will be applied, at least to buy time for a managed transition in which capital's economic nucleus is fully protected. The danger is that capital's rapacious need to expand will require increasing doses of SAI as atmospheric carbon concentration climbs toward 500 parts per million—with possibly catastrophic consequences. Even without the increasing doses, "as with all SRM technologies that only address global surface temperatures, dramatic perturbations in the climate system can be expected if SAI is deployed." Research studies suggest, for example, that sulphate-based SAI techniques "would likely cause droughts in Africa and Asia and endanger the source of food and water for two billion people." "Stratospheric Aerosol Injection (Technology Factsheet)," *Geoengineering Monitor*, June 11, 2018, http://www.geoengineeringmonitor.org/2018/06/stratospheric_aerosol_injection/.

6. "Principles of Energy Democracy," Energy Democracy, n.d., accessed January 28, 2020, https://www.energy-democracy.net/?page_id=870.

7. "The Plan," Reclaim Alberta, n.d., accessed January 28, 2020, http://www.reclaimalberta.ca/the-plan/; "About Us," Iron and Earth, n.d., accessed January 28, 2020, http://www.ironandearth.org/about_us.

8. As the authors of the manifesto write, "Moved by the treaties that form the legal basis of this country and bind us to share the land 'for as long as the sun shines, the grass grows and the rivers flow,' we want energy sources that will last for time immemorial and never run out or poison the land." The Leap Manifesto, 2015, https://leapmanifesto.org/en/the-leap-manifesto/.

9. "About," RAVEN, n.d., accessed January 24, 2020, https://raventrust.com/about/.

10. See "What Did We Hear at the Pact for a New Green Deal Town Halls?" Pact for a New Green Deal, n.d., accessed January 24, 2020, https://act.greennewdealcanada.ca/what-we-heard/. The page summarizes the themes that emerged at over 150 town hall meetings held across Canada in the spring of 2019.

References

Abramsky, Kolya. 2010. "Sparking an Energy Revolution: Building New Relations of Production, Exchange and Livelihood." In *Sparking a Worldwide Energy Revolution: Social Struggles in the Transition to a Post-petrol World*, edited by Kolya Abramsky, 628–57. Oakland, CA: AK Press.

Adkin, Laurie E., ed. 2016. *First World Petro-Politics: The Political Ecology and Governance of Alberta*. Toronto: University of Toronto Press.

———. 2017. "Crossroads in Alberta: Climate Capitalism or Ecological Democracy?" *Socialist Studies* 12, no. 1: 2–31.

Albo, Gregory. 2008. "The Limits of Eco-localism: Scale, Strategy, Socialism." *Socialist Register* 43: 337–63.

Baer, Hans A. 2019. *Democratic Eco-socialism as a Real Utopia*. New York: Berghahn Books.

Bellefontaine, Michelle. 2019. "Postmedia Hires Former Kenney Chief of Staff to Lobby on 'Energy War Room.'" *CBC News*, May 17, 2019. https://www.cbc.ca/news/canada/edmonton/postmedia-hires-lobbyist-alberta-government-war-room-1.5140631.

Berman, Tzeporah. 2018. "Why the Trans Mountain Fight Is Over More Than Just a Pipeline." *Opencanada.org*, October 4, 2018. https://www.opencanada.org/features/why-trans-mountain-fight-over-more-just-pipeline/.

Bond, Kingsmill. 2020. "Was 2019 the Peak of the Fossil Fuel Era?" Carbon Tracker Initiative. May 1, 2020. https://carbontracker.org/was-2019-the-peak-of-the-fossil-fuel-era/.

Bond, Kingsmill, Ed Vaughan, and Harry Benham. 2020. *Decline and Fall: The Size and Vulnerability of the Fossil Fuel System*. Carbon Tracker Initiative. June 4, 2020. https://carbontracker.org/reports/decline-and-fall/.

Brie, Michael. 2010. "Entry Projects to a Politics of Solidarity: A Radical Practice Test of Counter Hegemony in Times of the Crisis of Neo-liberal Financial Market Capitalism." Policy Paper. Berlin: Rosa Luxemburg Foundation. https://www.rosalux.eu/topics/global-power-and-resistance/entry-projects-to-a-politics-of-solidarity/.

Buci-Glucksmann, Christine. 1979. "State, Transition, and Passive Revolution." In *Gramsci and Marxist Theory*, edited by Chantal Mouffe, 207–36. Boston: Routledge and Kegan Paul.

Burke, Matthew J., and Jennie C. Stephens. 2017. "Energy Democracy: Goals and Policy Instruments for Sociotechnical Transitions." *Energy Research and Social Science* 33 (November): 35–48.

Canadian Press. 2020. "Total Writes Off $9.3B in Oilsands Assets, Cancels Canadian Oil Lobby Membership." *JWN*, July 29, 2020. https://www.jwnenergy.com/article/2020/7/total-writes-93b-oilsands-assets-cancels-canadian-oil-lobby-membership/.

Candeias, Mario. 2011. "Organic Crisis and Capitalist Transformation." Translated by Andrea Lenz and Anne Steckner. *World Review of Political Economy* 2, no. 1: 48–65.

———. 2013. *Green Transformation: Competing Strategic Projects*. Translated by Alexander Gallas. Berlin: Rosa Luxemburg Foundation. http://www.rosalux-nyc.org/green-transformation.

Carroll, William K. 2016. *Expose, Oppose, Propose: Alternative Policy Groups and the Struggle for Global Justice*. London: Zed Books.

Carroll, William K., Nicolas Graham, and Zoë Yunker. 2018. "Carbon Capital and Corporate Influence: Mapping Elite Networks of Corporations, Universities and Research Institutes." In *Corporatizing Canada: Making Business Out of Public Service*, edited by Jamie Brownlee, Chris Hurl, and Kevin Walby, 58–73. Toronto: Between the Lines.

Carroll, William K., and J. P. Sapinski. 2018. *Organizing the 1%: How Corporate Power Works*. Halifax: Fernwood.

CHRC (Canadian Human Rights Commission). 2011. *Now a Matter of Rights: Extending Full Human Rights Protection to First Nations*. Ottawa: Minister of Public Works and Government. https://www.chrc-ccdp.gc.ca/sites/default/files/nmr_eqd-eng.pdf.

Coburn, Elaine, and Clifford Atleo. 2016. "Not Just Another Social Movement: Indigenous Resistance and Resurgence." In *A World to Win: Contemporary Social Movements and Counter-Hegemony*, edited by William K. Carroll and Kanchan Sakar, 176–94. Winnipeg: ARP Books.

Corporate Europe Observatory. 2020. "A Grey Deal? Fossil Fuel Fingerprints on the European Green Deal." July 7, 2020. https://corporateeurope.org/en/a-grey-deal.

Cox, Robert. 1987. *Production, Power and World Order: Social Forces in the Making of History*. New York: Columbia University Press.

Daub, Shannon, and William K. Carroll. 2016. "Why Is the CEO of a Big Canadian Bank Giving Speeches About Climate Change and Pipelines?" Corporate Mapping Project. October 6, 2016. http://www.corporatemapping.ca/rbc-ceo-speech-climate-pipelines/.

Fossil Free Politics. 2019. *Big Oil and Gas Buying Influence in Brussels*. October 24, 2019. Brussels: Corporate Europe Observatory, Food and Water Europe, Friends of the Earth Europe, and Greenpeace EU.

Gorz, André. 1967. *Strategy for Labor: A Radical Proposal*. Boston: Beacon Press.

Graham, Nicolas. 2019. "Canadian Fossil Capitalism, Corporate Strategy, and Post-carbon Futures." *Canadian Review of Sociology* 56, no. 2: 224–50.

Gramsci, Antonio. 1971. *Selections from the Prison Notebooks*. Edited and translated by Quintin Hoare and Geoffrey Nowell Smith. New York: International Publishers.

Gray, Garry, and William K. Carroll. 2018. "Mapping Corporate Influence and Institutional Corruption Inside Canadian Universities." *Critical Criminology* 26: 491–507. https://doi.org/10.1007/s10612-018-9420-0.

Gunster, Shane, and Paul Saurette. 2014. "Storylines in the Sands: News, Narrative and Ideology in the *Calgary Herald*." *Canadian Journal of Communication* 39, no. 3: 333–59.

Hackett, Robert, and William K. Carroll. 2006. *Remaking Media: The Struggle to Democratize Public Communication*. London: Routledge.

Hall, Stuart. 1988. *The Hard Road to Renewal: Thatcherism and the Crisis of the Left.* London: Verso.

Hess, David J. 2018. "Energy Democracy and Social Movements: A Multi-coalition Perspective on the Politics of Sustainability Transitions." *Energy Research and Social Science* 40 (June): 177–89.

Heydari, Anis. 2019. "Jason Kenney Touts $30M 'War Room' but Provides Few Details." *CBC News*, June 7, 2019. https://www.cbc.ca/news/canada/calgary/jason-kenney-war-room-calgary-1.5167205.

Huber, Matthew T. 2013. *Lifeblood: Oil, Freedom, and the Forces of Capital.* Minneapolis: University of Minnesota Press.

Hughes, Tristan. 2019. "Trudeau's Climate Change Policy Is Strategically Inadequate." *The Tyee*, June 21, 2019. https://thetyee.ca/Opinion/2019/06/21/Trudeau-Climate-Policy-Inadequate/.

Kusnetz, Nicholas. 2020. "BP and Shell Write-Off Billions in Assets, Citing Covid-19 and Climate Change." *Inside Climate News*, July 2, 2020. https://insideclimatenews.org/news/01072020/bp-shell-coronavirus-climate-change.

Lee, Marc. 2019. "LNG's Big Lie." *Policy Note* (blog). Canadian Centre for Policy Alternatives, BC Office. June 17, 2019. https://www.policynote.ca/lngs-big-lie.

Löwy, Michael. 2018. Why Ecosocialism: For a Red-Green Future." Great Transition Initiative. December 2018. https://www.greattransition.org/publication/why-ecosocialism-red-green-future.

MacArthur, Julie L., Christina E. Hoicka, Heather Castleden, Runa Das, and Jenny Lieu. 2020. "Canada's Green New Deal: Forging the Socio-political Foundations of Climate Resilient Infrastructure?" *Energy Research and Social Science* 65 (July): 1–10. https://doi.org/10.1016/j.erss.2020.101442.

McCartney, Kevin. 2018. "Pricing Air to Starve the Fire: An Institutional Ethnography of Smart Prosperity." Master's thesis, University of Victoria.

McSheffrey, Elizabeth. 2017. "France's Biggest Bank Shuns Oilsands." *National Observer*, October 13, 2017. https://www.nationalobserver.com/2017/10/13/news/frances-biggest-bank-shuns-oilsands.

Marx, Karl. 1967. *Capital.* Vol. 2, *The Process of Circulation of Capital.* Edited by Frederick Engels. New York: International Publishers.

Mercure, J.-F., H. Pollitt, J. E. Viñuales, N. R. Edwards, P. B. Holden, U. Chewpreecha, P. Salas, I. Sognnaes, A. Lam, and F. Knobloch. 2018. "Macroeconomic Impact of Stranded Fossil Fuel Assets." *Nature Climate Change* 8, no. 7: 588–93.

Mookerjea, Sourayan. 2017. "Petrocultures in Passive Revolution: The Autonomous Domain of Treaty Poetics." In *Petrocultures: Oil, Politics, Culture*, edited by Sheena Wilson, Adam Carlson, and Imre Szeman, 325–54. Montréal and Kingston: McGill-Queen's University Press.

Neubauer, Robert. 2017. "Gateway to Crisis: Discourse Coalitions, Extractivist Politics, and the Northern Gateway Conflict." PhD diss., Simon Fraser University.

Poulantzas, Nicos. 1973. *Political Power and Social Classes*. London: New Left Books.

Rainforest Action Network, BankTrack, Indigenous Environmental Network, Oil Change International, Reclaim Finance, and Sierra Club. 2020. *Banking on Climate Change: Fossil Fuel Finance Report Card 2020*. March 18, 2020. http://priceofoil.org/content/uploads/2020/03/Banking_on_Climate_Change_2020.pdf.

Sapinski, J. P. 2015. "Climate Capitalism and the Global Corporate Elite Network." *Environmental Sociology* 1, no. 4: 268–79.

———. 2016. "Constructing Climate Capitalism: Corporate Power and the Global Climate Policy-Planning Network." *Global Networks* 16, no. 1: 89–111.

Sassoon, Anne S. 1982. "Hegemony, War of Position and Political Intervention." In *Approaches to Gramsci*, edited by Anne S. Sassoon, 94–115. London: Writers and Readers Publishing Cooperative Society.

Satgar, Vishwas. 2018. "The Climate Crisis and Systemic Alternatives." In *The Climate Crisis: South African and Global Democratic Eco-socialist Alternatives*, edited by Vishwas Satgar, 1–27. Johannesburg: Wits University Press.

Simon, Roger. 1982. *Gramsci's Political Thought: An Introduction*. London: Lawrence and Wishart.

Sum, Ngai-Ling, and Bob Jessop. 2013. *Towards a Cultural Political Economy: Putting Culture in Its Place in Political Economy*. Northampton, MA: Elgar.

Surprise, Kevin. 2018. "Preempting the Second Contradiction: Solar Geoengineering as Spatiotemporal Fix." *Annals of the American Association of Geographers* 108, no. 5: 1228–44.

Sweeney, Sean, and John Treat. 2018. *Trade Unions and Just Transition: The Search for a Transformative Politics*. TUED Working Paper No. 11, Trade Unions for Energy Democracy, New York, April 2018. http://unionsforenergydemocracy.org/wp-content/uploads/2018/04/TUED-Working-Paper-11.pdf.

Szulecki, Kacper. 2018. "Conceptualizing Energy Democracy." *Environmental Politics* 27, no. 1: 21–41.

Thombs, Ryan P. 2019. "When Democracy Meets Energy Transitions: A Typology of Social Power and Energy System Scale." *Energy Research and Social Science* 52 (June): 159–68.

Van Apeldoorn, Bastiaan, Nana de Graaff, and Henk Overbeek, eds. 2017. *The State-Capital Nexus in the Global Crisis*. London: Routledge.

Varcoe, Chris. 2020. "Varcoe: Deutsche Bank Move to Stop Oilsands Financing Sparks Pushback in Alberta." *Calgary Herald*, July 29, 2020. https://calgaryherald.com/opinion/columnists/varcoe-deutsche-bank-to-stop-oilsands-financing-triggers-pushback-in-canada.

VeneKlasen, Lisa, and Valerie Miller. 2007. *A New Weave of Power, People, and Politics: The Action for Advocacy and Citizen Participation*. Rugby, UK: Practical Action.

Wanner, Thomas. 2015. "The New 'Passive Revolution' of the Green Economy and Growth Discourse: Maintaining the 'Sustainable Development' of Neoliberal Capitalism." *New Political Economy* 20, no. 1: 21–41.

Willcocks, Paul. 2019. "Andrew Scheer's Real Bad Climate Plan." *The Tyee*, June 28, 2019. https://thetyee.ca/Opinion/2019/06/28/Andrew-Scheer-Real-Bad-Climate-Plan/

Williams, Michelle. 2014. "The Solidarity Economy and Social Transformation." In *The Solidarity Economy Alternative: Emerging Theory and Practice*, edited by Vishwas Satgar. Pietermaritzburg, South Africa: University of KwaZulu-Natal Press.

Contributors

Laurie Adkin is a political economist and professor in the Department of Political Science at the University of Alberta. Her main areas of research and teaching are political ecology, the populist radical right in Europe, and Alberta politics. Since 2002, she has studied the formation of climate change policy in both Alberta and Canada. She is the author of *Politics of Sustainable Development: Citizens, Unions, and the Corporations* (1998) and both the editor of and a contributor to *Environmental Conflict and Democracy in Canada* (2009) and *First World Petro-Politics: The Political Ecology and Governance of Alberta* (2016). Her recent work has focused on the political ecology of knowledge production in Alberta's universities and on innovation policy and discourse as responses to the global climate crisis.

Angele Alook is an assistant professor in the School of Gender, Sexuality, and Women's Studies at York University and a member of Bigstone Cree Nation. She specializes in Indigenous feminism, life course approaches, Indigenous research methodologies, cultural identity, and the sociology of family and work. She is interested in synergies and disjunctures between ways of being, knowing, and doing on her traditional territory. She is directing her research toward a just transition of Alberta's economy and labour force and the impact of climate change on traditional Treaty 8 territory.

Cliff Atleo (Niis Na'yaa/Kam'ayaam/Chachim'multhnii) is a Tsimshian (Kitsumkalum/Kitselas) and Nuu-chah-nulth (Ahousaht) scholar who researches and teaches Indigenous governance, political economy, and resource management at the School of Resource and Environmental Management at Simon Fraser University. He is interested in how Indigenous communities navigate and adopt and/or resist mainstream capitalism while at the same time working to sustain their cultural identities, practices, and world views. He is also interested in the revival of traditional economic practices as well as the exploration of new practices rooted in traditional Indigenous principles and values.

Emilia Belliveau is an organizer, artist, and researcher living on unceded Coast Salish territory. She holds a master's degree from the University of Victoria's School of Environmental Studies, where her research centred on environmental organizing among youth and, more broadly, on the political ecology of energy transitions.

John Bermingham is a graduate student in the School of Communication at Simon Fraser University. His work looks at the media coverage of climate and energy politics, with a particular comparative focus on the differences between corporate, public, and alternative news organizations and their journalistic approaches.

Gwendolyn Blue is an associate professor in the Department of Geography at the University of Calgary. Her research interests centre on the public deliberation of scientific findings and newly emerging technologies, with a focus on controversies surrounding climate change.

Paul Bowles is a professor who holds a cross appointment in the Department of Global and International Studies and the Department of Economics at the University of Northern British Columbia. His research areas include globalization, critical development studies, China's political economy, and extractivism in northern British Columbia. Among his publications are *The Essential Guide to Critical Development Studies* (co-edited with Henry Veltmeyer, 2018) and *Resource Communities in a Globalizing Region: Agency, Development and Contestation in Northern British Columbia* (co-edited with Gary Wilson, 2015).

Susan Cake completed a master's degree in sociology at York University before moving to the University of Alberta to pursue her PhD. In addition to her present research into union renewal and unions' communication structures, she has received training in strategic corporate research at Cornell University's IRL Worker Institute. She is currently the director of policy analysis for the Alberta Federation of Labour, where she focuses on occupational health and safety, workers' compensation boards, and pensions.

William K. Carroll is a professor of sociology at the University of Victoria and was the founding director of UVic's interdisciplinary Social Justice Studies program. Prominent among his interests are corporate power, global capitalism, social movements and the organization of dissent, policy alternatives, and the restoration of democracy. He is the author of numerous books, including, most recently, *Organizing the 1%: How Corporate Power Works* (with J. P. Sapinski); *Expose, Oppose, Propose: Alternative Policy Groups and the Struggle for Global Justice*; *A World to Win: Contemporary Social Movements and Counter-Hegemony* (with Kanchan Sarker); and *The Making of a Transnational Capitalist Class: Corporate Power in the 21st Century*. Since 2015, he has co-directed "Mapping the Power of the Carbon-Extractive Corporate Resource Sector," also known as the Corporate Mapping Project.

Shannon Daub is the director of the Canadian Centre for Policy Alternatives, BC Office, and co-director of the Corporate Mapping Project. In addition to environmental issues, her research interests include corporate power, social movements, and democratic capacity.

Jessica Dempsey is an associate professor in the Department of Geography at the University of British Columbia, where she works in the area of political ecology. Her current research examines the growing emphasis on economic and financial approaches to conservation and also explores the political economic drivers of biodiversity loss.

Emily Eaton is an associate professor in the Department of Geography and Environmental Studies at the University of Regina. She is the author of two books, *Fault Lines: Life and Landscape in Saskatchewan's Oil Economy* (with photographer Valerie Zink) and *Growing Resistance: Canadian Farmers and the Politics of Genetically Modified Wheat*. Her work concerns environmental, social, and economic aspects of oil and resource development as well as the prospects for energy transition in oil-dependent communities.

Chuka Ejeckam is Director of Research and Policy at the BC Federation of Labour. As a policy researcher and writer working in the labour movement, he has focused on automation, deindustrialization, precarious employment, and climate change. He is also a master's student in political science at the University of British Columbia, where his research centres on reparative drug policy, economic and political inequality, and structural racism.

Simon Enoch is director of the Saskatchewan Office of the Canadian Centre for Policy Alternatives and an adjunct professor in the Department of Politics and International Studies at the University of Regina. He completed a master's degree in labour studies at McMaster University before earning his PhD in communication and culture from Ryerson University. His interests include corporate social responsibility, political ecology, and media discourse.

Nicolas Graham recently completed his PhD in the Department of Sociology at the University of Victoria, where he is also a sessional instructor. His work in the areas of critical political economy and political ecology has appeared in the *Canadian Review of Sociology*, *BC Studies*, and *Capitalism Nature Socialism*. He is currently conducting research into competing political projects for energy transition.

Shane Gunster teaches in the School of Communication at Simon Fraser University and is also a research associate with the Canadian Centre for Political Alternatives. His research interests cluster around advocacy and news media coverage in the area of climate and energy politics. He is one of the co-authors of *Journalism and Climate Crisis: Public Engagement, Media Alternatives* (2017) and is currently working on a book about the climate crisis and populism.

Nicole Hill is a PhD candidate in sociology at the University of Alberta. She is interested in perspectives on culture, bodies, and gender that are informed by intersectional feminisms. Her current research explores the social and cultural dimensions of violence that birthing people experience in the context of maternity health care in Alberta.

Mark Hudson is an associate professor in the Department of Sociology and the coordinator of the Global Political Economy program at the University of Manitoba, as well as a research associate at the Manitoba Office of the Canadian Centre for Policy Alternatives and a researcher with the Corporate Mapping Project. His work primarily concerns the political economic mediation of human relationships with non-human nature, although he has written as well on community economic development, ideology in economics, and welfare state policy, among other topics. He is a co-author of *Neoliberal Lives: Work, Politics, Nature, and Health in the Contemporary United States* (2019) and of *Fair Trade, Sustainability, and Social Change* (2013), as well as the author of *Fire Management in the American West: Forest Politics and the Rise of Megafires* (2011).

Jouke Huijzer is a doctoral candidate and teaching assistant in the Department of Political Science at the Vrije Universiteit Brussel. He holds a graduate degree from the University of Amsterdam and worked at the University of Victoria in the fall of 2015, conducting research for the Corporate Mapping Project. He has a passionate interest in elites, their resources, and their ideas (or the lack thereof). He is currently writing a dissertation on the ideological "void on the left" in the Low Countries.

Ian Hussey is a research manager at the University of Alberta's Parkland Institute and a member of the steering committee of the SSHRC-funded Corporate Mapping Project. Before joining the Parkland Institute, Hussey worked for several international development organizations and was the co-founder and executive director of the Canadian Fair Trade Network. He holds an MA in sociology from the University of Victoria, and his PhD coursework and exams at York University focused on the sociology of colonialism and on political economy. His writing has appeared in the *Globe and Mail*, *New Political Economy*, the *Edmonton Journal*, the *National Observer*, and *The Tyee*.

Emma Jackson is an organizer with 350 Canada and Climate Justice Edmonton. Before joining 350 Canada, she worked with the Corporate Mapping Project as a research assistant at the Parkland Institute. She holds an Honours BA in geography from Mount Allison University and recently earned her MA in sociology from the University of Alberta.

Michael Lang is a PhD candidate in the Department of Sociology at the University of Victoria, where he also works as a research assistant with the Corporate Mapping Project. His academic interests lie with the politics and political economy of water and the environment more broadly. His SSHRC-supported doctoral research explores key historical moments in BC energy policy relating to hydroelectricity and shale gas development.

James Lawson is an associate professor in the Department of Political Science at the University of Victoria, where he is also the director of the Human Dimensions of Climate Change program. He teaches and researches primarily in the areas of Canadian political economy, environmental politics, and the political economy of resource extraction.

Marc Lee is a senior economist with the BC Office of the Canadian Centre for Policy Alternatives, where he has been based since 1998. For many years, he led the CCPA's Climate Justice Project (CJP), which has published a wide range of research on fair and effective approaches to climate action that integrate principles of social justice,. As one of Canada's leading progressive commentators on economic and social policy issues, he continues to write about climate and energy policy, as well as about strategies for affordable housing. Over the years, Lee has tracked federal and provincial budgets and economic trends and has published on a wide range of topics, from poverty and inequality to globalization and international trade to public services and regulation. He is past chair of the Progressive Economics Forum, a national network of heterodox economists.

Alicia Massie is a Joseph-Armand Bombardier doctoral scholar and a PhD candidate in the School of Communication at Simon Fraser University. She works as an educator, labour organizer, and community activist. In both her activism and academic work, she focuses on the intersections of gender, labour, and race in late capitalism, as well as investigating Canadian petro-capitalism from a socialist-feminist perspective.

Fiona MacPhail is a professor of economics at the University of Northern British Columbia. Her research program centres on inequalities, work, and public policy. As a member of the Corporate Mapping Project, she is interested in the political economy of fossil fuel projects, particularly in northern British Columbia.

Kevin McCartney is a PhD student in geography at the University of British Columbia. His work to date has focused on corporate power in climate denialist networks in Canada. His SSHRC-supported master's research examined corporate influence in energy policy development through ENGO sponsorship. His doctoral work, also SSHRC-supported, engages energy workers and resource communities on issues of climate change, energy transition, justice, and dignity, with a focus on petro-cultures and extractive subjectivities. He lives and studies on unceded Musqueam territory.

Robert Neubauer is an assistant professor in the Department of Rhetoric, Writing, and Communications at the University of Winnipeg. His work explores environmental and energy politics through the overlapping lenses of political economy, media studies, and ideology critique. He is particularly interested in the role of discourse coalitions—networks of civil society, industry, and state actors jointly advocating shared policy agendas—in promoting populist discourse in Canadian energy politics. His current work uses content, discourse, and network analysis to chart the development of industry-backed, pro–fossil fuel "echo chambers" and alternative media ecosystems on social media. He received his PhD from the School of Communication at Simon Fraser University and is, by most accounts, a pretty decent cook.

Éric Pineault is a professor at the University of Québec in Montréal, where he teaches political economy in the Department of Sociology and ecological economics in the Environmental Sciences Institute. His current research focuses on the political economy of the ecological transition in Canada, as well as of the extractive sector in Canada and globally. A core team member of the Corporate Mapping Project, he is the author of *Le piège Énergie Est* (2016), a book that critically examines the proposed Energy East pipeline project.

Lise Rajewicz served as a researcher for the Corporate Mapping Project while she was a student at the University of Calgary, where she earned a BA in human geography. She has since worked in a variety of settings that reflect her commitment to environmental stewardship, climate change advocacy, and public education. She recently joined the Calgary office of Bluesource, where she is responsible for coordinating projects designed to reduce methane emissions.

James K. Rowe is an associate professor in the School of Environmental Studies at the University of Victoria. His interests lie with social movement strategy, which he approaches from the perspective of political economy and political ecology, with a particular focus on the roots of injustice. He is especially concerned with the role of existential fears and resentments in the creation of injustice and the concomitant need for social movements to develop strategies capable of addressing these fears.

Karena (Kara) Shaw teaches in the School of Environmental Studies at the University of Victoria. where she is also a member of the Institute for Integrated Energy Systems. A political theorist by training, she is particularly interested in the political dynamics of environmental and social change. Past research has engaged with feminist, Indigenous, and environmental politics, all of which are embedded in her current focus on the political ecology of energy transitions. This research explores how communities are simultaneously resisting and embracing diverse energy technologies and, in the process, how they are reshaping political, social, and ecological possibilities.

Zoë Yunker is a student at the University of British Columbia's Graduate School of Journalism and a researcher and project coordinator with the Corporate Mapping Project. Her work focuses on issues of climate justice, Indigenous rights, energy politics, and the climate impacts of pension capital. She holds a master's degree in sociology from the University of Victoria.

a PROUD PARTNER in
Campus Alberta

A book in the Campus Alberta Collection, a collaboration of Athabasca University Press, University of Alberta Press, and University of Calgary Press.

AU PRESS

UNIVERSITY OF CALGARY
Press

Athabasca University Press
aupress.ca

Regime of Obstruction: How Corporate Power Blocks Energy Democracy
William K. Carroll, Editor
978-1-77199-289-3 (paperback)

The Medium Is the Monster: Canadian Adaptations of Frankenstein and the Discourse of Technology
Mark A. McCutcheon
978-1-77199-236-7 (hardcover)
978-1-77199-224-4 (paperback)

Public Deliberation on Climate Change: Lessons from Alberta Climate Dialogue
Lorelei L. Hanson, Editor
978-1-77199-215-2 (paperback)

University of Calgary Press
press.ucalgary.ca

Creating the Future of Health: The History of the Cumming School of Medicine at the University of Calgary, 1967–2012
By Robert Lampard, David B. Hogan, Frank W. Stahnisch, and James R. Wright Jr.
978-1-77385-164-8 (paperback)

Intertwined Histories: Plants in Their Social Contexts
Edited by Jim Ellis
978-1-77385-090-0 (paperback)

Water Rites: Reimagining Water in the West
Edited by Jim Ellis
978-1-55238-997-3 (paperback)

UNIVERSITY *of* **ALBERTA** PRESS

University of Alberta Press
uap.ualberta.ca

Dissonant Methods: Undoing Discipline in the Humanities Classroom
Ada S. Jaarsma and Kit Dobson, Editors
978-1-77212-489-7 (paperback)

Feminist Acts: Branching Out Magazine and the Making of Canadian Feminism
Tessa Jordan
978-1-77212-484-2 (paperback)

Keetsahnak / Our Missing and Murdered Indigenous Sisters
Kim Anderson, Maria Campbell and Christi Belcourt, Editors
978-1-77212-367-8 (paperback)